Foreign Aid and Development

Lessons Learnt and Directions for the Future

Edited by
Finn Tarp

Editorial Assistant
Peter Hjertholm

Routledge
Taylor & Francis Group

LONDON AND NEW YORK

First published 2000
by Routledge
11 New Fetter Lane, London EC4P 4EE

Simultaneously published in the USA and Canada
by Routledge
29 West 35th Street, New York, NY 10001

Reprinted 2002

Transferred to Digital Printing 2002

Routledge is an imprint of the Taylor & Francis Group

Typeset in Baskerville by Exe Valley Dataset Ltd, Exeter
Printed and bound in Great Britain by
TJI Digital, Padstow, Cornwall

British Library Cataloguing in Publication Data
A catalogue record for this book is available
from the British Library

Library of Congress Cataloging in Publication Data
Foreign aid and development: lessons learnt and directions for the future/edited by
Finn Tarp; editorial assistant Peter Hjertholm.
    p.   cm.
Proceedings from conferences held in Copenhagen, Denmark in Oct. 1997 and 1998.
Includes bibliographical references (p.   ) and index.
1. Economic assistance—Developing countries—Congresses.
2. Economic development projects—Developing countries—
Congresses. I. Tarp, Finn, 1951– II. Hjertholm, Peter.

HC60.F586 2000
338.91'1722—dc21   00–020816

ISBN 0–415–21546–3 (hbk)
ISBN 0–415–23363–1 (pbk)

Foreign Aid and Development

'Here at last is a comprehensive, stimulating, balanced and up-to-date analysis of the current state of donor debates and disagreements over the roles, effectiveness and future of foreign aid. Its broad coverage and variety of authors, and its consistently constructive, even when critical, approaches should make it an obvious starting-point for all students and policy-makers embarking upon work in this sphere.'

Gerry Helleiner, Centre for International Studies,
University of Toronto

Aid has worked in the past but can be made to work better in the future. In this book, leading international scholars and experienced aid practitioners re-examine foreign aid and its role in development. Introducing important new research material, the book combines analysis of post-war development aid policies with an assessment of current practice and recommendations for future policy.

The book is arranged into four thematic sections. Part I investigates major themes in the evolution of development doctrine, such as the role of govenment, and challenges the conventional wisdom about the impact of aid. Part II presents detailed analysis of aid instruments, including technical assistance, project and programme aid, and food aid. Part III opens up economic perspectives on aid design, and draws important conclusions on how such factors as environment, public sector reform and gender equality impact on the relationship between aid and development. Finally, Part IV takes a broader look at some of the most important contemporary issues in aid policy, such as armed conflict and the emerging global trade environment.

Foreign Aid and Development will be of essential interest to professional aid practitioners and those working in development studies, and invaluable to the student of economics or politics looking for new global perspectives.

Finn Tarp is Associate Professor of Development Economics at the University of Copenhagen. Formerly with the UN, he worked as an economist in southern Africa from 1978 to 1988. He is the author of *Stabilization and Structural Adjustment: Macroeconomic Frameworks for Analysing the Crisis in Sub-Saharan Africa*.

Peter Hjertholm is Assistant Research Professor at the Institute of Economics at the University of Copenhagen.

Contents

Tables

Figures

Contributors

Tony Addison, Lecturer in Economics, University of Warwick, United Kingdom

Irma Adelman, Professor in Graduate School, University of California at Berkeley, USA

Ole Mølgård Andersen, former Chief Economic Adviser (Development Economics), Ministry of Foreign Affairs (Danida), Denmark

Channing Arndt, Assistant Professor, Department of Agricultural Economics, Purdue University, USA

Elliot J. Berg, Visiting Professor, Centre d'Etudes et de Recherches sur le Développement International (CERDI), Université d'Auvergne, France

Bjørg Colding, Consultant, International Food Policy Research Institute (IFPRI), Washington, D.C., USA

Marion J. Eeckhout, Visiting Researcher, Africa Region, World Bank, former Head of Macroeconomic Analysis Department, Directorate General for International Cooperation (DGIS), Ministry of Foreign Affairs, the Netherlands

Henrik Hansen, Assistant Professor, Institute of Economics and Natural Resources, The Royal Veterinary and Agricultural University and Development Economics Research Group (DERG), Institute of Economics, University of Copenhagen, Denmark

John Healey, Senior Research Associate, Overseas Development Institute (ODI), United Kingdom

Rasmus Heltberg, Research Fellow, Development Economics Research Group (DERG), Institute of Economics, University of Copenhagen, Denmark

Peter Hjertholm, Assistant Research Professor, Development Economics Research Group (DERG), Institute of Economics, University of Copenhagen, Denmark

Raymond F. Hopkins, Richter Professor of Political Science, Department of Political Science, Swarthmore College, USA

Ravi Kanbur, T.H. Lee Professor of World Affairs and Professor of Economics, Cornell University, USA

Tony Killick, Senior Research Associate, Overseas Development Institute (ODI), United Kingdom

Jens Kovsted, Research Fellow, Development Economics Research Group (DERG), Institute of Economics, University of Copenhagen, Denmark

Mads Váczy Kragh, Economist, Confederation of Danish Industries, Denmark

Jytte Laursen, Technical Advisor (Economics), Ministry of Foreign Affairs (Danida), Denmark

Oliver Morrissey, Director, Centre for Research in Economic Development and International Trade (CREDIT), Economics Department, University of Nottingham, United Kingdom

Jørgen Birk Mortensen, Associate Professor, Institute of Economics, University of Copenhagen, Denmark

Paul Mosley, Professor of Economics, Director, Development Research Centre, University of Sheffield, United Kingdom

Uffe Nielsen, Research Fellow, Development Economics Research Group (DERG), Institute of Economics, University of Copenhagen and University Instructor, Institute of Economics and Natural Resources, The Royal Veterinary and Agricultural University, Denmark

Per Pinstrup-Andersen, Professor, Director General, International Food Policy Research Institute (IFPRI), Washington, D.C., USA

Lisa Ann Richey, Visiting Assistant Professor, Centre of African Studies, University of Copenhagen, Denmark

Sherman Robinson, Professor, Director, Trade and Macroeconomics Division, International Food Policy Research Institute (IFPRI), Washington, D.C., USA

Henrik Schaumburg-Müller, Associate Professor, Department of Intercultural Communication and Management, Copenhagen Business School, Denmark

Hans Peter Slente, Economist, Confederation of Danish Industries, Denmark

Finn Tarp, Associate Professor, Development Economics Research Group (DERG), Institute of Economics, University of Copenhagen, Denmark

Erik Thorbecke, H.E. Babcock Professor of Economics & Food Economics, Department of Economics, Cornell University, USA

Howard White, Fellow, Institute of Development Studies (IDS), University of Sussex, United Kingdom

Acronyms and abbreviations

AAWORD	Association of African Women for Research and Development
ABD	Aid Book Database
ACP	Africa, Caribbean and Pacific (countries)
AERC	African Economic Research Consortium
AFDB	African Development Bank
APEC	Asia-Pacific Economic Co-operation
ASDB	Asian Development Bank
BFWI	Bread for the World Institute
BIS	Bank for International Settlements
BMZ	Bundesministerium für Wirtschaftliche Zusammenarbeit und Entwicklung (Federal Ministry for Economic Co-operation and Development, Germany)
CAP	Common Agricultural Policy (of the EU)
CARE	Center for American Relief in Europe
CCPDC	Carnegie Commission on Preventing Deadly Conflict
CDC	Commonwealth Development Corporation
CDI	Centre for Development of Industry
CDM	Clean Development Mechanism
CEC	Commission of the European Communities
CEEC	Central and Eastern European Countries
CERDI	Centre d'Etudes et de Recherches sur le Développement International (France)
CFA	Communauté Financière Africaine
CGAP	Consultative Group to Assist the Poorest
CGE	Computable General Equilibrium (models)
CIDA	Canadian International Development Agency
CIP	Commodity Import Programmes
CREDIT	Centre for Research in Economic Development and International Trade (UK)
CVF	Counter Value Funds
DAC	Development Assistance Committee
Danida	Danish International Development Assistance
DAWN	Development Alternatives with Women for a New Era
DERG	Development Economics Research Group (Denmark)
DFID	Department For International Development (United Kingdom)

DGIS	Directorate General for International Cooperation (The Netherlands)
DRC	Democratic Republic of Congo
EBRD	European Bank for Reconstruction and Development
EC	European Commission
ECA	Economic Commission for Africa (of the UN)
ECDPM	European Centre for Development Policy Management
ECIP	European Community Investment Partners
EDA	Effective Development Aid
EDFI	European Development Finance Institutions
EIA	Environmental Impact Assessment
ER	Exchange Rate
ESAF	Enhanced Structural Adjustment Facility (of the IMF)
EU	European Union
Eurostep	European solidarity towards equal participation of people
EV	Equivalent Variation
FAC	Food Aid Convention
FAO	Food and Agriculture Organization (of the UN)
FDI	Federation of Danish Industries
Forex	Foreign Exchange
FSU	Former Soviet Union
GAD	Gender and Development
GATT	General Agreement on Tariffs and Trade
GDP	Gross Domestic Product
GDS	Globalization and Development Strategies (division of UNCTAD)
GEF	Global Environmental Facility
GHG	Greenhouse Gas
GNP	Gross National Product
G7	Group of Seven (industrial countries)
HIPC	Heavily Indebted Poor Countries (debt relief initiative)
IBRD	International Bank for Reconstruction and Development
ICVA	International Council of Voluntary Agencies
IDA	International Development Agency (of the World Bank)
IDS	Institute of Development Studies (UK)
IFC	International Finance Corporation (of the World Bank)
IFPRI	International Food Policy Research Institute (United States)
IFU	Industrialization Fund for Developing Countries (Denmark)
IIC	Inter-American Investment Corporation
ILO	International Labour Organization
IMAC	Institute for Management and Accounting
IMF	International Monetary Fund
INC	Canadian Industrial Co-operation
IRDP	Integrated Rural Development Project
IRR	Internal Rate of Return
ISS	Institute of Social Studies (The Netherlands)
IV	Instrumental Variable (estimation)
JI	Joint Implementation

JICA	Japan International Co-operation Agency
LIBOR	London Interbank Offered Rate
LIC	Low-Income Countries
LIRTA	Low-Income Country Regional Trade Agreements
LLDC	Least Developed Countries
LMIC	Lower Middle-Income Countries
MAI	Multilateral Agreement on Investment
MFA	Multi-Fibre Arrangement
MFI	Micro-Finance Institutions
NAFTA	North American Free Trade Agreement
NATCAP	National Technical Co-operation Action Programme
NATO	North Atlantic Treaty Organization
NDF	Nordic Development Fund
NGO	Non-Governmental Organization
NIC	Newly Industrialising Countries
NIS	Newly Independent States (of the former Soviet Union)
NOPEF	Nordic Project Export Fund
NORAD	Norwegian Agency for Development Co-operation
ODA	Official Development Assistance
ODI	Overseas Development Institute (United Kingdom)
ODM	Overseas Development Ministry (United Kingdom)
OECD	Organisation for Economic Co-operation and Development
OEEC	Organisation for European Economic Co-operation
O&M	Operations and Maintenance
OOF	Other Official Flows
PA	Poverty Assessment
PC	Performance Contract
PE	Public Enterprise
PER	Public Expenditure Review
PFP	Policy Framework Paper
PIP	Public Investment Programme
PL	Public Law
PR	Poverty Reduction
PREM	Poverty and Gender Network
PSD	Private Sector Development
PSM	Public Sector Management
PTI	Poverty Targeted Intervention
QDA	Quick Disbursing Assistance
QR	Quantitative restrictions
R&D	Research and Development
RDI	Relief and Development Institute
REPA	Reciprocal Economic Partnership Arrangement
RTA	Regional Trade Agreements
SADC	Southern African Development Community
SAF	Structural Adjustment Facility (of the IMF)
SAL	Structural Adjustment Lending
SAM	Social Accounting Matrix

SAP	Structural Adjustment Programme
SBS	Sectoral Budget Support
SDP	Sector Development Programme
SECAL	Sectoral Adjustment Lending
SIDA	Swedish International Development Authority (from 1962 to 1 July 1995, then transformed to Sida)
Sida	Swedish International Development Co-operation Agency
SIP	Sector Investment Programme
SME	Small and Medium-Sized Enterprise
SOC	Social Overhead Capital
SOE	State-Owned Enterprise
SPA	Special Programme of Assistance for Africa
SUNFED	Special United Nations Fund for Development
TA	Technical Assistance
TC	Technical Co-operation
TCPFP	Technical Co-operation Policy Framework Paper
TFP	Total Factor Productivity
UAP	Untied Aid Performance
UK	United Kingdom
UN	United Nations
UNCTAD	United Nations Conference on Trade and Development
UNDP	United Nations Development Programme
UNEP	United Nations Environment Programme
Unesco	United Nations Educational, Scientific and Cultural Organization
UNFPA	United Nations Population Fund
UNHCR	United Nations High Commissioner for Refugees
Unicef	United Nations Children's Fund
UNRRA	United Nations Relief and Rehabilitation Agency
UNSIA	United Nations System-Wide Special Initiative on Africa
UR	Uruguay Round
US	United States of America
USAID	United States Agency for International Development
USDA	United States Department of Agriculture
USSR	Union of Soviet Socialist Republics
VAT	Value Added Tax
WAD	Women and Development
WCED	World Commission on Energy and Development
WID	Women in Development
WIDER	World Institute for Development Economics Research
WFP	World Food Programme
WHO	World Health Organization
WTO	World Trade Organization
WWF	Worldwide Fund for Nature
WWI	World War I
WWII	World War II

Preface

This book is concerned with the role and effectiveness of foreign aid in development. It is part of a widespread and ongoing process of evaluations of past experience with foreign aid in the aid community, including recipient countries, researchers, and aid agencies. Much of the recent work reviewing the role of aid has been critical. While there is much to criticise, the papers in this volume approach aid from a variety of perspectives and try to come to grips in a constructive manner with the complexity of the aid-development nexus in both the short and long run.

The Second World War marked a point of major change in the evolution of the world economy, and the post-war experience with foreign aid should be seen in the context of the emergence of a large number of new nation states and the breakdown of the earlier colonial system. In the 50 years since WWII much has been learnt, and much has changed in the world: economic and political systems, motivating ideologies and the degree of integration of the world economy. The motivation for aid has evolved during this period and the turn of the century is an appropriate time to take stock:

- What lessons have been learnt about development policy and the provision of foreign aid?
- What are the key development issues facing the world community in the twenty-first century?
- What is the role of foreign assistance in addressing the problems of development in the future?

The last four to five decades of the twentieth century witnessed a massive outpouring of studies on foreign aid, and this flow intensified during the last few years. There are many reasons for this, including:

- The cold war rationale for aid disappeared following the demise of the centrally planned economies in Eastern Europe, and private capital flows to some developing countries surged during the 1990s. Aid objectives have gradually widened over the years, and the shifts in political coalitions are significant.

- There have been significant changes in our understanding of growth and development processes, appropriate development strategies and policies, and the design and delivery of aid.
- There has been continuing debate on the effectiveness of foreign aid, but recent work has benefited from the availability of a broader and more sophisticated array of analytical economic tools as well as more data.

The existing literature is of widely varying quality and accessibility and has often responded to specific institutional interests and needs. This book tries to provide a broad-minded and systematic overview. Moreover, the contributors to this volume can be characterised as a group of independent scholars and aid practitioners. They are mainly economists, but the group also includes political scientists. Some have extensive background in development economics and policy analysis, and have participated in the aid process for many years. Others have entered this field more recently, bringing with them fresh perspectives and technical skills.

The group of authors does not subscribe to a common set of economic policy recommendations, and the reader will find differences in emphasis and interpretation from chapter to chapter. The reader will also note a shared concern with how to improve the plight of the more than one billion poor people in the world who do not have acceptable standards of living. Foreign aid is mainly approached from the perspective of donor countries and institutions, but the fundamental goals of economic development are kept in mind throughout.

In addition to providing overviews of the evolution of development doctrine and the role of aid, this volume provides new empirical evidence on the effectiveness of aid. This evidence challenges key elements of the existing conventional wisdom, leading to more balanced policy conclusions. Fresh insights into the use of the various aid modalities, which are in a complex process of reform, are also offered. Taking stock and reflecting on how aid should be designed in the future to promote economic development (with a focus on growth, poverty alleviation and social justice) are core themes. To this come reviews of the past, present and future of aid as it emerges from analyses by political scientists. Finally, while much of what is said refers to a variety of poor countries in different regions of the world, particular attention is paid to the development challenges of Africa.

The original outline of the book was drafted in early 1997. During a one-day brainstorming meeting held at the Institute of Economics at the University of Copenhagen in October 1997, ideas were thrashed out in more detail, and a set of broad guidelines was agreed upon. An advisory editorial board was also established. The members include:

- Professor Sherman Robinson, Director of the Trade and Macroeconomics Division, International Food Policy Research Institute (IFPRI), Washington, D.C., USA.
- Professor John Toye, Institute of Development Studies (IDS) at the University of Sussex, Brighton, United Kingdom. He is currently on leave as Director of the Division on Globalization and Development Strategies (GDS), UNCTAD.
- Dr Howard White, Fellow, Institute of Development Studies at the University of Sussex (IDS), Brighton, United Kingdom.

These three experienced professionals have supported me throughout, and I would like to express my most sincere gratitude for the time and effort they put into this task. E-mail has made it easy to communicate in writing, but Sherman Robinson's several visits to Copenhagen over the past two years have facilitated deeper interaction and played a fundamental role in moving this project along.

During a second authors' meeting in Copenhagen in October 1998, draft papers were presented and discussed, and subsequently we have gone through a refereeing process of all papers. In this process, many valuable comments and suggestions have come up, and I would like to express my appreciation to those who took it upon themselves to serve in this function.

This book would never have come about without the organisational talent and editorial skills of Peter Hjertholm. He helped conceive the project, put in long hours of hard and dedicated work in reviewing and revising the individual chapters, kept track of all the files, and in the final phase played a central role in getting the complete manuscript together. I am deeply thankful to Peter for productive partnership and friendship.

Excellent research assistance was provided by Steen Asmussen, and Henning Tarp Jensen, and Vibeke Kovsted has in her quiet and well organised manner kept track of a wide range of administrative work and problems. They all in their way deserve major credit, and I am greatly indebted to them.

I am also grateful to Henrik Hansen, Rasmus Heltberg, Jens Kovsted, and Uffe Nielsen at the Institute of Economics. They are on the authors' list, as is Peter Hjertholm. They have, however, also contributed to the book through our many daily interactions from which I have derived a lot of inspiration. Moreover, they have never failed in making our common working environment both professionally stimulating and enjoyable.

During this project we have had excellent offices and meeting rooms, and the access to other facilities (such as computers) has been superb. I am therefore grateful to the Institute of Economics of the University of Copenhagen for providing this infrastructure. I also wish to acknowledge the financial support received from the Danish Development Research Council and the North/South Priority Research Initiative of the University of Copenhagen. The North/South Initiative is headed by Professor Holger Bernt Hansen, who encouraged the project from start to end.

Finally, I would like to express my most sincere appreciation to the group of authors. It has been both a pleasure and a great privilege to collaborate with such a distinguished and knowledgeable group.

FINN TARP
Copenhagen
1 September 1999

Foreign aid and development
Summary and synthesis

Sherman Robinson and Finn Tarp

Introduction and background

The evolution of the world economy over the past decades has been complex. There have been interrelated changes in resource accumulation, population growth, growth in knowledge, and improvements in production technology, all operating in an environment characterised by frequent and dramatic transformations in politics and institutions. In this overview we touch briefly on a number of these themes and their relationship to the ongoing debate about the role and effectiveness of foreign aid. The discussion draws on the chapters in this volume, which go into much more detail on particular issues.

Historical performance

Economic development after the Second World War has been spectacular. The developed world recovered rapidly from the ravages of war and went on growing on an unprecedented scale. The developing countries have also performed well on average. The World Bank, in a recent *World Development Report* (World Bank 1997a) lists data for 133 economies. It classifies 49 of them as low-income, 41 as lower-middle income, 17 as upper-middle income and 26 as high-income. There has been much movement in relative rankings and many of the current middle- and some of the high-income countries started out very poor in the post-war period. However, at the two ends of the spectrum there has been less change. The rich have stayed relatively rich and many of the poorest countries have not escaped poverty. Of the 49 low-income countries, most are African, a few are Asian, and very few are Latin-American.

While there are many examples of development successes, there is also evidence of a widening gap between the most and least successful; and the lagging economies are mostly African. Moreover, the numbers of poor and malnourished people have grown over the past decades, and more than one billion of the world's population have an income of less than a dollar a day. While most of the poor countries are African, most of the poor people are Asian. To the extent that aid is concerned with reducing poverty, there is a clear justification for focusing on Africa and Asia. Yet the two regions are very different – it appears that the underlying problems and impediments to growth are more intractable in Africa.

Even a cursory review of the data on economic performance also indicates that development in the last half century has been a complex and variegated process. In searching for lessons from this experience, one should be aware of the dangers of over-simplification. Single-cause theories have not fared well and simple policy recommendations are often inappropriate in a complex world. In economics, and particularly in development economics, it is very important to define the domain of applicability of a theory and related policy conclusions. The issue is not whether aid 'works', but how, and under what circumstances and economic policy environments. Generally, the papers in this book do not question if aid works, but most find that different modalities are more or less appropriate and effective at different stages of development and economic circumstances. In addition, justifications for aid have evolved since the 1940s, reflecting changes in both development theory and politics. How well aid works and should be allocated must be judged with reference to underlying goals.

Justifications for aid in the past

A number of alternative, but not mutually exclusive, justifications for aid have been articulated over the years.

- Altruism. Humanitarian concerns explicitly motivated many aid donors, reflecting concerns about the extent and degree of poverty and inequality in the world.
- Political ideology, foreign policy, and commercial interests. The cold war was used as a justification for providing aid to developing countries to stem the spread of communism. Similarly, aid from socialist governments was motivated by a desire to promote socialist political and economic systems. A number of donors support former colonies. They also pursue a variety of foreign policy and domestic commercial and private sector interests in the provision of aid. An example is the possibility of aid generating more exports, a justification that underlies the modality of tied aid.
- Economic development. This justification has been used both as a goal in itself and as a necessary condition for the realisation of other development goals such as: poverty alleviation, the spread of democracy, gender issues, social development, and the expansion of markets (including providing a hospitable environment for foreign investment).

On these criteria, the post-WWII experience with development has been remarkable. Income growth has been dramatic, although poverty remains a stubborn problem. The cold war is over. It also appears that many of the goals linked to economic development are increasingly being achieved. There are many encouraging cases of transitions from right and left wing authoritarian regimes to democratic systems. Social development is taking place, and markets are opening (including a greater role for foreign trade and investment). There is now much support for the earlier controversial argument that economic development would provide an enabling environment for such social and political progress.

The economic development argument for aid requires an underlying theory of the process of development and how aid can help foster that process. In Part I, Erik Thorbecke and Irma Adelman (Chapters 1 and 2) explore the evolution of economic development theory since the 1940s and express views on the role of government in both historic and post-war perspectives. Thorbecke describes how the term 'economic development' has incorporated many different concerns, reflecting changes in theory, existing data systems, and the world economic environment. His road map clarifies the interrelationships among development goals, development theories, strategies and policies, and the potential roles of aid. He starts with GNP growth, and then traces the gradual addition of issues over time, including balance-of-payments, employment, income distribution, poverty, stabilisation and structural adjustment, sustainability, and world financial management. As development concerns have broadened, aid in this schema has changed focus from a simple concern with resource mobilisation to a much more multi-dimensional role. Part II of this volume, in which alternative modalities of aid are reviewed, illustrates this evolution.

Most aid is channelled from government to government. Adelman outlines how the role of government in industrialisation has changed in the nineteenth and twentieth centuries. She also discusses ideological perspectives and the appropriate role of government in modern developing countries, and makes the argument that the government has a critical, and positive, role to play in the development process. In so far as aid supports government activities and policies, the two are closely related. This theme is picked up in many chapters in Parts III and IV, addressing the appropriate design of aid and broader issues, including conditionality.

Changing economic and political environment

Throughout the history of aid there has been interplay between the volume and character of economic aid, on the one hand, and the changing nature of the challenges facing recipient countries, on the other. In the immediate post-war period, the problem in Europe was lack of capital. The response was the Marshall Plan, which in part gave rise to many elements of the existing system for aid delivery. Peter Hjertholm and Howard White (Chapter 3) discuss institutional developments and provide historical data on aid flows, and Raymond Hopkins (Chapter 19) provides a political economy perspective on these issues.

After the success of the Marshall Plan, attention turned to developing countries. Aid flows grew in real terms until the early 1990s and represented a relatively constant share of the growing GNP of the donor community during the period 1970–90. After 1990, aid flows have fallen both absolutely and as a share of donor GNP. With this come changes in the relative importance of multilateral versus bilateral aid, the increasing importance of European aid, the changing role of commercial lending versus aid, the substantial increase in foreign direct investment, the extraordinary growth of short-term foreign exchange transactions relative to foreign investment and foreign aid, and the increasing role of trade versus aid.

The decline in aggregate aid flows can be attributed to a number of causes:

*   The fall of communism and the end of the cold war eroded support for aid given on ideological grounds. National security motives are still relevant in some cases (e.g. Israel, Egypt and parts of former Yugoslavia), but aid to countries in Asia and Africa attract less support.
*   The traditional support of development aid by liberal groups has been eroded by competition from other concerns (notably the environment) and distrust of the bilateral and multilateral aid agencies. These agencies, and more recent institutions such as the WTO, are seen either as instruments of commercial interests in the developed countries, seeking only to exploit cheap labour and natural resources in developing countries, or as self-interested, rent-seeking bureaucracies.
*   The widespread perception that aid has been ineffective in fostering growth at the macro level and many anecdotes about failed projects at the micro level have led to 'aid fatigue' in many donor countries.
*   The increasing awareness of examples of bad governance, corruption, and 'crony capitalism' has led to scepticism about the sincerity and credibility of aid receiving governments. The recent Asian financial crisis revealed such problems, and the inability of African countries to attract private capital is another evident reflection of such concerns.

These perceptions represent a serious challenge to the economic development rationale for aid, leaving only the humanitarian aid motive intact. This book focuses on economic development issues in the aid debate, challenges some of the negative perceptions, draws lessons from past experience, and discusses the requirements for successful aid programmes in the future. While often critical of aid in the past, the contributors to this volume are in broad agreement that there remains a valid economic development rationale for aid in the future, and delineate its components.

Aid from a macro perspective

The earliest work in the 1950s on economic development focused on aggregate growth and resource mobilisation. The underlying analytical framework was the Harrod–Domar growth model, linking growth to aggregate investment. This framework was extended in the 1960s to add a foreign exchange constraint in the Chenery–Strout two-gap model. The Harrod–Domar growth model provides the core of the underlying economic paradigm for analysing aid effectiveness at the macro level. Recent work on 'new growth theory', which attempts to endogenise productivity growth, has extended the paradigm and provides the analytical basis for a few recent empirical cross-country studies. These models and their influence are discussed by Erik Thorbecke (Chapter 1), Henrik Hansen and Finn Tarp (Chapter 4), Paul Mosley and Marion Eeckhout (Chapter 5), and Peter Hjertholm, Jytte Laursen, and Howard White (Chapter 15).

There have been many cross-country studies of aid effectiveness based on the simple macro growth models. The underlying causal chain runs from aid to savings to investment to growth. In the 'new growth theory' approach, the investment variable and productivity are assumed to depend on policy and institutional variables. The 'conventional wisdom' based on this work can be summarised as follows.

Results on the impact of aid on aggregate growth are mixed. Some studies find statistically significant links, some do not. The conclusion has been that there is no robust relationship between aid and aggregate growth. The 'micro–macro paradox' builds on this result and makes the stronger statement that while many studies conclude that aid is effective at the project level, no macro impact can be found. An influential recent study by Burnside and Dollar (1997) 'resolves' the paradox by concluding that aid is effective, but only when the macro policy environment is 'right' – a conclusion that supports the 'Washington consensus' view of appropriate development policy.

Henrik Hansen and Finn Tarp (Chapter 4) provide an encyclopaedic review of the cross-country literature. They conclude that the conventional wisdom needs to be qualified:

- Based on a survey of the actual regressions reported in the various studies, they conclude that the weight of empirical evidence is that there is a robust relationship between aid and aggregate growth. The conventional wisdom is based on over-emphasised or misinterpreted studies which have found a negative or insignificant relationship.
- The Burnside–Dollar 'solution' of the micro–macro paradox is statistically delicate, has been contradicted by other recent studies, and cannot be seen as robust.
- There is evidence that the marginal benefit of aid in recipient countries is higher when the policy environment is favourable.
- Non-linear effects between aid and growth appear important, which indicates that there is a need for more work on the underlying theoretical models and causal mechanisms.

There has been continuing debate on using aid effectiveness measures as criteria for the allocation of aid across countries. The 'Washington consensus' view is that more aid should go to countries with good policy environments.

Earlier debates were phrased in terms of allocating aid to countries where its 'marginal productivity' was the highest. It has long been recognised that mechanistic use of such criteria would lead to directing most aid to countries which need it the least. Conversely, aid is probably needed most in countries in which it is least effective. Maximising the marginal productivity of aid with respect to aggregate growth is not the only relevant criterion for aid allocation.

There is certainly merit in more sophisticated versions of arguments for selectivity, but they depend on a more complete understanding of the complex links in particular country circumstances between aid, growth, and development objectives such as poverty reduction. For example, it makes little economic sense to do structural adjustment lending, when the macro policy environment is 'bad' and there is little possibility for policy reform. On the other hand, it may well be possible to design effective modalities that direct aid to improving the situation of malnourished children even when macro imbalances continue. The same may be true for aid for long term institutional and human capacity building

Aid from multi-dimensional perspectives

As we move beyond the macro perspective with its focus on resource mobilisation, aggregate indicators, and macro relationships, we shift to different analytical frameworks. This makes it more difficult to generalise. A wider array of goals, instruments, and socio-economic and political variables and institutions appear on the scene, and it becomes necessary to develop more disaggregated data systems to support the analysis as discussed by Erik Thorbecke (Chapter 1). New issues include: poverty alleviation, inequality, employment, basic human needs, gender equity, macro stability, sustainability, environmental protection, and political and social transformation. Moreover, policy analysis and evaluation of the past performance and future potential role of aid become more subtle, since an intricate web of forces and constraints, which will vary from country to country, have to be considered. Analysis of these issues and their links to foreign aid requires the whole tool box of economics and also draws on other social sciences. There are, however, generalisations and lessons to be drawn from past experience, which most of the chapters in Parts II, III, and IV seek to distil, working within this broader framework.

Aid modalities

There has been a continuing debate in the aid literature on the relative merits of project versus programme aid. In recent years the distinction has become blurred. Paul Mosley and Marion Eeckhout (Chapter 5) document that the project component of aid budgets has declined dramatically from the early 1970s. A variety of other instruments have gradually grown in importance, such as policy-conditioned programme aid (e.g. structural adjustment lending), support for the private sector, NGO support, emergency assistance, and technical assistance and co-operation. There is also a move towards 'sector programme aid', discussed in detail by Ole Mølgård Andersen (Chapter 7). This shift represents an appreciation of the need to exploit synergies and externalities across projects within broad sectors. It can also potentially facilitate donor coordination to achieve an appropriate balance within sectors and across sectors within the economy. An understanding of how a collection of donor supported investment activities are linked within a coherent programme should also facilitate more effective policy dialogue and ownership by the aid recipient. Andersen covers the main issues, many of which are regularly missed in the aid debate, including the potential conflict caused by the dual origins of sector programmes, i.e. as a new way of running projects and as the latest incarnation of programme aid.

Technical co-operation is addressed explicitly by Channing Arndt (Chapter 6), and this aid modality also forms an important part of the analysis of poverty by John Healey and Tony Killick (Chapter 9) and the review of experiences with public sector reforms by Elliot Berg (Chapter 12). Such programmes have largely, and correctly, been phased out in the more successful developing countries, which have achieved the necessary level of knowledge infrastructure. This is not the case in low-income Africa and Asia, where knowledge transfer and institution building remain critical challenges. The authors discuss the many problems and mixed success of technical assistance programmes in the past. They all argue that while much of this critique is valid, it is crucial to expand the effort and find ways to manage this aid modality more effectively in the future. Based on past experience, they also suggest a number of specific ways to do so, recognising that this is a long run endeavour where there are no quick and easy fixes.

Food aid is an important component of aggregate aid flows in many low-income countries, and Bjørg Colding and Per Pinstrup-Andersen (Chapter 8) consider the pros and cons of this modality. Given the economic development focus of this book, they concentrate on project and programme food aid and argue that it can be an effective element of a broader food security strategy. Food aid must, however, be managed in such a way that it does not disrupt local agricultural markets, which would adversely affect poor farmers. They also argue that programme food aid be discontinued in cases where it is not additional – it is an expensive form of resource transfer and should be replaced by more cost-effective aid instruments. Issues of how to link relief to development are taken up by Tony Addison (Chapter 17).

Poverty, gender and the environment

Three chapters deal specifically with the fundamental goal of poverty alleviation and the increasing importance of understanding gender imbalances and the environmental dimension of development. Issues of poverty, income distribution, and basic needs were in focus already in the development debate in the 1970s. They slipped into the background in the 1980s when attention shifted to stabilisation, international financial flows, and structural adjustment. They re-emerged as important issues in the 1990s when old, but pushed-aside concerns were revived. John Healey and Tony Killick (Chapter 9) stress that anti-poverty action is difficult to achieve. The problem is complex and location-specific, with deep roots in the social fabric and distribution of economic and political power.

It is also argued that it is not evident that donors have a comparative advantage in this area, and it is difficult to imagine any aid programme having a significant short run impact on the overall functional and size distributions of income. There are, however, many opportunities where poverty alleviation objectives can be pursued in practice, focusing on programmes in education, health care, nutrition, social safety nets, sanitation, etc. that help ameliorate excesses of poverty and provide a basis for greater inter-generational income mobility in the long run. In their conclusion, Healey and Killick also link up with issues of selectivity, policy conditionality, and partnership. Given the fungible nature of aid resources in this field, donors can do little without domestic ownership and the active co-operation of aid recipients.

Gender as an issue in development economics is related both to the goal of equity between men and women and as an analytical category which is crucial for the understanding of how households operate and allocate resources. As an analytical category, gender analysis should therefore be an integral part of any analysis of how policy interventions – including aid programmes – affect the intra-household distribution of income, food, and leisure. Lisa Richey (Chapter 10) reviews these issues. She traces the different formulations of the 'woman question' and their meanings for development aid, discusses how aid programmes can support the goal of gender equity, and warns that the process of 'mainstreaming' gender analysis carries with it the danger that such concerns will not receive adequate attention. Four general recommendations on how to promote a gender agenda in practice conclude the paper. They range from strengthening gender commitment and support to attitudinal changes to the need for modified monitoring and evaluation procedures.

Environmental concerns entered the development discourse in the 1970s, focusing on issues of global resource depletion and 'Malthusian' population growth scenarios. Since then two strands have emerged. The first relates to global externalities such as global warming, reduced biodiversity, and resource degradation. The second relates to local, within-country, externalities such as soil depletion, degradation of water and other natural resources, and air pollution. These issues are discussed by Rasmus Heltberg and Uffe Nielsen (Chapter 11). They argue that the first kind of externality requires a global policy response with environmental transfers that should not be seen as development aid.

Local environmental problems involve externalities and incomplete markets in which government intervention is required. Aid has a significant role to play in developing countries which lack knowledge and resources to address such challenges effectively. In the past, developed countries polluted first and cleaned later. In many developing countries, with high population densities and fragile resource bases, it is necessary to deal with externalities sooner rather than later. We also now have knowledge about both the effects of environmental degradation and technology to deal with them that were not available in the early stages of modern industrialisation. Aid can play a positive role in transferring this knowledge.

Institutional and systemic reforms, and macro policy

The evolution of government and market institutions is an integral part of the development process. Institutional changes can hinder the development process if they do not take place in a flexible manner in response to emerging needs and priorities. Irma Adelman (Chapter 2) discusses the evolution of government institutions in a long historical perspective. In contrast, Elliot Berg (Chapter 12) reviews the experience with public sector reform initiatives since 1980. He argues that the lack of success in such reforms hinders the development process. In particular, he suggests that public sector reform is a prerequisite for the effective use of aid resources, which largely flow through government agencies. He reviews a number of aid-supported public sector reform initiatives, which have by and large failed, and places responsibility for this situation on both donors and aid-receiving countries.

Institutional development is also important in the private sector. A major theme in the development debate in the 1980s and 1990s has been how to encourage greater reliance on market mechanisms. Mads Kragh, Jørgen Birk Mortensen, Henrik Schaumburg-Müller, and Hans Peter Slente (Chapter 13) discuss a range of initiatives, which donors have taken in the past and could pursue in the future, to enhance the productivity and competitiveness of their private business sectors, including support to the development of private market institutions. They review a number of concrete examples in a variety of countries and conclude that there is a beneficial role for such direct private sector development aid to complement government-to-government aid designed to further the establishment of an enabling environment for private sector activity.

Following the Asian financial crisis there is renewed attention to the problems of inadequate financial systems in developing countries. Jens Kovsted (Chapter 14) reviews past experience with aid designed to strengthen the financial sector. He considers a number of issues: institutional development, modes of government regulation, and the development of new institutions such as micro-finance. He asserts that the combined presence of macroeconomic and social stability and an effective financial system facilitates efficient resource mobilisation and allocation, and therefore promotes growth. He also notes that increased globalisation of world capital markets puts growing pressure on the financial systems of developing countries.

Institutional development of the financial sector is an important part of increasing the capacity for domestic resource mobilisation in developing countries. It facilitates the savings side of the savings-investment gap. The trade balance is the second gap, and the government budget deficit has been introduced into the development literature as a third gap in the three-gap model. Peter Hjertholm, Jytte Laursen, and Howard White (Chapter 15) consider the role of foreign aid focusing on these three gaps. They also warn of potential macroeconomic problems whereby the link between aid flows, savings, and resource allocation gets distorted. At the macro level they note a potential moral hazard problem where the fiscal response to increased aid is to lower the tax effort and hence increase the government deficit. Second, aid may induce an appreciation of the real exchange rate leading to lower exports and higher imports – the Dutch disease. Third, they discuss issues of fungibility whereby aid resources lead to offsetting changes in government expenditure, limiting the net effect on real development expenditure patterns. Fourth, they note that aid in the form of concessional loans still represent a net increase in the stock of debt that must eventually be repaid. Finally, the potential role of aid in the future is discussed with reference to how to close, rather than fill, the three resource gaps.

Broader issues

The chapters in Part IV revisit some of the issues raised in previous chapters, but do so from different perspectives. They also raise additional issues not easily categorised elsewhere, but which are nevertheless important when thinking about the role, effectiveness, and future of foreign aid.

Oliver Morrissey (Chapter 16) discusses aid in the context of a more liberalised world trading environment. The world has seen successive rounds of global trade liberalisation since WWII, and the years since 1980 have seen dramatic shifts from inward-looking to outward-oriented trade strategies in a large number of developing countries, resulting in a greatly increased role for international trade. Trade shares have risen dramatically and the volume of world trade has grown much faster than output. Morrissey notes that not all countries benefit equally from increased trade, and there is evidence that the low-income countries may even lose from further liberalisation. In addition, even if a country gains in the long run, it will experience significant adjustment costs as it restructures its economy in the short to medium run. In addition to global trade liberalisation, many developing countries are joining regional trade agreements. Existing empirical evidence supports the view that this development may be beneficial, especially if a particular agreement incorporates a large, pre-ferably developed country (e.g. NAFTA). Morrissey argues that there are three implications of these trends for aid policy: (i) there is a need to finance adjustment costs, (ii) there is an argument for aid to compensate low-income developing countries that may lose out in the liberalisation process and (iii) support for the establishment of regional trading blocks may be warranted (e.g. the Southern African Development Community).

Emergency aid is an important component of aid flows, and there is increasing interest in devising ways in which such aid can be provided in a forward-looking, development-oriented manner. At the same time, the world has seen the emergence of many regional armed conflicts since the end of the cold war. Tony Addison (Chapter 17) discusses the role of aid before, during, and after armed conflicts break out. During conflicts, aid can play a limited role in humanitarian assistance and help in the transition from war to peace. There are, however, serious problems in operating in wartime environments. Addison notes that aid can complicate conflicts when it falls into the hands of belligerents. After war episodes, aid has a major role to play in very costly reconstruction and rehabilitation efforts. Finally, Addison considers the possibility for using aid to prevent conflict in areas at risk. He argues that we should build foreign policy support to use aid in conflict prevention. Such aid should be focused on reducing poverty and inequality to dampen social tensions and supporting institutions and processes for conflict resolution.

While we have argued that aid efforts should be focused on the poorest countries, most of which are in Africa, past experiences in this region have been disappointing. Ravi Kanbur (Chapter 18) characterises the current nexus of aid conditionality and debt regimes in Africa as dysfunctional. A major source of this situation is the unhealthy relationships between donors and governments in the region. The end of the cold war and the beginning of democratic transitions in African countries make Kanbur tentatively optimistic about future possibilities for aid impact. He lists four factors that will be central: (i) donors must be less intrusive and respectful of govern-ment prerogatives, (ii) donors must be consistent in defining and enforcing the terms of aid agreements, (iii) debt relief is important, and finally (iv) if such reforms lead to a fall off in the volume of aid it is less important than redefining the relationship between donors and aid recipients.

Finally, Raymond Hopkins (Chapter 19) reviews political economy reasons for the declining trend in aid. In addition to the end of the cold war and poor performance discussed above, he adds (i) dying patron–client ties, (ii) tight budgets in donor countries, (iii) smaller pay-offs for special interest groups in developed countries, and (iv) the ascent of a 'neo-liberal' outlook which sees a smaller role for government and seeks reductions in entitlement spending. In exploring the potential sources of support for aid in the future, Hopkins argues that three aid targets can appeal to overlapping domestic and transnational coalitions. These programmes are state strengthening, improved market management, and emergency safety nets. He concludes that in the future a major condition to generate support for aid is a belief in its efficacy. From a political science perspective, however, there are reasons to worry. Many of the potential aid recipients are what he calls 'anarchical states', characterised by terms such as 'patrimonial, shadow, rent-seeking, semi-sovereign, mafia-like and corrupt.' In this environment 'state failure' is the greatest threat to the success of aid. Those countries which need aid the most are precisely those countries where aid may be least effective, in this case for political rather than economic reasons.

Conclusion

There are many general lessons about appropriate development strategies that have emerged from post-WWII experience. We have learnt from both successes and failures, and the development agenda has expanded considerably. While lots of disagreements remain, important elements of consensus now exist about many of the components of successful development strategies. These include:

- development of market institutions, including supporting legal and regulatory structures;
- well-functioning government institutions;
- reliance on market mechanisms, reflecting that the command-economy model is no longer an alternative;
- investment to achieve critical levels of social and physical infrastructure (health, education, transportation, communication, etc.);
- maintaining a stable macroeconomic environment;
- achieving critical levels of resource mobilisation;
- reducing or eliminating gross distortions in incentive systems;
- increased role of foreign trade (both exports and imports);
- potential role of foreign private investment (including issues of short versus long term and portfolio versus direct investment); and
- transfer of knowledge and technology from developed countries.

Developing countries vary widely in initial conditions, which affects their potential for development. There are also trade offs and substitution possibilities among the elements listed above – there are many roads to success. However, these trade offs are undoubtedly not continuous. There are threshold effects and critical minima. There are also externalities and synergies across the different elements. Determining the appropriate balance among these elements and their sequencing over time defines much of the subject matter of modern development economics.

Since the 1950s, foreign aid has been associated with development successes and failures. With hindsight we can see that many of the failures were due to the pursuit of what we now know to have been inappropriate development strategies rather than to any deficiencies in aid modalities and implementation. It is crucial in evaluating the effectiveness of aid programmes to distinguish failures of the aid process from failures of overall development strategy. As an aside, it is worth noting that much of our present knowledge about what works and what does not work in development is based on research sponsored by aid agencies.

There are many examples where aid played a significant part in supporting what turned out to be successful development strategies. In that sense aid has worked, and worked well; and the cross-country evidence shows that on average successes have outweighed failures. Conversely, there are many examples where for various reasons aid has failed to support elements of a correct strategy.

One can distinguish two kinds of aid failure. The first is a failure in aid strategy. In this case, aid is pursued in spite of the fact that we know that it fails to support any of the elements of successful development strategies. Continuing structural adjustment lending to support macro reforms when they are not going to take place in the foreseeable future is an example. Another example is project or programme lending in an environment where the recipient simply diverts fungible aid resources to unproductive or outright harmful uses. The second kind of aid failure relates to aid delivery, including design, modality, or implementation. Examples include transferring inappropriate technology ('white elephants'), and relying on ill-trained technical assistance personnel. Not enforcing conditionality is a failure of implementation – imposing inappropriate conditionality is a strategy failure.

A successful aid programme requires matching one or more elements of a desirable development strategy with an appropriate aid strategy, supported by well designed modalities and effective implementation. A good aid strategy must take account of social and political forces in the recipient country that impinge on the possibility to pursue change. Prioritising among elements of the development strategy is not by itself an aid issue, but rather involves judgements about binding constraints on development. Designing an appropriate aid strategy not only takes account of such priorities, but also considers the feasibility of addressing them through the aid mechanism.

It is often argued that poor countries with good policies should get more aid than ones with mediocre policies. However, in an environment where it is not feasible to improve, for example, macroeconomic management, it may well be feasible and desirable to use aid to support other elements of a successful development strategy, although perhaps with a longer time horizon in mind. Indeed, in the very poor countries, development priority should be given to long run investments in social and physical infrastructure and institutional development. In these countries one should not expect quick fixes.

There is wide agreement that aid should in the future be focused on the poorest countries, which are mostly in Africa and Asia. In these countries, aid programmes have to be designed in an environment where it is difficult to set priorities and much remains unknown. This makes aid risky. One should expect failures and learn from them. The experience of the last 50 years of the twentieth century, however, should lead us to be confident that we will learn and that again successes will predominate.

Part I

Major themes

1 The evolution of the development doctrine and the role of foreign aid, 1950–2000

Erik Thorbecke

Introduction

The economic and social development of the third world, as such, was clearly not a policy objective of the colonial rulers before the Second World War. Such an objective would have been inconsistent with the underlying division of labour and trading patterns within and among colonial blocks. It was not until the end of the colonial system in the late 1940s and 1950s, and the subsequent creation of independent states, that the revolution of rising expectations could start. Thus, the end of the Second World War marked the beginning of a new regime for the less developed countries involving the evolution from symbiotic to inward-looking growth and from a dependent to a somewhat more independent relation *vis-à-vis* the ex-colonial powers. It also marked the beginning of serious interest among scholars and policymakers in studying and understanding better the development process as a basis for designing appropriate development policies and strategies. In a broad sense a conceptual development doctrine had to be built which policymakers in the newly independent countries could use as a guideline to the formulation of economic policies.

The selection and adoption of a development strategy – i.e. a set of more or less interrelated and consistent policies – depend upon three building blocks: (1) the prevailing development objectives which, in turn, are derived from the prevailing view and definition of the development process, (2) the conceptual state of the art regarding the existing body of development theories, hypotheses and models and (3) the underlying data system available to diagnose the existing situation and measure performance. Figure 1.1 illustrates the interrelationships and interdependence which exist between (i) development theories and models, (ii) objectives, (iii) data systems and the measurement of performance and (iv) development policies and strategies. These four different elements are identified in four corresponding boxes in Figure 1.1. At any point in time or for any given period these four sets of elements (or boxes) are interrelated. Thus, it can be seen from Figure 1.1 that the current state of the art, which is represented in the southwest box embracing developments theories, hypotheses

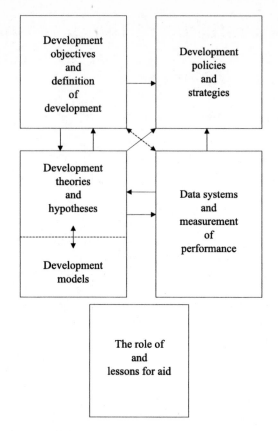

Figure 1.1 Key interrelationships between development theories, models, objectives, data systems, development policies and strategies and the role of and lessons for foreign aid.

and models, affects and is, in turn, affected by the prevailing development objectives – hence the two arrows in opposite directions linking these two boxes. Likewise, data systems emanate from the existing body of theories and models and are used to test prevailing development hypotheses and to derive new ones. Finally, the choice of development policies and strategies is jointly determined and influenced by the other three elements – objectives, theories and data, as the three corresponding arrows indicate.[1]

In turn, the role and function of foreign aid is influenced by and has to be evaluated in the light of the contemporaneous state of the art in each of these four areas. Clearly a deeper and better understanding of the process of development, based on the cumulative experiences of countries following different strategies over time, and empirical inferences derived from these experiences, helps illuminate how foreign aid can best contribute to development.

At the same time it is evident – and is well documented in other chapters of this book – that the socio-economic development of the aid-recipient countries is only one of the objectives of the donor countries. Political and commercial objectives play an important role in the allocation of foreign aid in the programmes of many donor countries. While recognising the role that non-developmental goals play in the allocation of aid, it would be overly cynical to dismiss altogether the developmental benefits of aid – whether they resulted directly from developmental motivation by donors or indirectly, as a side-effect of politically motivated resource transfers. Further-more, a significant part of aid is distributed through multilateral channels and is therefore less susceptible to being influenced by strictly political considerations.

Hence, in this opening chapter we explore how the concept of foreign aid as a contributing factor to the development of the third world evolved historically within the broader framework of development theory and strategy over the course of the last five decades of the twentieth century. The analytical framework presented above and outlined in Figure 1.1 is applied to describe the state of the art that prevailed in each of these five decades and, in particular, how the conception of the role of foreign aid changed as a function of the development paradigm in vogue entering a given decade.

The application of the above framework to the situation that actually existed in each of the last five decades helps to highlight in a systematic fashion the changing conception of the development process. Such an attempt is undertaken next by contrasting the prevailing situation in the 1950s, 1960s, 1970s, 1980s and 1990s, respectively. The choice of the decade as a relevant time period is of course arbitrary and so is, to some extent, an exact determination of what should be inserted in the five boxes in Figure 1.1 for each of the five decades under consideration.[2]

Figures 1.2–6 attempt to identify for each decade the major elements which properly belong in the five interrelated boxes. In a certain sense it can be argued that the interrelationships among objectives, theories and models, data systems and hypotheses and strategies constitute the prevailing development doctrine for a given time period. A brief sequential discussion of the prevailing doctrine in each of the five decades provides a useful way of capturing the evolution that development theories and strategies have undergone and of the changing role of aid. A final section sums up and concludes.

The development doctrine during the 1950s

Economic growth became the main policy objective in the newly independent less developed countries. It was widely believed that through economic growth and modernisation *per se*, dualism and associated income and social inequalities which reflected it would be eliminated. Other economic and social objectives were thought to be complementary to – if not resulting from – GNP growth. Clearly, the adoption of GNP growth as both the objective and yardstick of development was directly related to the conceptual state of the art in the 1950s. The major theoretical contributions which guided the development community during that decade were conceived within a one-sector, aggregate framework and emphasised the role of investment in modern activities. The development economists' tool kit in the 1950s contained such theories and concepts as the 'big push' (Rosenstein-Rodan 1943), 'balanced growth' (Nurkse 1953), 'take-off into sustained growth' (Rostow 1956) and 'critical minimum effort thesis' (Leibenstein 1957) (see Figure 1.2).

What all of these concepts have in common, in addition to an aggregate framework, is equating growth with development and viewing growth in less developed countries as essentially a discontinuous process requiring a large and discrete injection of investment. The 'big push' theory emphasised the importance of economies of scale in overhead facilities and basic industries. The 'take-off' principle was based on the simple Harrod–Domar identity that in order for the growth rate of income to be higher than that of the population (so that per capita income growth is positive) a minimum threshold of the investment to GNP ratio is required given the prevailing capital – output ratio. In turn, the 'critical minimum effect thesis' called for a large discrete addition to investment to trigger a cumulative process within which the induced income-growth forces dominate induced income-depressing forces. Finally, Nurkse's 'balanced growth' concept stressed the external economies inherent on the demand side in a mutually reinforcing and simultaneous expansion of a whole set of complementary production activities which combine together to increase the size of the market. It does appear, in retrospect that the emphasis on large-scale investment in the 1950s was strongly influenced by the relatively successful development model and performance of the Soviet Union between 1928 and 1940.

The same emphasis on the crucial role of investment as a prime mover of growth is found in the literature on investment criteria in the 1950s. The key contributions were (i) the 'social marginal production' criterion (Khan 1951 and Chenery 1953), (ii) the 'marginal per capita investment quotient' criterion (Galenson and Leibenstein 1955) and (iii) the 'marginal growth contribution' criterion (Eckstein 1957).

It became fashionable to use as an analytical framework one-sector models of the Harrod–Domar type which, because of their completely aggregated and simple production functions, with only investment as an element, emphasised, at least implicitly, investment in infrastructure and industry. The one-sector, one-input nature of these models precluded any estimation of the sectoral production effects of alternative investment allocations and of different combinations of factors since it was implicitly assumed that factors could only be combined in fixed proportions with

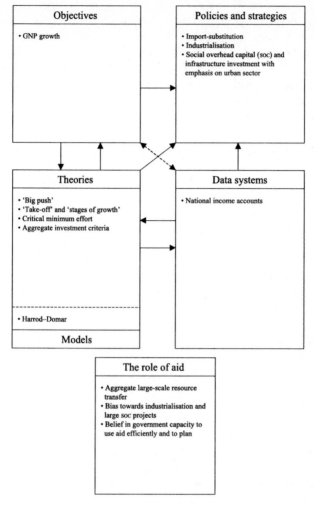

Figure 1.2 Key interrelationships in the 1950s.

investment. In a one-sector world GNP is maximised by pushing the investment ratio (share of investment in GNP) as high as is consistent with balance-of-payments equilibrium. In the absence of either theoretical constructs or empirical information on the determinants of agricultural output, the tendency was to equate the modern sector with high productivity of investment, and thus direct the bulk of investment to the modern sector and to the formation of social overhead capital – usually benefiting the former.

The reliance on aggregate models was not only predetermined by the previously discussed conceptual state of the art but also by the available data system which, in the 1950s, consisted almost exclusively of national income accounts. Disaggregated information in the form of input–output tables appeared in the developing countries only in the 1960s.

The prevailing development strategy in the 1950s follows directly and logically from the previously discussed theoretical concepts. Industrialisation was conceived as the engine of growth which would pull the rest of the economy along behind it. The industrial sector was assigned the dynamic role in contrast to agriculture which was, typically, looked at as a passive sector to be 'squeezed' and discriminated against. More specifically, it was felt that industry, as a leading sector, would offer alternative employment opportunities to the agricultural population, would provide a growing demand for foodstuffs and raw materials, and would begin to supply industrial inputs to agriculture. The industrial sector was equated with high productivity of investment – in contrast with agriculture – and, therefore, the bulk of investment was directed to industrial activities and social overhead projects.[3] To a large extent the necessary capital resources to fuel industrial growth had to be extracted from traditional agriculture.

Under this 'industrialisation-first strategy' the discrimination in favour of industry and against agriculture took a number of forms. First, in a large number of countries, the internal terms-of-trade were turned against agriculture through a variety of price policies which maintained food prices at an artificially low level in comparison with industrial prices. One purpose of these price policies – in addition to extracting resources from agriculture – was to provide cheap food to the urban workers and thereby tilt the income distribution in their favour. Other discriminatory measures used were a minimal allocation of public resources (for both capital and current expenditures) to agriculture and a lack of encouragement given to the promotion of rural institutions and rural off-farm activities. In some of the larger developing countries, such as India and Pakistan, the availability of food aid on very easy terms – mainly under US Public Law 480 – was an additional element which helped maintain low relative agricultural prices.[4]

A major means of fostering industrialisation, at the outset of the development process, was through import substitution – particularly of consumer goods and consumer durables. With very few exceptions the whole gamut of import substitution policies, ranging from restrictive licensing systems, high protective tariffs and multiple exchange rates to various fiscal devices, sprang up and spread rapidly in developing countries. This inward-looking approach to industrial growth led to the fostering of a number of highly inefficient industries.

It should not be inferred that the emphasis on investing in the urban modern sector in import-substituting production activities and physical infrastructure was undesirable from all standpoints. This process did help start industrial development and contributed to the growth of the modern sector. It may even, in some cases, have provided temporary relief to the balance-of-payments constraint. However, by discriminating against exports

– actual and potential – the long-run effects of import substitution on the balance-of-payments may well turn out to have been negative.

Role of foreign aid

The main economic rationale of foreign aid in the 1950s was to provide the necessary capital resource transfer to allow developing countries to achieve a high enough savings rate to propel them into self-sustained growth. The role of aid was seen principally as a source of capital to trigger economic growth through higher investment. Households in poor countries – hovering around the subsistence level – were seen to face the almost impossible task of raising their savings rates to a level sufficient to generate sustained growth rates. As Ruttan (1996) pointed out, in most cases developing areas lacked the physical and human capital to attract private investment so that there did not appear to be any alternative to foreign aid as a source of capital.

Two other interrelated factors made aid attractive as an instrument of growth: first, the faith that governments could plan successfully at the macro level as evidenced by the large number of five-year plans formulated during this period and, second, the simplicity of the Harrod–Domar model to calculate the amount of foreign aid required to achieve a target growth rate. In retrospect it was this totally aggregate planning framework and the focus on industrialisation-first that led to the neglect of the agricultural sector.

In any case, whatever the development rationale of aid in the 1950s, it was clearly already subservient to security objectives in the aid programmes of the US and probably Western Europe. The US aid was intended as a weapon to address the security threat of spreading communism (Ruttan 1996: 70).

The development doctrine during the 1960s

Figure 1.3 captures the major elements of the development doctrine prevailing in the 1960s. On the conceptual front the decade of the 1960s was dominated by an analytical framework based on economic dualism. Whereas the development doctrine of the 1950s implicitly recognised the existence of the backward part of the economy complementing the modern sector, it lacked the dualistic framework to explain the reciprocal roles of the two sectors in the development process. The naive two-sector models following Lewis (1954) continued to assign to subsistence agriculture an essentially passive role as a potential source of 'unlimited labour' and 'agricultural surplus' for the modern sector. It assumed that farmers could be released from subsistence agriculture in large numbers without a consequent reduction in agricultural output while simultaneously carrying their own bundles of food (i.e. capital) on their backs or at least having access to it.

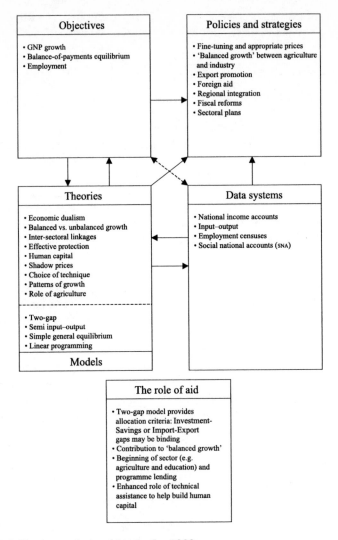

Figure 1.3 Key interrelationships in the 1960s.

As the dual-economy models became more sophisticated, the interdependence between the functions that the modern industrial and backward agricultural sectors must perform during the growth process was increasingly recognised (Fei and Ranis 1964). The backward sector had to release resources for the industrial sector, which in turn had to be capable of absorbing them. However, neither the release of resources nor the absorption of resources, by and of themselves, were sufficient for economic development to take place. Recognition of this active interdependence was a large step forward from the naive industrialisation-first prescription because the above conceptual framework no longer identified either sector as leading or lagging.

A gradual shift of emphasis took place regarding the role of agriculture in development. Rather than considering subsistence agriculture as a passive sector whose resources had to be squeezed in order to fuel the growth of industry and to some extent modern agriculture, it started to become apparent in the second half of the 1960s that agriculture could best perform its role as a supplier of resources by being an active and co-equal partner with modern industry. This meant in concrete terms that a gross flow of resources from industry to agriculture may be crucial at an early stage of development to generate an increase in agricultural output and productivity that would facilitate the extraction of a new transfer out of agriculture and into the modern sector. The trouble with the alternative approach which appears to have characterised the 1950s, of squeezing agriculture too hard or too early in the development process, was described in the following graphic terms: 'The backwards agricultural goose would be starved before it could lay the golden egg.' (Thorbecke 1969: 3).

The 'balanced' versus 'unbalanced' growth issue was much debated during the 1960s. In essence, the balanced growth thesis (Nurkse 1953) emphasised the need for the sectoral growth of output to be consistent with the differential growth of demand for different goods as income rises. Unbalanced growth, on the other hand, identified the lack of decision-making ability in the private and public sectors as the main bottleneck to development (Hirshman 1958). The prescription for breaking through this bottleneck was to create a sequence of temporary excess capacity of social overhead facilities which, by creating a vacuum and an attractive physical environment, would encourage the buildup of directly productive activities. Alternatively, the process could start by a buildup of directly productive activities ahead of demand, which, in turn, would generate a need for complementary social overhead projects.

The similarities between the balanced and unbalanced growth theses are more important than their apparently different prescriptions. Both approaches emphasised the role of inter-sectoral linkages in the development process. In a certain sense they extended the dual-economy framework to a multi-sectoral one without, however, capturing the essential differences in technology and form of organisation between modern and traditional activities. This was at least partially due to the type of sectoral disaggregation available in the existing input–output tables of developing countries during the 1960s. Except for the various branches of industry, the level of sectoral aggregation tended to be very high, with agricultural and service activities seldom broken down in more than two or three sectors. Consequently, any attempt at distinguishing traditional, labour-intensive activities from modern, capital-intensive activities in either agriculture or in service, could not be performed given the classification criteria underlying input–output tables. This example illustrates the interdependence that exists between the prevailing data systems and the conceptual framework in the actual formulation of development plans and strategies. This is an issue which is returned to subsequently.

Another contribution of the late 1960s which was imbedded in inter-sectoral (input–output) analysis is the theory of effective protection, which clarified and permitted the measurements of the static efficiency cost of import substitution when both inputs and outputs are valued at world prices.

Still another important set of contributions that appeared in the 1960s relates to the inter-sectoral structure and pattern of economic growth. Two different approaches provided important insights into the changing inter-sectoral structure of production and demand throughout the process of economic development. The first approach, based largely on the work of Simon Kuznets (1966), relied on a careful and painstaking historical analysis of a large number of countries. The second approach was pioneered by Hollis B. Chenery and based on international cross-sectional analysis which was subjected to regression analysis to derive what appeared to be structural phenomena in the process of growth (Chenery 1960 and Chenery and Taylor 1968).

The models that were designed in the 1960s can be divided into three types: (i) two-gap models, (ii) semi-input–output models and (iii) simple general equilibrium models. The first type tried to incorporate into a macro-economic model the role of foreign aid (Chenery and Strout 1966). The underlying logic of these models is that two independent constraints may limit economic growth. The first constraint on skills and savings, if it were the binding one, is described as the investment-limited growth. Alternatively, when the balance-of-payments constraint is effective, trade limited growth would follow. This is a disequilibrium-type model which assumes that developing countries are characterised by limited structural flexibility – with either the investment–savings gap or the balance-of-payments gap binding at any one point in time.

The other types of models (ii and iii above) rely on an inter-sectoral input–output framework. The semi-input–output method initiated by Jan Tinbergen distinguishes between international sectors which produce tradable foods and national sectors which produce non-tradable goods (Kuyvenhoven 1978). Hence, the required capacity expansion throughout the growth process can be computed for, at least, the non-tradable sectors. The general equilibrium models which appeared in the 1960s were either of a consistency or linear programming type. The main purpose of these models was to throw more light on the inter-sectoral linkages and the effects of alternative sectoral investment allocations on economic growth (Fox *et al.* 1972: ch. 13 and Manne 1974).

The conception of economic development in the 1960s was still largely centred on GNP growth as the key objective. In particular, the relationship between growth and the balance-of-payments was made clearer. Toward the end of this decade the increasing seriousness of the un- and under-employment problem in the developing world led to a consideration of employment as an objective in its own right next to GNP growth. The most noteworthy change in the conception of development was the concern for understanding better the inter-sectoral structure and physiology of the development process – as the preceding review of the conceptual state of the arts revealed.

The development policies and strategies that prevailed in the 1960s flowed directly from the conceptual contributions, development objectives and the data system. These policies fall into a few categories, which are reviewed briefly below. The first set embraces the neoclassical prescription and can be expressed under the heading of 'fine-tuning' and 'appropriate prices'. In a nutshell the 'fine-tuning' instruments embrace the use of an appropriate price system (including commodity, tax and subsidy rates), the removal of market imperfections, and appropriate exchange rate and commercial policies. It was expected that these measures would lead to a more appropriate output-mix between production activities and input-mix, or choice of technique, and thereby generate increased employment.

A second set of policies can be classified as essentially structural, emphasising the importance of inter-sectoral linkages. They include the allocation of investment and current public expenditures among sectors, so as to achieve a process of inter-sectoral balanced (or, in some instances, unbalanced) growth. More specifically, by the late 1960s agriculture was assigned a much more active role in the development process. The provision of a greater level of public resources to that sector – combined with less discriminatory price policies – were expected to result in a growth of output and productivity which would facilitate a net transfer back to the rest of the economy.

Role of foreign aid

The role of foreign aid, in the light of the two-gap models, was considered important in removing either a savings deficiency through an increased flow of foreign savings or a deficit in the current account of the balance-of-payments by providing the necessary foreign exchange. The faith in the capacity of foreign aid to break either one of these constraints appears, in retrospect, to have been somewhat misplaced – not the least because of the large balance-of-payments burden created, over time, by the need to service a cumulative sequence of foreign loans, even at concessionary terms (see Chapter 15). The increasingly binding foreign exchange constraint led to a critical reappraisal of import substitution policies and gradually to the encouragement of a mild form of export promotion, namely through the creation of regional custom areas and common markets. This process of regional integration in the developing world has, so far, been notoriously unsuccessful and may well be moribund by now.

Ruttan (1996: 104) summarised well the two directions in which development thought and foreign aid shifted in the 1960s:

First, shortages in domestic savings and foreign exchange earnings were identified as potentially limiting factors on growth. The counterpart in official policy was to extend programme-type lending to fill the foreign exchange gaps in the less developed countries. A second focus of the 1960s, influenced by the emergence of the dual-economy literature, was on sectoral development and, in the late 1960s, on sector lending for agriculture. As sectoral development processes began to be better understood, the importance of investment in human capital and of policies designed to overcome resource scarcities through technical assistance began to be appreciated.

The development doctrine in the 1970s

Figure 1.4 summarises the major development objectives, theories, data sources and policies prevailing in the 1970s. By the 1970s the seriousness of a number of development problems and issues, combined with the failure of a GNP-oriented development strategy to cope successfully with these problems in a number of developing countries, led to a thorough re-examination of the process of economic and social development. The major development problems that became acute and could no longer be ignored during this decade can be summarised briefly as: (i) the increasing level and awareness of un- and underemployment in a large number of developing countries, (ii) the tendency for income distribution within countries to have become more unequal or, at least, to have remained as unequal as in the immediate post-WWII period, (iii) the maintenance of a very large, and perhaps rising, number of individuals in a state of poverty, i.e. below some normative minimum income level or standard of living, (iv) the continuing and accelerating rural–urban migration and consequent urban congestion and finally (v) the worsening external position of much of the developing world reflected by increasing balance-of-payments pressures and rapidly mounting foreign indebtedness and debt servicing burdens. Largely as a consequence of these closely interrelated problems a more equal income distribution, particularly in terms of a reduction in absolute poverty, was given a much greater weight in the preference function of most developing countries compared with the objective of aggregate growth *per se*. Furthermore, this reduction in absolute poverty was to be achieved mainly through increased productive employment (or reduced underemployment) in the traditional sectors.

By the mid-1970s, GNP as a dominant all-encompassing objective had been widely, but by no means universally, dethroned. The presumption that aggregate growth is synonymous with economic and social development or, alternatively, that it will ensure the attainment of all other development objectives, came under critical scrutiny and was rejected in many circles.

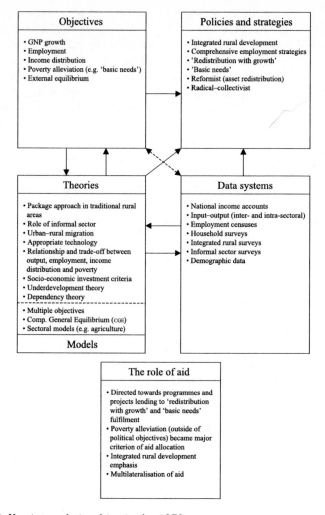

Figure 1.4 Key interrelationships in the 1970s.

The changing meaning of development as a process that should have as simultaneous objectives growth and poverty alleviation, both influenced and was influenced by a number of conceptual and empirical contributions. The first set of contributions comes under the rubric of integrated rural and agricultural development. A whole series of empirical studies at the micro- and macro-levels combined to provide an explanation of the physiology and dynamics of the transformation process of traditional agriculture. This body of knowledge provided a rationale for a unimodal strategy in the rural areas, which is discussed subsequently under the strategy box.

A second important concept that appeared in the 1970s is that of the 'informal sector'. Even though this concept had been around a long time and taken a variety of forms, such as Gandhi's emphasis on traditional cottage industries, it became revitalised in a more general and formal sense in the Kenya Report of International Labour Organization (ILO 1973). A number of case studies undertaken by ILO focusing specifically on the role of the informal sector concluded that it is relatively efficient, dynamic, and often strongly discriminated against as a result of market imperfections or inappropriate national or municipal regulations. These studies suggested that the informal activities represent an important potential source of output and employment growth.

A third contribution which surfaced in the 1970s includes the inter-dependence between economic and demographic variables and the determinants of the rural–urban migration. A number of empirical studies, mainly at the micro level, attempted to throw some light on the relation-ship between such sets of variables as (i) education, nutrition and health and (ii) fertility, infant mortality and, ultimately, the birth rate. The hypotheses that were generated by these studies highlighted the complex nature of the causal relationship between population growth and economic development.

With regard to the determinants of migration, the initial Harris–Todaro (1970) formulation triggered a series of empirical studies and simple models of the migration process. In general, migration was explained as a function of urban–rural wage differentials weighted by the probability of finding urban employment.

A somewhat parallel set of contributions at the micro-level consists of the attempt to incorporate socio-economic objectives – such as employment and income distribution – among investment criteria and in the appraisal and selection of projects (Little and Mirrlees 1974).

A review of contributions to the state of the art in development econo-mics would not be complete without at least a reference to the neo-marxist literature on underdevelopment and dependency theories. The essence of these theories is that underdevelopment is intrinsic in a world trading and power system in which the developing countries make up the backward, raw-material-producing periphery and the developed countries the modern industrialised centres. A neo-colonial system of exploitation by indigenous classes associated with foreign capital (e.g. multinational corporations) is considered to have replaced the previous colonial system.

After this review of major contributions to development theory, only a few words need be said about the nature of models which appeared in the 1970s. A major characteristic of these models was to explain, at the sectoral and multi-sectoral levels, the simultaneous determination of output, employment and income distribution. Most of these models were partial in the sense that they did not capture the complete interdependence among these variables.

The coverage and quality of the data available improved substantially in the 1970s as compared to the previous decades. By the mid-1970s, survey-type information on variables such as employment, income, consumption and saving patterns were becoming available. A variety of surveys covering such diverse groups as urban, informal and rural households started to provide valuable information on the consumption and savings behaviour of different socio-economic groups. In a number of developing countries it became possible, for the first time, to estimate approximately the income distribution by major socio-economic groups.

After having reviewed the changing development objectives, conceptual contributions and data sources which marked the 1970s, the next logical step is to describe and analyse briefly the new development strategies that emerged. From a belief that growth was a necessary and sufficient condition for the achievement of economic and social development, it became increasingly recognised that even though necessary, growth might not be sufficient. The first step in the broadening process of moving from a single to multiple development objectives was a concern with, and incorporation of, employment in development plans and in the allocation of foreign aid to projects and technical assistance.

One possible attraction of using employment as a target was that it appeared, on the surface, to be relatively easily measurable – in somewhat the same sense as the growth rate of GNP had previously provided a simple scalar measure of development. The real and fundamental issue was an improvement in the standards of living of all groups in society and, in particular, that of the poorest and most destitute groups.

Two partially overlapping variants of a distributionally oriented strategy surfaced during this decade. These were 'redistribution with growth' and 'basic needs'. The first one was essentially incremental in nature, relying on the existing distribution of assets and factors and requiring increasing investment transfers in projects (mostly public but perhaps even private) benefiting the poor (Chenery *et al.* 1974). The first step in this strategy was the shift in the preference (welfare) function away from aggregate growth *per se* toward poverty reduction. This strategy, which was favoured by the World Bank, focused on the redistribution of at least the increments of capital formation in contrast with the initial stock of assets. Since the bulk of the poor are located in the rural sector and the informal urban sector, this strategy had to be directed toward increasing the productivity of the small farmers and landless workers and making small-scale producers (mainly self-employed) in the informal urban sector more efficient.

The second alternative strategy inaugurated during the 1970s was the basic needs strategy, which was particularly advocated by the ILO.[5] It entailed structural changes and some redistribution of the initial ownership of assets – particularly land reform – in addition to a set of policy instruments, such as public investment. Basic needs, as objectives defined by ILO, include two elements: (i) certain minimal requirements of a family for private consumption, such as adequate food, shelter and clothing and (ii) essential services provided by and for the community at large, such as safe drinking water, sanitation, health and educational facilities.

A third type of development strategy follows from the neo-marxist under-development and dependency theories, which have been previously touched upon. This approach is radical, if not revolutionary, in nature. It calls for a massive redistribution of assets to the state and the elimination of most forms of private property. It appears to favour a collectivistic model – somewhat along the lines of the Chinese example – based on self-reliance and the adoption of indigenous technology and forms of organisation.

Role of foreign aid

The launching of the World Employment Programme by the ILO in 1969 signalled that the primary objective of aid should be to raise the standard of living of the poor through increased employment opportunities. The generation of new or greater productive opportunities was considered a means toward the improvement of the welfare of the poor.

Under the impetus of applied research undertaken under the auspices of ILO's World Employment Programme and the World Bank, focused on such issues as the relationship between population growth and employ-ment; appropriate labour-intensive technologies; the relationships between the educational system and the labour market and employment and income distribution; the informal sector; the determinants of rural–urban migra-tion and the role of traditional agriculture in the development process.

The fruits of the highly applied research endeavour encouraged and, ultimately, led to a fundamental re-examination of the function and goal of foreign aid. As Brown (1990: 115–6) put it,

> If development was no longer so closely identified with economic growth then aid should not be perceived so exclusively as a source of domestic and external savings. A greater focus on poverty, and on people's welfare in general, would require new types of investment and new forms of intervention.

The World Bank and USAID – two major donors – became very vocal in their advocacy of anti-poverty programmes. The major changes in their foreign aid strategies took two forms: first, a shift away from investment projects in power, transport and telecommunications and toward projects in agriculture and rural development and social services including housing, education and health (Brown 1990); and second, a much greater emphasis on direct interventions to benefit the poor and on technical assistance projects. Examples of direct interventions include food for the mal-nourished, mass inoculation programmes, adult literacy campaigns and credit provision for small farmers.

Thus, increasingly in the rural areas, aid was combined into a package of capital and technical assistance projects constituting integrated rural development programmes. This process of integrated rural development became even more successful as it was linked to the dissemination of the green revolution technology. In a nutshell, the new approach centred on lending and technical activities benefiting directly the traditional sector. This aid strategy conformed to a broader so-called unimodal agricultural development strategy (Johnston and Kilby 1975). The latter relied on the widespread application of labour-intensive technology to the whole of agriculture. In this sense, it was based on the progressive modernisation of agriculture 'from the bottom up'. This strategy can be contrasted with a bimodal strategy, which encourages the growth of the modern, commercial, large-scale, relatively capital-intensive sub-sector of agriculture while ignoring for all practical purposes the traditional subsistence sub-sector. Under the unimodal approach, agricultural development was spread relatively evenly over the mass of the people through a combination of appropriate agricultural research and technology, land redistribution, the provision of rural infrastructure, the growth of rural institutions and other measures.

In both instances (i.e. mono-type anti-poverty direct interventions and integrated rural development packages), the participation and involvement of the poor was considered an almost necessary condition of sustainability.

The shift in emphasis toward poverty-alleviation aid is evidenced by the share of poverty-oriented lending rising from 5 per cent of the total in 1968–70 to 30 per cent in 1981–3. Also, a relatively new instrument of channelling aid – sector loans (particularly to agriculture and education) – became more extensively used.

The development doctrine in the 1980s

A combination of events including an extremely heavy foreign debt burden – reflecting the cumulative effects of decades of borrowing and manifested by large and increasing balance-of-payments and budget deficits in most of the developing world – combined with higher interest rates and a recession in creditor countries, changed radically the development and aid environment at the beginning of the 1980s. The Mexican financial crisis of 1982 soon spread to other parts of the third world. The magnitude of the debt crisis was such that, at least for a while, it brought into question the survival of the international financial system.

Suddenly, the achievement of external (balance-of-payments) equilibrium and internal (budget) equilibrium became the overarching objectives and necessary conditions to the restoration of economic growth and poverty alleviation. The debt crisis converted the 1980s into the 'lost development decade'. Before the development and poverty alleviation path could be resumed, the third world had to put its house in order and implement painful stabilisation and structural adjustment policies.

Notwithstanding the fact that the development process was temporarily blocked and most of the attention of the development community was focused on adjustment issues, some important contributions to development theory were made during this decade (see Figure 1.5).

The first one greatly enriched our understanding of the role of human capital as a prime mover of development. The so-called endogenous growth school (Lucas 1988 and Romer 1990) identifies low human capital endowment as the primary obstacle to the achievement of the potential scale economies that might come about through industrialisation. In a societal production function, raw (unskilled) labour and capital were magnified by a term representing human capital and knowledge, leading to increasing returns. This new conception of human capital helped convert technical progress from an essentially exogenously determined factor to a partially endogenously determined factor. Progress was postulated to stem from two sources: (i) deliberate innovations, fostered by the allocation of resources (including human capital) to research and development (R&D) activities and (ii) diffusion, through positive externalities and spillovers from one firm or industry to know-how in other firms or industries (Ray 1998: ch. 4). If investment in human capital and know-how by individuals and firms is indeed subject to increasing returns and externalities, it means that the latter do not receive the full benefits of their investment resulting, consequently, in under-investment in human capital (the marginal social productivity of investment in human capital being larger than that of the marginal private productivity). The market is likely to under-produce human capital and this provides a rationale for the role of the government in education and training.

A second contribution based on a large number of quantitative and qualitative empirical studies – relying on international cross-sectional and country-specific analyses of performance over time – was the robust case made for the link between trade and growth. Outward-orientation was significantly and strongly correlated with growth. Countries that liberalised and encouraged trade grew faster than those that followed a more inward-looking strategy. The presumed mechanism linking export orientation to growth is based on the transfer of state of the art technology normally required to compete successfully in the world market for manufactures. In turn, the adoption of frontier technology by firms adds to the human capital of those workers and engineers through a process of 'learning-by-doing' and 'learning-by-looking' before spilling over to other firms in the same industry and ultimately across industries. In this sense, export orientation is a means of endogenising and accelerating technological progress and growth. Furthermore, to the extent that outward orientation in developing countries normally entails a comparative advantage in labour-intensive manufactures, there is much evidence, based on the East and Southeast Asian experience, that the growth path that was followed was also equitable – resulting in substantial poverty alleviation.

A third set of contributions that surfaced in the 1980s can be broadly catalogued under the heading of the 'new institutional economics' and

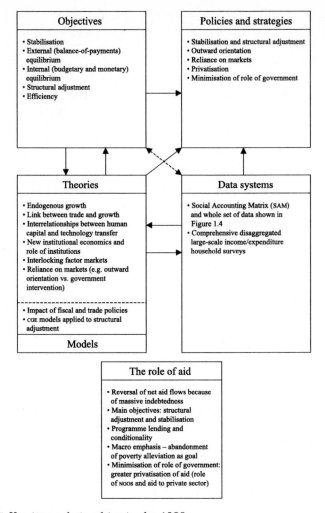

Figure 1.5 Key interrelationships in the 1980s.

collective action (North 1990, Williamson 1991 and Nabli and Nugent 1989). As de Janvry *et al.* (1993: 565) noted, 'The main advance was to focus on strategic behavior by individuals and organised groups in the context of incomplete markets. The theories of imperfect and asymmetrical information and, more broadly, transaction costs gave logic to the role of institutions as instruments to reduce transactions costs.' The neo-institutional framework, in addition to reminding the development community that appropriate institutions and rules of the game are essential to provide pro-development and anti-corruption incentives, also suggested broad guidelines in building institutions that reduced the scope for opportunistic behaviour.

Another contribution of this approach was to provide a clear rationale for the existence of efficient non-market exchange configurations, particularly in the rural areas. Prototypical examples of such institutions include intra-farm household transactions; two-party contracts (e.g. sharecropping and interlinked transactions), farmers' co-operatives and group organisations, mutual insurance networks and informal credit institutions (Thorbecke 1993). Those exchange non-market configurations – called agrarian institutions by Bardhan (1989) – owe their existence to lower transaction costs than those that would prevail in an alternative market configuration providing an equivalent good, factor or service. In most instances market imperfections or, at the limit, market failure (in which case there is no alternative market configuration and transaction costs become infinite) are at the origin of non-market configurations.

A final contribution worth noting – which can be subsumed under the 'new institutional economies' heading – is that of interlinked transactions (Bardhan 1989). An interlinked contract is one in which two or more interdependent exchanges are simultaneously agreed upon (e.g. when a landlord enters into a fixed-rent agreement with a tenant and also agrees to provide credit at a given interest rate). In a more general sense, this type of contract leads to interlocking factor markets for labour, credit and land. In retrospect it is somewhat ironical that during a decade dominated by a faith in the workings of markets – as is discussed subsequently – important theoretical contributions were made that highlighted market imperfections and failures.

Some important contributions to general equilibrium modelling appeared during the 1980s (Dervis *et al.* 1982). These models – calibrated on a base year Social Accounting Matrix (SAM) reflecting the initial (base year) socio-economic structure of the economy – proved particularly useful in tracing through the impact of a variety of exogenous shocks and policies (such as a devaluation, trade liberalisation and fiscal reforms) on the income distribution by socio-economic household groups.

Computable General Equilibrium (CGE) models became an important tool to simulate the disaggregated impact of structural adjustment policies on growth and equity. In fact, these models provided the only means to compare the impact of adjustment scenarios with the counterfactual of no- or limited-adjustment scenarios. Since most applied CGEs were built in the 1990s, they are discussed in the next section.

The 1980s witnessed a proliferation of statistical information on a variety of dimensions of development and the welfare of households. Besides more elaborate and disaggregated employment, manufacturing, agricultural and demographic surveys and censuses, large-scale household income and expenditure surveys produced by statistical offices of most developing countries – and often designed and funded by the World Bank (e.g. the Living Standard Measurement Surveys) – became available to analysts and policymakers. Perhaps for the first time, reasonably reliable and robust observations could be derived relating to the magnitude of poverty, the characteristics of the poor and the inter-household income distribution. In turn, the various data sources could be combined to build SAMs of a large number of countries.

The development strategy of the 1970s – centred on redistribution with growth and fulfilment of basic needs – was replaced by an adjustment strategy. The magnitude of the debt crisis and the massive internal and external disequilibrium faced by most countries in Africa and Latin America and some in Asia, meant that adjustment became a necessary (although not sufficient) condition to a resumption of development.

The main policy objective of third world governments became macro-economic stability, consisting of a set of policies to reduce their balance-of-payments deficits (e.g. devaluation) and their budget deficits (through retrenchment). Whereas stabilisation *per se* was meant to eliminate or reduce the imbalance between aggregate demand and aggregate supply, both externally and internally, structural adjustment was required to reduce distortions in relative prices and other structural rigidities that tend to keep supply below its potential. A typical adjustment package consisted of measures such as a devaluation, removal of artificial price distortions, trade liberalisation and institutional changes at the sector level.

Complementary elements of the prevailing adjustment strategy of the 1980s included outward orientation, reliance on markets and a minimisation of the role of the government. The outward orientation was meant to encourage exports and industrialisation in labour-intensive consumer goods. In turn, to achieve competitiveness in exports, vintage technology would have to be imported, which would trigger the endogenous growth processes described previously, i.e. investment in the human capital and knowledge of workers and engineers employing those technologies and subsequent spillover effects.

Under the influence of ideological changes in the Western World (e.g. the Reagan and Thatcher administrations) developing countries were strongly encouraged – if not forced – to rely on the operation of market forces and in the process to minimise government activities in most spheres – not just productive activities.

Inherent contradictions and conflicts arose among the elements of the broad adjustment strategy of the 1980s. The successful implementation of adjustment policies called for a strong government. Likewise, the rationale for a larger role of government in the education sphere to generate the social spillover effects and counteract the under-investment in education by private agents, which do not capture the positive externalities of their investment, ran counter to the objective of a minimalist state.

Another conflict was caused by the stabilisation goal of reducing the balance-of-payments disequilibrium, while simultaneously liberalising trade – mainly through elimination of quantitative restrictions and reduction and harmonisation of tariff rates. The latter measures would invariably lead to a significant rise in imports that would make it more difficult to restore balance-of-payment equilibrium. Here again, the successful implement-ation of somewhat conflicting measures called for a strong state.

Role of foreign aid

With the advent of the debt crisis and the debt overhang (discussed in Chapter 15), the role and conception of foreign aid changed in a funda-mental way. The primary purpose of aid became (i) a stop-gap measure to salvage the shaky international financial system – by allowing third world debtor countries to service at least part of their public and private debt and keep their creditors afloat – and (ii) to encourage the implementation of appropriate adjustment policies through conditionality attached to programme lending. The costs of servicing outstanding debt obligations of the developing countries (their total long-term debt was estimated at $1 trillion at the end of the 1980s) became so substantial that they tended to dwarf the inflows of concessional funds – leading to a net reverse flow (from the developing to the developed world) reaching about $15 billion annually during 1987–9 (Brown 1990: 132).

Nonetheless, the somewhat self-serving flow of aid from the rich coun-tries helped avoid, at least temporarily, the collapse of the financial system. In contrast, the conditionality strategy was only partially successful in 'buying' good policies – as is discussed in more detail in the next section.

In this decade, characterised by pro-market and anti-government rhetoric, there was strong sentiment to do away with aid altogether and have private capital flows substitute for it. Thus, in the early 1980s, the Reagan adminis-tration created a fertile environment for conservative critics of foreign aid who felt that 'economic assistance distorts the free operation of the market and impedes private-sector development.' (Ruttan 1996: 143). Clearly, the debt overhang put a damper on going too far in eliminating aid. Both public and private creditors in the industrialised world had too much at stake. Furthermore, private capital was not going to flow to African and Latin American countries until some modicum of macroeconomic equilibrium had been restored. In the meantime, there was an effort in many donor countries to privatise aid through channelling greater flows to NGOs and the private sector.

The development doctrine in the 1990s

In the first half of the 1990s, stabilisation and adjustment were still the dominant objectives (see Figure 1.6). While most of the Latin American countries (and the few Asian countries affected by the debt crisis) had gone through a painful adjustment process and were back on a growth path, the overall situation was still one of stagnation – largely caused by poor gover-nance in sub-Saharan Africa and most transition economies in Eastern

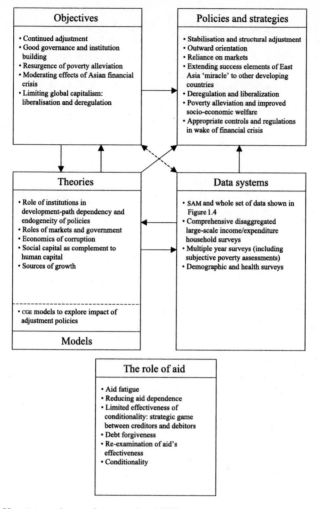

Figure 1.6 Key interrelationships in the 1990s.

Europe. It was becoming increasingly clear to the development community that fundamental and deep-rooted institutional changes to reduce corruption and facilitate a successful transition from socialism and command economies to market economies were a precondition to successful adjustment and a resumption of development in Eastern Europe and sub-Saharan Africa. Potentially the institutions and policies at the root of the East Asian 'miracle' could provide the model to follow.

In the second half of the 1990s the Asian financial crisis hit East and Southeast Asia with a vengeance, resulting in a sharp reversal of the long-term poverty reduction trend. Simultaneously socio-economic conditions deteriorated so drastically in the former Soviet Republics that poverty alleviation in its broadest sense – including improvements in health, nutrition, education, access to information and to public goods and a participation in decision-making – resurfaced as the major, if not over-arching, objective of development assistance. This conception of aid was strongly and unambiguously expressed by the President of the World Bank on numerous occasions in the recent past.

Another consequence of the financial crisis was to bring into question the Washington and IMF consensus of unbridled capital and trade liberalisation and complete deregulation of the financial system. A number of East and Southeast Asian countries are still suffering from the extreme deregulation of the banking sector and capital flows that weakened the supervisory and monitoring functions of central banks and other institutions. The international monetary and financial system that still relies on the outdated Bretton Woods rules of the game needs major revamping and a new set of rules befitting the contemporaneous environment. In the meantime, a number of affected countries are restoring controls on an *ad hoc* basis.

The conceptual contribution to development theory in the 1990s, in general, extended and further elaborated on earlier concepts. Perhaps the most fundamental issue that was debated during the 1990s is the appro-priate roles of the state and the market, respectively, in development. An inherently related issue is to identify the set of institutions most conducive to the acceleration of the process of economic growth and socio-economic development. Prior to the onset of the Asian financial crisis it was felt that the mix of institutions and policies adopted by the East Asian countries that gave rise to the East Asian miracle (World Bank 1993a) provided a broad model, with parts of it potentially transferable to other developing countries. The financial crisis led to a more sceptical appraisal – even whether the miracle, after all, was not a 'myth'.

In any case, the reliance on government actions in the previous decades to promote industrial growth on the part of East Asian countries (par-ticularly South Korea) appeared suspect and came under heavy criticism. Some critics argued that the already impressive growth performance would have been even better with less government intervention – and that even if those industrial policies had contributed to growth they required a strong state, an element sorely missing in other parts of the third world.

While the debate on the proper mix between the degree of government intervention and reliance on markets is still very much alive, the neo-institutional and public choice schools have helped clarify how the state can affect development outcomes. This can be done in a number of ways: (i) by providing a macroeconomic and microeconomic incentive environment conducive to efficient economic activity, (ii) by providing the institutional infrastructure – property rights, peace, law and order and rules – that encourages long-term investment and (iii) by insuring the delivery of basic education, health care and infrastructure required for economic activity (Commander *et al.* 1996).

Institutional capability as evaluated from the standpoint of entrepreneurs depends, in turn, on such indicators as predictability of rule-making, perception of political stability, crime against persons and property, reliability of judicial enforcement and freedom from corruption (Brunetti *et al.* 1997 and Chhibber 1998).

The role of institutions as a precondition to following a successful development path becomes even more critical if one subscribes to the new approach to political economy that takes institutions as largely given exogenously and argues that policies tend to be determined *endogenously* within a specific institutional context (Persson and Tabellini 1990). Thus, for example, if the central bank and the ministry of finance are not independent or are operating under loose discretionary rules, the monetary and fiscal policies that result will depend on political and social factors (or according to the political power of the different lobbies in society and the public choice formulation).

Two additional contributions worth highlighting in this decade are the concept of social capital and a better understanding of sources of growth (total factor productivity) and the need to explain the residual. Social capital was devised as a concept to complement human capital. If individuals are socially excluded, or marginalised, or systematically discriminated against, they cannot rely on the support of networks from which they are sealed off. Alternatively, membership in group organisations brings about benefits that can take a variety of forms (e.g. the provision of informal credit and help in the search for employment). The acquisition of social capital by poor households is particularly important as a means to help them escape the poverty trap.

The spectacular growth of East Asian countries prior to 1997 renewed the interest in identifying, explaining and measuring the sources of growth. Recent studies tended to demystify the East Asian miracle by suggesting that the rapid growth of these economies depended on resource accumulation with little improvement in efficiency and that such growth was not likely to be sustainable (Krugman 1994, Kim and Lau 1994 and Young 1995). This conclusion was based on estimates of total factor productivity (TFP) growth and depends crucially on the form of the production function used and on an accurate measurement of the capital and labour inputs. Whatever residual is left over is ascribed to technological progress. Some critics argue that typical TFP calculations significantly underestimate organisational improvements within firms or what Leibenstein calls x-efficiency.

The 1990s witnessed an increased interest in CGE-models used to simulate the impact of exogenous shocks and changes in policies on the socio-economic system and particularly income distribution. A key issue explored in those models was that of the impact of adjustment policies on income distribution and poverty. The general equilibrium models provide the only technique to compare the impact of alternative (counterfactual) policy scenarios, such as a comparison of the effects of an adjustment programme versus a counterfactual non-adjustment programme (e.g. Thorbecke 1991 for Indonesia and Sahn *et al.* 1996 for Africa).

This decade was marked by a proliferation of statistical information relating particularly to the socio-economic characteristics and welfare of households – in addition to the more conventional data sources previously collected (see data box in Figure 1.6). A large number of quantitative poverty assessments based on household expenditure surveys were completed, as well as more qualitative participatory poverty assessments. Furthermore the availability of demographic and health surveys for many developing countries provided information on health and nutritional status, assets and access to public goods and services to supplement information on household consumption. Also, perhaps for the first time, the availability of multiple-year surveys and panel data for many countries allowed reliable standard of living and welfare comparisons to be made over time.

In many respects, the development strategy of the 1990s was built upon the foundations of the preceding decade and retained most of the latter's strategic elements – at least in the first half of the decade. However, as the decade evolved, the adjustment-based strategy of the 1980s came under critical scrutiny that led to major changes – particularly in the wake of the Asian financial crisis.

In sub-Saharan Africa, the great majority of the countries were still facing serious adjustment problems. A widely debated issue was whether adjustment policies *per se* without complementary reforms – within the context of Africa – could provide the necessary initial conditions for a take-off into sustained growth and poverty alleviation. Two conflicting approaches to adjustment and diagnoses of its impact on performance were put forward. The 'orthodox' view, best articulated by the World Bank (at the beginning of the decade but subsequently modified), argued that an appropriate stabilisation and adjustment package pays off. Countries that went further in implementing that package experienced a turnaround in their growth rate and other performance indicators.

In contrast, the 'heterodox' approach – best articulated by the concept of 'adjustment with a human face', embraced by the Unicef (see Cornia *et al.* 1987) – while supporting the need for adjustment, argued that the orthodox reforms focus extensively on short-term stabilisation and do not address effectively the deep-rooted structural weaknesses of African economies that are the main causes of macro instability and economic stagnation. Accordingly, major structural changes and institutional changes are needed to complement adjustment policies to induce the structural transformation (such as industrialisation, diversification of the export base, the build-up of human capital and even land reform) without which sustainable long-term growth in Africa (and by extension in other developing countries facing similar initial conditions) is not possible.

The Unicef and heterodox critical evaluation of the impact of adjustment policies on long-term growth and poverty alleviation – even when it was not appropriately justified on empirical grounds – sensitised multilateral and bilateral donors to the need to focus significantly more on the social dimensions of adjustment. It made a strong case for the implementation of a whole series of complementary and reinforcing reforms, ranging from greater emphasis on and investment in human capital and physical infrastructure to major institutional changes – particularly in agriculture and industry – benefiting small producers. In turn, the orthodox approach has made a convincing case that appropriately implemented adjustment policies are not only a necessary condition to the restoration of macroeconomic equilibrium but can also contribute marginally to economic growth and poverty alleviation, in the short run.

In 1993, the World Bank published a very influential report on the East Asian miracle (World Bank 1993a). The report analysed the success elements of the high performing Asian economies and argued that many of them were potentially transferable to other developing countries. In brief, these success elements consisted of (i) sound macroeconomic foundations and stable institutions aiming at a balanced budget and competitive exchange rates, (ii) technocratic regimes and political stability that provided policy credibility and reduced uncertainty – an important factor for foreign investors, (iii) an outward (export) orientation, (iv) reliance on markets, (v) a more controversial set of industrial policies with selective government interventions often using 'contests' among firms as proxy to competition, (vi) high rates of investment in building human capital, (vii) high physical investment rates, (viii) a process of technology acquisition consistent with dynamic comparative advantage and (ix) a smooth demographic transition. In particular, the outward orientation, encouraging exports was applauded as a means of acquiring state of the art technology which in turn would trigger a 'learning-by-doing' and 'by-looking' (e.g. reverse engineering) process that would lead to spillover effects on human capital and positive externalities among firms within an industry and among industries.

The East Asian miracle also provided a convincing example of the essential importance of sound institutions (such as the balanced budget presidential decree in effect in Indonesia between 1967 and 1997) as preconditions to a sustainable process of growth with equity. The absence of institutions appropriate to a smooth transition from command to market economies in much of Eastern Europe and the fragility of existing institutions in much of sub-Saharan Africa provide painful counter examples of the enormous human costs of a weak institutional framework.

The Asian financial crisis that wrought havoc to much of East and Southeast Asia in 1997, forced a critical re-examination of an international trade and financial system based on excessive trade and capital liberalisation and financial deregulation. The large increase in the incidence of poverty that followed in the wake of the crisis sensitised the development community to again focus on poverty alleviation and improvements in the socio-economic welfare of vulnerable households as the overarching objective of development. Thus, at the end of the decade, the World Bank made it clear that poverty reduction – in its broadest sense – measured in terms of outcomes (e.g. health, education, employment, access to public goods and services and social capital) rather than inputs was the primary goal to strive for.

The crisis also triggered a re-examination of the role of government in protecting the economy from major shocks originating abroad (see Chapter 2). In particular, it pointed towards strengthening financial institutions and the provision of the minimum set of rules and regulations (e.g. improved monitoring and supervision of the banking sector) to reduce corruption and speculative borrowing from abroad; and the establishment of institutional safety nets that could act as built-in-stabilisers following a crisis.

Role of foreign aid

The decade of the 1990s was marked by a strong and lingering case of 'aid fatigue' evidenced by the absolute decline in net disbursements of official development assistance (ODA) after 1992 and the decline in the net ODA disbursements expressed as a ratio of donor GNP from 0.38 per cent in 1982 to 0.22 per cent in 1997. Private flows had largely replaced aid flows with the share of the former to net disbursement of ODA plus private flows rising from 26 per cent in 1987–92 to 55 per cent in 1993–7. Simultaneously, the sectoral composition of foreign aid switched towards a significantly larger proportion channelled to social infrastructure and services (e.g. education, health, water supply and sanitation) and economic infrastructure and away from productive sectors.

The above trends (considered in more detail in Chapter 3) reflected the strong faith in the operation of markets and scepticism regarding governments' (both aid donors and recipients) involvement in productive sectors such as agriculture and industry. Fatigue was also influenced by the rising fear that foreign aid was generating aid dependency relationships in poor countries and, as such, would have the same type of negative incentive effects that welfare payments have on needy households whose recipients might be discouraged from job searching.

A related issue that was critically debated in the 1990s was that of the effectiveness of aid conditionality (see also Chapter 18). First of all, given fungibility, is it really possible to use aid to 'buy' good policies, or even a sound programme of public (current and capital) expenditures from aid recipients? From the standpoint of the political economy of external aid, structural adjustment can be looked at as a bargaining process between bilateral and multilateral donors on the one hand, and debtor governments on the other. Both sides may have a vested interest in following soft rules in their lending and borrowing behaviour, respectively. This tends to foster and continue a dependency relationship that may well be fundamentally inconsistent with a viable long-term development strategy for the recipient countries (particularly in sub-Saharan Africa). The process of extending aid can be modelled as a strategic game in which the 'bureaucratic' interests of international organisations and the 'political' interests of the national governments are far from being contradictory. As Lafay and Lecaillon (1993: 13) indicated, 'each of the participants in their negotiation has a direct interest in defining a conditionality that is both economically effective and politically feasible.'

The conditionality debate fuelled a number of econometric studies of aid's effectiveness based on international cross-sectional data. Perhaps the most influential one was that of Burnside and Dollar (1997) which concluded that aid can be a powerful tool for promoting growth and reducing poverty but only if it is granted to countries that are already helping themselves by following growth-enhancing policies. In contrast, Guillaumont and Chauvet (1999) find that aid effectiveness depends on exogenous (mostly external) environmental factors such as the terms-of-trade trend, the extent of export instability and climatic shocks. Their results suggest that the worse the environment, the greater the need for aid and the higher its productivity. Hansen and Tarp (1999), using essentially the same cross-sectional data set as Burnside and Dollar, argue that when account is taken of unobserved country-specific fixed effects and the dynamic nature of the aid–growth relationship, the Burnside–Dollar conclusion fails to emerge. Country-specific characteristics of aid recipient countries – aside from the policy regime followed by those countries – have a major impact on aid's effectiveness.

The socio-economic havoc created by the Asian financial crisis engendered a fundamental re-examination of the role of aid and the uncritical acceptance of rules of the game, based on the somewhat outdated international trade and monetary system designed at Bretton Woods and the 'Washington consensus' no longer consistent with the contemporaneous conditions.

The sudden increase in the incidence of poverty in such countries as Indonesia, Thailand and South Korea, after 1997, and the lack of appropriate safety nets provided a strong rationale for redirecting aid flows to alleviate poverty and improve human welfare, and for using foreign aid to help build institutions that could help reduce recipient countries' vulnerability to exogenous shocks. Although very little progress has yet been made in revamping the international financial system, both the IMF and the World Bank are well aware of the need to modify existing practices. The strong economic recovery of most East Asian countries (between 1997 and 2000) and of Mexico, previously, suggests that the architecture of the international monetary system is better suited at helping countries recover from a crisis than preventing it from occurring in the first place.

Reflective of the trend towards using aid as an instrument to fight poverty is the recent study by Collier and Dollar (1999) that develops criteria for allocating aid when the objective is to maximise poverty alleviation.

Conclusions

The retrospective appraisal undertaken in this chapter revealed the close interdependence throughout the last five decades of the twentieth century among (i) development objectives, (ii) the conceptual framework and models, (iii) data systems and information, (iv) strategies and (v) the role of development aid. In each period, the nature and scope of the prevailing development strategy and the role of aid were largely predetermined by the conceptual state of the art, the available data systems and the prevailing conditions at the time. Thus, for example, a very limited analytical framework such as the totally aggregate (one-sector) model of the 1950s and the predominance of a data system relying almost exclusively on national income accounts, predetermined that the corresponding development strategy would be couched within a uni-sectoral setting. In contrast, the multi-sectoral framework of the 1990s, based on a much clearer understanding of the elements and mechanisms (some endogenous) influencing the development process and the availability of an extremely disaggregated set of socio-economic data, allowed the design of a stabilisation-cum-growth-cum-poverty alleviation strategy.

The conception of the role of aid evolved in parallel with the evolution of the development doctrine. In the 1950s, the role of aid was seen mainly as a source of capital to trigger economic growth through higher investment. Faith in the capacity of recipient governments to plan successfully and use aid efficiently was strong. In the 1960s, the role of foreign assistance, in the light of the two-gap models, was considered important in removing either a savings deficiency through an increased flow of foreign savings or a deficit in the current account of the balance-of-payments by providing the necessary foreign exchange. The 1970s witnessed a major change in the role of aid, i.e. that the primary objective of foreign assistance should be to raise the standard of living of the poor largely through increased employment. The focus on poverty alleviation required new types of investment and new forms of intervention.

With the advent of the debt crisis and the debt overhang, in the 1980s the role and conception of aid changed in a major way. The primary purpose of aid became twofold; as a stop gap measure to salvage the shaky international financial system and to encourage the implementation of appropriate adjustment policies in third world countries through conditionality attached to programme lending. In that decade, characterised by pro-market and anti-government rhetoric, there was strong sentiment to reduce aid drastically and have private capital flows substitute for it.

Finally, the decade of the 1990s was marked by a strong and lingering case of 'aid fatigue' influenced by the rising fear that foreign assistance was generating aid dependency relationships in poor countries. The issue of the effectiveness of aid conditionality was also critically debated. The socio-economic havoc created by the Asian financial crisis engendered a fundamental re-examination of the role of aid and the uncritical acceptance of the Bretton Woods rules of the game and the 'Washington consensus'. The World Bank, in particular, took the leadership in advocating poverty alleviation and improvement in human welfare as the overarching objective of development and of foreign assistance.

Notes

1 There are two additional reciprocal relationships denoted by arrows in Figure 1.1. The first one is the interaction between development theories and hypotheses and development models. Models are typically based on theoretical hypotheses, which often are of a partial nature. By integrating various hypotheses into a consistent framework, which the model provides, some new insights may be derived which could lead to a modification of the initial hypotheses. The second bi-directional arrow is the one linking development objectives and data systems. Clearly, the choice of development goals both predetermines the kind of data system that is required and is affected by it. Many concrete examples of these interrelationships are described and analysed next in the application of the conceptual framework in Figure 1.1 to the five decades spanning the period 1950–2000.

2 In particular, certain conceptual and theoretical contributions may have been formulated before they became part of the conventional wisdom. An example of this is the seminal article of W.A. Lewis (1954), that triggered the economic dualism concept which became a major element of the development paradigm of the 1960s rather than of the 1950s.

3 Here again the emphasis on industrialisation was greatly influenced by the Soviet model.

4 Public Law (PL) 480 refers to the *Agricultural Trade Development and Assistance Act* passed in the United States in 1954, marking the inception of food aid programmes.

5 Far from originating with ILO, the concept of basic needs and planning for poverty alleviation had already been expressed and formulated very clearly by the Indian planner Pitambar Pant as early as 1962 (see Pant 1974).

2 The role of government in economic development

Irma Adelman

Introduction

No area of economics has experienced as many abrupt changes in the leading paradigm during the post-WWII era as has economic development. These changes have had profound implications for the way the role of government has been viewed by development practitioners and their advisers in international organisations. There have been three phases in the dominant view concerning the optimal role of government in development.

The government as prime mover phase

In the first phase, lasting from 1940 to 1979, government was assigned a primary, entrepreneurial role. The intellectual roots of this view can be found in the writings of the pre-Marshallian classical economists and in their immediate post-WWII followers, Sir Arthur Lewis, Paul N. Rosenstein-Rodan, Ragnar Nurkse, Hans W. Singer, Raúl Prebisch, Albert O. Hirschman and Harvey Leibenstein. They viewed economic development as a growth process that requires the systematic reallocation of factors of production from a low-productivity, traditional technology, decreasing returns, mostly primary sector to a high-productivity, modern, increasing returns, mostly industrial sector. But, unlike the later neoclassical development economists who assume that there are few technological and institutional impediments to the requisite resource-reallocation, classical development economists assume that the resource reallocation process is hampered by rigidities, which are both technological and institutional in nature. Investment lumpiness, inadequate infrastructure, imperfect foresight, and missing markets impede smooth resource transfers between sectors in response to individual profit maximisation and provide the bases for classical, structuralist approaches to economic development. Technological external economies in infrastructural and 'basic' industrial projects would lead to co-ordination failures that would cause private agents to under-invest in them.

Classical development theorists recognised that long-run economic growth is a highly non-linear process. This process is characterised by the existence of multiple stable equilibria, one of which is a low-income-level trap. They saw developing countries caught in the low-income-level trap, which occurs at low levels of physical capital, both productive and infrastructural, and is maintained by low levels of accumulation and by Malthusian population growth. They argued that industrial production is subject to technical indivisibilities, which give rise to technological and pecuniary externalities. However, co-ordination failures lead to the realisation of systematically lower rates of return from investments based on, *ceteris paribus*, individual, profit maximisation than those that could be realised with co-ordinated, simultaneous investment programs. Uncoordinated investments would not permit the realisation of the inherent increasing returns to scale and, together with low incomes, which restrict levels of savings and aggregate demand, and Malthusian population growth, ensnare an economy starting at low levels of income and capital in a 'low-income-level' trap. Hence the need for government action to propel the economy from the uncoordinated, low-income 'no-long-run-growth' static equilibrium to the co-ordinated, high-income, 'dynamic-equilibrium-golden-growth' path. In his seminal work *Problems of Industrialisation of Eastern and South-Eastern Europe*, Rosenstein-Rodan (1943) posited the need for a government-financed series of interdependent investments, to take advantage of external economies and economies of scale and propel developing countries from a 'low-level-equilibrium' trap, with no growth in per capita income, to a 'high-level-equilibrium' path, characterised by self-sustained growth. Development could not be induced purely by market forces.

To remedy both the structural and co-ordination failures, government would therefore have to engage in an active role: subsidise investment, co-ordinate investment activities, and undertake direct investment itself from the government budget, despite the, it is hoped, mild inflationary pressures these actions would induce. Some development economists contended that a 'big push' of simultaneously undertaken investments would maximise the external economies generated by investment and generate self-sustained, growth faster. Others contended that 'balanced growth' would reduce the bottlenecks and import needs of the investment programmes and thereby raise the marginal efficiency of investment.

The 'government as prime mover' in development was reinforced by the realisation in the late 1950s that insufficient entrepreneurship was leading to serious absorptive capacity constraints to the provision of foreign aid and the undertaking of government-sponsored investment projects. There were simply not enough potential industrialists willing and able to undertake industrial projects to accelerate development, especially when commercial, import-license related, and 'non-productive' real estate investments provided such high rates of return in the inflationary and protected trade environments generated by government-sponsored policies.

Most classical development economists argued that, in the absence of private entrepreneurship, governments would have to continue to perform the entrepreneurial job while at the same time fostering the development of a cadre of private entrepreneurs willing and able to take over. Governments could foster the development of a cadre of private entrepreneurs by artificially increasing the rates of return from private investment through direct government subsidies; by engaging in joint government–private ventures, and by subsidising management training programs. Others, primarily Hirschman, argued that what was necessary was to economise on the need for private entrepreneurial talents by making the activities in which private investment would yield high returns more obvious through unbalanced growth.

The first rumblings against the 'government as prime mover' came in the early 1970s, when several International Labour Organization (ILO) missions were organised to analyse the employment situation in developing countries. Their reports concluded that, despite high rates of economic growth and industrialisation, overt unemployment and underemployment were very high, of the order of 20 per cent of the urban labour force. Not only was unemployment high but it had also increased with the process of industrialisation. The high rates of unemployment were in turn inducing an unequalising process of economic growth: the owners of capital (the rich) and the owners of skills complementary to government-sponsored, capital-intensive development (the professional and bureaucratic middle-class) were growing richer, while the owners of unskilled labour were not benefiting proportionately. Skilled and semi-skilled workers that had been absorbed in modern industry had become middle-class while the un-employed and underemployed workers in low-productivity sectors (agriculture and unskilled services) and in low-productivity enterprises (workers in small-scale firms using traditional technology) were falling increasingly behind.

Several different proximate reasons were offered for this development failure. But, fundamentally, all these explanations rested on the contention that the process of government-sponsored accelerated development had given rise to incorrect relative factor prices that did not reflect fundamental relative economic scarcities: the government-subsidisation of capital had led to capital being underpriced relative to its true scarcity and labour being overpriced both relative to capital and relative to its true scarcity. This had resulted in the adoption of too capital-intensive technology. In addition, too rapid rural–urban migration, induced by expected urban wage far exceeding actual rural per capita income, was swelling the ranks of the urban unemployed and underemployed. The migration was due to a process of industrialisation that was forcibly transferring resources from agriculture to industry by lowering the agricultural terms-of-trade through foreign aid financed imports of grains and government marketing boards thereby keeping rural incomes low. Whatever the reasons for the relatively high capital-intensity of development, the remedy was 'getting prices right', by reducing direct and indirect subsidies to industrialisation. Raising interest rates on loans to large-scale industry and reducing tariff protection to capital-intensive, import substituting industries and allowing grain prices to rise.

While the classical development economists realised this only imperfectly at the time, the 'getting prices right' school marked the beginning of ascendancy of the neoclassical school of economic development. Rather than argue for different forms of government intervention, the 'getting prices right' theory opened the door to the argument that government intervention should be curtailed, since its effects had obviously been counter-productive. The income distribution school continued to argue for a direct role of government in the economy, but called for a change in focus away from capital-intensive 'basic' industries towards labour-intensive consumer goods industries suitable both for domestic production and for exports. The day was carried however by the 'getting prices right' argument.

The government as a problem phase

This second phase, lasting from 1979 to about 1996, was a continuation of the neoclassical 'getting prices right' line of thought. Neoclassical trade theorists (e.g. Anne O. Krueger and Jagdish N. Bhagwati), who came to dominate the field of economic development, emphasised that international trade can provide a substitute for low domestic aggregate demand. They argue that the main thing governments need to do to position an economy on an autonomous, sustained-growth path is to remove barriers to international trade in commodities. According to this 'trade is enough' school of thought, export-led rapid economic growth would be the inevitable result. Comparative advantage, combined with the Heckscher–Ohlin theorem, would then do the rest. Governments should also remove price distortions in domestic factor and commodity markets ('get prices right') to induce suitable movement of factors among sectors, encourage the adoption of appropriate technology, and increase capital accumulation. In this view, domestic and international liberalisation programmes would suffice to bring about sustained economic growth and structural change. To the extent that economies are trapped in the low-level-equilibrium trap by deficient aggregate demand, international trade can indeed provide a substitute for deficient domestic demand. However, the moment one acknowledges that non-tradable intermediate inputs, such as transport and power, are needed for efficient domestic production in modern manufacturing, international trade cannot obviate the need for a 'big push' to lift the economy out of the low-level-equilibrium trap and hence provide a perfect substitute for a government-promoted investment programme into domestic infrastructure and interrelated industrial investments.

The culmination of the neoclassical counter-revolution in economic development that was initiated by the 'getting prices right' and 'trade is enough' schools was the 'evil government' school that, not coincidentally, started its life under the Reagan–Thatcher era of neo-liberalism. According to its view, government is the problem rather than the solution to underdevelopment. On the one hand, government interventions are not needed, as trade liberalisation can induce development, provide for economies of scale and make industries internationally more competitive. By the same token, greater domestic marketisation of goods and services, including public goods, would make development more cost-effective and efficient. Governments are bloated, they are corrupt, they accept bribes for economic privileges generated by government interventions into the market, and they operate by distorting market incentives in mostly unproductive, foolish and wasteful ways. Moreover, their discretionary interventions into markets, through regulation, tariffs, subsidies and quotas, give rise to rent-seeking activities by private entrepreneurs, which absorb large fractions of GNP and leads to significant economic inefficiencies. As a result, reducing the role of government in the economy would lead to more rapid and more efficient development.

Under these circumstances, they argued that the best actions governments can undertake to promote development is to minimise their economic roles. Liberalising domestic and international markets for both factors and products is the prescription of choice. Acts to promote the spread of markets and the rule of market incentives would improve the efficiency of the economy. Such acts would, in and of themselves, be taken as an indication of economic virtue, worthy of financial support by international agencies. A corollary of this view is that starving the public sector of resources is a worthwhile undertaking, in and of itself.

The 'evil government' period was one of general slowdown in the world economy. It was marked by a recession in Japan, Europe and the United States; a shift from growth-promoting to inflation-fighting policies in developed countries, a slowdown in the growth of world trade and an increase in trade restrictions in developed countries, a rise in world interest rates and an effective devaluation of currencies against the dollar, the second oil price shock and a severe debt crisis in developing countries. All of these ushered in a decade of drastic economic decline in developing countries. During the 1980s developing countries' average rates of economic growth either declined or became stagnant, balance-of-payments constraints became increasingly binding and priorities shifted from economic development to achieving external balance mostly through restrictive macroeconomic policies. Most developing countries experienced rampant inflation, capital flight, low investment rates, drastic declines in living standards and increases in inequality and substantial increases in urban and rural poverty. The average developing country transferred more than its entire growth of GDP abroad annually, for debt service. Nevertheless, the debt of developing countries has continued to increase, as two-thirds of them could not achieve a current account surplus sufficient to service their debts (more on foreign debt in Chapter 15).

As a result of the debt service crisis in Mexico, Turkey and Brazil, commercial banks in developed countries became unwilling to extend further loans to *all* developing countries. Therefore, developing countries became completely dependent on the Washington-based international institutions, the IMF and the World Bank, for their economic survival. These institutions, in turn, took advantage of this opportunity to enforce their 'evil government' philosophy on developing countries through their loan conditionality. The combination of 'marketise, liberalise and tighten-your-belt policies' dubbed the 'Washington consensus' became the slogan of development policy during this period. As a result, many of the economic and political institutions that form the core of capitalist development were created in a significant number of developing countries.

It is curious how completely neoclassical development theory came to dominate the policy agenda during this period despite its numerous theoretical deficiencies. First, neoclassical development economics ignored the fact that Marshallian neoclassical economics was never intended to be a growth theory; only a theory of static resource allocation. It therefore must be supplemented by a theory of accumulation and growth to be a complete development theory. It is possible for markets to be efficient for static resource allocation and be inefficient vehicles for accumulation and growth. Indeed, this is what classical development theorists would contend. Second, neoclassical development theory also ignored the fact that the postulates of neoclassical economics, which are needed to ensure the efficiency of neoclassical market equilibria, are not applicable to developing countries. Developing countries are hardly characterised by smoothly mobile factors, complete and well-functioning markets, comprehensive information and perfect foresight. In short, the institutional bases for a neoclassical economy are missing in most developing countries, and cannot be created overnight. But the absence of any of these characteristics implies that market equilibrium cannot be proven to be Pareto-optimal, and hence even statically efficient. Third, market equilibria depend on the initial distribution of wealth. If that distribution is not optimal, the Pareto optimality of a neoclassical economy will not maximise even static social welfare. Fourth, the advocates of neoclassical development also ignored the theory of the second best. Since it is impossible to remove all regulatory constraints on markets, it is quite feasible that, even when all neoclassical postulates hold, adding additional constraints on markets will improve, rather than reduce, market efficiency. Finally, all the objections to the 'trade is enough' theory also apply to the 'evil government' theory of development.

Rehabilitating government

Several forces coalesced to lead to a re-evaluation of the optimal role of government in economic development. First, economists and policymakers came to realise that the growth performance of most developing countries during the 1980s had been abysmal. Second, despite the poor growth of the overwhelming majority of developing countries, that of East Asian and some South Asian countries, in which governments continued to play an active role, had been remarkably good. Despite the unfavourable international environment of the 1980s, these countries were able to maintain, and, in some cases, even improve upon their previous development momentum. Rather than adopting deflationary government expenditure and macroeconomic policies and restrictive import and wage practices, the successful Asian countries exported their way out of the crisis. Their governments shifted from import-substitution to export-promotion regimes, devalued to promote expenditure switching among imports and domestic goods, undertook a set of market-friendly institutional and policy reforms, continued to invest in infrastructure and human capital, and engaged in the direct and indirect promotion of selective industrial policy. Third, there was a backlash in the OECD countries against the neo-liberal philosophy of the 1980s, which had led to slow growth and high unemployment, towards a more activist governmental stance. Democrats replaced republicans in the United States, labour governments replaced conservative governments in most European countries, and the international influence of Japan, whose government had always played a very active economic role, increased. Fourth, the mixed success of developing countries with market reforms during the 1980s led international institutions to understand that it takes capable, committed governments to promote and manage successful reform, even market-oriented reform. Otherwise, reform efforts will flounder and be derailed or captured by special interest groups of actual or potential losers from reform. The *problematique* therefore shifted from minimising the role of government towards making governments more effective.

A 'revisionist' school of economic development, dubbed the post-'Washington consensus' school appears to be now in the making. This school advocates a dynamically changing mix of state–market interactions, in which developmental governments play a significant role in investment, its finance, human capital formation, acquisition of technology, institution-setting and the promotion of policy and institutional reforms. And it is searching for ways to increase the capacity of governments to formulate development policy and implement it through a relatively capable and honest bureaucracy. Development economics is returning full circle, albeit somewhat sadder and wiser, to the view, held by the classical development economists, that government must play a strategic role in economic development. However, whether the post-'Washington consensus' school will survive remains an open question.

We now proceed to a description of the role governments played in developing countries. We focus on two major periods: the spread of the Industrial Revolution during the nineteenth century; and the development of developing countries during the golden era of economic development between the end of the Second World War and the first oil crisis.

The role of governments in economic history

This section is based on the systematic historical work on *Comparative Patterns of Economic Development*, carried out by Morris and Adelman (1988) and on the 200–odd references cited therein. Naturally, the drawing of policy conclusions from historical evidence applying to earlier periods is subject to obvious qualifications. Historical experiences cannot provide detailed prescriptions for contemporary development because of the differing international, technological, demographic and political contexts in which historical and contemporary growth take place.

During the nineteenth century, governments played a central and pervasive role both in establishing the economic and institutional conditions necessary for the occurrence of the Industrial Revolution and for promoting its spread to the follower European nations. Everywhere, governments reduced the risks of private transactions by promulgating laws that limited entrepreneurial liability, increasing the security of property rights and enforcing private contracts. For example, the most effective way of mobilising capital in Great Britain was the chartered joint-stock company with limited liability, introduced around 1830. Governments influenced incentives by setting and changing tariffs and determining monetary policies as needed. It is somewhat ironic in this context that the strongest advocates of free trade, Victorian Britain and post-war United States, were strongly protectionist during their own early development.

Governments increased the supply of factors by removing legal barriers to mobility of labour among regions and sectors, by establishing immigration laws and by setting the conditions for foreign investment and foreign capital inflows. Governments increased the domestic supply of skills by fostering investment in education and, where necessary, the import of foreign skilled workers. Governments increased the supply of domestic finance by promoting the establishment of investment banks, the formation of financial intermediaries and, where necessary, direct finance of industrial enterprises. Governments promoted the import of technology into the less-advanced European countries and hindered its export from the first-comers to the Industrial Revolution. In Britain, for example, the export of technology was forbidden by law and master technicians were arrested at the border if they wanted to emigrate. Governments were also a source of externality for private investment. They fostered the build-up of transport infrastructure through various means: direct investments in different transport modes, the provision of finance for building of canals and railroads and the granting of substantial incentives, such as rights of way, for the build-up of transport by the private sector.

In the comparative quantitative analyses of different aspects of economic development of 23 countries between 1850 and 1914, Morris and Adelman (1988) found that the extent of domestic economic role of governments explained significant portions of cross-country variance within groups similar in their initial conditions and in their choice of development paths. Inter-country differences in the extent of government sponsored investment in infrastructure and industry explained 50 per cent of the variance among countries in patterns of industrialisation, 28 per cent in inter-country differences in the extent of expansion of market institutions, 33 per cent in patterns of foreign economic dependence, 35 per cent of inter-country variance in the course of poverty, but only 11 per cent of variance in patterns of agricultural expansion.

In nineteenth century Europe, the degree of government promotion of industrialisation was positively, though not perfectly, correlated with the gap between Great Britain and the country in question. However, even in Great Britain and the United States, where the direct economic role of governments was least, governments played a pivotal role in promoting the Industrial Revolution. By 1870 in the United States and by 1850 in Great Britain, the governments of both countries had removed all pro-modern constraints on markets, had eliminated major legal barriers to national mobility of labour (such as slavery in the United States) and had commercialised land transactions. They had created limited-liability companies and had removed barriers to direct foreign investment. Nevertheless, self-financing remained the predominant source of most industrial capital. Both the British and US governments financed a significant, though not predominant, portion of investment in inter-regional transportation and granted large subsidies for the development of different transport modes (e.g. canals and railroads). But, by contrast with the follower countries, both the British and the US governments provided very little direct financing of investment in industry and agriculture. Before 1850, the British government had defended British entrepreneurs against outside competition through significant tariff protection and through discriminatory shipping rules. Moreover, throughout the nineteenth century, Great Britain supported and protected overseas trade by imposing free trade on its colonies and by promoting cheap raw material and food exports from the Commonwealth countries through its role in the development of inland transport and the improvement of its shipping. The British government opened up its overseas territories to British competition by investing in inland transport (e.g. Indian railroads) in the colonies, and it provided externalities for private British ventures overseas by paying an important portion of the security and administrative costs of the colonies, and by developing capital markets which enabled the export of large amounts of capital.

The role of government was especially active in the industrialising follower countries. Italy, Spain, Japan, Russia and Germany before 1870 were countries that were moderately backward but had administratively capable governments. There, governments responded to the military, political and economic challenges posed by Western European expansion by playing a significant role in eliminating existing restrictions on factor and commodity markets, by providing support for economic integration of urban–rural trade networks despite initial lack of effective political integration and despite significant economic dualism and by fostering education. Their efforts were closely and systematically associated with industrialisation and export growth, though not with the diffusion of the benefits from that growth, as they did not systematically raise agricultural productivity, wages in agriculture and industry or increase per capita, as distinct from aggregate, income.

Governments in the follower countries used a large variety of instruments to promote industrialisation: general and targeted subsidies, tariffs, incentives, monopoly grants, quantitative restrictions, licensing, tax privileges, and even forced allocation of labour (Landes 1998). Challenged by Britain's industrialisation, governments enlarged the size of the domestic market by unifying their countries politically; by investing in inland transport; and by abolishing customs duties and tolls to stimulate the evolution of national markets. They also added government demand for manufactures (e.g. military uniforms in Russia) to inadequate private demand. Governments substituted for missing domestic factors and undertook measures to enlarge the supply of skilled labour and finance. To increase the supply of skilled labour they invested in education, imported skilled technicians from more advanced countries, and, where necessary, removed restrictions on labour mobility (slavery and serfdom), and passed immigration laws favouring the influx of unskilled labour. Where the country was too poor to finance the banks required to finance industry, the state promoted the establishment of financial intermediaries, invested in industrial enterprises directly, or participated in industrial investment together with private entrepreneurs. In sum, the governments of the follower countries engaged in manifold entrepreneurial activities to catch up with Great Britain's Industrial Revolution, in an effort to reduce its military, economic and political power. Nevertheless, in the European follower countries, industrialisation and market expansion were dualistic. Before 1890, factories remained scarce and mechanised industry was limited to only some sectors and regions, with the rest of the economy largely untouched by modernisation.

The promotional activities of nineteenth century governments were not limited to the follower countries in the Industrial Revolution. In the land-abundant overseas territories settled by Europeans (Argentina, Brazil, Australia and New Zealand), governments undertook steps to remove institutional restrictions on export expansion by freeing market systems from institutional constraints on their operation, and by expanding specialised institutions facilitating land transfers, capital flows, foreign investment and commodity sales. In the land-abundant British colonies, governments removed restrictions on expatriate capital, entrepreneurship and immigration. These actions led to foreign-promoted primary export expansion and eventual modest industrialisation, the latter with a considerable time lag. But free immigration and rapid population growth slowed increases in domestic per capita incomes, in industrial and agricultural wages and induced a cyclical pattern (in contrast to a positive trend) in poverty reduction.

Naturally, then as now, the nature of the impact of governments on the economy and society depended on whose interests the government represented. In the follower Europe, it was only when the control over economic policies by landed feudal elites was weakened, that land institutions were changed to provide adequate incentives for small farmers and that the government's actions led to a wider diffusion of the benefits from growth. Similarly, in the overseas, white settler, land-abundant countries, it was only when and where the political dominance of large landowners declined that dualism diminished. Under those circumstances governments invested in education and transport, and changed land policies so as to help smaller farmers serve urban groups. In Australia, for example, a shift in political power led to land settlement laws that gave farmers greater access to markets in the 1850s and 1860s.

This stands in strong contrast to Argentina and Brazil, where landed elites continued to dominate politics and land ownership and the spread of benefits from growth remained highly concentrated. Finally, it also took a certain degree of political and economic autonomy from colonial powers for government initiatives to result in economic improvements of any kind. In the highly dependent, densely settled, colonial, peasant economies (Burma, Egypt and India) the construction of transportation systems by colonial governments and the foreign stimulated expansion of exports not only failed to lead to domestic economic benefits, but also led to backwash effects: the promotion of more market-oriented institutions by colonial governments caused wages in agriculture and industry to fall – a not surprising result in countries in which agriculture was characterised by low-productivity and concentrated land-ownership coupled with insecure tenancies, and where there was rapid population growth not accompanied by increases in productivity.

What we learn from nineteenth century development is that the state played a pervasive role in the initiation of development in all countries, particularly the late-comers to the Industrial Revolution. It used a large number of instruments, both direct and indirect, targeted and un-targeted. It intervened most directly in the least developed late-comers, by financing investment itself, by targeting these investments to branches of industry it wanted to develop for a mix of economic and political reasons, by substituting for missing factors and underdeveloped institutions and by working to increase their domestic supply. We also learn that the process took time and required continued commitment. That administratively capable governments were needed and that they required a certain degree of autonomy in setting policies and designing its interventions. Finally, we learn that the state's influence on the economy depended critically on who controlled the state. Governments controlled by feudal landed elites could only achieve narrow-based growth without development.

The changing role of the state in post-WWII developing countries

In a systematic, quantitative, comparative analysis of economic and institutional forces in economic development during the golden age of economic development in the nineteen 1950s and 1960s, Adelman and Morris (1967) found that the critical institutions for economic growth as well as the critical policy thrust changed systematically with the development process. The study indicated that the process of economic development was highly non-linear and highly multifaceted. We found that the interaction patterns among economic and institutional changes differed sharply among countries characterised by different institutional, social, and economic initial conditions. The implication is that the major functions of and activities of government must shift as industrialisation and institutional development proceed. Not only must economic institutions and the primary thrust of economic policy change but also the major functions of government must alter as development proceeds. We therefore divide our discussion of critical government actions by levels of development: least developed (the low group), intermediate transitional countries (the intermediate group), most developed developing countries (the high group), and the developed group of countries.

The low group

In the set of countries at the lowest end of the spectrum in socio-economic development, the economic growth process entailed principally an inter-related process of economic and *social* transformations. In 1960, the set of least developed states comprised mostly sub-Saharan African countries but also included the least developed countries in Asia and Libya and Morocco in North Africa. These countries were characterised by minimal degrees of development of market institutions and national polities, and by a predominance of social tribal influences over both individual allegiances and the economic activity of their predominantly subsistence agrarian economies. In the 1960s, Kuznets (1958) compared this group of countries to fourteenth century Europe in its economic, social and political development.

The statistical results found in Adelman and Morris (1967) for this low-development group, indicated that an important task of government, at this level of socio-economic development, is the build-up of social capital. Governments need to promote increases in the size of the professional, entrepreneurial and bureaucratic middle-class, remove social and educational impediments to entry into middle-class occupations, and champion increases in the degree of modernisation of outlook. They can increase the degree of modernisation of outlook by, *inter alia*, promoting the commercialisation of agriculture, reducing the overwhelming proportion of the population engaged in subsistence agriculture, and by investing in human resource development.[1]

The results show that the major economic means by which growth and social transformation were induced in this low-development group of countries during the 1960s entailed the dualistic development of a modern, export-oriented, primary sector. The development of primary exports, in turn, provoked significant transformations of social structure in rural areas, encouraged the diffusion of the market economy and induced a reduction in the sway of traditional tribal customs over economic activity.

Despite the fact that the promotion of industrialisation played a role in explaining inter- country differences in growth rates, industrialisation was not the primary force responsible for their economic growth. The industrial sectors of these economies remained highly underdeveloped, with handicraft industry and putting-out systems predominant in most countries. The highest levels of industrialisation achieved during the 1960s by the most advanced countries in this group, were the establishment of a number of small-scale, power-driven factories, and a very small number of modern, large-scale factories that were, however, foreign financed and foreign managed. Moreover, a large number of these countries were suffering from the 'Dutch disease' of deindustrialisation, due to their primary reliance on their export-oriented extractive sectors for their economic dynamism.

The governments of this group of countries also need to increase investment. They have to invest in physical infrastructure, primarily in transport and power systems. The physical overhead capital of even the most advanced countries in this group, while adequate for their small commercialised sectors, failed to provide continuous service in most parts of the country. And they have to invest in education.

The state should also start on the development of the critical economic institutions, their financial and tax systems, which, their efforts notwithstanding, remain rudimentary. In the 1960s, local financial institutions were foreign owned or directed; investment in food agriculture was either self-financed or financed through the unorganised money market; gross domestic savings rates were below 9 per cent and the ratio of demand plus time deposits to GNP was less than 15 per cent. And their tax revenues depended heavily on a foreign-owned extractive sector, their tax bases were extremely narrow, and they experienced severe difficulties collecting taxes.

Even though these countries shared common severe political barriers to growth and development, political influences exercised negligible impact on economic growth in the Adelman–Morris (1967) results because there was so little variation in their political characteristics during the 1960s. However, the results show that the performance of these many functions by the state requires increasing the administrative efficiency, professionalism and honesty of their bureaucracies; and a leadership that demonstrates greater than average degrees of commitment to national development.[2]

In sum, in this group of most underdeveloped countries, the primary functions of government consist of social development, and institution-creation, both economic and political. The early industrialisers had built up their market institutions during the 400-year proto-capitalist period. The countries in this set had never gone through a comparable process of proto-industrialisation, build-up of agricultural technology, and marketisation. Their governments therefore have to introduce the institutional changes required to strengthen responsiveness to market incentives – a process they accomplished by focusing on the expansion of commercialised primary exports. They have to eliminate legal and social barriers to factor mobility and trade, break down the sway of tribal influences, create domestically financed and managed credit institutions, and build institutions that facilitate the commercialisation of transactions in both land and labour. And they have to invest in infrastructure and education.

The intermediate group

In the next most developed group of transitional economies, that were intermediate in socio-political and economic degrees of institutional development, the process of social, economic and political modernisation had proceeded far enough by 1960 to profoundly disturb traditional customs and institutions without progressing far enough to set them on the path of self-sustained economic development. This set of countries was geographically diverse. It included Algeria, Tunisia, Iran, Iraq, Syria and Jordan in the Middle East and North Africa; Sri Lanka, India, Pakistan, Myanmar, Thailand, Indonesia and the Philippines in Asia; Bolivia, Guatemala, Ecuador, Honduras and Surinam in Latin America; and Ghana, Rhodesia and South Africa from sub-Saharan Africa. The countries in this group were also historically and culturally most heterogeneous. They were characterised by rapid and unbalanced social transformations, which had led to high degrees of social tensions and political instability. In the 1960s, they also had generally ineffective governments with weak administrative capacities.

The Adelman–Morris (1967) statistical results for this group of countries indicate that relatively narrow-based industrialisation, the build-up of economic institutions, particularly financial and tax systems, and investment in physical infrastructure dominated the explanation of inter-country differences in rates of economic growth. There was no longer evidence of a direct systematic impact of changes in social structure upon rates of economic progress, perhaps because the specific patterns of socio-economic progress, including specific social impediments to modernisation, varied substantially among clusters of countries in this transitional group. Furthermore, neither the precise form of the political system nor the extent of the leadership's commitment to economic development played an important systematic role in influencing growth rates in this transitional group, because the states were 'soft' and the countries were beset by high degrees of social tension and political instability.

For countries at this intermediate stage of development, the results indicate that the government should concentrate on providing the institutional and physical conditions and the policy environment necessary to promote the initial stages of industrialisation. It should invest in transport and power systems. It should raise the national investment rate, both through direct government investment and through subsidising and promoting private investment. It should champion the development of modern industry: foster an increase in the variety of consumer goods produced by power driven factory methods, encourage the domestic processing of natural-resource based exports, and strive to increase the proportion of manufactured goods in total exports.[3] The government should substitute for imported skills and capital by promoting domestic entrepreneurs in manufacturing, and by investing in education.[4] It should build up the domestic banking system and domestic credit institutions by adopting policies that boost private savings, channel them to the private banking system, and enhance the effectiveness of the banking system in performing its intermediation function between savings and investment. To avoid relying too heavily on inflationary finance, the government should build up its tax institutions by raising the ratio of government revenues to GNP, and by increasing reliance on direct, rather than indirect, trade-related, taxes. The government should create the conditions for a Lewis-type process of transfer of resources from agriculture to industry by raising the productivity of agriculture. It should make agriculture more responsive to economic incentives by expanding its degree of commercialisation while reducing the proportion of the population engaged in subsistence agriculture.[5] And it should encourage a reduction of socio-economic dualism by decreasing pervasive regional and sectoral cleavages in technology, types of economic organisation and styles of life between urban and rural inhabitants, large expatriate-managed factories and domestically owned and managed ones, and between export and domestic consumer goods production.[6] It should accomplish this not only through its investment patterns in infrastructure and education but also through the promotion of mass-communication media.[7]

The high group

The countries in this group comprise the socio-institutionally and economically most advanced developing countries. The majority of them had by 1960 a century or more of political independence and were well ahead of the intermediate group in social achievements (larger middle-class, higher literacy, more secondary and tertiary education, more urbanisation, more mass-communication, etc.), in degrees of industrial-isation, and in extent of development of economic and political institu-tions. The sample includes the sixteen most developed Latin American nations, the six most advanced Middle Eastern countries, and three East Asian countries – Japan, South Korea and Taiwan.

In this group of highly-developed developing countries, leadership commitment to economic development was the major political variable differentiating between economically more and less successfully developing nations. Indeed, this variable alone accounted for 77 per cent of inter-country variance in economic growth. The leadership commitment variable captures the contrast between the less successful, mostly low political commitment Latin American countries that had already achieved high levels of socio-institutional development and high incomes, on the one hand, and the high social-development but low income East Asian ones, whose leadership commitment to development was high, on the other.[8] In Japan, South Korea, Singapore and Taiwan, no correct reading of the role of government in the economy is compatible with a view that it acted like neo-liberal states. Leadership commitment is required to achieve the degree of autonomy the state needs to enable it to foster dynamic compar-ative advantage. This requires shifting direct and indirect state support among industries, changing trade and commercial policies towards specific sectors, thereby injuring some groups while benefiting others.

Once the social, human resource and physical conditions for develop-ment have been largely established, as they have for this group of countries, our results indicate that the primary function of government consists of the promotion of industrialisation while raising the productivity of agriculture. The performance of this function entails an activist government role in the adoption of an industrial policy that promotes dynamically changing comparative advantage: from resource-intensive, where still appropriate, to labour-intensive manufactures, to skill-intensive industries, to high-level manpower and capital-intensive sectors. During the 1960s, this transition entailed expansion of the quantity and variety of consumer goods pro-duced domestically in power-driven factories, at first largely for domestic consumption and then, in part, also exported and finally moving into the domestic production of intermediate goods that, initially, primarily sub-stitute for exports. Only the East Asian economies and Brazil had by 1960 reached a stage in which they were exporting consumer goods and none of them were exporting producer goods at that time. This process of progressive change in the thrust of industrialisation needs to be implemented through the formulation of appropriately changing international trade and commercial policies and the consistent direction of government finance, government investment and government incentives to this end. The general aim should be to make industries export-competitive and create a dynamic private sector. However, in each phase of the transition, initially infant-industry protection needs to be accorded to the key sectors; but the infant-industry protection *must be* gradually withdrawn and replaced by pressures and incentives to export. In support of the industrialisation effort the productivity of food agriculture must be raised to feed the urban population through investment in agricultural infrastructure and through agricultural technology and terms of trade policies leading to the increases in agricultural incomes required to boost home demand for domestic manufactures.

This phase also involves an increase in investment, public and private, domestic and foreign. It therefore presumes a greater level of development and more rapid improvements in both financial and tax institutions. In financial institutions, further institutional development entails reducing the degree of financial repression, raising gross domestic savings rates above 13 per cent, and improving the capacity of financial intermediaries to provide a fairly adequate degree of long-term finance for investment in both industry and agriculture. The improvement of tax systems entails expanding tax revenues, to avoid having to rely on more than *mildly* expansionary macroeconomic policies and modest foreign capital inflows, in the form of foreign direct investment and foreign aid. Furthermore, the reformed tax systems must also place greater reliance on direct rather than indirect, trade-related taxes. Otherwise, the needs of tax collection will conflict with the needs to ultimately foster internationally competitive domestic industries.

Developed countries

Finally, once the institutions of capitalism are mature and the growth, investment and savings habits are firmly entrenched in the entrepreneurial and household sectors, the scope of government policy should be diminished. By and large, the government ought to limit itself to providing the macroeconomic policy framework for rational economic calculus and full resource utilisation, the promotion of economic and political competition, the provision of a safety net and the protection of the weak in the marketplace, and the containment of negative social externalities, environmental and safety, inherent in unfettered profit maximisation. That is, the appropriate role of the government in the final phase, but *only* in the final phase, should change to that prescribed by the neo-liberal (Reagan–Thatcher) 'Washington consensus'.

However, it should be emphasised that this phase had not been attained by any countries in the 'high' groups in the 1960s and had been attained by less than a handful of the Newly Industrialising Countries (NICs) in the highest development group in the 1990s. Moreover, despite rhetoric to the contrary, even the United States and Europe are currently not pursuing purely neo-liberal policies. For example, the Clinton administration has been pursuing an activist industrial policy, aimed at accelerating the shift into a high-tech and service economy; an interventionist trade policy, aimed at pushing agricultural, service and technology exports through its bilateral and multilateral negotiations with other countries and through its participation in global institutions; and has been promoting a human resource investment policy aimed at providing the human capital needed by high-tech industries, generalising the ownership of human-capital, and increasing its rate of accumulation.

Common strands

We start by pulling together some very general common strands evident from both the nineteenth century continental European development and the post-WWII development of developing countries (see also Morris and Adelman 1989). These common strands have obvious implications not only for the role governments must play in economic development, but also for the changing role of foreign aid in assisting development and for the national and international institutions required to support it.

First, a reading of both economic history and contemporary development suggests that institutional readiness for capitalist economic growth is key to economic development, because it provides the conditions that enable technical progress and export-expansion to induce widespread economic growth. It also suggests that governments must take the lead in promoting institutional development.

The varied experiences of European countries during the Industrial Revolution period and those of developing countries during the golden age of economic growth underscore this point: those European countries that had achieved widespread economic growth by the end of the nineteenth century started with institutions better equipped for technological change than either the European dualistic-growth-turned-industrialisers or developing countries of the 1950s (Morris and Adelman 1989 and Kuznets 1958). They already had large preindustrial sectors well endowed with trained labour and entrepreneurs, governments that protected private property, enforced private contracts and acted to free domestic commodity and labour markets, and leaderships responsive to capitalist interests that adopted trade, transportation and education policies which fostered technological progress in either industry (the early industrialisers) or agriculture (the 'balanced growth' countries).

Similarly, those developing countries that in the 1950s were institutionally most advanced were the ones that benefited most from the growth impetus imparted by import demand from the OECD countries during the golden era of economic development. They had an average rate of economic growth 50 per cent higher than that of the average non-oil country at the next-highest, intermediate, level of socio-institutional development (Adelman and Morris 1967). Furthermore, by 1973, the overwhelming majority of the institutionally most developed countries in 1950 had become either NICs or developed countries while none of the countries that had lower levels of socio-institutional development had become NICs. Finally, upgrading financial and tax institutions was an important element in explaining inter-country differences in rates of economic growth at all levels of economic development in contemporary developing countries.

Second, both the overall investment rate and government investment, in infrastructure, human capital and industry, were important to development historically as well as contemporarily. Human capital and transportation made a significant difference to economic development. Indeed, in the Adelman–Morris (1967) statistical analyses, post-WWII and pre-WWI, human resource development was critical to technological dynamism in both industry and agriculture.

Historically, no country achieved successful economic development before 1914 without adult literacy rates above 50 per cent. And literacy was a foremost variable discriminating among more and less successfully developing countries during the nineteenth century (Morris and Adelman 1988: 211). Similarly, the historical results show that breakthroughs in inland transportation were necessary to advance agriculture in countries starting with severe transportation bottlenecks and having land institutions, human resources, and political structures that provided the potential for economic growth (Morris and Adelman 1988: ch. 5). Only where the structure of investment in transport accorded priority to domestic trade were technological improvements in food agriculture likely. Finally, the overall investment rate was important to historical development in all countries.

Analogously, in the 1960s, inter-country differences in infrastructure and human capital additions were important in explaining inter-country differences in rates of economic growth of developing countries as long as there still were major bottlenecks in internal transport and education and the overall investment rate was important at all levels of development. Furthermore, the development of the East Asian miracle countries also benefited from exceptionally high levels of human resource development. Indeed, starting from low levels of education and literacy, due to the legacy of Japanese colonialism, already by the mid-1960s, South Korea and Taiwan had attained levels of scholarisation that were triple the 'Chenery norm' for their levels of per capita GNP. And in South Korea, university enrolment rates exceeded those of Great Britain. The East Asian miracle-growth countries had both high rates of accumulation and high rates of economic growth. In fact, Krugman (1994), among others, find that in Taiwan and South Korea almost all of economic growth has, so far, been due to exceptionally high rates of physical and human capital accumulation and that the contribution of total factor productivity (TFP) growth to their income growth has been negligible.

Third, government-set trade policies and the international trade and payments regimes are critical for economic development. But, this does not mean that free trade policies are either necessary or optimal for industrialisation.

In nineteenth century Europe and Japan, tariffs were usually the cornerstone of industrialisation policies; nowhere except in Britain did initial factory-based industrialisation occur without some tariff protection. And even in Britain the period just preceding the Industrial Revolution was one of high tariff protection, as David Ricardo's tracts on the Corn Laws remind us. Thus the historical record of successful pre-WWI industrialisation suggests that Friedrich List and Hjalmar Schacht, rather than Adam Smith and David Ricardo, provide the appropriate guidelines for commercial policy in countries pursuing economic development.

A correct reading of the practice of the successful industrialisers, both historically and in current East Asia, indicates that *export orientation* rather than free trade are the critical ingredients of successful development policy. Historically, export expansion systematically speeded economic growth everywhere. But the export growth led to widespread economic development only where agriculture was at least moderately productive, and modernising governments fashioned institutional conditions favourable to technological improvements and undertook investments in education and transport favouring the development of a domestic market. Except for the first-comers to the Industrial Revolution, European countries did not adopt free trade policies. Rather, they obtained their start on industrialisation with tariffs and quantitative controls (Morris and Adelman 1988: ch. 6).

Similarly, both South Korea and Taiwan engaged in import substitution policies at the same time as they pursued export-led economic growth. But, unlike the Latin American countries, they used quantitative controls, more than tariffs and effective exchange rates, to achieve their selective industrial policies. They were thus able to maintain incentives for exports at the same time as they pursued selective import substitution. Indeed, quantitative import controls, which granted exporters a sheltered domestic market, were one of the mechanisms which made export orientation profitable to exporting firms. During the heyday of export-led growth in South Korea (1967–73), there were about 15,000 commodities on the prohibited list for imports. And in Taiwan, quantitative constraints on imports were specified not only by commodity but also by country of origin, with most labour-intensive imports from other developing countries barred in order to shelter domestic infant consumer manufactures from foreign competition. The critical difference between the second import-substitution phase into heavy and chemical industries in these two East Asian countries and the same phase of import substitution in Latin America was that, from the very beginning, the East Asian heavy and chemical industries were expected to export a large share of their output. Protection was withdrawn from heavy and chemical industries in about seven years after these industries were initiated and they were thereby forced to become export competitive.

As to the trade and payments regimes, periods of exchange rate stability, under either the gold standard or the Bretton Woods fixed exchange rate system of the golden age, were uniformly associated with high worldwide economic growth. By contrast, periods of widely fluctuating exchange rates, as during most of the 1914–50 period and since 1973 were associated, on the average, with slow economic growth. Similarly, liberal international trade regimes were associated with high rates of economic growth while protectionist regimes were associated with slow growth.

Fourth, the government has a critical role to play in promoting techno-logical dynamism, industrial policy, and in increasing productivity in both industry and agriculture. Historically, governments imported technology, financed and promoted different industries, and induced domestic industrialists to climb the ladder of comparative advantage. Technological dynamism was the essence of the Industrial Revolution. The productivity of resource-use, both newly accumulated and existing, and its rate of increase through technological change and resource reallocation among sectors, were crucial ingredients of long-term economic growth of developed countries. Technological dynamism was important in explaining contrasts in rates of economic growth during the nineteenth century in the Adelman–Morris (1967) results. And economists such as Kuznets, Abramowitz, Dennison, Solow and Krugman all find that there is a close association currently between TFP growth and rates of growth of GNP, just as both classical and endogenous-growth theories would imply.

In developing countries, the Adelman–Morris (1967) results indicate that the promotion of increases in agricultural productivity were important during the 1960s at all levels of development. Upgrading industrial technology became important once the major social and infrastructural bottlenecks to technical change were removed, and industrialisation that progressed from staple processing to consumer goods more generally and then integrated backwards into intermediate goods and machinery was the major instrument for development at all levels of development of develop-ing countries.

Fifth, as a result of the first four propositions, the government's eco-nomic policies, particularly with respect to institutions, trade, industrial policy, agriculture, investment and macroeconomic management, mattered. This point, which permeates the discussion in the previous two sections, would hardly be worth making were it not for the now Nobel-prize-hallowed 'rational expectations' school and were it not for the 'evil government'–'Washington consensus' school of economic development of the 1980s.

Sixth, the goals of economic policy matter. When, in the 1950–73 period, the OECD countries focused on economic growth, they got it. Similarly, when, after 1973, they focused on economic stabilisation, deliberately sacrificing economic growth and employment, they also got it. In the same vein, during the nineteenth century, developing countries that had suffic- ient political autonomy from their colonial rulers to be able to set their own economic policies so as to benefit domestic industrialisation (Australia, Canada and New Zealand) were able to translate the growth impulses from export expansion into widespread economic development; by contrast, those countries that were politically and economically so dependent on the centre that they had no control over domestic economic policies (India and Burma) achieved only dualistic, enclave, sporadic growth (Morris and Adelman 1988: ch. 6).

Seventh, institutional and policy malleability are key to sustained economic development in the long run. The Adelman–Morris (1967) historical study indicated that institutions and policies that were good for initiating economic growth were generally not appropriate for its continuation. For example, in the land-abundant non-European countries, foreign-domin- ated political institutions were a powerful force for the market-oriented institutional change that initiated strong primary export expansion. But the institutions that were good for export-growth brought about neither systematic agricultural improvements nor consistently rising standards of living. For ultimate success, however, the domestic economic institutions had to be transformed so that widely shared growth could ensue and a domestic market for manufactures could emerge. This required political transformation as well. At first, the establishment of political stability and political support for the promulgation of laws furthering market develop- ment were sufficient to promote rapid primary-export expansion. But unless the political institutions later adapted so as to provide support for the economic needs of rising domestic commercial and industrial classes, the translation of the initial impetus from exports into long-term economic development became blocked.

Similarly, in backward European countries, initially governments and international resource flows could substitute for the missing institutional requirements of economic growth. At first, government demand for domestic manufactures could successfully substitute for deficient home markets; government finance and foreign capital inflows could substitute for in- adequate domestic savings and financial institutions, and imports of skilled workers and technology could substitute for meagre domestic human resources. But after a certain point these substitutions became inadequate. To generate development, economic institutions had to change so as to enable the domestic provision of the capital, skills and broad-based domestic markets.

More specifically, the Morris–Adelman (1988: ch. 5) results indicate that the critical functions performed by agriculture in their countries' economic development change as development proceeds. Initially, agriculture must be capable of performing the Lewis function, of providing capital for industrialisation. In this phase, agricultural institutions must primarily be suited to the initial mobilisation of the agricultural surplus and its transfer to the industrial sector; large estates, worked with semi-attached labour, were best suited for this phase. Later, agriculture must be capable of providing food to the growing urban sector and markets for urban manufactures. In this later phase, the institutional structure of agriculture, terms-of-trade policies and investments in agricultural infrastructure must provide incentives for improvements in the productivity of food agriculture, and the agricultural surplus must be sufficiently widely distributed to enable widespread farmer-income growth and broad-based increases in demand for home-produced manufactures. At this stage, owner-operated farms of productivity and size sufficient to provide a marketable surplus were best.

In international trade, too, the Morris–Adelman (1988: ch. 4 and 8) results suggest that development requires policies to shift so as to enable structural change in the composition of domestic production and exports to occur continually. This, in turn, requires dynamic adaptations in trade regimes. Commercial policies necessary to initiate industrialisation, such as import substitution, are not good for its continuation, when shifts to export-led growth are needed to enhance scale and provide the impetus for efficiency in production. In both South Korea and Taiwan, the major thrust of government strategy with respect to trade and industrial policy shifted in rapid succession, with sometimes as little as four years spent in a given policy regime (Adelman 1999).

Not only economic institutions and primary policy-thrust but also the major functions of governments must shift as development proceeds. Initially, the primary roles of governments consisted of social development, institution creation, both economic and political, and infrastructural build-up. The governments of the European late-comers introduced the institutional changes required to strengthen responsiveness to market incentives during the early phases of the Industrial Revolution. The latecomers unified their countries and markets, as in Italy and Germany, eliminated legal barriers to trade and factor mobility, as in the Russian serf emancipation, created credit institutions and promoted joint-stock companies, as in Germany, and facilitated transactions, as in Italy and Spain.

Next, once the institutional and physical frameworks for development were established, the primary function of government consisted of the promotion of industrialisation while raising the productivity of agriculture. Both during the nineteenth and twentieth centuries, an activist government that promotes dynamically changing comparative advantage was needed to achieve successive stages of industrialisation. Climbing the ladder of comparative advantage required changing international trade and commercial policies and changing the thrust of government finance, government investment and government incentives. In each phase of industrialisation, initially infant-industry protection needs to be accorded to the key sectors;

but the infant-industry protection *must be* gradually withdrawn and replaced by pressures and incentives to export to generate an export-competitive industrial structure.

Finally, once the capitalist institutions are mature, the entrepreneurs have acquired investment attitudes and skill, and the household sector provides adequate savings and skilled labour, the scope of government economic policy should be curtailed. But, as indicated earlier, this stage has not been reached even now by most NICs. I firmly conclude from both European and East Asian development history, that, had the neo-liberal 'Washington consensus' been enforced on the East Asian miracle countries during the 1950s, 1960s and early 1970s, there would not have been an East Asian miracle.

Four corollaries

The importance of government policy to development, the importance of government goals to policy choices, and the need to be able to change the policy environment as development proceeds have four significant corollaries.

The *first corollary* is that a government with substantial autonomy, capacity and credibility is required for successful long-term economic growth. Does this mean that a strong, autocratic state is necessary to the adoption and maintenance of good economic policies? European growth during the golden age of the 1950s and 1960s suggests that it is not. However, the experience of the ultimately successful European followers during the Industrial Revolution, in which strong leaders transformed institutions and engaged in aggressive industrial policies, indicates that a strong state is needed to initiate economic development. Perhaps most importantly, as the literature on bureaucratic authoritarianism in Latin American countries emphasises, a state with a certain degree of autonomy from pressures emanating from entrenched economic elites, is necessary to implement switches among policy regimes (e.g. from import substitution to export-led economic growth) or engineer fundamental changes in economic institutions, such as land reform. Such policy regime switches, which, as emphasised above, are necessary to successful long-run economic development, inflict inescapable injuries upon some entrenched economic interests, such as entrepreneurs and workers in the protected import-substituting enterprises, while only promising to confer potential benefits on other groups, such as the would-be exporters and their workers, and that only after painful restructuring to become export competitive. Popular support for major policy regime switches is therefore unlikely, especially over a time-frame long enough for the new policy regime to become effective. Repeated abortive trade liberalisation efforts in Latin America and recent elections of communist leaders in some reforming Central European countries underscore this point.

To accomplish the variety of tasks required for development, the government has to raise the salience of economic considerations in its polity. It also must increase its own capacity by raising the training and professionalism of its civil service, the efficiency of its public administration and reduce the level of corruption of its bureaucrats. It also needs to mobilise its commitment to development by, *inter alia*, reducing the political influence of the landed traditional elite on the government's economic policies.

A government with substantial autonomy, capacity and credibility is therefore required for successful long-term economic growth. But such autonomy need not arise from repression of popular participation and civil rights. As long as the government is perceived as acting in the public interest, the requisite autonomy can be bestowed upon the government by: the government's independent popular support, such as enjoyed by governments led by national liberators or war heroes, or by the government's general credibility gained through successful economic and political leadership, or by popular values supporting hierarchic leadership roles, such as Confucianism, or arising from a perceived external threat to the country's national survival.

The *second corollary* derived from the importance of government policies and the importance of policy goals to long-run development is that of the nature of the state and its relation to civil society matters. Both historically and more recently, the structure of power represented by the government has determined the choice of policy thrust. Political history and economic history are closely related, as the contrasts in policies between 'Reaganomics' and 'Thatcheromics', on the one hand, and 'Clintonomics' and 'Blaironomics', on the other, indicate. In the late nineteenth century, when the landed political elites were modernising (as in Germany and Japan), they invested in education, agricultural extension and credit policies favouring family-owned farms. These, in turn, enabled techno-logical improvement in agriculture and the development of a home-market for industry. By contrast, where, as in Italy and Russia, the large estate owners who held political power were status quo oriented, they did little for education and agriculture and growth was dualistic, and poverty and illiteracy rampant. The critical importance of the political complexion of government to widespread economic development is also confirmed by the contrast in development paths, evident among European-settled land-abundant overseas territories during the nineteenth century. In Australia and New Zealand, when the sway of landed traditional elites over govern-ment policy eventually weakened, settlement laws favouring small farmers were passed and growth eventually became widespread. By contrast, in Argentina and Brazil, traditional elites remained strong throughout their histories, and the distribution of benefits from growth remained narrow. Thus, nineteenth century economic history confirms strongly that political institutions matter to the successful spread of economic development.

The crucial importance of the political complexion of government is also confirmed in post-war developing countries. The Adelman–Morris (1967) study found that leadership commitment to economic development was the major institutional factor differentiating among economically more and less successful nations in the group of countries that had already achieved high levels of socio-institutional development. Leadership commitment to development captures the contrast between most of Latin America, where commitment to development was mostly at best moderate and East Asia, where commitment to development was high.

The *third corollary* derived from the importance of government policy and policy goals is that a strong state that adopts self-serving, or simply misconceived economic policies and/or institutions can generate economic disaster. The indifferent economic growth in most African countries and in the non-defence sector of the former Soviet Union since the mid 1970s underscore this point. A non-activist government would have been preferable to a strong government promoting bad policies.

However, these are not the only alternatives. The economic histories of Japan, the four little tigers, the seven flying geese, and post-1980 China suggest rather strongly that the combination of a developmental state with good economic policy is unbeatable. Their experience underscores that a technocratically-influenced developmental state, with an economically-literate meritocratic bureaucracy, is key to long-run success in economic development.

The *fourth (and final) corollary* stemming from the critical and dynamically changing role governments must play in the development of their countries, is that they must have sufficient autonomy not only from domestic political constraints but also from international constraints on their economic actions.

After the end of the Second World War, the global economic system was designed so as to offer scope for increased economic interdependence while allowing national governments to pursue their own welfare and development goals. The architect of the post-war global system, Lord Keynes, knew well that the pursuit of national full employment required a global system that would permit governments to embrace anti-cyclical domestic policies, set wage policies and undertake anti-poverty measures that would be consistent with the particular government's social goals, and choose how fast it wanted to increase its rate of economic growth. He also knew that these pursuits required global economic stability and would be facilitated by enlarging the scope of world trade. The system he designed, known as the Bretton Woods system, was one of fixed, but adjustable, exchange rates with a lender of last resort and an international arbiter when national exchange rates were systematically under- or overvalued. The system stressed trade liberalisation but explicitly encouraged barriers to international short- and long-term capital flows. National governments thus acquired autonomy in setting the macroeconomic framework for their growth. They could choose the particular combinations of exchange rates, fiscal and trade deficits, domestic unemployment, inflation, interest rate, and wage and welfare policies that suited their special social traditions and current economic goals.

Between 1947 and 1973 (and for the first time in history) the global system extended the necessary degree of economic autonomy not only to developed countries but also to the newly decolonised underdeveloped nations. For them, the system offered even greater autonomy than it did for industrialised nations by designing national and international institutions to augment their meagre supplies of savings and foreign exchange earnings through multilateral and bilateral aid, and by exempting them, for a time, from free trade requirements. The result was a golden era of economic development. It combined full-employment growth in developed countries with development, consisting of a combination of economic growth and structural change, in the politically, socially and economically more advanced developing countries. The result was the emergence of about 25 semi-industrial countries, poised for entry into the club of industrialised nations.

This permissive, benign global economic system broke down abruptly in 1973, with the first oil crisis. Yet the seeds for its breakdown had been laid earlier. Toward the end of the 1960s, the liquidity needs of the world trading system could no longer be satisfied by the dollar-based Bretton Woods system. The supply of the international reserve currency (the dollar) became inadequate for the growing needs of international commerce. Also, there had been a slowdown in the growth of productivity in industrial nations; national wage settlements had started to exceed the growth of productivity, inflationary pressures were mounting, and a series of price shocks, in oil and grain prices, were imposed exogenously. The Bretton Woods system broke down and was replaced by a flexible exchange rate system with progressively more open capital markets and commodity trade, in which governments lost their economic autonomy.

Macroeconomic policies now had to become co-ordinated. For developed countries the co-ordination is accomplished through international negotiations among them. At the regular, periodic consultations among the G7 industrial nations, agreement is reached on the general thrust of national macroeconomic policies. They decide in a concerted fashion whether to stress macroeconomic stability (i.e. to fight inflation and achieve balance-of-payments equilibrium), or pursue full employment and growth. Recalcitrant nations that try to go it alone are severely disciplined by the world's financial markets. As to developing countries, under the new global system, those with relatively open capital markets, or those requiring economic assistance from international agencies, have to passively accept globally-established interest and exchange rates. This means that they cannot devalue strategically, in either nominal terms or through changes in domestic inflation, to encourage exports, and they cannot unbalance their government budgets or loosen monetary policy beyond modest degrees to subsidise or finance domestic investment. Otherwise they will experience large, disequilibrating short-term capital outflows or inflows, which can quickly turn into devastating financial crises, and greatly amplify cyclical swings in their real economies. The 1980s in Latin America, and the late 1990s in East Asia and Russia dramatically demonstrate the validity of this proposition.

Thus, in the post-Bretton Woods global payments regime, both developed and developing-country governments are precluded from pursuing independent economic policies. They cannot set an exchange rate which does not equilibrate the country's current account balance (i.e. is out of alignment with its international competitiveness), or an interest rate which is out of alignment with world market interest rates adjusted for a country-risk premium. Globalised financial markets preclude governments from having independent interest and exchange rate policies. With respect to interest rates, if, as happened in South Korea during the 1990s, the domestic interest rate is set significantly above world market rates, in order to mobilise more domestic savings, redirect them into the banking system, and fight inflation, then the result is a build-up of foreign private indebtedness. If, as happened in Japan and more recently in Canada, the domestic interest rate is set substantially below world market rates, the result is an outflow of domestic savings in the form of portfolio investment in foreign bonds and securities and of real investments abroad; the consequence is lower domestic economic growth.

By the same token, globalisation of short-term capital markets in a fluctuating exchange rate regime is also incompatible with an independent exchange rate policy, especially one that attempts to peg the exchange rate. Attempts to maintain an overvalued currency (as in Mexico and Turkey in the early 1990s and South Korea in the late 1990s) require using foreign exchange reserves to sell foreign currency to prevent a devaluation; eventually, the supply of foreign exchange reserves will be exhausted and the currency will devalue anyhow, frequently much below its equilibrium rate. Attempts to maintain an undervalued currency (as in Japan in the 1990s) will, in the absence of restrictions on currency outflows, cause an outflow of domestic currency with adverse effects on domestic investment and growth. Thus, financial globalisation imposes severe fundamental constraints on the policy levers which governments can exercise in their management of the domestic economy, thereby creating a crisis of the state. The new international environment thus has major implications for the future role of the state and the future potential for foreign assistance.

In view of the critical importance of governments to economic development, the current loss of autonomy imposed by the institutions of the current global financial system is scary. For it is evident from the above analysis, that the process of successful long-term economic development entails systematically changing dynamic interactions between institutional change, technological progress, structural change in the economy's production profile, and international trade and domestic accumulation patterns in which the government and its policies play a key role. Long-run success in economic development therefore requires that the dynamic restyling of all processes be mutually consistent and that it be embedded in a receptive international setting that is compatible with the shifting major thrust of domestic change. To enable governments to play their fundamental role successfully, they must thus have sufficient autonomy to shift among policy regimes as the requirements of economic development, domestic conditions and the international environment switch.

Conclusions

Developing countries wishing to become developed cannot renounce their policy autonomy. We saw in this chapter that government-led economic growth has been essential to the initiation of development both during the Industrial Revolution era and during the twentieth century. Furthermore, the nature of government–civil society relations must change dynamically through development history. But we also saw that the current global international financial architecture puts severe constraints upon government economic autonomy in pursuing developmental goals. So, what are developing-country governments to do in the post-Bretton Woods era? They have three classes of alternatives.

One, they can limit themselves to the instruments they retain. In particular, having lost control over more neutral indirect means of promoting structural change, they can rely increasingly on direct, targeted and untargeted means of achieving economic development. More specifically, they can use disguised subsidies to industry, through infrastructure investment, cheap food, and low-wage, anti-union policies.[9] They can use targeted subsidies in the form of tax rebates and/or monopoly privileges to specific industries, regions and firms. They can create generalised externalities in the form of investment in education, skill-import enticements, and tax holidays to promote local and foreign direct investment. They can build the physical and legal infrastructure for processing zones and industrial parks. The less developed among developing countries, that still retain the capacity to impose infant-industry protection under GATT/WTO, can use selective tariffs to promote climbing the ladder of comparative advantage. Finally, as was done in South Korea, Meiji Japan and communist China, they can create national commitment to development through the educational system, the use of the media and national campaigns to motivate workers, entrepreneurs, bureaucrats and households to exert themselves and save in the interest of the modernisation of their countries.

But the pace of modernisation developing countries will be able to achieve through the concerted (and co-ordinated) use of this battery of direct instruments will be much slower than it was during the Bretton

Woods era. It will be constrained to a balanced-budget, relatively restrictive monetary and fiscal regime. It will probably be costly, as some of the targeted efforts may be economically inappropriate, premature, ill-timed or of the wrong scale. It will also require state institutions for co-ordination of industrial policies, not unlike the development agencies of the 1960s and 1970s. This statist-capitalism approach will therefore not have much of a chance of success if the domestic political–bureaucratic environment is not capable, honest and committed to modernisation. It will also require that the international environment be committed to economic growth.

It is an ironic thought that this 'do what you can' approach, which is the most statist and interventionist, is stimulated by too liberal an international environment imposed on countries and economies that are not ready for it, either economically or politically.

Two, developing countries can work to convince the international community that the current global financial system requires reform. Their efforts along these lines can be augmented by lobbying the developmentally-oriented national and international aid establishments of OECD countries. International aid establishments can add their voice to those of developing country advocates of financial reform of global short-term capital markets in the international community. As we have learned from the almost 70 financial crises during the last 15 years or so, and as pointed out by Tobin (1974), international markets for foreign exchange are too smooth, permitting the transfer of vast sums to be carried out instantaneously. They are also much too large, enabling immense amounts of cash to be brought to bear on any currency at any moment in time.[10] And they also have an inherent tendency to overshoot, generating waves of over-optimistic risk assessments, leading to over-lending, followed by over-pessimistic risk assessments, leading not only to the cessation of new loans but also to huge withdrawals of foreign currency. They are thus pro-cyclical in nature, amplifying both domestic and international recessions and prosperity. The enormous swings in capital flows that ensue constitute the essence of financial crises. These crises penalise not only domestic institutional inadequacies and policy mistakes, but also the self-defeating efforts of governments to pursue policies of economic independence during the post-Bretton Woods era. No country, however large and however developed its domestic financial institutions (in terms of transparency and accountability), is immune from currency attacks. Indeed, of the 70 or so financial crises that occurred towards the end of the twentieth century, fully one third occurred in developed countries.

There is thus common ground for agreement among developed and developing countries that reform of short-term international financial markets to decrease their volatility and restrict the volume of largely speculative short-term foreign exchange transactions is desirable. Iconoclastic as it may sound, some mix of regulation, disincentives, or other impediments to short-term capital mobility is required to generate a global environment that is robust and friendly to economic growth and economic development.

Three, developing countries could unilaterally delink from international capital markets to preserve their economic independence and stability. They could either, like Malaysia and Russia, eliminate convertibility of their currencies on capital accounts entirely. Alternatively, as with India and China, they could delay convertibility of their capital accounts until their economic and financial systems are sufficiently mature. Or, like Chile, they could, unilaterally, themselves introduce differential taxes and higher reserve requirements on short-term capital inflows, and foreign deposits and controls on foreign borrowing. These measures would make it more expensive to engage in short-term foreign borrowing and exchange rate speculation, and thereby provide a greater degree of state independence.

None of these classes of approach are mutually exclusive. To my mind, the second, 'financial-system-reform' approach would be the most desirable. But it would also take longest to implement. Meanwhile, developing countries that want to develop will have to muddle through using a mix of approaches one and three. But, unless they stay within the monetary and fiscal constraints, or unless they adopt both measures of type one and three simultaneously, they will continue to suffer from periodic financial crises with devastating real consequences to the economy, to the people and to the state.

In the near future, OECD aid establishments can contribute most to the economic development of developing countries by adding their collective voices to developing country pressures for short-term global capital market reform. For, in the absence of reform of short-term financial markets, the effects of foreign aid are likely to be more than nullified by a succession of financial crises. And the ability of foreign aid to counteract financial crises once they start is like the effectiveness of applying band-aids to stem haemorrhaging, as the *annual* collective amounts of resources over which aid establishments dispose is only about one-eighth the value of the *daily* short-term speculative transactions taking place on the world's foreign exchange markets.

Notes

1 The variable representing the degree of improvement in the quality of human resources has a statistically significant, but only secondary, association with a factor explaining a large percentage of inter-country variance in rates of economic growth (Adelman and Morris 1967: tab. V.5).

2 The variables representing the degree of improvement in the administrative efficiency and in leadership commitment to development have statistically significant, but only secondary, associations with a factor explaining a large percentage of inter-country variance in rates of economic growth (Adelman and Morris 1967: tab. V.5).

3 The variable representing the diversification of exports and their shift away from primary-based exports (the structure of foreign trade) has a significant

correlation with the factor accounting for the largest percentage of inter-country variance in rates of economic growth (Adelman and Morris 1967: tab. VI.4).

4 The variable measuring the degree of improvement in human resources has a high (but secondary) coefficient on the factor explaining the largest proportion of inter-country differences in rates of economic growth at this level of development (Adelman and Morris 1967: tabs. VI.1 and VI.4).

5 The variable measuring the size of the subsistence agricultural sector has a high (but secondary) coefficient on the factor explaining the largest proportion of inter-country differences in rates of economic growth at this level of development.

6 The variable measuring the extent of socio-economic dualism has a high (but secondary) coefficient on the factor explaining the largest proportion of inter-country differences in rates of economic growth at this level of development.

7 The variable measuring the extent of mass communication has a high (but secondary) coefficient on the factor explaining the largest proportion of inter-country differences in rates of economic growth at this level of development.

8 The Latin American exceptions to this statement in the 1957–67 period represented in the Adelman–Morris (1967) data were Mexico, Venezuela and Brazil.

9 Open, direct subsidies are illegal under GATT/WTO agreements.

10 During 1993–5, the Bank for International Settlements (BIS) estimates that foreign exchange transactions averaged $13 trillion *per day*. By 1997, the daily volume of foreign exchange transactions had increased to about $2 trillion! Moreover, 40 per cent of these transactions are reversed within two days (and 80 per cent within seven days) and are thus clearly speculative in nature. The clearly speculative volume of daily foreign exchange transactions in 1997 was thus $800 billion.

3 Foreign aid in historical perspective

Background and trends

*Peter Hjertholm and Howard White**

Introduction

Aid is an international operation channelling tens of billions of dollars to developing countries each year and employing large numbers of people in a multitude of organisations.[1] This chapter first describes how aid has grown through various stages, from modest origins in the nineteenth century to being securely established following the Second World War, fuelled by the inertia of institutions created in the aftermath of the war (including the success of the Marshall Plan), the cold war and the wave of independence from 1945 onwards. Since then further changes have taken place in institutions (the rise of multilaterals in the 1970s and NGOs in the 1980s), types of aid (the decline of food aid and the rise and fall of financial programme aid) and aspects of donor ideology (mainly the perceived role of the state). These changes are discussed throughout the various chapters of this volume. Together with Chapters 1 and 2, this chapter provides the backdrop for the analysis by presenting an overview of the history of aid as well as the particular features of aid and their changes over time, considering volume, composition, allocation, tying and financial terms.

History of foreign aid

In this section we argue that, despite many changes over the years, there has been one constant in the history of aid, namely that the development objectives of aid programmes have been distorted by the use of aid for donor commercial and political advantage. This is not to say that aid has never been used for development nor achieved any beneficial effects. Yet this statement is conditioned by the modernist ideological stance of donors: they tend to believe there is a single model of development based on a particular conception of Western liberal democracy. We seek to illustrate these points in the following chronological discussion of the history of aid, following which we draw out some main issues. A schematic presentation is given in Table 3.1.

Table 3.1 Schematic overview of main developments in the history of foreign aid

	Dominant or rising institutions	Donor ideology	Donor focus	Types of aid
1940s	Marshall Plan and UN system (including World Bank).	Planning.	Reconstruction.	Marshall Plan was largely programme aid.
1950s	United States, with Soviet Union gaining importance from 1956.	Anti-communist, but with role for the state.	Community Development Movement.	Food aid and projects.
1960s	Establishment of bilateral programmes.	As for the 1950s, with support for state in productive sectors.	Productive sectors (e.g. support to the green revolution) and infrastructure.	Bilaterals gave technical assistance (TA) and budget support; multilaterals supported projects.
1970s	Expansion of multilaterals especially World Bank, IMF and Arab-funded agencies).	Continued support for state activities in productive activities and meeting basic needs.	Poverty, taken as agriculture and basic needs (social sectors).	Fall in food aid and start of import support.
1980s	Rise of NGOs from mid-1980s.	Market-based adjustment (rolling back the state).	Macroeconomic reform.	Financial programme aid and debt relief.
1990s	Eastern Europe and FSU become recipients rather than donors; emergence of corresponding institutions.	Move back to the state toward end of the decade.	Poverty and then governance (environment and gender passed more quickly).	Move toward sector support at end of the decade.

Note: Entries are main features or main changes, there are of course exceptions.

The origins of foreign aid

The roots of aid can be traced to at least the nineteenth century.[2] Two events in the history of US overseas aid at different ends of that century exemplify the tension in aid programmes between relief and assistance (illustrated by the 1812 Act for the Relief of the Citizens of Venezuela) and attempts to serve donor commercial or political objectives (illustrated, beginning in 1896, by the conscious use of US food surpluses for overseas market development).

The same conflict is evident in the early years of British aid; the 1929 Colonial Development Act allowed for loans and grants for infrastructure, the purpose of which was explicitly seen as obtaining inputs for British manufacturing. The 1940 Colonial Development and Welfare Act expanded the programme to allow funding of social sector activities. Nevertheless, the Minister of Food in the post-war Labour government stated that 'by one means or another, by hook or by crook, the development of primary production of all sorts in the colonial area . . . is . . . a life and death matter for the economy of the country.' (cited in Gupta 1975: 320). One Labour member of Parliament went so far as to call for the rapid development of the colonies so that Britain could become independent of the United States (ibid.: 321).[3]

The continued support of colonial powers, notably Britain and France, to their colonies after the Second World War is one of the three main features of the international aid scheme in that period. There was considerable continuity from colonial to post-colonial institutions. One example of this was the renaming of the Colonial Development Corporation as the Commonwealth Development Corporation in the 1960s. And aid-financed efforts drew from the experience of both British and French authorities (as in the case of the Community Development Movement).

International activities in the wake of the Second World War comprise the major basis for the development of today's aid machinery. Indeed, several institutions developed from organisations originally created to cater for the aftermath of war. For example: Oxfam first catered to refugees from Greece; CARE was originally the Center for American Relief in Europe (Europe later became Everywhere); and the development work of the UN began with the United Nations Relief and Rehabilitation Agency (UNRRA) founded during the Second World War (1943). Also, the International Bank for Reconstruction and Development, or IBRD (now commonly referred to as the World Bank), began with loans for war reconstruction, making its first loan to a developing country only in 1950 (to Colombia). And the success of the Marshall Plan, which involved the above institutions, provided the impetus for turning focus to the problems of the developing world.

A final feature of importance in the post-war international scene was the first wave of independence, creating a constituency for aid. The first meeting of the nonaligned movement in 1955 gave a focus to this voice, as did the various organs of the UN, notably the United Nations Conference on Trade and Development (UNCTAD). However, as argued below, whilst its existence is the rationale for aid, the recipient communities have not been successful in their attempts to affect donor aid policy.

From poverty to adjustment and back again

The 1970s saw two conflicting trends: the first oil price shock and falling commodity prices required quick disbursing assistance (QDA) made available in the first instance by the IMF, then by the emergence of import support aid and, by 1980, the start of World Bank structural adjustment loans (which is programme aid). These facts are part of the explanation for the increasing share of multilateral aid in the 1970s. Yet, at the same time, donors announced a reorientation towards a greater poverty focus. Notably the World Bank did so, under President McNamara, but so did bilateral donors, such as the United Kingdom in its white paper *More Aid for the Poorest* in 1975 (ODM 1975) and the United States, which established the International Development and Food Assistance Act in the same year. This bill stipulated that 75 per cent of PL-480 aid should go to countries with a per capita income less than $300.[4]

Although the poverty focus enjoyed a brief period of ascendency in the late 1970s, the advent of balance-of-payments problems at about the same time and the emergence of the debt crisis in the early 1980s, resolved this conflict in favour of adjustment and aid to adjustment (programme aid, including debt relief). As such, the increase in adjustment lending was not a response to a 'development crisis'. In general, there was no such crisis, although some African countries had begun a downturn. Rather, it was a response (though not exclusively) to balance-of-payments and debt problems, including the attendant risk of financial crisis in developed countries. The experience thus clearly illustrates how aid programmes may readily respond to the needs and interests of the major donors.[5] The initial focus on macroeconomic policy also gave the World Bank and the IMF, particularly the former, a preeminence they had not enjoyed before (hence the expression the 'Washington consensus'). The World Bank is without a doubt the most important development institution, leading both policy dialogue and increasingly the research agenda. Economic crisis in the West and changes in government also led some donors – again Britain is an example – to be more open about their intention to use their aid programme for their own commercial benefit (apparently not noticing the contradiction between this stance and the free market philosophy they espoused).

The eclipse of poverty was not without its critics, which found their most effective voice first in the Unicef report *The State of the World's Children* (Grant 1990) and the Unicef-financed study *Adjustment with a Human Face* (Cornia *et al.* 1987). These works argued that adjustment policies neglected the poor and should be redesigned accordingly.[6] By the late 1980s these arguments were having some effect and the World Bank began work on designing a poverty policy (assisted by President Barber Conable, who emphasised the issue), which culminated in the 'New Poverty Agenda' in the 1990 *World Development Report* (World Bank 1990a). This publication is often given as the starting point for poverty reappearing on the agenda of donor agencies (and agencies have based their strategies on that of the World Bank). As such it provides an example of how the World Bank can 'take over' activities even though the original initiative came from outside the World Bank and was initially resisted by the Bank.

Post-cold war era and donor domination

The end of the cold war may be expected to have heralded great changes for aid. There have been rather less (and different) changes than many expected, however. For example, aid budgets have declined throughout the 1990s, rather than growing as a result of the peace dividend as hoped. There *have* been two changes of note. First, the disappearance of Eastern Europe and the countries of the Former Soviet Union (FSU) as aid donors and their re-emergence as recipients. Second, donor concerns about governance. Although still inconsistently applied, donors have now awarded or withdrawn aid on the basis of governance issues, whereas in the cold war period they happily supported any 'friendly regime' (friendly to the West, not necessarily the bulk of the country's inhabitants). Some countries of former strategic importance are no longer so, and have seen their aid fall accordingly.

On the other hand, there has also been remarkable continuity in aid programmes. There were arguments in the early 1990s that aid would wither away, and be replaced by financing on issues of global importance such as the environment and international security. This does not appear to have happened, and there are not strong reasons to think that it is about to do so. It may be imagined that the low-income countries of the world, such as those in sub-Saharan Africa and South Asia, will continue to receive aid for some years to come – making the issues of aid effectiveness addressed in this volume of continuing importance (see Chapter 4). In Chapter 19 of this volume, the political economy aspects of these issues are pursued in further depth.

Donors have, as noted above, tended to dominate the aid scene. A number of examples may be given. From 1951 there was a campaign for a soft-loan special UN fund for development (SUNFED), that was not realised. Donors preferred instead to place the International Development Agency (IDA) under the World Bank. The UN applies one-country one-vote whereas the developed countries dominate the Bank. The Development Assistance Committee (DAC) of the OECD, which is the donor organisation responsible for monitoring aid performance, has no developing country members (even as observers); UNCTAD made several attempts to wrest control of aid policy from DAC but was unsuccessful. The main country-level co-ordinating mechanism is Consultative Groups (or Round Tables) at which the donor community presents the recipient with a report card and their latest concerns and conditions. The donor co-ordinating body for support to adjustment in Africa, the Special Programme of Assistance for Africa (SPA), has no African representation. Yet, it does not necessarily have to be like this. The Marshall Plan was administered by a committee (the Organisation for European Economic Co-operation, OEEC, which is the forerunner of the OECD) in which the donor had no special position over the recipients. Nevertheless, donors have not been willing to relinquish control of their aid programmes in developing countries. Although donors increasingly talk of partnership, and the need for recipient ownership, they in fact are reluctant to allow recipients more than a limited role.

A partial reason for this reluctance is in all likelihood the desire of donors to utilise aid for their own ends, a factor that also helps explain the persistence of bilateral aid despite widely aired arguments in favour of multilateral institutions. These ends are both political and commercial and affect who gets aid and what it may be used for. Hence, as described below, donors clearly do not allocate aid solely according to developmental criteria. This subordination of aid to other donor objectives is, however, at odds with the notion of policy coherence (or consistency), adopted by several donors in the second half of the 1990s.

Donor domination has also affected the largely modernist development thinking, which has been the basis of aid programmes. Thus, it has been accepted that there is a conception of the ideal societal state – basically Western liberal democracy, though the conception of this has changed over time – to which developing countries should aspire. The donor community has done little to support the search for alternative models of development and even less to promote them.

Aggregate trends in foreign aid

Aid volume and its components

Aggregate trends in official development assistance (ODA) to developing countries are presented in Figure 3.1.[7] A marked upward trend in the various indicators, including the real value of foreign aid, is clear since the 1960s, as is the peak in 1992. Since then, however, aid volumes have been characterised by a decided downfall. In 1997, aid in current prices stood at only $47.9 billion, a drop of 23.7 percent compared to 1992 ($62.7 billion). In real terms net ODA in 1997 was lower than in 1984.

As described above, this turnaround in aid flows in the 1990s followed the end of the cold war. New interests, problems and obligations successfully competed for the energies *and* financial resources of the industrial world. Donors also argued that a further factor was pressure on the national budgets of donors. A study undertaken by OECD (reported in OECD 1997) shows that aid has fallen fastest in those DAC members (e.g. Sweden, Italy and Finland) that have been running the largest fiscal deficits while, by contrast, the members with the smallest deficits (e.g. Norway, Japan and Ireland) all increased their aid in real terms. However, whilst by 1997 the average budget deficit amongst DAC donors has been reduced to 1.3 per cent of GDP, compared with 4.3 per cent four years earlier, aid volumes have continued to fall (German and Randel 1998).

For the reasons discussed previously, the share of multilateral aid rose from about 23 per cent in the 1970s to nearly 30 per cent in the 1990s (see Table 3.2).[8] Leading multilateral donors include the World Bank (which

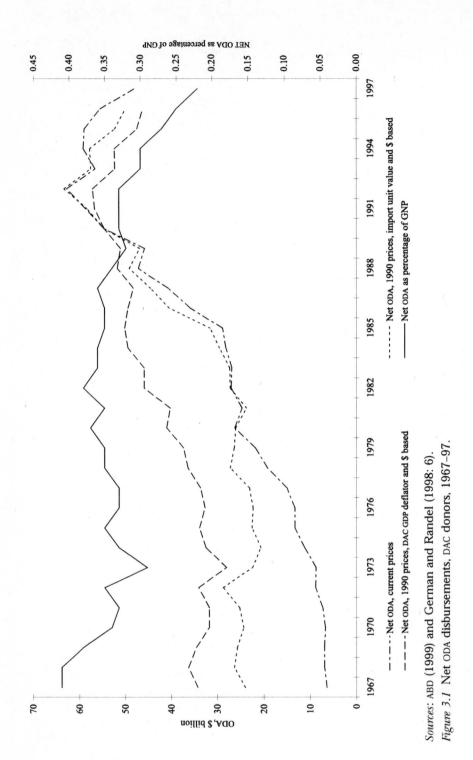

Sources: ABD (1999) and German and Randel (1998: 6).

Figure 3.1 Net ODA disbursements, DAC donors, 1967–97.

Table 3.2 Net ODA disbursements, by type and donor, all donors, 1973–96 (per cent)

	Average share 1973–80	*Average share 1981–90*	*Average share 1991–6*
ODA type			
ODA grants	61.6	71.1	77.4
ODA loans	38.4	28.9	22.6
Total	100.0	100.0	100.0
Donor			
Bilateral ODA[a]	77.2	75.4	70.1
Multilateral ODA	22.8	24.6	29.9
o.w. IBRD and IDA	5.6	7.7	8.3
IMF (SAF and ESAF)	0.0	0.1	1.3
United Nations Agencies	7.5	8.6	9.6
CEC	3.4	4.4	7.2
Other	6.3	3.8	3.5
Total	100.0	100.0	100.0

Sources: ABD (1999), except data for details on multilateral ODA, which is drawn directly from OECD (1998a).

Notes: There may be (small) discrepancies between the data shown here and the disaggregated data produced in ABD (1999), since the data in the appendix is drawn from OECD's *DAC On-line Database* (OECD 1999a).
o.w., of which.
[a]Including Arab donors.

has expanded its policy advisory role in the developing world side by side with its increased financial involvement), the UN agencies (notably UNDP) and the Commission of the European Communities (CEC). A further change is the increasing share of grant aid; more than 75 per cent of total ODA were in the form of grants in the period 1991–6, compared with just over 60 per cent two decades earlier (see Table 3.3 and ABD (1999) for further details on types of aid and other flows).

The relative importance of ODA among financial flows has changed over time. To a considerable extent, the decline in ODA flows to developing countries after 1992 has been compensated by an increase in private flows (ABD 1999). In fact, the surge in private flows has meant that they have become the most important source of financial flows to the developing countries as a whole. Having accounted for more than 60 per cent on average of total net disbursements during 1987–92 (and 70 per cent at its peak in 1990), the share of ODA has steadily declined to little more than a third of disbursements in 1993–7 (Table 3.3). Correspondingly, the share of private flows in net disbursements soared from an average of about 26 per cent in 1987–92 (with a nadir in 1990 of only about 12 per cent) to more than 55 per cent in 1993–7.

Table 3.3 Net disbursements of total official and private flows by type, all donors, 1987–97 (per cent)

	Average share 1987–92	Average share 1993–7
Developing countries		
Official development assistance (ODA)	61.6	37.2
Other official flows (OOF)	6.6	4.5
Private flows	26.4	55.1
Grants from NGOS	5.4	3.2
Total	100.0	100.0
	Average share 1987–92	Average share 1993–6
Sub-Saharan African countries		
Official development assistance (ODA)	89.5	90.2
Other official flows (OOF)	11.7	2.4
Private flows	−1.2	7.5
Grants from NGOS	n.a.	n.a.
Total	100.0	100.0

Source: OECD (1999a).

Note: n.a., not available.

However, if geography and income levels are taken into account, a somewhat different picture emerges, as exemplified by the case of sub-Saharan Africa (Table 3.3). As was the case for the developing countries as a group, net ODA flows to sub-Saharan countries also peaked in 1992 and then declined, although net disbursements at the end of the period were still larger (but only just) than in 1987. Yet, since private creditors and investors have been much more reluctant to increase their exposure in the sub-Saharan region, the shortfall in ODA flows has not been compensated by higher private flows (ABD 1999). In fact, in several years during 1987–96 private flows were negative. Consequently, ODA has continued to be the predominant source of financial resources for the poorest developing countries in sub-Saharan Africa (and elsewhere), with ODA shares accounting for about 90 per cent of net disbursements during the 1987–96 period.

The aid volume effort of the international donor community can be seen from Figures 3.1 and 3.2, where net ODA disbursements are expressed as a ratio of donor GNP. For DAC donors as a group, this ratio has nearly halved over the last three decades, and has been steadily declining since the early 1980s (from 0.38 per cent in 1982 to 0.22 per cent in 1997) (Figure 3.1). The UN target of 0.70 per cent thus seems more remote than ever. The individual donor effort underlying the poor aid record of 1997 is presented in Figure 3.2. Only four countries, Denmark, Norway, Netherlands and Sweden, have reached (and surpassed) the UN target of 0.70 per cent.[9]

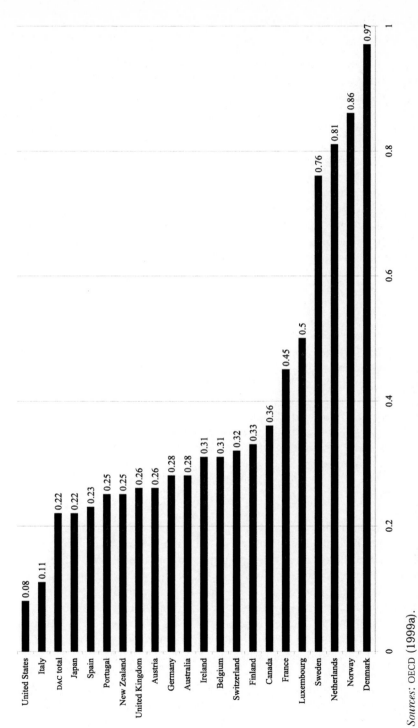

Sources: OECD (1999a).

Figure 3.2 Net ODA disbursements as a percentage of donor GNP, 1997.

Composition and allocation of aid

Aid composition

In Table 3.4, ODA commitments are presented by main sectors and purposes. A number of relatively clear allocative shifts have occurred during the period observed. There has been a marked switch toward more aid for social infrastructure and services (e.g. education, health, water supply and sanitation), in particular after 1992, a reflection of the strengthened emphasis by donors on the developmental role of human resource capabilities. In recent years more than a quarter of ODA has been committed to this sector. Likewise, economic infrastructure and services (e.g. energy, transport and communications) have received increased attention and flows (rising to more than 20 per cent of commitments by 1991–7).

Direct donor involvement in the productive sectors, such as agriculture and industry (and related activities) as well as trade and tourism, has, on the other hand, diminished significantly in developing countries since the 1970s and 1980s, accounting for only 12 per cent in 1991–7. The diminished role of aid in the area of production is in part explained by the increase in the 1980s of an ideological bias against direct support to the productive sector. Also, at least in the better-off developing countries, the decline is related to the increased importance of private financing through, for example, foreign direct investments or bond and equity issues (OECD 1997). Programme assistance (including food aid), after having played an important role in the 1970s and adjustment years of the 1980s, has been scaled down considerably (only 10 per cent in 1991–7). Finally, relative newcomers in the aid landscape, like multi-sector aid and (more permanent) debt relief have steadily expanded their share, accounting for around 5 per cent and 9 per cent of ODA commitments, respectively, to developing countries during 1991–7.

Allocation of aid

The allocation of aid across geographical regions and income groups is presented in Table 3.5 (detailed data in ABD 1999). A number of points can be drawn from these data. First, regarding geographical allocation, the sub-Saharan African region is, or has become, of high priority (although the large number of countries in this region implies that aid money is also more thinly spread), with 30 per cent of total ODA going this way in 1991–6 compared with about 20 per cent in 1973–80. The share of aid to this region from the four UN-target donors (Denmark, Norway, Netherlands and Sweden) has traditionally been much higher; more than 40 per cent on average in the 1980s, declining somewhat in 1991–6 to about 36 per cent (ABD 1999). The high priority given to the sub-Saharan region must be seen in the context of the deep-seated economic problems that have afflicted many countries in this part of the world since at least the early 1980s, in

Table 3.4 ODA commitments by sector and purpose, DAC donors, 1973–97 (per cent)

	Average share 1973–80	*Average share 1981–90*	*Average share 1991–7*
Social infrastructure and services	20.8	25.0	26.2
Economic infrastructure and services	13.9	18.7	21.8
Production sectors	22.0	19.7	12.0
Multisector (crosscutting)	2.2	3.0	4.7
Commodity aid and general programme aid	14.2	16.2	10.0
Action relating to debt	3.7	4.3	8.8
Emergency assistance	1.1	1.7	5.3
Administrative costs of donors	n.a.	3.8[a]	4.3
Support to NGOs	n.a.	2.2[a]	1.3
Unallocated/unspecified	22.1	7.1	5.7
Total	100.0	101.7	100.0

Source: ABD (1999).
Notes: n.a., not available.
   [a]Average numbers refer to 1984–90, explaining why the total does not add up to 100%.

Table 3.5 Net ODA disbursements, allocation by geographical region and income groups, all donors, 1973–96 (per cent)

	Average share 1973–80	*Average share 1981–90*	*Average share 1991–6*
By region			
North Africa	12.7	7.8	7.3
Sub-Saharan Africa	19.8	28.4	30.0
South America	3.7	3.5	4.5
Middle East	13.8	10.4	6.7
South and Central Asia	16.9	14.5	11.7
Far East Asia	10.7	10.4	13.4
Other[a]	22.3	25.1	26.4
of which Europe	2.0	1.7	4.2
Total by region	100.0	100.0	100.0
By income group			
LLDCs[b]	22.8	28.0	26.3
Other low income[c]	18.4	19.5	24.0
Low middle income[d]	33.2	26.1	25.4
Upper middle income[e]	3.6	3.2	3.3
Higher income[f]	6.1	5.7	4.0
Unallocated	15.9	17.5	17.0
Total by income	100.0	100.0	100.0

Source: ABD (1999).
Notes: [a]Includes Europe, Oceania, Central America and geographically unallocated.
     [b]Least Developed Countries.
     [c]Countries with per capita GNP < $765 in 1995.
     [d]Countries with per capita GNP between $766 and $3035 in 1995.
     [e]Countries with per capita GNP between $3036 and $9385 in 1995.
     [f]Countries with per capita GNP > $9385 in 1995.

combination with the stronger emphasis on the 'poverty orientation' of aid on the part of donors.

A number of other regions on the other hand (e.g. North Africa, the Middle East and South and Central Asia), have seen their share of aid flows diminish markedly, in large part a reflection of the decline in their earlier political and strategic importance for the allocative leitmotif of the larger powers. The lower shares of aid going to South America and Far East Asia are largely explained by the more pronounced extent of economic development as well as better access to alternative (in particular private) sources of finance. Regarding the allocation between income groups, donors have allocated roughly equal shares to the least developed countries (LLDCs), other low-income (LICs) and lower middle-income countries (LMICs) in 1991–6 (about a quarter of total ODA). The four UN-target donors, however, have since the early 1980s allocated a substantially higher aid share to LLDCs as compared to LICs and LMICs (ABD 1999).

Over the years various attempts have been made by economists (and by political scientists, see Chapter 19) to explain the allocative patterns of donor aid and their determining factors. Not only altruistic motives, but certainly also political, strategic and commercial concerns have been shown to play a part in shaping donors allocative motives and decisions.[10] Three aspects of the allocative pattern of aid have occupied economists in particular. One is the question of whether aid is appropriately allocated among recipient countries, the benchmark usually being that lower per capita income should generate higher per capita aid flows. This type of analysis is termed descriptive (or evaluative), and a variety of methods have been adopted in the literature to measure the performance of donors.[11] In general the Nordic donors (especially Norway) come out at the top of such evaluative performance rankings, while the United States is usually found among the worst performers.

The second type of analysis is explanatory in nature, asking why donors allocate aid the way they do.[12] Sharing often a common reference to the political economy literature, these studies usually treat aid as a foreign policy instrument applied to help achieve a range of political, strategic, economic, as well as genuinely humanitarian objectives. The basic assertion is that the pursuit of these objectives will motivate donors to allocate their aid so as to be conducive (in the eyes of the donor) to the attainment of these objectives. Since information on the motives themselves are not always readily available, explanatory analysis focuses on the decision making process of turning motives into allocations. A number of different modelling approaches have been attempted to identify the determining elements of aid allocation, usually involving two basically different sets of factors: those related to the development requirements of recipients and those related to the political, strategic and economic concerns of donors. The evidence suggests a general pattern where, for example, US aid appears to have been mostly guided by strategic considerations, Japanese aid by commercial objectives and Dutch and Nordic aid by recipient needs.

The third type of analysis is normative in nature, seeking to prescribe how donors ought to allocate their aid. Sharing the evaluative approach of the descriptive literature, the prescriptive studies go a step further by pointing out the discrepancy between observed performance of donors and the performance that ought to have been, based on notions of development requirements or good policy stance. Among the (still few) studies that attempt to arrive at such prescriptive conclusions one finds the supply-side models of aid allocation developed in McGillivray and White (1993b, 1993c). These involve various measures of recipient needs and absorptive capacity as well as the political and commercial concerns of donors. The results show a generally poor performance on the part of the donor community at large. A recent study by Collier and Dollar (1999), though using a different approach, reached similar conclusions, except that the World Bank appeared to perform above average.[13]

The strings attached: qualitative aspects of aid

Foreign aid may be tied in four ways: to payment, to procurement, to projects and to policies (the 4Ps). That is: (i) ODA loans are provided on the premise that the recipient country returns the money with interest according to the financial terms stipulated in the loan agreement, (ii) ODA grants and loans can be tied to procurement in the donor country or, in case of partial tying, in the donor country as well as a certain number of specified developing countries, (iii) ODA grants and loans may be tied for specific development projects under supervision of the donor and (iv) in the case of programme aid, the money is committed and disbursed in accordance with the recipient country's compliance with an agreed set of policies *vis-à-vis* the domestic economy. The two last Ps (project tying and policy conditionality) cannot be viewed as unambiguously bad features of aid delivery. By contrast, the two first Ps (payment and procurement) are generally seen (by development specialists, recipient country governments and many agency officials) as undesirable features of aid flows. Hence, we present here data on trends in the financial terms (measured by the grant element of aid) and tying status of ODA commitments by DAC donors.[14]

Financial terms

DAC has set out successive targets to ensure that the concessionality of aid flows remains as high as possible.[15] The present target stipulates an average grant element of total ODA commitments to all developing countries of at least 84 per cent.[16] In addition, for each donor to satisfy the DAC recommendations it is also required that the total aid effort should not be 'significantly below the DAC average.' To increase concessionality to meet these targets, donors can either increase the grant element of ODA loans or reduce the share of loans in total ODA. Table 3.6 presents summary data on financial terms for bilateral ODA commitments (full data, including details on the larger donors and the UN-target donors, are found in ABD 1999).

Compared with the 1970s, the average grant element of ODA commitments increased to 80 per cent in the 1980s, then dropped slightly in the 1990s, and has remained below the agreed target of 84 per cent. This outcome was the result of a markedly lower grant element of ODA loans, especially in the 1980s, not fully compensated by the otherwise considerable increase in the share of ODA grants.[17] The grant element of aid from the UN-target donors (Denmark, Norway, Netherlands and Sweden) on the other hand, has increased considerably since the 1970s, at that time already well above the DAC target, to reach almost 100 per cent in the 1990s. This development did not result from any improvement in the grant element of ODA loans, in fact they have worsened during the period observed, but from the reduction of the share of aid loans to a mere 1 per cent of total ODA by the 1990s.

Aid tying

Donor governments often feel justified to reduce the balance-of-payments cost of their aid by requiring recipient countries to purchase aid-financed goods from the donor country, subject to some safeguards of appropriate quality and prices (DAC guidelines allow a 10 per cent 'margin', i.e. mark up over world market prices, although data suggest rather higher margins are used in practice). It is believed that it is easier to maintain public and parliamentary support for aid programmes if immediate tangible benefits are seen to accrue to the national economy of the donor.[18] Economists and multilateral institutions have argued, however, that aid tying is a potential source of economic distortions, especially in cases where the donor is overly concerned with the promotion of home exports.[19] Moreover, tied aid is hardly compatible with OECD/DACs stated objectives in such areas as enhanced competition, reduced intervention in markets and withdrawal from subsidies. Ideally, aid recipients should have a free choice of the most appropriate and competitive source of supply, benefiting thereby from the advantages of international bidding (OECD 1985). Donors have therefore acknowledged (in principle) the higher value of untied aid for the recipient country and that economic distortions may thereby be reduced (OECD 1992a).[20]

In spite of this, the tying of ODA flows remains a prominent feature of the aid effort of many donors, as is shown in the Table 3.7. Although the share of total untied DAC aid has increased steadily from 40–5 per cent in the early 1980s to about 70 per cent in 1995–6 and even 88 per cent in 1997, a number of donors have been unable or unwilling to move decisively

Table 3.6 Bilateral ODA commitments, data on financial terms, DAC donors, 1973–96 (per cent)

	Average 1973–80	*Average 1981–90*	*Average 1991–6*
DAC donors			
Grant share of ODA[a]	33.9	55.0	48.7
Loan share of ODA	66.1	45.0	51.3
Grant element of ODA loans	61.0	55.4	59.5
Grant element of total ODA	74.3	80.0	79.1
UN-target donors[b]			
Grant share of ODA[a]	72.6	86.5	99.0
Loan share of ODA	27.4	13.5	1.0
Grant element of ODA loans	67.1	62.6	43.7
Grant element of total ODA	91.0	95.1	99.5

Source: ABD (1999).
Notes: [a]Grants refer to both ODA grants as well as equity investment and grant-like loans since these have a grant element of 100 per cent also.
[b]Denmark, the Netherlands, Norway and Sweden.

towards the DAC recommendations. Thus, they continue to tie often substantial amounts of their aid.[21] For example, if a 'good performance' in 1996 were to be defined as one where the donor ties no more than 30 per cent of its bilateral aid only eight donors (several of them quite small in volume terms) would qualify, and in 1997 only ten. Moreover, a number of the 'good performers' only became so recently, having tied substantial amounts of aid throughout the 1980s.[22]

The (un)tying performance tends, however, to change quite a bit over time, as the share of untied aid of individual donors is prone to considerable swings (ABD 1999). It is not an easy task to explain the variation of tying across time and donors, but if anything DAC recommendations are evidently not the only, let alone the main guiding principle. In many cases, changes in aid tying are probably closely linked to changes in the international competitiveness of home businesses, as suggested by White and Woestman (1994), with Japan in recent years (competitive and less tying) and the United Kingdom in the 1980s (less competitive and more tying) being good examples. In other cases, such as Germany (internationally competitive, but substantial tying nevertheless), other factors may be involved as well.[23]

A diagrammatic synthesis: aid diamonds

We can combine four important qualitative aspects of aid delivery (i.e. volume, concessionality, poverty orientation and tying) into a single figure called an aid diamond. Examples are given for Sweden and the United States in Figure 3.3 (diamonds for the other DAC donors are given in ABD

Table 3.7 Bilateral ODA commitments, share of untied aid, DAC donors, selected years 1981–97 (per cent)

	1981	1985	1989	1993	1997
Austria	3.4	3.0	3.1	44.8	60.6
Australia	60.0	53.4	10.4	41.9	63.1
Belgium	29.0	37.5	n.a.	n.a.	49.9
Canada	18.0	42.3	41.4	61.9	33.4
Denmark	63.6	60.4	n.a.	n.a.	71.6
Finland	84.9	80.9	20.8	59.0	76.8
France	42.5	42.5	47.8	31.5	n.a.
Germany	74.3	3.7	33.8	47.9	n.a.
Ireland	n.a.	100.1	n.a.	n.a.	n.a.
Italy	71.6	16.6	9.1	43.1	45.6
Japan	36.8	60.8	70.2	83.9	99.6
Luxembourg	n.a.	n.a.	n.a.	n.a.	95.2
Netherlands	57.3	60.3	45.8	n.a.	90.0
New Zealand	36.4	78.0	n.a.	n.a.	n.a.
Norway	73.6	70.3	71.3	81.8	91.1
Portugal	n.a.	n.a.	n.a.	63.8	99.1
Spain	n.a.	n.a.	n.a.	n.a.	n.a.
Sweden	84.0	68.8	71.1	85.0	74.5
Switzerland	50.1	67.3	74.9	91.4	94.9
United Kingdom	20.5	27.6	24.0	35.2	71.7
United States	33.4	40.9	34.9	37.4	n.a.
DAC donors total	44.1	47.3	43.8	57.9	87.6

Source: OECD (1999a).
Note: n.a., not available.

1999). There are four axes to the diamond. They represent: (1) aid volume, measured as a percentage of donor GNP; (2) the grant element; (3) the share to LLDCs; (4) the percentage of aid that is untied. The quality of aid delivery is seen to be higher the higher each of these numbers are. Thus, the better a donor's aid programme, the larger the diamond. Each figure combines donor performance with the DAC average and the DAC target. In the case of tying there is no DAC target (as there is, say, for 0.70 per cent of GNP for aid volume) so the target is set at 100 per cent. The DAC target for aid to LLDCs is 0.15 per cent of GNP. We have converted this figure to the share of a donor's aid which would have to go to LLDCs in order to meet this target by dividing through by the donor's ODA to GNP ratio. If a donor's ratio is less than 0.15 per cent of GNP (e.g. the United States in 1996), then more than 100 per cent of the aid should go to LLDCs to meet the DAC target. In such cases the diamond for the DAC target is 'truncated' at the 100 percentage point.

The examples given clearly illustrate how the quality of US aid delivery (the 'real' value of US aid, so to speak) has declined over time. They also show clearly the higher quality of Swedish aid delivery. Looking at the

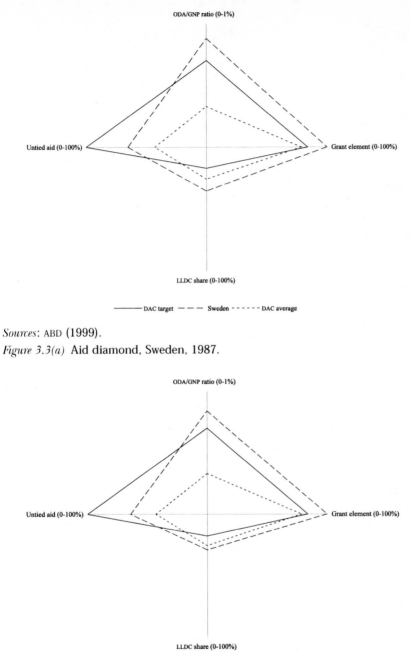

Sources: ABD (1999).

Figure 3.3(a) Aid diamond, Sweden, 1987.

Sources: ABD (1999).

Figure 3.3(b) Aid diamond, Sweden, 1996.

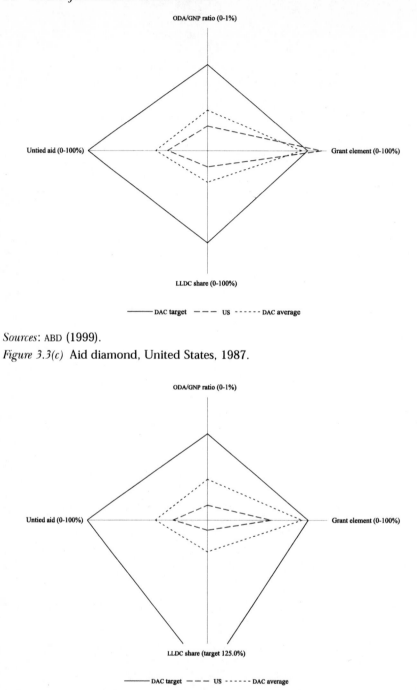

Sources: ABD (1999).

Figure 3.3(c) Aid diamond, United States, 1987.

Sources: ABD (1999).

Figure 3.3(d) Aid diamond, United States, 1996.

performance of all donors (as is done in Hjertholm and White 2000) within each of the four qualitative aspects of aid delivery, the diamonds depict plainly the extent to which a large number of donors are far removed from the recommendations and targets jointly set out by DAC. So when discussing the growth and development effectiveness of foreign aid (see Chapter 4), it is worth keeping in mind the generally poor aid delivery performance of donors.

It must be remembered that all four aspects of aid flows are identified precisely because of their implications for the economic growth potential of the donor effort. The aid volume effort (measured by the ODA/GNP ratio) derives its significance from its potential in filling (or closing) gaps in domestic financial resources (see Chapter 15). The concessionality of aid (measured by the grant element) derives significance from its role in determining the future debt servicing burden of recipients, a factor which has important ramifications for the development effects of macroeconomic management. The allocation of aid to the poorest countries (the LLDC share) derives its twin rationale from observing the disproportionate existence of needs in these countries, and the belief that higher aid-induced growth rates could yield disproportionately higher welfare gains for the poor. Finally, the untying of aid is seen as a way of increasing the cost-effectiveness of aid-financed imports.

Conclusions

Historically, foreign aid has served a multitude of objectives. For some of the smaller donors, the allocation and quality of aid flows have been largely, but not wholly, shaped by a concern for the development needs of the recipient community. By contrast, the foreign aid of several of the larger donors has been firmly established as a foreign and commercial policy tool, designed to achieve a range of political, strategic, economic, but also genuinely humanitarian objectives. This assertion is born by observing the historical origins of foreign aid and is supported by the empirical literature on aid allocation. Indeed, it seems that donor self-interest has been an enduring feature of donor–recipient relations since the 1950s, a relationship that has otherwise been characterised by many changes in terms of the volume, composition, types and objectives of aid flows. Yet, while this particular characteristic of aid flows may well have impaired the effectiveness of aid, by nature, there is no automatic contra-diction between donor and recipient objectives.

Perhaps the most important of recent changes in the aid picture is the clear reversal after 1992 of the historic upward trend in aid volumes. This may not be a big problem when declining aid flows are compensated by higher private flows, as has happened in several developing countries. Yet it may be a considerable problem in low-income countries without access to private capital and which continue to rely heavily on aid for financial resources. Clearly, the underlying premises of donor–recipient co-operation are very different when aid resources become more limited rather than more abundant, especially when debt service is still a factor of significance. Indeed, this is one of the rationales behind writing this book, and many of the themes touched upon in this chapter will be pursued in later chapters.

Notes

* The authors are grateful for useful comments on an earlier draft of this chapter from Paul Mosley and other participants at the aid book workshop at the University of Copenhagen, 9–19 October 1998, as well as from an internal referee The authors are also grateful for the data assistance provided by Jean-Louis Grolleau and the staff of the Development Assistance Committee of the OECD. The usual disclaimer applies.

1 No figures exist for how many people are directly employed in the aid business: one of the largest institutions, the World Bank, alone employs thousands of people and more than 40,000 aid-financed expatriates are estimated to be working in Africa.

2 Since our argument in this chapter is that aid programmes have always been characterised by their use for the political or commercial advantage of the donor, one could plausibly trace 'aid' back to gifts from one king or ruler to another in medieval or even classical times But there is a difference, in that aid as mentioned here was also seen as a general benefit to the population of the recipient country and that some continuity can be established with the present-day aid infrastructure.

3 Gupta (1975) argues that there were, however, forces in both the Colonial Office and amongst Labour members of the Parliament that held this drive to exploitation somewhat in check.

4 PL (Public Law) 480 food aid refers to the *Agricultural Trade Development and Assistance Act* (not to be confused with the *Agricultural, Trade and Development Assistance Act*) passed in the United States in 1954, which marked the inception of formal food aid programmes. While publicly announced at the time as a benign response to developing country needs, its primary purpose, as the name betrays, was to help develop new markets for surplus US agricultural output.

5 The differing responses of Western governments to the financial crises in East Asia and the natural disasters in Central America in late 1998 strongly bring this point home.

6 The authors of *Adjustment with a Human Face* did accept the need for adjustment, and they did not argue that adjustment policies had necessarily harmed the poor.

7 The data presented in this section is for the most part extracted from the Aid Book Database (ABD 1999), which is a set of companion appendixes prepared by Peter Hjertholm based on OECD/DAC sources. The ABD is available (in pdf format) at the Web site of the Development Economics Research Group (DERG) at the Institute of Economics, University of Copenhagen (www.econ.ku.dk/derg/pub. htm) as well as in a discussion paper by Hjertholm and White (2000). ODA is defined by DAC to include grants or loans to developing countries and territories which are: (i) undertaken by the official sector of the donor country, (ii) with promotion of economic development and welfare in the recipient country as the main objective and (iii) at concessional financial terms (i.e. if a loan, have a grant element of at least 25 per cent). In addition to these financial flows, technical co-operation is included in ODA, while grants, loans and credits for military purposes are excluded, regardless of their concessionality.

8 The share of multilateral aid going to sub-Saharan Africa has increased even more, to more than 40 per cent by 1994–6 (ABD 1999).

9 In 1996, these countries (referred to below as the UN-target donors) contributed almost 15 per cent of total net ODA disbursements.

10 See Hjertholm and White (2000) for an overview of the aid allocation literature.

11 See White and McGillivray (1995) for a recent survey of the methods and results of this literature.

12 The explanatory literature is surveyed in a paper by McGillivray and White (1993a).

13 Collier and Dollar (1999) use a combination of infant mortality rates and good policy indicators as allocative criteria, on the assertion that aid provided in a 'good policy' context leads to higher growth rates which in turn leads to less poverty and lower mortality rates.

14 The grant element is an indicator of the concessionality (i.e. softness) of the financial terms of a loan commitment, which combines interest rate, maturity (interval to final repayment) and grace period (interval to first repayment of principal capital). The grant element is calculated as the difference between the face value of the future service payments to be made by the borrower and the grant equivalent, and expressed as a percentage of the face value of the loan. The grant equivalent in turn measures the present value of a loan, conventionally using a discount rate of 10 per cent.

15 White and Woestman (1994) report on the history of these initiatives dating back to the late 1960s.

16 The DAC recommendations have in addition set out a number of targets (norms) for aid to the least developed countries (LLDCs): The average grant element of annual ODA commitments from each donor to each recipient country is set at least 86 per cent, or alternatively at least 90 per cent for the LLDCs as a group.

17 When the DAC target on financial terms (a grant element of 0.84) is combined with the UN target on ODA volume (0.70 per cent of donor GNP) a combined target of 0.59 is produced (White and Woestman 1994). Except for the UN-target donors, DAC donors have in general not met this combined target of 0.59 (see ABD 1999 for the data). It would thus appear that the donors which have been calling to attention their preparedness to substantially increase the grant element of their ODA (and have indeed done so), have also been the donors which have substantially reduced their aid effort in volume terms (thus the money may be cheaper now, but there is also a lot less of it!).

18 While the political rationale may be valid, it is uncertain, however, whether there are any significant macroeconomic benefits to the donor economy, given the relatively modest order of magnitude in most cases (OECD 1985).

19 The danger of economic distortions may arise from (i) a bias towards projects with a larger import content in areas of particular export interest to the donor, (ii) corresponding bias against projects and programmes with a lower import content, such as rural development projects, and in particular against local-cost financing, (iii) a bias against 'commercially interesting' developing countries, (iv) donor reluctance to co-operate and co-ordinate their aid activities with other donors who may be seen as competitors in the search for commercially attractive projects, (v) impaired credibility of donors in the development policy dialogue with recipients and (vi) donor reluctance to channel aid through multilateral institutions (OECD 1985: 241–2).

20 Estimates vary, but the extra costs that tied-aid recipients may incur as a result of uncompetitive (and thus over) pricing may be as high as between 10–25 per cent (see, e.g. Bhagwati 1967 and Riddell 1987), costs which can be expected to disappear once tying is discontinued.

21　As noted by the OECD (1994), the overall reduction of tied aid is more a result of an increase in the naturally untied components of aid, such as programme aid and emergency aid, than a reduction in tied project aid.

22　Analogous to the combined terms–volume performance considered before, the 'real' extent of DAC donors 'untied aid performance' (UAP) can be gauged by combining the amount of untied aid as a percentage of bilateral commitments with the ODA/GNP ratio, thus arriving at a 'volume corrected' ratio of untied aid Based on such combined data, Hjertholm and White (2000) compare donor rankings based on UAP and the performance 'corrected' by the volume effort of donors. The results show, for example, that the top UAPs of Japan and Portugal look a lot less impressive when account is taken of the fact that these donors do not provide much aid relative to the size of their economies. On the other hand, the UAPs of donors like Norway and the Netherlands, already far above the average, look even more distinguished when their high ODA/GNP ratios are considered. Denmark also performs substantially better when the UAP is held against the Danish ODA/GNP ratio of almost 1 per cent.

23　The extent to which less competitive home businesses can in practice influence the aid and tying policy of the donor government may be a factor here.

4 Aid effectiveness disputed

*Henrik Hansen and Finn Tarp**

Introduction

The past 30 years have witnessed a massive outpouring of studies on the effectiveness of foreign aid. The topic has been a central and recurring theme with which many economists, subscribing to the different paradigms of development thinking discussed in Chapter 1, have grappled. The question of whether aid works or not has been approached from different methodological and ideological perspectives. More specifically: (i) the impact of aid has been evaluated at both the micro- and macroeconomic level; (ii) cross-country as well as single-country case studies have been relied on; and (iii) aid effectiveness research includes broad surveys of a qualitative and inter-disciplinary nature as well as quantitative analyses. A comprehensive survey of the aid effectiveness literature is not feasible in this chapter.[1] Instead we will address a particularly thorny issue that has preoccupied aid protagonists and aid critics alike, namely the macroeconomic impact of aid on growth.

The choice of focus can be justified on several grounds. First, the existing literature lacks a strong analytical framework that can be used to compare and evaluate the causal relationships in the various studies. Aid is given for many different purposes, as discussed in Chapter 3, and in many different forms (see Chapters 5–8). From an analytical perspective, one can draw on both traditional growth theory and new growth models to illustrate how aid can potentially impact on economic growth through a highly diverse set of channels. For example, Cassen and associates (1994) argue that there is plenty of evidence to substantiate the view that development projects have often yielded respectable economic rates of return. Similarly, numerous case studies support the World Bank (1998a) observation that aid has, at times, been a spectacular success. It is neither analytically defensible nor empirically credible to argue from the outset that aid never works. A more constructive point of departure requires focused questions and well specified empirical hypotheses. The impact of aid on selected macroeconomic variables, including in particular savings, investment and growth, incorporates such a set of specific and testable propositions. In any case, it is desirable to explore the impact of aid in a wider macroeconomic setting (see Chapter 15).

Moreover, there is a need to resolve one of the most stubborn paradoxes in the aid effectiveness literature. This is the widespread perception that a contradiction exists between the results of microeconomic and macroeconomic studies. Literature surveys on the macroeconomic impact of aid covering the period up to the end of the 1980s tell a much less sanguine story than microeconomic project evaluations. Reviewers have found it difficult to generalise, and it is regularly argued that the traditional cross-country empirical work has failed to provide statistically significant insights. Michalopoulos and Sukhatme (1989) conclude that the cross-country evidence is ambiguous, and White (1992b) asserts that we know surprisingly little about aid's macroeconomic impact. He goes on to argue that the absence of a relationship between aid and growth is a fairly well established result. The seeming lack of a positive macroeconomic impact of aid in combination with the many favourable micro-based project evaluations is a puzzle. Mosley (1987) named it the micro–macro paradox.

The perceived lack of evidence on the macroeconomic effects of aid has generally been blurred by an associated critique of the econometric methodology applied. The conclusions drawn by Michalopoulos and Sukhatme (1989) as well as White (1992a, 1992b) have been particularly influential in shaping the common view of the aid–growth linkages. Yet these surveys concentrate on the conceptual, econometric, and data difficulties involved in cross-country analyses. While these difficulties must certainly be kept in mind, little guidance is provided in this work on whether empirical results (i.e. the signs of critical parameters, their statistical significance and their policy implications) are either robust or consistent with analytical models of the links between aid and growth.

A re-examination of the macroeconomic impact of aid is pertinent for other reasons as well. Debate has recently erupted once again following the cross-country regressions by Boone (1994, 1996) and Burnside and Dollar (1997). These studies are much cited contributions. In the colourful language of the *The Economist* (1994), Boone's work is claimed to show that aid is 'Down the rathole.' The Burnside–Dollar results are reviewed by the *The Economist* (1998) under the heading 'Making aid work,' and it is noted that aid will only work if it is spent on the right countries with low inflation, small budget deficits, openness to trade, strong rule of law and a competent bureaucracy.

In this survey we consider three generations of empirical cross-country work on aid effectiveness. We delineate the analytical underpinnings of each generation and provide an encyclopaedic survey of work in each. In this manner, we arrive at the conclusion that existing literature supports the proposition that aid improves economic performance. There is *no* micro–macro paradox to resolve, not even in countries hampered by an unfavourable policy environment.

Throughout this chapter, the underlying premise is that whether aid is effective or not is an empirical question. Theory, ranging from the early Harrod–Domar to the new growth models, has been important in influencing the specification of empirical relations estimated. Theory has also played an important role in influencing both the perceptions about how aid impacts on growth and the necessary conditions that must be in place for this impact to be positive. Nevertheless, Barro and Sala-i-Martin (1995) and Aghion and Howitt (1998) remind us that the growth process depends on an intricate range of interacting characteristics and lines of influence. The growth process cannot be fully captured in simple analytical frameworks. By implication, the same can be said for the macroeconomic impact of aid. While this may be discouraging to the purist, we try to demonstrate that useful insights can still be gained from the specifications adopted in the empirical cross-country literature when proper care is taken to do this in a coherent analytical framework.

Aid, savings and growth: first-generation studies

In the early literature on aid and growth in less developed countries, foreign aid was perceived only as an exogenous net increment to the capital stock of the recipient country. It was assumed by pro-aid development economists such as Rosenstein-Rodan (1961) that each dollar of foreign resources in the form of aid would result in an increase of one dollar in total savings and investment. In other words, aid was not treated as a component of national income adding to both consumption and investment. Hence, fungibility of aid resources was not allowed for, and aid for consumption purposes was skipped over in this type of macroeconomic aid-impact analysis.

The theoretical workhorse underlying this empirical work is the Harrod–Domar growth model with the causal chain running from aid to growth via savings and investment. Papanek (1972) characterised the highly optimistic aid-impact approach embedded in the Harrod–Domar growth model as 'curiously naive.' At the same time, he forcefully countered the arguments put forward in the late 1960s by Griffin (1970) and Griffin and Enos (1970). They held a sceptical view of aid and argued that the 'association is loose, but . . . the general tendency is that the greater the capital inflows from abroad, the lower the rate of growth of the receiving country.' (Griffin and Enos 1970: 318). A number of interacting reasons was listed to show why aid may retard development, but particular attention was paid to the observation that aid leads to lower domestic savings. Rahman (1968) had already made this observation, which was confirmed by Weisskopf (1972).

Papanek acknowledged that the so-called 'revisionist' contributions were useful in challenging overly optimistic views on the positive benefits of foreign inflows. Yet he also pointed out that, as long as the effect of an additional unit of foreign resources on investment is less than one, its effect on savings will appear to be negative. Newlyn (1973) elaborated on this and demonstrated that while negative values between 0 and −1 of regression parameters would normally mean a reduction in the dependent variable (in this case national resources used for investment to promote growth) no such implication can be drawn in the aid–savings context. Only if the negative parameter value exceeds unity can it be concluded that aid leads to an absolute reduction in the total amount of resources being used for investment. Newlyn argued that most writers had failed to make the above distinction.

The original Harrod–Domar model that assumes only a savings constraint on growth, as further discussed below, was expanded in the 1960s in the influential Chenery and Strout (1966) two-gap model. Import capacity (i.e. the trade balance gap) was introduced as a separate potential constraint on growth. The two-gap approach suggests that one or the other of the two gaps will be binding at different times in different countries. Inflows of foreign capital fill both gaps simultaneously, so *ex post* the two are necessarily equal. If the prospective trade gap is the larger of the two, actual savings are supposed to fall short of potential savings, and if the prospective savings gap is the larger, actual imports will be greater than those needed for growth (see Chenery and Eckstein 1970). There are several implications of the two-gap model. First, the impact of additional foreign finance will differ depending on which gap is binding. Second, while the aid–savings interaction is positive when savings are binding, this will not be the case when trade is binding. Third, when the trade gap is binding there is a direct impact from aid on growth that bypasses the Harrod–Domar aid to savings to investment to growth link.

A large body of empirical work in the two-gap tradition that focused on single country studies appeared in the 1960s and 1970s (e.g. Chenery and Eckstein 1970). Robinson (1971) took a cross-country approach and introduced the trade balance in a growth regression. He found that the trade balance variable was highly significant and that foreign exchange can operate as a limiting factor for growth, lending support to the two-gap model. Papanek (1972), arguing along the same lines, held that the two-gap model greatly increased analytical sophistication and connection with reality.

The issues debated in the first generation of empirical work have continued into the 1990s. To understand this approach, it is useful to lay out the underlying analytical framework. The core of the Harrod–Domar model is the Leontief production function and the assumption of excess supply of labour. No substitution among production inputs is possible, and output is linearly related to capital, the scarce factor of production. Capital accumulation is then the key to development. The only way in which savings, domestic and foreign (including aid), can affect growth in this model is through the accumulation of physical capital, i.e. investment. Assuming the capital–output ratio, v, is constant, the growth rate in production, g_{Yt}, is given as

$$g_{Yt} = \frac{\dot{Y}_t}{Y_t} = v\frac{\dot{K}_t}{Y_t}, \tag{1}$$

where Y_t is production in year t, K_t is the capital stock and a dot denotes changes over time. Relating changes in the capital stock to gross investment I_t and allowing for a constant depreciation rate of capital, δ, it follows that

$$g_{Yt} = v\frac{I_t}{Y_t} - \delta = vi_t - \delta. \tag{2}$$

In a closed economy, the investment ratio, i_t, can be replaced by the domestic savings ratio, s_t. However, in an open economy the relation between savings and investment is defined as

$$I_t \equiv S_t + F_t = S_t + A_t + F_{pt} + F_{ot}, \tag{3}$$

where F_t is the total inflow of foreign resources, including aid, A_t, as well as private and other foreign inflows, respectively F_{pt} and F_{ot}. Expressing domestic savings, S_t, and foreign inflows as fractions of Y_t, the following identity appears:

$$i_t \equiv s_t + a_t + f_{pt} + f_{ot}. \tag{4}$$

Assuming that $\partial f_{pt}/\partial a_t = \partial f_{ot}/\partial a_t = 0$, i.e. aid has no impact on private and other foreign inflows, the marginal effect of aid on investment reduces to:[2]

$$\frac{\partial i_t}{\partial a_t} = \frac{\partial s_t}{\partial a_t} + 1. \tag{5}$$

From (Eqn 5) it is clear that the impact of aid on domestic savings has implications for how the macroeconomic effectiveness of aid is assessed, as the aid–savings link, in turn, affects the investment ratio.

Going back to the early empirical literature, the following simple equation was often used in analysing the aid–savings relation:

$$s_t = \alpha_0 + \alpha_1 a_t, \tag{6}$$

where α_0 is the marginal savings rate and α_1 captures the impact of aid inflows (as a share of income) on the savings rate.[3] Moreover, f_t was regularly used as a proxy for a_t due to lack of appropriate data on aid flows. Level variables (rather than ratios) were relied on in a few instances, with Y_t explicitly included rather than implicitly present in the ratios. Equation (6) is a crucial relationship in the aid–growth debate. For example, White

(1992b) argues in his survey that there is no agreement as to the positive or negative relationship between aid and savings and suggests that the relationship may be positive.

Turning now to our survey of the empirical literature, we first look at how aid affects savings (i.e. the first-generation issue), and then move on to the different analytical model underlying second-generation estimations. Our survey is based on a comprehensive inventory, including 131 cross-country regressions identified in the literature published from the late 1960s to 1998.[4]

In what follows, the three dependent variables include savings (S), investment (I) and growth (G). Regarding the explanatory variables focus is naturally on aid inflows. However, in many of the early aid-effectiveness studies, aid flows are not identified separately from other foreign capital inflows. The 131 regression results are classified in two groups. In the first group, with a total of 104 regressions, the explanatory variables include a clearly identified measure of aid (A), roughly equivalent to the DAC (Development Assistance Committee) concept of official development assistance (ODA). The remaining 27 studies, in which aid cannot be separated from the various aggregate foreign inflow measures, were placed in a second group (F). The number of regressions in which the impact of either A or F on respectively S, I and G is analysed adds up to respectively 41, 18 and 72. Finally, we recorded the number of significantly positive ($+$), insignificant (0) and significantly negative ($-$) relations between the dependent and the explanatory variables.[5]

This survey approach is subject to pitfalls. Some regressions are more meaningful than others, and it is possible that many authors made the same mistakes. Our categorical analysis, however, is in line with Edward Leamer's 'extreme bounds analysis' (Leamer 1985) and the variation thereof used recently by Sala-i-Martin (1997) in his analysis of the robustness of parameters in growth regressions. One important difference between the extreme bounds analysis and our exercise is that we are not in control of the experiments, i.e. the variations in explanatory variables and samples. In our view this adds power and credibility to the results. In any case, the categorical analysis is one way of structuring the sample of empirical aid effectiveness results without too much selectivity and value judgement, and we think this is a necessary first step in the search for general conclusions about what the literature can really tell.

In our sample of 41 aid–savings regressions there are analyses where more complex functional forms than (Eqn 6) are used, and systems of equations have also been relied on to estimate the impact of aid on savings. Different empirical specifications of the aid–savings relationship carry with them distinct implications concerning the underlying savings behaviour in the economy, and a justified critique of much of the empirical aid–savings work is that these behavioural implications have not generally been recognised and explored.[6] Nevertheless, in trying to better understand the aid–savings debate, including the work of Griffin and Enos (1970), it is illustrative to summarise the available results as given in Table 4.1 (row 1). Here, the underlying null-hypothesis is $\alpha_1 = 0$. Thus, this summary of the aid–savings results follows the conventional path in which regressions have been presented and discussed in the literature, including the survey articles by Michalopoulos and Sukhatme (1989) and White (1992a, 1992b).

From Table 4.1, it is clear that there is only one study reporting an estimate of α_1 which is significantly greater than zero. Hence, arguments suggesting that the impact of aid on domestic savings is positive are speculative. More than 60 per cent of the observations in Table 4.1 (row 1) show a significant negative coefficient from aid to savings, which suggests that aid cannot be assumed to increase total savings on a one-to-one basis. There are plenty of empirical grounds on which to conclude that the early extreme pro-aid view of the macroeconomic impact of aid is not tenable.

At the other extreme of the debate, the negative parameter estimates in Table 4.1 (row 1) have been interpreted as a confirmation that aid is harmful to growth. In his counter-attack on this position, Papanek (1972) gave a number of reasons for expecting a negative link between aid and savings. The issue is not, however, whether the coefficient is negative, but whether it is between 0 and -1. Equation (5) clearly shows that Papanek and Newlyn were right in arguing that a negative α_1-parameter in the aid–savings relation in (Eqn 6) is consistent with a positive aid-impact on total investment as long as $\alpha_1 > -1$.[7] When $\alpha_1 = -1$, aid has no impact on investment, and only when $\alpha_1 < -1$ can it be concluded that the impact of aid on investment, and therefore growth, is harmful.

In assessing the investment implications of the aid–savings studies, which is what should ultimately concern us if we are interested in the growth impact of aid, it appears more reasonable to use as null-hypothesis that $\alpha_1 = -1$. Therefore, we derived the test statistics for this alternative hypothesis for 39 out of the 41 aid–savings analyses.[8] As shown in Table 4.1 (row 2), the number of studies with an α_1-estimate significantly less than -1 is limited to one observation. In contrast, there are 18 analyses where the aid impact is significantly greater than -1, leaving 20 regressions where α_1 is not significantly different from -1.

Robustness is an issue. Confidence bounds are in general very broad, partly reflecting the low number of observations in many of the first-generation studies. For example, there are six studies with no more than 10 degrees of freedom, and only four studies with more than 100 degrees of freedom. It is also evident that savings–investment behaviour is poorly captured in the studies surveyed. The end result is that the values -1 and 0 are inside the confidence bounds for α_1 in the majority of cases.

Some sound conclusions do emerge from the first-generation studies. Neither extreme view of the aid–savings–growth link is valid. There is no evidence for a positive impact, and in only one study does aid lead to lower total savings. The overwhelming evidence from these studies is that aid

Table 4.1 Impact of foreign aid and resource flows on savings, investment, and growth (131 cross-country regressions)

	Explanatory variable							
	Foreign aid flows (A)				Foreign resource flows (F)			
Dependent variable	(−)	(0)	(+)	Total [a]	(−)	(0)	(+)	Total
Savings Ho: $\alpha_1=0$	14	10	0	24	11	5	1	17
Savings Ho: $\alpha_1=-1$ [b]	1	13	8	22	0	7	10	17
Investment Ho: $\alpha_1=0$	0	1	15	16	0	0	2	2
Growth Ho: $\alpha_1=0$	1	25	38	64	0	6	2	8

Source: Extracted from the Appendix, Table A.4.1(a) and (b).
Notes: The null-hypotheses (Ho) are tested at a 5 per cent significance level against a two-sided alternative.
[a]The total number of regressions in the $\alpha_1=0$ and the $\alpha_1=-1$ savings rows are not the same (24 and 22) due to missing data on standard errors for two regressions.
[b]Since (Ho) in this row is $\alpha_1=-1$, the cells (−), (0) and (+) represent $\alpha_1<-1$, $\alpha_1=-1$, and $\alpha_1>-1$, respectively.

leads to an increase in total savings, although not by as much as the aid flow. Given the underlying Harrod–Domar model, the implication is that aid spurs growth.

Aid, investment and growth: second-generation studies

In the second-generation of empirical work, focus turned from the aid–savings relation to estimating the link between aid and growth. Some estimated the link via investment and some directly in reduced form equations. Insofar as there is an underlying structural model, focus remains on capital accumulation and is consistent with the Harrod–Domar model or a simple Solow growth model.

Regardless of the choice of growth model, the view is that investment is the major direct determinant of growth. The implicit assumption in the 18 cross-country aid–investment studies in Table 4.1 is that, if a positive relationship can be found between aid and investment, it is justified to conclude that aid makes a positive contribution to growth. Moreover, while the specifications of the aid–investment relationship in the regressions included in our sample vary, their core typically includes a behavioural equation linking investment to aid.

Papanek argued that focus in the aid effectiveness debate should shift away from the aid–savings relationship to examining the effects of aid on the various elements of investment and growth. Accordingly, he proposed a model in which the different financing components of investment – domestic

savings, aid and other foreign capital inflows – are separated. This advice
was followed in subsequent aid–investment studies, where the assumed
investment behaviour can generally be expressed as follows:[9]

$$i_t = h\left(s_t, a_t, f_{pt}, f_{ot}\right).$$

(7)

In the overwhelming majority of studies, analyses of the aid–investment
link are based on results where A, rather than F, is explicitly included
among the explanatory variables (Table 4.1, row 3). This is in contrast with
the aid–savings regressions, and reflects in part that second-generation
aid–investment studies generally consider domestic as well as foreign
sources of capital accumulation as separate explanatory variables in a
behavioural equation.

A linear regression form derived from (Eqn 7) is given by a reduced
form equation:

$$i_t = \gamma_0 + \gamma_1 s_t + \gamma_2 a_t + \gamma_3 f_{pt} + \gamma_4 f_{ot},$$

(8)

where the parameters are

$$\gamma_1 = \frac{\partial i}{\partial s}; \gamma_2 = \frac{\partial i}{\partial a}; \gamma_3 = \frac{\partial i}{\partial f_p}; \gamma_4 = \frac{\partial i}{\partial f_o}.$$

(9)

We return to (Eqn 9) below, as the widespread use of this behavioural
specification has critical implications for how empirical aid–growth results are
interpreted. In the studies in Table 4.1 (row 3), there is virtual consensus that
there is a significant positive impact of aid on investment, (the parameter γ_2).
Only one study, based on a very early pre-1970 sample period (Massell *et al.*
1972), found an insignificant coefficient. All other studies have a significantly
positive parameter. In sum, it is safe to assert that the investment enhancing
effect of aid is clear. The link to growth is a separate step.

A second strand of the second-generation literature explores the link
between aid and growth in reduced form equations. Over the past 30 years,
no less than 72 cross-country studies have tested whether or not a direct
impact of aid on growth can be identified. Some of these regressions have
taken a growth equation similar to (Eqn 2) as their point of departure, but
in most cases the investment ratio i_t has been substituted by a behavioural
specification such as the one in (Eqn 8). The typical second-generation aid–
growth regression is

$$g_{Yt} = \lambda_o + \lambda_1 s_t + \lambda_2 a_t + \lambda_3 f_{pt} + \lambda_4 f_{ot},$$

(10)

where $\lambda_0 = v\gamma_0 - \delta$ and $\lambda_i = v\gamma_i$, $(i = 1, \ldots 4)$.

This reduced form equation is consistent with a variety of alternative structural models. While the original derivation of the Papanek regression was based on the Harrod–Domar growth model, this regression is also applicable when the underlying model is of the Solow type where substitution among production inputs is allowed. In this case the auxiliary assumptions are that the growth rates in the labour force and technology and, especially, the capital–output ratio are constant over time. These assumptions hold in steady state, and in the small open economy model by Barro *et al.* (1995) in which the user cost of physical capital is constant and given from abroad. To the extent that the underlying assumptions do not hold, standard deviations on parameter estimates should increase even though the parameter estimates may still be unbiased. In empirical work, this implies a relatively higher share of insignificant estimates.

If it is assumed that γ_i equals unity, the corresponding λ_i parameter estimates in (Eqn 10) should all equal the capital–output ratio, v. However, interpreting (Eqn 8) as a reduced form, allowing for a behavioural relationship between gross investment, on the one side, and savings, aid and foreign inflows, on the other, leads to partial derivatives that may be different from unity. This implies that the regression coefficients may differ both from each other and from v.

In assessing aid effectiveness from the reduced form regression, the parameter of immediate interest is λ_2. An insignificant estimate of this parameter has in many studies led to the conclusion that aid does not affect growth. However, this statement involves a composite hypothesis: (i) $v \neq 0$ and (ii) $\gamma_2 = 0$. Not only the latter assumption regarding the marginal effect of aid on investment, but also the underlying model specification, impacts on the conclusions drawn about aid effectiveness. Yet, neither v nor γ_2 can be identified from the regression parameters without an additional, auxiliary assumption. A natural choice is that $\gamma_1 \neq 0$. This is equivalent to assuming that domestic savings have a positive impact on investment and growth whenever $v > 0$, and a minimum requirement to conclude that aid has no impact on growth in the reduced form regression is that $v_1 \neq 0$ while $\lambda_2 = 0$.

As shown in Table 4.1 (row 4), there is only one result in our survey that indicates a directly harmful effect of aid on growth. On the other hand, among the remaining 71 analyses, 40 show a positive impact of aid on growth, while 31 show no statistically significant impact. At first sight the evidence may appear mixed. A review of the 31 insignificant results reveals, however, that no less than 12 of these are based on regressions, which do not fulfil the minimum requirement for concluding that aid has no impact on growth (Table 4.2). When the aid coefficient is insignificant, so is the savings coefficient.

Some of the most widely cited results about aid effectiveness are those by Mosley *et al.* (1987, 1992). In these analyses and several others, it is concluded that aid does not seem to spur growth, giving rise to the suspicion

Table 4.2 Aid effectiveness results from Papanek regressions.

	$\lambda_1 \neq 0$ $\lambda_2 \neq 0$	$\lambda_1 \neq 0$ $\lambda_2 = 0$	$\lambda_1 = 0$ $\lambda_2 = 0$	$\lambda_1 = 0$ $\lambda_2 \neq 0$
Papanek (1973)	4	1	0	0
Stoneman (1975)	9	0	1	1
Dowling and Hiemenz (1982)	1	0	0	1
Gupta and Islam (1983)	3	2	1	0
Singh (1985)	1	1	1	1
Mosley *et al.* (1987)	1	3	6	2
Mosley *et al.* (1992)	1	0	3	0
White (1992b)	2	1	0	1
Snyder (1993)	1	1	0	1
Total	23	9	12	7

Note: From Tables 4.1 and 4.2 it follows that out of the 72 aid–growth regressions analysed here, 51 had a functional form that can be characterised as a Papanek regression. It also follows that there are 10 insignificant results among the remaining 21 non-Papanek regressions.

that there is a micro–macro paradox to be explained. In fact, in the large majority of their regressions, the savings coefficient is insignificant. Rather than emphasising that aid does not work, the real puzzle in their results is that savings do not work. This result raises the question of whether the underlying structural model is appropriate in their particular analysis.

Out of the 32 regressions where the identifying assumption is fulfilled (i.e. $\lambda_1 \neq 0$), there are 23 significant and only nine insignificant results (including three from the studies by Mosley *et al.*). The number of studies that find a significant link between aid and growth is impressive, especially given the simplicity of the reduced form equation and the quality of data relied on; and the reduced form Papanek-type regressions that found a significant aid–growth link are in general based on more observations than those that found insignificant links.

The observation that aid does not increase saving is not a puzzle within the two-gap model. In a two-gap model where the economy is foreign exchange constrained there would be no relationship between aid, savings and growth. However, aid would still be effective in furthering growth by relieving the import constraint. Such a situation is consistent with the results in column 4 of Table 4.2, which indicates a direct link from aid to growth, not operating via savings. Similarly, in a two-gap framework, one cannot use an insignificant parameter on the aid variable (see column 2 in Table 4.2) to conclude that aid is ineffective in furthering growth. Such a result may be caused by the economy being savings constrained so there is no room for picking up a direct impact of aid on growth. There may be an indirect effect through the impact of aid on savings, but that is not captured in the regression equation. The truly puzzling problem occurs (as in column 3 of Table 4.2) when neither the savings nor the aid parameter is significant.

A review of the 21 aid–growth reduced form regressions in our sample that have been classified as not relying on the Papanek approach shows that all of the ten insignificant results are from either very early and/or simple (correlation) regressions with few degrees of freedom or in studies where total foreign capital inflows rather than aid is being studied (Griffin and Enos 1970, Massell *et al.* 1972, Voivodas 1973, Bornschier *et al.* 1978 and Mosley *et al.* 1987). Recent analyses with a reasonable number of degrees of freedom report positive and significant results.

To summarise, we can draw a number of clear conclusions from second-generation studies. The aid–investment link is positive, consistent with the typical result from first-generation aid–savings studies. Moreover, the results from reduced form, aid–growth regressions suggest that there is a positive link between aid and growth whenever there is a positive link between savings and growth. This reduced form model is consistent with the aid–savings–investment–growth causal chain in standard growth models.

Aid, policy and growth: third-generation studies

Over the past few years, a new, third generation of aid effectiveness studies has appeared. Compared to earlier work they break novel ground in four areas. First, they work with panel data for a number of years and a large number of countries. The data cover a large share of developing country trade and other economic activity. Second, new growth theory has inspired the analysis in distinct ways, providing a different analytical basis compared to previous work. Measures of economic policy and the institutional environment are included directly in the reduced form growth regressions alongside traditional macroeconomic variables. Third, endogeneity of aid and other variables is addressed explicitly in some studies. Finally, the aid–growth relationship is explicitly seen as non-linear. While some of the earlier analyses addressed a variety of these issues, in our view, the third-generation studies represent a distinct step forward in empirical cross-country work on aid effectiveness.[10]

The studies by Boone (1996) and Burnside and Dollar (1997) have attracted particular attention, and they have both been reviewed and discussed extensively in a number of papers, including for example Feyzioglu *et al.* (1998), McGillivray and Morrissey (1998) and Tsikata (1998). The Boone study must be characterised as an outlier in the literature. He concludes that aid has no effect on investment and growth. This result Tsikata (1998) finds surprising, and it is indeed a result that is completely at odds with the broad range of investment studies we have surveyed above, including in particular the analysis by Feyzioglu *et al.* (1998). Careful reading of Boone's work also shows that he decides, in passing, to discard the result that aid does have an impact on investment when his full sample is used. Finally, while Boone endogenises aid, his results are subject to queries such as why he has not endogenised the growth rate of income per capita. For these reasons, and to keep the exposition manageable, we focus in what follows on Burnside and Dollar (1997) and three other recent aid effectiveness studies: Hadjimichael *et al.* (1995), Durbarry *et al.* (1998) and Hansen and Tarp (1999). Together these four contributions represent the present core of the new third-generation empirical analyses of aid effectiveness.

Overview

The third-generation studies in focus here share a common theoretical background, and even if the specific formulation of the growth relations and the choice of econometric technique differ, they have a lot in common from an analytical perspective. We briefly summarise these four contributions below, highlighting differences rather than similarities. Table 4.3 gives an overview of some of the parameters included in the estimated growth relations. The dependent variable is in all cases the average annual growth rate of real per capita GDP.

The main scope of the study by Hadjimichael *et al.* (1995) is to investigate the impact of macroeconomic policies, exogenous factors and structural reforms on growth, savings and investment in sub-Saharan Africa. This, and insights gained from empirical analyses of determinants of growth, savings and investment over the past decade, lead the authors to include specific policy variables in the regressions such as government investment, the public budget deficit and inflation. There are four novelties compared to earlier-generation work. First, the regressions include an intercept for each year in the sample.[11] Second, to account for country-wise heteroskedasticity, the parameters are estimated by weighted least squares. Third, the potential endogeneity of economic policy and aid is addressed by lagging most of the explanatory variables, including foreign aid, one year. Fourth, a squared aid term is included in the regression to capture possible non-linearities in the aid–growth relationship. The results in Table 4.3 (column 1) are based on an analysis of 31 sub-Saharan African countries for the period 1987–92. The main policy conclusion drawn is that the poor economic performance of sub-Saharan Africa stems from differences in economic policies, but the positive growth impact of aid is also recognised.

Turning next to Durbarry *et al.* (1998) (Table 4.3, column 2), they use a Papanek-inspired decomposition of investment as in (Eqn 4), but they allow for non-linear effects of aid on growth by including a squared aid term. This reduced form specification is not strictly in accordance with the Papanek investment specification but, referring to Hadjimichael *et al.*, Durbarry *et al.* argue that the possibility of non-linearity in the aid–growth relationship should be recognised from the outset. The main differences between these two studies relate to data coverage and estimation technique. Durbarry *et al.* analyse 58 developing countries over the period 1970–93. Annual data are used to construct four periods (averages over six years) and 238 observations. The results presented in Table 4.3 are from a mixed estimation procedure in which the time dimension is modelled using different intercepts in each period, while the cross-country dimension is modelled using a random error term.[12] The main conclusion is that there is robust evidence that greater foreign aid inflows have a beneficial impact on growth. The existence of an optimal aid allocation in terms of growth effects is also identified.

Burnside and Dollar (1997) (Table 4.3, column 3) draw, as is the case with the other third-generation studies, on the latest empirical results in the new growth literature. In addition to economic policy variables, they include several institutional and political variables that have appeared in growth studies in the mid-1990s (e.g. assassinations, ethnic fractionalisation and institutional quality). Furthermore, conditional convergence effects are captured by including the initial level of real GDP per capita. However, the major novelty in the Burnside–Dollar study – and the hottest issue in the debate – is the inclusion of an interaction term between foreign aid and economic policies. This specification is, as further discussed below, a different way of capturing non-linearity in the aid–growth relationship than the introduction of a squared aid term in the Hadjimichael *et al.* and Durberry *et al.* studies. Economic policies are grouped in a single policy index consisting of a composite measure of inflation, trade openness and the budget deficit. The interpretation of the aid–policy interaction term is that the effectiveness of aid in the growth process is directly dependent on the quality of economic policies. The results presented in Table 4.3 are based on data for 56 countries and 267 observations. The time dimension involves six periods based on four-year averages covering the period 1970–93. Endogeneity of aid is taken into account by using an instrumental variable procedure, while endogeneity of the policy variables is tested and rejected. As in the studies by Hadjimichael *et al.* and Durbarry *et al.*, the panel data structure is used to remove the world business cycle by including different intercepts in each of the six periods.[13] The main conclusion relates to the statistical significance of the aid–policy interaction term, which is used to argue that aid has a positive impact on growth in a good policy environment.

The last column in Table 4.3 presents results from the study by Hansen and Tarp (1999). They analyse the same set of countries as Burnside and Dollar and they use the same basic model formulation. The sample of 264 observations covers 56 countries over five periods for 1973–93. In addition, Hansen and Tarp take account of unobserved country-specific effects, conditional convergence and endogeneity of aid and policies by using an estimation technique for dynamic panel data models with country specific effects. They model the non-linear effect of aid by including a squared term as used by Hadjimichael *et al.* and Durbarry *et al.* Both aid and aid squared significantly affect the growth rate, and the same goes for all of the various policy variables. The conclusion is that aid has a positive impact on growth even in countries with a 'poor' policy environment.

Table 4.3 Comparison of recent growth regressions

	Hadjimichael et al. (1995: tab. 25)	Durbarry et al. (1998: tab. 3)	Burnside and Dollar (1997: tab. 3)	Hansen and Tarp (1999: tab. 7)
Aid	0.098**	0.101**	−0.580	0.938**
	(2.22)	(2.26)	(1.23)	(3.94)
Aid^2	−0.002**	−0.001**	-	−1.870**
	(2.57)	(2.01)	–	(4.61)
Aid x policy	–	–	0.320*	–
	–	–	(1.78)	–
Priv. investment	0.014	–	–	–
	(0.53)	–	–	–
Govt. investment	0.178**	–	–	–
	(3.43)	–	–	–
Domestic savings	–	0.064**	–	–
	–	(3.17)	–	–
Priv. net inflows	–	0.237**	–	–
	–	(3.80)	–	–
Other inflows	–	0.006	–	–
	–	(0.83)	–	–
Human capital	0.161**	–	–	–
	(3.36)	–	–	–
Pop. growth rate	−0.890**	–	–	–
	(2.54)	–	–	–
Terms-of-trade	0.029**	0.090**	–	–
	(1.99)	(3.29)	–	–
Real eff. exch. rate	−0.045**	–	–	–
	(2.94)	–	–	–
Openness	–	–	1.460**	0.027**
	–	–	(2.06)	(4.94)
Inflation	−0.034*	−0.001**	−1.160**	−0.011**
	(1.94)	(3.20)	(2.09)	(2.55)
Budget deficit	−0.168**	−0.066**	−0.080	–
	(4.61)	(2.00)	(0.01)	–
Govt. consumption	–	–	−2.590	−0.289**
	–	–	(0.30)	(2.88)
Financial depth	–	0.007	0.019	−0.073**
	–	(0.73)	(1.14)	(2.07)
Institutional quality	–	–	0.690**	–
	–	–	(3.70)	–
Initial GDP per capita	–	–	−0.950	−0.056**
	–	–	(1.11)	(2.62)
Sample period	1987–92	1970–93	1970–93	1974–93
Countries/periods	31/6	58/4	56/6	56/5
Observations	186	238	267	264
R^2	0.4	0.32	0.38	0.53

Note: Due to differences in the measurement of aid and growth (fractions/percentages), the parameter estimates are not directly comparable across the table. However, the effect of aid is directly comparable for the first two and the last two columns, respectively. * and ** indicate significance at 10 and 5 per cent, respectively.

The main results (Table 4.3) in comparative perspective are that Hadjimichael *et al.*, Durbarry *et al.* and Hansen and Tarp all find a significant impact of aid on growth, as long as the aid to GDP ratio is not excessively high.[14] In contrast, Burnside and Dollar find that the effectiveness of aid depends on economic policy and that aid has a positive impact on growth, but only in a good policy environment.

Given the differences in samples and estimation techniques, the results in terms of the effectiveness of aid are strikingly similar in the three studies by Hadjimichael *et al.*, Durbarry *et al.* and Hansen and Tarp. Moreover, it is of great policy relevance to sort out the reason for the apparent difference between the Burnside–Dollar study, on the one hand, and the three other studies, on the other, when it comes to the treatment of non-linearities in the aid–growth relation. We address this question below.

Analytical framework

There are many reasons for expecting a non-linear relation between aid and growth. Hadjimichael *et al.* argue that sub-Saharan African countries may have limited capacity to absorb foreign resources.[15] Durbarry *et al.* also refer to absorptive capacity and they add more recent results about optimal borrowing and Dutch disease problems. The analysis of absorptive capacity constraints is based on the Harrod–Domar and two-gap growth models. If the Leontief production function in this framework is replaced by a Cobb–Douglas production function, as in the Solow growth model, there is no longer a fixed capacity constraint (a threshold) but, instead, diminishing marginal returns to increased foreign aid. The decreasing marginal returns can in empirical work be approximated by a second-order polynomial in aid in the regression. In general, however, quadratic terms and interactions must be evaluated and interpreted with great care in regression models. They represent separate terms in a second-order approximation of what is really an unknown functional form.

A simple example that clarifies the role of squared terms and interactions is a linearisation of a Solow growth model with constant growth rates in population and technology, and a constant rate of depreciation. Assuming investments are financed partly from domestic savings and partly from foreign aid, the model can be formulated in several ways, with observationally equivalent first order approximations and second order approximations that (observationally) differ only with respect to the interaction term.

In a standard Solow model with convergence effects, growth in income per worker can be expressed as a log-linear relation, following Mankiw *et al.* (1992):

$$g_{Yt} = \alpha_o + \alpha_1 \log(i_t) - \rho \log(y_0),$$ (11)

where the last term is included to capture initial deviations from steady state.

Investments can be modelled as in (Eqn 8) (assuming private foreign flows are zero)

$$i_t = \gamma_0 + \gamma_1 s_t + \gamma_2 a_t. \tag{12}$$

Inserting savings and aid in the growth equation and linearising, using a first-order Taylor approximation, we obtain a familiar aid–growth relation:

$$g_{yt} = \tilde{\alpha}_0 + \frac{\alpha_1 \gamma_1}{\bar{\imath}} s_t + \frac{\alpha_1 \gamma_2}{\bar{\imath}} a_t - \rho \log(y_0) \tag{13}$$

where $\bar{\imath} = \gamma_0 + \gamma_1 \bar{s} + \gamma_2 \bar{a}$, in essence the sample mean, is used as the point of expansion. The linear relationship (Eqn 13) has typically been estimated using either least squares or instrumental variable estimators.[16]

A more precise, second-order Taylor approximation of the theoretical growth equation leads to an empirical reduced form where quadratic terms as well as an interaction term (e.g. a cross product) are present:

$$g_{yt} = \tilde{\alpha}_0 + 2\frac{\alpha_1 \gamma_1}{\bar{\imath}} s_t + 2\frac{\alpha_1 \gamma_2}{\bar{\imath}} a_t - \frac{1}{2}\frac{\alpha_1 \gamma_1^2}{\bar{\imath}^2} s_t^2$$

$$- \frac{1}{2}\frac{\alpha_1 \gamma_2^2}{\bar{\imath}^2} a_t^2 - \frac{\alpha_1 \gamma_1 \gamma_2}{\bar{\imath}^2} s_t a_t - \rho \log(y_0). \tag{14}$$

If savings and aid are assumed to provide different kinds of capital, the growth equation can be formulated as log-linear in each of the investment components. In this case no interaction term appears in the second order Taylor approximation, only squared savings and aid terms.

In the studies by Hadjimichael *et al.*, Burnside and Dollar and Hansen and Tarp, the savings rate does not enter directly in the regressions. However, savings can be substituted out either by government and private investment, as in Hadjimichael *et al.*, or by policy and institutional variables, as in Burnside–Dollar and Hansen–Tarp. In such cases, the non-linear terms in (Eqn 14) will include squared policy and aid terms, and, depending on the growth specification, an interaction between aid and policy as well.

As can be seen from Table 4.3, all the recent studies include either aid squared or the policy–aid interaction term from the second-order expansions, yielding better approximations to the underlying theoretical growth relation. Yet none of the four studies includes all second order terms. Further analysis is therefore required to understand the relative importance of the second-order terms. The question at issue between the Burnside–Dollar study and the other three is which combination of non-linear terms is statistically preferred. In any empirical model, interaction terms and squared terms may enter as 'proxies' for each other, unless all terms are included initially.

To illustrate, a stochastic variable such as the policy index used by Burnside–Dollar can always be decomposed into two terms: one which is perfectly correlated with aid, and another which is completely uncorrelated with aid:

$$\text{policy} = \kappa \, \text{aid} + \left(\text{policy/aid}\right). \tag{15}$$

is simply a regression coefficient, i.e. the sample covariance between the policy index and aid divided by the sample standard deviation of aid. The 'residual' (policy|aid) is the part of the policy index that is uncorrelated with aid. Using this relation, the interaction term between aid and policy can be reformulated as:

$$\text{aid} \times \text{policy} = \kappa \, \text{aid}^2 + \text{aid} \times \left(\text{policy/aid}\right). \tag{16}$$

This demonstrates that the interaction term may be significant in regressions even though it may well be that it is the aid squared non-linearity in the aid–growth relation that is in reality important. Reversing the argument (aid as a 'function' of policy) shows the other option; that aid squared is significant because of the importance of the aid–policy interaction. It is therefore very important in comparing and assessing the results of the four studies in focus here to test whether any of these two possibilities has empirical support.

Testing second-order terms

Table 4.4 presents results of re-estimations of the growth relation in which all three terms from the second-order approximation in aid and policy are included. The regressions reported in Table 4.4 are based on the same sample used in Hansen and Tarp (1999). The data in this sample differ slightly from the Burnside–Dollar data.[17]

Regressions 1 and 2 are identical in form and represent the Burnside–Dollar growth equation. In regression 1 we have excluded five outliers identified by Burnside–Dollar.[18] When the outliers are excluded, there is a significant effect on growth from the aid–policy interaction term as found in the Burnside–Dollar study. However, it is distressing to note how sensitive the results for the aid and aid–policy interaction terms are. Once the five Burnside–Dollar outliers are included in the sample, the interaction term becomes insignificant.[19]

Regressions 3 and 4 make use of the full data set and, based on the results in regression 3, we can evaluate the significance of the various aid

Table 4.4 Growth regressions with polynomial effects of aid and policy in 56 countries for five periods, 1974–93. Dependent variable: average annual growth rate of GDP per capita

Regression	1	2	3	4	5
Aid	−0.018	0.03	0.166**	0.165**	0.182**
	(0.40)	(0.88)	(2.00)	(2.09)	(2.21)
Aid × policy	0.085**	−0.004	−0.004	–	–
	(2.60)	(0.22)	(0.24)	–	–
Aid^2	–	–	−0.003**	−0.004**	−0.004**
	–	–	(2.22)	(2.32)	(2.26)
Policy^2	–	–	0.082	–	–
	--	–	(0.83)	–	–
Openness	1.498**	2.193**	1.466	2.07**	2.13**
	(2.60)	(4.13)	(1.47)	(4.03)	(4.07)
Inflation	−0.798	−1.323**	−1.338**	−1.217**	−0.979*
	(1.44)	(2.91)	(2.80)	(2.71)	(1.83)
Budget deficit	4.59	7.339	7.415	7.73*	8.70*
	(0.93)	(1.59)	(1.58)	(1.93)	(1.91)
Govt. consumption	−0.488	−2.095	−3.832	−3.014	−1.439
	(0.10)	(0.44)	(0.80)	(0.65)	(0.29)
Financial depth	0.009	0.016	0.014	0.013	0.008
	(0.67)	(1.22)	(1.03)	(1.01)	(0.62)
Institutional quality	0.73**	0.614**	0.675**	0.677**	0.718**
	(4.24)	(3.65)	(3.96)	(3.97)	(4.11)
Initial GDP per capita	−0.312	−0.302	−0.136	−0.137	−0.146
	(0.54)	(0.54)	(0.24)	(0.24)	(0.25)
Observations	238	243	243	243	238
R^2	0.38	0.38	0.39	0.39	0.38

Note: A constant and time dummies are included in all regressions. Regressions 1 and 5 exclude five observations as in Burnside and Dollar (1997); Nicaragua (1986–9, 1990–3), Gambia (1986–9, 1990–3), Guyana (1990–3). The *t*-statistics in parentheses are based on heteroskedasticity consistent standard errors. * and ** indicate significance at 10 and 5 per cent, respectively.

and aid–policy interaction terms. Neither the squared policy nor the interaction term are statistically significant. In contrast, aid squared is statistically significant at a 5 per cent level of significance, with or without the other terms.

As a simple test of robustness of the result we have excluded the five influential observations in regression 5. As seen by comparing regressions 4 and 5, these observations have no effect on the estimated parameters once aid squared is included. We take this as additional evidence in favour of modelling the non-linear relation between aid and growth using a second-order polynomial in aid.

Finally, to check the sensitivity of the results for endogeneity of aid, we have replicated the regressions in Table 4.4 using instrumental variable (IV) estimation. As shown in the Appendix, using IV estimation does not change any of the conclusions.

Summing up

The few third-generation studies draw on new growth theory and work with reduced form equations that go well beyond standard first- and second-generation analyses based on Harrod–Domar and simple neoclassical growth models. In the aid–growth literature, these empirical studies introduce aid and aid–policy interaction terms to new growth theory regressions. Consistent with results from second-generation models, there is a significant effect on growth, either alone or in combination with a policy variable. Non-linear effects are significant both statistically and empirically. The result that there is a link between aid and growth is robust and consistent with past studies. The Burnside–Dollar result that there is a significant interaction between aid and policy is delicate. The other studies find a significant non-linear relationship through squared terms which is robust and dominates the aid–policy interaction effect when the two types of effects are considered together.

Conclusions

What can we conclude from this survey of cross-country literature on a long and contentious debate on the macroeconomic effectiveness of foreign aid? Other literature surveys hold, in the words of the *The Economist* (1999), that 'countless studies have failed to find a link between aid and faster growth.' We have surveyed three generations of empirical work: early Harrod–Domar models, reduced form aid–growth model and new-growth-theory reduced form models. We find a *consistent pattern* of results. Aid increases aggregate savings; aid increases investment; and there is a positive relationship between aid and growth in reduced form models. The positive aid–growth link is a robust result from all three generations of work. As a corollary, using perceived ineffectiveness of aid as an argument against cross-country regressions at large is not substantiated. Important information is embedded in the similarities among countries, and cross-country work does provide clues to how aid interacts with savings, investment and growth.

The obvious question is why do other surveys find that the aid–savings evidence is mixed and that the evidence in favour of a positive aid–growth link is weak – or non-existent? A few highly influential studies in each generation of work have argued the negative. There has been a tendency for negative studies to dominate the debate. Our survey covers 131 first- and second-generation regressions and compares them with third-generation work in a common analytical framework. We find that in each generation of studies those arguing the negative are clearly in the minority. When all the studies are considered as a group, the positive evidence is convincing. The micro–macro paradox is *non-existent*. Microeconomic studies indicating that aid is beneficial are consistent with the macroeconomic evidence.

Third-generation work goes beyond earlier empirical studies to address the necessary conditions for (increased) aid effectiveness. Burnside and Dollar (1997) offer a solution to what has so far appeared as a Gordian knot, i.e. the *perceived* ineffectiveness of aid at the macro level. They argue that aid is effective, but only in a good policy environment. This intriguing result – which is broadly in line with the 'Washington consensus' view of development – is appealing to many. It suggests how donors and aid recipients can learn from mistakes in the past and improve aid effectiveness in the future in a straightforward manner. This simple message is very influential and has even made it to the pages of the *The Economist*.

Nevertheless, the basic Burnside–Dollar result turns out to be sensitive to data and model specification. The significance of the crucial aid–policy interaction term depends on five observations (an extension of the sample by about 2 per cent). In addition, Burnside and Dollar depart from the other three third-generation studies in that they do not report any regressions with squared aid terms in their empirical estimations. They only include the aid–policy interaction term to capture polynomial effects in the aid–growth relationship. This is in contrast with the by now common result in empirical growth modelling, where squared terms appear as the rule rather than the exception. This issue of specification is critical. The aid squared term is statistically significant and robust, while the same cannot be said about the aid–policy interactions term.

What general policy lessons can be drawn from this extensive literature? *The Economist* (1999) argues:

> Rich countries should be much more ruthless about how they allocate their largesse, whether earmarked or not. Emergency relief is one thing. But mainstream aid should be directed *only* to countries with sound economic management (emphasis added).

While the extreme view that aid only works in an environment of sound policy appears wrong, there is evidence that economic policies have an impact on the marginal productivity of aid. Yet, the world is heterogenous and noisy, and it may well be that many of those countries where aid works the best are, at the same time, among those that need foreign aid the least. In contrast, countries that are less fortunate in having good policies in place, may need help badly to help bring them on track. They may need different forms of aid, but such real-world dilemmas remain unresolved. Single-cause explanations and mechanistic aid allocation rules are neither robust nor useful guides to policy makers.

The third-generation work recognises that development is a complex process with interactions between economic and non-economic variables.

The past decade has seen enormous changes in the world economic environment and the economic systems in place in many countries. Using past performance as an indicator of future performance is especially dubious in this environment, given the existing limited understanding of the interplay between aid, macroeconomic policy and political economy variables. In sum, the unresolved issue in assessing aid effectiveness is not whether aid works, but how and whether we can make the different kinds of aid instruments at hand work better in varying country circumstances.

Notes

* Sherman Robinson provided extensive comments and drafting suggestions on earlier versions of this paper. They are gratefully acknowledged. The same goes for discussions with Irma Adelman and Erik Thorbecke among many others, who helped shape the approach adopted. Useful comments were also received from Gerry Helleiner and participants in four seminars at the University of California (Berkeley), Cornell University, the International Food Policy Research Institute (IFPRI) and the University of Reading, United Kingdom. Research assistance provided by Steen Asmussen, Henning Tarp Jensen and Søren Vikkelsø is appreciated. The usual caveats apply.

1 The reader may wish to consult Cassen *et al.* (1994) for a useful survey with a broader scope than the present paper.

2 This assumption is not always justified Aid may interact with foreign private flows in both positive and negative ways. If increased aid is interpreted as a signal that greater political stability can be expected in the recipient country, private flows may increase. In contrast, if more aid is perceived as a signal that a country is experiencing economic difficulties this may have a negative impact on other foreign inflows.

3 This equation can be interpreted as a behavioural relation where the level of savings depends on the levels of income and aid, so $S_t = \alpha_0 Y_t + \alpha_1 A_t$. The marginal impacts of respectively income (α_0) and aid (α_1) are in the formulation implicit in (6) allowed to differ. In case aid is perceived as a perfect substitute for other kinds of income (i.e. fully fungible), the two marginal effects on savings are equal.

4 The 131 cross-country regressions surveyed here were identified from the 29 articles, papers and books listed in the Appendix at the end of this chapter. Most books and papers included in the survey contain more than one empirical estimation. As such, they represent several observations regarding the impact of aid on economic performance. A list of the 131 regressions and all details about their classification is available from the authors.

5 The preparatory work behind the survey involved a series of cross-tabulations in which the 131 cross-country regressions were organised as a set of categorised data. The following classification scheme was used: region, sample period and analytical method. Ideally, it would have been desirable to study as well any impact arising from sub-sampling by income group. This was left for further research as information going beyond what is available in published sources would be required to reach solid conclusions.

6 It may be useful to recall here that understanding the determinants of savings is not just a problem in developing countries. Browning and Lusardi (1996) argue from a microeconomic perspective that even though numerous empirical studies of savings and consumption have been carried out and published, the question 'why people save' remains largely unanswered. A recent study by Masson *et al.*

(1998) approaches the issue from a macroeconomic perspective and examines possible savings determinants using both time-series and cross-sectional data. Interesting results emerge, but heterogeneity is characteristic.

7 If $S_t = \alpha_0 Y_t + \alpha_1 A_t$ and it is tentatively assumed that $Y_t = \beta_0 + \beta_1 A_t$, the implied investment effect is positive as long as $\alpha_1 > -1 - \alpha_0\beta_1$, which will normally be less than -1.

8 Due to missing data on standard errors for two regressions, no test statistics could be calculated for the alternative null-hypothesis.

9 Note that while (Eqn 4) is an accounting identity, (Eqn 7) is a behavioural equation in line with the assumptions in the literature surveyed here.

10 Note that Mosley (1980) is a forerunner when it comes to recognising the endogeneity of aid in empirical testing. Yet, while trying to address this problem at an early stage, he treated savings as exogenous.

11 These time–dummies are included to capture the effect of shocks that are common to all of the countries in each of the years, but not captured by other included variables (i.e. the dummies take account of the world business cycle).

12 Endogeneity of aid is not dealt with in the study.

13 Another difference between the Burnside–Dollar study and the other three studies is that Burnside and Dollar use a new measure of aid flows: effective development aid (EDA) (see Chang *et al.* 1998). However, in the World Bank (1998a) study it is stated that the choice between the standard aid measure (official development assistance, ODA) and the new measure (EDA) makes no significant difference in estimations.

14 In Hadjimichael *et al.* and Hansen and Tarp the turning point from which increased aid will have a negative effect on growth is an aid/GDP ratio of about 25 per cent. In Durbarry *et al.* this ratio is about 40 per cent. However, the empirical identification of a turning point should be interpreted with great care.

15 This argument can be based on the analysis of absorptive capacity constraints by Chenery and Strout (1966) and later followers.

16 This example illustrates a possible reason why so many studies have found large differences in aid effectiveness for low- and middle-income developing countries If the average investment rate, $\bar{\imath}$, around which the Taylor expansion is carried out, is correlated with the income level, the regression parameters in (Eqn 13) will be sample dependent.

17 We were unable to obtain all of the Burnside–Dollar data, although they kindly provided some. We filled in gaps based on other published sources. To our knowledge, the data sets are close, although we were unable to replicate their regressions. Our data set is available on request.

18 They are: Nicaragua (1986–9, 1990–3), Gambia (1986–9, 1990–3) and Guyana (1990–3).

19 To this end it should be noted that the five observations cannot be identified as outliers in regression 2. All regressions in Table 4.4 have the same extreme residual observations. Only three residuals are outside a three standard error band, while ten residuals are outside a two standard error band. The five observations excluded by Burnside and Dollar are not in any of these sets.

Appendix

List and classification of studies with cross-country regression results (exogenous aid and resource flows) summarised in the main text (Table 4.1). The 131 regressions identified in the studies below are classified as shown below in Table A.4.1(a) and (b).

[1] Ahmed, N. (1971) 'Note on the Haavelmo Hypothesis', *Review of Economics and Statistics* 53(4): 413–4.

[2] Areskoug, K. (1969) *External Public Borrowing: Its Role in Economic Development*, New York: Praeger Publishers. A later study by Areskoug (1973) contains identical results, so the original regressions are used in what follows.

[3] Bornschier, V., Chase-Dunn, C. and Rubinson, V. (1978) 'Cross-National Evidence of the Effects of Foreign Investment and Aid on the Economic Growth and Inequality: A Survey of Findings and a Re-analysis', *American Journal of Sociology* 84(3): 651–83.

[4] Dowling, M. and Hiemenz, U. (1982) *Aid, Savings and Growth in the Asian Region*, Economic Office Report Series 3, Manila: Asian Development Bank.

[5] Durbarry, R., Gemmell, N. and Greenaway, D. (1998) 'New Evidence on the Impact of Foreign Aid on Economic Growth', Research Paper 98/8, Centre for Research in Economic Development and International Trade, University of Nottingham.

[6] Feyzioglu, T., Swaroop, V. and Zhu, M. (1998) 'A Panel Data Analysis of the Fungibility of Foreign Aid', *World Bank Economic Review* 12(1): 29–58.

[7] Griffin, K.B. (1970) 'Foreign Capital, Domestic Savings and Economic Development', *Bulletin of the Oxford University Institute of Economics & Statistics* 32(2): 99–112.

[8] Griffin, K.B. and Enos, J.L. (1970) 'Foreign Assistance: Objectives and Consequences', *Economic Development and Cultural Change* 18(3): 313–27.

[9] Gupta, K.L. (1970) 'Foreign Capital and Domestic Savings: A Test of Haavelmo's Hypothesis with Cross-Country Data: A Comment', *Review of Economics and Statistics* 52(2): 214–6.

[10] Gupta, K.L. (1975) 'Foreign Capital Inflows, Dependency Burden, and Saving Rates in Developing Countries: A Simultaneous Equation Model', *Kyklos* 28(2): 358–74.

[11] Gupta, K.L. and Islam, M.A. (1983) *Foreign Capital, Savings and Growth – An International Cross-Section Study*, Dordrecht: Reidel Publishing Company.

[12] Halevi, N. (1976) 'The Effects on Investment and Consumption of Import Surpluses of Developing Countries', *Economic Journal* 86(344): 853–8.

[13] Heller, P.S. (1975) 'A Model of Public Fiscal Behavior in Developing Countries: Aid, Investment, and Taxation', *American Economic Review* 65(3): 429–45.

[14] Khan, H.A. and Hoshino, E. (1992) 'Impact of Foreign Aid on the Fiscal Behaviour of LDC Governments', *World Development* 20(10): 1481–8.

[15] Levy, V. (1987) 'Does Concessionary Aid Lead to Higher Investment Rates in Low-Income Countries?', *Review of Economics and Statistics* 69(1): 152–6.

[16] Levy, V. (1988) 'Aid and Growth in Sub-Saharan Africa: The Recent Experience', *European Economic Review* 32(9): 1777–95.

[17] Massell, B.F., Pearson, S.R. and Fitch, J. B. (1972) 'Foreign Exchange and Economic Development: An Empirical Study of Selected Latin American Countries', *Review of Economics and Statistics* 54(2): 208–12.

[18] Mosley, P., Hudson, J. and Horrell, S. (1987) 'Aid, the Public Sector and the Market in Less Developed Countries', *Economic Journal* 97(387): 616–41.

[19] Mosley, P., Hudson, J. and Horrell, S. (1992) 'Aid, the Public Sector and the Market in Less Developed Countries: A Return to the Scene of the Crime', *Journal of International Development* 4(2), 139–50.

[20] Over, A.M. (1975) 'An Example of the Simultaneous-Equation Problem: A

Note on Foreign Assistance: Objectives and Consequences', *Economic Development and Cultural Change* 23(4): 751–6.

[21] Papanek, G.F. (1973) 'Aid, Foreign Private Investment, Savings, and Growth in Less Developed Countries', *Journal of Political Economy* 81(1): 120–30.

[22] Rahman, A. (1968) 'Foreign Capital and Domestic Savings: A Test of Haavelmo's Hypothesis with Cross-Country Data', *Review of Economics and Statistics* 50(1): 137–8.

[23] Singh, R.D. (1985) 'State Intervention, Foreign Economic Aid, Savings and Growth in LDCs: Some Recent Evidence', *Kyklos* 38(2): 216–32.

[24] Snyder, D.W. (1990) 'Foreign Aid and Domestic Savings: A Spurious Correlation?', *Economic Development and Cultural Change* 39(1): 175–81.

[25] Snyder, D.W. (1993) 'Donor Bias Towards Small Countries: An Overlooked Factor in the Analysis of Foreign Aid and Economic Growth', *Applied Economics* 25(4): 481–8.

[26] Stoneman, C. (1975) 'Foreign Capital and Economic Growth', *World Development* 3(1): 11–26.

[27] Voivodas, C.S. (1973) 'Exports, Foreign Capital Inflow and Economic Growth', *Journal of International Economics* 3(4): 337–49.

[28] Weisskopf, T.E. (1972) 'The Impact of Foreign Capital Inflow on Domestic Savings in Underdeveloped Countries', *Journal of International Economics* 2(1): 25–38.

[29] White, H. (1992b) 'What Do We Know About Aid's Macroeconomic Impact? An Overview of the Aid Effectiveness Debate', *Journal of International Development* 4(2), 121–37.

Table A.4.1(a) Classification of regressions summarised in Table 4.1

Dependent variable	Explanatory variable: Foreign aid flows (A)		
	(−)	(0)	(+)
Savings[a] $H_0: \alpha_1 = 0$	**9**/5, **11**/2, **21**/1, **23**/2, **24**/1, **29**/3	**9**/5, **23**/2, **24**/2, **29**/1	
Savings $H_0: \alpha_1 = -1$[a,b]	**9**/1	**9**/7, **11**/1, **21**/1, **23**/3, **29**/1	**9**/2, **24**/3, **29**/3
Investment $H_0: \alpha_1 = 0$		**17**/1	**6**/2, **12**/1, **13**/1, **14**/1, **15**/6, **16**/4
Growth $H_0: \alpha_1 = 0$	**18**/1	**7**/2, **9**/3, **17**/1, **18**/10, **19**/3, **21**/1, **23**/2, **24**/1, **26**/1, **29**/1	**4**/2, **5**/5, **9**/3, **11**/2, **16**/2, **18**/2, **19**/1, **21**/4, **23**/2, **24**/2, **26**/10, **29**/3

Notes: The null-hypotheses are tested at the 5 per cent significance level against a two-sided alternative. The first number (in **bold**) refers to the study as listed and the second figure (after the forward slash) refers to the number of regressions in the study yielding the statistical result indicated.
[a]The total number of regressions in the $\alpha_1 = 0$ and $\alpha_1 = -1$ aid–savings estimations are not the same (24 and 22) due to missing data on standard errors for two regressions.
[b]Since H_0 in this row is $\alpha_1 = -1$, the cells (−), (0) and (+) represent $\alpha_1 < -1$, $\alpha_1 = -1$ and $\alpha_1 > -1$, respectively.

Table A.4.1(b) Classification of regressions summarised in Table 4.1 (*continued*)

Dependent variable	Explanatory variable: Foreign resource inflows (F)		
	(−)	(0)	(+)
Savings H_0: $\alpha_1=0$	1/3, **8/1**, **9/2**, **11/1**, **21/2**, **22/1**, 28/1	1/1, **8/1**, **9/2**, 10/1	20/1
Savings H_0: $\alpha_1=-1$[a]		1/3, **8/1**, **9/2**, **11/1**	1/1, **8/1**, **9/2**, 10/1, 20/1, **21/2**, **22/1**, 28/1
Investment H_0: $\alpha_1=0$			2/1, **12/1**]
Growth H_0: $\alpha_1=0$		3/5, 27/1	**11/1**, **21/1**

Notes: See Table A.4.1(a).
[a]Since H_0 in this row is $\alpha_1=-1$, the cells (-), (0) and (+) represent $\alpha_1<-1$, $\alpha_1=-1$ and $\alpha_1>-1$, respectively.

Table A.4.2 Instrumental variable growth regressions with polynomial effects of aid and policy in 56 countries for five periods, 1974–93. Dependent variable: average annual growth rate of GDP per capita

Regression	1	2	3	4	5
Aid	0.142	0.055	0.236*	0.230*	0.265**
	(0.25)	(1.19)	(1.75)	(1.75)	(2.00)
Aid×policy	0.079	−0.014	−0.012	–	–
	(1.61)	(0.55)	(0.42)	–	–
Aid²	–	–	−0.005*	−0.005*	−0.005*
	–	–	(1.70)	(1.78)	(1.81)
Policy²	–	–	0.078	–	–
	–	–	(0.77)	–	–
Openness	1.500**	2.183**	1.439	1.927**	2.016**
	(2.24)	(3.77)	(1.33)	(3.83)	(3.86)
Inflation	−0.799	−1.372**	−1.351**	−1.168**	−0.905*
	(1.41)	(2.68)	(2.55)	(2.55)	(1.70)
Budget deficit	4.81	8.304*	8.195*	7.853*	8.851*
	(0.89)	(1.73)	(1.67)	(1.92)	(1.86)
Govt consumption	−2.878	−3.825	−5.848	−5.040	−3.964
	(0.54)	(0.76)	(1.10)	(0.96)	(0.71)
Financial depth	0.014	0.02	0.016	0.015	0.011
	(0.95)	(1.51)	(1.14)	(1.11)	(0.75)
Institutional quality	0.727**	0.624**	0.717**	0.722**	0.760**
	(4.21)	(3.81)	(4.02)	(4.08)	(4.17)
Initial GDP per capita	−0.111	−0.163	0.041	0.038	0.098
	(0.18)	(0.27)	(0.06)	(0.06)	(0.14)
Observations	226	231	231	231	226
R^2	0.39	0.39	0.40	0.39	0.39

Notes: Instruments used are arms import (lagged), a dummy for Central American countries, a dummy for Franc zone countries, a dummy for Egypt, log(population), log(population)², log(population)×policy, log(infant mortality), log(infant mortality)², log(infant mortality)×policy, log(infant mortality)²×policy, aid (lagged), aid² (lagged), aid×policy (lagged), and aid²×policy (lagged). See also Table 4.4.

Part II

Aid instruments

5 From project aid to programme assistance

Paul Mosley and Marion J. Eeckhout

Introduction

Since 1980, overseas aid has transformed itself. Although seeking to perform the same purpose as in the early 1970s – the promotion of economic development, with an emphasis on poverty reduction, and with broadly the same resources (about $50 billion in 1998 prices) – it now uses different instruments to achieve that purpose. As illustrated by Table 5.1, the project aid component of aid budgets has declined severely from the early 1970s (sometimes to the point of collapse) and other aid instruments have expanded to fill the vacuum, notably technical co-operation, policy-conditioned programme aid, support for the private sector and for NGOs and emergency assistance.

These changes faithfully reflect the changing emphasis in development thinking (see Chapter 1) over the same period: from a single-minded emphasis on lack of capital as the key resource gap to a preoccupation with human, and finally social, capital shortages; from unthinking confidence in the ability of developing-country governments to compensate for market failure to complete disillusion with them, resulting in both policy conditionality on those governments and a search for alternatives to them as development partners; from a conception of war and internal disorder as exogenous to the development process to the view that donors, through the prevention and healing of conflicts, may be able to lay the foundations for the resumption of development. There is some evidence that the effectiveness of aid, as a consequence, may have begun to increase after a poor start and that its credibility may have begun to improve, as shown in Table 5.2. Ironically, this occurs at a time when aid volumes are beginning to decline, as discussed in Chapter 3.

Overseas aid, then, has lost its innocence. Having ignored questions of its overall impact for so long that both public and governmental support for it was beginning to dwindle, it is now seeking to repair the damage with an evolving mix of new instruments. They include financial programme aid in addition to food aid programme aid, which was used already prior to 1970 (see Chapter 3 for further historical background and Chapter 8 on

Table 5.1 Structure of bilateral British and multilateral World Bank aid, selected years, 1973–96

	1973	1980	1983	1996
United Kingdom				
Total aid amount ($ billion, 1996–7 prices)	2.3	n.a.	1.8	1.7
Aid types as a percentage of total amounts:				
Project aid[a]	38.0	n.a.	17.0	8.0
Programme aid	0.0	n.a.	9.0	7.0
Technical assistance	33.0	n.a.	42.0	51.0
Private sector aid	9.0	n.a.	8.0	15.0
Emergency relief	0.0	n.a.	2.0	9.0
Other[b]	20.0	n.a.	22.0	10.0
Total	100.0	n.a.	100.0	100.0
World Bank Group				
Total aid amount ($ billion, 1996–7 prices)	16.7	17.8	18.5	23.5
Aid types as a percentage of total amounts:				
Project aid[a]	n.a.	82.0	n.a.	48.0
Programme aid (adjustment lending)	0.0	2.0	n.a.	23.0
Private sector (through IFC)[c]	n.a.	15.0	n.a.	27.0
Other	n.a.	1.0	n.a.	2.0
Total	n.a.	100.0	n.a.	100.0

Sources: DFID (1999), Maxwell (1996) and World Bank, *Annual Report* (various issues).
Notes: n.a., not available.
        [a]Project aid here refers to aid provided to the recipient government.
        [b]Includes debt relief.
        [c]IFC is the International Finance Corporation.

Table 5.2 Statistical evidence on the effectiveness of foreign aid (dependent variable in regressions is the growth of GDP per capita and the independent variable is aid as a percentage of GDP)[a]

	Study and period investigated				
Country sample from	*Mosley et al. (1987) 1960–70*	*Mosley et al. (1987) 1970–80*	*Boone (1996) 1970–90*	*Mosley et al. (1987) 1980–5*	*Mosley and Hudson (1998) 1985–95*
Africa	−0.0104	−0.0889	–	−0.0890	–
	(0.27)	(0.63)	–	(0.41)	–
Asia	0.0985	0.4630*	–	0.6750*	–
	(1.31)	(2.03)	–	(2.49)	–
Latin America	0.0178	1.0100	–	1.9700	–
	(0.06)	(1.19)	–	(1.51)	–
Developing countries in general	–	−0.0300	0.0000	0.0100	0.3800*
	–	(0.32)	(0.03)	(0.07)	(3.24)

Notes: Student's *t*-statistics are given in parentheses under coefficients. An asterisk denotes significance at 5 per cent level.
        [a]Other independent variables include other types of financial flows, savings, growth in literacy and exports, except in Boone (1996), which adds population growth and area dummies to the variables listed.

food aid). This chapter examines two elements in the process of transformation which has been ongoing since the early 1970s: the decline of
project aid and the rise of programme, or 'policy-based' assistance. It
argues that the latter rose precisely because the former fell, but that given
the continuing morbidity of the bottom end of the capital market in the
poorest countries this may not always have been an appropriate long-term
development.

The rise and fall of project aid

When aid began in its modern form after the Second World War, poverty and
underdevelopment were seen as being caused by shortage of capital. The
'central problem in the theory of economic development', Sir Arthur Lewis
wrote in 1954, 'is to understand the process by which a community which was
previously saving and investing 4 or 5 per cent of its national income or less
converts itself into an economy where voluntary savings are much higher.'
(Lewis 1954: 155); and the process was seen as difficult and uncertain
because of the weakness and imperfection of capital markets in developing
countries. The 'savings gap' approach (later expanded with the 'foreign
exchange gap', whence the 'two-gap' approach) immediately defined a primary role for foreign aid: the provision of capital equipment, which developing countries were unable to finance through the market, and especially for
infrastructure, which private banks were particularly reluctant to support on
account of its long gestation period and the major uncertainties associated
with future demand patterns. As late as the mid-1970s, 52 per cent of total
OECD aid consisted of project aid, of which the majority (nearly two-thirds)
was for infrastructure: roads, railways, water and sewerage, ports, airports,
power stations and telecommunications (OECD 1997).

These investments had the advantage, from the aid donors' point of view,
of being highly visible and technologically straightforward in the sense that
they normally consisted of transplants of technology already available in
the donor country. Thus, from the point of view of the donor country's
business lobby, that was their attraction. Often these projects were designed
in such a way as to keep the role of the recipient government quite minor.
This was done, for example, by creating autonomous project authorities
with the financial ability to bypass central government, or by confining the
scope of the project to installation with maintenance left to be done by the
operating authority at some point in the future. In this way the problems
'at the bottom of the logical framework', of transferring the technology on
time and within budget, were kept to a minimum, thereby keeping outside
the realm of debate not only issues of ultimate impact, but also questions of
governmental ownership and sustainability that were to provoke such
extensive anxiety and debate later on.

The first big evolution of aid policy after the Second World War – the
move into poverty-focused aid, triggered by Robert McNamara's commit-

ment of the World Bank to poverty reduction at the World Bank–IMF annual meeting in 1973 – offered large opportunities for an expansion of the project mode of aid disbursement. The nettle of small-holder agriculture and credit, previously neglected because of the difficulty of disbursing aid in small amounts, was now grasped with enthusiasm. Urban infrastructure projects were moved down-market and expanded into slum improvement projects. Aid activities in the health and education sectors were, in most cases, moved away from the cities and towards the primary level. Most ambitiously of all, the decade of the 1970s saw the emergence of the integrated rural development project (IRDP), in which a range of activities – infrastructure, health, education, agricultural extension, rural finance – were financed in parallel within a particular underdeveloped region, in order to tackle the several interlocking causes of rural poverty at their root. In some regions IRDPs have failed to take root, but in others, notably South Asia, they have had long-term influence on the organisation of rural development and even on the decentralisation of government.

By the end of the 1970s, therefore, the project aid modality was established across all sectors in the portfolios of most donors. And the returns being obtained on those portfolios were perfectly respectable; some indicative data from the World Bank are provided in Table 5.3 below. However, even at that time, before the second oil crisis broke, there were symptoms of what we would now call unsustainability. These were basically of three types. In the first place, the new types of projects, more complex and government-intensive than the older civil-engineering variety, were causing ever increasing implementation delays and problems of absorptive capacity, making it difficult to speed the allocated aid budget and making urgent the creation of more flexible instruments of aid disbursement. It may be asked whether this matters as long as project benefits eventually get through to the poor. But as Wiggins (1985) pointed out, 'concern for the rural poor evaporates very rapidly when hard-pressed administrators are still emptying their in-trays at 7pm on a Friday evening.'

Second, it was increasingly perceived that the success of projects was determined not in the main by factors internal to the project, such as design or management competence, but by factors external to the project and especially policy. This is clearly illustrated by Table 5.3, which summarises rates of return for World Bank projects during the 1968–89 period, and shows that development projects in the private sector (such as those financed by the International Finance Corporation, IFC), and not only the conventional public sector operations, were hampered by policies of over-valued exchange rates, financial repression and high inflation.

Third and most disturbingly, it was becoming clear that evaluation methods such as internal rate of return which assessed only the direct effects of a project (such as those portrayed in Table 5.3) gave only a partial and almost certainly an over-optimistic view of the effects of aid. As will be recalled from Table 5.2, there are econometric estimates of the macro-

Table 5.3 Economic policies and average rates of returns for World Bank and IFC projects, 1968–89

Policy distortion index	All projects	All public projects	Public agricultural projects	Public industrial projects	Public projects in non-tradable sectors	All private projects
Trade restrictiveness						
High	13.2	13.6	12.1	n.a	14.6	9.5
Moderate	13.0	15.4	15.4	n.a	16.0	10.7
Low	19.0	19.3	14.3	n.a	24.3	17.1
Foreign exchange premium						
High	8.2	7.2	3.2	n.a.	11.5	n.a.
Moderate	14.4	14.9	11.9	13.7	17.2	10.3
Low	17.7	18.0	16.6	16.6	19.3	15.2
Real interest rates						
Negative	15.0	15.4	12.7	12.7	17.9	11.0
Positive	17.3	17.5	17.0	17.8	17.9	15.6
Fiscal deficits						
High (8 per cent or more)	13.4	13.7	11.7	10.3	16.6	10.7
Moderate (4–8 per cent)	14.8	15.1	12.2	21.0	16.8	12.2
Low (less than 4 per cent)	17.8	18.1	18.6	14.1	18.2	14.3

Source: World Bank (1991a).
Note: n.a., not available.

effectiveness of aid which suggest an overall impact (the partial regression coefficient of aid on growth) insignificantly different from zero; and yet the micro-estimates of effectiveness in Table 5.3 suggest project impacts which are respectable even by the standards of a private sector which has no developmental criteria to satisfy.[1]

The resolution of this so-called 'micro–macro paradox' (Mosley 1987: ch. 5) requires us, in our view, to take note of the indirect effects of aid which are in Table 5.2 but not in Table 5.3: first of all the knock-on effects of aid on the private sector (such as 'Dutch disease', buoying up of the exchange rate and depression of food crop prices by food aid) and second the knock-on effects of aid on public sector spending patterns, which may be minor in the case of an uncorrupt and developmentally-inclined recipient government but which in the case of a corrupt government may involve the switching of spending power made available by aid into political patronage.[2] Where aid accounts for most public spending and over 10 per cent of GNP, as in most of Africa since the 1980s, these moral hazard problems are potentially serious; the project mode of aid is powerless against them. Thus, independently of the existence or not of a 'micro–macro paradox', the objective of improving the effectiveness of aid leads to questions about the use and desirability of projects as a channel for foreign aid.

Although all of these problems with the project modality were perceived well before the great crash of the 1980s, it was that crash, and the debt defaults associated with it, which forced aid donors to come to terms with them. Specifically, they needed an aid instrument that was quick-disbursing, and project aid was not that. They needed an instrument that would bring about policy change, and project aid could not do that. They needed an instrument that would build governmental capacity, itself depleted by the consequences of the stabilisation measures of the 1980s, and project aid could not do that either, unless it came in the form of a project to re-habilitate, or replace, existing public sector functions and capacities.

As a consequence the main response by aid donors to the problems associated with the project aid instrument in the 1980s was not loyalty to that instrument, or even voice, but rather exit: in favour of financial programme aid (discussed in the next section), in favour of capacity-building technical assistance operations, or in favour of projects executed, not by the government, but by the private sector or by NGOs. When poverty focus came back into fashion in the 1990s, these non-state agencies, and not developing-country governments, took much of the responsibility for implementing it; through micro-finance and other small-business support measures, through support for non-state rural health and education services, and through grants to existing community organisations. As a result, the existing trend away from government-to-government transfers of capital equipment, apparent well before 1980 (Table 5.1), was accelerated thereafter.

The rise and transformation of financial programme aid

Financial programme aid, until the 1980s, was a thing of minor significance. There were of course programme operations, in the sense of money provided by international financial institutions for macroeconomic stabilisation purposes and not linked to any specific project of capital investment, but these were mainly provided on commercial terms by the IMF, as standby operations or, after 1975, from the Extended Facility or Compensatory Facility to deal with problems arising from the first oil crisis or more generally from secular commodity price decline. The conditions attached to such operations consisted, and still consist, essentially of deflation of aggregate demand, typically the public sector components of such demand such as public expenditure and its determinants such as credit creation by the central bank.

This money was of course provided at market rates of interest; the World Bank and bilateral aid donors did occasionally top up IMF loans with concessional aid of their own designed to achieve broadly the same purpose, but this was minor, more a way of getting rid of the unspent balance of the aid budget at the end of the financial year than a serious instrument of policy. The interesting question is what induced aid donors, at the beginning of the 1980s, to emulate the IMF and start providing programme aid of their own on an increasing scale (Table 5.1 above), often with a conditionality very different from the Fund's.

The answer contains both supply and demand elements. On the supply side, there was as we have seen widespread frustration with the project mode of aid disbursement, linked with a perception that good projects required good policy and good institutions to back them up, neither of which was forthcoming in the poorer developing countries at the onset of the second oil crisis. On the demand side, the long-drawn-out recession of 1980–5 triggered a series of defaults on sovereign debt which quite rapidly led to the withdrawal, transiently from the richer and permanently from the poorer developing countries, of most bank lending, portfolio investment and direct investment. This threw enormous demands on to the shoulders of the aid donors, but demands of a specific type: not for project aid of the old cumbersome slow-disbursing type, but for quick-disbursing balance-of-payments support which might help developing countries come to terms with an unprecedented emergency.

Eventually, this new kind of aid began to arrive from all quarters. From the World Bank in the form of adjustment lending, from bilateral donors as balance-of-payments support usually linked with the Banks operations, and even from the IMF itself in the form of the Enhanced Structural Adjustment Facility (ESAF), the first time that the Fund had involved itself in aid-giving. By the mid-1990s it was about a third of World Bank lending, and just under 20 per cent of the bilateral aid budgets of the OECD countries (OECD 1997). In general, such operations specified a conditionality that required the removal of elements of state intervention which were believed to interfere with the effective operation of markets, such as exchange controls, import quotas, taxation of farm prices by marketing boards, subsidies to public corporations, and price controls generally; a neo-liberal agenda which, of course, was being implemented voluntarily in industrialised countries as well as forcibly in the developing world through the medium of these structural adjustment operations, as the new form of programme aid became known. The purpose of this new conditionality was to move the aggregate supply curve downward and to the right, which if it could be done promised a more humane technology of stabilisation than the standard demand-deflationary (IMF) approach of moving the demand curve to the left, given that control of inflation and balance-of-payments deficits could, under the new technology, be in principle achieved without sacrifice of current output.

Adjustment lending was visualised by the donors as a short-term operation to deal with the macroeconomic emergency of the early 1980s, with equilibrium (implying the obsolescence of the programme aid instrument) being achieved over a period of about five years (Landell-Mills 1981). It happened in that way in a number of relatively flexible middle-income economies (e.g. South Korea, Chile, Thailand and Mauritius), but not in most. Some recipient countries, for a variety of reasons, did not commit themselves to programmes of economic reform until the beginning of the 1990s (for example, India, Argentina and the entire group of transitional economies in the former communist bloc); and others which began their adjustment on time in the early 1980s were still locked into adjustment programmes twenty years on. Essentially there were three problems with this first phase of adjustment-related programme aid, all of them unforeseen.

The first was a problem of *implementation*: about half of the first wave of adjustment reforms were not implemented (Mosley *et al*. 1995a and World Bank 1988, 1990b, 1992a, 1994a), because many governments realised that they could safely bow to political opposition to the removal of controls, and still keep conditional programme aid flowing. Another reason was that its suspension would have prejudiced the repayment of sovereign debt to donors and commercial banks (Mosley *et al*. 1995a and Mosley 1998).

The second was a problem of *effectiveness*: many countries which did implement adjustment programmes, especially in Africa, found that the supply response of the economy to the initial programmes of economic reform was negligible to the point of irrelevance.[3] The third was the problem of *social* (and to a lesser extent environmental) *side-effects of adjustment*: many countries which overcame the first two problems and implemented effective adjustment programmes, as well as many which did not, experienced deteriorations in poverty and human capital indicators that many ascribed (although the matter is not resolved) to the public expenditure cuts and reallocations which had formed the core of adjustment programmes. A preliminary balance-sheet on this first phase of programme operations is reproduced as Table 5.4: across over 80 recipient countries as a whole, trade performance certainly improved in adjusting relative to non-adjusting countries, investment certainly deteriorated, and the effects on both growth and poverty are ambiguous. This was certainly a worrying enough verdict to convince donors that further evolution of the programme aid instrument was required.

This evolution came in two forms. The first was exit: for example much aid intended, not only for poverty relief, but also for directly productive investment, is now conveyed, not through governments (either through project or programme aid) but directly to the private sector. The channel is either (at the small-scale end of the market) through NGOs or (at the large-scale end) through direct investment in private business, as shown by Table 5.1 above. In this way perceived defects in incentive structures are remedied, not through confrontation, but through avoidance. The second was voice, or reform: from 1992 onward all recipients of World Bank programme assistance must not only comply with specified policy reform

Table 5.4 Summary of effects of World Bank programme lending, 1980–96

Performance evaluation methods and studies	*Real GDP growth*	*Real export growth*	*Investment– GDP ratio*	*Poverty gap*
Tabular comparisons with control				
Mosley *et al.* (1995a: ch. 6)	neutral	positive	negative	n.m.
World Bank (1988, 1990b, 1992a)	neutral	positive	negative	n.m.
Sahn (1994) and Demery and Squire (1996)	n.m.	n.m.	n.m.	positive
Weeks (1997)	n.m.	n.m.	n.m.	negative
Multiple regression				
Mosley *et al.* (1995a: ch. 7)	(positive)	positive	negative	n.m.
World Bank (1994a)[a]	positive	positive	negative	n.m.
Mosley *et al.* (1995b)[a]	neutral	positive	negative	neutral
CGE or multi-market modelling				
Sahn (1994)[b]	n.m.	n.m.	n.m.	positive
Mosley *et al.* (1995a: ch. 8)[c]	positive	positive	neutral	neutral

Sources: As indicated. Original table format adapted from Mosley *et al.* (1995a: tab. 8.8).
Notes: n.m., not measured.
         [a]Results refer to Africa only.
         [b]Results refer to various countries.
         [c]Results refer to Morocco only.

conditions, intended to remove microeconomic distortions, but also by implementing an approved poverty strategy.

This initiative has been copied by a range of bilateral donors including all Scandinavian countries, the Netherlands and most recently the United Kingdom in its 1997 White Paper (DFID 1997). This helps to deal not only with the problem of side-effects but also with the problem of implementation, since if poor losers from an adjustment programme can be co-opted into supporting it as a consequence of the compensation they are given, that may take away an important barrier to reform. In some regions where the social costs of adjustment have been greatest, such as Russia and Eastern Europe, the lion's share of the programme aid budget of OECD donors consists of operations targeted at the social sectors (health, education and social services) designed precisely to counteract suffering which at the outset of the adjustment process had not even been recognised.

The initial function of financial programme aid, it will be remembered, was not to stand on its own, but to support the project aid operation, in particular by removing distortions which damaged aid projects. For example, an agricultural development project which suffered from too low a government purchasing price of maize or from a non-existent export market could be rescued by raising the price, or by dissolving the government monopoly marketing board, or by floating the exchange rate. Attractive though this logic is, comprehensive project audits such as that conducted by Willi Wapenhans on behalf of the World Bank in 1992 continued to show a remorselessly rising proportion of 'problem projects'. This information, quite apart from covering only a limited part of the aid budget, does not necessarily show that the logic was wrong. For example, there might be more 'problem projects' now because donors have moved experimentally into new types of operation (including adjustment lending, support for NGOs and relief operations) which require time before they can be made effective; the 'learning curve' argument. Donors, in an ideal world, suffer from a reverse moral hazard: they gravitate to where the difficulties are, and that may have costs for measured efficiency. But this provides only limited comfort. The evidence is that, although matters are improving, certain incentive problems, even after two waves of adjustment operations, continue to be embedded in the aid process itself. They are not specific to programme aid but will be discussed here because their remedy has been sought through different types of programme operation.

General moral hazard

If aid inflows are tied, as they usually are, to an indicator of need (such as a balance-of-payments deficit, or low income, or low investment) then the recipient has an incentive to lower performance in order to sustain the need for aid in order to make a case for continued aid (Pedersen 1996, Mosley 1996 and Mosley and Hudson 1998). Thus African economies, having reached through the 1980s' 'lost decade', the point where most of their public investment, and more than 10 per cent of their GNP, is being financed by aid, have an incentive not to improve performance to the point where aid is taken away and short-term losses result. A particularly import-ant example of this is taxation, which is negatively correlated with aid inflows (Moore 1997) and hence budgeting. For so long as a particular component of public expenditure is aid-financed, recipient governments can avoid the political cost of seeking the incremental public revenue which finances it through user charges or an extension of the tax net.

The specific moral hazard of corruption

Structural adjustment has reduced, but by no means eliminated, the scope for corruption within government. The apparatus of controls and permits has been partly dismantled, but all public expenditure is open to being corruptly allocated, and in the poorest countries most public expenditure is aid-financed. The World Bank, in a recent *World Development Report* (World Bank 1997a), has drawn attention to the efficiency costs of corruption and more generally of governance failings unreached by the processes of liberalisation. Many of these governance failings, it has become clear, arise not so much from rent-seeking as such, but from the damaging influence of civil war and international conflict.

The debt burden

Countries that owe a very high proportion of their export earnings as debt service have little incentive to undertake adjustment efforts, as a very high proportion of the proceeds of such effort, by assumption, benefits the creditor rather than the debtor. Indeed, the more debt is paid off, the less that debt can be used as a political weapon. This problem of the debt overhang is discussed at more length in Chapter 15 of this volume.

Co-ordination problems

The continuing co-ordination problems between the project and the programme instrument should, in principle, not occur, as the conditions attached to programme aid should all have the function of improving project performance. But in practice the choice of policy conditions may be dictated by considerations of what is politically feasible, rather than by the requirements of projects. There have even been cases where conditionality has been imposed in a directly opposite sense to that which project staff of the same aid agency were seeking.[4]

The above cluster of problems has sparked a third wave of programme aid operations, typically aimed at improving the incentive to use aid effectively both within the recipient government and within the nexus that binds it to the donors. The key initiatives within this third wave are:

- In response to the co-ordination problem, the device of sector investment programmes (SIP) has been introduced; this seeks to deal at the same time with the problems of dis-coordination and of under-budgeting of recurrent expenditure. This is done by specifying an interlinked package of investments and supportive policies for a particular sector (health, agriculture, education, etc.), the maintenance of which, according to a budget agreed between donors and recipients, constitutes the conditionality on the associated programme finance. In essence this is a fusion of programme and project lending, since under SIPs the (improvement of the) sector itself becomes the project in hand. The idea is only likely to work, and has only been tried, in highly aid-dependent economies such as those of Africa, and in some ways is an acknowledgement of the extent to which aid itself had undermined budgetary procedures in Africa, as noted under the general moral hazard problem. Early, somewhat intuitive evaluations (e.g. Jones 1997: 26) suggest some degree of success in sectors where the planning of public expenditure had been particularly poor in the 1980s (such as Zambian health and agriculture) but warn of a danger that 'what are universally recognised as weak administrations will be overwhelmed by the burden of SIP preparation.' Further ideas concerning what works and what does not work in the field of sector investment programmes are provided by the Appendix to this paper, which warns that the problems of donor harmonisation that SIPs were intended to cure have not yet been resolved. Chapter 7 of this volume also pursues these topics.

- In response to the debt problem, programme aid has been embodied in the form of debt relief initiatives, notably at the present time the Heavily Indebted Poor Countries (HIPC) initiative. This allows selected poor countries to receive cancellation of an unprecedented share of their foreign debt after a down-payment of stringent stabilisation and adjustment measures. The star beneficiary is Mozambique which if all goes to plan will have 80 per cent of its debt wiped out, but significant motivational benefits are also expected for Uganda and several other poor and indebted African countries.

- In response to problems of corruption, conditionality which is increasingly governance – rather than simply policy – related, has been observed, so that what is demanded is reforms of the political structure rather than of particular policy instruments. Up to the end of the twentieth century this had been applied exclusively by bilateral donors, and principally in Africa, though there is talk, but only that, of applying it to tackle the manifest governance and regulation problems exposed by the East Asian crisis of 1997–8. The right instrument of intervention in political conditionality is not always easy to identify: donors congratulated themselves on their efforts in getting a multi-party political system established in Kenya in 1992, only for the subsequent elections to come under suspicion, and when a somewhat cleaner election had been fought and won at the end of 1997, the central problem of corruption in the ruling party remained. Increasing attempts are being made by donors to tackle even this last bastion of rent-seeking, by measures which have become increasingly personal. For example, in the run-up to the last ESAF in Madagascar in 1995, the main conditionality which had to be satisfied was the sacking of the central bank governor, Raoul Ravelomana. But such feats of political muscle are typically attempted by the aid authorities only in small African countries, much though they might also wish to annul the reinstallation of the 'world's worst central banker', in the Russian Central Bank (in August 1998), it is improbable that they will attempt to do so.

In conclusion, readers will note that although much has been added to the conditionality menu since 1981, nothing has been taken off: conditional programme aid is thus now being expected to deliver stabilisation, pro-poor growth and now good governance, to say nothing of a whole array of supplementary agenda items not so far mentioned, including environmental protection, greater equity of provision between men and women, demilitarisation and conflict prevention. The ironic consequence of all this has been that financial programme aid, which was hoped to improve on project aid by imposing lesser burdens on hard-pressed administrators in developing country ministries, is now far from doing so and is arguably increasing those burdens, thus creating ample opportunities (Table 5.1 above) for another growing component of aid budgets not covered in this chapter – technical assistance (discussed in Chapter 6). The essence of the problem, in formal terms, is that Jan Tinbergen's rule has been breached – the one instrument of programme aid was from the beginning expected to hit two targets – quick disbursement and enforcement of policy conditions. To these two targets more have been added over the years, so that a serious problem of overload arises. In such a situation, donors need to choose which of their multiple targets they are seriously going to try to hit if they are to avoid being damned for missing them all.

The future

Mosley and Hudson (1998) provide preliminary results (see Table 5.1 above) that the supertanker really has turned around: having been neutral overall, the aggregate effectiveness of overseas aid has been significantly positive since approximately the mid-1980s. In that paper, responsibility for this welcome change is apportioned more or less evenly between three factors: (i) improvement in policies, which is associated with the switch from project to programme aid discussed in this chapter, (ii) a switch to technical assistance, also illustrated in Table 5.1, and associated with a development of skills and other elements of human and social capital and finally (iii) the erosion of fungibility, or scope for switching aid between uses, which was the direct consequence of the collapse of domestically-financed investment budgets in poorer countries in the 1980s.[5] Of these three factors, the last has self-evidently reached its limit, and we would inexpertly guess that technical assistance is unlikely to grow further in real terms either. This throws us back on the central question of this chapter: is the balance between project and programme assistance now right, and is there any scope for improving aid performance by switching aid between the two categories, or by obvious improvements in any one of them?

The widely-cited analysis of Burnside and Dollar (1997), now expanded into a book (World Bank 1998a) appears to suggest that a further switch to programme aid, or (not the same thing) selectivity in favour of countries with orthodox policy frameworks, would bring a dividend in terms of aid effectiveness.[6] Burnside and Dollar, it will be recalled, find that aid does not much influence policy – reinforcing our scepticism about the power of conditionality – but that where the policy framework is 'good', defined as low inflation, low budget deficit and an open economy, aid is effective in relation to growth. This finding is helpful but incomplete, since:

• Inflation and the budget deficit are obviously inter correlated, so that one of these terms could be dropped.

- There are many, not very well inter-correlated, definitions of openness on the market (see Edwards 1998) so that actions that open the economy on some criteria (like export subsidy) constitute closing it on other criteria. What is needed is a measure of the tendency of economic policy to promote competitiveness – such as the Sachs and Warner (1995) measure – and not, above all, a ratio of trade to GDP (see, e.g. Aziz and Wescott 1997), which is more a function of country size and resource endowments than of policy effectiveness.
- The analysis does not contain any discussion of the quality of growth or its ability to satisfy other criteria of aid policy – poverty reduction, reduction of infant mortality, environmental protection and so on. This lacuna has now been filled by Collier and Dollar (1999) who argue that with a more poverty-efficient aid allocation, with aid going only to countries that practise good economic policies, an additional 50 million people would rise above the poverty line.
- Most important, the paper implies that 'good' policy consists of only the three policy variables mentioned, in every country. This is simply false. Two of Burnside and Dollar's chosen policy variables – inflation and openness – have, as one might expect, greater leverage on growth in middle-income than in low-income countries, and inflation has no apparent leverage at all in Africa (Sarel 1996 and Mosley 1998). And a range of other policy variables, in particular the real interest rate, performance weighted protection, income distribution and policy instability, have been shown by several authors to influence growth across some or (in the last two cases) all developing countries (Rodrik 1990, Mosley *et al.* 1995b, Mosley 1998 and Stiglitz 1998) implying that a wider range of policy instruments is in fact needed.

The right inference, we believe, is that conditionality on programme assistance will continue to be an important condition for aid effectiveness, but that it should be *ex post*, project-linked, empirically based and country-specific. *Ex post* conditionality (the aid is handed over only after the necessary policy actions are taken) makes implementation harder to dodge, although not impossible, since there can still be backsliding after the money is received. The right conditionality for any country will be what works in that country, and it will enhance the credibility of the donors' policy dialogue if it is accompanied by empirical demonstrations that a recommended policy will work, rather than by a priori reasoning backed by threats. Often it needs to be gauged with other criteria than simple short-term growth maximisation in mind, for example poverty reduction or the prevention of internal conflict (Cramer and Weeks 1998). As an important special case of this principle, donor conditionality will gain credibility if it can be shown that compliance with it will increase the success of specific projects, as in the sector investment programme or hybrid loan approach. Finally, donor conditionality may well, in particular cases, contain some of the additional policy instruments listed above: the wider range of instruments recommended by Stiglitz (1998) as part of the post-'Washington consensus'.

Conditional programme assistance, thus amended, is therefore here to stay, and its recent rise should not be taken as purely a reflection of a periodic state of international financial emergency. At the same time, the utility of the traditional project aid instrument has not disappeared simply because of the implementation difficulties reported previously. Its function is to compensate for the ineffective working of the capital market both between countries and within poor countries. So long as that imperfection persists, there will continue to be a case for aid-financed projects that would be socially profitable under conditions of perfect knowledge, but that are not implemented. There is also, of course, an auxiliary case for investment by aid donors in improving the structure of capital markets in developing countries, especially at the bottom end of micro-finance (as discussed in Chapter 14 of this volume). This case has been widely accepted, and some countries – Bangladesh, Bolivia, Indonesia – are approaching the point where nobody, however poor, with a bankable project, however small, needs to be barred from access to loan finance. But most poor countries (and indeed some rich countries) are far away from that position. So long as that remains the case, the argument for old-fashioned project aid, sponsored either by official donors or by NGOs, will continue. As real aid volumes shrink, such project aid needs to concentrate on the areas of high priority – food crop research, small-scale renewable energy sources, informal sector manufacturing, primary health and education – until the overdue day dawns when these investments have borne fruit and aid finance is no longer needed.

Notes

1 See Chapter 4 for a comprehensive assessment of the economic literature on the effectiveness of foreign aid, with a somewhat different focus then the present chapter.
2 This potential for switching or 'fungibility', as it is often known, is investigated by Feyzioglu *et al.* (1998), who find extensive evidence of switching out of the originally intended use of projects in all sectors except (for reasons which are not completely clear) transport and communications. For a general discussion of fungibility, see Chapter 15 in this volume.
3 This is disputed by the World Bank's report on *Adjustment in Africa* (World Bank 1994a). Our reasons for being unconvinced by the Bank's analysis on that occasion are given in Mosley *et al.* (1995b).
4 A particularly emotive conditionality has been input subsidies, cuts in which are frequently sought by the World Bank and the IMF for fiscal reasons but which often underpin projects to upgrade small-farm and small-business technologies, especially in an imperfect capital market. For a case from Malawi, where input subsidy reduction was energetically sought by the World Bank's programme-lending staff and resisted by its project staff (on the national rural development programme), see Mosley *et al.* (1995a: vol. 2, ch. 15).

5 One suspects that this effect may increase over time, since per capita income growth has just (1995–6) turned significantly positive for a majority of countries in Africa, who are of course the biggest aid recipients.

6 The selectivity approach is the one now favoured by the British government's recent White Paper on international development (DFID 1997), entitled *Eliminating World Poverty*, which promises that the UK government will form 'partnerships', involving sectoral and programme assistance, with countries whose policy framework is acceptable, leaving the others forced to subsist on a diminishing volume of project and, if required, emergency assistance.

APPENDIX: Categories of sectoral assistance

Now that in most developing countries some sort of equilibrium has been reached at the macro level, structural weaknesses in these economies are coming to light. In most of the countries concerned, the private sector has not responded adequately to macro-level policy improvements by increasing production. Analysis of this stagnation at the country level indicates that the private sector simply cannot increase production when markets and/or institutions that mediate between supply and demand for services are not functioning reasonably well (i.e. are underdeveloped or even absent). Some donors have responded to the issues of second-generation reforms by shifting their focus to financing programme aid, generally on condition of satisfactory progress shown in the implementation of structural reform programmes. We argue in this appendix that sectoral support has advantages over traditional instruments, but that is not without pitfalls of its own. Moreover, if this instrument is not to be quickly discarded as the flavour of the month, bold changes in donor attitude will be necessary.

The roles of the government and the donors

The government has (as is further discussed in Chapters 2 and 12) a well-defined role to play in creating an environment conducive to private sector development at the meso level. Its instruments are sensible sector strategies based on clear priorities that take account of all major players in the sector, including NGOs and private actors. The main challenge of the government is to develop sectoral priorities that will effectively reach those stakeholders with limited access to services and income-generating opportunities. This is not to say that the government should control the sector, nor even need to have a direct stake in the sector. But the government is the only body with the prerogative to establish, and the means to enforce, the enabling environment (regulatory, security, etc.) that will unleash the economic activity of all participants. This means that the government needs to have appropriate policies for each of the priority sectors. It follows that the government must be in charge of the process of stakeholder consultation, that is, setting priorities and sectoral policy implementation.

Donors have an important, though a supporting, role to play by making funds available to enable expansion of priority programmes that are already in the government budget. In this era of relative macro stability in Africa there may be good reason to raise the funding of the budget considerably, disregarding the trend on the budget deficit before grants, in order to give the government the means to provide the level of services that is required. Often the normative level of services required is much higher than the budget resources allocated to a certain sector. There is good reason to finance the normative budget, as long as the financing available is of a medium-term nature and is reliable for planning purposes. In some cases this issue may take precedence over the 'appropriate' macro stance of budget deficit reduction (before grants) as a means of ending aid dependency over the medium term.

Comparable concepts but different impacts

Several donors have responded to the new financing requirements by developing a range of new aid instruments. Unfortunately, these largely similar but still significantly different instruments have also created considerable confusion. In this section the main categories of new instruments are discussed and in a later section good practices of hybrid financing are outlined.

Figure A.5.1 arranges adjustment lending instruments according to their locus of intervention, which in turn reflects the level of confidence that donors have in government policy. More confidence means fewer conditions and less confidence means more conditions. Thus, sectoral adjustment lending (SECAL) has least conditions, sectoral budget support (SBS) a moderate number of conditions, and sector investment programmes (SIPs) most conditions and entail most donor control.

The range appears much wider than it is because in other respects the instruments are rather similar. For instance, they all use the 'sector-wide' approach as the basis for sector strategy formulation and determination of priority programmes.

Differences mostly concern the nature and degree of bilateral conditionality. Such differences in modalities are important for the way the financing mechanism works through the budget and through the balance-of-payments. It also affects the receptiveness to the new concept of directly concerned government representatives. At stake is the considerable sway these managers generally hold over the application of project funds. They may well negatively perceive the increased freedom in applying the *ex ante* agreed upon budget funds within the *ex ante* negotiated broad terms of the programme financing agreement. Lastly, the modalities affect the fungibility of funds. Arguably, fungibility of funds need not concern donors when funds are neither tracked nor targeted. When, however, strict conditions are set, monitored, and reported on, aggregate and categorical

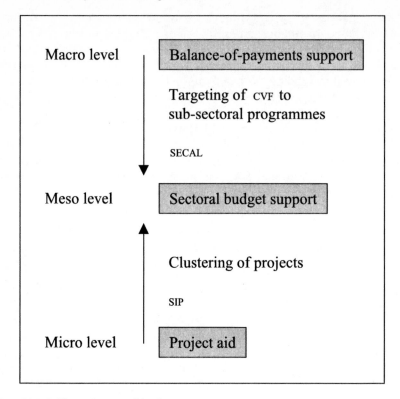

Figure A.5.1 View of sectoral budget support.

fungibility is an important issue (on fungibility, see also Chapter 15). As with the commodity import programmes (CIPs) of the 1980s, through which donors (thought they) directed imports to certain sectors.

From macro to the meso level and vice versa

Most bilateral donors increasingly recognise that aid should be given in whatever form contributes most to overcoming the key constraints on economic growth and sustainable poverty reduction. For instance, as discussed by OECD in its recent strategy paper (OECD 1996a), in cases where investments have run ahead of domestic recurrent resources, a dollar spent on the recurrent budget may yield higher benefits than a dollar spent on investment, thus contributing more to development.

Some donors have shifted focus from the macro to the meso level, and others from the micro (project) level to the meso level. Or, put differently, some shift from balance-of-payments support to budget support, while others move from 'stand-alone' projects to project 'clustering'. The end-result is not the same. Some sector support does not qualify as programme aid, since it retains a level of control that puts it squarely outside the programme aid category. In fact, in some cases the project approach is so ingrained that the transition leads to yet more control.

At the macro end of the spectrum, an understanding of fungibility should restrain donors in discussions and agreements with the recipient regarding the results attainable with the proposed financing. Donors with a micro tradition, however, tend to find it hard to jettison a long-held belief that control over detailed expenditures is necessary and can be exercised meaningfully despite its ample exposure as an accounting fallacy.

New instruments

Below we describe the main features of the new financing modalities. The SECAL is referred to simply to include the whole spectrum of modalities, but is not discussed further.

Sectoral budget support

Definition

Sectoral budget support is the only programme aid mode that makes it possible to unconditionally provide foreign exchange and still target poverty alleviation. The foreign exchange is sold by the recipient government for local counter value funds (CVF) which are included in the budget. The resulting increase in budget funding is used to expand, over a number of years, specific existing sector programmes to which the government accords high priority. A certain degree of macro stability is a precondition for any planning and any appropriate use of SBS.

Core elements

Core elements of SBS are additionality, fungibility and a normative, multi-year budget. The additionality of funds is a crucial aspect and is ensured by making multi-year financing commitments. This means that the financing is also closely linked to a medium-term expenditure framework. SBS objectives are measured by – and limited to – agreed performance monitoring indicators produced by a national management information system. National financial procedures are used for reporting on the use of funds. A certain degree of macro stability is a precondition for any planning.

If SBS focuses on programmes that the government are already planning to extend anyway, in the near to medium term, the government will have little difficulty guaranteeing the take-over of the expansion of the programme over a number of years. Put differently, the higher the programme's priority, the more apparent the fungibility of donor funds. The funds that would have been budgeted for, in the absence of SBS, can now be used for other, possibly non-priority expenses. A related risk is that when the time comes for the government to assume a substantial proportion of the additional funding, it may (have to) resort to cutting funding elsewhere in the sector budget, possibly hitting on other crucial expenditures, which are not 'protected' by donor agreements. It is therefore prudent not to cut all links with the macro framework. More specifically, monitoring of overall budget priorities (e.g. through public expenditure reviews) and maintaining a policy dialogue on priorities, will be necessary to avoid the potential fungibility pitfalls.

There are three possible scenarios for any sector or programme, namely (i) the desirable, (ii) the sustainable and (iii) the minimum budget. The desirable budget follows from the desirable level of service provision presented in, for example, a sector strategy document. Usually government resource availability – including grants – fall considerably short of these needs. The sustainable budget actually reflects the level of expenditures that available resources – from donors and own-government funds – over a number of years can finance. This usually includes a certain level of cost recovery. Seemingly at the other extreme, the minimum budget covers the resources needed to provide the absolute minimum acceptable level of services in the most cost-effective way. This may however still exceed the resources available. In fact, realising the minimum budget is often rather ambitious. The sector strategy dialogue needs to take account of these scenarios. The priorities in all sectors should be part of the macro budget dialogue which also sets the envelope for the sector budget.

The factors determining the feasibility of a transition to SBS include the extent of macro stability and the quality of sector policy implementation capacity. These are discussed below.

Macro stability

The assessment of a country's macroeconomic and social performance undertaken by donors usually largely focuses on the country's historical track record to which some forward looking elements are added. This takes into consideration the progress made on economic reform, social policy indicators and good governance considerations. In the Netherlands, for example, this annual review is called the 'macro exercise'. It puts the appropriateness of providing any form of programme aid into perspective. When considering sectoral assistance the same assessment is made but conditions are set less stringently since sectoral aid aims to improve these very aspects.

Sectoral policy

The quality of a sector strategy and implementation plan largely determines which programmes will be supported. Some issues need to be looked into more closely to ascertain that the process of formulating the strategy is appropriate and that all major stakeholders support the strategy. These include:

- Is the government fully in charge of the policy formulation and prioritising process needed to ensure a coherent programme?
- Do all stakeholders effectively participate in the setting of priorities, including NGOs and the private sector?
- Is an in-depth micro–macro analysis of the effects of macro level measures on the micro level of households a key element of the strategy preparation?

The quality of the sector policy is assessed in the same way as with SBS or sector development programmes (SDPs), considered below. Reviewed are the roles of the public sector and other stakeholders in the sector, the process of consultation of stakeholders and the setting of public expenditure priorities and the sustainability of the normative budget chosen for the sector.

Within the World Bank not everybody believes in the sector-wide approach. The evaluation unit, for instance, argues that poverty alleviation requires a holistic approach, which cannot be meaningfully broken down into sectoral issues. Preconditions often transcend the sector and they are of a cross-sectoral nature. Examples include the execution of a civil service reform (including reviews of the public payment structure and improving the management quality) or the establishment of a medium-term budget expenditure framework, in order to improve medium-term planning capacity (which involves all ministerial bodies in the development of such a framework).

Sector development programmes

The EU has developed its own mode of sector support which is a hybrid of import support (often for particular sectors) and financing of particular budget expenditures. CVFs generated by the sale of imports are put into a designated account and are released to governments against the appropriate expenditure receipts. EU staff maintain financial control and outside accountants report. This means that SDP funds are doubly tied, namely both at the foreign exchange stage and as local CVFs.

The EU now recognises this as a constraint and intends to relax its regulations in the future. It would like to be able to release the control over imported goods. For this to become possible, the import regime must have been liberalised and become transparent (providing equal access to foreign exchange at a free market price). Like the other instruments, SDP follows a sector-wide approach when assessing the quality of a sectoral policy it would like to support.

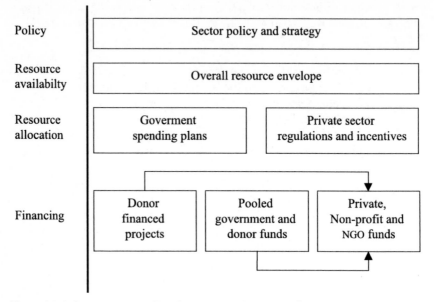

Figure A.5.2 Instruments within the sector-wide approach.
Adapted from: Cassels (1997).

Comparison and summary instruments

Figure A.5.2, which is adapted from Cassels (1997), illustrates where to position the instruments within the sector-wide approach.

SIPs emphasise investment financing and demand a common implementation procedure that puts the onus on achieving harmonisation of donor procedures. If desired, donors can earmark funds for specific programme components. The focus on investment ignores the increasingly recognised key role of recurrent expenditure as a constraint on expansion of most programmes. Because investment goods are generally imported, too much attention is often on import-procurement procedures. Moreover, import investment goods often are kept off-budget. Similar arguments apply in the case of SDPs, where import control may even lead to double tying (of imports and of budget expenditures).

SBSs finance a sector programme on the basis of prior agreements made with regards to expected results and financial reporting requirements to be met. SBSs rely on a reasonable level of confidence in the policy environment, mutual conditionality, the benefits of a long-term flexible partnership, and the recipient government being in charge. Where such conditions exist, SBSs provide a major step forward. In circumstances that fall short of the standard, it is quite likely to be a step too far.

This section argues that the scope of SIPS and SDPs is limited, that they are too conservative and concentrated on project-type controls. SBSs clearly will not be viable in all circumstances, but when they are, they will be considerably more appropriate, and thus beneficial, as they reflects a mature partnership between donor and recipient.

Conclusions

Case studies of sector adjustment show that programmes are country-specific and quite diverse. Formulation must be thorough in order to avoid foreseeable problems down the road. Bringing on board all major participants will go a considerable way to meet this objective. SIPs suffer problems of donor harmonisation. Donors resist accepting a common strategy that has not been jointly developed. SBSs seem to better reflect prevailing confidence levels, following increased ownership shown by governments, which make relying on up-front policy agreements and *ex post* financial reporting a viable option. Caution still needs to be exercised, however, if management capabilities are not to be overextended.

6   Technical co-operation

Channing Arndt

Introduction

Following the Second World War, Western Europe benefited from a massive infusion of public capital known as the Marshall Plan. This plan is widely credited with speeding up the recovery of war-torn West European economies. The success of the Marshall Plan generated optimism that very rapid economic development, fuelled in good measure by large volumes of foreign aid, was a real possibility. As West European economies regained their feet, attention turned to the less-developed economies of Africa, Asia and Latin America. Indeed, many of the same institutions involved in the reconstruction of Western Europe, notably the World Bank and the IMF, turned their attention more towards the developing world.

Since the 1960s, development assistance of the order of many Marshall Plans has been directed towards the less-developed economies (especially when viewed relative to the GDP of the recipient economies). However, the impact of this development assistance has not been as striking as the impact of the Marshall Plan. Human and institutional capacity lies at the heart of this dichotomy in performance. While physically ravaged at the end of the Second World War, West European countries still possessed a wealth of human and institutional capital. With a talented populace and well-functioning institutional structures suitable for a market oriented economy, development assistance under the Marshall Plan operated on fertile ground.

In contrast to post-WWII Europe, human capital in the less-developed countries in the 1960s was sparse – sometimes almost unbelievably so (see, e.g. World Bank 1981 and Fieldhouse 1983). As a corollary to low levels of human capital development, indigenous institutional capacity tended to be weak. Institutional capacity that did exist tended to focus on the pre-occupations of the colonisers. Independence often implied a realignment of priorities and thus a realignment of existing institutions. Given the paucity of trained manpower and the inadequate/inappropriate institutions present in the developing regions, it was clear to early development practitioners that significant efforts to build local human and institutional capacity would be required. Efforts to build local capacity were labelled 'technical assistance' or 'technical co-operation' (TC) and were enthusiastic-ally undertaken. As Elliot Berg states:

> technical assistance or technical co-operation was recognised as the indispensable handmaiden to capital investment. Technical co-oper-ation was needed not only to help build roads and universities but also to help develop the local capacity to maintain or run them.
>
> (Berg 1993: 243)

Despite technical co-operation grants totalling more than $300 billion (1992 prices) during the 1960–95 period, according to OECD data, weak cap-acity of local institutions remains a critical problem. This chapter addresses the goal of institutional development or capacity building and technical co-operation as an instrument for achieving this goal.

The problem: weak capacity of local institutions

Still a long way to go in developing strong institutions

Weak local institutions lie at the heart of the development problem. Many less-developed countries, particularly those in sub-Saharan Africa, lack adequate capacity to carry out even the most central functions. Analysis and formulation of economic policy is a prominent example (though gains have been made in this area in recent years – a point addressed in later sections). As a recent report from the UNDP on capacity building puts it: 'many [countries] are deficient in capabilities to address a problem with an appropriate policy and then transform the policy into a practical program.' (UNDP 1997a).

The costs of incoherent or inappropriate policies can be very high. Poor policy formulation is often blamed as the major explanatory factor for the relatively lacklustre economic performance of Africa, where institutional capacity to analyse and formulate economic policy is particularly weak (e.g. World Bank 1981 and Sachs and Warner 1997). Poor economic perfor-mance is strongly associated with an elevated incidence of poverty (UNDP 1997b). Furthermore, if human capital and institutional performance hinder the ability of a poor economy to grow, these same constraints, along with financial constraints, severely limit the capacity of that same economy to develop and implement targeted poverty alleviation programmes.

Weak institutions hamper the capacity of poor countries to effectively absorb or even spend the very aid monies designed to reinforce human and institutional capacity and speed economic growth.[1] Obviously, aid money cannot do any good if it is not even spent (much less well spent). The primary constraint on the use of the funds, according to the World Bank, has been recipient country institutional capacity. This highlights an often-cited paradox in aid: those countries most in need of aid monies tend to have the weakest capacity to effectively absorb the aid inflow. This simple proposition lies behind a wide range of donor strategies employed to implement aid programmes in weak institutional environments. These strategies, discussed further below, are widely viewed as being, at best, un-helpful to capacity building.

Existing capacity and the role of TC

While problems of institutional capacity clearly remain, particularly among the least-developed countries, gains in institutional capacity have been regis-tered in almost all countries. The 1997 *Human Development Report* states that:

> Since 1960, in little more than a generation, child death rates in developing countries have been more than halved. Malnutrition rates have declined by almost a third. The proportion of children out of primary school has fallen from more than half to less than a quarter. And the share of rural families without access to safe water has fallen from nine-tenths to about a quarter. These advances are found in all regions of the world.
>
> (UNDP 1997b: 2)

Vast increases in the capacity of developing countries to deliver health, sanitation, and education services were required to realise these gains. Improved energy, transportation, and communications infrastructure, including the capacity to manage these systems, were also required. The Cassen report (*Does Aid Work?*), which offers by far the most optimistic assessment of the impact of technical co-operation, argues that TC pro-grammes played 'a major role' in these accomplishments (Cassen *et al.* 1994: 145). Even the more critical study co-ordinated by Elliot Berg (which focused on sub-Saharan Africa) points to numerous gains:

> The past 30 years, for all their disappointments, have witnessed extra-ordinarily dense institutional growth in Sub-Saharan Africa, and growth in capacity to manage: central banks are now locally run, as are new school systems, agricultural research stations, power plants, airlines, armies, and universities.
>
> (Berg 1993: 14)

Unfortunately, in evaluating the impacts of technical co-operation for institutional development, vague terminology, such as 'a major role' and 'extraordinarily dense' is required. Quantifying increases in institutional capacity is, by itself, exceedingly difficult. Disentangling the exact role of technical co-operation in generating the increase from other factors is next to impossible. In this regard, formal project evaluations are of limited value. A series of projects, which failed to meet their proximate goals and thus were judged as failures, might have trained a group of individuals who later became the nucleus of a well-functioning institution. Evaluation of these cumulative effects would be extremely difficult, which explains why none (to the author's knowledge) have been undertaken.

Despite the measurement problems, a coherent impression of the impact of technical co-operation for institutional development seems to have emerged. Technical co-operation for institutional development has functioned best in environments where outputs are clear, measurable and relatively non-controversial. For example, the Cassen report cites meteorology as an 'example of a field where there is prima facie evidence of widespread impact of TC.' (Cassen *et al.* 1994: 146). While delivering weather forecasts, tracking hurricanes and providing meteorological services to civil aviation is technically demanding, the necessary inputs and required outputs are relatively well defined and basically non-controversial. Likewise, developing primary and secondary level educational systems is a daunting logistical task, but the output, a literate and numerate populous, is relatively easy to measure and not particularly controversial.

In environments where goals are amorphous, potentially conflicting and/or politically sensitive, the success record in capacity building has been much more mixed. Analysis and formulation of economic policy clearly falls within this category, likewise, the construction of well-functioning universities. The dichotomy is not hard and fast. In some instances, institutions with apparently clear-cut tasks, such as data collection, which have received years, even decades, of technical co-operation, function poorly and continue to rely heavily on external assistance. In other instances, institutions operating in a complex and amorphous environment function well with relatively little recourse to external assistance. Some central banks form a prominent example of this latter category.

Looking forward at institutional needs

While the consensus evaluations often find aid efforts to build indigenous institutional capacity wanting, the need for well-functioning institutions is almost certainly growing. Furthermore, the most pressing institutional needs almost invariably fall under the complex, amorphous, potentially conflicting and politically sensitive category. In particular, developing countries must forge links with a global economy, which is both volatile and unpredictable. The recent 'Asian crisis' and associated financial contagion is a prime example. The realignments brought on by the Asian crisis were both wrenching and extraordinarily difficult to foresee.[2]

Forging links with the global economy also implies participating in global (and often regional) trade negotiations with attendant institutional and analytical needs. Environmental issues, both global and local, pose complex problems with contentious trade-offs. Furthermore, these environmental problems will not sort themselves out in the marketplace; they require government action undertaken by competent public institutions. In the private sector, rapid technical advances, shortening product cycles, fickle consumer demand (particularly in products of importance to developing countries, such as wearing apparel, toys and some consumer electronics) and global competition shape the business environment. In short, the need for intelligent, forward-looking and adaptable institutions in both the public and private sectors is clear.

The World Bank's 1998 *World Development Report* (World Bank 1998b), which focuses on knowledge for development, addresses directly the challenge of operating effectively in a complex and global environment. The report cites human capital, knowledge institutions and knowledge networks (along with telecommunications infrastructure) as 'imperatives for developing countries'. However, for the World Bank and other donor agencies to be effective in the 'knowledge business', indigenous institutions capable of absorbing existing knowledge have to exist.

In sum, the need for capable indigenous institutions has been clear for some time. In addition, for a host of reasons, both the value of well-functioning institutions and the costs of substituting rote procedure for well-thought-out institutional responses to a given shock – as an institution lacking in capacity is bound to do – appear to be increasing. As such, aid donors are almost certain to be asked to deliver on institutional capacity building, a development goal that has proved even more elusive than most. The instrument to achieve this desired increase in institutional capacity will be technical co-operation in one form or another.

The instrument: technical co-operation

Formal definitions

Technical co-operation is a bit like poverty: difficult to define precisely; but one knows it when one sees it. Accordingly, there are a variety of definitions of technical co-operation employed by different agencies and individuals. For the purposes of this chapter, the definition of the Development Assistance Committee (DAC), which underlies OECD statistics on technical co-operation flows, will be employed. OECD defines TC (or so-called 'free-standing' technical co-operation) as:

> Activities financed by a donor country whose primary purpose is to augment the level of knowledge, skills, technical know-how, or productive aptitudes of the population of developing countries, i.e., increasing their stock of human intellectual capital, or their capacity for more effective use of their existing factor endowment.
>
> (OECD 1998a)

Unlike other organisations, such as the World Bank, which in practice use the terms technical co-operation and technical assistance interchangeably, the OECD has a separate and distinct definition for technical assistance (or so-called 'investment-related' technical co-operation), namely the:

> financing of services by a donor country with the primary purpose of contributing to the design and/or implementation of a project or programme aiming to increase the physical capital stock of the recipient country.
>
> (OECD 1998a)

Since OECD is the keeper of global statistics on technical co-operation, this distinction between technical co-operation and technical assistance is important. Technical assistance associated with investment projects is not included as technical co-operation in OECD statistics even if the goals of that assistance are very much in line with the definition of technical co-operation cited above. As indicated, the technical co-operation statistics refer only to 'free-standing' technical co-operation, defined as technical co-operation not associated with an investment project.

The link between technical co-operation and the goal of institution building has been increasingly highlighted. Accordingly, in a 1991 OECD publication, a definition, which addresses institution building goals more explicitly, stated that:

> Technical co-operation encompasses the whole range of assistance activities designed to improve the level of knowledge, skills, technical know-how, or productive aptitudes of the population in a developing country. A particularly important objective of technical co-operation is institutional development, i.e. to contribute to the strengthening and improved functioning of the many institutions essential for sustainable development through the effective management and operation of an economy and of society more generally.
>
> (OECD 1991)

Informal definitions

Behind these formal definitions lurks a more practical definition or basic technical co-operation model. Technical co-operation is essentially the provision of donor funded personnel to supply missing skills and train local people. The personnel are often foreign 'experts' who work in-country on either a short- or a long-term basis. These personnel are usually bundled with equipment such as computers, photocopiers and automobiles. In addition, most technical co-operation projects finance some training either through short courses delivered in-country or by sending local personnel abroad to engage in activities ranging from attending a conference to obtaining an advanced degree.

The goals technical co-operation personnel are meant to achieve vary widely. In some instances, performance goals, such as conduct of a study, take precedence. In other instances, TC personnel simply fill substitute roles for local personnel who are away undergoing training programmes. Some TC personnel play pure training roles. Finally, some are primarily charged with the more amorphous goal of catalysing institutional development.

With rare exceptions, some transfer of skills and know-how to locals is expected, either explicitly or implicitly, of technical co-operation personnel, regardless of their proximate goals. The predominant means for achieving knowledge transfer, other than formal training programmes, is the pairing of experts with local counterparts. Under this system, the foreign expert and local counterpart are expected to work together. In the process of this collaboration, counterparts are expected to learn by example.

The magnitudes: how much TC is there?

Amounts and caveats

The percentage of total development assistance dollars directed towards this basic model is, to many observers, surprisingly large. Total technical co-operation grants amounted to more than $18 billion in 1995. Technical co-operation grants comprised about 31 per cent of total official development assistance (ODA) in that year. For the period 1970 to 1995, technical co-operation grants comprised on average 25 per cent of annual total ODA. In addition, due to the distinction made by the OECD between technical assistance and technical co-operation, the official figures certainly understate the true volume (and quite likely understate the share in total ODA) of technical co-operation. The UNDP estimated in the early 1990s that adding technical assistance associated with investment projects into the figures on technical co-operation would increase total technical co-operation volume by 10–20 per cent. Berg (1993) points to three additional sources of significant under-counting. These are: (i) technical co-operation from non-OECD sources such as the former Soviet Union, (ii) technical co-operation financed by NGOs and (iii) loan-financed technical co-operation.

Geographical distribution and share of TC in foreign aid

Table 6.1 illustrates the distribution of total ODA and total technical co-operation grants by region for two time periods. Over the period 1970–95, Asia and Africa (North Africa plus sub-Saharan Africa) garnered roughly equal shares of global ODA. However, over the same period, sub-Saharan Africa alone garnered a greater share of global technical co-operation allocations than Asia. This implies that a greater share of aid to Africa was directed to technical co-operation than aid to Asia. The exact share figures are given in Table 6.2, which shows the share of technical co-operation in ODA by region. Over the 1970–95 period, technical co-operation grants comprised only 17 per cent of ODA to Asia. By contrast, for sub-Saharan Africa, the share of technical co-operation in ODA amounted to about 30

Table 6.1 Average shares of total ODA and technical co-operation (TC), by region, 1970–95 (per cent)

	Share of net ODA		Share of TC	
	1970–95	*1993–5*	*1970–95*	*1993–5*
Asia	36.0	32.0	27.0	29.0
Sub-Saharan Africa	28.0	31.0	28.0	24.0
North Africa	9.0	6.0	8.0	7.0
Americas	9.0	10.0	13.0	16.0
CEEC/NIS[a]	5.0	13.0	4.0	13.0
Other and unallocated	13.0	8.0	20.0	11.0
Total	100.0	100.0	100.0	100.0

Source: OECD (1998a).
Note: [a]CEEC are the Central and Eastern European Countries and NIS are the Newly Independent States of the former Soviet Union.

Table 6.2 Average shares of technical co-operation in net ODA, by region, 1970–95 (per cent)

	1970–95	*1993–5*
Asia	17.0	27.0
Sub-Saharan Africa	30.0	23.0
North Africa	24.0	35.0
Americas	34.0	44.0
CEEC/NIS[a]	n.a.	27.0
Total ODA	25.0	30.0

Source: OECD (1998a).
Notes: n.a., not available.
   [a]CEEC are the Central and Eastern European Countries and NIS are the Newly Independent States of the former Soviet Union.

per cent. This dichotomy in resource allocation across instruments reinforced the impression of overuse of technical co-operation in sub-Saharan Africa, which became widespread in the late 1980s and early 1990s (see Chapter 18).

Examining trends in TC disbursement patterns

Impression of overuse notwithstanding, sub-Saharan Africa has not received, historically, the highest percentage of technical co-operation grants in ODA. The Americas, particularly South America, received a higher share of TC. Moreover, more recent data paint a very different picture from the historical average. From 1993–5, total technical co-operation grants worldwide comprised a larger share of ODA than the historical average. This trend towards an increasing share of technical co-operation in ODA manifested itself, quite dramatically, in every region *except* sub-Saharan Africa, which exhibited a decline. In fact, by the period 1993–5, sub-Saharan Africa received a *lower* share of technical co-operation in ODA than any of the other major recipient regions (excepting South East Asia, which received a slightly smaller share).

Figure 6.1 illustrates these historical trends in TC as a share of ODA. The high initial share of TC explains much of the downward trend in sub-Saharan Africa. Nevertheless, by the late 1980s, the share of TC in ODA to sub-Saharan Africa was less than shares to the Americas and North Africa and comparable to shares to Asia. The stinging critique levelled against TC, particularly that going to sub-Saharan Africa, in the late 1980s and early 1990s probably contributed to the continuing downward trend in the early and mid-1990s.

The upward trends in the other regions are less easy to explain. The arguments posed above concerning the benefits derived from well-functioning institutions and the costs imposed by poorly functioning institutions, form a possible explanation. If one accepts that, over time and particularly in the late 1990s, both the benefits derived from competent institutions and the costs imposed by weak institutions have been increasing, then it is not surprising that recipients and donors alike would want to shift resources towards technical co-operation. Whatever the cause, sub-Saharan Africa appears to have been bucking a fairly well established trend towards technical co-operation in aid disbursement patterns. In addition, the trend towards an increased share of TC in ODA almost surely indicates that the critique levelled against TC resonated very little outside of sub-Saharan Africa.[3] We turn now to this critique.

Deep doubts about TC: critique and suggested reforms

Widespread dissatisfaction

By the early 1990s, dissatisfaction with technical co-operation had become widespread. A series of highly critical reports were published. Two prominent examples, among many, include a report by Forss *et al.* (1990), which focused on technical co-operation provided by Nordic donors to three countries in Africa (Kenya, Tanzania and Zambia) and a report by Buyck (1991), which focused on World Bank technical co-operation worldwide. These and other critical reports fuelled efforts to reconsider technical co-operation as an instrument.

For example, on the multilateral side, the UNDP launched an effort labelled the National Technical Co-operation Action Programme (NATCAP) designed to help recipient countries better manage the technical co-operation resources made available to them. As part of the NATCAP programme, each recipient was asked to draft a Technical Co-operation Policy Framework Paper (TCPFP). These papers provide, among a wealth of other information, a glimpse into recipient country sentiments *vis-à-vis* the technical co-operation resources made available to them. In addition, UNDP

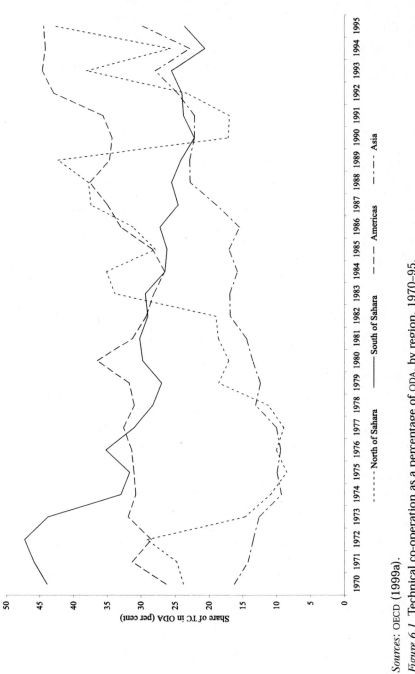

Sources: OECD (1999a).

Figure 6.1 Technical co-operation as a percentage of ODA, by region, 1970–95.

funded a comprehensive desk study of technical co-operation, which culminated in the publication of the book, referred to earlier, entitled *Rethinking Technical Co-operation* (Berg 1993). The World Bank, for its part, set up a task force in 1991 to examine the impact of its technical co-operation activities. As an example on the bilateral side, the Dutch government (along with a number of other donors) provided funding for the European Centre for Development Policy Management (ECDPM). The critique of technical co-operation, which emerged from these efforts, exhibited a remarkable degree of overlap across numerous reports from diverse sources. A broad consensus found that technical co-operation had performed least favourably in the category that is (or should be) its primary focus, namely institutional capacity building.

The main differences in opinion in the reports centred on degree of failure. Highly respected individuals, such as Edward Jaycox, then Vice President (Africa Region) of the World Bank, went so far as to assert a perverse effect. To wit, Jaycox states: 'it's my contention that the donors and African governments together have in effect undermined capacity in Africa; they are undermining it faster than they are building it.' (Jaycox 1993: 1). Elliot Berg, in his report, takes the somewhat less strident view that, while TC had built appallingly little capacity, it probably had not done very much harm. Perhaps for diplomatic reasons, the recipient country documents tend to be the least critical pointing to under-performance of TC with respect to capacity building and registering dissatisfaction with the form of technical co-operation.

Major elements of the critique

The diagnosis of the problems with TC are also remarkably uniform across reports. The following points, which are often inter-related, appear in report after report.

- TC is *supply driven*. Donors conceive, design and implement projects with too little input from recipients. As a consequence, recipients perceive little or no ownership in the projects. At the same time, the supply driven character of TC implies that projects often address low priority needs from the recipient country's perspective. These two problems have obvious negative implications for project sustainability.
- TC projects place *excessive emphasis* on tangible, measurable outputs as opposed to institution building. Donors like to have something to show for their projects. Technical co-operation personnel are often called upon to produce these measurable outputs. Recruitment of TC personnel usually proceeds accordingly. Furthermore, even if institution building objectives are clearly delineated, technical co-operation personnel have clear incentives to gravitate towards production of more tangible outputs, such as reports, as these are certain to endure beyond the

project cycle and are likely to serve as the primary basis for *ex post* performance evaluations of the TC personnel concerned.

- Weak recipient *country management* of TC. The aforementioned paradox of recipient country management comes into play here. Developing countries with weak institutions receive technical co-operation. However, that same TC comes from donors who frequently have their own agendas and a strong desire for measurable outputs within a limited time period. Because local administrative structures are weak, they are usually overwhelmed by a plethora of donors with their own agendas and tight timetables, not to mention complex administrative requirements. Weak recipient management structures impede progress towards proximate project goals. As a result, donors often search for ways to circumvent existing recipient management structures. This can serve to undermine the institutional capacity the project was meant to reinforce. This is particularly true in the least-developed countries, where administrative capacity is weakest and aid flows most important in relative terms. Finally, with expansive management responsibilities, donors have significant staffing needs. They often poach competent administrators from government, which further undermines local capacity.

- Insufficient emphasis on *training*. Training programmes are often appended to projects as an afterthought rather than treated as a central building block. In addition, if local staff are sent abroad for training, they are perceived as being far too likely to remain abroad rather than return and work in their home country.

- Excessive reliance on long-term resident *expatriate advisers*. Long-term resident advisers sit uneasily within local institutional structures. Relative to local staff, they are extremely well paid. Their 'adviser' status leads to, at best, ambiguous placement within the local administrative hierarchy. Since donors pay their salaries, ultimate authority clearly resides outside of the local administration. In addition, resident advisers almost invariably possess privileged access to office supplies, equipment and vehicles. Even in the absence of cultural factors, the combination of high pay, little accountability and privileged access to critical inputs could easily breed resentment and serve to demoralise local staff. When cultural factors are included, the breeding ground for negative dynamics between resident expatriate advisers and local staff becomes especially fertile.

- Failure of the *expert–counterpart model*. In many cases, experts and counterparts are simply never paired. For example, counterparts are often absent on training whilst the TC personnel are in-country. Even when they are, little transfer of skills and know-how actually occurs. Experts are often too busy producing outputs to bother with training counterparts. At the same time, counterparts often view accompanying experts as low status and off of the career fast track. Consequently, both tend to accord little importance to the relationship. Murky lines of authority between experts and counterparts further complicate matters. The notion of an equal partnership is belied by the pay and perks enjoyed by the expert. At the same time, experts typically lack the authority to impose a work plan, which might result in learning by doing; and counterparts lack the authority to demand the training to which they are supposedly entitled.

• Massive *distortions* in the market for TC. Recipients generally view TC as a free good. It is typically grant, rather than loan, financed. Furthermore, the supply driven character of TC leads to the perception of zero opportunity costs on the part of recipients. At almost every level, recipients behave as if more TC does not imply less of anything else. In a world of finite aid resources, this is clearly untrue. Nevertheless, given the perception of zero opportunity cost to TC, priority setting by recipients becomes pointless. This often leads to enormous resource misallocations. Two common examples follow. (i) Because resident advisers typically come bundled with equipment and some training, a full technical co-operation project can be accepted primarily to gain access to a few computers or a vehicle. (ii) Because TC is 'free', local administrations sometimes prefer to employ resident expatriates over trained nationals, who carry a direct budgetary cost. This occurs even though the total cost of the resident expatriate is of the order of 20 times (or more) the total cost of the trained national.

Reflecting the times, evaluations from the late 1980s and early 1990s generally fail to treat gender issues. A more recent perspective would add lack of gender awareness to the list of weaknesses of TC in general and TC personnel in particular.

The picture, that emerges from the standard critique of the early 1990s, is one of a large number of uncoordinated technical co-operation projects running roughshod over local administrative structures and pursuing a welter of goals. TC recipients have little incentive to decline the resources offered but also have very little say (or, at the very least, perceive that they have very little say) in the ultimate form and goals of the project. Under these circumstances, TC projects can easily end up addressing low priority needs. Since TC resources are so significant (spending on salaries for resident advisers can sometimes exceed the entire civil service wage bill), TC can inadvertently contribute to local administrative disarray with scarce local resources spread too thinly across an excessive range of activities.

Because donors require tangible results, excessive recourse is made to expatriate experts, especially long-term advisers. Due to the fundamental defects of the expert–counterpart model, little transfer of skills or knowledge occurs. In addition, the desire to obtain tangible results for their particular project commonly leads to the payment of salary supplements to talented staff. This mechanism serves to draw the attention of talented staff away from local administrations and towards projects to the detriment of institutional development. In the worst case, TC actually weakens local capacity by contributing to administrative disarray, demoralising local staff, hiring away the most effective staff members, and absconding with critical roles such as priority setting.

Reform measures

This bleak picture, which had emerged by 1993, led to no shortage of reform proposals. These proposals can be divided into three main groups:

- Donors should do a better job of managing technical co-operation.
- Recipients should do a better job of managing technical co-operation.
- Address the major distortions in the market for technical (e.g. make the recipients pay).

Most reform proposals fall within the first group. A non-exhaustive division of reform measures falling within the first group would include:

- Make the basic TC project structure work better. Institutional develop-ment goals could be better achieved through, for example, more specific terms of reference, greater weight to institutional development skills in hiring of experts, reduced emphasis on tangible outputs, greater care in project preparation to assure that priority needs are addressed, greater emphasis on training and more attentive pairing of experts with counterparts. More recently, improved gender awareness in the design of TC projects and among TC personnel has been added to this list buttressed by a rapidly expanding literature on gender issues and gender training.
- Modify the basic TC project structure. In particular, make much greater use of short-term TC personnel (often with multiple visits and contact by electronic mail in between visits) as opposed to long-term resident advisers, and expand the relative share of the training budget. In addition, where possible, consider 'twinning' of like institutions between developed and developing countries.
- Resort to comprehensive planning of TC. In this case, donors and the government would come together and agree on a comprehensive pro-gramme (see also Chapter 7 in this volume). Specific activities (projects) within the programme would then be paired with specific donors.

Under the second group of reform proposals, the NATCAP effort under-taken by UNDP is the most prominent example. The final group of reforms attempts to devise mechanisms that would ensure that recipients perceive some opportunity costs for TC. Before going into detail on the reform measures, a second look at the critique is merited.

A second look at the doubts

Two facts colour the critique of the late 1980s and early 1990s and by implication colour the proposed reform measures. First, outside of Asia, the economic environment throughout the 1980s and, in the African case, into the early 1990s was abysmal. The 1980s were coined 'the lost decade' for Latin America. For sub-Saharan Africa, the 1980s were simply disastrous in economic terms. Second, in the early 1990s, the world was at least perceived to be completely devoid of successful TC projects on which future efforts could be modelled. As a member of the team researching the book co-ordinated by Berg, the author spent months asking for examples of successful TC projects. Perhaps reflecting the mood of the moment, not one example was provided.

Both of these facts have changed. Economic performance in sub-Saharan Africa and Latin America was much better in the 1990s than in the 1980s. This has strong implications for the environment, both public and private, in which TC projects operate.[4] Also, some examples of successful TC projects are now available.

Role of the economic and administrative environment

Economic stagnation/decline and the economic restructuring that became a necessary corollary led to an environment, which prevailed more or less throughout the 1980s in many less-developed countries, essentially inimical to institutional development. The public sector environment, where most TC projects and personnel were placed, proved particularly harsh for the task of nurturing young institutions. In country after country, salary scales were low and highly compressed such that higher-level workers earned only marginally more than workers at the lowest administrative rungs. Rates of pay for even relatively high-level staff sometimes failed to cover subsistence needs. In many countries, public sector workers had no choice but to maintain multiple jobs. Despite the low salaries, the civil service wage bill absorbed an inordinate share of public sector expenditure due to severe budget constraints. As a result, operating equipment, including items as basic as pencils and paper, were in short supply.

Under these circumstances, even well-designed and executed institutional development efforts are unlikely to succeed. Most critiques of technical co-operation, Berg being the most prominent example, recognised both the need for a 'minimally congenial administrative environment,' (Berg 1993: 196) and the absence of that environment in many less-developed countries, particularly those in sub-Saharan Africa. Dealing with these public sector deficiencies is an enormous topic and the subject of Chapter 12 in this book. Nevertheless, the tight correlation between degradation of the economic and administrative environment in which many technical co-operation projects operated and the growth in dissatisfaction with technical co-operation as an instrument for institutional development casts doubt on some of the claims of TC's more strident critics.

Also, in the absence of a minimally congenial administrative environment, the logic of the much-maligned donor and TC personnel tendency to focus on tangible outputs must be conceded. If institutional development is doomed to fail, a focus on tangible outputs, particularly those outputs which might help to reverse, stem, or prevent further degradation of the economic/administrative environment, seems imminently sensible. This observation does not dismiss the criticism of an incentive structure within TC biased towards performance outputs. It does say that the criticism can be overstated, particularly when the environment is poor.

Finally, the disappointment associated with trainees, particularly those sent to obtain advanced degrees, who fail to return to their countries to work must also be viewed in the context of an abysmal administrative/ economic environment. It is hard to fault trainees unwilling to return to an environment where they feel that their skills will not be adequately employed. Furthermore, it is not clear that the actual magnitude of the 'brain drain' is unacceptably large. Powerful family and cultural ties draw trainees back to their home countries. An analysis of the Indian case concludes that 'the brain drain is not of a bewildering magnitude and the loss of educated manpower that individual developing countries have experienced on account of the brain drain is fairly small.' (Balasubramanyam 1993: 107). This study also points to evidence that significant numbers of those who do leave eventually return to their home countries (presumably this flow increases as local economic/administrative conditions improve).

Performance TC and corrosive TC

The dismissal or outright hostility towards performance technical co-operation (TC targeted towards producing some tangible outputs) is somewhat paradoxical given that most evaluations give performance TC relatively high marks.[5] Personnel exist who can function well in complex and chaotic developing country environments. In order to dismiss performance TC, one must either assert that the outputs are valueless (or not worth the costs) or that the process of producing the outputs is on balance corrosive to institutional development.

The latter argument stretches credulity. The critique contends that TC proliferates because of zero opportunity costs and simultaneously that TC undermines capacity due, in part, to the overwhelming administrative burdens imposed by TC projects. This is internally inconsistent if the recipient agency bears most of the administrative burden, which is almost always the case. Recipients would tend to balance perceived benefits of TC with the associated administrative burdens. In reality, for TC that has outlived its welcome or is accorded low priority by recipients, the administrative burdens imposed on recipients are probably not that high. Technical co-operation projects can be simply ignored or marginalised even if they cannot be shut down entirely.[6] The relative ease with which TC can be ignored or marginalised forms the primary counterpoint to the contention that TC contributes negatively to institutional development. Technical co-operation is either desirable or irrelevant, not harmful.

Regarding the value of performance TC outputs, it is easy to find examples where the value of performance TC has been small or zero. There are, without doubt, too many unread reports lying in drawers. It is also possible to point to TC projects, that had significant positive impacts. For example, recent calculations of the returns to agricultural research (a TC intensive activity) in the Sahel find substantial positive returns, with most of those returns occurring recently, that is, in the late 1980s and early 1990s (Masters *et al.* 1998). The authors of this study assert that policy reforms undertaken during the 1980s created an environment more conducive to adoption of technical advances. Agricultural research is a rare example relatively amenable to quantification. Other TC projects are more difficult to quantify. From personal experience, the author of this chapter is aware of three recent TC projects that had large impacts: TC personnel provided critical input to the privatisation programme in Morocco, to economic policy formulation in Ghana (post-structural adjustment) and in the elaboration of national accounts in Mozambique.

In short, critical skill shortages still exist in many developing countries, and the balance of evidence indicates that performance TC does a good job of filling these gaps. While there are many examples of failure, there are also many examples of success – with some of these success stories yielding very high returns. On balance, most evaluations find that TC does meet donor and recipient country needs for performance.

Technical co-operation and donor needs

Technical co-operation also meets more subtle, but very real, donor needs. Technical co-operation personnel serve as 'ears' within local administrations. They provide donors with some reassurance that project money is not being misappropriated. They serve as a contact point that can be approached without the confusion of cultural barriers. They assure that project reporting and disclosure requirements are met. These and other donor needs had already been observed in the mid-1970s (Tendler 1975). Proposals to reform TC that fail to account for these deep-seated needs on the part of donors are unlikely to succeed. For example, in line with arguments advanced by Tendler more than two decades earlier, Berg (1993) dismisses many proposed reform measures of TC to be undertaken by donors as calls for 'administrative leopards to change their spots.'

Impact of proposed reforms

As might be expected, the impact of the proposed reform measures appears to have been small to date.[7] The NATCAP effort appears to have fallen far short of the goals set for it, though no formal evaluation is available. With the difficulties experienced by NATCAP efforts, the prospects for comprehensive programming of TC seem distant at best. It is impossible to say whether exhortation for donors to design better TC projects and recruit better experts have had any effect. However, observers of technical co-operation at UNDP and the OECD are highly sceptical.[8] There has been no detectable move to attempt to establish a more rational market for TC as called for by Berg (1993). In fact, there is evidence to the contrary. As noted earlier, the share of grant financed TC in total ODA has been increasing in every region (except for Africa). Finally, though twinning has long had intellectual support as a possibly effective means for achieving institutional development, there remain few examples on the ground. This suggests the existence of barriers to establishment of these relationships.

On the brighter side, evidence from Mali indicates that there has been a shift towards short-term versus long-term technical co-operation (OECD 1998b). Short-term technical co-operation, defined as one to two years, replaced medium-term technical co-operation, defined as two to five years, as the predominant form of technical co-operation in 1991. The Malian experience seems to have been replicated elsewhere. Statistics are scarce; however, current wisdom in donor hallways, universities and consulting firms is that long-term resident overseas positions have become much more difficult to come by than in the 1970s and early 1980s. Thus, at least one reform proposal, a shift towards shorter-term assignments on the part of TC personnel, appears to have resonated with donors and recipients alike.

Two success stories

The relatively light impact of the reform measures emerging from the critique reflects both significant momentum in donor and recipient country practices and, as mentioned above, a lack of success models to guide future practice. Reform measures could be proposed, but, without success stories, they lacked both empirical substantiation and concrete models on which to build future practice. Some success stories are now available, which can guide future practice. We focus on lessons from a series of traditional institution building projects in Morocco and the more non-traditional success of the African Economic Research Consortium. Both of these examples come from the areas of economic analysis and policy.

The economic analysis division of the Ministry of Agriculture in Morocco went from a small, relatively obscure institution, in 1985, to a capable and highly influential entity by 1998. The quality of economic analysis undertaken in the Ministry of Agriculture, without doubt, increased enormously. However, the transformation took nearly a decade and a half to achieve. It involved advanced training abroad for more than 30 local staff members, resident expatriate advisers who undertook gap filling and coaching roles while critical staff worked on obtaining advanced degrees abroad, and, following the departure of the resident adviser approximately seven years into the process, a protracted series of short-term visits by TC personnel to collaborate on specific work projects with local staff. Often the same TC personnel who worked on a long-term basis in the Ministry undertook short-term assignments.

A host of external factors also contributed to the success of the project including:

- A reasonably congenial administrative environment.
- Consistent and dynamic leadership by the Moroccan director of the Economic Analysis Unit (the same individual throughout the life of the project).
- Strong support at high levels from within the Ministry of Agriculture and the Government of Morocco in general.
- The emergence of quality Master's degree programmes at local universities (also aided by technical co-operation), which provided a steady stream of competent younger staff.

Technical co-operation with the economic analysis unit helped set in motion a virtuous cycle of increased institutional competence, which increased institutional influence, which increased institutional prestige, which both encouraged existing staff to put in effort and attracted competent individuals from the outside, which further increased institutional competence and so forth. Long-term commitment by both the Government of Morocco and donors led to a relatively stimulating work environment. All of the individuals sent abroad for long-term training returned to Morocco and about 90 per cent of these still work in the Ministry of Agriculture.

It is important to highlight that the success in Morocco is not a refutation of many elements of the critique of TC summarised above. The success in Morocco underscores the usual exhortation concerning local government commitment and need to focus on institution building. In addition, the project incorporated many elements of the consensus (and non-consensus) reform proposals propounded by Berg (1993). The project placed training as a centrepiece (rather than an afterthought), resorted explicitly to gap-filling TC personnel while training was ongoing abroad, and then shifted to heavy reliance on short-term TC personnel with first a single resident expatriate adviser serving a co-ordinating role and then to all management of short-term TC personnel handled locally.

The second example of successful institution building is the African Economic Research Consortium (AERC). A recent evaluation of the AERC is so positive, it is practically fawning (Henderson and Loxley 1997). An evaluation the year before of the AERC research programme is no less upbeat (Thorbecke 1996). Evaluations this positive, with respect to institution building in sub-Saharan Africa, simply did not exist in the early 1990s. The principal objective of the AERC is to strengthen local capacity to conduct independent research into problems pertinent to the management of economies in sub-Saharan Africa by means of research grants, training programmes and dissemination of research findings.

The AERC supports individual researchers and selected universities as well as providing fora for review, discussion and publication of research results. It represents a significant break from past TC efforts in the area of economics and policy formulation in at least four ways. First, it is a regional organisation rather than a national organisation. Second, it seeks to support a profession, in this case the economics profession, rather than a particular government institution charged with economic analysis. Third, it seeks to influence the policy process by stealth rather than directly. The AERC believes that improved economic literacy will eventually lead to improved policy. Other than inviting policymakers to attend workshops, the AERC, as an institution, makes no direct attempts to influence economic policy. Fourth, it relies heavily on short-term TC personnel. Non-African economists attend AERC workshops, and opportunities exist for Africans and non-Africans to develop collaborative research efforts. Resulting collaborations are voluntarily formed and lack the baggage of the expert–counterpart model.

The approach has numerous advantages, most of which are replicable in the knowledge-building spheres with which TC for institutional development is concerned. The AERC structure and activities are highly diffuse regionally but tightly focused topically. Due to the diffuse regional structure, researchers and institutions (universities) are supported throughout Africa. Deterioration of economic or administrative conditions in one country or region has relatively little impact on the consortium as a whole. Also, rather than choose one institution and try to make it flower, the AERC provides opportunities for a large number of individuals and institutions to grow. Those that perform better tend to receive greater support. In this way, resources tend to be channelled towards the most productive individuals and institutions. Critically, this mechanism also provides correlation between effort and reward both for individuals and institutions. If a university increases the quality of its programme, the AERC is likely to respond by increasing funding for teaching and research programmes and by directing a larger number of AERC-supported students to that institution.

At the same time, the tight topical focus (large swathes of economics are excluded), combined with Internet access, e-mail and relatively frequent meetings, allows for generation of the critical mass of minds necessary to grapple with highly complex problems. Technology now enables this spatial diffusion but topical concentration. The formula has been immensely successful to date. The 1997 evaluation states: 'it is not too much to say that in the space of little more than seven years the Consortium has transformed the situation of economics and economists in Africa.' (Henderson

and Loxley 1997: 3). The annual budget for this achievement was approximately $7 million.

With less than a decade of experience, it is perhaps too early to conclude
that the AERC has made an enduring increase in the capacity of African
countries to manage economic policy. If donor funding to the AERC
disappeared, the consortium would be forced to substantially curtail
activities if not shut down entirely. Gains registered to date could prove
transitory. Moreover, external funding will be required for the foreseeable
future if the consortium is to continue to flourish and deliver on its
ambitious mandate. In addition, a number of specific factors are associated
with the success of the consortium. As in Morocco, quality local leadership
figures prominently among these factors. Nevertheless, the gains registered
by the AERC are impressive. There is no obvious reason why the basic
approach of the AERC could not be applied to a host of other critical
professions both within and outside of Africa.

Recent thinking on TC

The approach taken by the AERC also dovetails nicely with recent thinking
about good practice in institution building. Fukuda-Parr (1996) argues for
enlarging the scope of technical co-operation beyond the purview of public
institutions, which has been essentially its sole preoccupation. She also
argues for a shift in thinking from capacity *building* to capacity *utilisation*.
This shift is necessary because the nature of the institutional development
problem has changed over time. Relative to 1970, developing countries
now possess a large number of institutions and a large number of trained
people. These institutions function poorly and many skilled people are
underemployed or unemployed. Rather than creating new capacity, getting
this latent capacity to function better becomes the most pressing problem.
The AERC is a good example of an extension beyond the public sector and a
mechanism for improved capacity utilisation.

Grindle and Hilderbrand (1995) echo the call for capacity utilisation
over capacity building. They point out that:

> public servants in a broad range of countries regularly complain that
> they do not have meaningful work to do, that the skills they have are
> not effectively employed in their jobs, and that the quality of their
> performance is irrelevant to their career development. These
> complaints suggest that human resource constraints are more likely to
> derive from the failure to provide people meaningful jobs and utilise
> their skills effectively than from problems related to training *per se*.
>
> Grindle and Hilderbrand (1995: 444)

Prior to the establishment of the AERC, professionals in economics voiced
the same frustration. Doubtless many still do. Nevertheless, for many

African professionals in economics, the AERC has substantially improved the quality of the work environment. This was done in a quite cost-effective manner through small grants permitting researchers to actually carry out their projects and organisation of fora where quality work is recognised.

Conclusions

The critique of TC, which emerged in the late 1980s and early 1990s, was too dismissive of the roles of performance TC and training and too pessimistic regarding the capacity of TC to deliver institutional development. In developing countries, performance can matter a great deal and TC often delivers. In addition, training is critical. Without skilled people, institutional development has no chance. Technical co-operation finances formal training programmes, probably in insufficient amounts, which successfully produce trained people. If training occurs abroad, the available evidence indicates that the large majority of these trainees do return. In addition, those that do not return immediately often return eventually. Of the remainder that maintain permanent residence abroad, many keep close ties with their country of origin. Finally, if training is carried out in conjunction with effective capacity utilisation programs, such as the AERC, trainees are almost certain to be more likely to return following completion of the training and be more effective once back in place.

With respect to institutional development, disentangling the impacts of unfavourable economic/administrative conditions from the flaws in TC as an instrument proved exceedingly difficult. With the relative improvement in the environment in which TC operates, especially in Latin America and sub-Saharan Africa, more perspective can be gained. Beyond the success stories cited above, the OECD recently claimed that 'improved capacity for managing economic and social policies' belonged on the list of achievements of development co-operation (OECD 1996a). Institutional development is taking place, though not at as rapid a rate as many would like nor in as linear a manner as many appear to expect.

With this said, the critique does advance a series of coherent and relevant arguments. Few would argue against general exhortations to 'do a better job' and these will not be treated further. Also, few are opposed to the principle of improved recipient country management; however, this has proved difficult to achieve in practice and the way forward, at this point, appears to be poorly lighted at best. Finally, enthusiasm for introducing some market discipline into the allocation of TC appears to be practically non-existent, both on the part of donors and recipients.

The most practical contributions of the critique centre around the failure of the expert–counterpart model and the value of long-term resident expatriate advisers for capacity building. Experience indicates that the expert–counterpart model simply does not work. With respect to long-term TC personnel, institutional development goals are probably better achieved by placing resident expatriates in line positions with clear lines of authority within the local administrative structure. The advisor then deals with superiors and subordinates in much the same way (at least in principle) as the local personnel who are eventually expected to fill the post. In this way, some learning is likely as in any other institution.

The critique of the resident expatriate adviser also appears valid. Evidence indicates that resident expatriate advisers are in general a dubious means of achieving institutional development, especially when used in large quantities. Resident advisers can be expected to perform, play substitution roles, co-ordinate and fulfil a variety of donor needs. However, resident expatriates have not proven themselves particularly adept at fomenting institutional development. Groups of resident expatriates appear to be especially likely to isolate themselves from local administrative structures, usually in the name of achieving some proximate goal. As the critique rightly points out, this does little to build capacity. Short-term TC, meaning multiple visits of several weeks per year with electronic contact in the intervening periods as advocated by Berg (1993), appears better suited to fomenting institutional development. However, even this point must be nuanced. Effective short-term TC personnel often build upon a strong base of personal relationships and country knowledge, derived from a long-term experience.

Overall, institutional development has proven to be a long, fragile and expensive process. These three characteristics cannot be rescinded. Institutional development is also a crucial component of the overall development process. Consequently, technical co-operation can be expected to continue to absorb at least one-quarter to one-third of total ODA into the future. If anything, information technology and globalisation, with their concomitant demands for knowledgeable people and functioning institutions, bode a rise in the share of TC in global ODA. As such, greater emphasis, at least in relative terms, will be placed on institution building – one of the most elusive development goals.

With the large sums and large stakes involved, the need to use TC resources as wisely as possible is self-evident. While experience with TC for institutional development has been far from universally happy, real achievements have been made. Successes, as well as failures, now provide markers for the way forward. Increased emphasis on training and broad application of the concept of capacity utilisation, applied to both the public sector and civil society, appears to be the most promising avenue.

Notes

1 For example, the World Bank Group had $14 billion waiting to be disbursed to sub-Saharan Africa in 1993 (Jaycox 1993), while the total loan volume to sub-Saharan Africa at the time amounted to about $4 billion per year.
2 For example, for the 1950–90 period, Thailand and Indonesia exhibited higher and more stable GDP growth rates than the United States (Arndt 1996). Forecasts

by a wide array of respected institutions, such as the International Economic Analysis and Prospects Division of the World Bank, gave no indication that this trend would shift dramatically.

3 Not all critics of technical co-operation called for reductions in TC flows, preferring instead a restructuring of priorities within TC flows. However, calls for increases in the volume of TC flows were, to the author's knowledge, non-existent.

4 As discussed by Elliot Berg in Chapter 12, indicators, compiled by the World Bank and the IMF, of the health of the public sector administrative environment in sub-Saharan Africa have been basically static rather than improving in the 1990s. This is progress compared with the rapid degradation of the environment which occurred in the 1970s and 1980s. In addition, aggregate figures employed by the Bank could easily disguise increased resources channelled to priority areas. Poor statistics and conditionality imposed on pubic sector spending further muddy the waters.

5 The policy framework papers of the NATCAP programme are more critical of the performance aspects of TC. This might be mainly a matter of perspective. Recipients might judge the same average rate of incompetence or sloth on the part of TC personnel more harshly than donors due to the enormous salary disparity between local personnel and expatriate experts.

6 When TC projects pay salary supplements, they are more difficult to ignore as staff naturally gravitate to the increased incentives. Doubtless many developing country administrators succeed in extracting those elements they might want from TC projects, such as the salary supplements, vehicles and equipment, and marginalising any remaining unwanted elements. In any case, it is a long leap from the messy issue of payment of salary supplements, which is, at heart, intricately tied to the issue of a minimally congenial administrative environment, to TC as destructive force.

7 Little information is generated that might allow one to rigorously follow the evolution of the form of technical co-operation at an aggregate level. Consequently, the empirical basis for the discussion in this section is relatively thin. The discussion is thus couched in tentative terms.

8 Some donors have initiated gender training programmes for TC personnel. The impacts of these programmes remain to be evaluated.

7 Sector programme assistance

*Ole Mølgård Andersen**

A country is like a human being crossing the street. The objective is to cross the street within a reasonable time frame. However the tactics of safely crossing must be left to the individual: when to stop, when to dart across the street etc. Otherwise, listening too much to shouts across the street may cause an accident.

(Address by President Yoweri Museveni,
Consultative Meeting on Uganda, Kampala, December 1998)

Introduction

To several donor agencies the structural adjustment epoch of the 1980s had as a consequence that programme aid, in the form of balance-of-payment assistance, particularly to Latin America and sub-Saharan Africa, came to occupy a growing proportion of foreign aid budgets (see Chapter 5). Grave foreign exchange shortages made the so far dominating project approach rather meaningless, unless it could be supplemented with supplies of foreign exchange, or import support, to finance or cover vital imports and some debt servicing. To make a change into programme assistance several donors have relaxed certain donor restrictions, such as detailed control over the use of aid funds, and 'showing the flag'. These restrictions are by people in donor communities believed, or assumed, to be most likely realised through aid tied to projects, and through personnel assistance provided by nationals of the aid-delivering country.[1] The idea of moving from project to programme aid, in its pure and untied version, is not easily accepted in aid constituencies. Also, powerful commercial interests, and even career interests within and outside national and international aid bureaucracies, may militate against a general untying of aid programmes. As a sort of compensation for relaxing direct control over aid resources much programme aid was made conditional on recipient governments conducting 'sound' economic and other policies, following first of all the so-called 'Washington consensus', agreed between the IMF, the World Bank and the US government on behalf of the international donor community some time in the 1980s.

Different names for the same thing?

At the same time as these partial adaptations took place in the composition of aid programmes, it had become increasingly clear to members of aid constituencies that much of the foreign aid, in particular project aid to sub-Saharan Africa in the 1970s and early 1980s, had gone down the drain (see also Chapter 18), and that recipients together with donor governments and international aid agencies shared responsibilities for this to have happened. An essential lesson from these experiences is therefore that recipient and donor governments also share responsibilities for the design and future outcome of development co-operation (Lele 1991). This is also what a number of new or revitalised aid concepts, or aid rhetoric, is about: 'ownership', 'partnership', 'participation', 'institution-' and 'capacity build-ing', 'sustainability', 'aid co-ordination' etc. These concepts are also ingred-ients in what during the first half of the 1990s has become increasingly referred to as the 'sector-wide' approach. This approach includes, among others, sector investment programmes (SIP), sector programme support (or assistance), sectoral budget support (SBS) and sector development programmes (SDP). The different programmes can, in fact, be associated with different donor agencies. Thus although the multiplicity reflects a certain lack of donor harmonisation of terminology, it also reflects the fact that different donors, for various reasons, do emphasise different aspects in their aid programmes (see also the Appendix of Chapter 5). In what follows, the term sector-wide approach will be used as a general description of the phenomenon.

The new sector-wide approach to foreign aid can very much be seen as a reaction to a growing dissatisfaction with the project approach, in that an increasing number of aid projects became development enclaves during the 1970s. That was specially the case in sub-Saharan Africa where the socio-economic landscape had deteriorated and led to a growing isolation of donor projects from local realities, upon which the projects would make no or rather limited sustainable development impact. The adoption of the sector-wide approach has also been promoted in the context of the UN in the 1990s.[2]

Besides being a reaction to a widespread dissatisfaction in donor circles with the project approach to development co-operation, the sector-wide approach can also to some extent be seen as a reorientation of the policy-based balance-of-payment aid, which had come to play an important role in some of the more important aid programmes during the structural adjustment era. The relatively sizeable amount of balance-of-payment aid, which had been delivered under the so-called Special Programme of Assistance for Africa (SPA), orchestrated by the World Bank, and with inputs from most OECD bilaterals and the IMF, contributed very much to a removal of balance-of-payment constraints of the crisis years (World Bank 1997b).

Having come close to achieving this goal from about the mid-1990s, some leading donor representatives in SPA changed their attention from balance-of-payment issues to the implications of their programme aid on government budgets, including macroeconomic issues and budget policies (World Bank 1998c). Also there was a gradual change in emphasis from short-term stabilisation to medium- and long-term planning issues, and to the question of possible integration of donor programmes into medium-term budgeting and planning processes. Eventually these (explicit and implicit) approaches to sector programme aid will hopefully converge from their different entering points (i.e. the formerly dominating project mode and the more recent balance-of-payment approach) towards a co-ordinated and integrated support of sustainable development programmes and budgets of recipient countries.[3]

Guidelines from OECD

The subsequent and partial adaptation of aid modalities that took place in many donor agencies from the late 1980s was reflected in a new OECD development assistance manual (OECD 1992a). This manual was the result of close co-operation and consultation among the member agencies of the Development Assistance Committee (DAC), the World Bank, the IMF and UNDP. In the section on principles for programme assistance, there is the following general statement about sector programme assistance:

> For a number of donors sector assistance, including packages of inter-related project assistance, technical assistance, sector investment assistance as well as programme assistance, is an increasingly important mode of aid-giving and Members have agreed that they will plan and manage their aid increasingly in the context of co-ordinated support for larger sectoral programmes, objectives and policies.
>
> (OECD 1992a: 67)

At the time of the approval of the DAC principles by DAC members, there was no official attempt to propose a clear and unambiguous definition of sector programme assistance, but merely a reference to 'sector assistance' as something that could include any of the usual modes of aid deliveries, provided they were earmarked for a particular sector. However, as the quote suggests, DAC members had agreed to pursue co-ordinated support for larger sectoral programmes, objectives and policies, 'owned' by recipient countries. Five or six years after this agreement there was still no official reporting made in the DAC context, or elsewhere, on sector programme aid. There was, however, indication of an increasing number of donors attempting to live up to intentions of giving sector aid. The following presentation of the subject will mainly be based on published and unpublished donor reports, and it should be noted that not all of them are listed in the bibliography of this volume. At this stage, most available documentation on sector-wide approaches is prescriptive, or suggestive, rather than describing or analysing what may actually be taking place in aid-receiving countries. Most of the available evidence (e.g. Sida 1995 and Danida 1998a) – in the form of declared donor guideline manuals, co-operation agreements, and other information – almost invariably refers to African programmes, directly or indirectly.[4]

A World Bank version: sector investment programmes

It was staffs of the World Bank and the IMF who, in the early 1980s, designed the so-called structural adjustment programmes. The World Bank has since then been the unchallenged lead-donor agency as regards implementation of these programmes. It is therefore perhaps not surprising that it was the staff of the World Bank (Africa Region) who took the initiative to launch an initial attempt at a clearly designed and articulated blueprint for support of 'larger sectoral programmes' (Harrold 1995).

The proposed blueprint, which, somewhat misleadingly, was termed 'sector investment programme', assumed that in order to qualify as a SIP, certain conditions should be fulfilled. First of all an adequate macro-economic and sector policy framework should be in existence or be created. Second, the programme should be sector-wide in scope (or at least sub-sector-wide). Third, there should be a willingness on the part of the government to take the lead, and to consult with stakeholders. Fourth, an adequate government implementation capacity should exist, permitting a reduction in technical assistance. Fifth, there should be donor consensus and readiness to use common implementation arrangements. Perhaps most important, the proposal suggested incorporating, in operational terms, in particular two aspirations, reflecting what has become generally accepted as basic prerequisites for successful foreign aid. One is full *recipient responsibility* for the framework, and for preparation and implementation of (sector) programmes to be supported by donors. The other aspiration is effective *co-ordination* of donor inputs into such programmes. Both aspirations are easier to make statements about, on which all can agree, than to carry out in practice. Past experiences provide abundant evidence to that effect. Some of the numerous problems related to these conditions will be taken up in the following. Before doing so there is more to be said about the SIP proposal.

First, as to the definition of the sector concept in the SIP version, the World Bank blueprint maintains that 'it is not possible to provide a universal definition of a "sector", nor specific guidelines on where to draw sector boundaries.' (Harrold 1995: 6). The usual categorisation in various economic and social sectors may not always be a workable solution, even when they coincide with mandates of resort ministries. For example, the agricultural sector may be considered too large and diffuse to treat as one sector; a division between, say, animal husbandry and crop programmes may be more appropriate. The same necessity of splitting-up into sub-sectors may apply to, say, the transportation and educational sectors. The splitting-up of the sector approach into sub-sector programmes should not be understood as a decomposition of the sector approach in every respect. It is important that sub-sectors be defined and analysed within a comprehensive sectoral policy and budget framework. The sectoral frameworks should of course also be incorporated into a more comprehensive policy and resource framework, including all economic and social sectors, and eventually become associated with an overall expenditure budget framework (including figures covering donor contributions as well as own resources) leading to coherent overall multi-annual macroeconomic development planning.[5]

The World Bank outlook on SIPs, as presented in Harrold (1995), puts emphasis on ensuring recipient ownership of the programmes. It is thus assumed that, at least in principle, a starting point would be a 'home-produced' long-term vision. Following the setting of development goals and priorities comes the formulation of strategies, plans and budgets. In most developing countries which are clients of the World Bank, so-called public expenditure reviews (PER), and possibly also medium-term financial frameworks, have become important instruments for currently defining the amount and composition of expenditure budgets to be worked out for the various sectors. Ideally, the overall financial framework should not only set the expenditure targets, but also include estimates of public revenues to be generated from taxation, from loans and from grants. Based on the macro and meso planning and budgeting, one or several SIPs, depending on circumstances, may be prepared.

An important issue is the role of the national assembly in the planning process, particularly where a representative democracy is in existence (or under formation). Also, various interest groups – e.g. associations of farmers, industrialists, employers and employees – are supposed to be consulted. For preparation of the SIP programmes it is the ambition of the World Bank that ever more of the stakeholders directly involved should participate in the process. It is thus being suggested that:

> [A] particularly successful approach to this process seems to be for the government to form a task force to develop the sector programme, with working groups on the different aspects of the program, classified by functional or administrative groupings as appear most convenient . . . . These groups are entrusted with the development of the sector policy framework, development expenditure programme and accompanying budget requirements for their sub-sector, in line with overall policy and resource guidelines prepared in the central task force.

> (Harrold 1995: 24)

The arguments in favour of these strong stakeholder involvements (stronger than may be found in sectoral planning exercises in several highly industrialised countries) are ideological in part, but perhaps even motivated by a technocratic rationale, namely that this participation of stakeholders is likely to increase the chances of survival of the programmes.

The other fundamental prerequisite for a SIP programme is that it should provide a framework of effective and committed donor co-ordination within a sector. This is particularly important when there are several donors operating simultaneously within the same sector. In fact, in some countries more than 20 donors have been identified within the same sector. Some of these donors may be fairly important in terms of aid volume, others may represent relatively small contributions, as will typically be the case with most foreign NGOs. Since donor co-ordination may be time consuming, and be a heavy burden on recipient governments, not all donors need to be involved in every aspect of aid co-ordination procedures. It is suggested, as a rule of thumb, that 80–90 per cent of aid volumes should be covered by SIP co-ordination. Ideally the government should take the lead in donor co-ordination, but since this ideal may not always be possible to achieve, one of the larger donors, together with the government, could be expected to do it. Proper co-ordination implies that donors should participate in the same programme, which is either designed by the government or (at the very least), is the responsibility of the government. This responsibility is strongly underlined in the World Bank SIP blueprint, in that it 'requires a government with the willpower to say to donors: "Here is my program in this sector; if you wish to help me implement it, you are most welcome. If you wish to do something different, I regret that you are not welcome in this sector in this country".' (Harrold 1995: 13). For a government of a poor country to make such blunt statements *vis-à-vis* a major donor entails, of course, the risk of losing the aid money. Such confrontations are therefore likely to be an exception rather than the rule.[6]

Although it should be up to the recipient government to design sector programmes, with possible support of independent expertise from outside, it is, after all, for the donors to decide whether they will support a particular SIP programme or not, perhaps following lengthy negotiations. As is the case with project aid, the acceptability of sector programmes should be based on joint appraisals, where more specific issues – besides the question of economic efficiency – may be analysed. Such issues include, among others, the estimated impact on equity and poverty, gender issues, and the environment. It should, of course, also be carefully assessed what are likely to be the budgetary implications in the medium, and even longer term, of planned sector programmes. Following appraisal exercises, final decisions need to be made as to whether the government will accept, and whether donors will support, the programme. In such situations, donors may not only be influenced by considerations about the cost-effectiveness of the programme and about the likely meeting of environmental and social objectives. Other considerations, such as fear of under-spending in aid budgets, may ultimately influence donor decisions.

Having agreed on the support for a sector-wide programme, next comes the co-ordination of implementation arrangements. Important common components of direct relevance to donors include: procurement of inputs, accounting and auditing, disbursement, monitoring and evaluation and performance indicators. As will be discussed below, these are arrangements that are not simple matters for donors to co-ordinate. Here we shall mention only what may prove to be the most difficult issue for donors, namely the need for considerable flexibility in programme implementation. The strong need for flexibility may typically arise if the macroeconomic assumptions – on which the joint programme planning is based – undergo major changes, e.g. due to external or internal shocks. Consequently, the sectoral expenditure budget may have to be reduced to adapt to the new circumstances. And sudden changes in macroeconomic conditions are indeed likely to occur over the lifespan of a sector programme.

By way of example, one such change could be the impact of higher import prices, say, of energy, which may lead to requests for higher than anticipated government contributions to the recurrent budget. Subsequently the government may be unable to meet its financial obligations to the programme. Another example could be the emergence of a drought, which may require reallocation of government and/or donor funds for meeting emergency needs. Yet another example could be a deterioration, for whatever reasons, in the balance-of-payments, which may necessitate adjustments in public expenditure budgets – provided donors are not prepared to replace insufficient local funding by increasing aid transfers, or by reallocating support from other programmes of lower priorities. Unfortunately, administrative procedures in donor organisations may not easily allow for adjustments, at short notice, to rather unpredictable economic realities of recipient countries. As a result, co-ordinated implementation of programmes may be disrupted, and they may have to be reduced in scope, delayed or completely revamped.

Donor reactions to the World Bank blueprint

When the World Bank launched the SIP blueprint, a list of sector programmes under preparation was presented. Some of these programmes were at a fairly advanced stage, and offered useful lessons as regards the work with future sector investment and improvement programmes. The presentation of the SIP blueprint within the donor community was followed by seminar discussions about the feasibility of the SIP approach. In these seminars recipient governments were also represented. Among the conclusions that emerged from the discussions, the following are important (Jones 1997).

First of all it was found that the initial conditions for establishing a SIP often cannot be met. Since it will take time to fulfil these conditions, the donors, who might otherwise be prepared to allocate funds for SIP programmes, would have to make compromises, in order to ensure safe disbursements from their aid budgets. They would either have to disburse for traditional project aid, balance-of-payment assistance, debt reduction, or debt payments on behalf of recipient governments (e.g. through the Heavily Indebted Poor Countries (HIPC) debt relief scheme) – or through a combination of these modes of aid transfers. Some donors still wanted to opt for sector programme assistance, which was less ambitious than the strict SIP approach. The main question for them was what could be done to further promote a sector approach, based on a real partnership between donors and recipient governments, and within a conceptual framework similar to SIP. The possibilities are restricted not only by constraints on the recipient side, but equally important are the various donor constraints, being the same as those which constrained effective aid performance in the past. In the following we shall consider some key constraints to effective sector-wide co-operation on both recipients' and donors' side.

From ownership to ownership?

Ownership, meaning full recipient government responsibility for the design of development programmes, looms large in donor rhetoric. Until the 1980s recipient ownership was taken for granted by presumably all official donors. During the structural adjustment era in the 1980s, however, donors and recipient governments increasingly recognised that the autonomy of recipient governments in terms of economic and social policies should no longer be taken for granted. The decision-making power of African governments *vis-à-vis* economic policies was, more or less willingly, deposited in Washington, with the IMF and the World Bank.

A swing of the pendulum, at least in aid rhetoric, took place from about the early 1990s back to the position of post-colonial years. In part, this can be seen as a reaction to a state of affairs whereby, in the opinion of some critics, the former colonies (especially the poor debt-distressed sub-Saharan countries) had reversed into something that could be characterised as a semi-colonial status. There was another, perhaps more important, reason for the growing recognition that a semi-colonial status was untenable, namely the reduced ability of African governments and institutions to adequately manage their own affairs. Although the tide may now be changing – as highlighted in Chapter 6 – it will take time to develop human capacities to practise full ownership, including in a sector programme context. The process may be further delayed by the fact that it will also take time for at least some donors to change the problematic 'we know better' attitude, which some people in the donor bureaucracies and their representatives abroad adopted during the 1980s.

During the 1990s various official reports, including those from the UN system, have recommended an overhaul of the still large volume of technical co-operation (TC), and the ways it is being channelled (see Berg 1993 and Chapter 6 in this volume). There may be a growing recognition also among donors that much of the inputs delivered by TC personnel could just as well be provided by local personnel, provided conducive working environments could be established, including improved salaries for key civil service personnel. However, it will take years for recipient governments to be able to establish salary levels, that will ensure efficiency in public services. In the meantime, donor financial support is called for. Resources for common salary funds, in support of realistic civil service reforms, could be reallocated from donor spending on TC personnel, in most cases tied to nationals of aid-giving countries.[7] A study of Tanzania disclosed that total donor spending for TC personnel in that country (not including spending for external short-term consultancies) by far exceeded Tanzania's own spending on their total civil service (Berg 1993: 14). Until citizens of the recipient countries are equipped and allowed to take full responsibility of government functions, with limited and highly skilled expert assistance from outside, genuine ownership of the development programmes is unlikely to take root. In the meantime donors will continue to provide considerable personnel inputs, to some extent motivated by a wish to ensure control of the proper use of donor funds, even at disproportionately high costs.

Ownership of preparation of programmes

Ownership is of particular importance in the planning phase, because of the political decision-making and value judgements involved. The subsequent design of sector programmes is often handicapped by lack of specialised personnel, and sectoral planning units are either non-existent or very weak. As a result, donors are invited to assist in the process by making (it is hoped) competent experts available for helping with defining the policy framework as well as resource envelopes. This entails the risk that donor representatives may feel tempted to influence sectoral authorities to adopt policies and programme designs, and eventually insist on conditionalities, with which the government may not be in full agreement. It may nevertheless accept the interference in order to please the donor, as this may substantially increase the chances of getting financial support for a programme. Assuming that technical assistance for the preparation of programmes is inevitable, this does, however, not necessarily imply that assistance should be rendered by particular donors with specific interests in the programme design or implementation. Donors should rather be prepared to make earmarked funds available for the recipient government to recruit independent and professionally competent international advisers to assist with preparation of the programmes. Only after this exercise has taken place should representatives of potential major donors be invited to give their support, make their joint appraisals, and possibly assist with implementation, if there is a need for specialised expatriate personnel. However, as many functions as possible should be carried out by the national staff, if necessary with financial support from donors, as stated above.

Donor co-ordination and programme implementation

As stated above, donor co-ordination is a fundamental prerequisite for establishing a workable sector-wide approach. Effective donor co-ordination assumes pooling of (at least) major donor contributions for a jointly supported programme. The importance of a common understanding between the government and the donors regarding programme objectives and implementation is underscored by the fact that as much as half of central government budgets of some countries (and even more of sector budgets) may be financed from donor sources. Furthermore, the number of donors, even disregarding minor ones, may be very substantial. As indicated earlier, too many donors involved in the same sector may be a problem for governments striving to gain maximum benefit from donor resources. For instance, in the mid-1980s some 60 donor agencies were operating in Kenya, and a similar number in Zambia (van de Walle and Johnston 1996). The situation has probably not changed much since then, and is probably not different from that of some other African countries. The dispersed nature of the engagement of individual donors in various sectors is also significant, with the UN specialised agencies as a probable exception.[8] They are, in accordance with their mandates, technically confined to co-operate with one or two technical ministries. It should come as no surprise that in such circumstances co-ordination of donor interventions is limited and sporadic, and that understaffed sectoral ministries will not easily, if at all, be able to ensure co-ordination of several different contributions from donors with very different profiles. Where possible, successful efforts to co-ordinate donor and government inputs at sector level could therefore undoubtedly lead to substantial gains in aid and sector efficiencies.

In the following we shall make some comments as to the practical implications of donor co-ordination related to programme implementation. *First*, there is the overall management of the programme under the leadership of senior civil servants in the resort ministry, possibly organised as a separate management unit. This may differ from how things were organised in the past when parallel project management systems – established and managed by donors in order to circumvent problems of weak government capacities – was the rule rather than the exception. However, even without expatriate staffing, there may still be a risk of parallel structures. Other ministerial staff may see programme management as something apart from other ministerial functions, which in principle should be avoided.

Second, effective donor co-ordination during programme implementation assumes a common channelling of programme funds to a common 'basket', together with agreed contributions from the government's own resources. No funds should be channelled to sector programmes or sector ministries that have not been accounted for in the overall national planning and budgeting. Today, in several countries, less than half of official aid is properly recorded, if at all, in government budgets (IMAC 1996). Most funds bypass government accounts, instead of being channelled directly to projects or to accounts in sectoral ministries or local government agencies, or the funds are being converted into physical assets or aid personnel imported from outside the country (typically from donor countries), and without being recorded in respective government accounts. Even if funds are channelled directly to projects, as either monetary transfers or physical assets, this does not, of course, preclude transactions from being adopted in overall government budgets, under respective ministry allocations. Neither does it preclude subsequent expenditures from being debited against the respective expenditure accounts in the governmental account-ing system, and thus becoming subject to national auditing. But not even such proper bookkeeping is standard procedure, or at least has not been so in the past. For example, in one African country, receiving fairly substantial amounts of foreign aid, only an estimated 30 per cent of disbursements had been anticipated in the government budget. Since, in such cases, about half of all estimated resources available for government activities are aid resources, as much as 30–40 per cent of all resources bypass government budgets.

There are several reasons for such an unsatisfactory state of recording in recipient countries. Part of the explanation is slackness in budgeting and budget control in accounting procedures in ministries of finance and/or sectoral ministries. That may also be a reason why donors may lack incen-tives to adapt to local budget and accounting procedures. Another reason may be lack of compatibility with the reporting and auditing requirements of donor governments. In the past, this has unfortunately made donor agencies insist that aid-receiving governments should comply with donor accounting requirements. Donor agencies have also set up their own parallel project administration and control systems. A third reason why adaptation to recipient country budgets is often not practised is the fact that many aid transactions consist of physical items and services, the costs of which are not disclosed and therefore not registered in relevant govern-ment accounts. Besides negatively influencing overall and sectoral budget-ing and planning, these deficiencies obviously also impair the possibilities for effective co-ordination of inputs from various partners participating in the same operations. The chances of the recipient government eventually performing the role as overall co-ordinator of budget allocations, and subsequently controlling of resource use, are obviously limited under such circumstances.

Fortunately there are indications that some of the fundamental weak-nesses regarding adaptations of aid to national plans and budgets, are being increasingly recognised by donors and recipient governments as serious constraints. There seems to be a growing understanding that donor support for improving budgeting and accounting capacity in central and local government systems is essential if sector programmes are to become effective. There may also be a growing recognition that co-ordinated efforts to that effect are necessary, and that capacity enhancement of financial management should be given high priority, and possibly be included as an assistance component in sector programmes. No doubt capacity building within this crucial area of 'good governance' takes time, and requires more professional attention within governments as well as in donor agencies than has been the case in the past. It should be emphasised, however, that though capacity enhancement is mandatory for financial management to improve in recipient countries, it does not solve the problem that most donors do not systematically supply proper information on financial and other transfers to their co-operation partners.

Another important area for common procedures of implementation is procurement of goods and services, especially common tender procedures. At least in principle donors should accept the tendering procedures prescribed by legislation of the recipient country. That may not always be possible, because donor agencies may be restricted by their own rules and procedures, on which they may not be able to compromise. A still more severe restriction is, of course, where aid deliveries are also tied to purchases in the donor country.

A *third* area for co-ordination of implementation activities is joint reviewing and monitoring. For many years much criticism has been made of the lack of co-ordination of numerous monitoring and evaluation missions, who often review or evaluate the same projects or programmes, supported by several donors. Such missions, acting on their own on behalf of various donors, and doing the same or similar jobs, are very costly. More serious, however, is the yearly burden of several dozen visiting missions on scarce administrative and professional personnel in the recipient country, who will have to spend much of their time servicing all sorts of missions from several countries and aid agencies. Programme missions can and should be carried out as joint ventures, and with one common set of terms of reference, though making room for minor deviations to satisfy individual donor needs, where justified. Experiences with visiting missions involving more than two donor agencies have demonstrated that in practice donor co-ordination, including intra agency co-ordination, is difficult to obtain.[9]

In recent years performance indicators have become an increasingly important issue in many donor agencies. Demands for quantitative data on performance of individual aid programmes, to satisfy aid managers, financing authorities, ministers, or parliamentarians in donor countries, have been growing. That contradicts an also growing recognition that achievements of aid projects are more influenced by exogenous factors, over which donors have less (or no) control, than is possibly believed in donor countries.[10] This also applies to sector programmes, although it may be less of a problem here than with isolated projects, because some of the key variables, exogenous to a project, may become endogenous when included in a sector programme. For instance, an agricultural research project may show disappointing results in the field, because of a weak extension service. A simultaneous improvement of the extension service might completely alter the impact of the research project. In other words, the outcome of the research project can only be properly assessed when seen in conjunction with potential extension service improvements.

For these reasons it is not justified when donor agencies, or their constituencies, insist on measuring the performance of their particular contribution to sector programmes in isolation from what other donors or the recipient government may be contributing. To insist on measuring the results of the contribution of each individual donor runs contrary to the whole idea of a sector-wide approach, which implies that donors justify their individual contributions in terms of progress against jointly agreed sectoral objectives. Therefore, assuming that donors and recipient governments are prepared to accept the sector programme as a national programme, monitoring performance must be related to a *national* monitoring system already in existence or set up as part of the programme (or other programmes, for instance, in support of a national statistical system).

As performance monitoring is a crucial component in a sector programme, a framework for monitoring sectoral performance should be agreed upon by participants from the very beginning of the programme preparation. Such a framework may contain three main components relating to: (i) a budget (including sub-budgets) and accounts (including sub-accounts), (ii) a set of statistical indicators, possibly as part of a national statistical system, and (iii) a reporting system to keep track of institutional and systemic developments within the sector, and which is part of the programme. When a framework has been established, and its various components have been defined, donors should abstain from requiring additional information on performance. It is therefore important that agency-specific management instruments, such as log frames or other donor prescriptions, do not include indicators that cannot easily be verified using the agreed monitoring system.

Sector assistance in a decentralised government system

During the last decade decentralisation of government structures has taken place, or is about to take place, in many developing countries. One of the characteristics of a decentralised government system is the autonomy of decentralised governments as regards deciding on and managing public services according to rules prescribed in local government legislation. The revenue-generating capacity of local governments is limited, and local governments will receive considerable transfers from central government coffers. Some of these transfers are earmarked for meeting national minimum standards of education and health, and possibly also other services. The residual of non-earmarked block grants, together with locally generated resources, provide some leeway for local governments to decide which services could be provided in excess of national minimum standards.

The existence of decentralised governments may complicate the implementation of decentralised sector-wide programmes, because it raises questions as to whether and how foreign donors should become involved with decentralised local governments. However, if a donor is willing to provide budget support it should actually not matter whether decisions on resource use are made locally or centrally, so long as donor allocations do not exceed centrally agreed budget figures for the sector, or rather the part of the sector budget that the donor has agreed to cover. An example is a nationwide health programme, where donors may have agreed to finance a minimum health care service delivery package. If, as may be the case, a donor insists on supporting agreed sector programme activities in a particular geographical area, this should not complicate implementation of the national programme. Because of the fungibility of funds, the geographical concentration of donor allocations will merely substitute for a central government allocation, which may then be allocated to another area, or to other public services in the same or other areas. Alternatively, it may be 'used' for a reduction of budget deficits, for tax reductions, or debt service. Nevertheless, there may be situations where a donor wishes to finance specified public services in excess of minimum national standards in a selected geographical area. Even in such cases it would seem logical and justifiable, seen from a national and central government point of view, to make reductions in the block grant, equal to the donor financing of services. Historically, this is what has taken place in India, where donors, for whatever good or bad reasons, have earmarked their aid money to be administered by certain state governments, according to donor choice.

The sector-wide approach and the 2020 initiative

It may be a complication for co-operation on sector-wide programmes that donors want to emphasise different development goals in their aid programmes, and insist on certain conditions or conditionalities. Most people would probably agree in principle that donors should adapt their development visions as much as possible to those of recipient governments, particularly when it can be assumed that the government promotes a fair expression of the needs and social preferences of the population it is supposed to represent. A somewhat different situation may exist when both donors and recipient governments endorse certain universal economic or social goals adopted as resolutions at UN conferences, or which are encapsulated in, for example, the conventions of the International Labour Organization (ILO). In such situations, the sector-wide approach would seem to offer a unique opportunity for partners, through peer pressures, to ensure inclusion of universally accepted goals in sector programmes.[11]

The UN conferences on social matters that took place during the first half of the 1990s passed resolutions on several issues, which may be taken into account in the planning of sector programmes, or even at the overall national planning levels. They could also be taken into consideration when defining the contents of, say, a Policy Framework Paper (PFP), which in some countries is becoming a basic co-operation document between the government and its donors.[12] A well-intended attempt to promote actions to realise consensus decisions passed at various recent UN conferences was launched at the Social Summit in Copenhagen in 1995, where several UN organisations presented the so-called 2020 initiative. According to this proposal, developing-country governments should seek a restructuring of their government budgets, whereby certain social services should constitute at least 20 per cent of government budgets. At the same time donor countries should commit themselves to also contributing at least 20 per cent of their aid programmes to the same services. The initiative was favourably received by some governments, but not by others, among whom some argued that it would be too complicated to administer such, albeit well-intended, restrictions on aid budgets to be shared between many recipient countries.[13] The only operational and sensible reaction would seem to be that the 20 per cent target should be applied to a national budget that entails *both* donor *and* government contributions. That solution is, as a matter of fact, the crux of the matter in a genuine partnership on sector-wide approaches to development co-operation, as we have tried to argue in this chapter.

Notes

* My former colleagues in Danida, Anders Serup Rasmussen, Ole Winckler Andersen and Jytte Laursen made very useful comments on an earlier draft.
1 Because of the fungibility of donor funds, this belief is, of course, very much an illusion. For a thorough presentation of aid fungibility and its effects on development programmes, see World Bank (1998a: ch. 3). Fungibility is also discussed in Chapter 15 in this volume.
2 In 1996 the UN secretary-general launched the United Nations System-Wide Special Initiative on Africa (UNSIA). The purpose was to rationalise and maximise the impact of UN assistance, including that of the Bretton Woods institutions, through more effective co-ordination at headquarter and country level. The efforts were to be concentrated within certain sectors, of which education and health were the most important. Regarding the country-level activities it was recognised that donor co-ordination must be provided in support of programmes and strategies developed by African governments. After the first two years several African countries had allegedly responded to the invitation to participate, and even to being in the driver's seat. Particularly within the educational sector, several governments established sector strategies, in accordance with the World Bank promoted SIP blueprints. It is expected that

other (bilateral) donors, besides the World Bank, Unesco and Unicef, will join and provide their aid for education within these sector-wide frameworks.

3 In the next phase of the SPA effort (2000–4), a co-ordinated approach to integrating donor transfers into medium-term budgeting, and a strengthening of co-ordination of sectoral programme support are expected to be the two main items on the agenda, without doubt extremely important, but at the same time very ambitious enterprises in the SPA context.

4 A growing number of guidelines, manuals, handbooks, staff instructions, etc. are becoming available in donor agencies for staff and donor-selected consultants, engaged in preparing aid for sector programmes. A large part of this material runs contrary to the notion of recipient responsibility for preparing and managing programmes. The future magnitude and subject matter of this material may serve as an indicator of the degree of donor interference in the rights and competence of recipient governments to handle their development agenda, using their own national expertise (Mkandawire 1998), albeit with possible assistance of independent external expertise, according to their own choice.

5 The use of national development plans in developing countries was promoted in Africa by the World Bank in the immediate post-independence years. During the 1970s it was compromised by disruptive internal and external events. Today the somewhat looser and more liberal term 'strategy', historically stemming from the military vocabulary, seems to have replaced such plans, at least in development parlance.

6 The government of Ethiopia has become notorious among its donors for insisting on its sovereign right to determine its ways and means, even to the extent that visiting donor missions have had to return to their capitals, because they had insisted that 'something different should be done'.

7 In the 1980s, the donor community in Bolivia set up a common fund, which for a certain specified time period paid the salaries of 500 high-level government posts.

8 Still, since the mid-1990s, Danida has concentrated most of its bilateral aid on three or four sectors in each of the 20 countries with which Denmark has made a long-term co-operation agreement.

9 A joint donor mission, with eight donors represented, which visited the capital of a small West African country, did not perform very well, because government authorities had their hands full with servicing another visiting mission from a big international agency, also participating in the said joint mission.

10 Representatives of aid constituencies who visit aid-receiving countries may easily get the impression that the aid from their own country or international organisation is making footprints everywhere in the recipient country, at least everywhere they happen to appear, in accordance with a well-designed travelling programme prepared by local authorities in co-operation with respective embassies or agency residential representations.

11 In 1995, a DAC high-level meeting adopted a so-called path-setting statement, entitled *Development Partnerships in the New Global Context* (see OECD 1996b), which, besides a considerable amount of aid-rhetoric, also set various social goals for developing countries to be achieved by 2015. The most ardent advocates in support of this statement include DAC governments who are farthest away from the much quoted international aid volume target of 0.7 per cent of donor GNP. This makes the statement suspect as a reference for putting pressure on developing countries to adopt these social goals in their national plans. It has been suggested in OECD that donors should exert such pressures. Apart from that, what is agreed in OECD, even by high-level men and women of good will, can, of course, not commit governments in developing countries, not even morally, in contrast with UN (consensus) resolutions.

12 In the past, this document was produced in Washington It still is for some World Bank–IMF client countries, and is confined to the relationship with the Bretton Woods institutions.

13 Subsequently the 2020 proposal was adopted in *The Copenhagen Declaration and Programme of Action* as an option to be based on 'mutual agreement between interested developed and developing countries' (UN 1995a).

8 Food aid as an aid instrument

Past, present and future

Bjørg Colding and Per Pinstrup-Andersen

Introduction

The purpose of this chapter is to describe the history of food aid, to analyse the strengths and weaknesses of using food as a development instrument, and to propose a new 'food aid regime' for the future. Food aid is conventionally classified into three categories: programme; project; and emergency aid. The objective of programme and project food aid is to support economic and social development in recipient countries and both undergo the traditional project cycle of preparation, implementation, and evaluation. Emergency food aid, on the other hand, provides short-term relief in response to natural or man-made disasters. The objective is survival although the importance of prevention and rehabilitation is increasingly being emphasised by food aid practitioners. The chapter focuses on development food aid.

Food aid, particularly programme food aid, is a controversial form of foreign aid and has been the target of a disproportionate share of criticism concerning its effectiveness as a development resource. The possible disincentive effect of food aid on the agricultural sector in recipient countries is the single most widely treated issue in the food aid literature. The critics argue that food aid can encourage or enable governments to neglect agricultural production and investment and postpone, if not actually avoid, politically difficult policy reforms; food aid may cause a change in consumer preferences from local to imported goods, it can create economic and political dependency, it is often distributed for political reasons rather than needs, and the benefits can be poorly targeted to intended beneficiaries, taking the form of welfare handouts to the politically powerful with little impact on the long-term income of the poor.

Proponents of food aid, on the other hand, argue that in particular project and emergency food aid play a vital role in feeding the poor, saving lives in emergencies, and enabling countries to achieve economic growth and greater social equity. According to this point of view, food aid can: (i) increase resources for current consumption and capital accumulation, (ii) augment foreign exchange and fiscal resources, (iii) increase the income and improve the nutritional and health status and educational levels of the poor, thus directly alleviating hunger and poverty and adding to their human capital, (iv) serve as a wage-good, keeping wages low and promoting labour-intensive development, and (v) help ameliorate the adverse effects of policy reform and structural adjustment on lower-income population groups.

The evidence for and against food aid is inconclusive and mostly qualitative. Whether food aid furthers or hinders development in any given situation depends in large measure on the objectives of the donors and on their conditions for making food aid available. Also of importance is whether the policy environment and the institutional capacity of recipient countries are conducive to the effective utilisation of food aid as a development resource. A review of 21 empirical studies, conducted 20 years ago, concluded that it seems probable that a price disincentive effect on production can be (and has mostly been) avoided by an appropriate mix of policy tools (Maxwell and Singer 1979). Market segmentation – by region, commodity, or channel of distribution – to implement price discrimination and demand expansion in favour of the poor is one such policy tool. More recent research has found negative impacts in eight out of 12 African countries and there are many examples of negative effects where emergency or development food aid has been poorly handled (see Clay *et al.* 1996).

Most observers agree that cash aid (aid in the form of financial resources that can be used for some agreed purpose) would be preferable to food aid, if comparable amounts were available on similar terms. However, food aid has been wholly or partly additional to financial assistance for most major donors and supported by a separate and influential constituency in developed countries. An increase in financial aid to compensate for diminished food aid is therefore unlikely.

The food aid regime remained by and large unchanged until the late 1980s. Before 1990 the most important developments in food aid were changes in the quantity of food aid deliveries, the geographical distribution, and the constituencies supporting food aid. However, budget cuts, due to the economic crisis in developed countries in the 1980s, together with agricultural policy changes in Europe and North America in the early 1990s, and the signing of the Agricultural Agreement under GATT in 1993, have resulted in structural changes in food aid over the past decade. Cost and effectiveness have become issues of increasing concern. For these reasons, food aid deserves closer scrutiny as an aspect of official development assistance (ODA), as a financial cost, and as a resource transfer. The question is what the role of food aid will be in the future, with little additionality and smaller agricultural surpluses in donor countries. There are other factors, though not discussed in this chapter, that will affect global food production, demand, trade, prices and aid. These include the emergence of regional trading blocs, the underlying forces of technological change, climatic changes and rising population growth as well as commercial demand in developing countries as incomes increase (Pinstrup-Andersen *et al.* 1997).

The chapter is organised as follows. Next, the origins and developments in food aid deliveries over the past 25 years are reviewed. Then the strengths and weaknesses of programme and project food aid are analysed and their cost-effectiveness relative to other development instruments are discussed. Projections of future food aid needs and factors influencing future supplies are outlined in two further sections. Finally, a section proposes a new food aid regime, and the chapter concludes by listing a number of policy recommendations.

The origin and magnitude of food aid

Food aid has progressively declined as a proportion of total ODA from over 15 per cent in 1972 to less than 5 per cent in the 1990s. Global cereal deliveries were over 15 million tons in the mid-1960s, dropping to an all time low of 5.8 million tons during the world food crisis in the early 1970s, increasing steadily to 17 million tons during the food crisis in Africa in 1992–3 before plummeting to only 5.9 million tons in 1997. In 1997, cereal deliveries were 40 per cent less than the annual target of 10 million tons established by the World Food Conference in 1974. Bumper harvests in 1997–8, increasing grain surpluses, and food shortages in Russia and Indonesia are expected to result in an increase in food aid in 1998–9.

Institutionalised food aid was started by the United States in 1954 when a special government programme was enacted under the so-called PL-480.[1] As illustrated in Figure 8.1, the global trend in cereal food aid has largely followed developments in US food shipments, although the dominant role of the US food aid programme has declined significantly. Cereal shipments from the US in the 1980s averaged only one-third of the level of cereal aid provided in the 1960s. Nevertheless, cereal food aid from the United States still constituted one-half to two-thirds of global cereal food aid, down from 95 per cent in the mid-1960s. The lowest US shares were recorded in 1974–5, the early 1980s, and 1988–9. These reductions were associated with high grain prices and tight domestic supply. When the international market demand is strong, more will be sold and less given as aid. Food aid is a residual. As part of across-the-board reductions in US foreign aid in the 1990s, food aid deliveries were substantially cut from 8 million tons in 1994 to less than 3 million tons in 1997, equivalent to the level of US shipments during the world food crisis of the 1970s. The United States now accounts for only 41 per cent of global deliveries but remains the largest single donor.

The EU is the second largest cereal donor. Regular EU food aid programmes began following the signing of the first Food Aid Convention (FAC) in 1967.[2] The EU's share of global deliveries has risen from 0.5 per

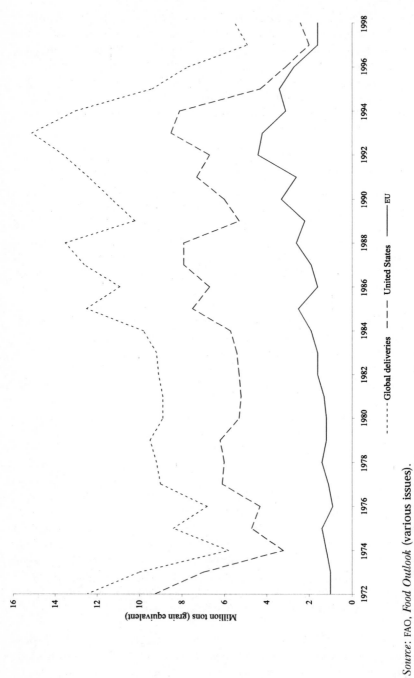

Source: FAO, *Food Outlook* (various issues).

Figure 8.1 Cereal food aid deliveries, selected donors, 1972–98.

cent in 1965 to as high as 21 per cent in 1974, before slipping to around 14 per cent in 1976. From the mid-1970s, EU annual shipments of cereal aid followed global food aid trends, with the so-called Community Action Food Aid Programme retaining its position as the world's second largest source (Clay *et al.* 1996). Record levels were reached in 1984–5, in response to food production shortfalls in Africa. With a further expansion in 1989–90, the EU's share rose to 29 per cent of global deliveries. Because of the cuts in American food aid in 1994–5 and 1995–6, the EU's share has risen to around 35 per cent of global deliveries. One of the most striking trends within the EU has been the increasing share of Community Action food aid, rising steadily from 22 per cent of EU cereal aid in the early 1970s to around 67 per cent during the period 1989–94, whereas the relative contributions of individual member states remained largely unchanged. Other major food aid donors are Canada, Japan and Australia, which together accounted for around 15 per cent of global deliveries from the early 1970s, with some variability in the relative shares of the three donors over time.

Globally, deliveries of non-cereals, such as milk products, fats and oils, pulses, sugar and meat products, have been of a much smaller magnitude than cereals. Non-cereal food aid increased steadily from 0.47 million tons in 1976 to 0.99 million tons in 1986. In the late 1980s, deliveries jumped to 1.2–1.4 million tons and peaked in 1992–3, when close to 2 million tons of non-cereal food aid were delivered before being cut to only 0.7 million tons in 1997. The largest donor has been the EU.

The main objective of US food aid is reflected in the geographical distribution of the food at any given time. During the 1950s, food aid was used in an attempt to weaken the dependence of Poland and Yugoslavia on the Soviet Union – Europe received about 51 per cent of total US food aid (in value terms) – and to strengthen the governments of South Korea and Taiwan. From 1957 to 1971, India received the largest US food aid grant, due to major shortfalls in food production and, to a lesser extent, because of India's strategic role in South Asia. In the late 1960s, Asia received more than two-thirds of US food aid. By fiscal year 1973, South Vietnam, Cambodia and South Korea accounted for 67 per cent of 'Title I' PL-480 food aid from the United States.

The food crisis in the early 1970s contributed to a growing emphasis in US foreign aid policy on meeting the basic needs of the poorest people in the poorest countries. A comprehensive restructuring of PL-480 according to these principles was introduced in 1975. Consequently, Africa's share of US food aid has gradually increased from 2 per cent in the 1950s, 12 per cent in the 1960s, 31 per cent in the 1970s, to 44 per cent in the 1980s, while Asia's share dropped to 28 per cent of deliveries in the 1980s.

Similar developments have occurred in global deliveries. Asia's share has decreased from more than two-thirds in the mid-1970s to one-third in the early 1980s. Africa's share increased from 21 per cent to around 50 per cent in the same period. Latin America accounted for 10–17 per cent during the decade ending 1991–2, up from 4–6 per cent in the 1970s. The large increase in the amount of food aid going to Africa reflected in large measure an increase in the need for emergency aid.

The pattern has changed dramatically in the 1990s; a significant proportion going to the republics of former Yugoslavia and Soviet Union rather than the traditional food aid recipient developing countries. In 1993, developed countries received a stunning 39 per cent of global food aid cereal shipments, of which the former Soviet Union accounted for over 80 per cent, while Africa received the lowest share in 20 years (29 per cent in 1993–4). Subsequently, deliveries to Eastern Europe and the former Soviet republics have steadily declined and represented 13 per cent of global deliveries in 1997, and Africa's share recovered to around 35 per cent. Still, in 1997, the quantity of food aid to sub-Saharan Africa decreased for the fifth consecutive year and amounted to approximately 2.3 million tons, the lowest level since 1983 and 62 per cent lower than the 1992 record level of 6 million tons.

Sharp jumps in the share of multilateral food aid and triangular transactions (in which a donor provides food aid from a third country) in global food aid constitutes another noteworthy development over the past decade. Multilateral food aid has increased from 12.9 per cent of total food aid in 1972 to between 20 and 25 per cent during the period from the late 1970s to the early 1990s. The share jumped to 35 per cent in 1996, due to cuts in US bilateral food aid and further increased to 41 per cent in 1997. A positive consequence of the triangular transactions (discussed further below) has been a rise in donor acquisition of commodities from developing countries to meet food aid commitments. In 1997, 20 per cent of global food aid was procured in developing countries, compared with 9.5 per cent in 1992 and 6 per cent in 1988.

The relative importance of the three food aid categories has changed over time. Until the end of the 1980s, programme food aid was the major form of food aid. In 1990, 58.9 per cent of total food aid was programme food aid, 20.3 per cent was emergency food aid, and 20.8 per cent was project food aid. The most recent data from the World Food Programme (WFP 1998) show that in 1996, the share of programme food aid had dropped to 41 per cent, making 1996 the third consecutive year in which programme food aid made up less than half of global deliveries. Emergency and project food aid accounted for 35 and 24 per cent, respectively, of global food aid deliveries. In 1997, programme food aid deliveries were almost halved, reducing its share to 25 per cent while emergency actions accounted for 42 per cent and projects for 24 per cent. This indicates a definite shift away from un-targeted food aid interventions.

This change is in part a deliberate policy decision by some donors to give higher priority to emergency and project food aid in order to promote food security and human resource development. However, it is also due to the fact that donors feel obliged to respond to an increasing number of unanticipated humanitarian crises and complex emergencies by reallocating already budgeted resources for emergency uses. This is clearly reflected in WFP's portfolio which consists of food aid projects and relief activities. Over the past decade, the share of relief operations in WFP's portfolio has increased from 25 per cent of total expenditures in 1987 to 68 per cent in 1996.

While emergency and project food aid are provided on a grant basis, programme food aid is also provided on a loan basis (on concessional terms). The share of total food aid donated as grants has increased from 61.7 per cent in 1972 to about 80 per cent in the 1990s. The United States is the only donor that continues to provide food aid as loans on concessional terms.

Development food aid

Food aid can further economic development through several channels. First, it adds resources that can be used for current consumption and accumulation. If monetised, food aid can be an important source of public revenue. Second, since most food commodities are internationally traded, food aid provides balance-of-payments support by reducing the foreign exchange spent on food imports. Third, it augments domestic availability of food (though not necessarily on a one-on-one basis). Fourth, to the extent it is targeted at the poor, it can alleviate poverty and food insecurity. By improving the health and nutritional status of the poor, it augments their human capital and future income earning capability. Fifth, to the extent it can be credibly tied to initiation of growth-promoting policies and reform of policies detrimental to growth, it can promote development. The question is whether or under what conditions food aid is more cost-effective than other development instruments in achieving the same objective.

Programme food aid

Programme food aid is usually provided directly to a recipient government or its agent for sale on local markets (monetisation). It is mainly delivered on a bilateral basis to reduce balance-of-payments deficits and to generate local currency to be used for public sector expenditure. The impact of this category of food aid on the agricultural sector of the recipient country and on poverty, food security and nutrition depends primarily on the supply and demand situation and the economic policies in the recipient country and how the proceeds from the food are distributed. The potential effects on dietary patterns and import dependency are not covered here.

The argument that food aid has a disincentive effect on the agricultural sector of the recipient country is based on the assumption that the recipient country is a closed-market economy in which prices are determined by supply and demand without intervention by the government or other agents. In this case, food aid would increase domestic supply resulting in depressed prices, decreasing agricultural earnings and consequently a drop in local production, unless demand was increased simultaneously. None the less, the resource transfer would unambiguously raise consumer welfare (Srinivasan 1989). However, there are very few countries where governments do not intervene in food prices, and most countries are open to international trade. In a small open economy, domestic prices are either determined by world prices or strongly influenced by them. Hence, an increase in domestic supply due to food aid would normally have a limited effect on domestic prices, even without government intervention.

Price disincentive effects have mostly been avoided by limiting the increase in domestic food availability through substitution of food aid for commercial imports and by increasing effective demand through market segmentation. Since donor countries do not wish to see their commercial sales reduced due to food aid, a common conditionality – which was hardly ever enforced and not at all nowadays – is that 'usual marketing requirements' should be fulfilled before food aid is allocated. Evaluation studies conclude that, on average, approximately 60–80 per cent of total food aid substitutes for commercial imports (von Braun and Huddleston 1988 and Saran and Konandreas 1991). In other words, the food aid received causes the food supply in recipient countries to increase by only 20–40 per cent of the volume of the food aid. This substitution reflects the fungibility of resources and the desire of recipient governments to maintain their overall policies and priorities. From a development point of view, a reduction in commercial food imports might be the optimal use of food aid because the foreign exchange saved can be reallocated to finance other needed imports, cover balance-of-payment deficits, or repay foreign debt, all of which can play an important role in support of economic and social development.

Sale of food aid in the domestic market has been a substantial source of income for many recipient countries. Since a large share of public sector revenue in low-income countries stems from the agricultural sector, proceeds from sale of food aid may be instrumental in reducing the tax burden for the agricultural sector and in increasing investments in this sector. On the other hand, food aid may induce recipient governments to postpone investments and policy changes benefiting the agricultural sector because of expectations that food aid will cover at least part of food requirements and solve any emerging food problems. Consequently, the disincentive effect of food aid on agriculture may work through policies rather than prices.

The effect of food aid on producer and consumer prices and agricultural production must thus be assessed on the basis of the specific economic policies of the recipient country, and not just on the basis of a neoclassical economic analysis of price formation in a closed-market economy without government intervention.

The impact of monetised programme food aid on poverty, food insecurity, and malnutrition depends on how the proceeds from the food are distributed. The proceeds from the sale of programme food aid are most often used as public budget revenue and the distribution of the benefits thus depends on the overall priorities of public expenditure. Hence programme food aid will often only have an indirect effect on the food security of the poor.

The effective food demand in many low-income countries does not reflect the actual need for food. The main reasons are low market integration which limits food availability and marketing in remote areas, and lack of purchasing power of poor households who cannot express needs as economic market demand. Market segmentation by geographical area, commodities, or channels of distribution can be a very effective policy tool to implement price discrimination and demand expansion in favour of the poor in remote areas, thereby limiting the price disincentive effect of food aid and increasing its impact on poverty and food insecurity. For example, some programme food aid is sold to target groups at subsidised prices, in which case the people who have access to the food aid get a share of the benefits while the sales proceeds make up the remainder of the benefits (see Table 8.1). These subsidies may or may not exclusively target the poor (Pinstrup-Andersen 1988). In the case of a gratis direct transfer in kind to target groups, which is most common in project food aid, the target group receives the entire resource even though the value of the resource transfer may not be the same to the recipient and the donor, as discussed below.

It is not easy to generalise about whether monetisation or a direct transfer in kind is the more appropriate means of distributing food aid. Monetisation is appropriate when balance-of-payment or budget support is the purpose of food aid and recipient and donor priorities and policies correspond. Monetisation of food aid is also likely to be appropriate when aid in cash is insufficient to cover non-food expenditures, such as administration and transportation costs necessary for the effective use of the food aid or when the food aid commodity is either too expensive or not culturally acceptable to target groups.

The cost-effectiveness of programme food aid is measured by how the donor costs of supplying food aid compare with the least-cost alternative of supply. The donor costs include the economic cost of the commodity and the transportation and storage/handling costs to the point of entry of the recipient country. The valuation of the economic cost of food aid commodities is not straightforward. If the donor buys the food aid commodity in the open market, the economic value is simply the market price. But if food aid comes out of surplus production, the economic cost of food aid could be valued at current world prices, the full budgetary outlays of donor governments, including costs associated with agricultural subsidy programmes and surplus storage, or at opportunity cost. Clearly, the choice of value will affect the assessment of the cost-effectiveness of food aid.

Table 8.1 Implications of food aid for selected variables under different price and market policies

	Food aid not additional to normal imports (open economy)	Food aid additional to normal imports	
		Sales on open markets at prevailing prices	Rationed sales below prevailing prices (support of farm prices)
Disincentive effects	0	+	0 or −
Food consumption	0	+	+
Foreign exchange savings	+	0 or −	0 or −
Fiscal resources	+	+	+ or 0

Source: von Braun and Huddleston (1988).
Note: 0 denotes no or small effect, + denotes an increasing effect, and − denotes a decreasing effect.

A recent analysis of the cost effectiveness of EU programme food aid compared the actual costs of delivering EU food aid to the point of entry of the recipient country, including only those costs attributable to the aid budget of the donor country and excluding costs refundable from the EUs agricultural budget, with the estimated reference cost for a hypothetical commercial transaction for the same commodity undertaken by the recipient country at the same time (see Clay *et al.* 1996). The analysis concludes that Community Action food aid was on average relatively more cost-effective than that of member states. Member states' programme aid costs were on average more than 70 per cent higher than the alternative commercial imports by the recipient which could have been aid-financed. The cost of the food aid administered by the EU was only 10 per cent higher than commercial imports. There were large variations in the cost-effectiveness of supply among donor agencies and the actions of individual donors. For example, food aid actions involving commodities procured on European markets are on the whole less likely to be cost-effective than commercial imports arranged by recipients, especially in Latin America, or triangular transactions and local purchases, although the latter is also sometimes problematic. Wheat flour, rice and sugar actions were particularly inefficient. The report also concludes that the revenue from monetisation of food aid was on average 23 per cent lower than the financial cost to EU donors.

These findings suggest that substantial savings could be made, or more food aid could be transferred, for a similar level of expenditure, if there were more flexibility in sourcing and choice of commodities or if some form of import or budget support were provided instead of food in kind. However, food aid may not be interchangeable with other aid instruments; if food aid were terminated recipient countries might not receive an equal amount of financial aid and the distribution among countries might change.

Project food aid

The WFP is the largest project food aid organisation. The overall objectives of food aid projects are to alleviate poverty and to improve the nutritional status of target groups. The most common food aid projects are supplemental feeding projects and food-for-work projects in which public works are undertaken by a labour force paid fully or partly in food. Food-for-work projects thus aim at achieving the additional, and at times conflicting, objective of infrastructure development. Food aid commodities are generally transferred in kind to target groups often located in remote areas. To a limited extent project food aid is monetised to cover non-food project costs or exchanged by donors for more appropriate commodities in local markets.

It is often argued that food transfers have a number of advantages over other types of development instruments (Katona-Apte 1993). Three of these are briefly discussed here. First, growing evidence shows that income in the hands of women contributes more to household food security and child nutrition than income controlled by men (Quisumbing *et al.* 1995). Since food is more likely to be controlled by women than cash it is argued that income transferred in the form of food is more likely to improve nutrition than if the equivalent income were transferred in cash. Further, food insecurity and malnutrition disproportionately affects women and small children, compared with household heads and other adult males, and women and children are also the most vulnerable household members to cuts in income and living standards. Food aid directed to women and children therefore has a natural poverty orientation. Alternatively, development efforts to enhance women's status through education, information, and improved access to technology and productive resources are likely to strengthen their relative power over household resources. This in turn would be expected to result in a higher household priority on the nutritional status of women and children in the long-run to the benefit of all household members (Pinstrup-Andersen *et al.* 1995b).

Second, it is argued that food is a more useful resource than cash to fund development activities in situations where food supplies are inadequate or unstable, and markets are inefficient. Food marketing has for many years been the responsibility of parastatals and public marketing boards which, in addition to performing all marketing functions, also were used by governments as an instrument to pursue political objectives, including price policies. The evidence clearly shows that these controlled public marketing systems have been expensive and highly inefficient in promoting sustainable agricultural growth, diversification and commercialisation. Although food and agricultural marketing has been liberalised in many countries in recent years, markets remain highly segmented due to continued inadequate public investments in economic infrastructure. In some food deficit areas, food transfers may thus be the only way to increase food access of vulnerable groups in the short-run.

Third, even in well-integrated marketing systems, food transfers may sometimes be preferred to a cash transfer because experience shows that most food-for-work projects have been better able to target the most vulnerable groups, particularly women, and avoid leakages. The reason is that deliveries of low-status foods such as coarse grains and foods with little market value are less likely to leak to unintended beneficiaries than cash transfers.

Others however have argued that food transfers are expensive, often composed of inappropriate products, bureaucratic in their operation, logistically difficult to deal with, and have been unsuccessful in improving the nutritional status and welfare of target groups. Negative effects on local market prices and farmer incomes are also mentioned.

Evaluations of the nutritional impact of feeding projects have shown that food aid is often a necessary, but not sufficient, intervention for improving the nutritional status of beneficiaries. Lack of measurable effects of single interventions, such as food supplementation, is largely a result of failure in project design and implementation to deal explicitly with complementary factors affecting nutrition (Pinstrup-Andersen *et al.* 1995b). These factors include hygiene, infectious diseases, nutrition knowledge, and access to and quality of primary health care. Substitution between individual interventions is also common. An example is school feeding projects which account for a considerable share of project food aid. Although the objective of these projects is to improve nutrition, there is reason to believe that the more important effect has been on the cognitive development of the children and on school attendance rates.

Interventions to improve nutrition can seldom be generalised across locations because the nature and determinants of nutrition, as well as the constraints to adequate nutrition and the opportunities for their removal, vary among households, communities, and countries. An important lesson learned is that household members behave rationally, given their goals and preferences, relative power, and the constraints within which they make decisions, particularly resource, time, information, and cultural constraints. Failure to seek compatibility between household behaviour and goals, on the one hand, and project design and implementation, on the other, is a major reason for project failure (Pinstrup-Andersen *et al.* 1995b). Past experience has shown that a high degree of participation by intended beneficiaries in problem identification, and the design and implementation of interventions greatly enhances the probability of success.

To ensure long-term, self-sustaining alleviation of poverty and malnutrition, policies and programmes to strengthen the income-generating capabilities of the poor are needed. Such interventions include employment generation, education and skill development, enhanced access to productive assets, and technological change to increase labour productivity. Food-for-work projects offer employment opportunities for disadvantaged groups during the off-season when employment and food are scarce and continue to play an important role in efforts to improve and develop rural infra-structure and in famine prevention. In their study of 14 African food-for-work projects, von Braun *et al.* (1991) conclude that food-for-work projects can result in increased earnings and improved food security among poor households. However, the effectiveness of the 14 projects varies consider-ably, mainly due to differences in the institutional capacity of the local government to manage the projects. Osakwe (1998) reaches similar con-clusions based on the analysis of a small open-economy model which demonstrates that increases in the stock of infrastructure due to food-for-work projects result in higher labour productivity in the agricultural sector, thereby increasing the demand for labour. Better employment opportun-ities in turn results in increased food production and improved food security. However, rural infrastructure development affects poverty and food insecurity and malnutrition not only because agricultural production and employment increases, but also because roads and markets are essential for the development of other complementary factors, including social infrastructure such as primary health services and education.

In addition to the appropriateness of project design and implement-ation and the institutional capacity of the recipient country, the impact of food aid projects on nutrition, employment and rural infrastructure develop-ment also depends on the extent to which the project's objectives and activities correspond to the government's overall development strategy. If they do not, the recipient country will adjust public expenditures to reflect the government's overall objectives and priorities. For example, WFP has found that some recipient countries reduce public expenditure to educ-ation more or less in equal amounts to the food aid contributions to school feeding projects.

Likewise, a rational food aid recipient will substitute all or some of the food received for other foods and non-food expenditure, in a manner that maximises her or his welfare, particularly if the food aid commodity is not culturally acceptable or other less expensive and/or preferred commodities are available in local markets. This monetisation of food aid by target groups does not necessarily reduce the impact of the food aid delivery on nutrition, food security or poverty. The net addition to energy and protein intake may be more or less than that contained in food aid, but the recipients' non-food expenditures, indirectly made possible by the added purchasing power released as a consequence of the food aid, may be just as important to the improvement of the recipients' nutritional status as added food consumption. The transaction costs to recipients associated with selling or bartering food aid will be low if local markets are efficient but the question then arises whether in such circumstances it is appropriate to transfer food in kind. If on the other hand local markets are inefficient, the transaction cost of monetising project food aid will be high, especially if food aid commodities are not indigenous, as will the cost of food aid deliveries.

Cost-effectiveness of project food aid, the so-called 'alpha-value', is defined as the unit value of the commodity to the recipient divided by the unit cost of delivery. The appropriate monetary value of the commodity to the target group depends on the food in the existing diet likely to be completely or partially replaced (Reutlinger and Katona-Apte 1987). The value would be the retail price, if the replaced commodity is normally purchased in the open market. If the food commodity potentially replaces a food obtained at a concessionary price in a food ration shop, the concessionary price would be the appropriate value. If the food aid commodity is supplied to a farming household and is used to replace a food that is marketable surplus, the appropriate value is the price the farmer receives for the additional food sold. The unit cost of delivery includes the donor costs to the point of entry of the recipient country as discussed above for programme food aid and in addition project related costs, typically inland transport, storage, handling, as well as on-site distribution and supervision, sometimes paid for by the donor. According to Katona-Apte (1986) commodities of highest cost to the recipient should be provided when food aid replaces other foods in the diet. Whereas if the food aid is additional to the usual diet, commodities with the highest nutritional content should be selected. That is, the energy or nutrient content should be divided by the delivery cost of the commodity. This alpha-value thus identifies the most inexpensive transfer of energy or nutrients.

Several studies of the cost-effectiveness of project food aid were conducted in the 1980s (see Fitzpatrick and Hansch 1990 for a summary). No clear overall pattern emerged; the cost-effectiveness of project food aid varies greatly among commodities, projects, regions, and countries. The absolute alpha-values in the various studies are not directly comparable because the benefits and costs are computed differently in each study. None the less, the studies yield the important finding that changes in the food basket alone can improve the cost-effectiveness of food aid projects significantly. For example, a study of WFP's food aid basket to Indonesia found that the alpha-value for pulses was only 0.04 while the alpha-value for rice was 0.87 (Katona-Apte 1986). Similarly, Reutlinger (1984) found that wheat transfers to Egypt had an alpha-value of 0.25, three times lower than the transfer efficiency of vegetable oil. In the studies, alpha-values above unity were found for vegetable oil in Nepal, Bolivia, Uganda and India, for dried skimmed milk in Bolivia and Botswana, for wheat flour in Bolivia, for rice in Ghana and for sugar in Sudan and Uganda (Fitzpatrick and Hansch 1990). Another important finding is that the objective of the food aid project determines which commodity basket is the most cost-effective. A comparison of the monetary and nutritional alpha-values of four alternative food baskets found that a food basket may rank high in monetary cost-effectiveness but low in energy or another nutritional alpha-value (Katona-Apte 1986).

These findings support the argument above that a thorough understanding of the nutrition problem and the characteristics of the beneficiaries is important for the efficient use of project food aid. Each project must necessarily be unique in its design and consequently the evaluation will be case-specific, taking into account the efficiency in the use of resources and the extent to which the project achieves its development objectives.

Future food aid needs

According to projections of food demand, supply, and trade until the year 2020 conducted by the International Food Policy Research Institute (IFPRI), the prospects of a food-secure world – a world in which each and every person is assured of access at all times to the food required to lead a healthy and productive life – remain bleak (Rosegrant *et al.* 1995 and Pinstrup-Andersen *et al.* 1997). The IFPRI global food model shows that under the most likely (i.e. baseline) scenario, 150 million children under the age of six – which is one out of every four children – will be malnourished in the year 2020, down from 33 per cent in 1993. Child malnutrition is expected to decline in all major developing regions, except sub-Saharan Africa, where the number of malnourished children could increase by 45 per cent to reach 40 million. The FAO projects that 680 million people, or 12 per cent of the developing world's population, could be food insecure in 2010, down from 840 million in 1990–2. Thus, although global food supplies will continue to grow faster than the world population, by 2010, every third person in sub-Saharan Africa is likely to be food insecure compared with every eighth person in South Asia and every twentieth person in East Asia.

The latest projections of future food aid needs, published by the United States Department of Agriculture (USDA 1995), were undertaken for three alternative scenarios to the year 2008. The projections are based on data from 66 lower-income countries. Food aid needs are defined as the amount of grain needed to fill the gap between what a country can produce plus its financial capacity to import commercially less non-food use, and a targeted consumption level. The consumption targets vary in the three scenarios: (i) per capita consumption is maintained at 1995–7 levels in the 'status quo gap', (ii) average consumption meets minimum recommended nutritional requirements in the 'nutrition gap' and (iii) food consumption brings each income quintile up to the nutritional requirements in the 'distribution gap'. The status quo gap is projected to increase 80 per cent to 19 million tons in 2008, while the nutritional gap increases 61 per cent to 28 million tons. Consequently, if food aid availability remains at the 1997–8 level, it will cover 28 per cent of the needs to maintain per capita consumption and only 19 per cent of the nutritional gap by the year 2008. The distribution gap is projected to rise 36 per cent to 38.4 million tons by 2008, of which sub-Saharan Africa is projected to account for 79 per cent.

These estimates strongly support increasing investments in agriculture to raise productivity in food production of low-income countries and to enhance access to food among the poor through poverty relief, broad-based economic growth, and lower unit-costs in food production.

Recent developments affecting the future of food aid

Global food aid deliveries have declined precipitously since 1992–3, principally because of cuts in US food aid, falling 67 per cent to 2.8 million tons in 1997. Several factors account for this steep decline. First, the main driving force behind the US food aid programme has always been disposal of domestic agricultural surpluses. European Union and Canadian food aid has also been closely linked to agricultural policies and surplus production. During the 1990s, global grain stocks have been falling due to changes in agricultural policies in North America and Europe. Agricultural subsidy programmes have been discontinued in an effort to reduce swelling fiscal deficits following the economic crisis in the 1980s. The 1990 and 1996 US farm bills require farmers to rely on market forces and curtail the build-up of government stocks, and the Canadian government discontinued its grain transportation subsidy and cut support levels for other grain programmes. The result was a decline in the wheat area during 1992–5 as farmers shifted to more profitable commodities. In 1992, the Council of Ministers of the EU reached agreement on the most extensive reform of the common agricultural policy (CAP) since its inception in 1962. Support prices were lowered and a land set-aside programme instituted in order to reduce stocks, increase domestic consumption (primarily to feed), and reduce budgetary expenditures. In all cases, a combination of external pressures, such as the signing of the Agricultural Agreement under GATT, and internal budgetary concerns, brought about the policy changes, and in all cases the changes resulted in large cuts in food aid contributions.

These recent policy changes in North America and Europe could permanently lower grain stocks as these governments will no longer need to hold large reserves to support agricultural subsidy programmes. With no surplus production, donor governments will have to purchase food aid commodities in domestic or international markets in competition with other buyers at full market price, as has been the case in the 1990s. This raises the question of whether food aid is still additional or whether it competes dollar-for-dollar with other aid instruments for available ODA.

Second, declining global grain production due to the above policy changes, stagnating grain yields in Asia, adverse weather conditions, civil conflict in sub-Saharan Africa, and low stocks, all resulted in an increase in grain prices in the mid-1990s (Pinstrup-Andersen and Garrett 1996). Since most donors fix their food aid budget in monetary values, an increase in the price of food aid commodities translates directly into lower tonnage of food aid deliveries.

Third, as part of the effort to reduce budget deficits, foreign aid has declined rapidly in the 1990s, falling about 30 per cent in nominal terms between 1990–1 and 1995–6 to $41 billion (see also Chapter 3). As the resources for international aid decrease, a number of donors have re-examined their aid policies and are seeking greater effectiveness for the development instruments used. In donor countries without a strong agricultural lobby, food aid supplies could be reduced further unless it is demonstrated that food aid can have a comparative advantage over other aid instruments in some development activities.

The agricultural sector has been hit disproportionately by the cuts in ODA. In real terms, aid to developing-country agriculture almost halved, from a peak of $19 billion in 1986 to $10 billion in 1994. This is partic-ularly unfortunate since the majority of poor people live in rural areas and depend either directly or indirectly on agriculture for their livelihood. These developments will have serious adverse effects on developing coun-tries' capacity to engage in broad-based and sustained economic growth and thereby to improve their food security in the future (Pinstrup-Andersen *et al.* 1995a).

Finally, it is unclear how the Agricultural Agreement of the GATT Uruguay Round, completed in December 1993, and the new negotiations planned to begin in late 1999, will affect food aid needs and availability. As shown in Figure 8.2, the European Commission projects rapidly increasing grain surpluses beginning around year 2001, unless further agricultural sector reforms are undertaken in Europe and North America. As subsidisation of exports is to be disciplined under the agreement, bona fide food aid may be the only outlet for surpluses from exporting countries (Shaw and Singer 1996). On the other hand a complete liberalisation of agricultural markets would eliminate the surplus disposal element since the remaining domestic subsidy policies that give rise to excess domestic stocks would disappear.

The more likely outcome is that the reform process will reduce future food surpluses. As these have determined food aid levels in the past, the agreement will probably lead to reduced food aid availability. Further recent analyses suggest that the impact of the agreement on food prices, although limited, may be sufficient to reverse a projected price decline for some commodities. As discussed above, higher food prices also result in lower food aid availability, given fixed budgets in monetary terms. This interpretation is supported by the large downward adjustment from 7.52 to 5.35 million tons of cereals, which donor countries made in 1995 to the minimum food aid commitment under the FAC, and by the decline in actual food aid deliveries documented above (Matthews 1998). Meanwhile, the increase in food prices and the expected increase in food price variation due to the reduction in global stocks are likely to have serious adverse effects on the import bill of the poorest food importing countries.

The GATT ministers agreed to guarantee that the implementation of the Uruguay Round of the GATT would not adversely affect food aid commit-ments to meet the authentic needs of developing countries and stressed the continuing need for bona fide food aid. However, the agreement is not

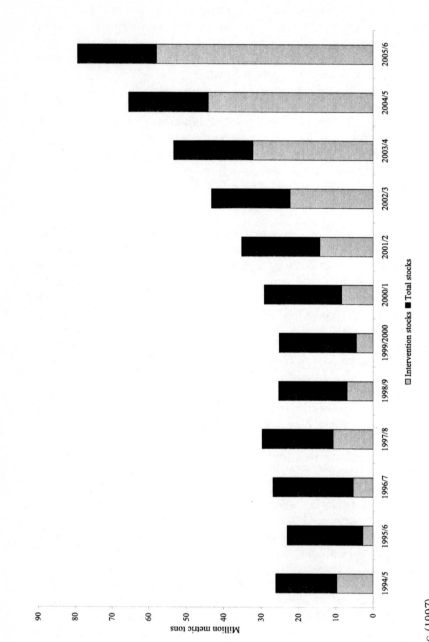

■ Intervention stocks ■ Total stocks

Source: EC (1997).

Figure 8.2 Total cereal stocks in EU-15, 1994/5–2005/6.

specific on how this is to be accomplished. No indication is given as to the level at which food aid should continue to be provided, whether that level should go beyond status quo demand to include the need to raise nutritional levels above their current status, what proportion of food aid should be provided as grants, and to what extent it should be channelled multilaterally. Equally, the food aid provisions of the Final Act are not very specific on what constitutes food aid, the steps to be taken to ensure reliability of its supply, or what is the appropriate forum to establish and review the level of food aid, and to ensure that it goes to the most needy countries.

A future food aid regime

There are several reasons why a review of the food aid regime is timely. Four such reasons are particularly important. First, the need for an integrated food security strategy for low-income countries is becoming increasingly obvious. The role of food aid in these strategies needs to be further discussed and refined. Second, foreign aid has been declining rapidly over the past decade, particularly in the agricultural sector, and that will have serious adverse effects on the capacity of developing countries to achieve food security in the future. The additional negative impact of cuts in food aid on total resource transfers has not been fully considered. Third, a decreasing share of food aid is originating from surplus production in donor countries due to recent policy changes in North America and Europe. Donor countries are increasingly purchasing food aid either in the domestic market or in third countries. If, consequently, food aid is no longer additional and thus competes with other aid instruments for scarce resources available, the use of food as a development instrument should be reconsidered. Fourth, the effect of the Agricultural Agreement on food prices and food aid availability is uncertain. Clear guidelines for future food aid deliveries should be established by the WTO.

Discontinuing or maintaining food aid?

This section addresses two related questions. First, under what conditions should food aid be continued or discontinued and, second, if food aid is to be continued, what major changes are needed in the design and implementation of food aid programmes?

Programme food aid should be discontinued and replaced with untied cash aid equal to the total donor costs of obtaining and shipping the food aid if the food aid delivery meets all of the following criteria:

- It is not additional to other aid. On the contrary, it competes with untied cash aid on a dollar-to-dollar basis.
- The opportunity cost to the donor is equal to or greater than the world market price of the food aid commodity.

- The transactions cost, including transport, handling, storage and administration, associated with the food aid is equal to or greater than the transactions cost associated with untied cash aid.

This is the extreme case where programme food aid beyond doubt should be terminated. If one or more of the criteria is not met, further analysis of the costs and benefits of the specific programme is required to establish whether it is an appropriate development intervention. Limited additionality, for instance, may not justify continued food aid. As discussed above, evidence suggests that programme food aid in general is not a cost-effective aid instrument compared with an untied cash transfer. None the less, if programme food aid is additional, donors should be encouraged to continue providing programme food aid because recipient countries need the resource transfer inherent in the food transfer, even if the alpha-value is small. However, donors should be extremely careful to avoid adverse effects on local agriculture and food habits; particular attention should be paid to the effect on local food prices and on policies and public investments benefiting the agricultural sector.

Food aid may be additional for several reasons, including the following:

- The opportunity cost to the donor may be less than the market value of the food, because food aid provides an outlet for surplus stock.
- Food aid enjoys stronger support than untied cash aid from special constituencies, such as farm lobbies, donor governments, and NGOs. The motives of the constituencies range from commercial and political self-interest to altruism.
- The perception of donor countries is that programme food aid is a more efficient means of influencing policy decisions and food allocation in recipient countries than cash aid, or donor country populations think that the benefits of food aid are more likely to reach the poor than cash aid.

Project food aid should be discontinued and replaced with untied cash aid if the three criteria pertaining to programme food aid are met and the recipient country possesses sufficient institutional, market and logistics capabilities, as well as the human resources necessary to design and implement the projects for which food aid is currently being used. However, as discussed above, low market integration, due to inadequate economic infrastructure, highly inefficient marketing systems, and weak institutional capacity in many developing countries, are among the main reasons why food aid may be superior to untied cash aid.

Single interventions, such as a food transfer, may have little effect on the nutritional status of the beneficiaries because the nutrition problem is usually determined by a set of complementary and mutually interactive factors. Since food aid alone cannot solve the nutrition problem, the concept 'food aid project' is obsolete and should be abandoned. The successor to the traditional food aid project is a more holistic food security approach that focuses on the specific needs and constraints of the intended beneficiaries.

The food security approach comprises the following steps: (i) food-insecure households or individuals are identified, (ii) the causes of the nutrition problem are uncovered and (iii) project activities to remove the constraints are developed. It is important to note that food transfers may or may not be included in this approach. If food transfers are included, they must be accompanied by efforts to develop an efficient local small-scale private food marketing system that will replace the project food delivery system, as well as efforts aimed at supporting agricultural development and increasing the purchasing power of food-insecure households. Historically, food aid distribution has bypassed local food marketing systems. Consequently, local capacity has not been developed and food distribution to food aid beneficiaries has not been sustained beyond the project duration. The food security approach, in contrast, has the advantage of addressing the causes and not just the symptoms of the nutrition problem.

Triangular transactions and local purchases

Since the 1980s, donors have increasingly used triangular transactions and local purchases (henceforth referred to as cash transactions) to improve the performance of food aid interventions. A triangular transaction means that a donor procures food commodities in one developing country to use as food aid in another, and a local purchase means that the donor procures food commodities in surplus areas for use as food aid in deficit areas of the same country. The documentation of the experiences with cash transactions is scarce. However, evidence from the late 1980s (RDI 1987, Clay and Benson 1990 and Fitzpatrick and Hansch 1990) confirmed that triangular purchases, in particular, appeared to have been cost-effective. For example, there is evidence that staples, such as white maize, white sorghum and millet, which are more in keeping with the food habits and customs of the beneficiaries, commanded higher prices locally than coarse grains and wheat available from bilateral pledges and the international market.

The studies argue that it is critically important to distinguish between purchases from countries that are regular exporters of the commodity in question, and purchases from countries that only periodically supply on world markets or have surpluses available for food aid export. The cost-effectiveness and timeliness of purchases in regular exporting developing countries are similar to those from developed countries, whereas the experience with purchases from non-regular exporting developing countries is more mixed, especially with regard to the timeliness of deliveries and assuredness of supply.

The stated objectives of triangular transactions include strengthening regional trade and production. However, they are usually limited to the acquisition of food in a developing country by means of short-term competitive tenders and the transport of the food out of the country in the most efficient manner using external personnel and equipment. An important future role of food transfers could be to exploit the trade and development opportunities associated with cash transactions in both the source and the recipient country.

Greater emphasis on the potential advantages of triangular transactions to source countries and complementary investments in institutional strengthening, physical infrastructure, and marketing and distribution, in both the recipient and source country, could stimulate sustained intra- and inter-country trade, thus contributing significantly to the long-term development of both types of countries. Another important benefit from strengthening inter-regional trade opportunities might be that the new regular exporting countries can supply food quickly and efficiently to emergency operations in the region. However, cash transactions can only encourage trade between developing countries to a limited degree; sustainable establishment of trade depends on national policies in trading countries.

Triangular transactions as proposed here are obviously more complex than traditional food aid deliveries, because the objective of benefiting a third party, the source region or country, is introduced into the operation. Donors should accept that to maximise the benefits of food transfers in the long run, projects might have to include a source country component, particularly if the source country is a non-regular exporting country, as well as a recipient country component. In addition, non-food expenditures could be significantly larger than in traditional food aid projects because of additional workloads involved in cash transactions. In most developing countries, the donor agencies will also have to invest in acquiring the considerable amount of information required for efficiently managing cash purchases.

The role of development organisations

The role of development organisations in the implementation of food transfers and cash transactions depends on the trade and marketing capacity of the source and the recipient country. When possible, the food should be channelled through existing local market structures. If the food distribution system in the recipient country and/or the source country is segmented and inefficient – due to insufficient physical infrastructure, inadequate institutional capacity, lack of market information or other necessary services – but the basic pillars of a private free market food distribution system are present, the role of donors should be to provide technical and financial assistance necessary to overcome the institutional constraints and to develop the necessary economic infrastructure. In this case, donors may not be directly involved in the procurement or handling of the food transfer. However, if more fundamental elements of the trade and marketing system are inadequate and more long-term interventions are required, it may be appropriate for the development organisation to procure and distribute food in parallel markets until the essential elements of the local marketing system have been established.

To avoid duplication of efforts and implementation of conflicting activities, one organisation should be made responsible for co-ordinating future government-to-government food transfer operations and for monitoring and documenting the experiences with the new food security approach. The WFP would be an obvious choice for the role as lead agency in future food transfer activities; the organisation has been responsible for the majority of food aid projects since 1970, it has been the single most important organisation involved in cash purchases, and WFP has substantial experience in procurement and logistics in which it is highly competitive internationally. The WFP could implement project activities itself or delegate the responsibility to local or international NGOs with country offices in the countries involved, whichever is more appropriate. For WFP to assume the role of co-ordinator and be able to implement food transfers efficiently, fundamental changes would be required, particularly with re-spect to funding procedures and staffing. Currently, most contributions to WFP's regular programme are tied to procurement in donor countries and more than one-third of total contributions are directed by donors to specific projects and countries. In the future, donors will have to provide WFP with cash donations and additional funding for management and administra-tion at headquarters would be needed. Also, additional professional and experienced specialists would have to be recruited because cash purchases require country staff with a certain level of knowledge and experience in procurement and logistics.

Conclusions and policy recommendations

In sum, based on the consideration put forward above, we recommend that:

- Future debates and decision-making about the magnitude and compo-sition of foreign aid incorporates all aid instruments, including food aid.
- The monetary equivalent of reductions in food aid in the 1990s be added to financial aid budgets to compensate for the decrease in overall resource transfers to developing countries caused by the cuts in food aid.
- Any future reductions in food aid be compensated by equal increases in financial assistance.
- Programme food aid be discontinued in cases where it is not additional, provided that the funds are reallocated to more cost-effective develop-ment instruments.

- A strengthened commitment to improve food security be promoted and adopted.
- The concept 'food aid project' be abandoned and a new food security approach be pursued. This new approach should focus on the needs and constraints of the intended beneficiaries and search for sustainable solutions to their nutrition problems. Food transfers may or may not be included in this approach.
- In order to achieve sustainable improvements in the food access of poor and food-insecure households and individuals, food transfers should be accompanied by efforts to develop an efficient local small-scale private food marketing system as well as efforts to increase the purchasing power of the intended beneficiaries.
- Food commodities for food transfers should be, to the extent possible, imported commercially. If, for political reasons, the aid is tied to donor-country commodities, a foreign currency facility could be made available, whereby foreign currency is put at the disposal of the public or private sector in recipient countries which can then import food and/or agricultural inputs commercially from the donor country.
- Food transfers should be, where possible, channelled through existing private marketing systems, with donors limiting their role to providing technical and financial assistance for institutional strengthening and economic infrastructure development. Only where more fundamental long-term restructuring of the local marketing system is required should donors be directly involved in food procurement and distribution and then only in the interim period until local capacity has been developed.
- Expanded use of triangular cash transactions should be pursued, when donors are responsible for procurement and distribution of food commodities. There are strong arguments for relying substantially on cash purchases in developing countries in food transfer activities both from a cost-effectiveness and from a development point of view.
- Triangular cash transactions should focus, not only on transferring food, but on generating sustainable economic development among small farmers in the developing countries where the food is purchased (source countries). Furthermore, these transactions should focus on fostering the conditions for future international trade between developing countries by strengthening institutions, infrastructure, and marketing and distribution in both the recipient and the source country.
- The WFP should be appointed the lead agency for co-ordination and monitoring of government-to-government food transfers in the future. For WFP to be effective in this important role, future WFP contributions should be donated in cash or import facilities and larger contributions would be required to fund the additional administrative and personnel costs associated with cash transactions.

Notes

1 Public Law (PL) 480 food aid – which refers to the *Agricultural Trade Development and Assistance Act* (not to be confused with the *Agricultural, Trade and Development Assistance Act*) passed in the United States in 1954 – contains three articles. Prior to 1990, activities were organised under the articles according to form of aid (loans or grants): Title I authorised concessional sales of surplus agricultural commodities to 'friendly' nations, Title II authorised bilateral donations of food for famine and other urgent relief programmes, and Title III authorised donations of food through non-profit voluntary organisations. In 1990, the articles were reorganised by objective.

2 These conventions are fora for pledging of food aid (in volume terms), but they do not as such handle food aid. This is left to individual donors, who decide on how to allocate their pledges. The EU made a commitment of 1.3 million tons a year in wheat equivalent, representing 30 per cent of total global commitments of 4.2 million tons under the 1967 FAC. The EU divides its FAC commitment into two parts: the so-called Community Action Food Aid Programme, and the national action programmes in each member state.

Part III

Economic perspectives on aid design

9 Using aid to reduce poverty

*John Healey and Tony Killick**

Introduction

This chapter sets out to describe and analyse attempts by aid donors to use their assistance for poverty reduction (PR), against an assessment of the current state of knowledge concerning poverty in developing countries. The two following sections present brief surveys of the state of knowledge on the nature of poverty and on the effectiveness of policies for combating this, and draw out potential implications for donors and for the remainder of this paper. A section then describes and evaluates the objectives and records of donors. The limited evidence on the effectiveness of past donor PR interventions is then examined and a final section concludes by suggesting ways of increasing the PR effectiveness of aid.

The nature of poverty

If aid interventions are to contribute effectively to the reduction of poverty they need to be firmly grounded in an understanding of the nature of the problems addressed. This section presents a set of propositions which summarise our understanding of the contemporary state of knowledge of the nature and causes of poverty in developing countries. Some of these are fairly trite; others perhaps less so.

Poverty is multi-dimensional

Material deprivation is at the core of poverty. This includes low income and consumption levels, leading to poor food and poor nutritional status; inadequate clothing and housing; and substandard access to health and schooling. It also includes deficient command over productive assets, both material (land, equipment and other inputs) and human (education, training, health). Vulnerability and resulting insecurity are further characteristics, aggravated by inability to make provision against emergencies: vulnerability to droughts, floods and other natural disasters; to human disasters such as the death or illness of a bread-winner, as well as war and civil disturbance; and to economic phenomena such as inflation or market collapses.

Poverty has important less material aspects too. Among these is dependency, e.g. arising from unequal relationships between landlord and tenant, debtor and creditor, worker and employer, man and woman. A further relational dimension is labelled as social exclusion, referring to inferior access to state services and other collective provisions; inferior access to the labour market (resulting in low mobility, low security of employment and particularly high risk of unemployment); inferior opportunities for participation in social life and collective decision-making; lack of decision-making power. Hopelessness, alienation and passivity are thus common among those living in poverty. Finally, we should record the socially relative nature of poverty. People can be said to be poor when they are unable to attain the level of well-being regarded by society as constituting a reasonable minimum. Poverty thus relates to an individual's (or family's) standing in society and to her or his self-esteem. 'Absolute' measures of poverty are thus insufficient because they ignore this societal context.

Alternative conceptualisations yield differing inferences

While there is no serious disagreement anywhere that poverty is a multifaceted state of deprivation, nor that it cannot be wholly divorced from its social context, there remain considerable disagreements about where the balance should be struck, particularly as between income- or consumption-based measurements and other indicators, and between absolute (objective) and relative (subjective) conceptualisations, with substantially differing policy conclusions being drawn by the protagonists. Questions of definition and measurement cannot be divorced from issues of policy. Advocates of income-based approaches, for example, place more reliance on the indirect benefits of policies for accelerating economic growth, while those stressing basic needs often favour more direct pro-poor interventions. Different approaches are varyingly sensitive to successful PR policy interventions. Thus, it is complained about income or consumption-based 'head-count' measures of poverty (which record the proportion of a population living below a poverty line) that they are not very useful for identifying specific groups to target for policy purposes, and that agencies given the task of reducing head-count poverty may be tempted to neglect the particularly difficult plight of the very poor.

Similarly, those identified as poor differ appreciably according to the definition used. One study of the Côte d'Ivoire (Glewwe and van der Gaag 1990) applied varying definitions, confined to material and other objective indicators, to the same set of data and found that they did not choose the same people, even though all definitions were set so that a fixed proportion of people were classified as poor. The disparities would surely have been even greater had the range of definitions employed included the more subjective indicators of dependency, insecurity and social exclusion. This presumption is strengthened by 'Jodha's paradox', derived from a study of two Indian villages between 1964 and 1984 (Jodha 1989). Objective measures showed that real incomes had declined during these 20 years, but when villagers whose incomes had declined were asked about their well-being they reported their situation as having improved, citing decreased dependence on low-pay jobs and on patrons and landlords, improved mobility, and better consumption patterns.

However, one should not exaggerate the extent of the differences. Although they did identify materially different poverty groups, most of the Glewwe–van der Gaag definitions were quite strongly correlated with each other. More generally, the subjectively-based participatory approaches to poverty identification, while yielding valuable additional insights of their own, produce results consistent with those of household expenditure surveys, with the poor stressing the importance of access to jobs and assets such as land and education – all income-related. Similarly, there is broad correlation between the cross-country results of income-based poverty line measures and the human poverty index developed by the UNDP which excludes income variables, particularly for Southern Asia and sub-Saharan Africa, although there are important differences too (UNDP 1997b).

The poor are heterogeneous

It is almost always misleading to talk of 'the poor' as a single category of people. Poverty affects various socio-economic groups and policy measures are likely to affect these groups differentially. A major distinction is between urban and rural poverty. Most of the poor of developing countries live in rural communities but the share of urban poverty is rising. Among the urban poor, it is useful to distinguish between the working poor and the unemployed. Within the rural population, we can similarly differentiate between those who or do not have land; and, among those who do, between those who participate in the production of cash crops and those who are exclusively food farmers; and, among the latter, between those who produce a surplus for sale and those who are net food importers.

Two other important differentials are those between temporary and permanent poverty, and between poverty and destitution. On the first, there is evidence (mainly based on income-based measurements) of substantial mobility in and out of poverty. A study of Pakistan found very few households remained poor (or non-poor) throughout the three-year period studied (Alderman and Garcia 1993); a study of Côte d'Ivoire found comparably high mobility (Grootaert and Kanbur 1995). It seems that the incidence of permanent poverty is much lower than of total poverty. On the other hand, the distinction between poverty and destitution (or between the poor and the poorest) turns on whether an individual or household has sufficient resources and capacity to function in a sustainable way, albeit at a sub-standard level. It is far harder to reach and assist the destitute than the less disadvantaged poor.

Regularly recurring causes of poverty

Despite the above heterogeneity, there are regularly recurring causes of poverty, which can be organised under three headings: (i) low income and productivity, (ii) socio-political factors and (iii) inequalities. As regards income and productivity, since the growth of average income is the domin- ant influence on trends in poverty, it follows that poverty is substantially a function of the inadequacy of income (and therefore productivity), partic- ularly in agriculture and other rural activities, and in the urban informal sector. The poor have inadequate access to educational and other economic and social services, leaving them with few modern skills. Largely as a result of this, the assets of the poor have low productivity, partly reflecting weak ability to participate in modern production processes and little access to formal sector credit.

Under the heading of socio-political factors, economic dependency is a factor perpetuating poverty, i.e. a concentration of the un- and under- employed in poor households, and exceptionally large family sizes, result- ing in heavy child dependency. Political fragmentation and civil strife are other potent forces. There is also the issue of power. The poor have little market power and this, in combination with often undemocratic political structures and limited governmental accountability, feeds into weak political power, resulting in the neglect of agriculture and other pro-urban policy biases, and low priorities for anti-poverty measures. Additionally, political traditions are often centrist, top-down, excluding participation of the poor even in programmes intended to assist them.

As regards the influence of inequalities, the basic point is obvious: for a given total national income the amount of poverty will be a rising function of the degree of inequality. Measures of inequality typically show high levels in many African and Latin American countries, with a more mixed picture in Asia. Capital-intensive growth paths, with a corresponding weak growth in the volume of formal-sector employment, perpetuate poverty because access to employment is of enormous importance to the poor, both as a direct source of income and as the basis of the urban-to-rural remittances upon which so many (often female-headed) poor rural households rely to augment their incomes.

Inequalities within households are a further aspect. These often dis- advantage women, who frequently have fewer rights to productive resources and household income, are expected to shoulder a disproportionate share of household work, have lower consumption standards, suffer from greater insecurity and dependency, and have often inferior participation in household decision-making. In consequence, the gender dimension of poverty is now universally accepted as requiring special attention.

What could donors do?

Given that most donors have now embraced poverty reduction as a prime goal, albeit with varying degrees of enthusiasm, what policies and specific interventions might they adopt for this purpose? Here again, the following paragraphs are intended to reflect the existing consensus.

Promote economic growth

External funds, skills and influence can support faster economic growth. This includes efforts to support improved policies for macroeconomic management and for what has become known as 'structural adjustment'. Evidence suggests that foreign aid flows assist growth most effectively where the policy environment is appropriate, but that the aid itself has limited revealed ability to influence the quality of policies.

Recognise that growth is often not enough

Most cross-country econometric studies that decompose the influences of growth and income distribution on poverty find that growth dominates. A rough rule of thumb is that growth 'explains' about half of all changes in poverty. Either growth is associated with improved or unchanged income distributions or, if inequality increases, this generally does not happen at a sufficient rate to cancel out the PR benefits of growth. Moreover, growth expands the revenue base of the government and thus enhances its ability to execute directly poverty-reducing measures. However, the power of growth to reduce poverty is strongly influenced by where it occurs, both geographically (e.g. whether it is urban- or rural-based) and sectorally (e.g. agriculture *vis-à-vis* industry; labour- versus capital-intensive). Moreover, growth has a weaker poverty-reducing effect when initial inequalities are large (as is the case in much of Africa and Latin America) and when prospective growth rates are likely to be low (especially in sub-Saharan Africa). Hence, accelerated growth in Africa (the only major region where poverty is a proportionately increasing problem) is unlikely to bring satisfactory improvements in poverty (World Bank 1996a and Demery and Walton 1998). Note also that growth does not necessarily do anything to reduce the non-material dimensions of poverty.

The limitations of growth as a means of reducing poverty have led to consideration of how it could be made more labour-intensive and pro-poor. Orthodoxy on this looks to the avoidance of large macroeconomic disequilibria (particularly rapid inflation, against which many of the poor are unable to protect themselves); the promotion of export growth (which the evidence suggests would produce particularly strong anti-poverty responses); the promotion of other sectors likely to bring particularly large benefits to the poor, most notably in the area of rural development; and measures to improve the efficiency of factor markets, particularly to remove distortions which make capital cheap relative to labour, accompanied by 'structural' measures to raise the, often slight, responsiveness of employment to changes in factor-price relativities.

Redistributive measures desirable

The power of economic growth to reduce poverty will be enhanced if, in the face of major inequalities, there is an initial redistribution of assets and incomes in favour of the poor and if growth is accompanied by further redistributive measures. There are, however, constraints on what can be achieved by this route. To some extent, these limits are defined by the revenue base of many developing country governments, because the most direct poverty-reducing policy instruments available to them – e.g. education, health, transfer payments and other social service provisions – demand large resources if they are to reach most of the poor. Political constraints are likely to be more fundamental, however, limiting what the state can do through tax-and-spend policies and by asset redistribution measures such as land reforms.

Blend direct and indirect measures

This largely follows from the two propositions above. Growth- or productivity-promoting measures can be thought of as indirect PR measures; redistributive measures are obviously direct. As already suggested in relation to Africa, growth-promoting measures will often not alone result in an acceptable rate of poverty improvement, so redistributive measures will also be required. There is an even wider range of circumstances where, given the practical constraints, redistribution alone will not be able to achieve desired results. The best hope, then, lies in striking a balance between the 'trickle-down' effects of growth and more direct approaches to improving the resources, security and empowerment of the poor.

Donor interventions

External agencies can make specific poverty-focused interventions. These can be targeted to benefit identified poor groups directly and exclusively. More widely targeted programmes can be designed to provide the poor with a disproportionate share of benefits. These include sector-wide approaches as yet largely untested in PR terms. Donors can also act as innovators in PR approaches through specific interventions since, with their greater resources and ability to take risks, they can support pilot ventures. These can establish approaches and activities which, if successful, can be 'scaled up' and replicated by domestic authorities. Donors can also help to improve domestic institutions – particularly central, regional and local administrative systems – and their capabilities for design and implementation of the needs of poor groups. They can also contribute to the reform of the political system to make it more accountable and responsive to the needs of poor people, while changes in law and practice can reduce the degree of exclusion and discrimination against vulnerable groups such as women or minority ethnic groups.

Mixed experience with direct measures

Studies that attempt to identify the beneficiaries of state-provided social services find in most cases that the richest participate proportionately more than the poorest. Social services tend to be poorly targeted at the poor, although educational and health benefits still have some egalitarian tendency because they are more important to the poor than to the rich, relative to income.

Employment-creation (e.g. public works) programmes have a particularly poor record, with only a small net creation of wage employment, major leakages of public resources to unintended beneficiaries such as contractors, and a tendency to exclude the poorest and women. A common part of the problem is a top-down approach to programme design and execution, with minimal beneficiary participation. Similarly negative conclusions are reached about food-for-work programmes (discussed in Chapter 8 in this volume).

Micro-credit institutions and schemes aimed at the poor can bring real benefits. Micro-credit schemes can graduate rural households out of poverty, by injecting capital to generate a virtuous circle from low income, credit and investment, to more income, more credit, more investment. Well-designed lending programmes, like those of the Grameen Bank, have been successful in improving the incomes of poor people, moving a substantial number of households above the poverty line, although it has been suggested that the income-generating credits have not been 'scale neutral' and that they have failed to promote sustained growth of income in the long run. They are most likely to be useful for 'middle and upper' poor households; the destitute require a more comprehensive approach to financial service provision. In Chapter 14, financial sector aid is discussed at more length. There are also doubts about the transferability of projects like the Grameen Bank in different social situations.

A variety of safety-net instruments has been employed in recent years, particularly in attempts to reduce the negative effects of adjustment programmes: targeted subsidies and transfers of various kinds; employment-creation and retraining schemes; special infrastructural development schemes in poor areas. These have made little impression, however. They have generally reached only a small fraction of the poor, being too small and poorly targeted, although they have created useful infrastructure, albeit on a small scale. Another source of weakness is that safety nets tend to be add-ons, not built into broader programme provisions, and there is often a tension among the objectives of safety net provisions, between using them to assist those in poverty or to compensate politically powerful groups who stand to lose from adjustment measures.

In sum, therefore, the apparent simplicity of direct measures is misleading. They can bring real benefits, and there is surely scope for doing better in the future, but not too much should be expected of them.

Targeting sometimes appropriate

Those who would provide state services to raise the welfare of the poor, say, with food subsidies, must choose between universal provision or targeting on defined poverty groups. There is a strong case in principle for a targeted approach. Targeting sets boundaries around the extent of the government's commitment and safeguards against the tendency for the relatively well-to-do to capture a disproportionate share of universal benefits.

There are, however, some important contrary considerations. One is that targeting distorts incentives, encouraging the ineligible to misreport their incomes (or whatever other characteristic the benefit is targeted on) in order to take advantage of the subsidy, and quite possibly discouraging people from improving their earnings in ways that would raise them from the eligible to ineligible category. Another is the potentially high cost of administering a targeted scheme; the narrower the target group the higher the per-beneficiary costs of executing and policing. There are also practical problems with defining target groups in ways that are operationally feasible – a task made the more complicated by the often quite high short-term mobility of households in and out of poverty, reported earlier. A possible solution to some of these difficulties is to design schemes so as to be self-targeting on the poor, e.g. to confine food subsidies to 'inferior' (but nutritious) goods or to offer only low wages in employment-creation schemes.

Political considerations may also prompt caution in the use of targeting: confining benefits to the poor may alienate the not-so-poor, who are the more politically influential. The danger is that excluding this segment from benefits will breed opposition, undermining their willingness to pay taxes, distorting implementation of anti-poverty measures and generally undermining the sustainability of the provision. If the opposition engendered is great enough, it is possible that the end-result might actually be reduced provisions for the poor, as has happened in Colombia, Sri Lanka and other countries.

In short, the resource-rationing and egalitarian benefits of targeting need to be considered alongside its unfavourable practical and political ramifications. In a specific situation, a careful balance has to be struck between exclusivity and universality. Policies that have the greatest impact on poverty are not necessarily the most narrowly targeted ones. In striking this balance – indeed, in deciding whether targeting is worthwhile at all –

one key factor is the extent of poverty. If most are poor there is an only weak prima facie case for targeting. The smaller the proportion of the population who are poor the stronger is the case for it, especially if it is the permanently poor and/or the destitute who are the main target. In such situations, it is for the government to manage the political resistance to directed assistance, which places the strength of the government's own determination at centre stage.

Some measures are doubly blessed

Some measures are doubly blessed because they bring both direct and indirect (pro-growth) benefits. Included here are the provision of education (especially primary) and training, as well as preventive health measures. Access to good quality education and health is of the greatest importance to the poor in raising their income-earning potential and combating various other dimensions of poverty. This draws attention to the crucial importance of government expenditure priorities. Rural development policies, addressed both to raising agricultural productivity and off-farm sources of income, are also likely to enhance both output growth and PR, subject to a similar caveat that they need to be designed so as to benefit poor small holders and the landless.

In some countries land reform, a way of utilising underemployed and usually poor labour for more intensive cultivation of land, can similarly benefit both output and poverty, although the outcome depends crucially on country circumstances and on how well the change of ownership is managed. In the macroeconomic area, measures which correct distortions in relative prices that have led to capital-intensive growth are also highly desirable, for it is hard to exaggerate the importance to the poor of access to jobs.

Working through others

Donors will almost always have to operate through others. The main candidate is usually the recipient government. Donors are used to dealing with governments and it is important that they should do so. Working through governments is desirable because of the importance of local 'owner-ship' for successful implementation, especially in face of the essentially political nature of the PR task. It is hence important that donors engage in constructive policy dialogue with recipient governments in this area. However, because of the importance of the state in the PR task, there are limits on what donors can achieve when governments are indifferent – a not infrequent situation – and probably little scope for effective action when the government is actually hostile.

Working through central government is not the only possibility, however. Depending on the local political system and the realities of power within it, donors can also work through local government agencies, who are closer to the problems. There should be particular scope within federal systems. Another, already quite widely practised, possibility is to work through charities and other NGOs, both local and from the donor country. NGOs have a proven record of working successfully with poverty groups because they are closer to the problems, are more likely to adopt participative approaches to the design and execution of their programmes, and often have stronger anti-poverty motivation than official agencies. NGOs offer a way of operating in countries with an unsupportive political climate. This modality has limitations, however. Many NGOs are essentially ameliorative and often have a quite narrow remit, not geared to tackling the causes of the poverty they address, although others are active campaigners against the status quo. A few are opportunistic, existing largely because of the availability of donor and private monies. It is also difficult to channel large sums of assistance through NGOs without changing their nature, diminishing their grassroots credibility and other advantages. NGOs therefore do not offer a satisfactory substitute for a sympathetic government.

Against the above background on donor options, we turn now to examine the policies and experiences of various donors.

Donor approaches in the 1990s

Revival of the poverty objective

After an upsurge of interest in the poverty problem in the 1970s, attention shifted in the 1980s to a preoccupation with macroeconomic stabilisation and then issues of economic efficiency and market reform. The 1990s have seen poverty reduction restored to the main agenda. Thanks to its highly influential 1990 *World Development Report,* on the theme of poverty, the World Bank (1990a) took the lead. Its three-pronged pro-poor operational strategy formed a benchmark for other donors.

The first prong was to be the pursuit of labour-intensive or broad-based policies that would generate a pattern of growth in which the poor would participate more fully. Particularly favoured here were market reforms that eliminated bias against unskilled labour and removed discrimination in markets against small-scale producers (especially women) and improved incentives for them. Second, the intention was to create assets for poor people to improve their productivity, especially by investing in their human development, mainly through greater access to primary education and health, preventive health, nutrition and other basic services. Third, for those who could not take advantage of these policies, there should be safety-net measures, especially for the old and disabled and those temporarily affected by shocks and adjustment measures.

Is there now a consensus among donors (bilateral and multilateral) on the importance of poverty reduction? An important landmark was a general commitment by the major donors to international targets to reduce poverty by half by the year 2015, as well as certain sub-targets, set out in OECD (1996a), although there are differences among donors about the priority given to this. For some, PR is an overarching goal, for others it is one goal among several; and there remain some (like France, Italy and Spain) who have no explicit PR objectives. Virtually all donors now give prominence in their public pronouncements to the reduction of gender discrimination and the importance of gender sensitivity for PR.

There is now wide acknowledgement of the importance for the poor of services such as primary health care and education, drinking water and sanitation. Some donors explicitly favour efforts to reorient public expenditures in favour of basic services, as well as providing financial support directly or via counterpart funds. And various donors have adopted the 1995 *World Social Summit* commitment to devote 20 per cent of their aid budgets to basic services which benefit the poor disproportionately (UN 1995a). In other respects, however, donors show limited interest in redistributive fiscal policies, even in public policy statements, although some favour higher user charges for tertiary services, such as higher education, which largely benefit the less poor, and support the principle that the poor should not be required to pay user charges for basic services. Very few donors face up to the issue of more egalitarian access to land or natural resources, yet there is increasing evidence that the higher the initial inequality in countries the more constrained is the speed of poverty reduction from growth.

What now of the actual record of donors in the PR field, as distinct from what they say their policies are? Information is not easily available on country operations and the impact of donor interventions on the poor. While we are able to draw on the previously mentioned results of the Europe-wide study (Cox *et al.* 2000), other donors are not adequately covered because of a dearth of independent research and limited donor evaluation studies. The following therefore largely concentrates on the donor agencies of the EU countries, augmented by information provided by the World Bank.

Poverty understanding of donors

To take first the World Bank, its Poverty Assessments (PAs) have become the main source of information about poverty used by donors in-country. Despite delays, the number of PA's completed and their quality has improved in the 1990s. Participatory analysis surveys have given a better understanding of the needs of the poor (especially in Africa) and new information has been obtained about which income groups benefit from public expenditures.

However, marked weaknesses and variability in quality remain (Toye and Jackson 1996 and Hanmer *et al.* 1996), especially in sub-Saharan Africa, where the conceptual framework for addressing the poverty problem is particularly problematical. The World Bank's approach to the measurement of poverty is seen as too dominated by a quantitative income approach which takes insufficient account of the personal characteristics of the poor, the household as a unit (especially in subsistence activities), gender relations and the social context. Poverty Assessment coverage of asset distribution is seen as weak and there is inadequate focus on socio-economic groups and the structure of poverty. A perceived lack of attention to structural and institutional aspects affecting poverty, results in fewer operationally relevant conclusions. Furthermore, the link between descriptions of poverty situations and policy recommendations is considered weak, particularly in establishing links between micro and macro measures. The analyses are criticised as lacking a historical–cultural context and as insufficiently aware of the political dynamics that constrain structural and policy changes.

Whatever the limitations of the World Bank approach, European donors have gone much less far in conceptualising and analysing poverty, and formulating pro-poor policies. They have done little in-depth analysis, although they may sometimes assist in strengthening local capacities for this purpose. Sometimes, but not always, they use World Bank data.

Donor strategies for poverty reduction

Starting again with the World Bank, in 1996 a task force pointed to considerable weakness in the World Bank's Country Assistance Strategies for most sub-Saharan African countries. There appears to have been no clear perspective, objectives or strategic vision, with little emphasis given to PR *per se* or to specific actions that might benefit the poor (World Bank 1996a: 53). It is not clear whether these criticisms hold equally for other regions. Independent analysts have also been critical of World Bank country policy and programme assessments in Africa, observing that few operational conclusions seemed to stem from the characterisation of poverty and much pro-poor content is lost between initial poverty assessments and the implementation of lending programmes. Criticisms centred on pre-occupation with macroeconomic policy, lack of clarity about how labour-intensive growth can be achieved, inadequate attention to institutional and market structures, and too little attention to measures to reinforce the over-stretched network of support in communities or to safety nets. However, recently increased efforts have been made by the central management of the World Bank and the Poverty and Gender Network (PREM) to strengthen the poverty orientation of country assistance strategies.

European donors who use the country strategy and programming instrument and which have a global PR strategy also often do not have a well formulated poverty-focused content. Examination of the country operations of seven of the principal European donor agencies in a total of seven poor countries revealed the following broad characteristics:

- Contrary to headquarters' statements of support for the value of participatory approaches and local ownership, country strategies were usually drawn up by donors in a 'top-down' way, with little consultation within the recipient country.
- Donors rarely established clear prioritisation between PR, other development objectives and (often conflicting) commercial objectives.
- Strategies were sometimes too vague to provide operational guidance and did not provide sufficient benchmarks for judgement about performance in implementation.
- The link between donor interventions and their PR objectives was usually weak.
- There was very limited cooperation on PR between European donors (sometimes not even exchange of information), although there was some co-operation with the World Bank.
- Although some donors are introducing a sector approach instead of *ad hoc* projects, there is limited evidence yet that sectoral approaches have substantially or successfully incorporated poverty objectives.

There was, in other words, a rather large gap between the headquarters' statements described above and the reality in recipient countries. Changes are occurring, however. The European Commission has recently circulated guidance on how to incorporate PR objectives into its country programming, and Germany, Ireland, Sweden and the United Kingdom (since 1998) are donors who have undertaken measures to integrate PR goals into country programming.

Donor–government poverty-related dialogue

Here again there is a large rhetoric–reality gap. The World Bank's poverty-focused adjustment operations are defined as those which eliminate distortions and regulations, that limit income-generating opportunities for the poor, that reallocate public expenditures in favour of the poor, support safety nets and assist in data and analytical work on poverty. On these criteria, about half of the World Bank's structural and sectoral adjustment loans had a poverty orientation (24 out of 49 in 1992–3 and 14 out of 27 in 1995). The World Bank has increased the proportion of policy conditions in its adjustment operations intended to protect or raise expenditure in the social sectors to benefit the poor (from 18 per cent in 1988–90 to 42 per cent in 1992–5). However, these conditions are normally monitored by observation of budget estimates which, however, do not necessarily reflect actual spending patterns.

With some exceptions, European donors agencies have had little meaningful bilateral dialogue with recipient governments at the national or macro level on poverty policies, nor have they worked together collectively to seek a consensus on an appropriate 'single strategy'. Where national commitment to pro-poor positions has not been strong, donors have sought pro-poor alliances at intermediate levels of government, for example in line Ministries. Consultative groups and consortia have proved more effective vehicles for sectoral than for national level dialogue but have not focused much on the poor. Conditionality has rarely been applied in favour of pro-poor policy change, with most donors considering that domestic ownership of such strategies is the only way forward. This means that external pressures can only be applied through their criteria for selection or non-selection of partners for support, and by engaging in local dialogue.

Donor poverty reduction portfolios

There were some shifts in the World Bank's portfolio during 1992–5, partly in a pro-poor direction. The proportion of (annual) aid commitments for poverty targeted interventions (PTIs) rose from 18 per cent to 24 per cent in the World Bank as a whole but remained static at 28 per cent for the IDA during this period. Interventions with specific mechanisms for targeting the poor, which are usually participatory and community based, remained limited (in 1995 only one out of 24 of the PTIs in sub-Saharan Africa and three out of eight in South Asia.). During 1993–5 there was an increase in the proportion of spending commitments for primary education, while the proportion of social sector interventions aimed at women and girls also rose. The percentage of funds targeted on poor farmers for improvement of agricultural productivity also increased. However, over the same period, programme composition in sub-Saharan Africa did not always shift in a pro-poor direction. There was still limited agricultural assistance and little of it was targeted and there was a further decline in rural spending on water and roads.

Most European donors do not publish information on specific poverty-focused interventions. No agencies publish the pattern of their operations for individual recipient countries. None the less, available information suggests that, notwithstanding their stated objectives, the European agencies' role in PR is modest, measured by the share of specific poverty-focused interventions in total bilateral aid portfolios. The share for the Netherlands in 1994–5 was 19 per cent, while for the United Kingdom those projects with a direct (targeted) poverty focus accounted for 11 per cent of classified expenditure during 1995–6 to 1996–7. Germany provides technical co-operation for self-help projects which have a mainly PR focus and the share of expenditure on this mode rose from 8 per cent in 1991 to 19 per cent in 1995. It is estimated that poverty-focused expenditures by Italy were a mere 7 per cent of total grant aid in 1995. It is unlikely that the proportions were significant for France or Spain.

Commitments for basic education and health can be used as a proxy for anti-poverty orientation. Incomplete information indicates that as a proportion of their total bilateral commitments (unweighted average), OECD

Table 9.1 Estimated share of PR interventions in country portfolios of major EU donors, 1997

	Directly PR targeted	*Indirectly PR targeted*[a]	*Other interventions*	*Total*
India	21.0	30.0	49.0	100.0
Zambia	3.0	23.0	74.0	100.0
Zimbabwe	9.0	31.0	60.0	100.0

Source: Cox *et al.* (2000).
Note: [a]By 'indirect' is meant interventions for which it is reasonable to expect a substantial proportion of poor beneficiaries to be included although the interventions are not targeted directly on poor communities.

bilateral donors' contributions to basic education were negligible in 1990 and even by 1996 constituted less than 3 per cent of total aid. For basic health care, nutrition, infectious disease control and health education, the picture was similar (under 3 per cent usually), although some agencies achieved considerably higher levels. Among the multilateral agencies, only the World Bank's IDA window appears to have achieved a high commitment (over 10 per cent) in recent years. Overall, the effort appears very modest.

Systematic information on the balance of pro-poor interventions is scarce but a few country cases give some idea, summarised in Table 9.1. In Zambia the European donors gave low priority to interventions focused on PR, although the proportions ranged from 54 per cent (Finland) to 5 per cent (United Kingdom). In Zimbabwe too only a few projects were directly targeted on the poor, although adding in the 'indirectly targeted' interventions raised the overall average to 40 per cent, again with considerable variations across donors. There was a stronger poverty orientation in India and a rising trend over time. The large variations between agencies in the same country and across different countries suggests that there is ample scope for donors to increase the PR share of their country programmes.

Assessing donors' practices in poverty reduction

How do the activities of donors relate to the best practices on targeting, participation and gender? To take first the World Bank, the majority of its PR interventions have been indirectly targeted – providing basic services where the poor are assumed to benefit disproportionately. Direct targeting has been fairly slight, adopted in countries where poverty is rather isolated, geographically concentrated, well understood and a government with the capacity to use targeting mechanisms, e.g. for social services in unserved and tribal areas, and improved sanitation, drainage and water supplies in poor urban areas. Targeting is mainly based on location, with about half targeting the poor in agricultural and rural development projects.

As regards participatory approaches, according to the World Bank (1996a: 28), about 40 per cent of projects approved in 1995 involved the participation of people who would be directly affected and an additional 14 per cent of projects included participation by NGOs or other interest groups. A study of 67 IDA projects by Carvalho and White (1996), concluded that the early 1990s saw more World Bank projects seeking systematically to involve beneficiaries or stakeholders in project design and implementation. However, the information they provide suggests that, while more than half of the health family, planning and nutrition interventions utilised participatory approaches, this approach was employed in only a minority of primary and secondary education programmes. World Bank projects for extension services were judged to have reached a much higher proportion of women farmers than was true of government schemes (e.g. in Gambia).

For European donors there is independent evidence from the study by Cox *et al.* (2000). The 90 projects and programmes selected for examination in this investigation were largely those which the donors themselves considered to have a particular poverty focus. They were not, therefore, a random sample. Concerning targeting, out of the projects for which information was available, 38 per cent revealed no particular attempt to target benefits on the poor. Only 21 per cent of projects were closely targeted on the poor, with a third showing a moderate level of targeting.

What determines the balance between direct targeting and broader based interventions in a country? The World Bank undertook few narrowly targeted projects, which may have reflected bias in their poverty assessments or their concern about the intensity of staff inputs and time involved. The European bilateral donors did not seem to have had a clear strategy on this issue. They were poor both at identifying clearly defined groups of poor people and at designing interventions to focus on such groups.

When examined for participation and gender sensitivity, about half of European interventions demonstrated moderate levels of participation by poor groups with a further fifth showing high levels of participation. Participation at the particularly important identification and design phase was weaker than at the implementation stage. It was often difficult to determine the extent to which gender relations had informed project design and implementation. Nearly two-thirds of this sample of projects paid attention to gender relations although in only a fifth was this thorough. Gender has probably enjoyed an increasing profile over time, in the newer projects. No individual agency emerged as leader in this area.

Effectiveness and impact

How much difference have the donors made to the welfare of the poor in practice? The evidence here is particularly weak, because most donors' monitoring and evaluation systems have not given much attention to the distributional impact of interventions. For the World Bank, there has been evaluation of the performance ratings of 67 IDA poverty reduction projects approved in 1988–90. As a group, these had better ratings than other projects, in terms of achievement of objectives and overcoming problems of implementation (World Bank 1996a). There were some cases of model PR projects, such as IDA's national leprosy elimination programme in India, which, although in its early stages, already manifested clear impact in reducing infection among poor people. The latest evaluation for pro-grammes in 1995 concludes that progress has been made in reducing poverty but that the gains are modest when set against the challenge (Morra and Thumm 1997).

European agencies have very little evidence on the effects of their interventions on poor people. Impressionistic evidence from the European comparative research project suggested that nearly three-quarters of all the selected PR interventions had brought, or were likely to bring, some benefits to the poor. Of these, a quarter were judged likely to have a large impact. If these judgements were correct, donor PR interventions were far from having being a failure. However, the figures also underlined the consider-able scope for improvement, given that a quarter of the projects were thought to have had a negligible impact on the welfare of the poor, even though the projects studied were those selected by donors as having a poverty orientation.

It was possible to judge different elements in the overall judgement of impact: the extent to which the poor benefited from improvements in their livelihoods, from improved access to resources, from enhanced knowledge and skills, and improved rights and empowerment. Table 9.2 presents evidence on more than 70 European projects.

As can be seen, the greatest impact was through increased access of the poor to resources: over 90 per cent of all sample interventions contributed in some degree to access to resources. Projects were also judged to have made a significant impact on levels of knowledge. Nearly a third of all projects were regarded as having substantially raised levels of knowledge and skills, and only a fifth as having made no contribution at all. However, under a quarter of projects were viewed as making a large contribution to increasing livelihoods, with two-fifths making no impact. Unsurprisingly, given the difficulties external agencies are bound to experience in such sensitive areas, the record was the weakest in relation to enhancement of the rights of the poor, with only about one project in seven thought to have empowered the poor substantially, although half of the projects were judged to make some contribution.

What explained these variations in the degree of impact? Although there was considerable variation between countries, the sample was not large enough to test whether country context was a dominant influence. How-ever, impact emerged as positively associated with the degree of targeting, as did the use of participatory approaches (see Table 9.3). Other possible influences not systematically confirmed were the degree of past experience

Table 9.2 Nature of impact of poverty (per cent of observations in each class)

	Size of impact			Sample (no. of projects)
	Large	Moderate	Negligible	
Overall impact	25.0	48.0	27.0	73
Livelihoods	24.0	36.0	40.0	72
Resources	34.0	57.0	9.0	77
Knowledge	31.0	49.0	20.0	71
Rights[a]	15.0	51.0	33.0	72

Source: Cox *et al.* (2000).
Note: [a]Numbers do not add to 100.0 due to rounding.

Table 9.3 Impact related to degree of direct and indirect targeting (per cent)

	Type of poverty orientation		
	Direct	Indirect[a]	Other
Degree of impact			
High	73.3	16.1	7.7
Moderate	26.7	71.1	34.6
Negligible	0.0	12.9	57.7
Total	100.0	100.0	100.0

Source: Cox *et al.* (2000).
Notes: 17 interventions for which data were unavailable were excluded, leaving 72 observations.
[a]Numbers do not add to 100.0 due to rounding.

of the donor in the country and the shortness of the gestation period of projects.

Several donors have decided to switch to more sector-wide approaches for their PR interventions because of problems with *ad hoc* project approaches. The problems of projects include the heavy demands they make on donor skills, the tendency for donors to pursue a 'hands-on' management approach and off-budget support plus the difficulties of sustainability when the wider context is unfavourable. While sector approaches offer scope for greater domestic ownership and wider approaches, there is as yet little evidence on sectoral approaches designed to benefit the poor. European agencies' support for sector interventions in India have so far proved encouraging. Here, local ownership was important. In Africa the record so far has been much more mixed.

When we looked at the sustainability of the European interventions, the evidence suggested that most European donors only became concerned themselves with the sustainability of their interventions towards the middle of the 1990s. Overall, likely sustainability was low in African countries but more encouraging in India. Some problems arose from adverse budgetary conditions exogenous to the projects. Elsewhere, inherent weaknesses in design and excessive external management limited the scope not only for sustainability but also for replication or scaling-up, of which there was little evidence.

In sum, taking an overall view of donor aspirations, practices and results, there is, at least for the European donors on which we have reasonable evidence, a wide gap between their stated commitment to poverty reduction and actual practices in the field. Except for Germany, most have paid little attention to the conceptualisation and analysis of poverty, and have been particularly weak in the translation of the PR objective into operational guidance and through country assistance strategies. Their aid portfolios in poor countries have only a modest PR content, although that varies across donor and recipient. Their main instrument has been a series of *ad hoc* projects, including support for NGO projects. In these specific interventions they have made improvements over time in their approaches to participation by beneficiaries and gender sensitivity, although best-practice approaches are still rare and the evidence suggests that few donors have concerned themselves with sustainability, although there are exceptions. More positively, a high proportion of the PR projects which the European donors had initiated had brought benefits to poor people, chiefly by improving their access to income-raising resources. Nevertheless, the wider poverty issues have been rather neglected since the European donors have not had a worked-out approach to pro-poor strategies and policies and have been slow to engage recipient governments in policy dialogue on poverty issues. Poverty reduction only started to gain more dynamism in negotiation and implementation from about 1997.[1]

Conclusions: lessons and recommendations

Drawing both on the wider literature and on the experiences described above, what lessons and recommendations might be derived?

Perhaps the overriding inference to be drawn is that effective anti-poverty action *is* difficult to achieve. The problem is complex and location-specific. Its roots go deep into the social fabric and into the distribution of economic and political power. The resource and other practical constraints on effective intervention are considerable, and there is an ever present danger that provisions intended to raise the welfare of the poor will become captured by the less poor. Moreover, it is not obvious that foreign donor agencies have a comparative advantage in the PR area. There is a danger that, in a specific country context, they will not know enough about the local situation and its causes, will be too remote from local socio-political realities, will be too centralised and top-down, willing and able to devote too few manpower resources to the task. Against this, we have reported above a not negligible rate of success for donor specific PR interventions. Donors should not withdraw from PR but should be realistic about the severity of the difficulties they are likely to face and the scale of the effort needed if these are to be overcome. As ingredients of such an effort, the following guidelines can be suggested:

- In any specific country, donors need to have a clear *conceptualisation* of the nature of the poverty that they wish to redress and of the poverty groups they are seeking to aid. Recall here both the multi-dimensional nature of the problem and the heterogeneity of 'the poor'. In countries where poverty is endemic, a donor will have to make choices among poverty groups. The PR measures adopted should be consistent with the chosen view of the nature of the poverty problem, because of the connection between conceptualisation and choice of intervention.
- Actions which leave the *causes* of poverty largely untouched are unlikely to be effective in the long run. Indeed, any ameliorative effects might, at the political level, actually delay action upon causes.
- In most poor-country situations, reliance on the PR effects of growth alone will *not be enough*. There are still donor officials who argue that 'all our aid is poverty-reducing' because it is intended to raise economic efficiency and growth. We reported earlier that in many cases, especially in Africa, generalised growth is unlikely to result in satisfactory rates of PR and that the sectoral and factoral nature of the growth path is crucial to the impact of economic expansion on the welfare of the poor. This points away from aiding activities biased towards urban development, high-potential agriculture and capital intensity in favour of 'twice-blessed' interventions, such as the provision of primary educational and health services, and pro-smallholder rural development policies and promotion of non-traditional exports.
- The particular *style of intervention* makes a lot of difference to the probabilities of successful poverty reduction. It has long been recognised in the literature that programmes that include intended beneficiaries in the processes of design and delivery have a substantially better prospect of success than the mediocre record of standard top-down approaches, and that conclusion was reinforced by our own evidence on the experiences of European donors. The participatory approach is also desirable for its own sake, contributing to the empowerment, self-confidence and useful experience of target groups. This principle is also closely related to the desirability of local ownership.
- As regards *monitoring* and *evaluation*, because of the difficulties of reaching poverty groups, the resulting risks involved and the absence of any effective way of monitoring results in the absence of a special design, it is important that donor interventions should embody data collection and other modalities to permit outcomes to be monitored and subsequently evaluated.

A further major lesson is that effective PR requires careful *political management* but a lot of governments do not give this high priority. As was seen in the discussion of targeting, formidable political opposition can be ranged against PR measures, which therefore require careful management. This, in turn, means that governments need to be determined in their anti-poverty goals and to be willing to take risks in their furtherance. Unfortunately, some governments have proved indifferent, occasionally hostile, as argued in World Bank (1996a), with few African governments apparently giving high priority to PR; some exceptions are Uganda and Mozambique in the late 1990s. The practical implication of this for donors is the importance of *selectivity* in the choice of governments to assist.

When considering the issue of selectivity, we must recognise the fact of fungibility in the utilisation of aid resources. This has long been recognised as an important consideration but the evidence of this as a pervasive factor has recently been persuasively assembled by the World Bank (1998a: ch. 4). This report argues (p. 66) that 'aid is largely fungible' as between reducing taxation or increasing spending, as between consumption or development expenditures, and across particular categories of spending (see Chapter 15 for more on fungibility). We can link this factor with another, namely the demonstrated inability of policy conditionality to induce recipient governments to undertake measures they do not favour (Killick 1998a). Despite donor efforts to tie their assistance to preferred categories, governments can use the extra resources provided through development assistance largely as they choose, so that what difference aid makes depends on how recipient governments respond to the resources thereby provided. Ownership is all. To an important degree, aid finances a time-slice of a government's total spending.

At the same time, the policy environment has a pervasive influence on the well-being of the poor. So, in attempting to devote their assistance to the goal of PR what matters most crucially is that donors should choose as their partners those governments that share their concerns with the poverty problem, are anxious to adopt pro-poor policies and have the capacity to do so. A good many aid-receiving governments do not behave as if they give high priority to an attack on poverty, with those categories of state spending with the greatest potential for PR (education and health) often skewed in favour of middle-class beneficiaries. Selectivity in the choice of recipient governments is hence central to any serious attempt to shift the allocation of aid resources in favour of the poor. Are donors willing to withdraw support from governments that do not share their PR priority? To ask this question raises the familiar problem of donors' multiple motives in the allocation of aid.

The ineffectiveness of conditionality and the pervasiveness of fungibility also draw attention to the importance of policy dialogue with governments sympathetic, or at least not antipathetic, to the PR goal. On this, judging from the experience of the European donors, there is much unexploited scope for bilateral dialogue on poverty issues. Always subject to the overriding importance of local policy ownership, aid agencies need to do more of their own analysis to develop a well worked out view of what constitutes a pro-poor strategy for each recipient country. This is clearly most important where the partner is sympathetic but has no real PR strategy. To help the recipient to formulate a possible strategy ideally requires strengthening its technocratic capacity, which donors do not seem to have done systematically.

The pursuit of relationships of 'partnership' based on mutual commitment and ownership should be pursued preferably between all the agencies and not just bilaterally. The ultimate objective must be consensus among them on a single strategy for the country. There need to be institutional mechanisms through which such exchanges of views can be focused nationally (of course involving high-level political and societal involvement). While local ownership of PR policies and programmes is the key, the use of conditionality may be effective where there are pockets of domestic commitment in a more generally unsympathetic environment and where donor leverage can tip the balance among domestic policy makers in favour of reformists.

Field evidence shows that co-ordination between donors, even at the most basic level of information exchange, is given low priority (with a few exceptions like the UNDP). In part, this is related to donor levels of decentralisation and devolution since co-ordination is likely to be meaningful only when it reflects and influences local realities and is thus essentially a country-based activity. Since many donors have low staffing levels in-country or lack specialist skills, they may simply not have sufficient time or the right kind of knowledge.

As an instrument of consensus-building, as well as for a more coherent utilisation of aid resources, donors' country strategies and portfolios could become far more effective, through changes to both process and content. Possible improvements include:

- Agency personnel need to better understand the local cultural and historical context of poverty. Agencies should improve their own analytical capacity and co-operate more in supporting local research on poverty and pro-poor policy.
- Agencies should provide more assistance to recipient governments for the formulation and, even more importantly, the implementation and monitoring of pro-poor strategies.
- Agencies need to formulate more precisely their own country strategies for achieving PR, draw them up with wide local consultation processes and use them more effectively as a management instrument for PR.
- Agencies' contributions should complement government plans and budgets where these are genuinely pro-poor.
- Agencies' own country strategies should give clear operational guidance to programme managers for drawing up their portfolios and monitoring performance.

- The PR interventions could constitute a more substantial element of bilateral total portfolios, taking a share nearer to the 50 per cent which is the average that some European donors have achieved in India.

If the anti-poverty objective is to be given higher priority, the design of structural adjustment programmes should also be revisited. Of course, these are primarily intended to promote economic adaptation but there is an obligation, at the very least, to see that this is achieved at minimum costs to the poor. Although the anti-poverty effects of adjustment programmes have often been exaggerated, few of these programmes had been designed with the interests of the poor prominently in mind (Killick 1998b) and the IMF in particular still does not take seriously its own rhetoric about protecting the poor in the design of its programmes (Curto 1998).

Project interventions are unlikely alone to solve the problem of poverty reduction. Concern about the scale of impact of projects, their sustainability, and their skill and human-resource intensity for donors, has led some agencies to look to sector-wide approaches (see Chapter 7). These approaches can combine policy reform and institutional support as well as provision of substantial budgetary funds through the selected public sector organisations such as ministries of health or community development. In particular they can be designed to create a supportive policy environment for the delivery of services to clients, including the poor, and in this way to have wider potential impact than projects. However, this approach demands considerable changes in the behaviour of donors and recipient governments to be effective. First, donors need to work according to a locally owned strategy and follow a less 'hands-on' management style for projects than they have often pursued. Second, the sectoral approach requires provision of budget support, including perhaps recurrent budget funds in co-ordination with other donors. Third, donors need to follow flexible long-term approaches with partner governments who share the same poverty objectives. The major challenge is to ensure that attention to central administration reform does not undermine sensitivity to and focus on, the needs of the poor. Of course, where governments do not share the PR objective, fungibility robs choices between project or sectoral approaches of much of their meaning.

This brings us to the need for a strong conscious effort by donor organisations to ensure that the PR focus remains at the forefront throughout. Even among donors with explicit PR objectives, few seem to drive them operationally from the top. There is thus a need for better systems of management, guidance and incentives. The mechanisms for transmitting PR objectives to the field need strengthening. As the World Bank (1996a) has recorded, it is all too easy to start with good intentions but to have lost the PR focus by the time an intervention is executed. Even for donors that publicly embrace a PR goal, most provide weak operational guidance and inadequate training, yet PR remains a vague objective for many programme managers and is indeed a complex challenge. Only the World Bank and the German agencies seem partial exceptions to this generalisation.

Incentives for programme managers and their staff, or at least minimum disincentives, are vital to encourage them with the difficult problems of understanding poverty and designing effective PR interventions. Agencies often lack benchmarks for judging the PR performance of their managers, so that managers who make a more serious attempt to increase the poverty impact of their interventions may go unrecognised and unrewarded. Furthermore, an effective approach to PR is usually participatory, often benefiting from an extended phase of awareness-creation and institutional development prior to investment in physical infrastructure. Since such approaches are time consuming, this runs counter to another incentive characteristic of donor agencies, the need to disburse country aid budgets and often within an allotted time.

Notes

* The authors wish to thank Roli Asthana at Overseas Development Institute (ODI) for valuable research assistance, particularly in the preparation of materials for the poverty survey. Other sections draw mainly from material published by the World Bank and, for the European donors, from a synthesis of a major collaborative research study of their operations in seven poor countries (see Cox *et al.* 2000).

1 Since this chapter was completed, there has been a major OECD review of the PR policy and practices of all its members (OECD 1999b). The conclusions of this study do not differ greatly from those above. However, the study has led to follow-up work by the donors and the preparation of new guidelines to help strengthen the focus and effectiveness of donor country operations for PR. In addition there is a current (1999) review of the PR orientation of the World Bank's Country Assistance Strategies by its Operations Evaluation Department. Conclusions are not yet published but provisional results indicate that about two-thirds of these strategies cover all three elements of the three-pronged 1990 agenda and had a satisfactory 'relevance' rating for the content of their strategy. Performance was weaker on operations and particularly weak on monitoring the implementation of their PR operations.

10 Gender equality and foreign aid

Lisa Ann Richey

The advancement of women and the achievement of equality between women and men are a matter of human rights and a condition for social justice and should not be seen in isolation as a women's issue. They are the only way to build a sustainable, just and developed society. Empowerment of women and equality between women and men are prerequisites for achieving political, social, economic, cultural and environmental security among all peoples – Conference Platform for Action.

(UN 1995b: 19)

The commitment referred to in the Declaration, therefore, constitutes a general commitment to undertake meaningful implementation of the Platform's recommendations overall, rather than a specific commitment to implement each element of the Platform . . . As the United States has stated on a number of occasions . . . it cannot agree to an increase in funding for matters dealt with in the Platform for Action . . . .

(Reservations and Interpretive Statement submitted by the US delegation)
(UN 1995b: 173)

Introduction

In the heterogeneous and noisy world of development, described in Part I of this volume, it may be that countries where aid works best are those that need it least, and in countries where aid is most needed, it is difficult to implement and show 'success'. Gender is an area where achieving results from aid interventions is difficult, and when progress is made it is not easily measurable. However, gender and development, 'an area of great need, but small progress' (Longwe 1991), is a critical aspect of aid. It is often the very lack of 'successful' gender interventions that spur many mainstream policymakers and implementers to view gender relations as culture-specific or personal, and thus beyond the scope of foreign aid. Yet, it may be precisely these areas of inequality that are most in need of intervention.

This chapter examines a new goal of foreign aid – 'gender equality' – and a new means of achieving it – 'gender mainstreaming'. After placing gender and development in a historical context, I analyse why mainstreaming can be a problem for development interventions and what the implications are for foreign aid in the future. This work is an attempt to heed the call of feminist theorists of development, such as economist Diane Elson (1998), to 'stop talking only to ourselves' and initiate an engagement with those of the 'inside' of the policy process.[1]

In this work, I trace the emergence of 'gender' as a part of how we understand the development process and as a site for development interventions.[2] Without asserting that 30 years of academic and policy-oriented research has led to a clear identification of women's interests in development, I examine historically and ideologically differing formulations of 'the woman question', and their meanings for foreign aid. Gender objectives are important to development practices in their own right, but historically they have been taken into consideration for their role in shaping and being shaped by economic forces.[3]

Recognition that supposedly gender-neutral or gender-blind policies have significant gender impacts was an important step for policy development and implementation. To the extent that these interventions exacerbated existing inequalities between women and men, these were cause for concern among feminists. However, the greater concern for conventional development planners and practitioners was the ways in which gender outcomes inhibited the intended development goals.

As suggested by the first quotation introducing this chapter, women's 'equality' has become a widely accepted goal of development.[4] Equality is used to indicate two kinds of meaning: first, a kind of justice or fairness in treatment, and second, a notion of sameness, conformity and homogeneity. Equality in the sense of fairness is distinguished in feminist theory by using the term 'equity'. Achieving gender equity is understood through two antithetical poles of an absolute dichotomy: equality and 'difference'. Fraser (1997) defines gender equality as treating women exactly like men, while difference means treating women differently in so far as they are different from men.[5] Therefore, the common use of the concept of 'gender equality' in international development is equivalent to that of equity, and refers to both notions of equality and of difference. This chapter adopts the popularised use of equality in reference to goals of gender equity.

As the second introductory quote suggests, this goal of equality must be achieved within a context of increasing scepticism about the effectiveness of aid, coupled with decreasing resources for its implementation. It is important to understand how gender will be interpreted both conceptually and materially. What does it mean that gender equality has gone from the trenches of the women's movement to the discussions and documents of perhaps every development agency? Is it the case that feminist activists were 'right' all along and a realisation about the importance of gender has taken place in all corners of the development community, or is it that gender has come to mean something different over time and as it is incorporated into different contexts?

Women as a development constituency

Within development theory and aid interventions, there has been a constantly changing cast of approaches to the issue of women and development. The 'high turnover' in this conceptual realm may indicate both successes and failures of previous approaches. As assumptions about the roles women play in development have changed, the interventions designed to target them have adapted to new understandings. However, the strategies used within foreign aid as well as the goals for which they are used have not been consistent, and have even been at odds with each other. In the following, I trace in chronological order, the ways women have been considered to constitute a development constituency. The Appendix at the end of this chapter summarises policy approaches to women and development issues and their underlying assumptions about the relationships between gender, development, poverty and aid.

Women in Development (WID)

Women in Development (WID) approaches concerned themselves with adding women into the interventions aimed at promoting development. The following discussion analyses early approaches to women as part of a 'vulnerable group' – the earliest WID approach. Then, I discuss attempts at achieving women's equity, anti-poverty and efficiency within the development process. Finally, I briefly summarise the critiques of WID that led to a new generation of approaches.

Welfare approach to women as a vulnerable group

Historically, women have become a 'development' constituency through their bodies. In the colonial discourse, third world women were viewed as the embodiments of the exotic, as sex objects, and as the most backward members of a backward society (de Groot 1991, see also Mohanty 1991). Parpart notes that 'during the colonial period, missionaries, colonial officials, and settlers put forward a blend of information, imagination, pragmatic self-interest and prejudice to explain why third world women were inferior beings, bound by tradition – either unable or unwilling to enter the modern world.' (1995b: 257).

Early 'development' planners accepted these assumptions uncritically and, considering women as obstacles to progress, virtually ignored them in their productive capacity. Women were not considered as constituents for interventions during the first two post-colonial decades when 'development' came to replace 'colonialism' as the defining parameter of the relationship between the West and the third world. It was assumed that once men became attuned to the needs of development and their corresponding, and not coincidentally, Western forms of political, economic, and social organisation, that their women would naturally just 'follow along' (see Afshar 1991).

However, like the disabled and the sick, poor women were understood to constitute a vulnerable group to whom relief would be offered based on the assumption that, as wives and mothers, they would provide care for their families. This 'welfare approach' as described by Bulvinic (1983) has been the oldest development strategy for women, and still underlies the formulation and implementation of policies in many organisations.[6]

Along with relief aid, early foreign aid to women consisted primarily of family planning. The conceptualisation of third world women as reproducers, together with a growing international consensus on the 'problem' of population, coalesced to bring a large proportion of aid in the form of contraception. Much of the aid community's concern with women's reproductive behaviour was driven by US foreign policy concerns and by concerted lobbying by neo-Malthusian groups.[7] Population control came to be linked with US foreign policy at the end of the Second World War, responding to fears created by the Axis powers' use of population pressures (*lebensraum*) as a justification for their expansionist policies (Sharpless 1997). Population became a development problem with family planning as its solution – intensifying the focus on third world women's reproduction.

Moser (1989) suggests that the welfare approach has been based on three problematic assumptions: (i) women are passive recipients of development rather than participants in it, (ii) motherhood is the most important role for women and (iii) that child rearing is the most effective role for women in all aspects of development. Moser concludes that 'intrinsically, welfare programs identify women rather than lack of resources as the problem, and place the solution to family welfare in their hands, without questioning their "natural" role.' (1989: 1809).

Equity approach

Questions of how to deal with 'productive' women began to enter the discourse of development in the 1970s with the work of Danish economist Ester Boserup (1970). Boserup 'discovered' that development, identified as increasing levels of economic growth, could have negative consequences for women and children by increasing already existing inequalities between men and women. Her book provided insights into the relationship between colonialism and women's status, but she has also been criticised for accepting the prevailing evaluations attached to the work done by men and women (Scott 1995).

Boserup's book sparked demands by liberal feminists for the inclusion of women as workers and producers into the process of development.[8] According to Kabeer (1997), WID brought up the 'first wave of official feminism within the international development agencies.' Proponents of this approach sought to bring the inefficiency of women's lost development contributions to the attention of planners and policymakers. After decades of constricted concern, the 1970s saw an upsurge of interest in third world women: the United Nations declared 1975–85 the 'Women's Decade', 1975 was the International Women's Year, and 1973 marked the Percy Amendment in the US Congress which said that US foreign aid should try to improve the status of women in developing countries by integrating them into the development process.[9]

The policy approaches taken by WID departed from earlier notions of 'welfare' and extended into new approaches characterised by Bulvinic (1983) as equity and anti-poverty. The equity approach, the original WID tactic, recognises women as active participants in the development process. Equity approaches have been concerned with reducing the inequalities between men and women in both public and private spheres of life – in the marketplace as well as the home.

Anti-poverty approach

The anti-poverty approach shifts the emphasis from reducing inequality between men and women, to reducing income inequality and targeting poverty. This strategy was adopted by development agencies in response to two different problems with the equity strategy. First, donor agencies and developing country governments were, and continue to be, reluctant to become involved in the relations that are understood to be 'cultural'. Second, by the 1970s, a failure of modernisation theory to tackle issues of income distribution or poverty had become apparent to donors (Moser 1989). The anti-poverty approach coincided with the 'basic needs' strategies that came to dominate development thinking in the 1970s (see Chapter 1). Anti-poverty focused on increasing the productivity of women in low-income households, and was based on the assumption that women's poverty and inequality with men could be attributed to their lack of access to ownership of capital and land, and to sexual discrimination in the labour market (Moser 1989).

The types of projects implemented within the anti-poverty strategy tend to be small-scale, income-generating projects. These encourage sex-specific activities in which it is assumed that women are already participating, and which will not challenge pre-existing notions of a gendered division of labour. These projects assume that women's time is elastic and, thus, they do not provide any relief, such as socialised child and elder care, from women's other activities. Furthermore, anti-poverty projects often reflect the prevailing attitude among development organisations that women's productive work is supplemental income, and is, therefore, less important than men's wage labour (Moser 1989).

Efficiency

As a response to the economic crises from the mid-1970s, efficiency became the next dominant approach. This approach 'shifted the emphasis away from women and toward development on the assumption that increased economic participation for third world women is automatically linked with increased equity.' (Moser 1989: 1813). The objective of the efficiency approach is to utilise the formerly untapped potential of 50 per cent of the workforce by successfully incorporating women into national development efforts. However, critics of this process have shown that the efficiency approach actually shifts the costs of development from the paid (and traditionally male) economy to the unpaid (and predominantly female) economy (see Moser 1989 and Elson 1995, 1998). As the gender-arm of structural adjustment programmes, the efficiency approach is subject to many of the criticisms that have been levied at the impact of adjustment policies on vulnerable groups.[10] None the less, efficiency has become the most popular approach to women's issues in foreign aid, and, despite a change in terminology, still provides the underpinning of many contemporary approaches.

Criticism of WID approaches

Women and Development approaches have been criticised as a sort of ladies' auxiliary to modernisation theory. It stresses Western values and rationality, embraces ethno-centric notions of linear progress, and targets individual women as actors responsible for their own condition. Women's development is considered primarily as an economic, not an equality issue.

Jaquette and Staudt argue that women in this context were still viewed primarily as 'at risk reproducers' and that 'Despite the 1973 congressional mandates that AID [United States Agency for International Development] promote "growth with equity" to the "rural poor majority" and "integrate women in development," it is virtually only through population policy and related maternal/child health programs that AID reaches women.' (1985: 236).[11] So, even with the supposed expansion of 'the woman question', foreign aid still targeted third world women first and foremost as reproducers. Parpart and Marchand sum up the retrospective critique of WID. They note that 'while some exceptions occur, WID discourse has generally fostered development practices that ignore difference(s), indigenous knowledge(s) and local expertise while legitimating foreign "solutions" to women's problems in the South.' (1995: 18).

Despite the shortcomings of many interventions under the WID rhetoric, it was, as described by Simmons, 'a genuine effort by women to raise the issues of discrimination and equality.' (1997: 246). Similarly, as Stamp (1990) has warned, we should not consider all aid agencies as monolithic institutions nor their interventions as equal, and we should recognise that some useful research did come out of WID projects.

Gender and Development (GAD)

In the late 1970s, a new approach to issues of women and development originated from the supposed recipients and beneficiaries of foreign aid.[12] Unlike previous approaches, the empowerment approach to Gender and Development situates gender domination within the structures and institutions of society itself, and thus seeks to completely restructure these institutions in dramatic ways (see Kabeer 1997, Parpart 1995b and Young 1997). However, at the end of the 1990s, GAD has taken on new proponents and has changed both its critique and its constituency.

Some feminist development theorists use this approach to simultaneously deconstruct both 'gender' and 'development' as they have been previously interpreted. The extent to which either of these categories is allowed to remain as a legitimate concept for research or intervention is the subject of ongoing debate. Can we (and who is the 'we' that speaks?) speak of 'women'(which women?) in any meaningful sense? Recently, some scholars and activists from the South have begun to incorporate aspects of post-modern critique, such as the focus on language, dualistic thinking, and the construction of a colonial 'other' in development discourses (see Chowdhry 1995). Many of these scholars see development, as it has been conventionally understood, as a narrow scope of modernisation projects which are a cause of mal-development in the third world (ibid.).

This powerful impetus for questioning previously narrow conceptualisations of women as a unified sisterhood and development as western modernisation came from third world women themselves.[13] The organisation DAWN (Development Alternatives with Women for a New Era) – a network of researchers, activists and policymakers from the third world – noted that the Western women's movement gained strength during the late 1960s and early 1970s when their own countries were relatively insulated from the shocks in the world economy, and thus, their main concern was in achieving parity with men. For poor women in the developing world (or oppressed groups within rich countries), 'equality with men who themselves suffered unemployment, low wages, poor work conditions and racism within the existing socioeconomic structures did not seem an adequate or worthy goal.' (Sen and Grown 1987: 25). Thus, the notion of gender equality was inseparable from improved livelihoods for both men and women.

Issues of diversity among women themselves and their relationships to men need not preclude attention to a goal of gender equality. Most feminists working in development would support the perspective raised by

Mehta when she questioned 'why is it that challenging gender inequalities is seen as tampering with traditions of culture, and thus taboo, while challenging inequalities in terms of wealth and class is not?' (1991: 286) Historically, donors have been reluctant to influence cultural change directly. Therefore, because the social relations of gender have been considered to fall into the realm of culture, 'strong advocacy for a rethinking of gender relations' has been often been ruled out as 'unwarranted "cultural interference".' (Rathgeber 1995: 207).[14]

In spite of the internal critiques within feminism, most feminists still view gender as a structural principle of the division of labour, and 'as such, it disadvantages women as aggregate.'(Fraser 1997: 201). The manifestations of this disadvantage may differ in relation to women's position within the economic structure. However, with increasing globalisation, we will see a more uniform structuring of gender as an economic ordering principle. This gives us a stronger claim for dealing with gender as a legitimate issue for aid, even when 'women' constitutes a highly contextualised and stratified group. For some development theorists and practitioners, these considerations have been taken as an incentive to make conceptualisations and intervention more circumspect. Limited claims to the 'truth' about women that are situated in a historical and geographical context set the stage for appropriate interventions.

Gender and Development has popularised a distinction between different kinds of gender needs and interventions designed to meet them. Moser (1989, 1993), drawing from the work of Molyneux (1985) distinguishes between women's 'practical gender needs' and their 'strategic gender needs'.[15] Practical gender needs are needs identified by women and men from their own experiences within socially accepted roles in society. These needs are practical and often a response to an immediate perceived necessity such as adequate housing, food, water, health care and employment. While these needs arise from existing gender relations, meeting them does nothing to call these gender relations into question.

In contrast, 'strategic gender needs' are formulated from the analysis of women's subordination to men and these needs will vary according to the particular context in which they are situated.[16] Meeting strategic gender needs requires policies to improve women's status, promote equity and remove biases against women in both the public and private spheres; they are clearly a challenge to the gender status quo. Moser argues that meeting strategic gender needs has been difficult for aid interventions because these are best challenged by the 'bottom-up' struggle of grassroots women's organisations. However, Moser's gender training strategies suggest that organisations that implement gender planning attentive to both women's strategic and practical needs, will be able to serve as important actors in the reshaping of gender relations.

Gender roles, often inaccurately referred to as the 'sexual division of labour', are now recognised as socially defined and contingent, and thus amenable to change.[17] Moser (1993) has popularised the notion of the 'triple role' of women: (i) the reproductive role, comprising childbearing/ rearing responsibilities and domestic tasks undertaken by women, required to guarantee the maintenance and reproduction of the labour force, (ii) the productive role, comprising work for payment in cash or kind (including market production with an exchange value, and subsistence production with an actual user-value, but also a potential exchange value) and (iii) the community managing role, consisting of activities undertaken primarily at the community level as an extension of women's reproductive role. Community management ensures the provision and maintenance of scarce resources and is voluntary and unpaid work (ibid.).

Distinguishing between the roles women play is an important step in recognising the potential for competing responsibilities, shifting priorities, and unanticipated burdens placed on women by new opportunities. However, these distinct categories may obscure the relations of power which determine the prominence of one category over others at any given time. They do nothing to question the unequal burden assumed by women in productive and community managing roles. Also, as with any overarching categorisation, the meanings given to women's roles may not be adequately comparable from one context to another.

In contemporary thinking and practice, the GAD approach is being pushed into two different, perhaps even opposite, directions. First, it is used as a springboard for a radical reconsideration of the possibility of identifying a single gender or development agenda. Second, GAD is used as a new linguistic signifier for the old conceptualisations of the WID approach, but with the added twist that men are in some way responsible for incorporating women into 'modernity'. Interpreting what the new agenda of GAD will mean for aid is a critical issue for donor agencies who are often forced to confront competing agendas both within their own institutions and within those of their development partners.[18]

Impact of gender and development on foreign aid

Mainstreaming to implement GAD

Gender first appeared in official development discourse in the 1980s, but the GAD approach gained momentum only in the 1990s. During this time several UN-affiliated international meetings promoted and strengthened the institutionalisation of gender as a component of development. These included meetings on children (1990), the environment (1992), human rights (1993), population (1994), social development (1995) and most prominently, the Fourth World Conference on Women: Action for Equality, Development and Peace (known as the Beijing Conference) (UN 1995b).[19] The popularised version of GAD known as the 'equality approach' came from the Beijing Conference, and it is now the prevailing approach for aid agencies.

'Gender mainstreaming', a phrase coined by Jahan (1995), is the strategy embraced by both government and private development institutions for specifically incorporating gender issues into all stages of policymaking, programme design and implementation.[20] Mainstreaming can promote changes in (i) the partner country (through changes in institutions, laws, government policies and programmes), (ii) the development co-operation programme (with partner governments, multilateral organisations, or NGOs) and (iii) the aid agency itself through changes in its operating procedures and structures (see Schalkwyk *et al.* 1996). However, the transition made by GAD from the context of third world women's organisations and their academic supporters to the mainstream of development has not been a smooth one.

Jahan (1995) identifies two types of mainstreaming strategies: (i) the 'integrationist approach', which adds gender issues into the existing spectrum of development sectors and (ii) the 'agenda setting' approach, where the agenda of women, as opposed to women as individuals, gets recognition in the mainstream of development. The Working Party on Gender Equality of the Development Assistance Committee (DAC) of the OECD states that 'the agenda-setting approach . . . holds the greatest potential to support equality between women and men.' (OECD 1998c: 26). However, evidence suggests that the agenda setting approach to mainstreaming is not the one used in practice. Jahan's (1997) follow-up case study of four donors dealing with women's issues concludes that 'There was slow progress toward agenda-setting.' While the language has shifted from WID to GAD, it is still primarily women as individuals who are being incorporated, neglecting the potential for transforming aid from a gender perspective.

The GAD approach calls into question not simply the ways in which women are incorporated into development thinking, but the entire system into which they are being brought. Parpart notes that 'while this approach [GAD] has had considerable influence on academic development discourse, its willingness to consider fundamental social transformation does not sit well with the large donor agencies who prefer government-to-government aid, with its respect for the sovereign rights of member states.' (1995b: 260).[21] The result is that the language of GAD has been embraced, but in practice, underlying WID approaches prevail.

GAD *potential for incremental change*

By shifting the focus from women to gender, the GAD approach provides opportunity for opening up the arena of development players, or, as Elson (1998) puts it, 'talking to the boys' about gender issues. Some pragmatic proponents of even a 'watered down' version of GAD support including women first, and rethinking gender later. They argue in the words of Gordon (1996: 80) that 'empowering women to compete and become "integrated in development" will give women access to the institutional positions and authority that is arguably the only way women can challenge, modify, or transform capitalism and patriarchy.'

Similarly, some GAD allies argue that attention to gender can improve the ways that aid is currently conducted – even in the absence of a critical rethinking of development goals. They believe that an instrumental approach to gender will put these issues into the budgets and activities of development agencies, while appeals on grounds of ethics or equity will not.

For example, Elson and Evers (1996: 2) begin from the premise that 'reduction of gender inequality is not only a goal in its own right, but also is a contribution towards sustainable and equitable economic growth,' and suggest that foreign aid can be provided in ways that reduce gender-based distortions in prices and patterns of resource allocation. Similarly, Standing (1997) proposes a framework for considering gender implications of health sector reform by including specific gender issues within an existing framework. Like Evers and Elson, Standing is engaging in a dialogue between neo-liberal policies and their likely impact on women. Both of these examples suggest sites for aid intervention within the limited parameters of mainstream organisations. While this type of approach can be criticised for its appeal to a 'lowest common denominator' of agreement on gender goals, it also represents one way gender researchers can bring about change within bureaucracies where development interventions take place.[22]

The recent attention that GAD has brought to the gender 'variable' has provided ample evidence of why supporting gender equality makes economic sense.[23] Yet, instrumentally promoting gender equality as a means for achieving other ends may be counter-productive. Jackson (1998) shows how using gender to promote the poverty agenda does not tackle issues of gender injustice, and often results in unintended consequences for policies. Also, as suggested by Baden and Goetz (1997), instrumental arguments run the risk of being discredited, and they do not take into account the gendered nature of institutions themselves which determine the ways in which information is collected, analysed and prioritised.

Does GAD *imply advantages for men?*

When 'gender' replaces 'women' in development discussions, it may be used in ways that are quite different from those envisioned by feminists who first pushed for the examination of gender roles. For example, Kabeer (1997) notes that some scholars and practitioners have understood the shift from women to gender as one to include women and men as WID targets. Kabeer relates comments she received during a workshop on gender-aware planning in Bangladesh, when one of the women participants asked her, 'do you think we are ready for gender and development in Bangladesh when we have not yet addressed the problems of women in development?' (1997: xii).

In this context, abandoning women as the unit of analysis was resulting in the appropriation by men of any privileged space in development. Including men as individuals is not the same as critiquing masculinity. This linguistic shift can be used to deny women-specific disadvantage and serves as 'an excuse to abandon any measures intended specifically to benefit women.' (Kabeer 1997: xii).

For example, in a Tanzanian family planning project that included income-generating activities, men were brought in as local participants in what previously had been an all-woman project (Richey 2000 (forth-coming)). This shift satisfied both donors' concerns with increasing levels of 'male involvement' in family planning and the desire of local men to have access to project spoils. Including men in women's projects, such as this one, may, in theory, expose them to more progressive ideas on women's health issues and women's empowerment. However, as I discuss elsewhere (ibid.), women participants were at a disadvantage when it came to setting the project agenda and competing for scarce resources because of the local hierarchy of gender relations.

While the project's stated intentions were to improve women's status and empowerment, its outcome was to integrate men into the project in ways that reinforced gendered relations of power. Not challenging such inequities was beneficial in gaining project acceptance among powerful local interests. This example speaks to the difficulties of promoting both 'popular participation' and gender equality (ibid.). While these are both important goals of development projects – and can be embraced by a variety of development promoters – they are not easily commensurable in grassroot implementation. Nighat Khan summed up the perspective of many third world women: 'the focus on gender, rather than women, had become counterproductive in that it had allowed the discussion to shift from a focus on women, to women and men, and, finally, back to men.' (Goetz 1997: 39).

Is gender lost in mainstreaming?

In the new rhetoric of gender mainstreaming, it is important to examine the institutional space for gender issues. How well informed are individuals at all levels of foreign aid about the role of gender relations within the issues on which they are working? How strong is the institutional commit-ment to addressing gender inequality in practice? Research in a variety of contexts, such as the contributions in Goetz (1997), argues that develop-ment institutions themselves are deeply gendered in their own structure and policies. Therefore, we need to focus on 'getting institutions right' if polices, programmes and projects are likely to address gender needs. Traditionally, women's issues have been dealt with in a specialised unit that ensured a concentration of gender focus and experience. However, these gender units may be regarded as top-down, 'culturally coercive sources of gender-related recommendations,' (Wallace 1998) that lack the capacity for enforcement.

Gender issues may be actually implemented only when individuals herald them. Rathgeber's (1995) research shows that progress toward implementation of GAD within aid agencies has often been due to the efforts of progressive individuals within those institutions. Gender and Development has been located primarily at the level of gender training (Parpart and Marchand 1995). This training is usually voluntary and typically consists of short-term exposure to gender issues during a half-day seminar.

Even in the more 'progressive' donor organisations of the Nordic countries, GAD must rely on the commitment of a few individuals, not on an institutional enforcement mechanism. A Danida representative summarised: 'you won't have any negative sanctions if you don't have women and gender in a programme, but you would if you don't have proper reporting on expenditures or environment issues.'[24] The lack of a formal enforcement mechanism, and the difficulty of implementing one if it were in place, speaks to the conflicting ideas on the issue underlying an institution's stated gender policy.[25] In a study of 17 British NGOs, only four were found to incorporate gender awareness into their policies and procedures by allocating time, staff and resources (Wallace 1998).

A review of a Unicef gender training manual, which was part of a survey of various manuals considered for use by USAID, strikingly illustrates the dissonance between competing interpretations of GAD. It reads:

> Drawbacks. Persons uncomfortable with women's equality and empowerment as a goal in international assistance efforts, or those for whom efficiency is primary, may dislike the approach taken in this manual.
>
> (Pfannenschmidt *et al.* 1997: 17)

It is ironic that 'persons uncomfortable with women's equality and empowerment' as goals for aid policy would be responsible for conducting gender training or gender analysis. There is also an implied contradiction between the primacy of 'efficiency' as a development goal and that of 'equality and empowerment'. Why would foreign aid that works for equality and empowerment be inherently inefficient, and on which criteria is efficiency defined? The type of 'gender practitioner' in the audience for this review is one who might use 'equality' and 'empowerment' as terms of convenience; admirable goals for international assistance efforts only in so far as they contribute to the more primary goal of economic efficiency.[26]

One danger of the GAD consensus on the importance of gender equality is that it is no longer an issue for debate.[27] Thus, disagreements or differing interpretations no longer have a legitimate voice. This limits the opportunity for dialogue, and may channel disagreements into less-direct channels. For example, individuals may engage in passive resistance where gender issues are not given adequate attention, even while they are supported rhetorically. As Goetz's (1996) research in Bangladesh demonstrates, fieldworker discretion plays a large role in implementing GAD policy in both state and NGO contexts, and a fieldworker's own biases worked to constrain gender goals. Therefore, sensitisation to gender issues is important for all cadres of development workers to ensure that gender does not get lost within aid bureaucracies.

In theory, mainstreaming calls for bringing gender into every aspect of foreign aid, but in practice, gender issues may suffer from the 'tragedy of the commons' and its agenda may become more diluted as everyone becomes a supposed 'gender specialist'. One disturbing trend is the assumption that practitioners can become sufficiently well-versed in gender issues after a half-day training session. No one would suggest that expertise in farming systems, water management, or environmental degradation would come so readily. This is not to call for an end to short-term gender training, but to suggest that dealing with gender takes as much time and commitment as dealing with other critical development issues. Furthermore, some individuals within donor institutions, host governments and co-operating agencies may be uncomfortable with the goals of women's empowerment. Agencies should consider whether these individuals are in a position to mainstream gender into their policies, programmes and projects.

Are politics left out of gender mainstreaming?

The concept of gender can be used in a descriptive way that removes it from issues of power relations (Baden and Goetz 1997). There is a concern that gender language is being hijacked from its feminist agenda and used as a bureaucratic tool. Jackson argues that 'the many strands of feminist thinking and varieties of gender analysis have not been equally absorbed by development agencies.' (1998: 39). Gender becomes a series of variables in the guidelines for development, but the ways in which these are operationalised have little resemblance to the larger gender concerns usually promoted by GAD activists and scholars.

As the equality rhetoric of GAD has come to dominate mainstream approaches to aid, it is still not a single unified approach.[28] Rathgeber's (1995) examination of GAD in aid projects shows that most approaches to development interventions arise out of 'an essentially separatist mentality' where issues are identified as being left out of previous approaches, and then these are taken out of context as the sites for future donor support. Rathgeber (1995: 205) describes the pattern of development interventions as: (i) identification of the problem, primarily from a macro perspective, (ii) identification of economically efficient approaches to redress the problem and (iii) implementation of technologically-based solutions to the problem.

GAD is being used to 'add gender in' just as WID tried unsuccessfully to 'add women in' to development. Baden and Goetz describe how the main-streaming agenda has been criticised for being donor driven and for focusing on 'process and means rather than ends, leading to a pre-occupation with the minutiae of procedures at all levels, rather than clarity or direction about goals.' (1997: 38).

Changing gender inequalities is a question of altering power relations which is inherently political. Furthermore, the most commonly used approaches, economic efficiency and equality, are not necessarily synergistic goals. The efficiency approach is defined by the World Bank as focusing on gender differences with a 'key' objective of economic growth, yet 'this approach does not implicitly assume that gender inequality is an issue; therefore, it is *not seen as confrontational.*' (emphasis added) (World Bank 1998f: 15–6). Any approach that does not recognise the existence of gender inequality is incompatible with an approach whose key objective, as the same report claims, is 'to reduce gender-based inequality and thus to achieve greater inclusion and social justice.' (ibid.).

Promoting a gender approach that is 'not confrontational' is inherently contradictory. If, as is now commonly accepted, gender relations are sites for struggle, and gender inequality is based on unequal power relations between socially defined men and women, then any intervention that serves to shift this balance of power must confront the existing power relations. When the Bank refers to efficiency as being non-confrontational, it is speaking to an audience with vested interests in maintaining the unequal status quo. Its non-confrontational approach is legitimating and reproduc-ing such relations, which those at the bottom of the hierarchy may certainly find confrontational. However, gender interventions almost never mention political outputs and are rarely designed to foster political action (Parpart 1995a).

Can GAD change what counts as development?

Insights from GAD could contribute to a rethinking of development inter-vention. As Jackson argues:

> Indeed, one of the main features of gender analysis is the insistence that gender identity patterns all social life and that therefore gender awareness is not about 'adding women' but about rethinking develop-ment concepts and practice as a whole, through a gender lens. This insight is one of many which appears to have been lost in translation.
>
> (Jackson 1998: 43)

Examining gender processes, power and relationships within a context of persistent inequality converge with a new emphasis on 'participation', 'accountability' and 'empowerment'. These more political issues are over-taking gender as legitimate concerns for aid policy. Development interventions can be reconceptualised from their inception to reflect goals of gender equality: what is the development goal to be met, who brings about development and what process do they use? These are relevant questions to be asked at all levels.

In this process, the role of the 'expert' must be reconceived. Parpart (1995a) argues that the formalities of planning reproduce, intentionally or not, hierarchies within the development enterprise that privilege formal development credentials over the expertise of indigenous people. Local expertise is far more likely to be under the control of women than is expertise acquired through a formal and usually Western education. The expert can be an important change agent for empowerment when equipped with critical skills and attitudes. Rowlands describes the necessary approach as one including 'complete respect for each individual and for the group; humility and an eagerness for learning to be mutual; flexibility; and commitment to the empowerment process.' (1997: 136). Gender plays an important role in access and participation in development, but participation also facilitates the push for gender equality. With reference to Zambia, Frischmuth (1997) argues that gender should be inherent in a participatory approach to development, but it is not automatically addressed without a particular effort to do so.

Development objectives such as empowerment and participation are difficult to monitor.[29] Most aid organisations rely on quantitative indicators for regular monitoring and evaluation, and qualitative indicators have rarely been used. For example, Birgit Madsen, a senior social advisor to Danida, developed a series of project-specific indicators for measurement and assessment of the qualitative processes of empowerment and participation. She notes that 'it is important to keep in mind that the significance of assessment of qualitative indicators is not validity and reliability in the conventional methodological sense, but impact on the perceived participation and empowerment for social development and sustainable livelihoods.' (Madsen 1998: 6). However, these indicators were not ever actually used in the project, and these long-term measures of difficult concepts like empowerment or sustainability have been overshadowed by political interest in 'quantitative targets such as expenditures and physical, visible targets.'[30] One of the potential pitfalls of GAD objectives is that they are not short term and are difficult to measure (see Wallace 1998). These sorts of goals can not simply be added into existing schemes for development. Therefore, GAD calls for a rethinking of development 'success' to reflect different kinds of goals and progress, which may not be measurable with quantitative indicators alone.

Integrating GAD in aid policy

Changing attitudes is necessary, but not sufficient for achieving gender equality.[31] A recent OECD report provides a snapshot of the current thinking on gender and foreign aid; donors recognise that 'a focus on gender equality and women's empowerment in development co-operation (WID) is a means to enhance the total effectiveness of aid.' (OECD 1998d).

This key aspect of gender equality is achieved through empowering women. However, many interpretations of empowerment refer simply to a change in attitude. For example, the definition of DAC states: 'Women's empowerment generally refers to the recognition that women legitimately have the ability and should, individually and collectively, participate effectively in decisionmaking processes that shape their societies and their own lives' (OECD 1998d: 12). No doubt, the notion of empowerment has become, as suggested by Jane Parpart, a 'motherhood term', i.e. something comfortable and unquestionable, with which everyone categorically agrees, even when understandings of the term are different.[32]

However, the fact that representatives from the world's richest nations are giving third world women the permission and the responsibility for effective participation in their own lives and societies, lacks a recognition of the complexities and difficulties faced by such women in their personal or political realms. Most striking is the disregard on the part of OECD of the role donors can play in realising or impeding the goal of women's empowerment. Empowerment is a question of allocating power, and aid brings resources that can be used to increase power. Obviously, it is not enough to tell women to empower themselves; realistic contexts must exist at global and household levels, and foreign aid can enable such an environment.

In 1995, the OECD 'endorsed gender equality as a vital goal for development and development assistance efforts,' and recognised that 'adequate institutional and financial arrangements are crucial' and 'increased financial resources are essential.' (OECD 1998d, annex 1). Yet, estimates of resource flows from DAC donors and multilateral agencies show that funds have been steadily decreasing, as described in Chapter 3 of this volume. In a context of decreasing resources from wealthy countries, the admonition by OECD that third world women can and should be empowered can be interpreted with some scepticism.

Similarly, a study on trends in aid flows from five donor agencies suggests that declared strategies, frameworks and annual reports are often more relevant as public relations tools and do not necessarily reflect the agencies' priorities for funding; 'all sectors "grow" in development reports, although the tables tell another story.' (Agarwal *et al.* 1999: 36). The study gives the example that in 1995, the Asian Development Bank (ASDB) declared improving the status of women as one of its five strategic development objectives. However, by 1997, the ASDB did not have a single project in which gender and development was its primary objective.

Conclusion

Gender inequalities are often conceptualised as if they were bits of archeological matter – social relations that were formed in some distant past but have remained fundamentally unchanged. In many discussions on gender and inequality, these relations are taken as a 'given', as if they were already forged by some unfortunate coincidence of things, but can now be altered once they are 'unearthed'. Hence, inequality is 'discovered' by one study after another. This approach fails to recognise that the social relations and their corresponding actors are living, dynamic, and thus, re-creating gender inequality. One of the most useful such discoveries, emerging from Esther Boserup's work, is that foreign aid itself can exacerbate gender inequality. Because gender inequality is based on unequal distributions of power (be it capital, physical, social or other), and because aid by nature intervenes at power axes with the provision or potential of some 'good', there is no way of providing foreign aid without interacting with gendered power relations. Insights from the Gender and Development approach can draw attention to these inequalities and can engender development of alternative interventions – specific, focused, long term and cognisant about local and global gender realities.

Indeed, gender relations have always been important to foreign aid, even when they went unnoticed by development planners. Gender issues suffer from the misconception that because they are present in, and interact with, all other development arenas, they require no particular financial commitment in their own right. Indeed, mainstreaming gender into existing aid policies is likely to suffer from many of the same drawbacks that plagued earlier attempts at incorporating women into development. Gender language will become a common part of policies, programmes and projects, but the nature of foreign aid will remain essentially the same.

The structures that currently set the agenda of aid policy without sufficient participation by women, and then exclude women from receiving an equitable share of any spoils from development are unlikely to change as long as GAD means taking a gender perspective on the same old notions of development. As I have shown in this chapter, GAD, as a radical critique, remains outside of the structures of mainstream development, while GAD as a mainstreaming tool becomes completely diluted as gender is subjected to bureaucratic standardisation and projectisation. However, a middle ground, that incorporates some of the difficult critiques of GAD into the existing aid framework, can make a positive contribution to dealing with gender inequality. The challenge of GAD is to recognise where power imbalances exist – from inside aid institutions themselves to the local communities with whom they interact – and to mobilise resources to act against them.

If gender equality is not realised as a priority of aid policy through extended and specific financial commitments, then it simply becomes yet another development goal competing with other goals, such as poverty reduction or environmental protection. Given the history of unequal participation by women at all levels of development co-operation, from donors to local government, there is no reason to expect that gender issues will fare well in competition with other development priorities. In fact, there is ample reason to suspect that unless donor priorities toward gender equality are taken beyond rhetoric at international conferences, convened to deal with 'women's issues', it will remain merely 'gender terminology' and not 'gender equality' that is actually mainstreamed into development.

Directions for promoting GAD in aid policy

Among the lessons learnt from GAD is the need to tailor interventions to meet the complexity of divergent local needs, and that no group of un-differentiated women exist as targets for aid. Yet, nearly a decade of experience in most aid agencies' organisations has pointed to consistent difficulties in promoting a gender agenda in practice. The following is a summary of general directions that can form the basis of effective GAD implementation.

Commitment to gender equality

The commitment to gender equality should be assessed and strengthened within donor agencies. Gender issues must not be 'pigeonholed' into 'ghetto' areas where a token woman or gender project is included as a symbolic statement. Yet, mainstreaming at only a superficial level without adequate training at all levels of aid policy risks adopting the rhetoric of GAD while ignoring the substantive critique. Individual commitment to GAD should be rewarded, as meeting gender equality goals become an important part of aid policy.

Rethink scope and methods

Gender and Development's effectiveness comes with the ability to go beyond simply adding 'gender' in place of 'women' in development. Context-specific, longer-term interventions that allow for flexibility of design and implementation, along with greater participation by aid recipients, would shift the development process in ways that promote gender equality. Mainstreaming should not become assimilation, where gender exists as another variable in a rigid preconception of development.

Redesign monitoring and evaluation

Monitoring and evaluation procedures should be redesigned to reflect a process instead of a discrete intervention. If, as I have shown, GAD goals are different from those of previous approaches, the mechanisms used to meet these goals must be understood differently. Both qualitative and quanti-tative data are needed to examine such change. Monitoring and evaluation of progress toward gender equality must be redesigned to include the subjective experiences of aid participants.

Attitude and commitment

Support for attitudinal change should go hand in hand with increased material commitment. Changing the attitudes of women and men involved in all parts of the aid process is necessary if gender issues are to be considered as a serious aspect of development. However, attitude change alone is not enough. The most significant indicator of the importance of an issue for aid policy intervention is the amount of funding allocated. Gender equality is cost-effective, and aid should be invested so as to ensure that women are beneficiaries of both gender and development.

Notes

1 The 'feminist' term has taken on contentious meanings in both popular and academic discourse Feminism will no doubt be a rallying cry for some readers and a stumbling block for others. None the less, as I understand it to encompass a particular, if broad and amalgamate, perspective that is relevant to this chapter, I will use it. To bracket theoretical debates over types of feminisms, I use Kathleen Staudt's synthesis that feminists 'recognize power and value imbalances between men and women' and 'they look toward active women to foster more balance.' (Staudt 1998: 30).

2 Whereas 'sex' refers to the biological state of being male or female, 'gender' refers to the social aspects of the interpretation of this biological state. Gender is understood to be culturally and historically specific, and thus, both changing and changeable. However, when data is disaggregated on the basis of men and women, this is usually termed 'sex-disaggregated' data because 'while the hope is to capture differences due to gender, the way that gender is operationalized in a given context is through the respondent's sex.' (Pfannenschmidt *et al.* 1997: 7).

3 Of the objectives for which aid is a foreign policy instrument – political, strategic, economic and humanitarian (see Chapter 3 in this volume) – the relevance of women and/or gender was first articulated as humanitarian and now is also considered to be of economic interest.

4 See Lummis (1993) for a critique of the notion of 'equality' as it is used in contemporary development discourse.

5 Fraser summarises: 'proponents of "difference" have successfully shown that equality strategies typically presuppose "the male as norm," thereby disadvantaging women and imposing a distorted standard on everyone. Egalitarians have argued just as cogently, however, that difference approaches typically rely on essentialist notions of femininity, thereby reinforcing existing stereotypes and confining women within existing gender divisions.' (Fraser 1997: 44).

6 The welfare approach has its roots in the nineteenth century European Poor Laws These laws were based on the notion that individual participation in the marketplace should be sufficient to satisfy social needs, and social welfare institutions should become necessary only when the normal structure of supply, the family, and the market broke down (Wilensky and Lebaux 1965 and Hardiman and Midgley 1982, cited in Moser 1989).

7 Without diverging into an in-depth history of the population problem, we should note that at the same time that the welfare approach was directed at third world women, certain American demographers were describing a population 'explosion' that threatened to block economic development efforts (Hodgson and Watkins 1997).

8 For a comprehensive review of liberal feminism, see Tong (1989), and for a description of different feminisms linked with development, see Staudt (1998: 22–31).

9 WID made its way into bilateral institutions over a period that ranged from Sweden's initiation in 1968 to Germany's in 1986 (Staudt 1998: 182).

10 For gender critiques of structural adjustment, see Cagatay *et al.* (1995), Bourginon *et al.* (1991), Commonwealth Secretariat (1989) and Cornia *et al.* (1987).

11 Jane Jaquette and Kathleen Staudt worked in the Women in Development office at USAID from 1979 to 1980.

12 Another approach known as Women and Development (WAD) preceded GAD as a WID alternative. However, WAD was embraced by some NGOs, but was not taken up by mainstream development agencies because of its roots in a Marxist structural critique, coupled with a radical feminist critique of patriarchy (see Visvanathan 1997). WAD called for small-scale, women-only projects designed to avoid male domination. WAD's contribution to later approaches was its recognition that women have always been a part of development processes; therefore, we need to focus on their relationship to development, not try to incorporate them.

13 In the early 1980s, the Association of African Women for Research and Development (AAWORD) issued a sharp critique of the role of Western feminism in development (AAWORD 1982) Similarly, DAWN (Development Alternatives with Women for a New Era) published a challenge to 'development feminists' that is considered to be the articulation of a 'different voice' in WID debates (Sen and Grown 1987). However, Hirshman (1995) criticised this text for sharing certain premises with earlier WID perspectives about the 'sexual division of labour', decontextualising women's lives in an attempt to build a 'broad-based' movement, and the primacy of material needs in development.

14 For a further discussion of the construction of gender as part of culture and therefore outside the scope of the development mandate, see Parpart (1995b) and Stamp (1990).

15 Radcliffe and Westwood (1993) suggest that 'practical' and 'strategic' are often aligned with notions of 'private' and 'public' and assumed to be universal and linear in such a way that suggests a hierarchical relationship where women must progress from practical to strategic interests. Marchand (1995) argues that we should consider practical needs and strategic needs on a continuum as they play out in actual practices.

16 Examples of strategic gender needs include: gender-based discrimination in the division of labour in the household or market, access to credit or property, freedom of choice over childbearing, and adoption of adequate measures to eradicate violence against women.

17 Of course, other than childbearing and breastfeeding, none of these activities are actually related to one's sex although they have become related to one's gender.

18 The collections by Staudt (1997) and Goetz (1997) analyse constraints and opportunities for promoting gender redistributive policies within bureaucracies from multinational organisations to states and NGOs.

19 For a review of gender issues in these conferences, see UNFPA (1998).

20 There are three main theoretical frameworks that form the basis for GAD in aid work (see Pfannenschmidt *et al.* 1997 and World Bank 1998f): (i) the Harvard Framework (Overholt *et al.* 1985), (ii) the Moser Methodology (Moser 1993) and (iii) the Longwe Framework (Longwe 1991).

21 The GAD push for development alternatives has not received universal support even among feminists working in development. For example, the case study by Booth (1998) of the WHO stresses the link between the reluctance on the part of 'femocrats' (feminist technocrats) to embrace a globalist strategy, on the one hand, to institutional norms embedded in nationalist ideology, on the other.

22 Because my point is to recognise work toward gender equality from within the rubric of development, I am purposefully not critiquing these approaches for what they have 'left out'. For other examples of how aid bureaucracies and individuals within them can and cannot empower women, see the contributors in Staudt (1997).

23 For example, a recent cross-national study by Swamy *et al*. (1999) argues that policies designed to increase the role of women in business and politics may have an efficiency payoff of lowering corruption.

24 Interview with the author, July 15, 1999.

25 Another donor informant explained that she would use in-house contacts to express concern if gender were an important policy concern in a given intervention. 'You couldn't work with people if they knew that you were above them [to enforce compliance], but of course, you could have a formal requirement from the board [of directors] that you have to do something on gender.' (interview with the author, August 5, 1999).

26 Similarly, Kardam's (1997) interviews with World Bank staff showed that gender issues were considered justifiable only when WID was linked to economic productivity and returns on investment.

27 The adoption of a gender policy by development organisations sets a baseline position that all must accept. Thus, it will necessarily be all-encompassing, perhaps to the point of having little real impact. Wallace's (1998) study of NGOs also shows that a slick policy façade can be used to conceal conflict and a lack of commitment to gender equality.

28 Even within single organisations there is often a lack of clarity about the terminology used or the goals of gender analysis, and the constituent parts falling under the rubric of GAD may not be fully compatible in practice. For example, an analysis of gender mainstreaming within the World Bank found that commonly used terms such as 'sex', 'gender', 'gender roles' and 'gender division of labour' held no consistent meaning throughout the institution (World Bank 1998f).

29 Attempts have been made at defining, modelling, and measuring aspects of empowerment such as those by Stein (1997) on women's health, Karl (1995) on women's participation and decision-making, and the contributions in Afshar (1998) on issues of who empowers whom.

30 Birgit Madsen, Danida, e-mail message to the author, July 28, 1999.

31 I am not suggesting that gender equality is simply a matter of focusing on 'bread and butter' issues. A strictly materialist approach to GAD must be continually relinked with the contexts in which these 'needs' arise. Failure to do so will result in a naive assumption that once these basic needs are taken care of, other non-economic needs will simply fall into place (Hirshman 1995).

32 For a critical look at empowerment, see Parpart *et al*. (2000 (forthcoming)).

Appendix: Policy approaches to gender and foreign aid

Table A.10.1 WID approaches to gender and foreign aid

Policy approach	Gender—development relations	Mechanisms generating gender imbalances	Gender—poverty interactions	Role of foreign aid
Welfare (1950–70: still used in practice)	Women as wives and mothers responsible for reproductive labour	Not considered in this approach	Poor women targets of food aid, malnutrition interventions and family planning projects	Bring women into development as better mothers through top-down provision of aid
Equity (1975–85)	Women as producers left out of the development process due to gender discrimination	Lack of political and economic autonomy for women; unequal relationship between women and men in the family and workplace	Poor women not being reached by development projects targeting poverty. Women therefore the most disadvantaged of poverty target groups	Encourage direct government intervention to bring women into economic and political equality with men; top-down aid; positive discrimination policies; challenge discrimination from the household to the government
Anti-poverty (1970s; continues in some agencies)	Women as producers left out of the development process due to them being disproportionately poor	Lack of economic development such as access to private owner-ship of land and capital, and to sexual discrimin-ation in the marketplace	Because of lack of economic opportunities, or inability to take advantage of existing opportunities, women are unable to pull themselves or their families out of poverty	Target the working poor, the informal sector; income-generating options for low-income women
Efficiency (post-1980s, since the debt crisis; continues in some agencies)	Increased participation by women in the development process automatically linked with increased equity between women and men (assumes that development helps all men)	Lack of education; under-productive technologies; culture	50 per cent of the human resources available for development are being wasted or under-utilised	Support more efficient and effective projects making use of women's productive potential; 'investing in women' who are the most effective conduit for improving household welfare

Sources: OECD 1998d, Moser 1989, Kabeer 1997 and World Bank 1998f.

Table A.10.2 GAD approaches to gender and foreign aid

Policy approach	Gender—development relations	Mechanisms generating gender imbalances	Gender—poverty interactions	Role of foreign aid
Empowerment/ Autonomy (1975 on; accelerated during 1980s as the equity approach failed)	Oppression of women differs according to race, class, colonial history and position in the international economic order. Thus, women must challenge oppressive structures simultaneously at different levels	Power identified less in terms of domination over others (with a gain for women and loss for men) and more in terms of the capacity of women to increase their own self-reliance and internal strength	Poverty linked with global economic inequalities, racism and sexism. Household income cannot be equated with women's individual well-being	Legal and institutional changes, together with consciousness raising, political mobilisation, education; focus on women's organisations; support the agenda of grassroots; bottom-up, instead of top-down development
Equality (From the Fourth World Conference on Women (1995); now the most common approach)	Inequalities between women and men are not only a cost to women, but to development as a whole	Unequal gender relations recreate and reinforce inequalities between women and men	Poor women must be empowered to participate in decision-making at all levels in order to pursue strategies addressing their situation and to bring about socio-economic change	Inequality in gender relations an objective rather than women as such. Inequality can be reduced by attention to gender disparities at all levels of development, i.e. gender can be 'mainstreamed' into all parts of development

Sources: OECD 1998d, Moser 1989, Kabeer 1997 and World Bank 1998f.

11 Foreign aid, development and the environment

*Rasmus Heltberg and Uffe Nielsen**

Introduction

Economics has, since Malthus and Ricardo, had something to say about the relationship between growth and natural resources. However, not until the 1980s did the environmental economics of development become an area of major interest and research, sparked by the Brundtland report on *Our Common Future* (WCED 1987), which promoted sustainable development as a universal goal. The 1980s also witnessed a shift in emphasis from depletion of exhaustible resources to problems related to degradation of renewable resources. The debate on environmental sustainability has profoundly impacted on international environmental concern and rhetoric as well as on external aid funding for environmental purposes.

The rise of environmentally related transfers is the result both of a growing recognition of the importance of the natural resource base for development, and of developed country concern with deterioration of the global environment, including climate change. Environment and development are interlinked, and environmental degradation jeopardises development prospects (World Bank 1992b and Dasgupta and Mäler 1995). Degradation of the natural resource base reduces the productivity of agriculture, fishery and forestry and can be associated with a negative spiral of increasing poverty; pollution of air, water and food has negative effects on human health and well-being; and pollution of the global environment can alter the climate and harm production capacity. Concern over the poverty-resource degradation nexus (Dasgupta and Mäler 1995) has led many donors to finance technical assistance towards enhanced productivity and improved natural resource management by poor rural communities. Also, it has been recognised that development assistance can have adverse environmental side-effects (Reed and Sheng 1998). For project and sector programme aid this has lead to the adoption of environmental guidelines for different phases of the project cycle. For programme aid, however, the links between macroeconomic reform and the environment are complex and not well understood, and environmental concerns remain poorly integrated in macroeconomic policy making (Munasinghe *et al.* 1996).

Financial transfers for environmental purposes are becoming an important part of development co-operation. For a variety of reasons, it is difficult to document the magnitudes and trends in environmental transfers: there is a lack of data for environmental disbursements before 1990 (Franz 1996); many projects have been reclassified as 'environmental' in recent years; definitions differ; and many projects have multiple purposes. The World Bank is the largest multilateral donor in the environmental area. In recent years, between 1 and 4 per cent of total World Bank lending has been primarily environmental. During 1986–97, loans totalling $11.6 billion were approved to 153 environmental projects (which were still active in 1997) spanning 62 countries. Of these loans, 60 per cent of the funds went to projects related to pollution and urban environment, 31 per cent to rural environment and 8 per cent to institutional capacity building (World Bank 1997c). Among bilateral donors, Japan, for example, spent 16.9 per cent of its total 1992 official development assistance (ODA) on the environmental sector, while Norway allocated 18 per cent of its ODA on environmentally related activities between 1991–3 (Franz 1996).

Two important characteristics make aid for environmental purposes different from other types of aid. First, many environmental problems are international or even global. Resources such as the global atmosphere, oceans and biological diversity (biodiversity) are *global public goods*. This entails a free-rider problem in relation to efforts at conserving global resources: individual countries have incentives to avoid the costs of environmental actions, but cannot be excluded from sharing in the benefits of environmental conservation. Global environmental problems is a new challenge donors have embraced in recent years – undoubtedly because environmental action has become popular with developed country electorates, and because donors have a comparative advantage doing this – who else should pay?

A second characteristic of environmentally related aid, partly related to the first, is strongly differing priorities between donor and recipient countries. Industrialised and developing countries disagree on the importance of environmental objectives *vis-à-vis* other development needs, and on the relative priority of different environmental problems. While global environmental problems are often the least urgent from the point of view of developing countries, they receive much more attention from donor countries.

These two characteristics are important factors influencing the role and design of environmentally related transfers. Thus, a recurring theme throughout this chapter will be the political economy of environmental aid, i.e. the implications of differing objectives of donors and recipients, as well as the importance of the global/local environmental dichotomy. The primary purpose of the chapter is to critically assess the concept of environmental aid, both in general and with respect to specific transfer mechanisms and strategies. First, in order to systemise this analysis, a taxonomy of environmental transfers as well as an overall discussion of the objectives and scopes involved in environmental aid is offered in the following section. In the subsequent sections, this discussion is extended towards specific mechanisms and strategies for disbursement of environmental transfers, concentrating on the global environment (i.e. activities under the Global Environmental Facility (GEF), debt-for-nature swaps and environmental conditionality) and on the local environment. Thereafter, key issues related to the environmental side-effects of general foreign aid are reviewed. Conclusions are provided in a final section.

Objectives and scope of environmentally related transfers

Taxonomy of environmentally related transfers

The purpose of this section is to conceptualise and discuss environmental aid. First, it is useful to distinguish between transfers primarily aimed at environmental improvement *per se*, and transfers whose primary objective is economic development with environmental sustainability as a secondary or derived effect. In the following, the first type of transfer is referred to as 'environmental aid', while the second type of transfer is termed 'sustainable foreign aid'. Second, an important distinction can be made between transfers whose main scope is the global environment (biodiversity, the atmosphere, the climate and the oceans) and transfers targeting the recipient country environment, including its natural resources and human health. Superimposing these two distinctions – objective and scope – gives rise to the taxonomy of transfers shown in Table 11.1.

It is clear from Table 11.1 that there is a remarkable difference between local and global environmental improvement in terms of the distribution of benefits. Improvements in the local environment benefit today's inhabitants of the developing countries directly and immediately, e.g. through a cleaner and healthier urban environment or through protection of natural resources necessary to sustain agricultural productivity. In contrast, the benefits from conserving the global commons are invariably much more dispersed, uncertain, indirect and long-term. For example, biodiversity conservation is surrounded by a great deal of scientific uncertainty, but benefits may accrue to future generations and to genetic researchers, pharmaceutical companies and conservation-oriented people in the developed countries.

As discussed in more detail below, the differing distribution of benefits from global and local environmental improvement has important implications for the role of environmentally related transfers. For the global environment, the role of aid donors is to represent and express the disparate and future benefits which are neither captured by market forces, nor by individual actors or recipients. By doing so, donors play a crucial and new role as providers of global collective action. When it comes to local environmental action, the role of donors is more traditional as 'gap fillers'

Table 11.1 Taxonomy of environmentally related transfers according to objective and scope

Objective:	Environment	Economic development
Term:	Environmental aid	Sustainable foreign aid
Scope: global environment	Support for improvements in global com mons (atmosphere, biodiversity, oceans), e.g. through: financing incremental costs debt-for-nature swaps environmental conditionality joint implementation of CO2 reductions	Transfer of clean and efficient energy technologies
Scope: local environment	Support for: pollution control clean water and sanitation waste management environmental capacity building	Support for: improved soil and water management sustainable rural development agricultural research land reform

and providers of knowledge, technology and expertise. Donors are facing a new requirement, though, that aid projects and programmes do not contribute to environmental degradation in recipient countries. Most donors have therefore introduced environmental guidelines, as described below.

Although illustrative, the taxonomy in Table 11.1 is not always clear-cut and does not cover all features of environmentally related transfers. First, there may be multiple objectives and scopes involved in a given transfer. This is for example the case with forest protection, which both conserves biodiversity (global commons) and improves soil and water management and biomass availability in surrounding agricultural areas (local resources). Also, aid for clean water and sanitation, which improves the local environment, also has positive effects on health and worker productivity. These complementarities between local and global environmental goals and between environment and development can be called 'win–win' options and, as argued in this chapter, they ought to be utilised strategically by donors to a larger extent. Second, even when donors are motivated by environmental concerns, whether local or global, the motive for the recipient government to accept the transfer can be very different, as discussed below.[1]

Third, there are important regional cross-border environmental issues, which are not included in Table 11.1. Trans-border pollution, control over river water and fishing management present intermediate cases between local and global environmental issues (Mäler 1990). As with global commons, regional environmental problems cannot be handled by a single country. But the benefits of environmental action are not as dispersed, and regional environmental issues are therefore not open-access situations. Bilateral bargaining can be used to find solutions, possibly involving some form of side payments or compensation.

If an environmentally related transfer imposes strict environmental standards which constrain development in the recipient country, can this transfer then be classified as 'environmental aid' (as in Table 11.1)? Singer and Ansari emphasise that 'resource transfers, the cost of which [to the recipient country] exceeds their contribution to the development process of the recipient country, cannot be classified as economic assistance.' (1988: 173). This definition of aid may not be very operational – it is difficult to assess the net impact of transfers a priori. But it raises an important issue, whether environmental transfers to protect the global environment impose net costs on the developing countries. In the case of biodiversity conservation, for example, developing countries bear most of the costs, mainly opportunity costs of forest conservation, but may only receive a small fraction of benefits. At the aggregate level, the possibility that environmental transfers impose net social costs is taken seriously by developing country policymakers, who fear that environmental standards might hamper economic growth. They argue that, historically, development and industrialisation in today's rich countries entailed large-scale pollution, forest conversion and natural resource degradation, and that development should take priority over environment. In contrast, better protection of the local environment (e.g. improved natural resource management and pollution control) often entails net social benefits.

There are, nevertheless, a number of arguments for labelling the transfers in the left-hand column of Table 11.1 as 'environmental aid'. First, if a recipient country government accepts a given transfer, it is presumably because it perceives the transfer to entail positive net benefits. Second, there is an alternative view that 'environmental aid' is assistance to the environment as such. This view, however, is at odds with the understanding of 'aid' as involving altruism and a net transfer to fellow human beings (Singer and Ansari 1988). It raises fundamental questions about whose environmental concerns are being addressed (soil conservation versus rare species) and on which conditions. Third, environmentally related transfers can be regarded as altruism on behalf of future generations, a kind of 'inter-generational' aid – in line with the goal of sustainable development. The concept of inter-generational aid is somewhat peculiar, though, as it entails transfers to *potential*, rather than existing, people. Furthermore, the concept of inter-generational transfers raises the issue of whether inter-temporal equity is improved. From this perspective, there is no rationale for inter-generational assistance unless future generations are likely to be poorer than the present.

Differences in objectives

Differences in objectives between donors and recipients arise to some extent whenever aid is tied to specific purposes. But the differences are larger and more common for environmental tying. At the early stages of development, countries focus on managing natural resources such as soil, water and forest, on which incomes and exports depend. As industrialisation proceeds, the health implications of the urban environment gets increasing attention and relatively affluent countries attach importance to global environmental issues while maintaining a focus on natural resources and urban environment (UNEP 1997). There are many reasons why donor and recipient priorities differ with respect to environmental issues. Implications for the role and design of environmental transfers depend on which of the reasons, discussed in the following, dominate in a specific setting.

First, basic economic reasons can often explain environmental priorities. As mentioned above, the distribution of benefits and costs from environmental protection are often aligned such that developing countries are less keen than developed countries to undertake environmental improvement. A low level of environmental protection might be optimal from the point of view of developing countries, and imposition of environmental and labour standards can undermine developing countries' comparative advantages in labour and natural resources (Mohamad 1995). In the face of this type of divergence in priorities, environmental efforts can only succeed if compensation is provided for locally incurred costs. The persistent demand from developing countries that environmental transfers should be additional to existing aid budgets have to be seen in this light – environmental aid is perceived to divert financial resources away from other, growth-oriented, development goals.

Second, the underlying preference structure of donors and recipients can be similar, but priorities may still differ as developing countries, due to lower incomes, are on another segment of their welfare function where they have higher marginal utility of wealth and lower marginal utility of environment as compared to donors. To the extent developing countries have higher discount rates than donors, this will also cause a different perception of the costs and benefits of environmental interventions. Thus, interests may eventually converge, but do not at present. In this situation, imposing some form of conditionality or aid tying is necessary to achieve environmental goals, while additionality remains vital for recipients.

Third, preferences for environmental goods and amenities may differ fundamentally between countries, for example due to cultural reasons. To many developing country observers, sustainability must seem like yet another fashionable idea of donors, bending to environmental lobbies in order to justify and protect aid budgets, distracting from urgent poverty problems and other development needs. As before, compensation for costs imposed on recipients is necessary.

Fourth, priorities may also differ for reasons related to lack of know-ledge and awareness of the short and long-run consequences and costs of pollution and resource degradation; lack of adequate technology to remedy the situation; lack of financial resources and/or administrative capacity to formulate, monitor and enforce environmental legislation at the regional, national and local level in the developing countries; and due to the considerable scientific uncertainty surrounding all ecological systems. The role of environmental aid is more uncontroversial and traditional when faced with this type of priority divergence; to co-operate with recipient governments on mutually agreed priorities; to transfer knowledge, exper-tise and technology; and to support capacity building in environmental administrations. It is interesting, though, that cases of priority divergence understood by donors as knowledge differences frequently occur where recipients make reference to cultural differences.

Fifth, a great deal of environmental degradation is not optimal from any perspective, and appears to be caused by irrational policies and institu-tional failures. Environmental destruction caused by government failure, although sometimes due to neglect or ignorance, can often be explained by the lobbying of influential resource extracting sectors such as mining, timber, ranching, fishing and energy industries. Poor people in rural areas do not exert such influence on government policies, and get hurt from natural resource degradation. For donors wishing to address this, policy conditionality on transfers is vital, and strategic support to environmental groups in recipient countries is warranted to help strengthen environ-mental voices.

In practice, it is difficult to uncover the dominant reason for any divergence in priority, as donor and recipient priorities may differ for one or more of the reasons given above. It is an important point, however, that not all divergences in priorities are due to lack of information. Thus, the explicitly stated donor sub-goal of transmitting environmental awareness, concern, and to promote long-term thinking is not always warranted as a goal in itself. In many situations, recipient priorities and interests are bound to remain different from those of donors.

Implications of different objectives

Differences in objectives critically affect issues of fungibility, incentives and additionality. As discussed in Chapter 15, fungibility arises when a donor-financed project would have been implemented by the recipient even in the absence of external funding. For most environmentally related transfers fungibility is not a critical issue, since donor-financed environmental programmes and projects are rarely top priorities of recipients, and therefore would not have been implemented in the absence of aid. Instead, diverging objectives cause incentive problems in that recipients may accept environ-mental transfers but fail to support the projects, fail to pass agreed changes in policy or obstruct the environmental effort through other initiatives.

The issue of additionality – i.e. whether environmentally related transfers are additional to existing aid allocations – arises for environmental interventions with a global scope.[2] Here, the role of aid is partly to compensate developing countries for the costs they incur in providing a global environmental good. Much of the global environmental action is prescribed by international conventions that set up funds for financing developing country efforts through mandatory payments by the industrialised countries. Developing countries have demanded that contributions from donor countries to international environmental funds should be additional to existing aid budgets and many OECD countries have, on paper, accepted the need for additionality (OECD 1992b). In practice, though, transfers tend to be financed over existing (shrinking) aid budgets, and hence can hardly be regarded as compensation by the developing world as a whole. With total aid falling in recent years (see Chapter 3), environmental transfers are probably not additional in the aggregate, and hence crowd out aid for other purposes.[3]

It is also important whether environmentally related transfers are concessional. It could reasonably be argued that environmental transfers should primarily be financed by grants rather than by loans. The reason is that 'soft' projects in the environmental, social, health and education sectors, which are not directly for productive purposes, do not enhance the recipient's export capacity, at least in the short run. Hence, loan financed projects in these sectors do not help generate the foreign exchange needed to repay the loan, and may thus worsen the burden of debt. This holds true even if a standard project appraisal has revealed a positive net present value (Korten 1994).

Mechanisms for global environmental transfers

There are a number of different mechanisms through which donors make transfers to developing countries related to global environmental action. In light of the incentive problems caused by differing donor–recipient priorities, all global transfer mechanisms involve tied payments. In this section, two significant transfer mechanisms are discussed in detail: the incremental cost mechanism and debt-for-nature swaps. Subsequently, other types of mechanisms are briefly introduced.

Financing the incremental costs of global environmental action

The Global Environmental Facility (GEF) was established in 1990 with a mandate to finance projects and programmes addressing key international environmental problems. The four focal areas of GEF are climate change (greenhouse gas emissions), depletion of the ozone layer, loss of biodiversity and international ocean resources. The principle underlying the working of GEF is illustrated in Figure 11.1 (World Bank 1992b and Tisdell 1991), using

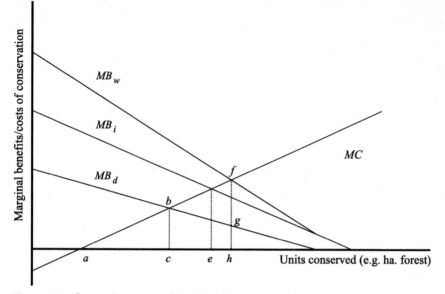

Figure 11.1 Optimal amount of biodiversity conservation.

biodiversity conservation as example. Assume for simplicity a world consisting of a developing country endowed with plentiful biodiversity and a developed country with little biodiversity, to whom the biodiversity of the developing country is potentially valuable, e.g. for pharmaceuticals.

In Figure 11.1, the MC curve shows marginal costs to the developing country of undertaking environmental action such as biodiversity conservation, the MB_d curve shows marginal benefits accruing to the developing country from conservation, MB_i are conservation benefits accruing to the industrialised country, and MB_w (the sum of MB_d and MB_i) are global conservation benefits. Assuming that no externalities from conservation can be internalised by individuals, an unregulated market would conserve amount a of biodiversity, while a rational developing country government would conserve amount c, where marginal costs of conservation equal the marginal benefits accruing to the country. However, this is less than the globally optimal level of conservation h, where marginal global conservation benefits (MB_w) equal marginal conservation costs. Thus, environmental action in the developing countries to protect the global commons generates positive externalities to the industrialised countries. Figure 11.1 underscores the dichotomy described earlier between global and local environmental problems. Achieving conservation up to level c can be regarded as a national problem, while conservation beyond c is basically an international challenge. Nevertheless, donors still can (and do) play a powerful role in assisting developing countries with local projects up to c, where win-win options are more prevalent.

The Global Environmental Facility awards grants for environmental action corresponding to the amount necessary for the activity to break even for the recipient. This amount is known as incremental costs. It can be understood with reference to Figure 11.1. If the amount h of biodiversity is conserved, incremental costs are the area bfg, i.e. the net additional expenses occurring to the developing country from its environmental effort. Thus, in theory the entire net benefits of the effort accrue to the industrialised countries, while the developing country is kept on its *ex ante* utility (Heltberg 1995). In practice, though, there are considerable difficulties in developing operational definitions and methods for measuring incremental costs, especially as environmental functions are highly non-linear and uncertain (Fairman 1996).

The main advantage of GEF from the point of view of the developing countries is that it consists of grants. These grants are additional in the sense that the global component of projects is financed by a separate grant, which does not subtract from the funding for other project components. But the money flowing into GEF's trust fund will often come from existing aid budgets; GEF funding is therefore not additional in the aggregate. The GEF trust fund is provided mainly by donations from the developed countries; $1.2 billion was pledged by donors in the period 1991–4 and $2 billion in the period 1994–7.

The developing countries have criticised GEF's mandate to finance only activities related to the global environment, rather than local environmental problems such as soil erosion, which they perceive to be more urgent. As a compromise, it was decided that the incremental costs of land degrading activities could also be financed by GEF, but only to the extent that these activities relate to one of the four global focal areas (Fairman 1996). Thus, the grants awarded by GEF to a large and evident extent reflect donor priorities. Moreover, as transfers are designed to finance only the incremental costs, recipients are left with no net benefits.

Debt-for-nature swaps

Debt-for-nature swaps involve a commitment by a developing country to undertake a specific environmental action – often the creation of protected areas for biodiversity conservation – in return for debt relief (Hansen 1989). At the height of the debt crisis in the 1980s, NGOs were able to buy developing country commercial debt on the secondary market with a heavy discount. This debt was cancelled in exchange for conservation in the debtor country. Thus, the developing country government had a fraction of its debt cancelled, and in return it would either directly finance environmental projects over its budget, or issue bonds in the name of a local NGO executing the project (Jakobeit 1996). Between 1987–93, $983 million was raised for these swaps, including $46 million from NGOs and the rest from the German and American governments. About $1.1 billion worth of developing country debt was cancelled through these transactions (Franz 1996 and Jakobeit 1996). Use of this mechanism has now declined as the Latin American debt crisis has become less critical.

The main idea behind debt-for-nature swaps is that if commercial debt can be purchased at, say, 20 per cent of face value, one dollar invested by the donor cancels five dollars of outstanding debt. This leverage is an implicit donor benefit – donors get more environment for their money. However, the leverage is normally shared with the recipient in that only a certain fraction of the domestic currency equivalent of the debt is allocated to conservation purposes. This, together with the fact that debt-for-nature swaps are based on grants, ensures a high implicit grant element. However, this aid is conditional, and recipients have limited degrees of freedom as to the use of released funds. The real advantage to recipients is lower pressure on foreign exchange reserves, as the funds earmarked for conservation purposes are spent entirely in domestic currency.[4] Some domestic trade-offs are involved, in that public funds are reallocated for purposes dictated by donors, and other government projects are crowded out. Of course, this has to be weighted against the benefits from reduced international debt.

Initially, debt-for-nature swaps were used by environmental NGOs such as the Worldwide Fund for Nature (WWF).[5] This makes it likely that these debt-for-nature schemes consisted almost entirely of additional funds. When bilateral donors later embraced the idea, they probably to a lesser degree applied additional funds. Differences in preferences between donor and recipient are inherent in debt-for-nature swaps, but do not necessarily pose a problem. In fact, differing objectives make both parties better off from the transaction. Donors pursue their own conservationist priorities, while the recipient achieves debt relief.

Other mechanisms and summing up

The mechanisms discussed above are important examples of types of global environmental transfer mechanisms. There are, however, numerous other types, which we will not discuss in detail. Examples are transfers under the Montreal protocol on ozone-depleting substances (DeSombre and Kauffman 1996); international parks agreements involving government-to-government payments (World Bank 1992b); transferable development rights, a proposed scheme whereby individuals can pay for the non-development of conservation areas in developing countries (Panayotou 1994). A more prominent example is the greenhouse gas (GHG) emission reduction mechanisms of the Kyoto Summit in 1997 – i.e. the joint implementation (JI) and the clean development mechanism (CDM). The exact design of these mechanisms is not yet finalised. Here, it is sufficient to note that in principle there is no element of aid or concessional terms in JI, and that the CDM consequently is intended as a means to ensure that developing countries benefit from participating in GHG abatement. Also, environmental conditionality, which links financial aid with environmental policy reform, has proven an important mechanism for ensuring compliance with global (as well as local) environmental goals. Here, even if recipients perceive environmental conditionalities as economic constraints, the benefits from the accompanying grant or loan may outweigh the costs from the conditionality, thereby making the overall package attractive to both parties, although for quite different reasons (environmental versus financial objectives).

It is clear that many of the global environmental transfer mechanisms discussed above to a large degree are compensatory schemes, which offset the negative global effects of developing country policies, but which do not in a strict sense assist these countries, as their priorities differ widely from those of the 'donors'. This is most evidently the case for the incremental cost mechanism of GEF (and probably also for the JI mechanism), but also to some extent for e.g. debt-for-nature swaps. Hence, these mechanisms should only be viewed as aid in so far as they contribute directly to the development process of the recipient country and consist of additional funds.

Targeting the local environment

The benefits from improving the local, as compared to the global, environment are less dispersed and more immediate. Recipient and donor priorities more often coincide for local environmental issues. Moreover, even when priorities differ for some reason, development efforts can be designed to simultaneously address development and the environment. This is the idea of win–win strategies which, in the terms of Table 11.1, can be understood as both 'environmental aid' and 'sustainable foreign aid'.[6] In a win–win strategy, incentive problems are less likely to arise, making transfer mechanism design more straightforward than for global environmental aid. In this section, the main focus is therefore on win-win strategies more than on transfer mechanisms *per se*.

One type of win–win strategy is based on the idea of a vicious circle between poverty and environmental degradation. The vicious circle hypothesis is that poor people are forced to degrade the natural resource base on which they depend. According to this hypothesis, poverty alleviation will automatically lead to environmental improvement through better incentives and ability to manage the resources. The vicious circle is caused by three factors. One is lack of liquidity (own savings and credit) which makes it hard for the poor to finance conservation investment (e.g. soil management and tree planting). A second factor is that the priorities of the poor may focus on short-term subsistence rather than on long-run resource management. Lack of liquidity and short-term priorities combine to make the discount rates of the poor high (Holden *et al.* 1998). An additional factor is high fertility, caused by the desire for a family work force and for insurance substitutes. High fertility and population growth can lock families and countries in poverty and may contribute to environmental degradation.

Another type of win–win argument is based on the environmental effects of a country's development level. There is some evidence suggesting that middle-income countries tend to have worse pollution indicators than low and high-income countries. This is captured in the so-called environmental Kuznets curve, which postulates a U-shaped relationship between GDP and environmental quality. These curves have been estimated econometrically for environmental indicators such as deforestation, urban air pollution and river contamination (Grossman and Krueger 1995, Shafik and Bandyopadhyay 1992 and Cropper and Griffiths 1994).

However, it is a misconception to believe that growth and poverty alleviation by itself leads to environmental improvement. Development interventions should be aimed towards specific and direct win–win options, where synergy effects are certain and immediate. To identify these options, detailed knowledge of local resources, people's resource use and management institutions is required.

There are a number of ways in which donors can assist developing countries in improving their local environment and capitalise on win–win strategies. First, donors can finance projects and programmes that help conserve natural resources, curb pollution or reduce environmental health hazards. Another possibility is to strengthen local environmental agencies by supporting environmental capacity building. A third avenue is to exercise environmental conditionality to change government policies.

Examples of win–win options include support for income generation and consumption smoothing in rural areas; tree planting and improved resource management; research in sustainable and yield-increasing agricultural technologies (improving both agricultural productivity and soil conservation); giving local people a share in conservation revenues (e.g. eco-tourism, hunting fees); land and tenure reform aiming at increasing tenure security; and transfer of cleaner and more efficient energy and manufacturing technologies.

Thus, there is a wide range of win-win policies available to donors and recipients. However, there are some critical constraints to more widespread donor support for win-win policies. First, commercial and military interests in donor countries may not always favour these options, especially those that do not involve physical investment: where infrastructure and manufacturing projects can be tied to purchases in the donor country, this may not to the same extent be possible with environmental and rural development projects. Second, many donors are under-staffed and under pressure to reduce administration costs. Small-scale complex rural development-cum-environment projects require more preparation and administration per dollar of on-site costs than larger projects such as infrastructure. Third, low environmental capacity in the administration of developing countries can constrain co-operation.

Nevertheless, as donors have crucial experiences with interventions designed to systematically exploit win–win options, some important policy lessons will be learned. If foreign aid is to become an effective component of the struggle to achieve environmentally sustainable development, seeking out the win–win gains will be indispensable.

Environmental side-effects of aid

There are a number of cases where foreign aid has damaged the environment of the recipient country, sometimes irreversibly. In this section, environmental side-effects of foreign aid are dealt with, looking first at project aid and environmental assessment, and next at programme aid, especially structural adjustment programmes.

Impact of project aid on the environment

Environmental NGOs have been a strong force in criticising environmentally harmful donor projects. For example, World Bank financed projects in the Amazon area have been accused of destroying the tropical rainforest (Mikesell and Williams 1992). A Finnish financed forestry project in Tanzania that provided sawmills in areas adjacent to the unique Usambara rain forest led to increased logging, deforestation and loss of biodiversity (Larsen 1989). Japanese aid to Indonesia has helped promote a trade pattern where Indonesia exports pollution-intensive goods to Japan, whose domestic environment is thereby spared (Lee and Roland-Holst 1997). Large dams, such as the proposed projects in India's Narmada River, which flood huge areas and displace many people are also highly controversial.[7]

Starting from the 1980s, donors are increasingly seeking to incorporate environmental considerations into aid operations. This is to avoid development programmes and projects damaging the local or global environment, endangering medium-term development prospects or adversely affecting resource-dependent local populations. Donors are adopting environmental guidelines that call for screening of proposed projects for their environmental consequences. The objectives of environmental assessment are (i) to avoid undertaking projects that provide negative net benefits once social and environmental consequences are taken into account; (ii) to help mitigate and minimise adverse environmental effects in project design and implementation;[8] (iii) to identify and consider environmental effects which are important for project success in financial terms.

An important tool for systematic screening of the environmental effects of development interventions is environmental impact assessment (EIA). The projects and programmes which have the biggest environmental impacts, and where an EIA is most required, are in land clearing, forestry, livestock, large dams, population resettlement, water management, large-scale irrigation and most infrastructure (Mikesell and Williams 1992). Environmental Impact Assessment describes the expected positive and negative effects on pollution, natural resources and human health, estimating, when possible, the magnitudes of the impacts (in physical terms). In practice, the environmental team is often under pressure not to recommend excessive alterations to the original project plan and to maintain projects on track (Adams 1990). Mikesell and Williams (1992) are unable to find a single example where one of the multinational development banks entirely abandoned a proposed project following an unfavourable EIA exercise. Some donors have moved towards using EIAs at an earlier stage of the project cycle, facilitating the incorporation of environmental considerations as part of project identification, planning and design, equal to technical and economic feasibility.

The cost-benefit framework can be extended to include environmental economic analysis. This allows the environmental effects to be explicitly compared with other project costs and benefits. It requires that opportunity costs can be estimated for the major pollutants, natural resource impacts and health effects which were identified in the EIA. A reasonable criterion for project selection is to select the projects with the highest net social benefits after inclusion of environmental effects, and to implement only projects with positive net social benefits.

A variety of techniques can be used to estimate the opportunity costs of environmental amenities, natural resources and human health, including (i) the impact of the environmental change on output and incomes, (ii) hypothetical mitigation or prevention expenses, (iii) replacement costs (cost of restoring natural resources to previous standard), (iv) contingent valuation techniques (including willingness to pay) and (v) hedonic valuation (such as induced variation in house and land values) (Dixon *et al.* 1994). Much resource degradation in the developing countries has an immediate bearing on production and income in sectors such as agriculture, fisheries, forestry and tourism. This influences the choice of valuation technique as projects' environmental impacts can then be estimated directly as the induced change in producer surplus. Such direct valuation techniques are probably more robust and easier to implement than hypothetical contingent valuation techniques, which are sometimes criticised for imprecision and irrelevance for developing countries (Diamond and Hausman 1994). For example, the social costs of a project that adversely affects a coastal area can be estimated as the loss in producer surplus from the expected decline in fish catch and tourism, without the need for resorting to hypothetical valuation exercises.

Impact of programme aid and structural adjustment on the environment

The current pressure on the environment and natural resources of the developing countries are of such a magnitude that a limited number of individual environmental projects cannot be expected to achieve sufficient improvements. Environmentally benign projects are easily offset by macroeconomic and sectoral policies that create incentives for resource degradation. Thus, debt, pricing policies, taxes, subsidies, trade policies and land tenure affect the environment in a number of important and complex ways. The natural resources, through export resources and agricultural production potential, also have important bearings on macroeconomics. Therefore, in order to achieve a more environmentally sustainable pattern of development, increased attention on the complex interrelationships between macro-economic and sectoral policies, the institutions of the economy and the environment is necessary (Pearce and Warford 1993).

The structural adjustment programmes (SAPs) of the World Bank and the IMF have been criticised for paying insufficient attention to environmental issues (Reed 1992, 1996). The World Bank has reacted to the criticism by maintaining that SAPs have a number of beneficial effects for the environment, but acknowledging that unintended adverse environmental effects could take place and that mitigating measures are warranted (Munasinghe *et al.* 1996). Nevertheless, systematic integration of environmental policies and targets in adjustment programmes and macroeconomic policies is yet to materialise.

Structural adjustment affects the environment in a number of complex ways, both positive and negative. First, economic liberalisation programmes often help to correct policy-induced environmental problems. Bringing prices of goods and services more in line with their opportunity costs promotes a more efficient and less wasteful utilisation of resources. This is clear, for example, in the energy and water sectors where government subsidies and underpricing in many countries lead to excessive use, waste and environmental degradation, often at the expense of most poor people who may be cut off from these services anyway (Meier *et al.* 1996). The slashing of water and energy subsidies during adjustment can therefore improve the environment as well as efficiency and equity as big landowners are the largest beneficiaries of cheap water and electricity. However, introducing marginal cost pricing of water and electricity has major distributional implications and is therefore politically difficult in practice. Likewise, reduction in subsidies for agricultural inputs such as pesticides and chemical fertilisers can help reduce pollution due to overuse and runoff and curb human health hazards associated with excessive and improper use.

Second, currency devaluation and price deregulation have important implications for the crop composition and income of rural producers. The environmental outcome depends to a large extent on the ecological properties of the affected crops. Many exportables are perennials such as coffee, tea and fruits, which have good soil conserving properties, and a shift towards those crops brought about by increased outward orientation under structural adjustment can reduce soil degradation. Other exportables are soil degrading, as for example groundnuts. There may also be a shift of labour and capital into the natural resource sectors, where the export potential often lies. Compounded by insufficient management and/or lacking property rights, this may lead to higher pressure on soils, forests and fisheries and pollution from mining.

Third, fiscal reform can adversely affect the environment. In many adjusting countries, public environmental agencies have seen their budgets disproportionately reduced, causing a severe decline in the quantity and quality of environmental regulation (Panayotou and Hupé 1996). Cuts in environmental infrastructure spending, such as water supply, waste disposal, public transport, protected area management and agricultural research and extension also have negative environmental effects (Reed 1992). Fourth, balance-of-payments targets can lead to increased extraction of timber, fish and mineral resources for export, causing increased deforestation and overfishing. Fifth, poverty sometimes worsens during SAPs, which may induce poverty-related environmental damage.

The environmental effects of SAPs are difficult to evaluate empirically. Most work attempting this is not based on explicit modelling of the counterfactual scenario, and conclusions tend to be weak (see Reed 1992, 1996). Macro reforms have positive environmental effects in some countries and negative ones in others. Some environmental indicators may improve while others worsen. To what extent is it reasonable to blame adjustment programmes, aimed primarily at restoring macroeconomic balance and growth, for failing to address environmental problems? Certainly, it is not reasonable to blame the early reforms in the 1980s, implemented at a time when environmental knowledge and concern was far less than today.

The interaction between macroeconomic policy and the environment is highly complex, uncertain and conditioned by a number of institutional, market and policy failures. Although effects can no doubt can be large and important, present knowledge about macroeconomics and the environment is too limited to formulate simple operational frameworks that can environmentally safeguard macroeconomic reform. Environmentalists argue that environmental sustainability ought to be an overriding operational imperative for all policy making, including macroeconomic reform, and that market and government failures related to the environment are just as important to address as the market failures traditionally addressed in structural adjustment. However, from a practical point of view, adjustment lending is already ripe with unfulfilled conditionalities, and additional environmental conditions may not achieve much, unless shared by recipient governments, While focusing on macroeconomic aggregates, SAPs ought to pay attention to the environment, and as a minimum consider and, where relevant, address major environmental effects. More policy research on macroeconomics and the environment is warranted.

Conclusions

It is often unclear whether 'environmental aid' is regarded as aid to the environment as such, as inter-generational aid, as foreign aid through environmental sub-goals, or as foreign aid with environmental side-effects. A precise and operational definition of environmental aid would be desirable.

As a step towards this, a taxonomy was developed in this chapter that distinguishes between transfers targeting the global and the local environment, as well as between objectives of development and environment. The taxonomy captures important aspects of environmentally related transfers, and distinguishes between 'environmental aid' and 'sustainable foreign aid'.

It was argued that transfers for the global environment, and also to some degree transfers with the environment as a direct objective, are more susceptible to incentive problems caused by differing priorities between donors and recipients. Certain global environmental transfers do not classify as 'aid'. Transfers targeting the local environment that have positive development impacts are more likely to be jointly acceptable to donors and recipients. Systematically exploiting win–win synergies, both between environment and development objectives and between global and local environmental objectives, has the potential to maximise the impact of transfers as well as to minimise incentive problems.

Yet it needs to be recognised that resource degradation and pollution in many developing countries are caused by adverse policies, rapid population growth and social and institutional conditions which are not easily changed by inflows of foreign capital, however large. Instead, it is required that foreign aid donors, recipient country governments, NGOs and the private sector co-operate to create sustainable long-run development.

What should be the role of environmental transfers in the future? In our view, environmental considerations are not just another temporary 'fad' in the development debate, but reflect a lasting and important change of knowledge and attitudes. Environmental outcomes have important implications for poverty alleviation and economic growth, which donors can ill afford to ignore. Environmental aid for both local and global environmental purposes should be maintained in the future. Problems of divergent objectives need to be addressed through greater reliance on win–win policies as well as through incentive-compatible design of transfer mechanisms. For efforts targeting the global environment, the compensatory role of transfers ought to be widely recognised, and the effective additionality of such transfers should be assured.

In a decade of stagnating and declining aid budgets, there is reason to believe environmental transfers have crowded out aid for other purposes. It appears problematic that funds for global common goods are diverted from poverty-alleviation and development. The Danish solution to this has been to enact a separate budget framework for environmental aid, which is by law additional, aimed at 0.125 per cent of GNP. This approach seems worth replicating in other donor countries.

Notes

* Comments from Jens Kovsted, Anil Markandya, Irma Adelman, Channing Arndt, Anne Olhoff, Jørgen Birk Mortensen, Christian Friis Bach, Jørgen Peter Christensen, Claus Pörtner, Peter Hjertholm, Finn Tarp, an anonymous reviewer

and participants at two workshops on foreign aid at the Institute of Economics, University of Copenhagen are acknowledged.

1 Admittedly, there are heterogeneous interests within recipient and donor countries. Throughout most of this chapter, internal differences in interest are downplayed, focusing instead on conflicts between 'donor' and 'recipient' (government) objectives, assumed to be well-defined.

2 For transfers targeting the local environment, where benefits accrue domestically, issues of compensation and additionality do not arise.

3 An exception is Denmark, whose budget for environmental aid is separate from that for other aid.

4 However, if the developing country was not initially servicing its debt, debt-for-nature swaps do not improve the *de facto* foreign exchange position.

5 The World Wide Fund For Nature was formerly known as the World Wildlife Fund.

6 A different type of win–win gain occurs from spillover effects of local environmental action on the global environment. Forest conservation, for example, benefits both the local and the global environment. Also, cleaner and more efficient energy sources reduce both local air pollution, global GHG emissions and fuel costs.

7 In no case has the discussion about the environmental and social impacts of development projects been as intense as in the case of large dams. Environmentalists are fiercely opposed to dam projects. Flooding due to reservoir construction leads to displacement of former inhabitants and loss of agricultural land, forests and wildlife habitat. Relocated people have often not received adequate compensation for loss of land, property and livelihood. The World Bank financed more than 400 large dams between 1970 and 1988, including some of the world's largest (Mikesell and Williams 1992), dropping to a rate of approximately four every year in the 1990s (World Bank 1996b). The criticism has led the Bank to adopt a number of guidelines, and to tighten existing ones, on resettlement, indigenous people, natural habitats, dam safety, and environmental assessments, to which all new projects must conform (World Bank 1996b). Some large dams, such as China's three gorges project, go ahead without World Bank funding and the environmental scrutiny that implies. However, the net environmental effect of dams is more ambiguous than admitted by environmentalists. It is possible that some dams may be a net improvement for the environment, as well as for development, once the counterfactual is taken into account. Hence, in the case of dams for hydro power, the alternative is often coal-fired power plants, with ensuing emission of greenhouse gases, smog and other pollutants. In the case of irrigation projects, the counterfactual often involves continuation of low-productivity rainfed agriculture or intensified pressure on groundwater reserves. Thus, it is not environmentally sound to stop financing large dams altogether. Instead, adverse social and environmental effects should be minimised through proper attention to resettlement and adequate compensation to displaced people, and through alterations in project design and location (Goodland 1996).

8 In view of the considerable uncertainties surrounding ecological systems and any interventions affecting them, continued environmental monitoring during implementation ought to be routine in most projects in order to help address unforeseen events.

12 Aid and failed reforms

The case of public sector management

Elliot J. Berg

Introduction

Much of the recent thinking on aid effectiveness and on economic growth has given priority to the role of the policy environment in the aided countries. But stress on policy has not crowded off centre stage the other basic determinant of aid effectiveness and growth, namely the administrative or institutional environment. Foreign aid cannot make much of a contribution to equitable growth when public sector management of national resources is ineffective and wasteful, when public services are too few and badly delivered, budgeting disorderly, investment priorities dubious, civil services in deep disarray, policy formulation unsystematic, and, often, corruption endemic.

The critical importance of these problems has drawn a good deal of aid money into programmes for reform of public sector management (PSM): capacity-strengthening in key ministries, reform of the public enterprise (PE) sector (including privatisation), strengthening of public expenditure management, civil service reform and, more recently, general governance improvement, which bears indirectly but strongly on public management. Estimates of the total volume of aid money devoted to reform of PSM do not exist. Part of the problem is that the data for many of the donors active in this area are not at hand. There is also ambiguity about what to count. However, some indication of the nature and magnitude of PSM reform efforts can be derived from World Bank lending data.

The major vehicle for PSM reform has been World Bank adjustment lending. From the late 1970s to the early 1990s, the World Bank financed 245 adjustment operations, about half of which were in sub-Saharan Africa (Jayarajah and Branson 1995). Of 99 structural adjustment loans, 90 per cent had public enterprise reform components (ibid.).[1] More than 230 loans (in 68 countries) contained measures related to privatisation, and half of these were in Africa (World Bank 1994b).[2] Public expenditure reform operations (more than 200) were introduced in 83 countries (Huther *et al.* 1998).[3] Civil service reforms were targeted in loans to 88 countries as of the end of 1991; two-thirds of these were African (Nunberg 1994).[4]

World Bank spending on PSM programmes, according to their classification, averaged more than a billion dollars a year between 1995 and 1997,
or 5.4 per cent of total Bank lending (World Bank 1997c). This was a 70
per cent larger share than in 1988–92. The real total and share is undoubtedly much larger. The World Bank figures not only understate their
own effort, but of course also omit activities of other donors, some of whom
are highly active in PSM. In any case, the available numbers make clear that
donors, especially the World Bank, have made substantial investments in
PSM reform.

The impacts of these reform programmes are hard to measure with
precision, and experience varies between countries and types of reform.
But it would be hard to find dissenters from the view that their success has
been generally very modest, especially in relation to the resources they have
absorbed. Public enterprise sectors remain large and usually inefficient.
Budgets remain ineffective instruments for the allocation of public resources.
Public service provision continues to suffer from poor financial management and weak civil services.

These general conclusions regarding results, or more precisely lack of
results, in PSM reform are demonstrated in detail in the next section of this
chapter. This is a compilation of findings and conclusions in evaluations of
specific PSM areas: public enterprise reform programmes, civil service
reforms, and efforts to improve the efficiency of public expenditure management.

The third section considers the donor role in explaining PSM reform
failures. It is an aspect of the aid effectiveness problem that is often
neglected in the literature on reform, which tends to explain failure (or
slow progress) as stemming from such factors as lack of government
commitment, uncongenial economic and ideological environments, political
obstacles, technical difficulties, and lack of skilled implementers (e.g.
Shirley and Nellis 1991 and World Bank 1995). These are certainly
pertinent. But more needs to be said about aid donor contributions to
reform failures.[5] After all, in most reforming countries, it is the donors
(especially the World Bank) who conceive, define, implement and champion
PSM reforms. The quality of reform-mongering has to be a factor of some
importance in explaining results.

That donor reform-leadership in this area has been of low quality is the
main theme of the third section. Two dimensions of bad donor reform-
mongering are explored. First, the fact that donors introduced PSM reforms
as part of conditioned policy loans, and second, their poor implementing
capacity. Donor shortcomings are not the whole story of course; often they
are not even the main part of the story. Other factors contributing to slow
progress in reform are important and are acknowledged. But the purpose
of this chapter is to highlight the donor role, which has been underplayed
in the reform literature. Most of what is said is well known by many aid
agency staff members; indeed this overview draws heavily on donor self-

evaluations. It is in fact a tribute to aid agency self-awareness that donor sources, especially World Bank reports, themselves document both the slender achievements in this reform area, and the donor contributions to this poor performance.

The main focus is the experience of low-income countries, especially in Africa. This is where most aid donor PSM efforts, in terms of number of projects and breadth of attempted reforms, have taken place. Also, because these countries have longer experience with PSM reform programmes, more is known about them. Furthermore, excepting e.g. India and perhaps China, weakness in national economic management capacity is a particularly critical bottleneck to equitable growth in these countries. Experience in low-income countries, then, inspires most of the generalisations made in what follows.

Although the most intensive reform activity, in terms of number and breadth of project, has been in low-income countries, this is not true in terms of aid volumes. The biggest share of World Bank PSM spending has been in Latin America and the transition economies in Europe and Central Asia.[6] The concentration on Africa has changed somewhat in recent years; adjustment operations have declined and transition economies receive much more donor attention.[7]

The analysis and conclusions in this chapter have to be understood in this context. The extent of PSM reform failures appears to be less general in middle-income and transition economies than in low-income countries. This indicates the need for some prudence in generalising, though, as will be seen below, many robust generalisations emerge from existing evaluations. A second caveat may be more significant. Some of the approaches and instruments that are reviewed have been dropped or strongly modified since the mid-1990s. This seems to be the case for public investment programming, for example, and perhaps for civil service reform. But it is not clear just how much change has really taken place and in any case most of the analysis remains relevant.

The record of failure

Evidence for the paucity of positive outcomes is abundant in recent evaluations and studies of specific reforms. Three major targets of reform are reviewed: (i) public enterprise sectors, (ii) civil services and (iii) public expenditure management.

Public enterprise reform

The main reform objectives have been to make state-owned enterprises (SOEs) more efficient and effective providers of goods and services, and to reduce subsidies from the national budget. Instruments are financing of restructuring, reduction in surplus workers, clarification of enterprise objectives and of relations with governments via performance contracts, strengthening management and improving management incentives, and substituting *ex post* for *ex ante* government controls. Divestiture (privatisation or liquidation) is a major component. Results of the almost two decades of reforming public enterprises and shrinking the size of the PE sector are, by almost all accounts, slender.

A study undertaken by the IMF in 1993 analysed the experience of 19 countries under its Enhanced Structural Adjustment Facility (ESAF). The study concluded that 'only a few countries, Bolivia, the Gambia, Guyana, Senegal, Sri Lanka and Togo, made significant inroads into the problem of public enterprise reform.' (Schadler *et al.* 1993: 14).[8]

In 1994, the World Bank published an intensive review of adjustment lending in sub-Saharan Africa (World Bank 1994a). The report notes that financial control of SOEs remains rudimentary. Even strategic enterprises are rarely audited by independent accountants; in only four of 29 countries (Zimbabwe, Malawi, Gambia and Burundi) were many firms audited annually, and there was a long delay in publishing any accounts at all. Accounting for external funds on-lent to the SOEs is unsystematic, as is tracking of repayments and arrears. The general assessment is that despite a few encouraging stories there is little evidence of successful SOE reform. Few rehabilitated PEs have made significant and lasting improvements, and many are being rehabilitated for a second and third time. That the African story is not atypical is suggested by the results of another recent worldwide evaluation. It concludes from examination of project completion reports that implementation of PE reform programmes was satisfactory in only five countries (Argentina, Chile, Peru, Gambia and the Philippines), and weak in 20 countries (Datta-Mitra 1997).[9]

Privatisation, a major thrust in PE reform programmes, has made limited and uneven progress in low-income countries. The privatisation record in Africa is of special interest because donor interventions have been especially intensive there. A recent World Bank review (White and Bhatia 1998) shows that many transactions have occurred – 2600 by the end of 1996 – which is a reduction of one-third in the number of SOEs. But three-quarters of the countries in the region have done very little divesting, and the economic weight of successful privatisation is limited. As of 1996, privatisation activity was concentrated in ten countries and effective in fewer.[10]

The World Bank report entitled *Bureaucrats in Business* (World Bank 1995) provides striking general evidence of the limited progress in PE reform, at least until the early 1990s. The report assembled data on outcomes for 40 developing countries. It found that between the late 1970s and the early 1990s there was little or no shrinkage in public enterprise sectors. The share of public enterprise sectors in GDP was unchanged and even increased in middle-income countries. Public Enterprise shares in paid employment also increased, substantially so in Africa.[11] Moreover, after 1985, state enterprises in low- income countries took a larger share of domestic credit; as direct budget subsidies declined, bank credits often increased, providing indirect subsidies.

Civil service reform

Civil service reform programmes have been particularly intensively studied. In addition to generating better information and strengthening personnel management agencies, the main goals were reductions in employment, reduction of the aggregate wage bill, creation of better incentive structures by raising real wages and 'decompression' (i.e. raising higher level staff salaries more than those of unskilled staff). Virtually all assessments agree that these goals have been met in very few countries.

The *Adjustment in Africa* report of the World Bank (1994a) found that few adjusting countries had effective control over the payroll system; all but six had significant problems. Only a handful of countries cut the number of civil service employees by more than 5 per cent since they began structural adjustment. Moreover, personnel cuts usually had little fiscal impact, because they disproportionately affected low-paid employees at the bottom of the civil service, and salary erosion continued.

The outcomes of the African experience, as of 1994, are summarised in another comprehensive World Bank assessment (Nunberg 1994: 147ff). With respect to employment the study concluded that of 'the fourteen countries for which data are available, seven were able to reduce government employment,' though there were some reversals in three countries. With respect to cost containment, in only four countries did the wage bill decline in absolute terms. In half the countries the salary to GDP ratio rose over the period, and the ratio of salary to non-salary costs did not improve. On decompression, the salary structure became more compressed in 10 of 13 countries.

The most recent assessment comes from the IMF (Lienert and Modi 1997). Its analysis covers 32 countries, from 1986 to 1996. With respect to nominal wages, it found that there was no change in the average civil service wage bill to GDP ratio until 1993. Some reduction occurred after 1993. In 1996 the ratio was 6 per cent, 1 percentage point lower than a decade earlier. Most of the declines occurred in the CFA countries, following the January 1994 devaluation.

The study also indicated that incentive structures had shown little improvement over the decade (1986–96). Real wages per civil servant continued to fall – by 2 per cent a year on average in 20 countries excluding Uganda. 'The available evidence suggests that there was little desirable change in the salary structure in the countries that experienced decreases in real wages.' (ibid.: 28–9). In only a very few countries was there any decompression of salaries; differentials rather were further compressed in many countries. Nor were differentials between public sector and private salaries improved. In the CFA countries the 1994 devaluation led rather to a widening in favour of private employees.

Finally, regarding employment, a fall was observed in a third of the 19 countries with data. In six countries the number of civil servants declined by more than 10 per cent (Benin, Central African Republic, Guinea, Madagascar, Mali and Uganda). Uganda was the champion 'down-sizer', but there were significant cutbacks also in Tanzania and Sierra Leone.

Barbara Nunberg, probably the World Bank's leading specialist on civil service reform, has recently summed up her conclusions in plain language:[12]

> Does civil service reform as currently supported by the World Bank make a critical difference in helping governments develop the capacity to achieve sustainable performance improvements? In reflecting upon nearly a decade and a half of operational experience in civil service reform, the answer is, despite some isolated successes and significant lessons learned, probably not. We cannot be confident that our projects have either significantly boosted effectiveness (i.e., through strengthening government capacity to carry out essential public tasks), or efficiency (i.e., through reducing the cost and dimensions of government in relation to output). Civil service pay and employment reforms have seen only limited achievements, and there have been difficulties of government ownership and oversight capacity, especially in Africa.
>
> (Nunberg 1997: 5)

Public expenditure management

Between 1986 and 1991 the World Bank had 81 financial management operations in adjustment and technical assistance loans (Shirley and Nellis 1991).[13] The reform of public investment procedures was the most frequent intervention. The World Bank encouraged governments to set up rolling (usually three-year) public investment programmes (PIPs). The aims were to generate better information about investment activities, make development budgets comprehensive, improve investment selection procedures, concentrate national resources on priority projects (that is, reverse the practice of overloading development budgets with too many projects) and encourage adoption in PIPs of 'realistic size' investment programmes whose present counterpart and future recurrent costs could be adequately financed.

About the same time that the World Bank introduced PIPs, it attached conditions to adjustment loans that required governments to submit investment programmes for World Bank review. This evolved into the widespread practice of World Bank organised public expenditure reviews (PERs), i.e. examinations of all public expenditures. The rationale was that investment could not be isolated from overall public spending. From the early 1990s, emphasis has been put on medium-term expenditure programmes, or enhanced forward budgeting. Comprehensive sectoral investment programmes became prominent after 1995. Assessments of the public expenditure management reform efforts are fewer than those available for public enterprise operations. But those that exist offer severe judgements about their effectiveness and impact.

A major World Bank report on fiscal reform, which looked at the 250 adjustment loans to 86 countries between 1979 and 1994, found few positive outcomes (Datta-Mitra 1997). With respect to reductions in budget deficits – one of the major objectives of these reform programmes – the report noted that 'low-income adjusters, severely indebted adjusters, and primary exporters showed no improvement.' 'Success has been limited', the report went on to say, 'in restructuring current expenditures away from wages and subsidies and toward non-wage O&M (operations and maintenance), and attempts to cut public employment have generally been short-lived or modest.' Also, 'the record on budget process reform is poor . . . . Few countries that had planned to refine estimates of O&M requirements by evaluating capital budgets have yet done so.'[14]

The World Bank's comprehensive 1994 study of adjustment in Africa contains a number of pertinent observations (World Bank 1994a). On public investment management, the authors point out that as of late 1993, 18 of the 29 adjusting countries in their study had not put in place an effective tracking system for projects in their investment programmes. Budget processes and allocations remained poor. The attempt to put a ring around high priority projects by protecting core programmes has been only partially effective.

The experiences of Kenya and Senegal illuminate the difficulties of budget reform and the limited impacts of reform efforts; PIP-based reforms have made little headway in these two countries. Achievement of information objectives lags. Total project cost estimates prove beyond reach, hampered by lack of access to foreign-aided project agreements, among other factors. (Kenya's agriculture ministry could locate only 12 agreements out of 56 projects.) Introduction of PIPs makes budgets more comprehensive, in that externally funded projects are included, but not all projects are included. Effective appraisal by core agencies remains rare. Operationally useful priorities are lacking, there is a shortage of trained staff, projects are too numerous, PIP preparation is hurried, and responsibility for preparation, implementation, and monitoring of PIPs is diffuse.

Budgetary stress has led to stronger budget discipline and white elephants are fewer. But since it is easier to get projects into the PIP than into the regular budget, many low-priority projects find their way into the PIP. Moreover these come to be heavily loaded with recurrent items; 35 per cent of the total PIP in the Kenyan case. Recurrent budget projections remain unreliable, usually unusable for financial planning. The core project concept gives rise to adjustments in definitions of projects, and other tactics are adopted that severely dilute its effectiveness. Casual observation in other low income countries suggests that progress in Kenya and Senegal, which have relatively strong administrative systems, is better than average.

Public expenditure reviews (PERs) are another major donor reform vehicle. These are non-project instruments. They are studies, initially done by World Bank staff alone, later with other donor participation, of the level and composition of a client government's overall public expenditures, their intra-sectoral and inter-sectoral allocations, PIPs, budget policies and institutions. They were a follow-on from investment programme reviews, which were done in connection with the introduction of the PIPs. The rationale was that public investment spending was only the tip of the expenditure iceberg; expenditure reform had to consider all public spending, the bulk of which took place outside the PIP.

The PERs have a long history, though their place in the public expenditure reform arsenal has grown in the 1990s; their number grew from 12 a year in the 1980s to 18 a year in the 1990s (Pradhan 1996). Between 1987 and 1993, 113 reviews took place. More than 100 reviews were completed between July 1993 and February 1998. A hard-hitting evaluation of the PERs was completed recently (World Bank 1998d). It concluded that PERs have had very little impact even on World Bank thinking, policies or programmes, or on the IMF. More important, the PERs were judged to have had insignificant impact on other donor participants, who in many cases never even received copies of the completed PER. The effect on overall aid co-ordination was thus hard to discern. And most important of all, except for some Anglophone African countries, the effects on the policies of low-income borrowers have been negligible.

The evaluation noted that the PERs are getting more diverse and better, and proposes changes that could improve them further. But there is no escaping the central conclusion: the results of PERs in terms of strengthening public expenditure management have been dismal.

Donor responsibility for failure in PSM reforms

Three sets of factors account for the poor record in PSM reform. The first consists of internal obstacles to reform, those having little to do with aid. The second is indirectly related to donors; it consists of general fallouts from the aid presence. The third is directly aid related: inadequacies of the aid agency reformers. This last set is what the remainder of the chapter is about. We note the first two briefly, in passing.

Many endogenous factors help explain the limited success of PSM reform efforts.[15] First, among the most important are the enormous difficulty of reforming administrative systems everywhere, and the special difficulties in low-income countries. These are typified by political fragility, ethnic diversity, deep poverty and strong aversion to employment-reducing measures, eroded administrative institutions and dysfunctional civil services with resulting weak implementing capacity, lukewarm intellectual and political conviction among elites that proposed reforms are really right for their countries, uncongenial economic environments. The weight of this set of factors varies between countries and between type of PSM reform, but is generally considerable.

Second, many aid practices erode local institutional capacity and hence work against PSM reform in an indirect or general way. This is most visible in heavily aided poor countries, notably in Africa, where aid-GDP ratios are high, more than 10 per cent in two-thirds of the countries in the continent, according to World Bank data.

Most of these capacity- and reform-undermining effects are well known to aid practitioners and noted in the aid literature (e.g. Sida 1996 and Berg 1997). Aid management absorbs local officials and turns their attention outward. Budget constraints are softened; aid inflows permit hesitant governments to put off hard decisions. Local policy initiatives tend to disappear; officials know that what counts is what donors think and want, so technocrats become passive and politicians 'deresponsibilised'. Incentive structures are distorted on several levels. Donor staff needs, for their offices and their projects, hiring and salary practices create dual salary structures. And austerity measures and planning that would normally be imperative become questionable where the aid presence is significant. This point is taken up later, in connection with the recurrent cost problem in expenditure management.

These two sets of factors – the inherent difficulties of administrative reform and structural change, and the unsettling effects on general administration and the incentive to adopt reforms caused by the aid presence – are central to an explanation of reform results. The focus in this chapter, however, is on the third source of failure: the fact that reforms were sponsored by aid donors.

In almost all poor countries, PSM reform is a donor import. To a degree unparalleled in history, outsiders have introduced, even imposed, reforms intended to change the way that sovereign governments organise themselves and spend their money. Donor agencies crafted the reforms, financed them, and played a big role in their implementation. Donor involvement has numerous positive effects. It provides ideas on how to proceed, technical help and money for training and implementation. In many countries, without the donor impetus reforms might not have been undertaken at all, or would have been long delayed. But donor sponsorship has also had a down side. It contributed directly and significantly to reform failure, in two ways. First, PSM reform was introduced as part of structural adjustment programmes and came laden with conditionality. This undermined local ownership of the reforms and had other reform-weakening effects. And second, donors have proved to be imperfect designers and implementers of PSM reform. Each of these sources of reform failure is considered in turn.

Negative effects of the adjustment connection

Most PSM reform in the low-income countries came packaged in adjustment loans, as part of general structural adjustment programmes, in sectoral adjustment loans, or as related free-standing technical assistance. They came with conditionalities attached. The process by which most adjustment loans were introduced practically guaranteed that local ownership and commitment would be minimal. It also gave content to the reforms that was less than optimal and led to game-playing that reduced reform credibility.

The PSM reform instruments were crafted in donor headquarters, usually with little local input. Governments usually accepted these reform programmes because they were hard pressed for money. Their leaders did not believe in the reforms, or believed in them half-heartedly. Nor was there much possibility to develop local backing. Public debate over the rationale and content of reform programmes was rare; the specific conditionalities in adjustment loans were usually unknown to the general public, and were often not revealed even to fairly senior officials. Almost everybody regarded these conditioned reform programmes as imposed by the Bretton Woods institutions. It is hard under these circumstances to have the kind of general and open dialogue that nourishes true ownership.[16]

A 1994 study on World Bank privatisation assistance worldwide included a survey of privatisation project task managers (World Bank staff). The managers were asked to rank the host country motivations for privatisation. The third highest ranked reason was 'to please international donor agencies' (World Bank 1994b: 16). In fact, numerous respondents ranked this first. The report's authors note laconically: 'This certainly seems to suggest that privatisation programmes, imposed from outside, may well fail for lack of sufficient local support.' (ibid.).

The fact that PSM reforms were incorporated in adjustment loans also shaped programme priorities and choice of instruments. In civil service reform, containment of the wage bill came to dominate the programme because of its link to fiscal reform and macroeconomic stabilisation. This was so even though many reformers knew that for deeper reform and sustainability other components should take priority, such as stronger personnel management systems, and efficiency-based reductions in staff.

The criteria for success were also shaped by the adjustment environment. Evaluators often rebuked PSM designs as containing too many 'soft', process-based conditionalities. Programme designers therefore searched for more 'monitorable', that is quantified, conditions. Thus SOEs and governments had to sign a given number of performance contracts; governments had to divest a specific number of companies (or, later, a given portion of the value of state assets); 'budgeters' had to estimate rates of return on some percentage of projects in the PIP and reject those falling below a specified floor return; and wage bill and employment ceilings became standard features of civil service reform projects and programmes.

These quantified conditionalities invited *pro forma* agreements by governments, and half-hearted or mechanistic implementation. Performance contracts between SOE management and governments were routinely signed, but both parties failed to deliver on their promises. The requirement in

Senegal to do rate of return analyses on 80 per cent of PIP project requests and reject those with less than 10 per cent return, for example, led to mechanistic analyses. Project costs and output data, put together by the operating agencies (or by donors), were accepted by the core ministry screeners virtually without question, despite their invariable over-optimism. And, anyway, projects that did not meet the 10 per cent floor rate of return were frequently approved on 'social' grounds or because they met one of the many priorities established by government. The finance/planning ministry evaluators were so busy doing the rate of return arithmetic that they rarely had time (and little incentive) to find out if proposed projects really made sense. Along the same lines, conditionality (as in Kenya) that required operating ministries to designate only a small number of projects as 'core' or high priority, led to agglomeration of smaller projects into bigger ones, meeting the conditionality but defeating its purpose.

The defects of conditionality-laden adjustment loans as vehicles for PSM reform were exacerbated by the weakness of the traditional project framework into which they were fit. Even without conditionality the classic project is an inappropriate instrument for PSM reform (Nuadet (forthcoming)). These kinds of reforms often do not have a clear beginning and end. Their outputs are not easily measurable, and monitoring is difficult. Blueprint types of project planning do not fit. The objectives are long term and non-specific. Also, contradictions arise in practice. Putting hurriedly in place a formal system of project screening, usually with technical assistance, is not the same as developing an effective, sustainable set of procedures for raising project quality. In the end, given the adjustment environments, priority was given to the shorter term, quantified, and monitorable instruments and objectives. Institutional development or capacity-building objectives were neglected.

The inclusion of PSM reforms in adjustment vehicles had two other anti-reform effects, which are related. It encouraged game playing rather than serious efforts at joint problem solving. And it undermined the credibility of the reform effort. None of the parties to a structural adjustment programme wants to see it fail. A cessation of disbursements is a personal defeat for responsible donor staff and the organisations they work for. It is the same with relevant local officials. And since structural adjustment programmes were (and still are) parts of resource-gap-closing exercises involving many donors and the IMF, the punishment for non-compliance (possible cutoff of all aid) was too awful to invoke. The World Bank operated in the worst of two worlds. It negotiated harsh looking conditions at a cost in good will and ownership, but couldn't use the resulting big stick. World Bank cancellation of adjustment lending was rare until the mid-1990s, despite many delays in tranche release. To avoid it, donors accepted *pro forma* compliance with conditionalities.[17]

Such arrangements kept the adjustment money coming. But they also contributed to the creation of a no-sanctions atmosphere, diminished the credibility of specific reforms, and contributed to the persistence of a soft budget constraint in general. By reducing the avoidance costs of non-compliance, they shifted decision-makers' calculations of the costs and benefits of reform implementation in the direction of non-implementation.

Poor choice or faulty adaptation of reform

Even taking account of the tremendous difficulty of the task and the formidable internal obstacles to reform, it is hard to avoid the conclusion that aid organisations have done a generally poor job of designing and implementing PSM reforms. Developing country reform histories are littered with false starts, with examples of donor reliance on approaches and instruments that did not work or stopped working after donors dropped their support.

It can be argued that some donor initiatives were doomed from the start because of their lack of fit with the specific features of client countries. But most reform programmes that have ended badly were not based on bad ideas. They were brought down not because of basic conceptual flaws, but because of failure to foresee or adapt to blockages in implementation and in the post-implementation environment. The general problem has been aid agency failure to adapt programmes to fit country-specific conditions. The main donor weakness has been inflexibility, a sluggish response to emerging implementation difficulties, and an inability to tailor programmes to the special features of low income country environments.

Three examples are described here: (i) the reliance on performance contracting in public enterprise reform, (ii) the use of PIPs for investment planning reform and (iii) the resort to public expenditure reviews (PERs) for budget reform.

Performance contracting

This has been the principal World Bank instrument for improving performance of SOEs that remain in the public sector. The basic idea is deceptively simple. The rights and duties of governments (as owners) and enterprise managers should be clearly spelled out and put to paper. The goal is to increase dialogue, eliminate the problem of unclear or conflicting SOE objectives, diminish the interference of oversight agencies, and help ward off claims from various stakeholders in the enterprise. The SOE management undertakes to meet explicit targets in production, pricing and employment. The government on its side commits itself to pay off arrears, pay its future bills, allocate agreed-to subsidies, finance a given level of investment, and grant tax relief or other privileges.

The World Bank introduced these agreements in Senegal in the early 1980s. By 1990, they had become a standard fixture in adjustment operations with SOE reform components. They were present in 10 countries by the mid-1980s, and a decade later there were almost 600 of them in 32 countries, mostly in Asia and Africa (Cissé 1994).[18] Verdicts on the effectiveness of this instrument were not long in coming. A 1988 evaluation of the Senegalese experience painted a discouraging picture. The negotiations often failed to come to terms, agreements took a long time to negotiate, contained few incentives for management performance improvement, and government frequently failed to comply with its promises (Nellis 1988).[19]

The World Bank (1995) study contains the results of a more intensive Bank investigation that inventoried existing performance contracts (PCs). The authors found little to cheer about in the way performance targets are set, the effectiveness of information flow, the provision of incentives, or the commitment of governments. The overall conclusion is that performance contracting does not work, and might cause more harm than good. A parallel, more recent, paper puts it forcefully, stating that it is clear that, if the contracts in our sample are representative of the performance contracts in use with natural monopolies worldwide, then considerable time and effort is being expended on an exercise with neither theoretical nor empirical justification (Shirley and Xu 1997).[20]

World Bank analysts of PCs singled out from the start 'lack of commitment' as the principle reason for their poor results. The authors of World Bank (1995) follow in this tradition.[21] Governments are said to have reneged on their obligations under the contracts because it was politically too costly to meet them. This is surely one of the reasons for failure, but by itself is not illuminating. Governments renege, also, because in many instances performance contracts were signed to meet donor conditionality, but no sanctions were imposed for reneging.[22] The balance of costs and benefits was tilted in favour of backsliding.

Reasons more fundamental than lack of commitment were at work. Some of them are listed in World Bank (1995) itself: the problem of too low and too numerous targets set by opportunistic managers in a situation of information asymmetry; the relative weakness and low status of government negotiators and monitors; the limited autonomy of managers in the face of continuing government control of key decisions; and the fact that good performance by managers rarely affected their careers, which were politically determined. It seems utopian to think that PCs could work in environments with these features. It should have been evident that these elements make up a formula for failure in these circumstances, the performance contract approach was wrong for low income countries.

Even more basic flaws in the PC instrument should have been recognised, flaws that should have turned donors away. A fundamental premise of the PC is that it is both feasible and desirable for governments to commit themselves financially to SOEs in the framework of a negotiated agreement. But firm commitment is not feasible in countries with unstructured budget systems, usually running on a cash management basis. Spending agency requests for new money invariably exceed what is available; budget directors routinely put in the budget only a small percentage of what agencies ask for. Moreover, agencies routinely receive actual allocations that are less than budgeted; and given the heavy weight of salaries, capital expenditure requests are particularly vulnerable. Commitments generated via PCs are treated like other government commitments in the budget process; cut if cash management requires it.

Even if feasible, firm commitments would have been undesirable. It is technically easier for many SOEs to develop investment projects, and they have easier access to consultants than most ministries. When PCs are in operation, SOE managers have no incentive to limit project proposals. On the contrary, they use them for negotiating purposes, and in a donor rich environment, financing is always possible. The vetting process, which should sort out high priority needs from others, is weaker in the SOE channel than in central government. The supervising technical ministries to which SOEs 'belong' have no interest in trimming their expenditure requests, which are usually shipped up the ministry of finance without question. With the PC in hand, and World Bank conditionality behind it, the SOE investment proposals would have a better chance of approval than would those in other operating units. If government commitments made in the PCs were in fact held to, then the probable result would have been a deterioration in the quality of public spending.[23] The choice of the PC as the major instrument of public enterprise reform in low income countries was clearly a mistake.

Public investment programming

The rolling (usually three-year) public investment programme (PIP) was the World Bank's chosen instrument for improving investment planning and implementation. The earlier summary of evaluation results and the Kenya and Senegal case studies made clear that PIP effectiveness was limited. The PIP has certainly fallen out of favour. The World Bank's budget reform specialists are very harsh in their judgement of the concept. The World Bank's most recent statement of best practices says, in effect, that the PIP approach was a terrible idea, and lists its deficiencies (World Bank 1998e: ch. 2).[24]

Most of the criticisms are on target. But some part of the poor record of PIPs stems from their poor implementation. Their great potential was to provide time for more measured evaluation of project proposals. This was not exploited. Too much emphasis was put on comprehensiveness, on encompassing all projects, and on *pro forma* calculations of rates of return. Too little energy went into real improvements of the project vetting process. The idea that high priority development expenditures could be cordoned off, protected as 'core', was beyond donor capacity to implement and too remote from political reality to succeed. And finally, too much time and energy was wasted in the recurrent cost quagmire.

Public investment programmes became, over time, more and more concerned with forward budgeting. Spending agencies were urged, cajoled, implored to take into account more accurately the future operating costs of projects under way or in preparation. Forms were prepared and revised, and spending agency replies were summed. The hope was that investment programmes would be more realistic (smaller) and completed projects would work better since the necessary operating and maintenance costs would be available. But it did not work.

As the Kenya and Senegal stories indicated, and other experience seems to confirm, usable recurrent cost estimates have almost never been produced in these budget exercises or reviews. This was partly because there are conceptual problems. What assumptions should be used about staffing levels, salaries, productivity? What about projects that generate no incremental operating costs but merely replace old physical facilities? What level of maintenance is to be assumed, what level and type of service or goods production? Should you estimate capital replacement costs?

In PIP preparation, spending agencies are rarely or never given operational guidelines on these definitional questions. Even if such guidelines existed, ministry officials would still be in the dark about how to apply them. This is one reason why forms are so frequently filled out perfunctorily or not all, and often with non-credible numbers. All the estimates are biased, generally too low, so as not to scare off donor funding of capital projects.[25] Recurrent cost figures produced in these circumstances are unlikely to be usable for meaningful expenditure projections.

There is another reason why this is so. Operating ministries are being asked to act against their own interest, which is to accumulate the most projects they can. These bring staff, activity, prestige and money for operating costs that they no longer find in the regular budget. Even if a conceptually clear basis existed for projecting recurrent costs, heads of operating agencies would not submit an honest estimate if it threatened project approval. If international donors are willing to support investment projects today, in the form of grants or near grants, poor country decision-makers would be foolish to refuse them because of likely revenue scarcities in future. The future is uncertain; the economy may be better, or aid flows more abundant. Donors may in any case be persuaded to pick up all or part of the running costs of completed projects. As for future repayments of non-grant financing, debt relief is always possible, even probable. If economic officials and politicians really operated on the principle of cutting back projects to levels that can be supported by future revenues, aggregate public investment would shrink, unless they had credible donor promises that excised projects would not mean lower aid volumes.

Rational bureaucratic and political actors cannot therefore be faulted for following the rule: gather rosebuds while you can. Nor can they be blamed for playing recurrent cost games to that end. And at the spending agency level there is another factor working in the same direction, notably the inter-agency competition for new activities and new money. It is not in the individual agency's interest to worry about recurrent cost implications while his colleagues do not.

Despite its common-sense appeal, then, the persistent strong donor emphasis on the need to calculate recurrent costs was (is) a mistake. Alternative estimating methods might have sufficed, though this would mean reduced aspirations for accuracy in medium term expenditure planning. Other process reform priorities merited much more attention than they typically received, such as cutting back the number of projects evaluated, using more rough and ready evaluation methods, enhancing dialogue with donors and technical ministries, strengthening procurement and bottleneck-removing procedures and improving procedures for determining the annual allocation of uncommitted government resources.

Public expenditure reviews

Of all the instruments of PSM reform this one comes closest to being an inherent non-starter. How could a donor investigation into public expenditures be regarded by targeted governments as anything other than an audit? How not be taken aback by the intrusiveness of the process; donors looking into expenditure closets, many with old skeletons, in their search for activities that donors regard as unproductive and of low priority.

There could be no mistaking that this was a donor operation, one of whose objectives was the hunting up of new conditionalities. Its incompatibility with local ownership was overwhelming. Nor for a long time did this seem to be much of a worry. Of the 113 PERs between 1987 and 1993, only three had local participation (in Bangladesh, India and Indonesia). Donors apparently believed that the two putative PER objectives (technical advice and independent assessment of public finance) were reconcilable, so that the PER could be an effective instrument despite its lack of ownership and its inherent intrusiveness.

That they were wrong is evident from the modest to negligible impacts uncovered by the first formal World Bank evaluation of PERs, summarised earlier (World Bank 1998d). Its descriptions of what went wrong are unsettling. The PERs, it states, do not meet the needs of any well-defined end-user. They often overlook areas of critical importance: public sector performance as service provider, sub-national expenditures, tax expenditures. Their prescriptions are often dogmatic, their recommendations formulaic. Many of the recommendations and analyses are so general they could apply to any country. Institutional issues receive little attention.

The evaluation notes that with very few exceptions the PERs have acquired little or no local ownership. Governments see PERs as 'nothing more than a prerequisite for donor funding.' The PER reports are not circulated widely in host governments. They take too long to produce and do not coincide with budget cycles. They contain too many recommendations, rarely prioritised, and these often parallel existing but unsuccessful government programmes, without indicating why they should end up differently.

These conclusions confirm those of an earlier evaluation (van der Windt 1995) sponsored by the Special Programme of Assistance for Africa (SPA).[26] This evaluation noted the perception of many local government officials that PERs are an externally driven exercise used to formulate condition-alities for structural adjustment credits and donor funding. It pointed out that many of the PER processes worked systematically against the develop-ment of internalisation or ownership. The World Bank set the agenda for the review. Issue papers were drafted with too little lead time to allow discussion with the recipient government (or with the bilateral donors who wished to join the mission). The status of the *aide-mémoire* that the mission left behind was not clear to governments (or to other donor participants either). Report preparation was entirely done by the World Bank (Ghana being the only exception.). The contents of PER documents were barely known outside the circle of people directly involved in the review process. Capacity building spin-offs were negligible. Host government officials said follow-up of PER recommendations was ineffective.

Conclusions

Two main arguments have been presented. The substantial donor efforts to reform PSM in low-income countries during the past 15–20 years can justifiably be called failures. And a significant share of the responsibility for these dismal results has to be attributed to donor deficiencies as reformers.

Various objections can be raised. It might be said that mistakes and slow progress are to be expected, given the enormity and the novelty of the task, and the many environmental obstacles to success. That is certainly right. But however much non-aid-related factors contributed to the poor record in PSM reform, that record gives little evidence of donor creativity, adaptability or flexibility. In general, donors failed to adapt programmes and practices to the circumstances of low-income countries with weak administrative institutions. Their response to implementation problems appears to have been generally inadequate. In these senses they have been unimpressive architects and implementers of PSM reforms.

It might be objected also that the analysis has dwelt excessively on the World Bank, and may not be representative of donor experience generally. It is true that examples of poor donor performance are taken mainly from World Bank experience. But the World Bank is after all the flagship institution in PSM reform, the main designer, financier, implementer and evaluator. And the World Bank's record is well documented. Plenty of corroborating examples can be culled from other donor experience. The missteps in technical assistance, which have reduced its capacity building impacts, have been abundantly documented (see Chapter 6 in this volume).

A major UNDP effort, the National Technical Co-operation Action Pro-gramme (NATCAP), which was intended to provide a structure for aid management, generated some useful information but never was able to make operational the proposals in its diagnostic/analytic studies (e.g. Williams 1991 and World Bank 1991b).[27] It faded away. A long list of false starts and failed initiatives could undoubtedly be drawn up from the PSM reform portfolios of other donors.

It can be objected, finally, that the critique in this chapter is no longer relevant. It is concerned with first generation reforms, which have been abandoned or much modified since the mid-1990s. It is true that there have been changes. The pace of privatisation has picked up. The so-called Medium Term Expenditure Framework has displaced the PIP as the centerpiece of budget reform. The PER has become a more diverse instru-ment. Civil service reform approaches have been broadened; there is much talk about administrative reforms in the direction of the 'New Public Management'.

But it is far from clear how much these new ideas have been translated into operating reality in low-income countries. Some of the 'old' reforms seem to linger. And even if it involves some beating of dead horses, analysis of the results of the first round of PSM reforms is useful. Understanding their nature and shortcomings may improve prospects for future success.

There remains a final question. What organisational factors explain the poor performance of donors, particularly the World Bank, in designing and implementing PSM reforms? Only a few summary observations on this complicated question can be given here. One factor is the well-known organisational inclination in the World Bank to give much greater weight to analytic issues than to the softer matters of process such as concern with ownership and nurturing of local capacity. A recent evaluation of World Bank fiscal reform programmes is indicative (Datta-Mitra 1997). It puts the blame for the modest achievements of these programmes almost entirely on analytic shortcomings, as though the poor past results in fiscal reform derive from inadequate knowledge and technical ineptness. But process deficiencies are probably more important, and they are ignored. The word 'ownership' does not seem to be mentioned even once in this document. Moreover, the recommendations give little place to local participation, ownership and commitment. They call for expansion of reform scope and a deepening of supporting analysis, which means greater World Bank intrusiveness.

Related to this is World Bank staff discomfort with institutional matters. Awareness of institutional weakness should permeate all reform activities in low-income countries. But sensitivity to country-specific institutional constraints has never been a strong point in World Bank operations. For example, fully a third of World Bank staff working on privatisation replied to a 1994 questionnaire that the greatest weakness in World Bank oper-ations was inability to customise programmes to country-specific needs

(World Bank 1994b). The 1998 evaluation of PERs (World Bank 1998d) found neglect of institutional issues to be a major failing; it observes also that the African PERs show less awareness of institutional constraints issues than do those in other regions, despite the generally higher level of institutional sensitivity among staff in that region.

Another factor is the natural tendency to resort to off-the-shelf solutions. Confronted with extremely difficult and complex problems, crafters of reform almost never have the time or the specialised skills and experience needed to develop customised approaches. They rely on what is available – 'best practices' or what other countries are doing.

Then there is the inadequacy of communication, learning failures, within the World Bank. The weaknesses of many PSM reform instruments and approaches were flagged early in their evolution by World Bank staff. The poor performance of performance contracts was underscored as early as 1989, and repeatedly thereafter. Yet the signing of these contracts continued to be centrepieces of the conditionality in structural adjustment and public enterprise reform credits. And they still may be, even after they received a devastating evaluation in the World Bank (1995) study. One of the main reasons given for cancellation in 1996 of a public enterprise reform credit (in Guinea) was failure to meet the conditionality on performance contracts.

It is the same with PIPs. Some sector specialists sounded alarms about the dangers of dual budgeting and other deficiencies as PIP implementation unfolded in the 1980s. Yet rolling PIPs remained popular, the World Bank supplementing them with public investment reviews and, later, PERs. Although now depicted as a terrible idea in the World Bank's *Public Expenditure Management Handbook* (1998e), limited observation suggests that many countries continue to produce PIPs, with or without World Bank support.

Why do these messages circulate so slowly in the World Bank? Lack of horizontal communication is one often-cited factor. Poor vertical communication may be as significant. Supervision has always been an orphan in the World Bank, often carried out reluctantly and perfunctorily. The messages transmitted upward may be superficial or vague; most of the information is contained in summary project ratings, which illuminate little as to institutional development or capacity building effects. The World Bank's institutional instability is undoubtedly a factor. Task managers change frequently, as have division chiefs and directors since the reorganisations of the 1990s.

Thus it may be that in PSM reform, candid and probing evaluations are rare in supervision reports and are slow to come in general, that their messages are transmitted imperfectly and that staff reshuffling severely dilutes the impact of these messages. Learning is slow, capacity to adjust impaired.

A complicating factor seems to be the hubris to which World Bank staff is prone. Overreach, over-ambition is endemic. Institutional weaknesses are noted, then passed over with a reference to technical assistance. Basically sound instruments are expanded and made more complex, pushing them beyond the implementing capacity of low-income countries. One example (not discussed in this chapter) is the comprehensive sector investment programme. The PIP is probably another.

Recent changes in World Bank structure may take care of these organisational problems. If so, and if organisation behaviours more generally are reviewed for their institutional development implications, the prospects for improved World Bank performance as a leader of public sector management reform will be much enhanced.

Notes

1 These included making state-owned enterprises (SOEs) work better and divestiture (privatisation). Of the total of 245 adjustment operations (including sectoral adjustment lending, SECAL), two-thirds had such components. About 60 per cent were in sub-Saharan Africa and 20 per cent in Latin America. Of almost 1,500 conditionalities in these adjustment loans, 20 per cent referred to divestiture, and half were for PE restructuring.

2 Some indication of the magnitudes involved emerges from a recent study which estimates that between 1988 and 1995, privatisation-related credits to sub-Saharan Africa totalled $10 billion, almost $7 billion from the World Bank, and over $3 billion from other donors (White and Bhatia 1998).

3 In 52 of these countries World Bank loans included conditions aimed at better public investment programming and the streamlining of general budget processes.

4 Nunberg (1994) identified 90 World Bank projects with prominent civil service reform components between 1981 and 1991; of these, 55 were African.

5 A notable exception is World Bank (1995: 259–61), which gives explicit attention to the donor role.

6 Half of total 1995–7 PSM spending according to World Bank classifications went to Latin America, more than a quarter to transition economies in Europe and Central Asia and only 12 per cent to Africa, a decline from nearly 20 per cent in 1988–92 (World Bank 1997c).

7 Adjustment operations declined in the mid-1990s to 15 per cent of total World Bank Group lending, though they rose in 1997 to 20 per cent of the somewhat lower ($20 billion) total. Low-income countries have a smaller place. For example, in 1997 there were only 14 adjustment operations in sub-Saharan Africa, most very lightly financed, as compared with more than 30 in the late 1980s (World Bank 1997c).

8 See also World Bank (1995: 2), which states that 'only a few countries have reformed their state-owned enterprises successfully'.

9 Later in the same report somewhat different (worse) numbers are given: implementation of (public enterprise) reforms is said to be incomplete or weak in 25 (of 27) countries (ibid.: 37).

10 Of the ten main privatisers, only Zambia, Ghana, Mozambique and Benin earn good grades as effective in process and outcomes.

11 The PE sector share in GDP remained at a little over 11 per cent for the whole sample of countries, and over 14 per cent in low-income countries. The sector's share of paid employment remained at 10 per cent overall, increased from 15 to 16 per cent in low-income countries and from 19 to 22 per cent in Africa. There

were some positive changes; government investment shares did decline, and net financial transfers from the PE sector to the government decreased, though they remained positive through most of the decade.

12 For similar conclusions, see Dia (1993) and Klitgaard (1997).

13 The main donor public expenditure management activities, judging from World Bank projects, have been in public investment programming (28 per cent of operations), tax administration (22 per cent) and budget management (29 per cent). The remainder were in such areas as accounting/auditing, debt management and procurement. Of these, 46 were in sub-Saharan Africa, 19 in Latin America, nine in Europe, the Middle East and North Africa and seven in Asia. The geographical distribution changed during the 1990s, as noted.

14 Examination of completion and audit reports for 97 operations revealed that implementation has been weak in budgetary process and public enterprise reform and in the reduction or restructuring of current expenditures.

15 See Shirley and Nellis (1991), World Bank (1995) and White and Bhatia (1998) on public enterprise reform. For civil service reform, see Dia (1993) Lindauer and Nunberg (1994) and Klitgaard (1997).

16 During a 1994 visit to Uganda, the author met with the Economic Committee of the Parliament to discuss reform issues, especially privatisation. Committee members said that debate over such policies was negligible. When parliamentarians questioned members of the administration they were told that it was pointless, since executive branch members had no influence over privatisation policies. These were negotiated with donors and incorporated in policy loans. Parliamentarians were not involved. Moreover, they couldn't find out much about issues and problems. When officials or outsiders came before the committee they invariably spoke as defenders of the existing programme.

17 An example from Senegal in the late 1980s is illustrative. One of the conditions of second tranche release in Senegal's third structural adjustment loan was the government's offer of selling shares in 10 public enterprises by September 1987. Nothing had been done by the due date. The government proposed to meet the condition by announcing in the local press that 10 enterprises were for sale. However, none was really ready for sale, in the sense of having a complete dossier (audit, asset valuation, and so forth). Even the decision to privatise the firms in question had not been fully discussed within government; later reflection led to the removal of the two largest enterprises from the list. The World Bank in any case accepted the announcement of intention to sell as equivalent to putting up for sale, and thus as meeting the condition for tranche release.

18 The Chinese contracts have been variously estimated to number more than 100,000 and 450,000.

19 The critique was broadened in Shirley and Nellis (1991). The 1994 World Bank study *Adjustment in Africa* dismissed the approach in one sentence: 'With a few notable exceptions, performance contracts and other attempts to boost the efficiency of enterprises remaining under state ownership have failed.' (World Bank 1994a: 103).

20 A significant United Nations study (Bennett 1994) is somewhat less bleak in its conclusions, but from the substance of the text and the attached case studies, it is not easy to know why South Korea is depicted as the outstanding success, but the World Bank (1995) comments that enthusiasm for performance contracting is waning there. The UN study gives good marks to Pakistan and Gambia, but Indian experience is disappointing, that of Bangladesh unimpressive, and the other two African cases ineffective.

21 'The failure of contracts, in our sample, adequately to address the commitment problem may be the most important explanation for the evident failure to

improve performance' (World Bank 1995: 128). Nellis (1988: 49) argued that 'the governments' failure to pay is the problem.'

22 One example: a condition of third tranche release in adjustment lending was that the government meet its financial obligations to the SOEs as agreed in signed performance contracts. The government could not raise the sums involved from available budget resources. Instead, as the deadline for third tranche release approached, it unilaterally reduced the amounts committed under the agreements, paid them, and declared it had met its obligations. The World Bank agreed and released the adjustment money. This experience naturally nourished cynicism about the meaningfulness of performance agreements.

23 Other conceptual flaws exist in the PC approach. Many SOE problems could be addressed at the enterprise level, without the complexities of a PC. And some problems require attention at the sectoral level, which means that other actors beside the SOE had to be at the table. This is clear, for example, with urban transport enterprises.

24 The *Public Expenditure Management Handbook* (World Bank 1998e: ch. 2) points out among other problems that projects in the PIP cannot be ranked by economic rates of return; that internal rates of return are not comparable across sectors, and for many projects cannot be calculated. If they could, few poor countries have the capacity to cover all projects; insufficient attention is paid to recurrent costs; and most fundamental, the PIP has encouraged dual budgeting, and the 'dual budget may well be the single most important culprit in the failure to link planning, policy, and budgeting, and in poor budgetary outcomes.' Development budgets have a lower hurdle for entry, so operating agencies put less sound projects or those containing many O&M costs into the PIP.

25 Biases in the estimates depend on the nature of the budget environment. If there is no serious medium-term expenditure plan or forward budget, estimates are always low so as not to alarm the donors, or occasionally, the finance ministry. In the rare cases where such plans or budgets exist, and are credible, it may pay ministry officials to put in a high estimate in an effort to establish a bigger claim on future resources. The likelihood that the forward budget proposals will be cut back further encourages exaggerated estimates in this case.

26 The study included field visits to nine countries: Burkina Faso, Côte d'Ivoire, Ghana, Mali, Mozambique, Senegal, Tanzania, Uganda and Zambia.

27 There was also an initiative, apparently now dropped, that aimed at 'comprehensive country programming', the weaving together under UNDP auspices of sectoral programmes that would include all projects, however financed.

13 Foreign aid and private sector development

Mads Váczy Kragh, Jørgen Birk Mortensen,
Henrik Schaumburg-Müller and Hans Peter Slente

Introduction

After structural adjustment

Many developing countries affected by the economic crises in the 1980s have undertaken structural adjustment programmes (SAP). These programmes aim at enhancing the efficiency of the economy through deregulation, liberalisation and privatisation. The private sector is now widely recognised as the main engine of growth.

Structural adjustment programmes have often disappointed by not creating the expected supply response in the private sector. Thus, as a next step in the process of creating a competitive market economy, governments are now focusing on creating a favourable climate for the private business sector with more direct measures. These measures have been termed second generation reforms (Camdessus 1997).

With a more prominent role for the private sector in developing countries, foreign aid has taken new forms in order to support the transition process and in the longer run support the private sector in creating growth. In recent years, aid to the private sector has become more widespread; at firm, sector and macro level.

Several reasons come together in explaining the increase in private sector aid (see also Chapter 1). First is the redefinition of the role of the state; a large number of countries have moved towards market economy and the role of the state has been redefined from being directly involved in production and marketing to being a regulator and provider of a stable macroeconomic climate and an appropriate framework for business activity (see Chapter 2). Foreign aid accommodates this policy change.

Second, the slow supply response of the private sector of SAPs has led to the introduction of more active instruments to boost competitiveness and thereby private employment. SAPs alone will not enhance productivity enough; this must be addressed through industrial policy measures at macro, sector and micro level.

Third is the identification of barriers to growth in the private sector, e.g. inappropriate laws and regulation, underdeveloped financial markets (see Chapter 14) and lack of skills required in a market economy.

Fourth, as the private sector grows, imperfect markets and externalities will become increasingly visible, suggesting a role for private sector development (PSD) aid. Lack of information and high transaction costs can be addressed through PSD aid. Likewise, environmental depletion, unemployment and uneven income distribution can be addressed through a PSD aid programme. A control and regulatory system that addresses such negative externalities will in most cases benefit the overall economy (Riddell 1987).

Fifth, as discussed in Chapter 15, the need for filling the savings gap remains relevant in most developing countries even though the primary issue is now private, not public, savings. Diminishing flows of official development assistance (ODA) and increasing private capital flows have prompted thoughts and experiments on how foreign aid can act as a catalyst for private capital flows.

Sixth, there is an ongoing debate on aid effectiveness (see Chapter 4) and donor agencies see PSD aid as a way of testing new and possibly more growth-oriented aid instruments.

Definition

Private sector development has become a popular term in developing countries and among aid agencies, but what does the term actually mean? According to the OECD, the definition and scope of PSD is as follows:

> 'Private sector' is conceived by the donor community as a basic organising principle for economic activity where private ownership is an important factor, where markets and competition drive production and where private initiative and risk-taking set activities in motion. The private sector principle can be applied in all economic activities – agriculture, industry and services (including the delivery of public services). Donor motivations for supporting PSD are based on promoting economic efficiency and social welfare. Donors agree that PSD is fundamentally about people: releasing and harnessing their productive potential and satisfying their human needs and desires; and creating pluralistic societies which provide both human freedom and human security.
>
> (OECD 1995)

This definition clearly shows the broad scope of the PSD concept. The main difference from traditional aid is that the immediate beneficiary of PSD aid is the private, productive sector: enterprises and entrepreneurs. However, improved efficiency and growth in the private sector also benefits the population at large; labour through increased employment and wages and consumers through lower prices and better quality of goods and services.

This chapter focuses on the industrial sector, leaving out agriculture. However, a number of the findings of the chapter also apply for private agriculture and many of the instruments also benefit the agricultural sector, e.g. credit instruments for small entrepreneurs (see Chapter 14). The chapter provides an overview of the experience with PSD aid. The next section briefly overviews concepts and analytical approaches. Then follows a description of a range of private sector aid instruments and an assessment of experience. Finally, the outlook for future PSD aid is discussed.

Concepts and features of private sector development aid

What is the theoretical rationale for giving aid to the private sector? Overall, PSD aid can supplement the domestic industrial policies of developing countries; it can smooth the transformation of the economy; loosen constraints on enterprise growth; and strengthen factors that determine the competitiveness of enterprises.

In order to formulate and assess private sector aid and its potential, it is useful to adopt an appropriate analytical framework. The PSD issue can be addressed at different levels: (i) macro (economy), (ii) sector (industry) and (iii) micro (enterprise). When using macroeconomic theory to generate policy advice, the solution usually offered is a structural adjustment programme (SAP). After such SAPs, developing countries have often found their manufacturing sector unable to compete with foreign imports. Global trade liberalisation is also rapidly eroding preferential trade arrangements for developing countries' export, which has been a popular instrument at the macro-level used both in bilateral and multilateral agreements. In this chapter we will mainly deal with what comes after stabilisation and structural adjustment to spur efficiency and competitiveness of the enterprise sector. The framework presented below is not a model, but it does provide an overview of the rationale underlying different types of PSD interventions by donors and recipient country governments.

Sector level interventions

At the theoretical level, 'industrial organisation' is a neoclassical expansion of the 'structure–conduct–performance' paradigm, which analyses how market structures influence the conduct of companies and the performance of markets (e.g. Ferguson and Ferguson 1988). Industrial dynamics have roots in the 'evolutionary' school, in which the scope is dynamic and agents are assumed to exhibit 'procedural rationality' (as opposed to the assumption of full rationality and information of neoclassical theory). This school of analysis has mainly focused on innovation, invention and diffusion of technology.

Another way of systematising the competitiveness of a certain sector in a certain country is offered by Porter (1990), who integrated many aspects of industrial organisation and industrial dynamics into a single system. Porter seeks to identify the sources of growth by answering the question: 'why do certain countries become a base for successful industries?' The framework is not a theory in the strict sense but provides a framework or a 'checklist' for analysing industrial sectors by drawing upon many different theories. It is argued that the sources of competitiveness are to be found in the inter-relation between four determinants within a sector.

First, *factor conditions* consist of human resources, physical capital, know-ledge resources, capital resources and infrastructure. Aid to all kinds of education, research, technology transfer and credit schemes will help upgrade these factors. Infrastructure is also an obvious investment target for aid donors.

Second, *demand conditions* are crucial to growth. Domestic demand is usually very important to companies in most countries despite growing international trade. Efforts to expand local markets by establishing regional trade blocks help companies attain a minimum efficient scale of produc-tion. Demand conditions can also be upgraded by linking-up companies to markets through export promotion. Structural adjustment programmes, in particular, have focused on liberalising trade and on strengthening exports.

Third, *related sectors* are about vertical and horizontal linkages. The existence of efficient links to sub-contractors influences the costs and quality of production. Positive dynamic effects can be obtained through co-operation within a sector on technology, education etc. These sector group-ings are also termed 'clusters'. Foreign aid can support creation of linkages, networks and business associations by enabling companies to exchange technologies and to draw on common services.

Fourth, *strategy, structure and competition* relate to the behaviour of companies and individuals. Competition and rivalry between companies are necessary preconditions for the creation of firm competitiveness. Only competition makes companies specialise and invest in upgrading their own factor conditions. The government must put proper legislation and control in place to ensure that domestic firms compete. Adjustment programmes have emphasised the need for creating a competitive environment. Further-more, at the institutional level, foreign aid can help create an enabling environment for PSD.

The importance of these four determinants will differ from one sector to another. Firms in a cluster are characterised by the same determinants, i.e. sharing the same market and factors of production. Upgrading the determinants has a positive impact on the cluster as a whole, but not necessarily on other clusters within the economy. Another feature is the dynamics of the determinants, which is obtained by describing the mutual reinforcement of the determinants over time and how companies and the government can upgrade them. The government, assisted by aid agencies, can influence the competitiveness through policies directed at one or more of the determinants. In the discussion below of aid instruments, the ways in which PSD aid can impact on these determinants will be identified and assessed.

Micro level interventions

In the neoclassical theory, the firm is simply regarded as a production function in a rational explanatory perspective. Micro level theories explain how firms are formed, organised and managed, and they offer insight into the company making possible the analysis of the various actors involved, recognising their different interests, resources, uncertainties, risk assessments and asymmetric levels of information.

The evolutionary theory focuses on the dynamic evolution and creation of competitiveness within firms through innovation. The neoclassical assumption of rational behaviour is replaced by procedural rationality, where the firm is described by routines rather than by optimisation. Nelson and Winter (1982), building on evolutionary theory, introduced the concept of capabilities within the firm. Lall (1993) analyses managerial, organisational, technical, marketing and financial capabilities within firms. At low levels of technological development, the core capabilities comprise equipment selection, quality control, process and product technology, basic industrial engineering and efficient procurement of input.

An important aspect is the learning mechanism that describes how firms acquire and introduce new technology. This holds important lessons for technology transfer. Traditional neoclassical theory views technology as 'a broad range of techniques which the firm can choose from without problems.' (Knudsen 1991). In contrast, evolutionary theory specifically describes the acquisition and adaptation of new technology. Technology choice is not seen as a discretionary change, but as an adaptive and incremental process within the firm (Evenson and Westphal 1995).

The evolutionary theory reiterates the point that there are large positive effects of education and training because firms cannot upgrade their technology without in-house capabilities. The evolutionary approach also brings to the forefront the point that companies often develop in co-operation with other firms (clusters). Private sector aid therefore can also aim at supporting links and networks.

Network theory and other recent business theories in the tradition of economic sociology, similarly emphasise how firms that co-operate in network relations are able to upgrade and renew (Grabher 1993). Inspired by the industrial development in Italy, much work has been done to explain successful industrial co-operation (Swedberg 1993). Sharing the assumptions of evolutionary theory, network theory provides useful concepts such as flexible specialisation and trust that are useful for understanding not only co-operation between firms but also relations between firms and the broader supporting and regulatory institutions created by the government.

Problems

As reviewed below, there are several problems related to extending foreign aid to the private, productive sector. These problems must be taken into consideration when planning and evaluating PSD aid. For instance, market distortions can easily occur when supporting individual enterprises. They can be minimised by supporting activities outside the core business, e.g. environment or occupational health above the legal requirements.

The issue of who controls funds might also cause problems when co-operating with companies rather than the government. The government has, in principle, a one-stringed decision-making structure, e.g. from the ministry of health down to the local health clinics, whereas the private sector is of a more ungovernable nature. To counter the control problem, it is necessary to build simple disbursement procedures and appropriate control mechanisms.

Incentives are different in private companies not pursuing the social goals of the government or the donor, but aiming to maximise profits. The means of influencing their behaviour is through market-oriented mechanisms and incentive structures. Support should only be given if there is consistency between the company's objective and the social (development) objective. To ensure this, a minimum requirement is a competitive market. Other social goals within the companies can be pursued through direct incentives for investment in training and environmental measures over and above the level the company would have chosen through profit maximisation.

Donor co-ordination is easier in the public than in the private sector. When giving aid through the public sector, a master plan of one sector can be laid out in a ministry and each donor can take on some of the tasks outlined in the plan. The private sector has no master plan – and it should not have one. Given the decentralised and competitive nature of the private sector there is no natural forum for donor co-ordination. The lack of co-ordination can lead to duplication of efforts and thereby inefficient utilisation of resources. Sometimes donors compete in supporting business associations, providing advisory services, credits or training for the same groups of enterprises.

Rent-seeking behaviour also occurs in the private sector. Inefficient companies and private sector institutions might be kept alive only by foreign aid, and the constant inflow of donor money makes it difficult for efficient entities to compete without aid. Recipients might start spending more time on pleasing donor agencies than on pursuing their primary business goal.

Finally, corruption among public servants should be limited through privatisation programmes. On the other hand, there are windfall gains to be had during the privatisation process if companies are sold to preferential investors in exchange for illegal commissions. Nevertheless, donor support of privatisation programmes often aims at enhancing the process and making it as transparent as possible.

These problems must always be checked when planning and evaluating PSD aid. There will often be a choice of placing, say, service providers to

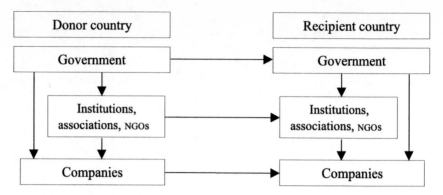

Figure 13.1 Channels of PSD aid.

private industry in either public or private entities. The above problems must be considered in making this choice, and they are part of the critical review of PSD aid below.

Channels of PSD aid

Private sector development aid has the enterprises as the immediate beneficiary. The interventions can be at macro, sector, or enterprise level, and the aid can go through various channels that might differ from other traditional aid instruments. In this respect, PSD aid is similar to aid to NGOs. The flow to the private sector can take many forms on the way from donor to a private enterprise. It is possible to summarise the recipients under the following headings: (i) local public institutions, e.g. for vocational training, extension service and policy reform, (ii) local private institutions, associations or NGOs, such as banks, business associations or grass root groups, e.g. for organising, assisting and training entrepreneurs, (iii) local companies directly, e.g. for investment and training, (iv) donor country institutions, associations or NGOs, e.g. for project management and technical assistance to their local counterparts and (v) donor country enterprises, e.g. direct partnerships with local enterprises involving transfer of technology, know-how and investments. The various channels of PSD aid are illustrated below.

One flow-example is government-to-government-to-business. Here, the local government receives aid which is then directed towards PSD. Such support may be directed at four different areas: (i) the political level (policy), (ii) private sector regulations, (iii) promotion of private business and (iv) alleviation of the negative impact of the market economy. In this case, it is important to stress that although emphasis is on the private sector, the government plays an important role. Consequently, support to government on how to handle a market economy can also be regarded as private sector aid. Private sector development aid is not necessarily equivalent to downsizing, but rather redefining, the public sector.

Private sector development aid instruments

A range of instruments exists at macro, sector and enterprise level to assist in developing the private business sector. The following is a presentation of a number of these instruments, their application by different donors, and their effects. The different types of aid can be divided into four main categories: (i) investment support programmes, (ii) enabling environment support programmes, (iii) privatisation and commercialisation programmes and (iv) business partnership programmes. We consider each in turn.

Investment support programmes

Objectives

In the late 1960s, a number of European countries directed part of their foreign aid towards national venture capital funds in order to enable them to stimulate and participate in private sector investments in developing countries. The funds normally participate in joint venture investments between firms in the donor and the recipient country. The rationale for transferring aid to venture capital funds is that risk capital, especially in foreign currency, is limited in most developing countries. Theoretically, the investment support programmes are rooted in the two-gap models, where either domestic savings or foreign exchange act as a binding constraint on economic growth (see Chapter 4 and 15).

In addition to the direct effects of capital inflows, donors visualise a significant transfer of technology from the donor country through private companies – either in the form of training or the introduction of new techniques and machinery. The upgrading of factor conditions has been estimated to be as significant as the direct effect of capital transfer.[1]

Finally, foreign exchange earnings are expected to increase from transfers between companies in donor and recipient countries. This will occur through trade between subsidiary and parent company or alternatively by the parent company being able to promote the products of the subsidiary on new markets. The capital directed towards the venture capital fund often works as an alternative banking system where loans or share capital in hard currencies can be obtained which will ease the credit squeeze many companies are facing in countries with poor financial infrastructure and, consequently, high interest rates.

The development aspects are, beside higher growth, increasing employment and decreasing poverty. It can be argued that some of the funds reserved for investment support instruments are primarily focused on assisting companies in donor countries in their internationalisation effort. The funding organisations have two objectives: (i) a return on their investment and (ii) economic development in recipient countries. An additional aim for national venture funds based in donor countries is to support national companies in their process of internationalisation.

Methods and initiatives

The grant transferred to a venture capital fund cannot strictly be regarded as foreign aid. However, due to the fact that many of these institutions may be willing to take a higher risk than do traditional investors, an *indirect* grant element exists, which helps eliminate financial market externalities in recipient countries where financial markets may be either non-existing or inefficient (see Chapter 14). The international and national venture funds have attempted to target these externalities by providing loans, equity (and quasi-equity) or guarantees. In some cases grants can also be provided in the form of training or environmental facilities related to such funds. Some agencies are also funding feasibility and technical studies. The tendency has been to provide support in the implementation phase rather than in the preparatory phase (FDI 1992).

At national level, a number of European countries have formed venture funds that offer long-term finance by way of equity and loans to private enterprises in developing countries. The loans are typically in foreign currency, given on semi-market terms (LIBOR plus a risk margin), whereas the equity is risk bearing for 4–7 years whereafter the shares are sold on market terms. Since the mid-1990s, European donor funds (joined in the European Development Finance Institutions, EDFI) have experienced a large increase in investments and the total amount committed for projects in the developing world, mainly in Asia and Latin America. Africa is clearly lacking behind (EDFI 1998).[2]

The most significant multilateral venture fund is the International Finance Corporation (IFC) which is part of the World Bank group. The IFC is the largest multilateral source of loan and equity financing for private sector projects in the developing world. In terms of policy, IFC can assist governments in creating conditions that will stimulate both foreign and domestic private investments in developing countries. The activities of the IFC have expanded quite considerably in both Asia and Latin America, with the portfolio of the IFC to a wide extent directed towards areas with high growth rates and countries with strong purchasing powers like Brazil, China and India.

A number of regional development banks have created their own venture funds.[3] They typically provide loan and equity to joint venture companies. Furthermore, they might support feasibility studies and training activities related to the establishment of a joint venture. These funds are typically invested in smaller projects than those involving the IFC. The number of venture capital funds incorporated in developing countries increased rapidly in the late 1990s. They are typically funded by donor agencies, national venture funds, regional development banks and private investors.[4]

Experience

The investment support instrument has become popular among donors. It has primarily worked as a financial instrument for the private sector in developing countries. Although a demand for social development and technical transfers to the recipient country has been attached to most funds, the majority of 'aid' generated cannot be characterised as foreign aid according to the definition the Development Assistance Committee (DAC) of the OECD.

Assistance through the investment support programmes has in many cases, especially in Asia, been successful in terms of investment returns. In 1999, the Danish Industrialisation Fund for Developing Countries (IFU) investigated the internal rate of return (IRR) on all investments in Africa, Asia and Latin America. The results indicated a negative IRR in Africa, a positive IRR in Asia and a mildly positive IRR in Latin America (IFU 1999). The IFC has made the same type of analysis with similar results (IFC 1998). Compared with other types of investment, sustainability seems to have been acceptable. The experience of IFU shows that out of 350 projects from which IFU has withdrawn, only 78 projects have stopped (IFU 1999).

It is, however, doubtful whether the broader development objectives have been reached, and the more 'soft' issues, in particular, are seldom addressed directly by the above mentioned funds. Many venture funds try to distance themselves from the aid community by focusing more narrowly on the economic return on their investment. But more of them are interested in parallel funds to support softer issues like the environment and training. More recently, emphasis has been on combining capital, training, environmental awareness and technical transfers, rather than on the isolated economic support for private investments. This type of aid is typically generated through partnership programmes as described below.

A second problem with venture funds is that they may create unfair competition *vis-à-vis* the finance systems of developing countries. In that way the experience gained from venture funds is not rooted in the local community. This is one of the main arguments for supporting regional and national funds based in the developing countries with local money involved. A third problem is that the local companies will always bear the foreign exchange risk. A recent example of this is the current financial crisis in Asia, where many companies are practically bankrupt due to loans in foreign currencies.

The number of new institutions and the amount of money committed have increased rapidly in the late 1990s. This indicates a growing demand from companies in developing and developed countries. It clearly reflects the fact that a larger proportion of production now takes place in the private sector. Cassen points out that this process started in the early 1970s (Cassen *et al.* 1994). Though an overall growth has been experienced, the regional differences are evident.

Enabling environment support programmes

Objectives

Most agree that it is desirable to create an enabling environment for private enterprises, but what is actually an enabling environment? The host of things covered under this heading translates into what we would normally term industrial or business policy. An enabling environment concerns rules, regulations, information, physical and financial infrastructure, research and development, education, training and other resources, created outside the company but affecting operations inside the company.

The enabling environment is supported at macro or sector level and should in principle not interfere with individual firms, which distinguishes it from the other support measures discussed in this chapter. This type of intervention at sector or macro level does not create unfair competition between firms, if it is available for all, which is generally the case.

Adjustment programmes have supported the creation of an enabling environment through liberalisation and deregulation, thereby creating a level playing field on which all firms can potentially compete. They have also assisted in laying down the foundation for a stable macro environment. These reforms can be termed *first-generation* reforms. *Second-generation* reforms are more specifically targeted at certain economic activities and sectors (Camdessus 1997). There is a natural progression in the reforms; if overall macro stability is not at hand, other reforms might not work.

Among bilateral donors there is a tradition for supporting the environment in which private firms are operating. Much of this support has been directed towards the small- and medium-sized enterprise sector, very often in the form of vocational training and credit programmes. Support to an enabling environment can be organised in the public sector, the private sector (firms, business associations or other entities) or in partnerships between the two. In the process of going from planned to market economy, a range of public institutions will be closed down and replaced with new ones – or they will have to change their focus and improve their services. Thus, second generation reforms entail a 'better state' rather than 'less state' (Camdessus 1997). Public administration can be targeted with support to improve the legislative system, public services and public administration in areas related to business.

Private organisations also play a new role within a market economy and can be targeted with donor support to better understand and fill out this role. These organisations can be business associations, private business support organisations, market institutions or organisations for the promotion of exports, investment, education, research and technology development, etc.

Methods and initiatives

The World Bank is the largest single donor supporting an enabling business environment, often within a broader programme approach to PSD. Over the ten years from 1989, many bilateral donors also developed programmes and projects within this category of private sector support.

Within its PSD department, the World Bank has established a business environment group, which assists countries in the design and implementation of strategies and individual reforms to enhance productivity and foster private sector competitiveness. The group operates with four mutually reinforcing areas: (i) market framework institutions and policies, (ii) consensus building: private–public partnerships, (iii) export development and external linkages and (iv) training and technology access.

The World Bank often conducts a private sector assessment study, which identifies barriers and obstacles for PSD and forms the basis for the design of support activities including both policy and regulatory work and investment initiatives. Other donors make the same kind of overall analysis of the business environment as a basis for their support to the business environment, but a range of donors just support an enabling environment on an *ad hoc* basis with small grants for projects that are presented to them. The Asian Development Bank (ASDB) and the other regional development banks have policies and strategies that support the private sector business environment, although these organisations' private sector programmes are more focused on assisting individual enterprises or industries.

At an early stage, German aid agencies created a tradition for support through German business associations to sister organisations in developing countries. This has benefited chambers of commerce and industry and other sector institutions in a range of developing countries. The support to these organisations has mainly been directed to commercial activities and less to institution building. The European Union will support national and regional business associations under the next Lomé-Convention to start in the year 2000 (CEC 1996). Other donors are also supporting business associations in order to build an effective voice of business within the countries in transition and for these associations to deliver business services to their members as well as providing a policy and business network for enterprises.

National export promotion agencies receive substantial support for their efforts to promote and diversify exports of the country. The support is often given to capacity building within the agency for trade regulation, export credits, export promotion, seminars, collection and dissemination of market intelligence. Trade regulation issues have high priority among the developing countries, because their enterprises may have grown very dependent on a protected trade regime and they now realise the challenges posed by free trade promoted under the WTO.

Vocational education and training is supported by many donors, either through national authorities or private organisations supplying technical or managerial training. With the introduction of market economy, new concepts such as marketing and modern management are taught to middle and top management. With the opening up of the economies, new demands arise on the quality of products and competitiveness of the work force. This reveals a huge need for vocational education and training. Environmental protection as well as occupational health are also aspects addressed by donor financed education programmes.

Sub-contracting and networking between firms is encouraged. The rationale is that a protected home market and inadequate incentives for private enterprises, has created a few large (former parastatal) firms with a high degree of vertical integration, and a group of small, informal firms. In other words, there is a 'missing middle' which is unhealthy for the dynamics of the sectors. Sub-contracting can increase the efficiency of the larger firms and increase demand for the products of small and medium-sized enterprises (SMEs). Sub-contracting opens SMEs up for technical and managerial upgrading because they need certain skills to qualify as sub-contractor to a formal company. Demand driven programmes like these are the most efficient way to provide services to SMEs (Humphrey and Schmitz 1995).[5]

Many donors still adopt an *ad hoc* approach to the private sector while others try to make coherent programmes. Denmark is supporting the enterprise sector in Tanzania through a sector programme containing the following components: (i) credit institutions: bank, venture capital and micro credits, (ii) vocational training: public owned, private financed, (iii) strengthening of business associations: industrial association and labour unions, (iv) establishment of a commercial court and (v) capacity building within the Ministry of Industry and Commerce.

Experience

There are still only few evaluations of how effective donors have been in supporting enabling environments. In many Asian countries, PSD has benefited from a very active industrial policy supported by government and donors. In many African countries, where governments have a lower capacity, it is still difficult to draw conclusions about the experience. But basic institutions in African countries, including financial ones, remain weak.

Most of the traditional support programmes within vocational training and business support services have no doubt had a positive impact. A relative success story, Danida's tool room projects in India, started in the early 1970s. However, part of the earlier support to an enabling environment, like training schools and credit institutions, has not been very successful. One reason is that aid was not targeted enough to the needs of the business sector because the companies were not involved in the design. Thus, the activities became supply driven instead of demand driven. This is why the dialogue with the private sector must be strengthened. Adverse macroeconomic conditions have often overshadowed the positive effects of the efforts to create an enabling business climate. An important lesson is that without the overall macroeconomic framework being in order, money may be wasted on second-generation reforms.

There is clearly a lack of donor co-ordination within this type of activity that leads to rent-seeking and duplication of efforts among local business associations and business support organisations – often this competition may even occur between government and private agencies within the same service area. Many support activities, such as the sub-contracting schemes or training of entrepreneurs, are not commercially viable and therefore require a subsidy. A number of suppliers compete for the funds available. Competition is healthy, but at the same time much donor effort and money is wasted in building separate systems.

Privatisation and commercialisation programmes

Content and objectives

The objective of privatisation and commercialisation is the restructuring of the public sector in order to improve efficiency and to concentrate on services complementary to private activity. Privatisation is part of public sector restructuring whereby state-owned enterprises (SOEs) are transferred to the private sector, normally for the purpose of increasing efficiency and reducing public expenditure. Privatisation has often been part of an adjustment agreement with the World Bank. The motives of privatisation have primarily been that the private sector works more efficiently than the public sector and in that way – from an economic point of view – there should be benefits from privatising public sectors where there is no natural monopoly (Nellis and Kikeri 1989).

Another measurable benefit may be a decrease in public expenditure associated with loss-making public enterprises. It was estimated (by the World Bank) that the deficit of state owned enterprises averaged more than 4 per cent in the 1970s and increased during the 1980s in all developing countries (Gillis *et al.* 1996).

Commercialisation (or public enterprise reform) is also part of public sector restructuring and covers measures to strengthen the commercial operation of state owned enterprises. There are arguments that it is not necessary to change the ownership of state owned enterprises to make them effective, but to separate management of the enterprises from the political level and introduce market conditions (a hard budget constraint) in these companies (e.g. FDI 1992). In recent years, donors have widely agreed that privatisation and commercialisation programmes could enable developing countries to develop faster. Privatisation was critically viewed as one of the ten headings of the 'Washington consensus'. However, Williamson (1993) points out that privatisation is less wanted among the recipients than among donors.

One can argue that firm efficiency does not depend upon the ownership structures but on whether there is free and fair competition. If state-owned enterprises operate on market terms, there is no efficiency gain in changing their ownership. From this point of view, commercialisation is as good as privatisation. However, in practice it has been very difficult to exclude political interests in the day-to-day operations of SOEs.

Methods and initiatives

The World Bank is the leading institution in the preparation and support of privatisation programmes, providing advice and loans to cover costs associated with privatisation, and also providing investment loans to help restructure privatised enterprises. It also supports in the post-privatisation phase by assisting governments to set up the facilitating and regulatory framework for the privatised sectors, by assisting the enterprise sector to adjust to the new situation, and by assisting the financial sector to deal with the new private enterprises.

Many bilateral donors have supported the privatisation and commercialisation process in various ways. Traditional foreign aid has often been directed to public infrastructure and utilities, to prepare them for privatisation or at least commercialisation. Donors have also contributed to cover expenditure and clear debt in the privatisation processes. Debt-for-equity swaps have been facilitated by donor funds, and sometimes donors have provided funds to finance the privatisation. Bilateral donors have also supported government directly in the privatisation process, as did USAID in Egypt, helping to create an optimal environment for privatisation and assisting with technical assistance and capital. The USAID programme also included identification of relevant US enterprises for matching with Egypt enterprises.

Experience

Privatisation efforts have taken place across all economic sectors and developing countries. Privatisation is often part of a larger economic reform programme, which makes it difficult to identify and measure the overall effects of privatisation. While output and employment effects are difficult to quantify, efficiency gains have been reported at company level (see Hjertholm 1997b for a survey). It is therefore difficult to draw general conclusions about the outcome of these efforts and their effect on the development of the countries concerned. However, it is fair to say that the outcome has been more successful in Asia compared to Africa because of greater economic flexibility and generally more favourable business conditions, including the availability of investment capital. Likewise, the commercially most attractive sectors such as telecommunication are easier to privatise than other sectors, e.g. water and sanitation.

In most African countries, SOEs have dominated in many sectors and have been a heavy burden on public finances. However, privatisation programmes have been slow and only a limited part of SOEs has been privatised (World Bank 1993b). The procedures of privatisation have often been lengthy and it has been difficult to find buyers (van de Valle 1989). This is partly because a large proportion of the SOEs put up for privatisation are loss-making and commercially unviable (Larsson 1994). A common problem is the new owners' obligations to old company debt and to the work force. Private investors have also been reluctant to bid as conditions and policies for future business operations have been uncertain.

In many cases there has been widespread resistance among politicians, public servants and employees to privatise. Often the public servants have used the excuse of protecting the interests of employees and consumers. Another motive is fear of losing privileges or even income from kickbacks and corruption (van de Valle 1989). Finally, selling SOEs that are natural monopolies (for example railways) can generate inefficiencies if legislation and control mechanisms are not in place. Donors have helped establish such mechanisms, anti-trust laws, commercial courts, etc.

Typically the adjustment programmes are implemented over a period of five years or more (Corbo and Fischer 1995) and the privatisation process will in most cases be the one with the slowest pace.

In terms of privatisation experience, the best data available are analyses of privatisation in Eastern Europe. The results from Eastern Europe show that privatisation creates higher efficiency and larger growth rates but, adversely, creates unemployment and poverty (Gillis *et al.* 1996). The experience is that donors, particularly the World Bank, are crucial in the design of privatisation programmes and the legal and administrative reform to back it. Many privatisation programmes move ahead only very slowly, but without support, they would have been even slower and less transparent.

Business partnership programmes

Objectives

Traditional investment projects have been criticised for focusing more on equipment export from the donor country than on training of the local company in using it. The idea of partnership programmes is to involve companies from donor countries on a more permanent basis than just being suppliers, thereby transferring their knowledge and skills to the partner in the recipient country. The donor's objective with this partnership can be to provide the company in the recipient country with capital, technology and know-how, management skills or access to foreign markets. Most partnership programmes support projects with some of the following features: (i) creation or safeguarding work places, (ii) increase in production and productivity, (iii) generation of exports, (iv) introduction of higher environmental and occupational health standards and (v) improvement of the livelihood of women.

This kind of programme addresses individual companies and, thus, works at the micro level with the firm's capabilities. It upgrades knowledge at worker and manager level, it provides capital, and it can give market access to the donor country's market.

Methods and initiatives

A number of donors have engaged in business-to-business programmes. One of the most comprehensive programmes is the Danish PSD programme, which started in 1993 and presently comprises six countries in Africa and Asia. The aim of the programme is to assist individual companies in the preparation and first implementation phases of commercial co-operation.

In order to be eligible for assistance, co-operation must be long-term and commercially viable, and both companies must take a commercial risk. These conditions are meant to ensure a serious commitment to the project from the companies. The project must be documented through a feasibility study and business plan. The co-operation can be a joint venture, a management agreement or another long-term, mutually binding agreement regarding production, not merely sales. The programme can support firms of any size within the manufacturing and service sectors.

The PSD programme co-finances the initial phases of a co-operation, which include: (i) mutual contact visits between the potential partners, (ii) elaboration of feasibility studies: technical, commercial and financial, (iii) training of the recipient country firm workers and management, (iv) investment in environmental and occupational health measures above national standards and (v) loans to overcome credit market imperfections and enable the local partner to buy their share in the joint venture.

The donor agency does not become an active part of the project and withdraws fully after the initial phase leaving the full commercial risk and incentive with the two companies. They stand to gain if the project succeeds and will lose if the project fails. This programme provides only co-financing for most elements. The companies' own investment up-front assures the donor of their serious commitment. Another important feature of the programme is that it is decentralised, which means that it does not actively develop business ideas but responds to ideas generated in companies in the recipient countries and Denmark.

The Norwegian Enterprise Contact Facility supports the establishment of contact between Norwegian, Indian and Sri Lankan enterprises which can lead to technological co-operation, licensing agreements, joint ventures, etc. The main target group is small- and medium-scaled enterprises in both countries. Only sectors where Norwegian companies have a strong position are eligible for support. Costs of mutual visits and preparatory studies are supported through NORAD.

The Canadian Industrial Co-operation (INC) programme is the business part of the overall Canadian Partnership Branch, which supports PSD in developing countries by supporting the efforts of Canadian firms, universities, professional associations, municipalities and NGOs. This programme provides assistance to Canadian companies on a cost-sharing basis in support of their own initiatives in developing countries to form joint ventures (OECD 1995).

The EU finances the Centre for Development of Industry (CDI) under the Lomé Convention. The CDI can support companies in ACP countries with their own feasibility studies and business plans. An extra component of this programme is the possibility of sponsoring the linking up of these companies with a relevant counterpart from an EU country. The European Community Investment Partners (ECIP) facilitate the creation of joint ventures between EU enterprises and enterprises in developing countries outside the ACP group. The ECIP support feasibility studies and provide loan and equity to joint venture companies. Furthermore, ECIP supports training activities related to the establishment of a joint venture among small- and medium-sized companies.

A range of other more loose partnership programmes exists. They typically aim at building technical competence with technical assistance from a company in the donor country. The assistance can be either 'hardware' or 'software' such as training. This type of programme can be used when the commercial risk in the country is so high (or the potential so low) that no companies from the donor countries would join a programme that entails taking a commercial risk (Pedersen 1994).

Experience

The business partnership programmes are still relatively new, so there is little literature on their success in meeting commercial and development goals. Some of the highlights of existing evaluations are presented below.

- The programmes can alleviate poverty through their generation of jobs, private incomes, export earnings and tax revenue (Danida 1995).
- Programmes can be an effective catalyst of private capital. The total investment in the partnerships supported by the Danish PSD programme is 3–4 times the value of the donor support.
- The success of the programmes depends on the overall macroeconomic conditions and the existence of attractive business opportunities.

Adverse macroeconomic conditions in Tanzania during the 1980s ruined the Swedish Sister Industry Programme (Olsen 1995).

• A genuine interest in business partnership programmes is registered among companies in several countries. Marketing, simple rules and flexibility are vital to attract serious private companies of the right quality.

• Involving donor country companies as active business partners is a more efficient way of transferring their know-how than the traditional role as a supplier. The success rate increases with company size and with the companies' previous international experience (Danida 1995).

• There must be a genuine interest in the business idea at the highest management level in both companies to ensure that the co-operation succeeds.

Problems such as market distortions and rent-seeking behaviour have not been subject to evaluation. It is obvious that both problems may occur, but the basis of the programmes is the companies' own commitment and risk-taking, which ensures that the elementary business idea is sound. It may well be the case that some of the established partnerships would have occurred without assistance. But the prevailing idea is that this type of programme helps draw attention to the target countries that they would not have got otherwise. The existence of a partnership programme may convince some companies that would otherwise have invested elsewhere or stayed home, to invest in that particular country.

Conclusions and perspectives

Private sector development aid has grown significantly during the 1990s as a consequence of structural adjustment in many countries and ideological changes. However, it still accounts for only a very small part of the total amount of foreign aid. This is puzzling because, when looking at the developmental activities of developing countries, a large proportion today take place in the private sector. One reason is that not only 'private sector aid' targets the private sector. Many other activities such as agricultural programmes also largely target private entities.

One explanation of a lower level of PSD aid than might have been expected is that the overall decline in foreign aid has led to a reorganis- ation of aid from large infrastructure projects to focusing more directly on poverty alleviation, efficient public service delivery and institutional reforms for good government management (World Bank 1998a). Another reason why PSD aid is still limited is that the private sector in many developing countries is small, underdeveloped and with a limited absorp- tion capacity, in which case huge inflows of aid could do harm, distorting basic incentive structures and fragile markets.

Developing countries focus increasingly on market economy principles and therefore require assistance to see this through. Responding to this demand, more donors elaborate strategies, programmes and projects within PSD. It is the authors' expectation, that private sector aid will increase in the future, although the majority of aid will still be for the public sector. During the 1990s, many new PSD aid instruments have emerged in the search for new flexible tools that can stimulate the private sector. It is expected that the successful ones will become mainstream aid in the future.

In practice, PSD aid has many similarities with other types of aid. Donors must draw upon similar methods and take the same precautions as in traditional aid. As with other types of aid, its impact depends on a good framework in the recipient country and a capacity to receive. That is why, for example, Asia performs better than Africa, generally, and in terms of productively using PSD aid.

Opponents of PSD aid have often pointed out that PSD aid disregards objectives other than growth of the private sector. This chapter has pointed out that this is not so for the majority of PSD aid programmes. Although few evaluations have been conducted, most of them conclude that, for example, poverty and environmental objectives are met through PSD aid.

Today's question is not *if* private sector development should be strengthened by donor support, but *how* it can be done in an optimal way: how to increase private savings and attract investment through aid, how to reach social goals through enterprise growth, how to avoid market distortions by supporting enterprises and how to regulate and dialogue the business sector.

Notes

1 As argued by Groth (1990), this corresponds with the 'Solow result': increases in savings will have only marginal effect on growth, whereas an increase in productivity will have a significant effect on growth rates.
2 The members of EDFI are venture funds from the following countries: Denmark, Sweden, United Kingdom, Spain, Austria, Neherlands, Germany, France, Belgium and Italy. The EDFI members can invest in all independent developing countries included in the OECD/DAC list with a GNP per capita not exceeding $5,445 in 1999.
3 These include the Asian Development Bank (ASDB), the African Development Bank (AFDB), the Inter-American Investment Corporation (IIC) and the European Union. All support one or more regional venture funds (see ASDB 1998, AFDB 1988 and IIC 1998 for details). At the Nordic level, the Nordic Development Fund (NDF) and Nordic Project Export Fund (NOPEF) have been established for similar purposes.
4 The Commonwealth Development Corporation in London, for example, has a strategy of building local venture capital funds throughout developing Commonwealth countries (CDC 1998). The IFU has invested in similar funds (IFU 1998).
5 USAID and NORAD support such a Business Linkage Programme in Zimbabwe with the Confederation of Zimbabwe Industries as the executing agency. A similar programme of business advisory services to SMEs, the Business Growth Centre, has been supported by UNDP in Ghana through the Association of Ghana Industries.

14 Financial sector aid

*Jens Kovsted**

Introduction

The combined presence of social and macroeconomic stability and an efficient resource allocation is generally recognised to promote economic growth. The strategies and instruments employed towards establishing these growth conditions have, however, changed over time. In recent years, the financial sector has been identified as a market-based, cost-effective facilitator of the efficient resource allocation. International donors have consequently displayed a growing interest in financial sector assistance and financial sector reforms. The pivotal role assigned to the financial sector can be attributed to the following five factors.

First, the relative and absolute size of official development assistance (ODA) has diminished drastically compared with international private flows in the 1990s (Chapter 3). This has prompted donors to reconsider the role of foreign aid *vis-à-vis* private capital flows. Should aid be used to complement or substitute for private capital flows, and should donors seek to influence private capital flows?

Second, financial liberalisation has increased the need for donor assistance to the financial sector. Partly because liberalised financial systems are in many respects more demanding on regulatory and supervisory agencies than a centrally directed system (Gelb and Honohan 1991), and partly because financial liberalisation has reduced the level of government engagement especially in the rural financial markets. The reduction of government involvement has created a vacuum, which is left unfilled because neither corporate nor informal financial sectors have incentives or capacity to act (Aryeetey 1996 and Ghate1992).

Third, international financial crises and in particular the recent East Asian financial crisis have focused the attention not only of donors but also of almost all governments and international agencies upon financial sector issues. Since the early 1980s, a number of developing countries have experienced severe episodes of financial crisis and unrest, resulting in drops in the levels of investment and consumption and the bankruptcy of fundamentally sound firms. The overall objective of financial sector aid is thus perceived to be to develop and strengthen the financial sector while simultaneously minimising the risks of systemic failure and safeguarding the economy against excessive volatility and contagion from both domestic and international financial markets.

Fourth, changes in economic thinking have enhanced donor interest in the role of the financial sector *vis-à-vis* economic development. Empirical analyses of the relationship between financial sector development and economic growth have established a positive correlation between the two. Moreover, compared to previous generations of monetary growth models, the recently developed theoretical models accord real significance to the financial sector and financial intermediation. The inclusion of uncertainty, asymmetric information, transaction costs and economies of scale provides a rationale for modelling endogenous financial institutions and sectors, and opens up the prospect of financial intermediation permanently raising the level of economic growth. A stable and efficient financial sector should thus assist the private sector with the mobilisation of funds and venture capital, with the identification of investment projects, and with the diversification of risk.

Fifth, two- and three-gap models identify a shortage of domestic savings as a possible constraint upon economic growth (see Chapter 15). If this is the case, foreign aid can either fill the savings gap through a direct transfer of funds and/or seek to develop domestic financial sectors in order to enhance the mobilisation of savings.

Rather than providing an overview of the empirical evidence of impact and implementation of financial sector aid and reform, this chapter reviews the issues, principles and problems of financial sector aid. The analysis is organised as follows: next is a brief review of past principles and methods of providing aid to (and through) the financial sector; recent donor practices of assisting the development of national financial systems and individual financial market institutions are then covered in two separate sections, after which the much publicised possibility of aiding micro-finance institutions is presented; a conclusion is the final section.

Financial sector aid in the past

Historically, a substantial share of the aid given to financial sectors from World War II to 1980 was conceived as a means rather than an end. This reflected a general perception of the financial sector as being instrumental and subsidiary to other sectors. This conception legitimised donor use of commercial banks, credit co-operatives and development finance institutions as channels of funds to productive sectors. The autonomous development of the financial sector received little or no attention, and the predominant logic was that of the productive sector. This reduced the financial sector to a supplier of one input, capital.

The overall performance of donor supported initiatives in the financial sector was frequently poor. Stated donor intentions of providing credit to the poor failed as funds were secured by well-off individuals taking advantage of their political connections, local power and access to collateral. Moreover, donor interventions typically lead to the range and prices of financial services being supply led rather than demand driven. The combination of subsidised lending rates and high rates of inflation frequently lead to negative real interest rates, which in concert with a scarcity of basic financial accounting data and financial management capacity undermine borrower incentives to pay back loans. In addition, individual institutions had little (if any) influence upon the allocation of loans, and were often not dependent on the performance of these loans for their economic survival. Consequently, the attitude on arrears was lenient, and deliberate defaults and institutional failures were widespread. The result was a sustained dependence of financial institutions on donor funds – a development which stemmed from limited progress in building financially self-sufficient institutions, discrepancies between the objectives of the donor agencies and the financial institutions, or both (Argyle 1983 and Garson 1996).

The sudden curtailment of foreign lending in connection with the international debt crisis of the 1980s, the deteriorating terms-of-trade and the rising international interest rates in the early 1980s revealed the magnitude of (and worsened) the problems in financial sectors of developing countries. This prompted a revision of donor strategies towards the financial sector. The philosophical basis for this revision was the McKinnon–Shaw paradigm of financial liberalisation. As a result, donor support to subsidised interest rates and directed credit was abolished.[1] The systemic perspective – focusing on the entire financial sector – was reinforced by and nested in the structural adjustment lending (SAL) programmes which were introduced during the 1980s (see Chapter 5).

From a slow start, the number of financial sector adjustment lending programmes, and financial sector related conditionality, increased rapidly through the 1990s. In 1995, financial sector and related conditionality accounted for almost one-third of all conditionality in SALs (Jayarajah and Branson 1995). Three main components of financial sector reform can be identified. First, as financial systems in most developing countries are dominated by banks, measures to strengthen the solvency and financial management of banks are common (often in concert with initiatives to consolidate and improve the supervisory and regulatory agencies). Second, steps are taken toward dismantling controls on interest rates and allocation of credit. Third, efforts to improve the efficiency of existing markets for capital as well as to create new financial markets are also present.

The policies of financial liberalisation have been subject to a severe critique for failing to recognise (i) the importance of the informal financial market in developing countries, (ii) the prevalence of market failures and (iii) that government interventions under some conditions can improve a situation (Fry 1995). But the distance between proponents and critics of financial liberalisation has diminished as the importance of addressing problems of macroeconomic instability and fiscal deficits precipitating (or coinciding with) financial sector reform has become evident. It is now widely recognised that financial reforms are not overnight events. Donor agencies and domestic institutions must deliver sustained efforts to restructure financial institutions, improve the regulatory framework, and increase the stock of human capital.[2] Financial liberalisation is not perceived as an end in itself but rather as a means towards the establishment of efficient and sustainable financial institutions and markets.

Recently, financial market turmoil in Mexico, Argentina and East Asia has raised the question of whether the process of financial liberalisation has proceeded too rapidly compared to the level of integration of developing countries into global financial systems. One should in this context take note of the gradual expansion of donor perspectives on financial sector aid over time, from the local, institutional level to the international level. However, as will become clear, donor attentiveness towards a higher level of financial markets does not exclude the lower levels – rather the contrary.

Aid to institutions regulating the financial market

The analysis in what follows draws upon the artificial, but heuristically useful, distinction between institutions *regulating* the financial market (regulatory institutions) and financial *market* institutions. Regulatory institutions include finance ministries, central banks and supervisory agencies for banks, insurance companies and capital markets. Financial market institutions cover banks, insurance companies, credit co-operatives, etc. This section concentrates on issues pertaining to aid to regulatory institutions, while aid to financial market institutions is the topic of subsequent sections.

Motivation

It is possible to identify two interdependent factors underlying donor interest in aiding regulatory and supervisory institutions on the financial markets in developing countries. First, the increase in the level of exposure to global financial markets heightens the demands upon the technical and managerial capacity of the regulatory institutions, on the level of transparency, and on the adherence to recognised standards of auditing and accounting. Moreover, because of the increased interdependence of financial markets, the probability of regional or global fallout from domestic financial crises in developing countries has increased. Donor support to regulatory institutions in developing countries thus in part originates from a desire to protect financial sectors and investors in donor countries.

Second, the poor performance of aid to financial market institutions has underscored the difficulties associated with circumventing the overall problems of the financial sector by dealing directly with selected financial market institutions. Accordingly, donors have recognised the necessity of complementing the provision of institutional support with a systemic perspective and systemic support. Partly this is because the performance of financial institutions is likely to be adversely affected by weak, inefficient regulatory institutions and structures, and partly because systemic aid may decrease the need for aid to financial market institutions. Furthermore, the above mentioned poor record of aid to financial market institutions, leads donors to prefer the more indirect approach of supporting financial systems over the direct involvement with individual financial market institutions.[3]

Methods

Addressing shortcomings in the accounting, legal and regulatory frame-work, donors *must* confront and involve the governments of the recipient countries. The reasons are fourfold: (i) despite recent financial liberalis-ation and privatisation, the level of direct and indirect government inter-vention in financial markets in developing countries is substantial, (ii) the liberalisation of financial markets intensifies calls upon governments to provide regulatory institutions with resources and training to counter the often accompanying increase in financial sector activities, (iii) governments are the only agencies with legislative power and (iv) only governments potentially have access to all relevant information. In short, domestic governments are part of both problem and solution.

Ensuring government compliance with donor initiatives may involve any combination of direct remunerations, persuasive new arguments in favour of change, and implicit or explicit pressure. While the required combin-ation differs according to the political and economic realities of the country, the establishment of consonance and co-ordination between donors and the government is a must. Lack of political consensus behind reforms of regulatory and supervisory structures and institutions drastically reduces the chances of success.

The probability that donors and recipient governments agree has, how-ever, increased as a more balanced view of governments as regulators and facilitators of financial markets and institutions has evolved in recent years. Still, substantial differences of opinion and potential areas of conflict may remain, as vested interests in maintaining the status quo are frequently strong due to high levels of political engagement and the considerable government revenues often raised in financial markets (Fry 1995 and Zank 1990).

If consonance is established, the actual transfer of aid can take place. Contrary to aid given to financial market institutions, which primarily has been focused on crisis management, a substantial share of aid targeted at the financial system and the regulatory institutions is aimed at crisis prevention and capacity enhancing measures. The different donor options include:

- Support for the provision of comprehensive, timely and accurate financial information, which adheres to internationally accepted principles of accounting and auditing.[4] Although questions related to improvements in the provision of information are operational rather than questions of principle, it must be emphasised that accurate and relevant information is a necessary but not a sufficient condition for efficiency.[5] It is, moreover, important that different agencies do not promote different standards of information, but agree upon, and adhere to, one (or very few) international standard(s), e.g. the Dissemination Standards Bulletin Board of the IMF (IMF 1998).
- Donor agencies can play an important role in the analysis and dissemination of international experience. Donors can observe past experiences over a wide range of different circumstances and countries, and may thus provide information about best practices.
- Donors can invest in the initial phase of the establishment of a new regulatory institution. As such initiatives are frequently fraught with risk, and as the social benefits of introducing new institutions often exceed private benefits, the case for agency intervention is strong. Donors are, moreover, frequently in a position where they may provide valuable advice and assistance which could accelerate the establishment of the institution.
- Donors can support existing regulatory structures with a direct transfer of funds and technical assistance. Apart from the direct benefits derived from this transfer, the public knowledge of donor involvement may augment the credibility of institutional reforms. This could prove beneficial as the reputation of governments may be low due to past interventions and breaches of faith. It is of course necessary that donors enjoy good reputations, and that market participants perceive the relationships between governments and donors to be stable and credible. Donors should, however, be aware of possible market misinterpretations of their engagement. If the market is yet to realise potential or actual risks, the announcement of donor support could inspire all the confidence of seeing an ambulance outside your door. Consequently donors must assess situations carefully in order to avoid the very incidents they are trying to contain or prevent, namely financial panic.
- Donors can finally choose to support institutions and markets which complement and assist financial sectors, such as legal systems, rating agencies, business press, and land registration offices.

The effectiveness of the above measures are, as mentioned previously, contingent upon the degree to which donors can make recipient governments share (or abstain from obstructing) the objectives and the implementation of the donor initiatives (BMZ 1994, Danida 1998b and Sida 1997). The primary contribution of donors could therefore be the initiation of a constructive dialogue with the government as well as the identification and establishment of sources of government revenue outside the financial sector.

Problems

A major source of problems is lack of co-ordination between donors and between donors and recipient governments. Credibility and the maintenance of a good reputation plays a central role in financial markets. The possibility of reputation spillover effects in concert with the interdependency of financial markets and institutions creates an environment where 'one rotten apple can spoil the entire basket.' Donors must consequently insist upon the professionalism of all agencies active in the financial sector and co-ordinate their work as well as the standards they promote.

The establishment of a new regulatory institution is likely to be associated with considerable difficulties. Both market participants and customers have to learn how to interact with the new institution, and already established institutions may oppose and obstruct any deviation from the status quo. As a consequence, the introduction has to be gradual and prudent. Furthermore, previous institution-building experiences underscore the importance of determining and publicly announcing the conditionalities behind each tranche of assistance as well as the final expiration date for aid transfers to the institution in question (see Chapter 6).

Donors must also consider whether the new institution supplies a hitherto unmet demand or merely reflects donor considerations and requirements. As the market mechanism is either temporarily suspended or has failed to generate such an institution, donors should possess considerable and detailed knowledge about the financial markets and the needs of the targeted group(s). Knowledge can be obtained through field studies and co-operation with local groups and experts. Finally, donors should consider whether financial sustainability of the institution is feasible within a reasonable time limit, and whether they are prepared to provide the necessary funding.

Efforts to reform the regulatory and supervisory structures are, however, ineffective if financial market institutions are insolvent and inefficient. Support to regulatory institutions can rarely be regarded as a substitute to support to financial market institutions. In the majority of cases the provision of aid to individual financial institutions is complementary to efforts towards strengthening the regulatory system. Direct aid to financial market institutions is the topic of the next section.

Aid to financial market institutions

Commercial banks dominate the financial markets in developing countries (Fry 1995, Goldstein and Turner 1996 and World Bank 1997d), and any attempt to reform and provide assistance to the financial institutions has to consider the role of banks. Consequently the present analysis is concentrated around issues related to bank recapitalisation and restructuring, while readers interested in characteristics of aid to other types of financial institutions (except support to micro-finance, which is dealt with in the next section) should consult other sources (e.g. World Bank 1997d and Sida 1997).

Motivation

Three factors motivate the provision of donor support directly to financial institutions (i.e. banks) in developing countries. First, improvements in the regulatory and supervisory frameworks are rarely sufficient, on their own, to enable banks to operate efficiently under market conditions. Historically, governments in developing countries have used banks to support faltering state-owned enterprises, to secure votes, and to the private benefit of politicians, bank managers and clients. This has left many banks unprofitable and *de facto* insolvent with large portfolios of non-performing assets. Rather than foreclose on bad debts, these banks typically have chosen to accrue unpaid interest and reschedule portfolios of old loans. Such neglect, caused by political pressure or lack of ability to take the loss, constrains the banks' ability to move into profitable positions. Consequently many banks in developing countries need to be recapitalised and restructured before they are able to operate under market conditions.

Second, giving aid to banks enables donors to directly address two prominent financial sector shortages in developing countries, namely the virtual absence of long-term finance and certain classes and segments of the population's lack of access to financial services. In both cases, donors give direct support and guarantees to improve these areas. This provides donors with a direct channel of influence as well as an indirect presence in financial markets. Another motive is that donors obtain an ability to pursue objectives external to the financial sector (such as poverty eradication or gender equality) more efficiently.[6]

Third, donors may support individual banks based on the conviction that they could become a catalyst for further financial sector development. If the supported banks are able to expand their business or introduce new financial services and instruments, this could force or tempt other institutions to follow suit.

Methods

Problems frequently do not restrict themselves to one bank but are shared by the entire sector. Hence donors have to consider whether to provide assistance on a case-by-case basis or initiate across the board assistance. The latter entails changing the overall conditions for financial sector activity, e.g. changes in liquidity conditions, central interest rates and financial sector legislation. At face value, across the board assistance may appeal to donors as it minimises the distortion in terms of competition on the financial markets. It furthermore represents a departure from historic donor failures of direct institutional support. If donors co-operate with domestic governments, across the board assistance can be pursued through macroeconomic and financial sector policies of the government, and may consequently appear to be a less demanding form of assistance. Across the board assistance to financial institutions generally has, however, proved to be ineffective and imprecise (World Bank 1989), resulting only in temporary improvements without affecting the underlying problems of distorted incentives and poor management.

This leaves donors with little choice: if they wish to deliver aid to financial market institutions, they must provide it on a case-by-case basis. Banks in developing countries face three types of problems: (i) problems associated with the quality of the portfolios of the banks, (ii) problems originating from lack of bank autonomy and the incentives offered to bank personnel and (iii) problems related to staff quality and quantity. Clearly, the three types of problems are interdependent and frequently resemble compounds of the three, but the classification is useful for analytical purposes.

The problems associated with the portfolios of banks, can be solved relatively quickly through a direct infusion of funds (often in the shape of a donor guaranteed swap of government bonds for non-performing loans). Unless accompanied by profitability-improving measures this is rarely a sustainable improvement. To improve sustainability donors can choose to infuse funds through the purchase of equity in the financial institution. This ensures that infusions of funds are made according to legally regulated and transparent procedures, and simultaneously place the supported institutions under an obligation to ensure a return on the capital. Packaging donor funds as market funds disciplines bank management more than direct transfers of funds or gifts.

Historically, the design of bank restructuring packages has been unbalanced with 'an emphasis on the solvency improving measures rather than on profitability improving measures.' (Dziobek and Pazarbasioglu 1997). A possible explanation may be that assistance to individual banks beyond recapitalisation leads to more hands-on involvement than most donors prefer, since this conflicts with donor intentions of creating the prerequisites for market liberalisation. But a failure to address the underlying problems which caused the insolvency in the first place is to invite a repetition.

The deterioration of bank portfolios can be ascribed to a mix of factors that are both internal and external to bank management. The latter connects bank reconstruction with reconstructing other sectors and enterprises in the economy. If a reconstructed bank discontinues servicing the unprofitable and inefficient firms and, in addition, seeks to recover overdue debts and non-performing loans, it will almost inevitably cause problems for these clients. Thus, donors may have to adopt a comprehensive, holistic approach to bank reconstruction, which in some cases even involves addressing the problems of bank clients.

Moreover, governments of developing countries have not limited themselves to using banks to cover operating losses of state owned enterprises. Often banks and financial systems are a considerable source of revenue for the government – partly through direct taxation and partly through indirect taxation in the form of high reserve requirements remunerated below the market level, or forced investments in government securities. Any attempt to restructure banks must address such problems. This again underscores the importance of involving the domestic government.

This leads to the problems related to lack of bank autonomy and incentives offered to bank employees. Again, a dialogue with the government is imperative. The overall objective is to increase both autonomy of individual banks and to increase competition among banks. This does not necessarily involve the creation of new institutions nor does it have to include the removal of barriers of entry. In many cases it can be achieved by bestowing already existing banks with greater freedom to set interest rates, choose their clients, and influence the range of financial services offered. To minimise the risks of repeating previous mistakes donors should seek to ensure that supply of financial services and products is demand driven rather than supply led.

In addition to the already mentioned ways of securing government compliance, donors can apply additional pressure on the government by channelling all donor funds through foreign banks or by initiating twinning arrangements between financial institutions in donor and recipient countries. Such measures are, however, secondary to a constructive dialogue with the governments.

Twinning arrangements can also contribute towards a solution to the problems concerning the quality and quantity of bank personnel. Banks and financial institutions are labour intensive institutions. This is especially true in developing countries where banks are often over-staffed and operate without the benefit of a formal planning process or efforts to control costs. The quality and training of bank personnel is of crucial importance, and is an area where donors often have a comparative advantage as agencies that understand and work within financial systems of both developed and less developed countries.

In this context, the significant costs associated with restructuring the labour force of a bank make considerable demands upon the funds and commitment of donor agencies. In most cases, aid is delivered as transfers of technology and administrative practices or as technical assistance and training. But the efforts are ineffective unless banks are able to offer competitive salaries and attractive career potentials. If these are absent, donors have to ensure that profitability-improving measures, such as operational restructuring measures, are undertaken, and that management objectives and strategies are coherent with these objectives. This emphasises that in the majority of cases the three types of bank problems identified earlier have to be addressed simultaneously. Partial donor involvement in bank reconstruction and recapitalisation is rarely an option.

Problems

Problems associated with giving aid directly to financial institutions can be divided into (i) operational problems, (ii) problems of principle and (iii) fundamental problems. Operational problems involve issues related to design and implementation of aid. Problems of principle arise in connection with disparities between overall donor principles for giving aid and the special conditions associated with aid to financial institutions. Fundamental problems are challenges which to some degree remain, regardless of changes in the conditions or principles for aid.

Operational problems

Among the operational problems is the problem of whether donors possess the necessary flexibility and capacity for immediate action if they are to advise bank management. Another operational problem is whether bank management acts as expected by donors. Both problems can to a large extent be solved by increasing the level of donor involvement in the financial institutions. This would provide donors with flexibility, inside information and direct control over management dispositions to enable them to address these problems. It would, however, also lead to what most donors would consider an undesirably high level of involvement. To avoid this, donors will tolerate some operational problems.

If the expansion of credit to the private sector is among the objectives of donor aid, then the discrepancy between dispositions of bank management and donor objectives can assume alarming proportions. Despite donor support, bank management is frequently equipped with an outdated stock of basic financial skills and unreliable and sparse information about a largely unknown (to bank management) private sector. This often leads managers to limit bank lending to investments that yield relatively secure returns (e.g. trade credit and government bonds). Thus, public sector deficits and trade credits will effectively displace credit to productive investments. Problems of this type are common and underscore how dependent financial sector initiatives are on the general macroeconomic climate. Donor co-operation and co-ordination with the domestic government can provide a start, but without a relatively stable macroeconomic climate and a limited government budget deficit, expanding credit to productive investments (without resorting to past practices of allocating credit) is difficult.

Problems of principle

Problems of principle primarily stem from the high degree of donor involvement which is almost imperative when giving aid directly to financial institutions. This is undesirable for some donors, as it exposes them to negative publicity and makes it difficult to maintain donor neutrality in other contexts. To achieve distance, donors should credibly pre-commit themselves to certain operating procedures and principles. One method could, as outlined previously, be to infuse donor funds through the purchase of equity in the bank, another could be to refrain from employing expatriate labour in the bank. In each instance the increase in distance between donors and recipient institutions comes at a cost, measured in donor abstinence from using a potential channel of influence and control. On the other hand, bank clients should not have the impression that a financial market institution is underwritten by donors (even though this might *de facto* be the case for a period of time), as this can adversely affect client behaviour and incentives.[7]

Fundamental problems

Almost any transfer of direct institutional aid creates a constituency of beneficiaries among recipients who: (i) wish aid flows to continue, (ii) expect donors to provide additional support when future problems arise and (iii) adapt dispositions and behaviour accordingly. The last two problems, which involve moral hazards, is at the centre of the fundamental problems associated with the provision of direct institutional aid. Expecting donors to continue to underwrite their institution, bank management may be tempted to disregard market signals, to deviate from best practices, and to take excessive risks. A possible solution is to hold bank management accountable for inefficient, unprofitable dispositions by letting the bank incur associated losses. However, this increases risks of bankruptcy – an often unacceptable event in light of possible systemic disruptions and overall drops in the confidence in the financial system. Bank managements are frequently aware of these concerns, and some take advantage of them.

The difficulties associated with achieving a sufficiently high level of management commitment and proficiency tempt donors to accept management responsibility. This is, however, an expensive approach which often results in very little domestic capacity building. The result could be permanent aid dependence, and donors have to carefully spell out (and abide by) credible conditions for the tranches and termination of aid prior to any direct institutional engagement. Otherwise, donors will time and again choose to give additional portions of aid, partly because previously given aid would otherwise be lost, and partly because donors feel obligated towards the institution.

The underlying problem is that whenever a crisis hits, actual and perceived risks of systemic failure almost invariably dominate any principle of non-intervention. Hence, the question is not whether governments and donors will intervene, but whether they intervene before or after the crisis. The absence of co-ordinated, effective preventive measures consequently makes it almost impossible to avoid problems of moral hazard.

Another fundamental problem is distortions in the terms of competition on financial markets. Concern varies among donors over this issue. In this respect, it is important to note that very few financial markets in the developing world can be characterised as competitive (in many cases not even remotely so). Although a widespread lack of competition on financial markets does not imply that donors may disregard stated principles of avoiding excessive interventions, it can make it less of a problem.

Aid to micro-finance institutions

The donor community has over the last decade supported a large number of micro-finance programmes in a wide variety of forms and contexts. Micro-finance is here defined as the provision of small-scale credit and savings facilities to low-income groups. The high level of donor interest in concert with micro-finance institutions (MFI), which is distinctly different from other financial institutions, merits the inclusion of a section devoted to micro-finance.

Motivation

Donor engagement in micro-finance is motivated by the fact that micro-financial services are often scarce and highly valued among the poor in developing countries. A number of studies confirm that low-income groups can enjoy considerable benefits from access to savings and credit facilities alike (e.g. Chaves and Gonzalez-Vega 1996 and Christen *et al.* 1994). Frequently, the unsatisfied demand for formal financial services has become larger in recent years, and micro-finance is among the principal instruments used by donors in the attempt to fill the vacuum in financial markets (see above).

Another factor contributing to donor support for micro-finance is the perception that micro-finance is capable of simultaneously meeting the, often conflicting, donor objectives of providing assistance under market conditions while reaching the poor and the marginalised. As a consequence, donors often attempt to pursue a number of overall objectives through micro-finance programmes, including poverty reduction, gender equality, nutritional education, community empowerment and balanced sectoral development (BMZ 1994, Danida 1998b and Sida 1997).

Donor interest in micro-finance is heightened by multiple accounts of successful MFIs. Micro-finance has been found to work in both urban and rural areas and over a wide range of absolute levels of development. In a widely quoted study, Christen *et al.* (1994) found that MFIs were able to achieve success even when economies grew slowly and irregularly, when financial markets were heavily regulated, when interest rates in the formal sector were fixed below market clearing rates, and when legal frameworks for collecting defaulting loans were weak.

Further contributing to the attractiveness of micro-finance from donor perspectives is widespread dissatisfaction with methods and instruments used to provide assistance to the financial sector in the past. Micro-finance is viewed as new and different, which enhances donor interest. There appears to be a micro-finance bandwagon effect: donors feel obliged to establish micro-finance programmes because everyone else is and vice versa. Finally, accounts of the successful MFIs have reached a wide audience. Reports from institutions such as the Bank Rakyat Indonesia Unit Desa and the Grameen Bank in Bangladesh have disseminated the knowledge of micro-finance to the general public. Thus, apart from being viewed as an effective, precise tool in the pursuit of both financial sector and overall development, micro-finance is perceived as a success, and donors want and need to be part of a success.

Methods

The number of donor agencies engaged in micro-finance has increased markedly since the mid-1990s. The newcomers include both established agencies moving into micro-finance and institutions created specifically to operate in micro-finance. Among the stated objectives is sustainability and outreach of MFIs. As regards sustainability, a distinction is made between operational efficiency (defined as covering administrative expenses and loan losses out of interest income and client fees) and financial self-sufficiency (defined as covering all costs and raising capital without external subsidies, i.e. operating under market conditions). Outreach is frequently defined with reference to a specific population or social mission, and is as such intimately related to the previously mentioned use of micro-finance programmes to pursue donor objectives external to financial sector issues (see Chapter 9).

In recent years, donors, practitioners and analysts have been divided over whether priority should be given to sustainability or outreach (Garson 1996 and Montagnon 1998). One group stresses the importance of getting micro-finance 'off the donor dole'. Proponents of this view emphasise that donors should give overall priority to financial sustainability. Accordingly, the role of donors is restricted to the initial phase of setting up micro-finance enterprises and experimenting with the development of new institutions and instruments.

The other group emphasises the importance of the social mission and outreach of micro-finance, which is considered to be impaired if too much emphasis is placed on sustainability and reliance upon commercial funds. According to this point of view, emphasis on sustainability will: (i) place the

MFI in a position similar to any other financial institution – irrespective that methods and spirit of MFIs are frequently different from other financial institutions and (ii) result in a loss of the comparative advantage of MFIs, namely social intermediation with the poor offering them a range of services and products for which the costs cannot necessarily be recovered (Dichter 1996).

The instruments favoured by donors are grants and soft loans. The funds are used for (i) the purchase of technical and managerial assistance and training, (ii) the requisition of new operating systems and procedures and (iii) direct institutional support. In the latter case, an often stated condition is the exclusion of donor support to the maintenance of interests rates fixed below commercial rates. The lessons of financial repression imply that no donor explicitly will support a suppression of on-lending rates below market rates (as discussed earlier). Implicitly, however, it occurs quite frequently due to the fungibility of funds (Yaron 1992).

The vehicles and procedures used to deliver aid to MFIs differ according to donor type. Bilateral donors frequently choose to channel funds through NGOs, and multilateral donors often shift funds through the governments of recipient countries. Recently many multilateral donors have opened special micro-finance disbursement windows which co-operate directly with the MFIs, such as the Consultative Group to Assist the Poorest (CGAP) of the World Bank and the MicroStart programme of the UNDP.

Once the overall objectives and the vehicle is decided upon, donors have to make the following decisions: (i) whether they should facilitate or initiate the creation of MFIs and (ii) whether they should follow the 'minimalist' (credit only) approach or the 'credit plus' approach, which includes direct support, technical assistance, and advice to targeted populations in *addition* to micro credit and savings facilities. If the choice is made to operate as facilitator, the overall objective is strengthening the linkages between existing financial institutions and individuals with an interest in micro-finance facilities and services. If, on the other hand, the choice is made to act as initiator, the level of commitment rises considerably as engagements typically will be on a larger scale and of a longer duration.

There is also increased donor awareness of the need to change regulatory frameworks to accommodate and support efforts of MFIs to mobilise savings and leverage external funds assuming full commercial costs (Jansson and Wenner 1997, Rock and Otero 1997 and Vogel 1994). Donors work to enhance supervisory capacities and powers of regulatory agencies and to inform domestic regulatory agencies about: (i) experiences of other countries, (ii) differences between MFIs and other financial institutions and (iii) how regulation should be adapted to accommodate these differences. This is of particular relevance in connection with efforts to aid regulatory institutions and structures, donor consonance and co-ordination is essential as donor initiatives otherwise could counteract each other.

Problems

Donors have, as stated previously, embraced micro-finance because it appears to solve the dilemma of providing sustainable assistance to marginalised populations using market mechanisms. But the saturation of micro-finance institutions with subsidised funds without strings attached may be the greatest danger currently facing the micro-finance movement. When subsidised funds are ample, there is a tendency to ignore or devalue the importance of financial management capacity and fundamental principles of accounting within MFIs. Furthermore, the large infusion of aid into micro-finance can create a lack of high quality information.[8] Donors do not always require that information provided by MFIs adheres to standard financial accounting and auditing methods. The reason is that funds are supplied as grants or soft-term loans in which case this kind of information may appear irrelevant.

This was visible when the World Bank collected information for a worldwide inventory of micro-finance institutions (World Bank 1996c).[9] Several administrators of international NGOs warned about sending questionnaires directly to their affiliates. Instead, administrators requested that it was sent to the international office where experts would fill it out. The reaction of the author of the micro-finance inventory was that 'if some managers of micro-finance institutions are unable to answer questions about their own costs and arrears without the help of outside experts, how can they be expected to run sustainable financial institutions?'

The provision of reliable and accurate information is a precondition for commercial market interest in micro-finance, as it should be for the provision of donor funds. If MFIs are to become independent of donor support they need technical assistance to enhance financial management capacities and donors have to package aid as commercial funds. In addition, ample supplies of donor funds moderate MFI vigour in the pursuit of bad debts. This may result in a deterioration of the local credit culture, to the detriment of all financial institutions in the region. Another implication could be an impairment of the incentives to mobilise savings.

Donors have historically tended to neglect the mobilisation of micro savings partly out of the now refuted perception that 'the poor do not save', partly because focus has been on the productive use of credit, and partly because donors frequently measure success by the amount of funds spent – a success criterion which is met more easily with an extension of credit than the establishment of savings facilities. Compared to the disbursement of credit, the mobilisation of savings generally involves a considerable degree of institutional build-up, the establishment of a public reputation for being reliable and significant staff training (Robinson 1997). All raise the necessary level of donor commitment and may prolong donor involvement – factors which discourage less committed donors.

Lack of good quality information is not the only obstacle to the creation of linkages to other financial institutions. Another impediment is differences in the attitudes and procedures in MFIS compared to those of other financial institutions, differences which in some cases are actively promoted by donors. More specifically, most MFIS practise project based lending and several (mainly Asian) MFIS offer group lending. Banks, on the other hand, practice asset based lending and tender individual loans. In addition, the self-image of many MFIS is that of a compassionate alternative to the market – a perception that contributes to the (in)voluntary isolation of the MFI in financial markets.

This is not an argument for donors to give priority exclusively to financial sustainability, but rather a caveat. If donors pursue the financial sustainability of MFIS, then conditions of funding as well as attitudes and procedures actively promoted in MFIS must be consistent with the drive towards financial sustainability. The probability of a successful transformation to an integrated, autonomous financial institution is raised if donors and MFIS emulate procedures and attitudes of such institutions.

When implemented, the main problem facing MFIS is the very high transaction costs associated with the delivery of micro-financial services. The large number of small financial transactions, frequently taking place in geographically remote areas, accentuate the need for simple administrative procedures and relatively cheap labour. If donors rely on expensive expatriate labour and employ complicated schemes of accounting and registration, it is highly unlikely that the enterprise will develop into a financially sustainable enterprise.

Finally, donor initiated creation of MFIS to target specific populations can cause problems. Some degree of targeting can be achieved comparatively easily through choice of geographic location, types of services and products offered, and size of loans, which can be chosen to encourage the self-selection of the targeted population.

But if the degree of targeting obtained through self-selection is unsatisfactory, donors typically attempt to exclude certain populations (such as men) from participating in micro-finance programmes. Reaching women and achieving a low default rate on loans is, however, not equivalent to empowering women – it may even under some circumstances worsen the situation of women (see also Chapter 10). Consequently, donors may have to settle for the degree of targeting achieved through self-selection. This is, however, not without problems. If, for example, the size of loans is restricted to increase the proportion of women borrowers (women typically need smaller loans than men), this can limit the scope for this MFI to expand on the market and to become financially sustainable. As before, donors have to choose between sustainability and being operationally feasible.

Conclusions

The combined presence of macroeconomic and social stability and an efficient resource allocation promotes economic growth. The analysis in this chapter has underlined that obtaining efficient resource allocation by means of the financial sector is crucially dependent upon the other two growth accommodating conditions. A main lesson is thus that the efficiency of aid to the financial sector is subject to the performance of other sectors (most notably the productive sector and the government) as well as upon the overall enabling environment. Donors must consider whether the conditions are favourable for the provision of financial sector assistance, or whether the effort and funds would be better spent attempting to improve the conditions for financial sector assistance.

Throughout, the scope has shifted from the national to the micro-economic level – steadily increasing the proximity of the financial institutions and markets to the individual clients. A structure chosen to stress the importance of linkages and the interdependence between the different layers has been emphasised. In this context, the East Asian financial crisis illustrates that direct proximity of financial institutions and markets is not necessarily proportional to the real impact upon individual clients. Inter-national capital flows and financial markets can have pronounced effects upon even marginal financial institutions and clients. Donors have taken this into account by adopting a systemic and holistic approach when giving aid to the financial sector. Frequently this implies involving the government of the recipient country, but it also implies that donors have to consider influences originating from the international financial markets.

By ensuring that the development of the financial sector and the supply of financial services is demand driven and not supply led, donors minimise the funds wasted because the sophistication and range of products offered by the financial sector exceed those that can be efficiently utilised by the clients in the economy. This approach entails that the financial sector supports rather than generates economic growth.

Common to almost all forms of financial sector aid is the required long-term commitment by the donor. A long-term commitment that originates partly from the frequent occurrence of institution building efforts, and partly from the significance attached to the establishment of credibility and a good reputation on financial markets. Donors who cannot plausibly pre-commit themselves for a longer period should consider providing support to other sectors. If donors terminate aid to financial sector institutions prematurely or disregard financial market principles (abandoning the collection of issued loans, slacking the conditions for issuing loans, etc.), it is likely to be to the detriment of other donor agencies active in the financial sector. Systemic contagion is an important factor in financial sector aid. Consequently donors have to insist on the professionalism and long-term commitment of all agencies active in the financial sector. The key concepts are consonance and co-ordination – among donors and between donors and governments.

Among future developments that could increase the effectiveness and level of aid to financial sectors are: (i) the progress in and increased proliferation of information technology in the delivery and administration of financial services and products, and (ii) the related increase in the global integration of financial markets. These concomitant developments are likely to result in a sustained increase in private capital flows relative to ODA funds, which again accentuates the importance of using aid to complement and attract private capital flows (domestic and foreign) instead of attempting to substitute for these.

Notes

* Useful comments by Rasmus Heltberg, Jytte Laursen, Torben Lindquist, Alan Matthews, Oliver Morrissey, Uffe Nielsen, Jørn Olesen, Anders Serup Rasmussen and seminar participants at the University of Copenhagen are gratefully acknowledged. The usual caveats apply.
1 Notwithstanding a recent trend towards deregulation, most governments of developing countries still place restrictions on interest rates and to a lesser degree direct credit (World Bank 1989).
2 An extensive literature exists about the precise nature and timing of financial reforms as well as the interaction with other reform and adjustment programmes (Gelb and Honohan 1991, Jayarajah and Branson 1995 and Zank 1990).
3 One could argue that donor engagements in the field of micro-finance represent the reappearance of targeting. See further below for an elaboration of this argument.
4 The importance of reliable and detailed information is accentuated by the virtual absence of equity markets in developing countries.
5 As an example, publicly available data from the Bank for International Settlements (BIS) showed increased dependence of the East Asian economies on short-term international bank loans prior to the financial crisis. International banks were, however, largely unconcerned and continued such lending up until the eve of the crisis (BIS 1998).
6 The inclusion of a 'social mission' when aiding financial institutions is discussed below.
7 Note the difference from the case of regulatory and supervisory institutions which can use donor credibility to enhance their own.
8 See, e.g. von Stauffenberg (1996), World Bank (1996c) and Vogel (1994).
9 The criteria for inclusion in the survey were that the institution should: (i) offer micro-financial services, (ii) be founded in 1992 or earlier and (iii) have more than 1,000 clients.

15 Foreign aid and the macroeconomy

*Peter Hjertholm, Jytte Laursen and Howard White**

Introduction

The traditional macroeconomic rationale for foreign aid is, as discussed in Chapter 4, that aid can help fill savings and trade gaps. In the next section, we therefore briefly review the simple gap approach. Nevertheless, it has become abundantly clear that the macroeconomic role and effect of aid are complex in a variety of ways which are not explicitly captured in gap models. Some of these complications are discussed, namely: (i) the effects of aid on government behaviour (including the tax effort of aid-receiving governments and the fungibility of aid), (ii) foreign debt problems and (iii) the relationship between foreign aid and the exchange rate (Dutch disease). Thus, aid does much more than fill gaps, and a major argument of this chapter is that aid should not be perceived simply as a measure to *fill* gaps in the short run. Instead aid should be given in such a way that the gaps will *close* over time so that growth and development can be sustained without aid. In the next to last section, we discuss the ways in which aid may be used to close both the external and fiscal gaps, considering both macro-level interventions and project-level activities. A final section concludes.

The macroeconomic rationale for aid

The gap models of the 1950s and 1960s had in common the Harrod–Domar tradition of stressing physical capital formation as a central driving force of economic growth. In the Harrod–Domar model, output depends upon the investment rate, and on the productivity of that investment. Investment is financed by savings, and in an open economy total savings equal the sum of domestic and foreign savings. A savings gap is said to arise if domestic savings alone are insufficient to finance the investment required to attain a target rate of growth (Rosenstein-Rodan 1961 and Fei and Paauw 1965). It should be stressed that the idea of a gap only makes sense given an exogenously determined target growth rate. A distinction is thus made between the *ex ante* savings gap (the difference between desired investment and domestic savings) and the *ex post* savings gap (the difference between actual investment and domestic savings).

In addition to the savings gap there is also a trade gap, based on the further assumption that not all investment goods can be produced domestically. A certain level of imports is required to attain desired investment (i.e. once again the investment required to achieve the target growth rate). The import bill is financed either from export earnings or foreign capital inflows (e.g. aid). If exports are not sufficient to cover the whole bill, the availability of foreign exchange (forex) to purchase imported capital goods (rather than the supply of domestic savings) may become the binding constraint on growth. Once again a distinction is made between the *ex ante* trade gap (the difference between desired imports and exports), and the *ex post* gap (the difference between actual imports and exports). Critics of the approach argue that this difference between *ex ante* and *ex post* can only emerge if markets are suppressed through a fixed exchange rate regime: if the exchange rate is flexible there can be no gap. This argument misses the point that the gap is defined with reference to a target growth rate, in which case a gap may be present even if markets are liberalised (though the 'gap' may be less if controls held back exports). The trade gap formed the basis of much of the planning work carried out by the United Nations in the 1950s.

The two gaps are combined in the two-gap model, put forward by Chenery and Strout (1966) and others. Growth will be constrained by the larger of the two *ex ante* gaps. If aid is insufficient to fill the larger of these gaps the desired growth rate cannot be attained. That is, the gaps are not additive: aid simultaneously fills both gaps (by paying for imported capital equipment, a single aid dollar relaxes both the savings and the forex constraint). If the larger gap is filled then the non-binding gap is 'over-filled' (the *ex post* gap exceeds the *ex ante* one).[1]

The traditional two-gap model sees imports as aiding capital accumulation, whereas more recent statements of the three-gap model (see below), reflect the fact that output may be constrained by low capacity utilisation due to lack of spares and intermediates rather than lack of investment (e.g. Nalo 1993, Ndulu 1991, Shaaeldin 1988 and the country studies in Taylor 1993). These models thus disaggregate imports, so that import composition matters as well as the level of imports.

Chenery and Strout also raised the possibility that there would be a skills gap at early levels of development, whereby a lack of technical expertise would constrain the level of investment that could be attained. Over the years, other gaps have been proposed, such as technology, food, gender and environment. More narrowly related to the tradition of the two-gap model have been recent concerns over a third 'fiscal' gap between government revenue and expenditures, as illustrated by the three-gap models by Bacha (1990) and Taylor (1991, 1993). Although the fiscal gap is a subset of the savings gap, the former may be binding if there is some limit on public spending (say, through a borrowing target) and private investment is linked to public investment through a crowding in (or out) relationship. Thus, government efforts to stimulate private investment may be curbed when government resources for investment and imports are insufficient, *inter alia*, as a result of public debt service; indeed, evidence is available suggesting that government expenditures in the sub-Saharan African region have been curtailed by foreign debt service (e.g. Fielding 1997, Gallagher 1994 and Sahn 1992). The closing of this fiscal gap could thus be facilitated by external resources directed to the government budget.

In sum, the gap models predict a positive role for foreign aid whereby it supplements domestic savings, export earnings and government revenue, increasing investment, imports and government expenditure, and thereby growth. However, the empirical record of aid (Chapter 4) does not confirm the above simple picture. A number of complications have been advanced in the literature to help explain why there is no one-to-one relationship between aid, on the one hand, and economic performance on the other. In the next section we discuss three such areas, before proceeding to discussing ways in which aid may help close macroeconomic resource gaps.

Macroeconomic complications in foreign aid

To analyse aid's macroeconomic impact we need to study aggregates such as growth, output, investment, savings, etc. with aid, and compare them with what they would have been without aid. It may seem that such an analysis need simply (i) classify aid in various ways – for example, as being for investment or consumption, types of government expenditure supported and imports versus local costs – and then (ii) add these aid amounts to the amounts which originate from domestic resources (and non-aid capital inflows). This is the approach inherent in the two-gap model. Yet, such analysis is not satisfactory since it is based on the assumption that domestic savings, government expenditure and revenue, foreign borrowing, the exchange rate, etc. are not affected by aid inflows. We illustrate below how some of these economic complications may interfere with the simple aid–growth relationship in the two-gap model.

Aid and government behaviour

An important complicating factor, which has not been explicitly accounted for in the gap literature, is the fiscal behaviour of governments which receive foreign aid. It is, in particular, of considerable interest to understand how aid inflows affect government expenditure and financing patterns. This is so since the aid recipient may of course have other objectives than the aid donor. Two distinct, but inter-related, strands of the development literature have attempted to deal with these issues, both having the concept of aid fungibility as a central issue. The first approach is explicitly concerned with the fungibility of aid as regards government spending patterns. The other, so-called 'fiscal response' literature, adopts a more theoretical approach and attempts to analyse how aid impacts on various categories of expenditure and financing sources (including taxes). Both approaches form the broader context in which government behaviour *vis-à-vis* foreign aid is analysed (McGillivray and Morrissey 2000).

Aid fungibility

The traditional fungibility argument – not conceived within the fiscal response literature – was first advanced by Singer (1965). He argued that aid's impact should not be evaluated against the projects said to be 'aid-financed'. His point may be illustrated as follows. Suppose a government has $100 million to be allocated between two activities (both costing exactly $100 million): rehabilitating rural health clinics or buying some military hardware (say, nice shiny tanks). After some deliberation the government decides to prioritise the health clinics. Subsequently a donor offers the government $100 million for any development project. Clearly the tanks are not eligible for donor finance, but the health clinics are. So the government may ask the donor to finance the latter, freeing up its own resources to buy the tanks. The actual impact of the aid (a comparison of with versus without) is therefore to increase military rather than health expenditure (Table 15.1). No diversion of funds is involved, but funding an activity that would have happened in the absence of aid frees up resources to be used elsewhere. It is this marginal expenditure which is effectively related with the impact of the aid.[2] Fungibility among different types of expenditure is therefore observed when the item for which aid is intended does not rise by exactly the amount of the aid inflow.[3] It is obvious that if the government initially intended to buy military equipment, aid will clearly be beneficial, and there are in any case limits to fungibility, as discussed below.

The fungibility problem can also be illustrated using the more narrow concept of fungibility inherent in the analysis by Griffin (1970). He looked at the relationship between aid and domestic savings. Accordingly, Figures 15.1 and 15.2 illustrate inter-temporal consumption decisions with and without aid. Income may be consumed in the current period (C_t) or saved, invested and consumed in the next period (C_{t+1}). Future consumption will be $(1+r)$ times the value of savings in time t (r being the return on capital). For a given level of income in Figure 15.1 the budget constraint is KL, and assuming standard preferences, the consumption bundle is at point P, with domestic savings of $L - C_t^1$.

Now suppose there is an aid inflow of value A, equal to LN. This shifts the budget constraint out to MN. In the two-gap model, there is no fungibility. Thus, it is assumed that aid is used to increase investment only, so consumption in period t remains unchanged at point P'. In contrast, it can be argued, as does Griffin, that aid will in reality be treated like any other income and shared between consumption and savings according to their

Table 15.1 Expenditure patterns with and without aid

	Health expenditure (e.g. rural health clinics)	Military expenditure (e.g. tanks)
Without aid	100	0
With aid	100	100

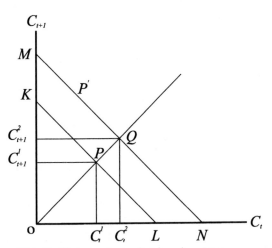

Figure 15.1 Griffin's analysis of aid and savings.

respective marginal propensities. This would move consumption in period t to point Q, and domestic savings fall to $L-C_t^2$. As such there is no longer a one-to-one relationship between aid and savings–investment; aid is fungible.

One underlying assumption behind the above argument is that it treats aid as a free resource (i.e. as part of income) which may be allocated exactly as the recipient wishes.[4] Assume instead that the donor directs the aid towards investment in such a way that the budget constraint with aid changes from being MN in Figure 15.1 to MNL as shown in Figure 15.2. From Figure 15.2 it follows that aid remains fungible as long as the preferred consumption bundle lies along MN. Yet, if preferences dictate that a point to the right of N should be chosen, this is no longer feasible. In this case, aid fungibility is limited. Such situations appear, *ceteris paribus*, when aid finance is large relative to domestic resources, or if few resources would be devoted to investment in the absence of aid. At the limit, assuming L is chosen without aid, there are no domestic savings. In this case, aid geared at investment will result in a one-to-one increase in investment, i.e. there is no fungibility. This also illustrates that aid will tend to be fungible if it is allocated to a use to which the recipient accords high priority.[5]

In sum, it is clear that the fungibility of aid is an important issue in understanding how aid impacts on government behaviour and growth in aid receiving countries (see Feyzioglu *et al.* 1998 and Pack and Pack 1993 for recent studies). It should be highlighted, however, that fungibility may

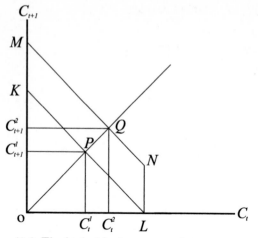

Figure 15.2 The kinked budget constraint.

not necessarily be a problem. If the aid recipient has more knowledge about how to maximise the impact of aid, then fungibility may in fact be growth-enhancing, assuming, of course, that the aid recipient pursues growth and development objectives in an effective manner. Thus, whether fungibility should be seen as a positive or negative feature of aid depends upon country-specific circumstances and the interplay between donor and aid recipient objectives.

Fiscal response models

The fiscal response literature relies on more formal modelling to identify how aid inflows may result in government behaviour that undermines the intended growth effects of aid (McGillivray and Morrissey 1999b). A number of studies on this subject have appeared following the seminal paper by Heller (1975), including Mosley *et al.* (1987), Gang and Khan (1991), Binh and McGillivray (1993) and White (1993). The standard point of departure is a government utility function, where targets have been set for expenditure types (e.g. recurrent and capital), revenue (tax and non-tax) and borrowing (domestic and foreign). The government tries to maximise the utility function by attaining these targets, subject to a budget constraint in which aid inflows have traditionally been included as an exogenous variable (on the ground that aid levels are supply determined). Recent specifications of the utility function include aid as an endogenous variable (e.g. Franco-Rodriguez *et al.* 1998 and McGillivray and Morrissey 1999a).[6] Estimation of the model is performed after deriving reduced form equations for each endogenous variable.

Recent empirical evidence for Pakistan generated along these lines indicates that foreign aid has led to somewhat higher capital expenditures (investments), markedly lower recurrent expenditures (consumption), and a markedly lower tax effort during the 1965–95 period (Franco-Rodriguez *et al.* 1998) than would have been the case without aid. This result appears also to be characteristic in a number of other studies (McGillivray 1999), implying that the aid–investment link is firm. In contrast, the World Bank (1998a) puts more emphasis on the potential consumption enhancing effects of aid. Turning to the lower tax effort of aid recipients, this may be seen as an undesirable consequence of aid, though some may point to the removal of the distortionary effects of taxation, or argue that this is a channel for global redistribution from developed country taxpayers to developing country ones.

Aid may either increase or decrease the budget deficit, or even leave it unchanged, depending on the difference between incremental expenditures and revenue. In theory, the deficit may increase if the government has to commit its own additional resources to complement project aid or if tax revenue falls sharply. On the other hand, programme aid, the local currency countervalue of which is often not tied to any particular expenditure, can reduce the deficit (for evidence of which, see White 1999a).

In spite of the insights gained from fiscal response models, a number of theoretical and methodological problems limit the scope for clear-cut conclusions about the fiscal behaviour of governments *vis-à-vis* the aid–growth link, as discussed in more detail in McGillivray and Morrissey (1999a) and White (1992a, 1994). Important among these are the estimation problems that arise from inadequate data. More important, these models do not specifically link the fiscal effects of aid to growth, or macroeconomic aggregates more generally. This implies, *inter alia*, that the impact on savings and taxes, transmitted through the feedback effects of aid on current and future income, are not accounted for even though they may be of real significance (White 1993). Only indirect inferences can therefore be made about how government fiscal behaviour affects the aid–growth relationship, and thus how donor policy can be designed or re-designed so as to maximise aid's growth potential. As noted by McGillivray and Morrissey (1999a), this points to a combination of (preferably country-specific) growth and fiscal response theory as an avenue of future research.

Aid and foreign debt

Gap models provide a macroeconomic rationale for aid. Yet, if aid is debt creating – i.e. a loan and not a grant – it may have adverse implications for the savings, forex and fiscal gaps in the longer-term, and for macro performance more generally. Two types of debt problems have occupied debt analysts. First, debt payments are a further demand on foreign exchange and, often, government revenue. Where these items are constrained there may be problems of debt capacity. Second, there are other channels by which a large debt may adversely affect economic development. We consider each of these in turn.

Debt capacity problems

Three different approaches to the analysis of debt capacity can be found in the literature: (i) whether output growth is sufficient to support foreign borrowing; (ii) external solvency; and (iii) the fiscal dimension of debt.

The first ('growth-cum-debt') approach argues there is a 'debt cycle', which is linked to the course of economic development (e.g. Avramovic *et al.* 1964 and McDonald 1982). As development proceeds, changes in domestic income, rates of savings, accumulation of capital stock, and rates of return on investment can be expected to alter the volume and direction of financial resources. Hence, over time, countries are expected to move through a number of formalised balance-of-payments and debt stages, from a debtor position to that of the creditor. However, there is no automaticity in this process; a number of conditions must be met. The most important condition is a satisfactory rate of economic growth, so the various conditions have often been submerged into the single condition that the growth rate of output should exceed (or at least equal) the rate of interest, thus generating the resources to service the debt (e.g. Hernandez-Cata 1988 and Greene and Khan 1990).

But as debt payments must be made in foreign exchange, preservation of debt capacity requires more than growth. 'Debt dynamics' models directly address this issue of external solvency and provide a further rule, namely that the rate of growth of exports must exceed (or at least equal) the rate of interest (e.g. Cooper and Sachs 1985 and Simonsen 1985). Hence a loan aid inflow may fill the trade gap today, but necessitates a faster rate of export growth in the future for the country to become independent of foreign inflows. As we argue below, aid can usefully be directed toward activities that will help close the trade gap.

The debt dynamics model has an important shortcoming as it ignores internal constraints on debt capacity, such as the import and agricultural dependence of these countries. Of particular importance is the dichotomy between private assets and public liabilities in countries with predominantly public debts, which creates an internal transfer problem. For example, Kharas (1981) considered the problems faced by governments engaged in foreign borrowing to finance public expenditures, and which are constrained in their ability to collect revenue to service the acquired debt. If the government uses most of the borrowed funds for investments in such areas as infrastructure, education, health services, etc., the sustainable level of debt the government can take on will depend on the government's ability to collect sufficient domestic resources for debt service. Debt capacity requires an expanding tax base.[7] Reisen and van Trotsenburg (1988) analysed empirically the internal transfer problem in the context of the theory of international transfers, arguing that the fiscal transfer problem had been one of the main obstacles to a return to international credit-worthiness for most of the major (commercial) debtors in the first half of the 1980s. With respect to the indebted low-income countries in sub-Saharan Africa, a study by Hjertholm (1997a) similarly found that fiscal debt burden indicators played a significant role in explaining the poor debt servicing performance of a large number of sub-Saharan countries. This suggests that the issue of debt service capacity cannot be separated from the issue of the government budget constraint. Moreover, as discussed below, the fiscal implications of debt may undermine economic performance.

Foreign debt and economic development

Empirical evidence suggests a robust statistical relationship between debt indicators and poor economic performance, such as low growth, investment and human development (e.g. Cohen 1996, Ojo and Oshikoya 1995, Oshikoya 1994 and Greene and Villanueva 1990). A main channel for the adverse effects of large debt burdens are fiscal effects, namely: (i) effects from reduced public expenditure and (ii) disincentives associated with a large debt overhang.

Public expenditures may crowd-in private investment, especially where the latter is impeded by structural bottlenecks such as weak infrastructure (e.g. Díaz-Alejandro 1981 and Taylor 1983). The generally poor state of infrastructural, educational and health facilities in developing countries thus provides considerable scope for realising positive externalities from government expenditures (e.g. Hadjimichael and Ghura 1995 and Hadjimichael *et al.* 1995). These opportunities will be missed, and so growth foregone, if expenditures are squeezed by debt service, which empirical evidence suggests has been the case in sub-Saharan Africa (e.g. Fielding 1997, Gallagher 1994 and Sahn 1992).

A closely related cash-flow problem associated with public debt service is import compression, which can occur for two reasons (Ndulu 1991). First, if the ability of the economy to substitute between imported and home produced capital goods is limited, a cut in capital goods imports will lead to a decline in growth.[8] Second, following Hemphill (1974) and Moran (1989), import compression can occur in cases where import volumes are determined by import capacity rather than relative prices. Clearly the magnitude of debt service matters for import capacity. Import compression can occur both at the balance-of-payments level and at the budgetary level (i.e. the effect of public debt service on the import content of government expenditures). Reductions in the import capacity of the government, as a result of debt service, can thus reduce government investment activity, whereby the comple-mentarity effects mentioned above are lost. That such cash-flow effects have indeed been at work in poor indebted countries is confirmed (for 20 sub-Saharan African countries) in the empirical study by Hjertholm (1997a).

In addition to these direct effects from reduced public investment and lower imports, a high debt burden may undermine growth performance on account of the debt overhang. Debt overhang effects may be classified in two ways: (i) the narrow approach focusing on tax disincentives; and (ii) the broad approach related to macroeconomic instability. The fundamental notion of the narrow debt overhang theory is that the future debt service burden of a country will weigh heavily on the increase in the country's future economic output, which will have to go to foreign creditors. Hence there will be a tax on investment returns which will discourage investors (Borensztein 1990). Besides the possibility of disincentives working through taxation, there may be further disincentives through general macroeconomic instability which is seen as particularly bad for private investment (see Hjertholm *et al.* 2000 for an elaboration of the adverse effects that may result). Public debt overhang can affect macro stability through several channels: (i) an increase in the fiscal deficit; (ii) exchange rate depreciation; (iii) monetary expansion and inflation from monetising debt service obligations; and (iv) recourse to exceptional financing (such as payment arrears and debt reschedulings), which tends to maintain uncertainty about the future debt servicing profile of the public sector. Public debt-induced fluctuations in such macro indicators as inflation, exchange rates and exceptional financing may thus signal fiscal distress and an inadequate ability on the part of the government to control fiscal events. Such signals may in turn heighten investor uncertainty about the future direction of the macroeconomy and thus reduce the incentive to invest. In sum, the broad debt overhang hypothesis asserts, and is supported by available evidence, that one or more of the macro stability indicators discussed are likely to capture part of the investment disincentives of a foreign debt burden.[9]

Aid and the exchange rate

A third complicating area of concern in analysing the macroeconomic impact of foreign aid has been the effect of aid on the exchange rate of the recipient country, and thus on the general competitive stance of the export sector. Originally observed in connection with booming primary exports, this phenomenon has been labelled 'Dutch disease', deriving its name from the unhappy experience of the Netherlands after the discovery of major natural gas reserves in the 1960s.[10] Since then, examples of the syndrome include Zambia (copper), treated in Kayizzi-Mugerwa (1990) and what Gillis *et al.* (1996: 479) has labelled 'a bad case of Dutch disease', namely the case of the oil boom in Nigeria (treated in, e.g. Bienen 1988 and Nyatepe-Coo 1994).[11] Dutch disease effects associated with booming exports were originally analysed by Corden and Neary (1982) and Michaeley (1981), van Wijnbergen (1986) and recently Rattsø and Torvik (1999) have formulated theoretical models of aid-induced Dutch disease effects.

The Dutch disease phenomenon basically describes a situation where an inflow of foreign exchange in any form (i.e. from export earnings, private capital flows or foreign aid) puts upward pressure on the real exchange rate of the recipient country by stimulating more rapid domestic inflation. A large inflow of foreign aid may therefore result in a loss of competitiveness of exports, counteracting other efforts to increase exports.

The inflationary effects of foreign aid, however, may to some extent be mitigated by the inflow of foreign commodities purchased by foreign aid. Aid that increases the supply of commodities in general or eases supply bottlenecks in the economy, can be assumed to have a deflationary impact, which may or may not exceed the upward pressure on the real exchange rate as a result of the aid. Furthermore, an inflow of aid may raise the productivity of the traded-goods sector – for example, by lowering transport costs or raising the educational level. Aid that increases overall productivity in the traded-goods sector serves to improve international competitiveness, i.e. to increase the supply of traded goods at any given price (determined by world market prices, if the country is a price taker).

Since there are counteracting effects, it is not possible *a priori* to determine what effects an increase in foreign aid will have on the recipient country's exchange rate, and hence, on the competitiveness of its exports. This is an empirical matter. The study by van Wijnbergen (1985), for instance, of six sub-Saharan African countries, to some extent confirms the hypothesis that increases in the volume of foreign aid can cause an appreciation of the real exchange rate in recipient countries, as did the study by White and Wignaraja (1992) of Sri Lanka. A study on Ghana similarly found that Dutch disease effects had posed problems for macroeconomic management in the 1980s (Younger 1992). Evidence for Tanzania, on the other hand, suggests that foreign aid inflows had caused a real depreciation, a result that runs contrary to the Dutch disease hypothesis (Nyoni 1998).[12] There are several ways in which aid may support exchange rate depreciation, mainly through support for a change in exchange rate regime through policy dialogue and the provision of aid funds to support the more liberalised regime (see White 1999a, 1999b).[13]

However, in countries where foreign aid plays an important role in covering external deficits, there is good reason to be aware of the dangers of an aid-induced real appreciation of the rate of exchange. It remains, however, more a question of appropriate management of the inflow of foreign exchange; it is clear that the release of foreign exchange into the domestic economy needs to be in accordance with the absorptive capacity of the economy.

Foreign aid for gap closing

It follows from the above review that the channels through which aid impacts on macroeconomic performance are complex, and further complicating issues such as political economy problems are addressed in, for example, Chapter 18, where explicit reference is made to the situation in Africa. Looking ahead, we would argue that it is equally important to understand how aid can help close resource gaps in the long run, rather than merely filling these gaps in the immediate future. While foreign aid may well be needed for a considerable amount of time to help finance investment, imports and public expenditures, aid should also be used to boost recipient countries' ability to mobilise their own resources. Provision of financial and technical support for mobilisation of domestic savings is a measure directed at closing the savings gap (see Chapter 14 on financial sector aid). Here we consider measures directed at enhancing the import capacity by using aid for export promotion (i.e. closing the trade gap), as well as aid supported initiatives intended to strengthen the capacity for revenue and expenditure management of recipient country governments (i.e. closing the fiscal gap).

Closing the trade gap

Foreign aid helps fill the trade gap in the short run, where import reducing initiatives may also be considered in order to pursue economic stabilisation. However, the long-run development objective is that a country's own export earnings should be more or less sufficient to meet import requirements. Since import reduction is not conducive to the long-run growth process, this objective has to be pursued through export promotion (or, more precisely, achieving growth in export receipts in excess of that of import payments). Accordingly, while import substitution was widely supported by donors in the 1960s and 1970s, far greater emphasis in aid policy should in future be placed on measures geared at export promotion.[14]

Export promotion consists both of raising export levels for existing products and of diversification into non-traditional exports. The latter is important since many countries remain reliant on a narrow range of primary products. Developing countries export only half as many products as developed countries, and Africa in turn only exports half the number of that of other developing regions (Table 15.2). Primary products are subject to greater price fluctuation than manufactured products and they are believed by many to be subject to a secular decline in their relative price.[15] Diversification allows branching out into higher value added activities and reducing exposure to price fluctuations.

Foreign aid can help promote exports through three main channels: (i) supporting a conducive policy environment; (ii) financing infrastructural development; and (iii) direct support to export promotion. Each of these is discussed in turn.

The policy environment

Since the early 1980s, programme aid has been conditional upon implementing policies agreed with the World Bank and the IMF. These policies promote a market-oriented development strategy and are intended to increase the production of tradable goods, and more specifically exports (as discussed in more detail in Chapter 16).

Most studies of the effect of adjustment policies find that export performance is the one area in which a positive impact is most likely to be felt. The World Bank, in its study on *Adjustment in Africa* found that 'countries with the largest improvements in macroeconomic policies enjoyed the highest median growth in exports and had by far the largest surge in export growth.' (World Bank 1994a: 153). This result is largely confirmed by other studies, such as Mosley *et al.* (1995a) and Lensink (1996). Yet, it can be asked what role aid has played in supporting the reforms which have by now taken place in most developing countries. Whilst there is a feeling that aid has failed to buy reform, this conclusion is nuanced in relation to the type of reform. The policy measures of most interest here – notably liberalisation of the foreign exchange market, but also export and import duty reductions – are amongst those where there does appear to have been a degree of influence in many countries. Indeed, as argued earlier, there are reasons to think that aid may have assisted the move to more liberalised forex regimes, and the associated exchange rate depreciation, in several countries.

Two caveats should be made to this positive picture. The first is that some argue that the export increase is not of the sort that will bring widespread benefits. For example, Gibbon *et al.* (1993) argue that increased exports have come from extractive foreign investment and are prone to the fallacy of composition (increased output will reduce prices and so not raise incomes), and criticisms of footloose labour-intensive industries are well known. Second, diversification has not been that great, especially in Africa and Latin America and the Caribbean. Indeed, classifying countries by policy stance (using the classification from *Adjustment in Africa*) shows that countries with the largest improvements in macro policy have become more concentrated rather than less (Table 15.2).

The main recommendation in terms of aid policy emerging from the above review is that, to the extent aid impacts on policy, the implications for export promotion need to be carefully considered.

Improving infrastructure

'Getting prices right' is a necessary but not sufficient condition for restoring growth in exports or output more generally. Adequate infrastructure is also required for a supply response to occur. Such investments have been a traditional part of aid, accounting for around 20 per cent of commitments in the 1980s and 1990s (Chapter 3, Table 3.4). Aid may finance general infrastructure, notably roads, which open areas up to commercial production, or more specifically export-oriented infrastructure, such as that for export zones. Infrastructure is, with the exception of railways, something

Table 15.2 Export diversification, 1980 and 1994

	1980		1994		Change	
	Number of exports	*Conc. index*	*Number of exports*	*Conc. index*	*Number of exports*	*Conc. index (%)*
Overall						
Developed countries						
Mean	208	0.169	210	0.169	2	0
Median	226	0.109	225	0.120	−1	10
Developing countries						
Mean	95	0.499	105	0.420	10	−16
Median	83	0.467	90	0.375	7	−20
Developing countries by region						
Africa						
Mean	58	0.565	57	0.544	−1	−4
Median	47	0.534	43	0.565	−4	6
Asia and Pacific						
Mean	115	0.350	135	0.296	20	−15
Median	97	0.303	152	0.241	55	−20
Latin America and Caribbean						
Mean	106	0.436	112	0.323	6	−26
Median	98	0.399	104	0.316	6	−21
Middle East and North Africa						
Mean	109	0.704	130	0.562	21	−20
Median	104	0.802	134	0.642	30	−20
Sub-Saharan African countries classified by policy change						
Large improvement in macro policies						
Mean	80	0.500	81	0.547	1	9
Median	83	0.476	73	0.600	−10	26
Small improvement in macro policies						
Mean	61	0.550	57	0.519	−4	−6
Median	47	0.501	47	0.565	0	13
Deterioration in macro policies						
Mean	55	0.544	45	0.545	−10	0
Median	43	0.456	37	0.485	−6	6

Source: UNCTAD (1996).

Note: Concentration index ranges from 0 to 1, with lower values for less export concentration.

donors can do reasonably well. A World Bank review found infrastructure projects (except railways) to have consistently performed better than the average (Morra and Thumm 1997, vol. 2: 41). As such, this area appears as a promising area of aid intervention also in the future.

Direct export promotion

Finally, donors may give direct support to export promotion, usually focusing on non-traditional exports. Such projects typically comprise management and technical support to selected export firms, provision of market information and other support to market penetration (e.g. particip-ation at trade fairs),[16] and institutional development of relevant bodies, such as exporters' associations and standards' offices. Credit may also be provided, although cheap credit is usually frowned upon (though the management and marketing services are subsidised). Synthesis studies of US support to export promotion (Bremer *et al.* 1994 and McKean and Fox 1994) present a generally positive picture, though it is stated that such support is only worthwhile if the policy environment is right and there is a suspicion of too great a role for public sector bodies.[17] Export markets are most successfully secured by establishing links with a foreign partner, and indeed such projects often combine trade and investment promotion.[18] Critics of aid might therefore argue that if the market is allowed to function, and foreign investment flow in, then these supply chains will develop so as to increase developing country exports. More generally, the value of increased exports that may be ascribed to such projects, is not as yet sufficient to be of macroeconomic significance.

The overall picture with respect to past experience is therefore mixed. Policy reform does appear to increase exports, although there remain questions as to the extent to which reform can be attributed to aid, and diversification is proceeding only slowly if at all. Support through infra-structure and direct export promotion can claim some success, but their macro significance should not be overstated.

Closing the fiscal gap

The largest share of foreign aid is provided in support of public expend-itures. Aid therefore helps fill the fiscal gap – a situation which is likely to continue in the short- to medium-term. Accordingly, much of the rationale for the programme aid provided during the 1990s has been focused on filling gaps. Nevertheless, the long-run objective of aid is that a country's revenue efforts should be – more or less – sufficient to cover its public expenditures. With the successful reforms of trade and exchange rate regimes undertaken by many developing countries in the 1980s, increasing emphasis has therefore been placed on closing the fiscal gap in structural adjustment programmes during the 1990s. Apart from reducing aid dependence, the rationale for this emphasis involves that a reduction of the fiscal deficit, in particular a reduction of the domestic financing of such a deficit, has been and remains key to achieving and maintaining macro-economic stability, which is needed to promote long-term growth.

Closing the fiscal gap involves (i) increasing government revenue in a manner which minimises the distortionary nature of taxation and/or (ii) promoting the effectiveness and efficiency of expenditures. While reduction of public expenditures may be pursued in the short run with a view to economic stabilisation, expenditures are in the longer run likely to rise if government is to perform the necessary activities in support of sustainable growth. As noted above, public spending aimed at reducing the impediments to growth implied by inadequate economic infrastructure (such as lack of access to electricity or an inadequate road structure) and insufficient social services (such as education and health) is of major importance in developing countries. In sum, closing the fiscal gap is of critical importance, but focus must be on revenue and the effectiveness of public expense rather than on mere size.

Increasing government revenue

In the early years of structural adjustment, particular focus was given to rationalising the export duty and import tariff regime in line with the liberal economic trade policies pursued. Such efforts can reduce revenue collection in the short run, but the expectation is that tariff rationalisation, including the reduction of evasion and avoidance, will be revenue-enhancing in the longer term. Simultaneously, efforts were made to switch from taxes on external trade to domestic taxes (e.g. increasing excise taxes on certain items, such as petroleum, alcohol and tobacco).

The most widespread of these efforts has been the introduction of value added tax (VAT) to replace traditional sales taxes in a large number of developing countries over the past decade. The VAT has a number of distinct advantages, including that it reduces economic distortions, since traditional sales taxes at all levels of production and sales introduce a bias towards vertically integrated firms. Such a firm only pays the sales tax once. An element of self-control is also involved as firms have an incentive to require VAT paid on their purchases in order to subtract this from their own VAT due. As the VAT is more complicated to administer than traditional sales taxes, it has been argued that developing countries with limited administrative capacity should not introduce this tax. Experience to date shows, however, that despite initial opposition to the VAT from the taxpayers and some loss of revenue during the first six months of operation, this tax has been successfully introduced in several countries. Finally, in addition to the VAT, efforts are being made in many developing countries to increase revenues from direct taxation, such as business and corporate taxes and some form of personal taxation, typically payroll taxes.

Despite the above efforts to increase public revenues, tax revenue in developing countries remains low; the average of total tax revenue is about 20 per cent in sub-Saharan Africa, far below the average for OECD countries of about 35 per cent. Thus, the key challenge faced is, as already alluded to above, to increase taxes while at the same time trying to minimise their distortionary nature. This is so since the negative growth impact of inadequate provision of public services may well thwart growth in the long term. It follows that expanding the tax is also an important challenge, and substantial efforts are required to enhance the effectiveness of tax administrations in many countries. This includes the introduction of self-assessments, substantial training of staff in revenue authorities, and computerisation of, e.g. tax registers to allow checks of taxpayer information across different types of taxes. Such efforts at institutional capacity building are costly and of longer term duration, and as such open up many avenues for aid, including technical assistance, to be of use in furthering growth.

Expenditure management

The other way to close the fiscal gap in the longer run is to make public expenditures more effective. Expenditure reduction was at the forefront of adjustment programmes from the start. This was due – in part – to the fact that substantial expenditure reductions can be achieved at a faster rate than increasing revenues and hence, was the only way to quickly alleviate the fiscal gap and the attendant stabilisation problems. It also reflected the consensus that some expenditure items were not conducive to growth, including, for example, the support given to state-owned enterprises. On the other hand, privatisation was pursued as an efficiency enhancing policy, and in this area there have been notable achievements. In many developing countries a large number of enterprises have been privatised and the most important of those remaining are public utilities, such as electricity and water. The extent to which the private sector can be involved in the provision of 'public' services in future remains a much debated issue.

Turning to the public sector wage bill, there has been retrenchment of civil servants in many developing countries. Yet, the need for increasing the numbers of, say, nurses and school teachers has in many cases become apparent. In addition, the need to increase remuneration is by now critical, as salary levels are typically too low to attract professional staff for the civil service.

It is difficult to draw general lessons from civil service reform in developing countries, as the critical issues of further reforms of the public administration vary widely from country to country (see also Chapter 12). Nevertheless, consideration of public expenditure issues can usefully be split into three levels: (i) the issue of aggregate fiscal control, i.e. controlling the size of the fiscal deficit to be within a realistic short-run macroeconomic framework; (ii) the strategic allocation of expenditures across different sectors; and (iii) the effectiveness and efficiency of expenditures within a given sector or sub-sector. Much success has been achieved regarding aggregate fiscal control during the 1990s, but many challenges still remain in addressing the last two points.

This can be illustrated by the fact that the cash budget system that has enabled many countries to maintain aggregate control has in many cases had an adverse impact on budget planning and implementation. Actual expenditure allocation has varied substantially from month to month, implying the budget process in many aid dependent developing countries has more or less broken down. The result is that the state budget does not work as a planning tool, as actual expenditures within any given sector tend to be very different from the budgeted allocation. In addition, most budgets in aid dependent developing countries do not account for all or even most foreign aid. It is channelled directly to end-uses, completely bypassing the government. It has therefore become very difficult for political decision-makers to play their role in ensuring that government policy priorities are reflected in the strategic allocation of actual public expenditures across different sectors. Furthermore, the break-down of the budget process has made it difficult to develop the necessary transparency over public expenditures and maintain accountability for these. Public expenditure reviews (PER), typically led by the World Bank, have been the main instrument with which to try to address such issues, and this instrument has already been discussed in Chapter 12.

Longer-term planning of all expenditures are key to improving the effectiveness and efficiency of public expenditures and hence, to improving the results obtained (such as increases in the number of children who receive primary education or health care). In aid dependent countries, foreign aid finances more than half of all expenditures and donors may therefore appear to be legitimate stakeholders in the process of budget planning and implementation, although their role is properly confined to ensuring transparent procedures and accountability to the local people. With the move to new aid modalities, particularly the adoption of sector programme support by many donor agencies (see Chapter 7), external assistance is becoming an integral part of public expenditures. While the allocation of total public expenditures, including both governments' own resources and foreign aid, has always been important in any assessment of public expenditures, these new aid modalities bring out such issues much more clearly. Moreover, efforts are now being made in a number of countries to include sector programmes in a medium-term fiscal framework, which includes all public expenditure financing and attempts to ensure consistency with the macroeconomic framework being pursued.

As has been indicated above, the role of foreign aid in filling the fiscal gap is very large indeed, particularly in aid dependent countries. Furthermore, it is beyond doubt that foreign aid will continue to play a key role in helping close the fiscal gap for some time to come. Increasing the level of tax revenues takes a long time and needs to be carefully balanced with the objectives of encouraging economic growth. This requires skills and experience which many countries do not possess. Thus, aid has a role to play. The same goes – as is clear from this section – for the management and control of public expenditures.

Conclusions

The traditional macroeconomic rationale for foreign aid relates to its ability to supplement domestic savings, foreign exchange and government revenue, thereby contributing to higher economic growth. The economic processes envisioned presumes a simple Harrod–Domar context in which economic growth is driven by physical capital formation. However, as this chapter makes clear, the macroeconomic reality of foreign aid recipients is much more complicated. Three examples of complicating factors have been discussed: (i) the effects of aid on government fiscal behaviour, (ii) the problem of foreign debt and (iii) Dutch disease effects.

Over the longer term, rather than merely filling gaps, foreign aid should play a role in closing gaps. The merit of being increasingly able to finance investment with domestic savings, imports with export earnings, and government spending with government revenue, is obvious: reliance on foreign aid and (perhaps especially) foreign borrowing is diminished and economic policy autonomy is increased. Closing the savings gap entails, on the part of aid donors, financial and technical support for mobilisation of domestic savings (as discussed in Chapter 14). Closing the forex gap entails export growth in excess of import growth (so the gap can be closed without reducing imports from present levels). Donors can support this endeavour by supporting a macroeconomic environment conducive to export growth, by helping to expand and improve the physical infrastructure, and by direct support for export activities, notably those of a non-traditional nature.

With respect to the fiscal gap, this can in the longer run be closed by increasing government revenue and improving expenditure management. But, unlike the savings and forex gaps, fiscal closure is a more delicate task; public expenditures may be critical for growth, but at the same time taxes come along with distortions. When closing the savings–investment gap, emphasis is on 'ever' higher savings, so productive investments can be expanded. Similarly for the forex gap; since maintaining productive import is important, emphasis is on 'ever' higher exports. In terms of the fiscal gap, however, where maintaining productive government spending is also critical, government taxation cannot simply be 'ever' expanding since it brings about distortions and thus economic disincentives. Thus, closing the fiscal gap is a much more difficult job to do, and one in which donors and recipient governments will have to carefully balance the disadvantage of lower-than-needed government spending against the disadvantage of higher government taxation.

Notes

* The authors are grateful for useful comments on an earlier draft of this chapter from Oliver Morrissey and other participants at the aid book workshop at the University of Copenhagen, 9–19 October 1998, as well as from an internal referee. The usual disclaimer applies.

1 This fact of course requires some adjustment in the model variables. Chenery and Strout assumed that there would be additional consumption if the savings gap is over-filled and additional imports if the forex gap is over-filled.

2 Thus if the donor does not specify the use of funds it makes no sense to talk of fungibility. Programme aid funds (discussed in Chapter 5) are often called 'very fungible', but that is a mis-use of the term since there are no conditions as to what these funds should be used for. Aid which has no designated purpose is best referred to as free resources. Aid which does have a designated purpose is effectively free resources if it is fungible.

3 White (1998) elaborates this definition to cover aggregate and categorical fungibility (see also Hjertholm *et al.* 2000).

4 See White (1998) for further critiques.

5 Figure 15.2 may be adapted to analyse other allocations: for example developmental government expenditure on the vertical axis and other expenditures on the horizontal, or capital and intermediate imports and consumer imports respectively. The same argument regarding the limits of fungibility will apply in these cases.

6 Including aid as an endogenous variable is based on the premise that, once donors have committed the aid money, recipients can in practice determine actual disbursements (total and among different expenditure types).

7 An important point to emerge from this line of argument, and one that departs from conventional debt capacity analysis, is that the critical link between debt service and government taxation makes it possible for debt problems to occur even if all inflows of foreign resources are used for investment, and if the marginal product of capital is greater than the real rate of interest.

8 Since some substitution away from imports may take place, the decline in investment will probably be proportionally less than the decline in imports. And yet, the remarkable stability of the relationship between real capital imports and real investments observed in sub-Saharan Africa in the 1980s, suggests that the fixed proportional relationship is not that far off, and the imperfect substitution phenomenon is indeed partly responsible for the import compression observed in this region.

9 The study by Hjertholm (1997a) for sub-Saharan Africa, for instance, while not generating strong evidence for the narrow debt overhang hypothesis, showed clear evidence of the 'extended' version, in that public debt burdens had several (indirect) effects that were transmitted through macroeconomic variables, such as inflation, exchange rates and exceptional financing.

10 In the 1970s, after substantial natural gas reserves had been discovered in the 1960s, the ensuing export boom and balance-of-payments surplus promised increased welfare for all Dutch. Instead, the 1970s saw a Dutch economy suffering from rising inflation, falling manufactured exports, lower growth rates and rising unemployment (Gillis *et al.* 1996).

11 There are also cases where the export booms have not led to Dutch disease problems, notably diamonds in Botswana (Hill 1991) and oil in Iran (Majd 1989).

12 A study testing the Dutch disease hypothesis in the context of the 1976–7 Tanzania coffee boom similarly did not find supportive evidence (Musonda and Luvanda 1991), and neither did a similar study of the Dutch disease effects of the 1976–9 coffee boom in Kenya (Bevan *et al.* 1992).

13 Furthermore, by financing an exchange rate anchor, aid has an anti-inflationary effect.

14 However, critics of aid from a dependency perspective argue that the focus of international agencies on increasing developing country exports illustrates the role of aid in forcing these countries to a subordinate position in the world economy (e.g. Hayter and Watson 1985).

15 Of course, so long as prices are not perfectly correlated, a country experiences less earnings variation by producing two crops with variable prices rather than one.

16 Typical of the conflicting objectives of donor agencies is the fact that aid also supports penetration of the recipient market by donor country firms.

17 Another report on US aid finds that government export promotion services in South Korea had 'minimal impact on export expansion' (Rock 1993).

18 The evaluation of CIDA's Jamaica Export Promotion Project, which had not included investment promotion, recommended it be included when the scheme was replicated elsewhere in the region (CIDA 1993).

Part IV

Broader issues

16 Foreign aid in the emerging global trade environment

Oliver Morrissey

Introduction

The global economic environment has changed significantly in the 1990s. An important element of this has been the conclusion of the Uruguay Round and the inception of the World Trade Organization (WTO). Trade liberalisation at all levels (multilateral, minilateral and unilateral) has proceeded apace and the remit of the WTO has broadened to consider social and environmental dimensions of trade, and new issues such as intellectual property rights, trade in services, investment and competition policy. Importantly, for low-income countries, agriculture is being brought into multilateral trade liberalisation. Concurrently, many countries have liberalised their foreign exchange regime and financial sectors, and the volume and speed of global capital flows has increased significantly (a contributory factor to the East Asian crisis according to most commentators, see Chapter 14). There have also been moves, such as the aborted Multilateral Agreement on Investment (MAI), to establish a more liberal global environment for foreign investors. All of these are important matters of concern to developing countries, and have implications for future demands on foreign aid, especially in so far as they may impact on poverty.

Increasing globalisation and liberalisation over the past 25 years have seen expanding flows of trade, technology, capital and foreign direct investment between countries in both the developed and the developing world. Concerns have been expressed that this increased openness leaves developing countries more vulnerable, and indeed may have an adverse impact on income distribution and poverty. Even if the impact of trade and technology on growth is positive, there is recent evidence from Latin America suggesting that they tend to increase inequality (Wood 1997), although 'growth in household incomes, even if it is associated with increasing inequality, can nevertheless bring about poverty reduction.' (McKay 1997: 672). In this chapter, concern is not directly with the links between globalisation, growth and poverty although this must be implicit in the discussion as poverty reduction is a primary (if not the primary) objective of foreign aid (see Chapter 9).

Greater openness to trade, capital and technology will almost certainly have distributional consequences, both at a global level (between countries) and within countries (depending on initial conditions, economic structure and government policies). These in turn will have implications for future aid flows in a number of ways. Fundamentally, if globalisation increases poverty, because some countries or groups within countries are losers, the case for aid will be strengthened, either to compensate losers or to assist the (newly) impoverished. Alternatively, if some countries benefit, for example from trade liberalisation, this could enhance growth and export earnings, thereby reducing their need for aid. A further possibility is that volatility associated with increased capital mobility may give rise to new forms of aid for affected countries. A remit to address the implications for aid of all elements of the changing global economic environment would be too broad; attention is restricted here to the implications for aid of the changing global trade environment. Although this chapter limits attention to trade policy, similar implications (in terms of aid) arise in respect of technology and capital flows.

Ever since the seminal contribution of Chenery and Strout (1966), the principal economic justification for aid has been to fill financing gaps that constrain attainable growth rates in developing countries (discussed in Chapters 4 and 15). Of particular relevance in the context of trade is the foreign exchange (forex) gap that arises if export earnings are insufficient to finance needed imports of investment goods. The existence of a financing gap *per se* does not imply a case for aid, and the original argument was in terms of the need for foreign capital inflows. Foreign direct investment can be effective in filling a savings–investment gap, and alleviates the forex constraint in so doing, but has proved of limited benefit to low-income countries. Commercial borrowing is another option, but the debt burden may be a problem in itself, rather than a solution, for low-income countries (see Chapter 15). Consequently, the (residual) case for aid financing in low-income countries is strong; often it is the only viable option.

Arguably, the forex gap is the primary gap. If export earnings are high, sufficient investment goods can be imported and any domestic savings constraint can be alleviated. Provided the government gains adequate revenue from export earnings, any budget constraint is alleviated. Indeed, if exports are an engine of growth, the dynamic gains to the economy will relax domestic savings and revenue mobilisation constraints in the long run. This line of reasoning lies at the root of the so-called 'trade not aid' argument. Whilst one may contest the 'trade as an engine of growth' hypothesis, there is now a convincing body of evidence that outward-oriented (exporting) countries exhibit superior economic performance to 'inward-oriented' (import substituting) economies. This is not an argument for exporting *per se* as the growth benefits arise from (the combination of) a number of factors. Encouraging exports is helpful, and openness attracts foreign investment, but the real benefit may be in technology transfer through the ability to increase imports (for a lucid exposition of this argument see Rodrik 1999).

The particular focus of this chapter is whether global trends in trade policy (and, by implication, trade flows) enhance or retard the ability of low-income countries to increase their export earnings, and thereby reduce their reliance on aid. Not all low-income countries can expect to 'export their way out of aid reliance', to coin a phrase. Some countries are severely resource-constrained and have very limited export capacity; this is true of many small island economies, such as the Windward Islands. A more general problem for low-income countries is their dependence on primary commodity exports. Deteriorating terms-of-trade, fallacy of composition and inelastic demand all constrain the ability of such countries to improve export earnings (McKay *et al.* 1997). Even if the trade environment improves, so that there are strong incentives to export, many countries will still require aid support. Furthermore, although multilateral donors increasingly require trade liberalisation as a condition of granting aid (Greenaway and Morrissey 1993), donor policies often have the effect of discriminating against the export sector in recipient countries (Morrissey and White 1996). Changes in the global trade environment may reduce some recipients' need for aid, but will increase the needs of others (who lose from liberalisation), and can also affect donor attitudes towards aid.

In the long run, trade liberalisation would be expected to benefit low-income countries (LICs) by increasing global efficiency and permitting them to benefit from increased export earnings. Not all LICs will benefit, and those that do will not benefit equally. Furthermore, in the short-run, trade liberalisation is likely to impose costs on LICs. These issues are addressed below, considering each type of liberalisation. Multilateral trade liberalisation, the implementation of the Uruguay Round, will have effects on world prices. It is shown that, according to existing estimates, LICs derive the least benefit from such liberalisation, and many will suffer welfare losses (there is an argument for using aid to provide compensation). Unilateral trade liberalisation, within LICs, is treated next; there is a case for aid support, given the short-run adjustment costs. Minilateral liberalisation, through regional trading agreements, is also addressed; this may have the effect of attracting aid and investment to the region. A final section presents the conclusions.

Multilateral trade liberalisation[1]

Changes within the multilateral trading system will affect developing countries; on one level, these effects come through changes in world commodity prices, on another, through new multilateral rules that constrain domestic trade policy (in general, countries are obliged to be less protectionist). There are two elements of multilateral trade liberalisation post-Uruguay Round that will have especially important implications for LICs; liberalisation of trade in agricultural commodities and of trade in textiles and garments, the phasing out of the Multi-Fibre Arrangement (MFA). These are the specific focus of this section.

Tropical agricultural commodities and textiles (broadly defined) constitute the greater share of LIC exports. For those LICs without mineral resources, these commodities typically account for more than 75 per cent of merchandise exports (UNCTAD 1995). Most LICs are importers of temperate agricultural commodities, and many are net food importers. Prior to the Uruguay Round, the agricultural sector was treated as a special case in the GATT framework, with generous scope permitted for government intervention. Consequently, agricultural protection has been high in most developed countries, where also export subsidies have been widely used. The aggregate effect has been to depress world prices for temperate agricultural products. If the developed countries liberalise their agricultural policy regimes, as committed to in the Uruguay Round, the effect will be to depress producer prices in those countries but to increase the world price of the foods they export (as subsidies are removed).

There have been numerous economic studies projecting the effects of implementing the Uruguay Round on commodity prices (e.g. Martin and Winters 1996). While estimates of the magnitude of price effects vary from study to study, there is one point of general agreement. The world price rises induced by agricultural trade liberalisation are likely to be much lower for tropical agricultural commodities (the cash crops exported by LICs) than for temperate agricultural commodities (the food crops exported by developed and some developing countries). This is because trade barriers against tropical products are generally quite low in developed countries, as domestic farmers do not compete with these products. Sugar is perhaps the major exception.

The effects of liberalisation of trade in textiles is more complex. World textile prices are expected to fall, but some countries will benefit because the abolition of quotas will permit them to expand output and exports. The principal losers will be countries that currently benefit from large quotas; none of these are LICs. The principal beneficiaries are expected to be LICs in South and East Asia: Bangladesh, India, Pakistan, China, Vietnam and perhaps some others. These have very low wage costs and can expect to gain a larger share of the world market. The LICs in Africa are expected to lose, as they will be unable to compete with Asian exporters (except perhaps in certain niches). With the exception of those LICs that can expand textile exports in a post-MFA world, most LICs are likely to lose from multilateral trade liberalisation.

It is difficult to be precise about the impact of multilateral trade liberalisation on specific countries or groups of countries. The impact depends on how prices of particular commodities are affected, how important these commodities are to specific countries (especially the net trade balance), and the ability of countries to respond and adjust to changing world prices (which will depend largely on domestic policies). Existing estimates suggest that there will be distributional effects, i.e. some countries will gain but others will lose. The largest gains in value terms are likely to be among the developed countries that tend to export temperate foods (the prices of which will rise) and import textile products (the prices of which will fall). The impact on low-income countries (LICs) depends crucially on their net trade balance in foodstuffs and textiles, the two commodity sectors likely to be most affected. Illustrative estimates of the impact of liberalisation, as proposed in the Uruguay Round, are provided in Table 16.1. It is salient that LICs, notably in sub-Saharan Africa, are projected to incur net losses, while the major gains accrue to rich countries.

These short-run losses to developing countries in sub-Saharan Africa are primarily caused by higher world food prices following agricultural trade reforms and loss of preferences due to the general liberalisation and the abolition of the MFA. The losses could be countered by long term dynamic gains, but in the short term there will be adjustment costs. The effect of agricultural liberalisation on a specific developing country depends crucially on whether, for example, the country is a net food importer or exporter, and how important agricultural commodities are as a share of exports (and which particular commodities). Nevertheless, the results in Table 16.1 are indicative and make the important point that there will be losers from multilateral liberalisation, that the losers are most likely to be among the poorest countries (already major recipients of aid) and that their need for aid is likely to increase.

The potential gains and losses from trade liberalisation are not likely to be evenly shared among all developing countries. Developing countries can be categorised into a few 'representative types' to identify likely impact. One categorisation distinguishes net food-importing from net food-exporting developing countries; for reasons already given, the former will lose but the latter will gain. A second grouping analyses developing countries according to region (Anderson and Tyers 1990, UNCTAD 1990 and Zietz and Valdes 1990). Latin America is expected to be the 'big' winner of agricultural trade liberalisation and sub-Saharan Africa the 'big' loser. Results for Asia differ among studies and usually depend on which countries have been included.

The third grouping isolates low-income developing countries from middle- and higher-income ones (Zietz and Valdes 1990), effectively a further decomposition of the first approach. Low-income food-importing developing countries (among which are many African countries) suffer most from higher world prices for agricultural commodities (particularly cereals). Under the Uruguay Round agreement, the GATT recognised that these countries 'may experience negative effects in terms of the availability of adequate supplies of basic foodstuffs from external sources on reasonable terms . . . and provides for the establishment of appropriate mechanisms to rectify this possible situation including a recognition that the Members concerned may be eligible to draw on the resources of international financial

Table 16.1 Regional welfare gains of Uruguay Round (UR) reforms (estimated in terms of equivalent variation, EV)

	Full UR reforms		Agricultural liberalisation	
	EV in $ billion	EV in % of 1992 income	EV in $ billion	EV in % of 1992 income
Australia and New Zealand	1.04	0.36	0.96	0.33
Canada	1.57	0.30	1.03	0.20
United States	21.46	0.41	2.65	0.05
Japan	26.65	0.84	5.16	0.16
European Union	24.86	0.42	11.37	0.19
China	6.13	1.37	0.11	0.02
Taiwan and South Korea	1.57	0.47	0.70	0.21
Hong Kong and Singapore	−1.68	−0.23	−0.29	−0.04
Economies in Transition	2.50	0.52	3.93	0.82
Other middle-income	−3.21	−7.11	0.01	0.02
Brazil	−8.43	−0.34	0.18	0.00
Other low-income	6.22	1.49	0.15	0.04
Sub-Saharan Africa	−0.49	−0.33	0.00	0.00
World	78.20	0.39	25.94	0.13

Source: Blake *et al.* (1998).

institutions.' (GATT 1993: 86). The principle of compensating losers, and using aid to do so, is recognised; we return to this in the concluding section.

To alleviate or reverse the potential losses, LICs have only a combination of three options. First, they can try and expand the volume of tropical agricultural exports to increase earnings. This is difficult if all developing countries are attempting the same expansion simultaneously. Second, they can try to diversify into non-agricultural exports. Again, this is difficult to achieve, especially in the short run. Third, they can try to reduce food imports. This offers the most potential, but requires liberalisation of domestic agricultural policies to improve incentives and opportunities for domestic food production (McKay *et al.* 1997). Many developing countries have domestic policies biased against agriculture and would actually gain from liberalising their own agricultural sector. This issue is addressed in the next section. However, at least in the short run, many LICs will suffer a deterioration in their trade balance following agricultural trade liberalisation, and the case has been made that they may require compensation, in the form of aid, at least to maintain food imports (GATT 1993).

Trade liberalisation in developing countries

Trade liberalisation, the removal of restrictions on imports and reduction of discrimination against exports, has become an increasingly common policy reform. Whether independently or as part of a World Bank structural adjustment programme (SAP), the majority of developing countries have attempted some degree of trade liberalisation since 1980. The prevalence of trade reforms as elements of SAPs renders it difficult, and perhaps pointless, to separate the two. The success of the many liberalisation episodes, on their own or as part of a SAP, has been very mixed. This is true whether reforms are evaluated according to the amount of liberalisation actually undertaken or the impact on economic growth (see Corbo *et al.* 1992, Greenaway and Morrissey 1993, 1994, McGillivray and Morrissey 1999b, Mosley *et al.* 1995a and Papageorgiou *et al.* 1991).

There is no concise and generally agreed definition of trade liberalisation in the literature (Greenaway and Morrissey 1994 discuss alternatives). We adopt a simple definition of trade liberalisation as *any* reform or set of reforms that reduce the bias against exports. On this basis three types of liberalisation can be distinguished. First, import liberalisation includes any reforms that reduce protection, generally the removal of quantitative restrictions (QRs) and the reduction of tariffs. Such reforms reduce the price of imports and importables (domestic goods that compete with imports), and increase the relative price of exports. Second, export promotion reforms increase the return to exporting and make it easier to export, and encourage domestic resources to be redirected to the exportables sector. Third, exchange rate liberalisation, devaluation and removing exchange controls so that the exchange rate is 'market determined' helps to keep relative domestic incentives in line with relative world prices for importables and exportables. Devaluation itself increases returns to exporters (who receive more domestic currency for a given world price) and is intended to bring the exchange rate closer to its equilibrium level. Easing access to foreign exchange makes it easier to import, effectively by reducing transaction costs and/or rent-seeking, and thus could be considered an element of import liberalisation. Permitting exporters to retain export earnings is often an important (and simple) export promotion measure.

It is not unusual for all three elements to be present in a trade liberalisation episode. In the 12 cases summarised in Table 16.2, five used all three elements. Exchange rate liberalisation was evident in nine cases, as was tariff reduction, while reduction of QRs was present in eight cases. Direct export promotion was the least frequently used measure, in only half of the cases. The advantage of considering pre-1980 liberalisations, as in Table 16.2, is that we have evidence on export and growth performance after the liberalisation episode. In general, liberalisation had the expected beneficial effects.

There are, however, problems with the evidence and some fairly fundamental problems with the way in which liberalisation episodes in the Papageorgiou *et al.* (1991) study are identified and measured (Greenaway 1993). In particular, it is not always clear that 'liberalisation' in any of the senses discussed above has occurred. In some instances it is only stabilisation combined with devaluation that has been implemented. This is important because these may be key causal ingredients in stimulating

Table 16.2 Elements of pre-1980 trade liberalisations

	Policy reforms present or not[a]				Post-reform growth[b]	
	QRS	Tariffs	Exports	ER	Exports	GDP
Argentina	–	yes	yes	yes	+	?
Brazil	–	yes	yes	yes	+	+
Chile	yes	yes	–	–	+	+
Colombia	yes	yes	yes	–	−ve	+
Indonesia	yes	yes	yes	yes	+	+
South Korea	yes	yes	yes	yes	+/−ve	+/−ve
Pakistan	–	–	–	yes	+	+
Peru	yes	yes	–	–	–	–
Philippines	?	?	–	yes	+	+
Sri Lanka	yes	–	–	yes	−ve/+	?/+
Turkey	yes	yes	yes	yes	+	?
Uruguay	yes	yes	–	yes	+	+
No. of countries	*No. of 'yes' countries*				*No. of '+' countries*	
12	8	9	6	9	8	7

Source: Adapted from Greenaway and Morrissey (1994: tabs. 14.1 and 14.4–5).
Notes: These are broad indications of diverse reform packages from a variety of countries and time periods, and are no more than indicative.
[a]Policy areas: QRS: reduction in the number/extent of quantitative restrictions on imports; tariffs: reduction in average level or range of tariffs; exports: direct measures to promote exports; ER: rationalisation and/or devaluation of the exchange rate. The keys 'yes' indicate reforms were present, '?' that reforms were ambiguous or very limited and '−ve' opposite reforms (e.g. export disincentives or increases in tariffs).
[b]Comparison of annual average growth rates for the three years prior to reforms with the three years after reforms. The keys '+' indicate a growth increase after reform, '−ve' that growth slowed and '?' that minimal difference occurred. Two keys imply significant differences between reform episodes.

export and output growth. When the evidence is examined in greater (econometric) detail, the link between liberalisation and growth is found to be weak (Greenaway *et al.* 1998). Such econometric evidence must be interpreted with extreme caution, however, as cross-country studies are limited to using simple measures of liberalisation (such as whether or not a reform episode was in place, or changes in average tariffs); these measures are often inaccurate and misleading (Milner and Morrissey 1999).

Onafowora and Owoye (1998), in a time series analysis of 12 African countries over 1963–93, offer more encouraging results. For about half of the countries, they find evidence that exports are positively related to growth. Using a trade policy index, they find some evidence that growth is higher in more outward oriented economies. They conclude that trade liberalisation, interpreted as outward orientation, does offer potential for some sub-Saharan countries to increase growth rates. They acknowledge the results are not fully generalisable; the commodity composition of exports, in particular, can limit the contribution of exports to growth. Nevertheless, the findings offer some comfort to proponents of trade liberalisation.

There is a shortage of convincing evidence that trade liberalisation increases growth. Rather than discuss the literature at length, we make two important points. First, there is no evidence that trade liberalisation retards growth. Second, the objective of liberalisation as we define it is simply to remove the bias against exporting; this in itself appears thoroughly desirable. Trade liberalisation as implemented may reduce but not remove the bias, hence there will be little if any export response. More importantly, there may be other biases not directly related to trade policy. The case of agriculture is particularly relevant to LICs that are predominantly exporters of agricultural commodities. In such countries the bias against agriculture is often severe (Bautista and Valdes 1993), but the bias against (agricultural) exports is only a component of this. Trade liberalisation alone will be insufficient to remove the bias against agriculture, hence we may not observe any export response (McKay *et al.* 1997). This is an important reason why one may not observe any relationship between trade liberalisation and growth, including export growth, in LICs. This does not imply that such countries would not be better off by liberalising the trade regime.

A more general point can be made regarding the link between trade liberalisation and openness. Often the two are treated as almost the same, but effectively the former is only an element of the latter. Trade liberalisation need not imply free trade, rather it requires increasing the incentives to exporting *and* increasing the openness of the economy to imports. While the latter may give rise to concerns regarding the competitiveness of domestic producers of importables, access to imported investment goods and the technology embodied in imports may be very beneficial. On a broader dimension, openness implies being receptive to ideas and tends to attract foreign investment (admittedly a mixed blessing if appropriate controls are not in place). Although no panacea, openness broadly conceived does appear conducive to growth, conditional on appropriate domestic policies and institutions (Rodrik 1999).

Having argued the case for trade liberalisation, we can ask if much has occurred. Table 16.3 provides some evidence on trade liberalisation since 1985 in 25 of the countries covered by Dean *et al.* (1994). The tariff ratio (the ratio of the post-reform average nominal tariff to its pre-reform level) provides a summary measure of liberalisation: a ratio above unity implies an increase in average nominal tariffs while a ratio of, for example, 0.5 implies a 50 per cent reduction. As a summary measure it has problems and may even be misleading regarding the direction of change in trade policy orientation (Milner and Morrissey 1999).

Nevertheless, changes in average nominal tariff are indicative and some general patterns emerge. Tariff reductions were greatest in Latin America: the eight countries in this region reduced tariffs by 50 per cent or more; South Korea was the only other country in the sample to reduce tariffs by more than 50 per cent. About a third of the total sample reduced nominal tariffs by more than 50 per cent. Some 40 per cent of the countries reduced

Table 16.3 Elements of recent trade liberalisations

	Average nominal tariff [a]			
	Pre-reform	Current	Ratio	ER[b]
Bangladesh (1989; 1992)	94	50	0.53	−5.3
India (1990; 1993)	128	71	0.55	−7.7
Pakistan (1987; 1990)	69	65	0.94	−11.7
Sri Lanka (1985; 1992)	31	25	0.81	−0.5
South Asia (average)	**80**	**53**	**0.66**	
China (1986; 1992)	38	43	1.13	−43.9
Philippines (1985; 1992)	28	24	0.86	1.8
Indonesia (1985; 1990)	27	22	0.81	−23.2
South Korea (1984; 1992)	24	10	0.42	13.1
Thailand (1986; 1990)[c]	13	11	0.85	−0.5
East Asia and the Pacific (average)	**29**	**25**	**0.86**	
Côte d'Ivoire (1985; 1989)	26	33	1.27	CFA
Ghana (1983; 1991)	30	17	0.57	−11.1
Kenya (1987; 1992)	40	34	0.85	−5.4
Madagascar (1988; 1990)	46	36	0.78	−11.2
Nigeria (1984; 1990)	35	33	0.94	−71.2
Senegal (1986; 1991)	98	90	0.92	CFA
Tanzania (1986; 1992)	30	33	1.10	−145.2
Zaire (1984; 1990)	24	25	1.04	−13.1
Sub-Saharan African (average)	**41**	**38**	**0.93**	
Colombia (1984; 1992)	61	12	0.20	−36.1
Peru (1988; 1992)	57	17	0.30	106.7
Costa Rica (1985; 1992)	53	15	0.28	−15.8
Brazil (1987; 1992)	51	21	0.41	9.5
Venezuela (1989; 1991)	37	19	0.51	0.2
Chile (1984; 1991)	35	11	0.31	−14.5
Argentina (1988; 1992)	29	12	0.41	43.7
Mexico (1985; 1987)	29	10	0.34	3.7
Latin America and Caribbean (average)	**44**	**15**	**0.34**	

Source: Derived from various tables in Dean *et al.* (1994).
Notes: Years given in parenthesis are pre-reform and current, respectively.
   [a]Unweighted average nominal tariff (tends to be biased upwards), rounded. The
   ratio is current number divided by pre-reform number (a lower ratio implies
   greater tariff reductions). Figures in average rows are simple averages for each
   region.
   [b]Percentage real exchange rate depreciation between the first year of reform and
   1992.
   [c]Import-weighted average nominal tariff.

tariffs by between 10 and 50 per cent; three reduced tariffs by less than ten per cent; and four actually increased average nominal tariffs. One should exercise caution; Morrissey (1996) demonstrates that at least in the case of Tanzania these results are misleading. Nevertheless, it is clear that tariff reductions were least in sub-Saharan Africa, where only Ghana achieved a significant reduction.

Perhaps the most instructive message to emerge from Table 16.3 is that trade liberalisation tends, quite strongly, to be least in the poorest countries. In terms of per capita incomes, the poorest countries are those in sub-Saharan Africa, South Asia and East Asia excluding South Korea (and perhaps Thailand). None of these countries reduced average tariffs by more than 50 per cent, few attained reductions of more than 20 per cent, and all the countries that increased tariffs are in this category. Partly, this may be because poor countries are more reliant on trade taxes. Partly, it may be because the average nominal tariff is a poor measure of liberalisation. Indeed, for poorer countries, that tend initially to be highly protected, it is likely that other forms of import liberalisation, such as removal of QRs, are more important (as measures to reduce protection) and easier to implement. Furthermore, Table 16.3 shows that most of these countries undertook at least some devaluation. Nevertheless, progress on trade liberalisation in LICs has been limited (Uganda, not included here, is one major exception).

To conclude this section, trade liberalisation offers benefits to LICs as it reduces the bias against exports. As such countries, especially those that are dependent on aid, tend to be primarily exporters of agricultural commodities, complementary agricultural liberalisation is essential. Few LICs, however, have achieved significant progress in trade liberalisation (although more has been achieved in the 1990s than is reflected here). One reason for this is that there are costs to liberalisation. Aid can play an important role here, either to compensate for revenue losses when adjusting to lower tariffs or to avert import compression following devaluation. Another reason, not to be underestimated, is that trade liberalisation can be politically difficult to implement (Morrissey 1996). Aid can play a role here also. Trade reform conditions associated with adjustment loans have played a role in encouraging liberalisation; donor support for the administrative and institutional capacity to implement trade reforms would be constructive. However, unilateral trade liberalisation by LICs does not in itself offer the prospect of increasing export earnings. As such, in the short term at least, it does not offer the prospect of reducing aid dependence. In fact, to compensate for the costs, the process of liberalisation may increase aid reliance in the short term.

Regional integration

The 1990s have seen something of a revival of interest in regional trade agreements (RTAS), globally and among low-income countries. This is not the place to review individual RTAs in any detail; the task would be massive (e.g. on sub-Saharan Africa, see Oyejide *et al.* 1997; on Central America, see Bulmer-Thomas 1998). Lyakurwa *et al.* (1997) identify seven RTAs in sub-Saharan Africa alone. To this can be added South Asia, Pacific Islands, the Caribbean, Central America and the Andes, not to mention RTAs comprising industrialised and middle-income countries. We have only space here to review the motivations underlying RTAs and to consider the potential economic benefits to members. We will consider the potential impact of RTAs on exports and aid for low-income countries.

The new regionalism

There has been a remarkable proliferation in RTAs since the Second World War and more than 100 agreements have been ratified. Essentially there have been two waves of regionalism, the first in the 1960s, the second in the 1990s (often referred to as 'the new regionalism'). There are a number of distinctive characteristics of the recent phenomenon. First, while the 'old regionalism' typically involved RTAs that were 'North–North' or 'South–South', the new regionalism includes many 'North–South' arrangements like NAFTA and APEC. This characteristic offers obvious potential in terms of gains from trade. It also creates the potential for adjustment problems and trade tensions. Second, whereas with the old regionalism RTAs typically involved (near) neighbours, many recent arrangements have been intercontinental. Third, many recent arrangements are not mutually exclusive: multiple membership is not problematic. Finally, whereas all arrangements under the old region-alism promoted shallow integration, liberalisation of border measures only, many recent agreements have aspired to deep integration with commitments to harmonisation of regulatory measures, freeing up of factor movements and so on. We can note that the first two characteristics have not generally applied to RTAs comprising low-income countries.

There are a number of explanations for the resurgence of popularity of RTAs. A popular view sees their proliferation as a reaction to frustrations with the GATT in general and the Uruguay Round in particular. However, many RTAs post-date the successful conclusion of the Round. A more sophisticated version of this explanation is associated with, among others, Krugman (1993) along the lines that RTAs are easier to negotiate and implement than multilateral agreements. This is partly a consequence of the number of negotiating parties involved, and partly of the fact that multilateral agreements are no longer simply about tariffs but a much wider range of measures. RTAs typically involve fewer negotiating parties reaching agreement on a narrower range of issues. Bhagwati (1993) advances a related argument in putting the new regionalism down to US interests in RTAs, which the EU has also promoted.[2]

As an alternative explanation, Baldwin (1997a) puts forward his 'domino theory' of regionalism. This exploits the fact that any RTA results in some trade and investment diversion, that in turn creates a desire for excluded nations to be included, the more so the greater the number of nations included. A single initial agreement, if it is important, triggers a domino effect. A similar, though not identical, explanation is often cast in terms of defensive regionalism (e.g. Greenaway 1999). Here it is not trade and investment diversion from growing blocs that is the threat, but the fear of market exclusion and the need to provide countervailing bargaining power.

Benefits of regional integration

There is a very extensive literature on the economic effects of RTAs (Baldwin 1997b provides an excellent review). The pioneering work of Viner (1950) developed the concepts of trade *creation* and trade *diversion*. The former is essentially the outcome of liberalisation within the region; when this results in more efficient suppliers replacing less efficient suppliers, the union as a whole is better off. Trade diversion, by contrast, arises if imports from an efficient global supplier are replaced with (diverted to) a less efficient regional supplier enjoying the protection of common external trade barriers. Whether the RTA is welfare improving or not depends on the balance between trade creation and trade diversion.

Subsequent analysis of the effects of integration incorporated consumption benefits (even trade diversion may reduce consumer prices), the impact on factor flows (labour and capital) and scale economies. That focus was on static benefits, i.e. those associated with the reallocation of resources. The most important benefits may be dynamic, associated with accumulation rather than reallocation. Ultimately, the best way to improve living standards is by increasing real incomes. A key feature in achieving this is technical progress, which directly affects factor productivity; spillover effects or externalities associated with capital accumulation. This could arise through investments in infrastructure or public intermediate inputs or through spillovers from one form of private sector investment to another. Alternatively, following Romer (1990), it could arise through endogenous innovation. A third possible channel is through human capital accumulation. More highly trained/better educated workers are not only more productive themselves, they may also enhance the productivity of those with whom they work. Moreover, as increased investment in schooling and training enhances the current stock of knowledge, that too has beneficial implications for the productivity of future generations.

Several ways in which economic integration can play a role can be suggested. First, as the pool of scientific knowledge affects the productivity of future R&D, economic integration can be beneficial by enhancing the size of the pool. Second, economic integration can enhance the pool of human capital, as free movement of labour regionally is more achievable than free movement globally. A third potential channel for integration relates to its effects on market structure and the incentives to innovate. Domestic markets often shelter monopoly providers when the minimum efficient scale of production is high relative to the total market. In such circumstances monopolists do not have a strong incentive for innovation. Free entry in an integrated market makes for a more competitive environment and also increases the potential rewards to innovation. This market size effect is a fourth potential link between economic integration and endogenous growth.

Finally, it has been argued by many that 'institutions' matter for long-run growth (e.g. Rodrik 1999 and Williamson 1994). Good institutions need to underpin a clearly defined regime of property rights as well as embedding arrangements for contract enforcement. Such arrangements reduce uncertainty and thereby contribute to investment and innovation. When any integration takes place there is a need for some institutional innovation, even if only mutual recognition. Regional integration may provide a conducive environment for the development of such institutional arrangements, given the smaller number of players involved compared to the multilateral level and the likelihood of greater cultural similarity.

Benefits of RTAs for low-income countries

All of the potential benefits from RTAs identified above are applicable to RTAs among low-income countries (LIRTA), but the magnitude may not be great. The central problem is that as the economic size of the individual countries is so small, the LIRTA is likely to be small. Crucially, the potential benefits of market size (scale economies, eliminating monopoly power and encouraging innovation) may not be realised. Furthermore, it is often the case that one economy dominates the LIRTA market, especially in manufactures, such as Kenya in East Africa and South Africa in Southern Africa, while the smaller members produce primary commodities not demanded by the large member. This implies trade and market benefits often accrue to only one member, increasing tension within the LIRTA (one factor in the collapse of many LIRTAs, see Lyakurwa *et al.* 1997). This is compounded by the fact that cultural and political differences are often intense between neighbouring low-income countries (this is true for almost all African LIRTAs and South Asia). Significant economic gains can often compensate for political costs. In LIRTAs this may not happen.

For most LIRTAs, the static gains from integration are slight and, where they arise, are likely to be concentrated in one member country. The smaller members may have to be convinced of the dynamic gains to entice them into the agreement. There are three important and related potential dynamic gains. First, increased factor mobility. Even if the static gains are concentrated in one country, smaller countries can benefit if their labour is able to migrate to where jobs are. Alternatively, mobility of capital and labour may induce firms to relocate activities to some of the smaller countries (initial location may have been motivated by higher protection in the large country). Second, integration may attract investment. This may be from foreign investors or within the region. In the latter case, economies of scale and externalities in public investment (for example on infrastructure) could benefit smaller countries. Third, the RTA may help the regimes to establish policy credibility (Fine and Yeo 1997). Establishing and maintaining an RTA may signal a credible policy commitment to liberalisation, that in turn will attract foreign investment (it may also, of course, be a necessary condition for attracting foreign aid).

Attracting increased investment may be the key to the success of LIRTAS. Levels of investment will obviously depend on expected returns. The fact that LIRTA markets are currently small limits the expected returns of investments in production activities geared to the domestic market. Increased levels of investment then are most likely to occur in sectors producing for international markets. By increasing their exports to the much larger world market, LICS may have their best opportunity of increasing their growth rates. We have previously noted that their ability to increase exports may be limited, but it is not non-existent. Sectors engaged in the production of tradable goods for export potentially offer the highest returns to investors. Investors may be most concerned about security of access to global markets and stability of trade policy. This is especially true of foreign investment, where the investors may have several countries to choose between. Establishing an RTA can help here.

Similar arguments apply to securing continued aid flows. Although integration has never featured in aid conditionality (it is however something that the EU is willing to support), maintaining a commitment to liberalisation is a cornerstone of conditionality. As noted by Collier *et al.* (1997) many African countries that have undertaken trade liberalisation subsequently reversed some of the policies. The reasons obviously vary from case to case, although the revenue consequences seem to have been an important factor in several instances of reversal. Again, establishing an RTA sends a positive signal. Furthermore, aid is an important source of funds for investment. This could be important in the context of public investment that benefits all members of a LIRTA.

The most important potential dynamic benefit of a LIRTA is investment; encouraging domestic investment, attracting foreign investment and appealing to donors. This benefit may be enhanced if the LIRTA is likely to form an agreement with an RTA of industrialised countries (such as the EU or NAFTA). If, for example, Lomé trade preferences were deemed illegal under GATT, the only way countries other than the least developed could avail of preferences would be if they formed an RTA which then reached a reciprocal economic partnership arrangement (REPA) with the EU. This scenario is quite realistic. Most low-income countries are among the Africa, Caribbean and Pacific (ACP) countries benefiting under the Lomé convention. The EU is considering the potential of REPAS to maintain trade preferences towards ACP countries (NAFTA may also consider them). A REPA requires that the LIRTA grants the EU preferential (essentially tariff-free) access, in return for which the LIRTA gets free access to the EU. The static gains would accrue largely to the EU, which would become the competitive supplier of most manufactures (and perhaps also of temperate agricultural products). However, perhaps more important are the dynamic impacts. If for example the formation of a REPA was to lead to higher levels of investment and growth in the LIRTA than would occur in its absence, then this might be a sufficiently important effect to outweigh any possible adverse static impacts. This is quite probable, partly because the EU itself may grant investment funds (aid), partly because the REPA locks the LIRTA into trade liberalisation, and partly because access to the EU will attract investment.

Conclusions

Multilateral agricultural trade liberalisation, by increasing international competition, improving access to foreign markets and inducing more efficient resource allocations, is expected to produce large dynamic gains in terms of economies of scale, technical changes and economic growth. In the long run, trade liberalisation (in its various forms) would be expected to benefit LICs by increasing global efficiency and permitting them to benefit from increased export earnings. Whether a particular country is likely to benefit will depend on what goods it imports and exports. Most countries are likely to benefit, but three types of countries will probably lose. First, are net food importers, who will face higher food prices. Second, countries that import temperate foods although they export tropical foods. Third, countries that export low volumes of textiles and are likely to be uncompetitive in a more open world market. Most low-income African countries fall into one or more of these categories, and are the most likely to be losers. Other small poor countries, such as Nepal or tropical island states, are also likely to be net losers.

There are a number of implications of the changing global trade environment for future aid flows. First, as has often been implicitly recognised in structural adjustment loans, unilateral trade liberalisation imposes short-run costs. The most obvious of these are potential losses of (tariff) revenue and an increased import bill following devaluation. Foreign aid can be, and has been, used to alleviate these costs. Such use should only be temporary. Second, low-income regional integration arrangements may attract aid support, especially to finance shared infrastructure or for institutional capacity-building. Again, such use should only be temporary (although investment effects should be long-run). Regional integration offers the potential to attract investment and expand exports, which should ultimately reduce aid dependency.

The forms of foreign aid just discussed could be described as functional, and fully in keeping with the general notion of using aid to cover financing gaps, especially where foreign exchange earnings from exports are low. However, the fact that multilateral trade liberalisation will generate losers suggests a more redistributive role for aid. How this may work in practice could be central to how aid develops in the future (and will be related to the multi-faceted effects of globalisation on growth and on poverty). Multilateral trade liberalisation can be a Pareto welfare improvement if the winners compensate the losers. We know that the largest winners are the industrialised nations of the donor community, and the main losers are the least developed countries. We also know that a major source of losses is the potential increase in world food prices. One possible way forward is to monitor food prices and import needs for low-income countries (which should of course be encouraged to implement policies to support their own farmers). This is not intended as an argument for food aid, but rather for aid linked to the incremental cost of food import requirements. Nor is this proposed as an alternative to other aid channels, but as a particular form of aid intended to address the distributional implications of multilateral trade liberalisation.

It is not the aim of this chapter to present the details of an aid scheme to compensate losers in the process of globalisation, although this could become a fundamental argument for aid in the future (both from recipients seeking help and from interests in donor countries seeking to reverse aid fatigue). It is emphasised that there will be losers from multilateral trade liberalisation, that the principle of compensation is established, and that doing so through a scheme linked to the cost of food imports is one option. Monitoring the impacts on poverty adds another dimension to this. Structural adjustment loans have effectively compensated recipients for the adjustment costs of economic policy reform, including unilateral trade liberalisation. Regional integration arrangements typically include schemes to compensate losers. The same principle can be applied, with care, to multilateral trade liberalisation where the probable losers are the low-income countries of the world, while the largest gains accrue to the already wealthy industrialised countries. Globalisation will have losers so some people are likely to become poor, or poorer. This will give rise to new redistributive claims for aid in the future. Supporting the process of globalisation, such as integration, or assisting countries' ability to adapt, such as through institutional capacity-building or meeting adjustment costs, will also give rise to claims for aid. These distributional and functional claims will be mutually reinforcing as they apply to the same countries, and will be an important element in the evolution of aid policy in the early decades of the twenty-first century.

Notes

1 The author acknowledges the suggestions of Christian Friis Bach who contributed to a provisional draft of this section.
2 For example, the EU has been quite pro-active in promoting regional integration amongst African countries, specially in Southern Africa. Although not explicitly a condition of aid, it was clear that the EU would look favourably on granting aid support for integration efforts.

17 Aid and conflict

*Tony Addison**

Introduction

The last decade of the twentieth century saw the disintegration of the former Yugoslavia, genocide in Rwanda and the collapse of Somalia, to name only three tragedies. At least 43 major conflicts occurred in the 1990s – the exact number depending on how we define a 'major' conflict – with Africa accounting for 17 of these (Brogan 1998 and CCPDC 1997). These have included inter-state wars (most notably the Gulf War of 1991), but the majority are intra-state in nature (see Wallensteen and Sollenberg 1997). Such horrors are not unique to our time – the 1970s saw genocide in Cambodia – but the number of intra-state conflicts in the 1990s suggests a deterioration in the mechanisms of conflict management in many societies. How to prevent and end violent conflict, deal with its humanitarian debris, and help countries recover, is now *the* most important set of issues facing the donor countries and their development, foreign policy, and military institutions.

At present aid is being put to a considerable number of uses. These range from emergency relief in Africa and the Balkans to reconstruction and development assistance in, among others, Guatemala, Bosnia and Herzegovina, and Mozambique. Aid can be used as a sanction; reconstruction aid is presently denied to Serbia and the United States threatened to block aid to India and Pakistan in order to dampen their nuclear escalation. Aid can also be used as an inducement; food aid is currently delivered to North Korea to defuse tensions on the Korean peninsula. All these demands on aid must be met from declining aid budgets; aid is now under 0.22 per cent of OECD donor GNP – its lowest level since the Marshall Plan of 1947, the world's first aid-financed reconstruction programme.

Needless to say, aid in conflict situations is both complex and controversial. This chapter reviews the subject, starting with the role of aid during and after conflict. Humanitarian aid, assisting the war-to-peace transition, aid to sustain and rebuild livelihoods, and balance-of-payments and budgetary support are discussed in turn. The next section then identifies critical tasks to improve aid in conflict situations. In particular, the impact of insecurity in reducing the effectiveness of both humanitarian and reconstruction aid is highlighted. The chapter concludes by recommending three ways in which aid can contribute to preventing conflict. These are: (i) focus aid on reducing inequality as well as poverty as a means to dampen social tension and violence, (ii) use aid to help countries channel conflict into institutions and processes for its non-violent expression and resolution, as well as to assist peaceful secession and (iii) build a coherent foreign policy framework to support the use of aid in conflict prevention.

Aid during and after conflict

Humanitarian aid

Despite considerable success in reducing the number of victims through humanitarian assistance, severe problems have been encountered which have led some observers to doubt the fundamental value of emergency relief. This section provides a brief review of what is a complex and multi-dimensional issue.

Some 70 million people have become international refugees or have been internally displaced by conflict since 1990, and 15 countries have had more than 20 per cent of their population displaced. Donor countries provide food, medical assistance and shelter to the needy *in situ* and to refugees through NGO, WFP, UNHCR and Unicef programmes. These have been major logistic exercises with very large coverage; for example, two-thirds of Bosnia's population was receiving humanitarian aid at the height of its crisis. Relief to cope with flood and drought is also provided in conflict situations; in 1998, Somalia and Sudan saw major operations to cope with the effects of the El Niño. The modalities of delivery depend on the type of emergency, ranging from Mozambique, where a functioning government existed, to Somalia, in which the state had collapsed. Under-funding has in recent years hampered relief operations in Africa; only 25 per cent of UNHCR's total requests were met in 1999.

Operations in conflict countries have placed heavy demands on food aid. In 1990, emergency food aid accounted for 19 per cent of global food aid; its share has now risen to 42 per cent (IFPRI 1998). The number of people receiving WFP food aid increased by 17 per cent over 1996–7. There is now much experience in targeting food relief to the needy (see the review in Chapter 8 in this volume and also Stewart 1998).

Despite the need to focus on emergency relief in conflict situations, donors can also help to keep some basic services running. Unicef conducts vaccination campaigns in conflict countries; for example, it used the 1998 cease-fire in southern Sudan to restock clinics with basic drugs, thereby containing a major diarrhoea outbreak among children. Unicef also supports community-based education initiatives in Taliban-held areas of Afghanistan (thus partially counteracting discrimination against girls in formal education) and continues to work with education authorities in the few remaining areas outside Taliban control (Unicef 1999). Moreover, the rehabilitation of victims and psycho-social support are essential both during and after war. Women need considerable help; in Mozambique 44 per cent of women witnessed a murder and a quarter were separated from their children (Cairns 1997). In Cambodia, Norwegian and Swiss-based NGOs are supporting mental health programmes for refugees. In Sierra Leone, NGOs are working to release child soldiers from the militias (Unicef 1998). In these ways, aid can relieve human suffering as well as sustain and rebuild social capital.

Nevertheless, humanitarian aid can prolong and intensify conflict when it falls into the hands of belligerents. The UN secretary-general has argued that this is one of the greatest challenges facing humanitarian assistance (Annan 1998). During its 1993 Somalia operation, only 50 per cent of UN relief reached the target population; the remainder went to warlords (Ramsbotham and Woodhouse 1996). In Bosnia, militias commandeered UNHCR relief, and Sudan's rebels covertly tax UN relief (Duffield 1999). In 1996, Liberia's warlords looted over $8 million worth of relief supplies much of which found military use (Annan 1998). Moreover, humanitarian aid can be diverted to combatants based in refugee camps. This is a longstanding problem; relief supplied the cross-border operations of Afghan fighters based in camps in Pakistan and Cambodian fighters based in Thai refugee camps. Indeed, major powers covertly supported rebels in this way during the cold war (Barber 1997).

These, and other problems, have led some commentators to reach very strong conclusions. For example, Alex de Waal asserts that 'most humanitarian aid in Africa is useless or damaging and should be abandoned.' (de Waal 1997: xvi). Others have argued that the ancient medical principle – 'do no harm' – should be the guiding light for humanitarian aid, implying that help should be withheld if there is a chance of it falling into the wrong hands. Luttwak (1999) alleges that NGO assistance helps to prolong warfare, by resourcing combatants and thus preventing mutual exhaustion from forcing an earlier political settlement.

But such views have met forceful rebuttal. The Overseas Development Institute in London argues that: 'In most, if not all, conflicts the role of humanitarian aid as a source of support for warring factions has probably been slight. Rather, in those situations where relief is blamed for supporting a particular group this is often the result of political and military failings.' (ODI 1998: 6). Thus, unintended support to combatants arises not from a failure in humanitarian aid as such, but from a failure to provide security for its delivery (an issue that we return to below).

In eastern Zaire in 1996, for example, 5 to 10 per cent of the displaced Hutu population from Rwanda were not bona fide refugees (ODI 1998). The 1951 Refugee Convention, requires refugees to be screened to verify their status. But this could only be done with military peace-keepers, which the major powers were unwilling to provide. As a result, 1.2 million refugees were left under the control of the 'genocidaires' who benefited from the humanitarian aid. Cairns (1997) highlights the dilemmas that this posed for the NGOs; some stayed on, others felt they had no choice but to withdraw.

Agencies have now redesigned their relief programmes to reduce these dangers. The WFP contracts Somali businessmen to deliver food aid to needy communities. Contractors must deposit a bond for the value of the food aid and the cost of any food that goes astray is deducted. Their profitability therefore depends on success in negotiating safe passage for the food; WFP claims that only 2 per cent of the value of the food is lost in this way. Agencies have also redesigned their programmes to reduce the value of their relief to belligerents. Following the looting of relief supplies in Liberia, international NGOs agreed to use only locally available inputs in their programmes, thereby limiting the availability of new resources to looters (Cairns 1997). When insecurity is high, many NGOs cease to use dry food rations which are easily stolen. By reducing the incentive to loot, these measures permit humanitarian aid to continue in otherwise highly insecure situations. But they are obviously not a substitute for creating security itself.

Assisting the war-to-peace transition

If a cease-fire can be secured, then war-to-peace transition can begin. The tasks involved include electoral assistance, justice, security and institutional investment. The livelihoods of shattered communities must be rebuilt and balance-of-payments and budgetary support used to assist social and economic reconstruction.

Democratisation

Competitive elections are widely seen as essential in preventing a return to violent conflict. Krishna Kumar identifies three main objectives for post-conflict elections: (i) to transfer power to a government with national and international legitimacy, (ii) to start and then consolidate democratisation so that democratic institutions embed themselves and (iii) to promote reconciliation between former opponents by replacing violent conflict with political competition – 'ballots take the place of bullets.' – (Kumar 1998: 7). Most peace accords include an agreement to hold elections and a timetable. Examples include Bosnia and Herzegovina, Cambodia and Mozambique. Aid is usually conditional on competitive elections being held (Eritrea, Rwanda and Uganda are exceptions). Assistance is provided to draft electoral legislation and to organise and monitor the voting process.

But the role of national and regional elections in resolving conflict is controversial. In some cases, elections may have been too hastily implemented and in the absence of basic pre-conditions for peace (Angola and

Sierra Leone, for example). There is no single electoral system that is best for all divided societies (Reilly and Reynolds 1999). Moreover, early elections may simply legitimise nationalist and racist elites which were responsible for conflict (Chandler 1998). Civil society institutions must expand for democracy to embed itself. Since nationalist and racist interests may dominate some civil society institutions, donors should target progressive institutions which can bridge ethnic and racial divides. But this is more easily said that done (Engberg and Stubbs 1999).

Justice

The international community is financing the international criminal tribunals for the former Yugoslavia and Rwanda. These may deter potential war criminals, and they represent an important innovation in the 'globalisation' of justice. Pressure can be put on governments to respect human rights and to clean up their judiciaries by threatening the withdrawal of aid (although aid as a sanction has had limited effectiveness). For example, some donors have sought to link aid to Cambodia to judicial reforms, including an international trial for Khmer Rouge leaders, but this pressure is weakened by a lack of unanimity among Cambodia's bilateral donors.

Security

Land mines increase demands on overstretched health services, disrupt transportation, and deny the use of land for farming and grazing (Heiberg 1998). Private and public aid to de-mining is now extensive; Canada alone has pledged $64 million over five years. Despite the problem's high profile, delays in clearance are common. Bureaucratic wrangling between UN agencies and lobbying for lucrative contracts stalled large-scale clearance for over a year in Mozambique, although NGOs cleared many mines in the interim (Barnes 1998). The marginal cost of complete clearance is prohibitive – hence the importance of mine-awareness campaigns – and fresh mines were laid when war resumed in Angola and Ethiopia/Eritrea.

Peace agreements require the disarmament and demobilisation of combatants and, in some cases (Mozambique, for example), the creation of new national security forces by fusing together government and opposition armies. The United Kingdom provides military aid to restructure and reduce armed forces, and to train 'democratically accountable' armies. Aid to demobilisation reduces the fiscal burden of military spending, allowing public money to shift from military to development spending. For example, military spending was 35 per cent of total public expenditures during Djibouti's 1991–2 civil war, and aid-financed demobilisation helped to raise development and social sector spending after the war.

Institutional investment

Some conflicts end with state institutions largely intact (for example, El Salvador, Ethiopia and Mozambique) while others create new countries which require major institutional investments (for example Eritrea and East Timor). In extreme cases state institutions are smashed and require complete reconstruction (Cambodia in 1979 and, eventually, Somalia). Technical assistance is therefore necessary to build or rebuild public administrations, judiciaries, and central banks and to introduce new currencies. The IMF and UNDP are the lead agencies in these tasks. The plethora of donor and NGO programmes and their need for skilled and professional labour can impede institutional rehabilitation when they siphon off scarce personnel from core government institutions – a problem in poor countries such as Mozambique.

Peace agreements may result in complex political outcomes and thus complex institutional arrangements; the Palestine Authority and its relationship to Israel is one example. Aid agencies in Bosnia and Herzegovina must work with three administrations: (i) the state of Bosnia and Herzegovina itself and its constituent parts, (ii) the Muslim–Croat Federation of Bosnia and Herzegovina and (iii) the Serb-run Republika Srpska. Co-operation between the latter two entities has been sporadic, forcing donors to push a 'quick start package' of laws covering state institutions, including the budget, the central bank and the customs service (EBRD 1997: 157).

Aid to sustain and rebuild livelihoods

It is possible in some conflicts for community projects to provide livelihoods and basic services for the poor in cities safe from war thereby mitigating the impact of forced urbanisation. Some 40 per cent of Angola's population is now packed into Luanda, for example, and community projects are one of the few means to help them. Development projects may also be possible in safe rural areas – these were undertaken in Mozambique, and ameliorated a desperate food security situation. Aid to sustain livelihoods in enclaves protected by outside military forces is possible; the rehabilitation of social and economic infrastructure in Iraqi Kurdistan is an example.

Once peace is secured the immediate task is to help refugees return and rebuild their livelihoods. Aid helped two million Mozambicans return and provided seeds and tools to restart farms and micro enterprises. Security in post-war Mozambique was relatively good, thus easing the resettlement and the work of donors. But genocidaires continue to terrorise northwest Rwanda. Rwanda's army has moved Hutus into inadequately equipped camps from where they will eventually be relocated to specially constructed villages under army protection – a classic counter-insurgency technique. Donors are rightly wary of contributing to a programme that includes forced resettlement, and have largely confined themselves to pilot projects.

Since poverty is a cause of conflict, broad-based (poverty reducing) reconstruction and growth are critical to sustaining peace (see below). Guatemala is one example. The distribution of land is highly skewed against indigenous people and human development indicators are amongst Latin America's worst. This fuelled 36 years of insurgency against successive military regimes. The World Bank is targeting project aid to rural road construction in the poorest zones (thereby improving market opportunities), and to rural basic education, female education and bilingual education – thereby improving the livelihoods of indigenous people.

Women and their livelihoods are often neglected when the first priority is to find employment for demobilised men. Projects can help bridge the ethnic divide by enabling women to see themselves as having common interests in rebuilding communities. The Bosnia Women's Initiative, a programme of income-generating projects (including micro-credit), has this objective (Hunt 1999). More generally, support to civic organisations builds social capital; this is an explicit aim of UNDP projects in Bosnia and Herzegovina (Engberg and Stubbs 1999).

Donors face a real dilemma in keeping aid out of the hands of war criminals. In some areas of Bosnia and Herzegovina war crime suspects own the companies most able to undertake reconstruction work; in the Republika Srpska, these include officials who ran the notorious Omarska and Keraterm prison camps (Paul 1997). European bilateral aid is alleged to have gone to these companies. Human rights organisations favour denying aid to municipalities whose leading officials are under investigation while donors conclude that contracts cannot be blocked unless company owners are officially indicted for war crimes. Moreover, the distribution of aid across ethnic communities may create tensions. Boyd (1998) notes that only 2 per cent of reconstruction aid goes to the Republika Srpska, a distribution that intensifies ethnic animosity.

Conflict causes massive damage to the infrastructure that facilitates livelihoods; the cost amounted to $25 billion in Lebanon and $20 billion in Bosnia and Herzegovina. In assigning a role for aid, priority should be given to infrastructure in poor regions, primary schools and basic health services, and infrastructure which can be rehabilitated using labour-intensive methods. The latter creates much needed employment when jobs are scarce in the early years of peace, especially for demobilised combatants who may otherwise resort to crime. Directing aid together with public money to that objective is not easy; it requires sound budgetary institutions, a supporting fiscal framework, and plentiful external finance. So, it is to the macroeconomic dimensions of aid that we now turn.

Balance-of-payments and budgetary support

Conflict depresses export earnings and raises the demand for imports of otherwise domestically produced goods. As such, the complexity of the resource mobilisation issues, discussed in Chapters 14 and 15, is reinforced. Severe import rationing will typically result unless export production is secure from fighting – Angola's offshore oil industry, for example – or donors are willing to finance the balance-of-payments deficit through food aid and/or programme aid such as structural adjustment loans (as in Mozambique and Sri Lanka). The deficit will stay high in war's aftermath, reflecting the large excess of reconstruction investment over domestic savings and may rise if aid increases to finance reconstruction. For instance, Bosnia and Herzegovina's trade deficit was 40 per cent of GDP in 1997.

Access to international commercial borrowing will typically fall during conflict and will remain low until the country's credit rating recovers unless the government is able to mortgage oil revenue (the Angolan case). Moreover, many conflict countries are included in the group of Heavily Indebted Poor Countries (HIPCs); examples include Ethiopia, Mozambique and Nicaragua. Relief has been granted on past bilateral aid loans, and some progress (although not enough) has been made under the HIPC initiative to reduce their multilateral debts. Debt workouts are complex in the case of states that have broken apart (e.g. former Yugoslavia).

Conflict reduces the economy's tax base, and revenue from trade taxes falls as import compression occurs (and this effect is magnified by international trade sanctions in the cases of Iraq and Serbia). Social sector and development spending are cut back as revenues fall and military spending grows. Unless programme aid is available to provide budgetary support, large fiscal deficits are usually monetised (leading to the hyperinflation characteristic of wartime economies). The IMF and the World Bank attach fiscal conditionality to their support (which is generally available to only a few wartime economies) but stabilising a war economy is generally a very difficult undertaking (see e.g. World Bank 1996d, for an evaluation of adjustment lending to Sri Lanka).

Economies generally emerge from war with low and distorted public revenues, a highly distorted structure of public spending, very large fiscal deficits and high levels of public debt. Increased public investment together with matching recurrent spending is necessary to start reconstruction. This in turn requires the reduction of military spending, the reform of public expenditure management, careful privatisation of loss-making public enterprises and increased revenue mobilisation (on fiscal issues, see also Chapter 15). Few governments are able to manage this complex set of tasks satisfactorily and political pressures to over-spend may increase with democratisation. Therefore fiscal crises are common in the early years of peace.

International Monetary Fund fiscal conditionality typically requires the reduction of the budget deficit before grants. A tight budget deficit target may preclude essential recurrent spending to match aid-financed investments, thereby disrupting donor programmes. The World Bank and bilateral donors have in some cases criticised the IMF for applying over-restrictive fiscal conditionality (see Addison and de Sousa 1999, for the case of Mozambique). The World Bank's chief economist is among those arguing for an easing of the IMF's fiscal policy conditionality when aid inflows to finance the fiscal deficit are reasonably stable, and when aid and public money are being used to finance high-return investments in social and economic infrastructure (Stiglitz 1998). Moreover, war precludes diversific- ation and thus increases the vulnerability of low-income economies to fluctuations in primary commodity prices, an effect that has negative fiscal effects; Guatemala and Rwanda have both suffered recently. It is unclear whether this constraint is adequately incorporated into IMF policy advice or conditionality at present.

The threat of future conflict exacerbates fiscal fragility. In Burundi, military spending accounts for 38 per cent of budget expenditures: this exceeds combined spending on agriculture, health and education, which total 24 per cent. In Rwanda, military expenditures were 40 per cent of the 1996 budget (Oxfam 1997). This is a serious problem given the fungibility of much programme aid. The fiscal burden of military spending is a growing problem in Uganda – one of Africa's largest aid recipients – reflect- ing its involvement in the civil war of the Democratic Republic of Congo (DRC), continuing insurgency in the north, and the incursion of Rwandan genocidaires intent on destabilising the country. Defence spending increased by 26 per cent to $131 million in the 1998–9 budget. Insecurity therefore blunts donor-supported reallocation of spending to basic services, and limits the developmental impact of Uganda's recent qualification for debt relief under the HIPC debt relief initiative.

Budgetary and planning institutions are exceptionally weak in conflict countries, and this slows their ability to translate increased spending into improved local services and infrastructure. Despite Uganda having one of the strongest public administrations among Africa's conflict countries, much of the social sector budget is still not reaching local services (Ablo and Reinikka 1998). Moreover, many donors have run their projects off-budget thereby undermining public expenditure management (see e.g. Wuyts 1996, on Mozambique). The adoption of sectoral approaches to bring all expend- itures, both government and donor, into a common framework is improving matters, but there is still a long way to go before public expenditures become truly focused on broad-based development (Gould *et al.* 1998).

Unresolved issues

Implications for the development community

For the development community, the rise in incidence of violent conflict has had a number of implications. These include:

New institutional structures and partnerships

There is a need to create new institutional structures and partnerships. The UN has reorganised its humanitarian operations, the World Bank has created a post-conflict unit (World Bank 1997e) and the bilateral donors and the EU have expanded and refocused their humanitarian activities. NGOs are very active in conflict situations – over 200 were present in the Great Lakes region during 1994–5 – delivering aid financed by charitable donations as well as acting as sub-contractors for the UN and bilateral donors (see e.g. Barnes 1998 on NGOs in Mozambique). They too have innovated in order to cope with the new demands. Conflict has led to new and sometimes uneasy partnerships with the foreign policy and defence institutions of the donors including, most recently, NATO.

Increased complexity in aid co-ordination

Co-ordination between donors has always been a problem (see also Chapter 18); it has increased with the number of agencies working in the field. In Bosnia and Herzegovina, for example, over 100 agencies operate ranging in size from the World Bank to the NGO, Norwegian Women for Bosnia. Agencies have different organisational structures, reporting procedures and perspectives on conflict and reconstruction. A lack of co-ordination between the agencies concerned with framing economic policy, the IMF and the World Bank, and those engaged in the peace process and its aftermath, the UN agencies, is sometimes a problem (for contrasting views, see Boyce 1996 on El Salvador and Marshall 1998 on Mozambique). Co-ordination between donors must also cope with the complex political arrangements that peace agreements establish; Bosnia and Herzegovina, and its constituent parts, is one example.

Weaknesses in implementation capacity

Donors use local and international NGOs for implementation when the state is weak (see Barnes 1998 and Goodhand and Hulme 1997 for reviews). While this is often necessary in the short term – and NGOs can be highly effective – donors may neglect investment in rebuilding and reforming state capacity. International agencies often see local NGOs as a means for cheap service delivery, leading to little investment in their sustainability, and local NGOs tend to be urban-focused; in Bosnia and Herzegovina, for instance, there are few organisations serving rural areas (Engberg and Stubbs 1999).

Increased demands on shrinking aid budgets

Humanitarian aid budgets came under pressure in the second half of the 1990s; starting in the mid-1980s, relief and humanitarian expenditures rose six-fold to peak at $9 billion in 1994 and then declined to $3.75 billion in 1997, partly reflecting the fall-out from Rwanda (Duffield 1998, citing Oxfam data). Farm subsidies have also been reduced under recent world trade agreements, thus cutting the supply of food aid (Barrett 1998 and Cohen and Pinstrup-Andersen 1998). Donors supplied 15 million metric tons of food aid in 1992–3 but this fell to 6.7 million metric tons in 1996–7, with the fall in US food aid accounting for most of the total decline (IFPRI 1998). Moreover, some large reconstruction programmes are under-way; Bosnia and Herzegovina is one of the biggest – aid is financing a reconstruction programme with a budget of $5.1 billion for 1996–2000. These demands intensify pressure on budgets for foreign aid elsewhere.

Reorganisation, time, and enough resources can overcome these problems – but only if the political will exists to support and resource the develop-ment agencies. It is to this issue that we now, briefly, turn.

Ending war

At the start of the 1990s, US President George Bush spoke of a 'A New World Order' in which the UN Security Council would sanction 'armed human-itarian interventions.' (Weiss 1999). But with no unanimity amongst the five permanent Security Council members, UN operations were increasingly diluted or compromised by insufficient political support (Parsons 1995). Eventually NATO's members bypassed the UN to intervene in Kosovo in 1999, an action which had major implications for the international management of conflict.

This is not the place to rehearse the dismal story of the 1990s: the slow reaction of Europe and the United States to ethnic cleansing in the former Yugoslavia; the collapse of the US-led 'Operation Restore Hope' in Somalia; and the failure to prevent genocide in Rwanda, among other events (see instead Clarke and Herbst 1997, Gourevitch 1998a, Ignatieff 1998 and Weiss 1999). Suffice it to say that both the United States and the Europeans are still groping for a coherent strategy (Babbitt 1999 and Moïsi 1999). After the Somalia debacle, the United States limited itself to operations in which it had 'clear' interests. But its foreign policy establishment continues to argue over what this means and the broad bi-partisan consensus on foreign policy that existed during the cold war is yet to re-establish itself (Hoffman 1999). But the glimmer of a new strategy is starting to emerge, and many in the development community will find it uncomfortable. Former Assistant Secretary of Defence, Joseph Nye Jr., for example, identifies 'A' list threats to American survival (tensions in US–China relations, for instance), 'B' list 'imminent threats' to US interests but not to its survival (North Korea and Iraq) and a 'C' list of situations that get media attention but which only indirectly affect US security and do not threaten its interests; Kosovo, Bosnia, Somalia, Rwanda and Haiti are examples (Nye 1999). With the end of the cold war, Africa is now strategically unimportant and its conflicts are almost certainly well to the bottom of any list of US priorities.

During his 1998 visit to Rwanda, President Clinton concluded that 'the international community, together with the nations of Africa, must bear its share of responsibility for this tragedy. We did not act quickly enough after the killing began. We should not have allowed the refugee camps to become safe havens for the killers. We did not immediately call the crimes by their rightful name: genocide'. Despite such lamentations, the response remains weak. For instance, during the cold war, the major powers committed substantial diplomatic resources to ending Namibia's war and, in parallel, to removing Cuban troops from Angola in the 1980s. In contrast, Angola's worsening crisis over 1998–9 commanded little of their attention.

To fill Africa's peacekeeping void, many look to regional powers – especially to South Africa – and military assistance to train African armies in peacekeeping increased in the 1990s (Herbst 1998). However, South Africa's intervention in Lesotho in 1998 was badly managed, and budgetary pressures limit its involvement as a peacekeeper. Nigeria committed a quarter of its army to the West African peacekeeping force in Sierra Leone. But its own internal conflicts, and the need to secure the transition from military rule, have cut into Nigeria's peacekeeping operations. Moreover, Angola and Zimbabwe claimed a SADC (Southern African Development Community) peacekeeping mandate to intervene in the DRC to disguise the pursuit of national and commercial interests.

Thus Africa's wars continue in the absence of credible regional peacekeeping and the lack of interest of the major powers. This has dire consequences for the delivery of humanitarian aid. First, insecurity raises the cost of relief delivery (airlifts rather than ground transportation), people in desperate need cannot be reached – the situation in Angola and Sierra Leone today – and agencies must constantly negotiate safe passage. Second, conflict endangers aid workers themselves. In 1998, casualties among the UN's civilian personnel exceeded its military (peacekeeper) casualties for the first time in UN history. Belligerents target aid personnel, hoping to force them out so that genocide can proceed unhindered and unobserved. Third, aid falls into the hands of belligerents, thereby resourcing war, as noted earlier. In sum, the political failure to use diplomatic and military resources to end Africa's wars reduces the effectiveness of humanitarian aid and compromises its basic principles.

Incomplete peace

When the fighting stops we cannot know for sure whether peace will sustain itself. We can only look to the particular circumstances; are the belligerents still able to make war? Do they have the motivation? Can third parties prevent a return to war? Do formal and informal channels permit the peaceful expression and resolution of conflict? It may take a decade or more to conclude that peace is embedded.

Mozambique looks unlikely to return to war. Central America may stay at peace if social injustice is addressed. But, formal peace agreements have not prevented Angola from returning to war, the Eritrea–Ethiopia war has restarted, and unrest in the former Yugoslavia continues. Moreover, Rwanda's ethnic reconciliation remains precarious, and although Cambodia is relatively stable, its government is highly authoritarian. Therefore the label 'post-conflict' is often a highly misleading description of these societies, especially when violence and insecurity continue long after a formal peace agreement is signed (Crisp 1998). Donors may also phase out their assistance in the mistaken belief that the underlying problem of conflict is somehow resolved.

For countries, 'incomplete peace' keeps investment low, and perpetuates the unbalanced economy of war time; activity concentrates itself in commerce which has immediate returns and few sunk costs, and stays away from production which has longer term, but less secure, returns. Military spending continues to crowd out development spending. For donors, incomplete peace lowers rates of return on project and programme aid, raises the financial risks of aid loans (by increasing default), and cuts into the government recurrent spending needed to match aid-financed investment spending. Incomplete peace thus reduces aid effectiveness and makes constant demands on humanitarian budgets (leaving less for development aid). The ability of donors to meet what is now their primary objective, the rapid reduction of poverty, is therefore undermined.

Moreover, conflict threatens stable countries in unstable regions, and thus reduces the effectiveness of aid to them. In particular, their military budgets remain high (the case of Uganda has been discussed), they must cope with the refugees of their neighbours, regional transport networks and trade are disrupted, and foreign investment is deterred. The Kosovo war hit Bulgaria and Romania, and economic recovery in Macedonia, the poorest republic in the former Yugoslavia, was disrupted by trade sanctions against Serbia during the Kosovo crisis, and the region's instability reduced the effectiveness of World Bank and IMF stabilisation support (World Bank 1998h). Conflict avoidance would therefore improve the success rate of aid-supported stabilisation efforts.

Conclusions: using aid to prevent conflict

This chapter has reviewed a large set of issues. Many remain unresolved and events over the first few years of the twenty-first century – especially post-Kosovo – may generate a new framework for using aid in conflict situations. But we should be wary of seeing aid as some kind of simple lever that can be pulled to either prevent or end conflict. Nevertheless, at the risk of over-simplification, we conclude by setting out three key mechanisms by which aid, if wisely used, might contribute to conflict prevention.

Focus aid on poverty and inequality

Foreign aid should focus on reducing inequality as well as poverty as a means to dampen social tension and violence. Widespread poverty nurtures crime and social conflict. For sure, many triggers are needed for day-to-day violence to escalate into genocide, but, to take one example, rising poverty acted as the recruiting sergeant for the Hutu leaders of Rwanda's Interahamwe militias. Rwanda suffered from years of political and economic discrimination by a Hutu elite against the Tutsi population, with the donors unwilling to recognise the true nature of the regime which they assisted (Uvin 1998).

Conflict prevention increases the urgency of concentrating aid on poverty reduction (see also Chapter 9). But since poverty reduction is hard to achieve when initial income and asset inequalities are high, and since inequality by social class, region, and ethnicity feed insurrection and genocide, the reduction of inequality itself must be a goal for aid. This requires close attention to the structure of public spending, and donors are now pressing for a better focus on basic services. However, donors should also encourage and assist well-designed land reform and the construction of progressive taxation systems, including the taxation of wealth, through, for example, land taxes.[1] The donors to transition economies have pushed rapid privatisation which, when badly designed, has in turn contributed to a marked concentration of wealth (enabling elites to use fragile democratic processes for their own purposes) and a socially destabilising fall in output and employment (Stiglitz 1998). Closer attention to the social consequences of economic reform, and the basic design of reform itself, should be a high priority, both for poverty reduction but also for conflict avoidance.

Aid support for non-violent conflict expression and resolution

Foreign aid should be used to help countries channel conflict into institutions and processes for its non-violent expression and resolution, as well as to assist peaceful secession. All societies experience conflict over political and civil rights, employment opportunities, and access to social and economic provision. Successful societies invest in institutions that allow the peaceful expression and resolution of conflict. This imparts stability, but also helps societies overcome the tensions that inevitably arise from economic growth (usually attended by uneven regional development even in the best run economies), urbanisation (and the resulting reduction in 'traditional' norms and values), and differences in opportunity and wealth by ethnicity, religion and gender.

Creating such institutions takes skilful leadership, resources and (above all) time for trust in institutions to develop. Democracy's development in the United States was, for example, interrupted by bloody civil war, and racism was institutionalised in the southern states as late as the 1960s. We should not therefore be surprised by the difficulties of democratisation in young nations. Democracy is not, however, a 'luxury' that can only be enjoyed once societies become rich. India's democracy, despite its many imperfections, has sustained economic growth and, at least in states such as Kerala, democracy has helped to achieve significant human development.

Donors should reinforce democratisation by assisting countries to hold regular competitive elections and to build institutions that decentralise political and economic power (critical to resolving regional and ethnically based tensions). At the same time, donors must be realistic about what they can achieve. Elections are an important institution of a democracy, but they do not by themselves make a democracy; that requires investment in civil society, an independent media and an independent judiciary. How far aid should be used as a sanction to encourage democratisation remains problematic (Wintrobe 1998, discusses alternative strategies for different types of tyranny). Multilateral aid to Burma (Myanmar) is presently contingent upon democratisation but has not, so far, had much success.

The number of internationally recognised states was 74 at the UN's foundation; it is now 193. World trade liberalisation has reduced the economic advantages of being a large nation; success goes to those nations able to use investment in education and information technology to bend globalisation's forces to their advantage, and not to nations with large internal markets that they can protect (see Chapter 16 for further discussion of trade liberalisation). If regional security can be improved, then the security benefits of being a large nation will also diminish. This, together with globalisation, will almost certainly lead to more secessions, and thus increased demands on aid to help new countries create their economic and political institutions. Indonesia is likely to be a test case. The UN's funding and its reform must be resolved if the world is to pass peacefully through future turbulence.

Foreign policy coherence

A coherent foreign policy should be built in order to support the use of aid in conflict prevention. Aid can only fulfil its promise if the foreign policy and strategic frameworks of the donor countries are supportive. That means using diplomatic and military power to (i) prevent and end conflict, (ii) direct aid to governments that respect human rights, and (iii) concentrate aid on countries in which corruption is low. Progress is at best hesitant for all three issues.

First, as noted earlier, despite their rhetoric, the major powers assign a low priority to Africa's wars (which account for over half of all war-related deaths worldwide). While these are complex – often involving shifting alliances of loosely organised forces – they are no more so than those of the Balkans in which NATO intervened. The problem is rather a failure of political will. In 1997 the Canadian general, Roméo Dallaire, the UN force commander in Rwanda at the start of genocide (and whose repeated warnings were ignored by the Security Council), expressed the feelings of many when he said:

[t]o be very candid . . . who the hell cared about Rwanda? Who really comprehends that more people were killed, injured and displaced in three and a half months in Rwanda than in the whole of the Yugoslavian campaign, in which we poured sixty thousand troops and more. The whole of the Western world is there – we're pouring billions in there. . . . Who is really trying to solve the Rwandan problem?

(cited in Gourevitch 1998b: 46)

Second, history warns us that strategic interests can overwhelm consider- ations of human rights and development in aid allocation. While some donors, notably the Scandinavians, have traditionally emphasised aid's humanitarian and development objectives, strategic interests were critical in motivating aid from the United States, the Soviet Union and their allies during the cold war (see Graham and O'Hanlon 1997 and Chapter 19 in this volume). Using multivariate analysis, Schraeder *et al.* (1998) show that the existence of a security alliance with the United States resulted in the generous provision of US aid. As a result, both sides of the cold war sent aid to tyrannies. The Horn of Africa bears witness to the ravaging effects of the cold war (Lefebvre 1991). Somalia received $492 million in bilateral US aid and $194 million in military aid in the 1980s despite congressional criticism of Siad Barre's regime. From 1962 to 1992, Mobutu's Zaire was the second largest recipient of US aid to sub-Saharan Africa. Other strategic motives have also had pernicious effects. French government complicity in Rwanda's genocide, through the provision of military aid, has been alleged (and rejected by a French parliamentary committee in 1998, which many observers regard as a whitewash).

It would be naive to believe that strategic interests will fade away in aid allocation. Alesina and Dollar (1998) find that strategic alliances remain important in explaining the cross-country distribution of aid, although at the margin democratisation tends to be rewarded by increased aid. Global aid flows have declined in real terms since the early 1990s, in part because much of the developing world is now strategically unimportant to the major powers (see Chapter 19). Ruttan concludes that 'efforts to develop new sources of political motivation – new rubrics such as "environmental security" and "democratisation" – have failed to generate the same political force as the Cold War.' (1998: 572). There is some scope for arguing that since poverty and inequality breed conflict, aid to broad-based develop- ment does enhance the security of donors. But ultimately it is up to pro- development legislators and groups to press the development case for aid as opposed to dressing it up in a security rationale. The latter distorts the allocation of aid and becomes a slippery slope in which objectives become muddled; this is unacceptable even at the risk of reducing the political vote for aid, and thus the level of national aid budgets.

Third, aid must be directed to governments that have high levels of transparency as well as to communities and civil society organisations that can best use it. Despite all their rhetoric about good governance, donors still need to get serious about corruption in recipients. Alesina and Weder (1999) find that according to some measures of corruption, more corrupt governments receive more aid than less corrupt ones (the allocation of Scandinavian aid is the exception). While corruption is not necessarily inimical to either democracy or development, rising corruption certainly contributes to conflict in most cases, especially in societies that are natural-resource rich and in which the resource rents represent a considerable 'prize' for corruption and, ultimately, outright war (Angola, Congo-Brazzaville and the DRC for instance). Moreover, the corrupt redirection of aid may also contribute to eventual conflict: in Somalia the state was eventually 'mined out' in a contest over resources and aid (Maren 1997). The World Bank has belatedly responded to the massive misuse of its aid to Indonesia, amidst rising social conflict.

In summary, future historians will see the 1990s as a critical decade for foreign aid and its relationship to the foreign policy and strategic goals of the major powers. Donors must develop coherent foreign policy and military frameworks to support their aid agencies and their NGO partners together with the multilateral agencies. The decline in aid resources must be reversed and aid redirected to assisting broad-based development, including the reduction of inequality as well as poverty. Otherwise aid cannot fulfil its humanitarian and reconstruction objectives, and the new decade will be no more peaceful than the 1990s.

Notes

* The author acknowledges the useful comments and suggestions by Peter Burnell, Raymond Hopkins, Philippe Le Billon and Finn Tarp. The usual disclaimers apply.
1 Land taxation raises revenue for basic services and increases the supply of land in the market for purchase by community projects, which can themselves be financed through a portion of the land tax revenue.

18 Aid, conditionality and debt in Africa

*Ravi Kanbur**

Introduction

The years since the early 1980s have seen an exhaustive, and exhausting, debate on foreign aid, conditionality and debt. The post-WWII consensus on aid flows to fill the investment–savings 'gap' in the less developed countries has collapsed, under attack from both the political right and the political left. Closely tied in to this debate were the disagreements on conditionality, and on debt. The Latin American debt crisis of the 1980s launched the arguments for and against debt relief with different degrees of conditionality – both for the debt relief and for subsequent new flows. But it is in Africa that the current debate finds its centre of gravity. Despite massive foreign aid, with inflows far exceeding debt servicing outflows, and despite much resented conditionality on this aid, Africa has failed to achieve significant progress in the well-being of its population. Some lay the blame on Africa's foreign debt burden. Others on conditionality. But on conditionality, there seems to be a three-cornered fight: between those who believe aid conditionality would work if only it were targeted towards the opening up of markets and rolling back the frontiers of the state, those who believe it would work if only it were targeted towards better allocation of public expenditure and programmes toward the poor, and those who believe that the carrot and stick of aid is powerless in the medium term to shift the domestic political equilibrium in a direction other than the one in which it wants to go.

Africa is the test case. It is the last remaining region of the world where official aid inflows outstrip private capital inflows, and they do so by a large margin, even after debt service outflows have been netted out. Africa is aid dependent, some African countries grotesquely so, not only in terms of the quantity of aid but in terms of the institutional mechanisms of this aid flow. And, at least for now, this massive quantity of aid does not seem to be helping African development. This chapter argues that aid has failed in Africa, that aid conditionality has failed in Africa, and that there is very little chance of recovery from this failure under current institutional arrangements. It presents a diagnosis, and proposes in preliminary fashion a direction of movement which includes simultaneous heavy debt relief and major institutional reforms which reduce African aid dependence and put the accountability for African performance not on outsiders but on the people and their governments, in Africa. One implication of such a shift might be a reduced volume of conventional foreign aid to Africa; it is argued that this is a price worth paying for reduced aid dependence.

The failure of aid

It hardly bears repeating that development has not lived up to expectations in Africa. After the initial post-independence boost in per capita income growth, serious decline set in. An overview of African economic performance is provided by Collier and Gunning (1997), but the comparison of Ghana and Malaysia is emblematic. Both countries became independent in 1957, and both are countries of similar size and resource base. At independence, Ghana's per capita GDP was several times that of Malaysia – four decades later, the situation is reversed. While many social indicators have been on a long-run trend improvement in Africa, the process has been much slower than in other parts of the developing world, and there may have been further slowing down since the 1980s.

This is a chapter on foreign aid in Africa and so, quite naturally, aid will be centre stage in discussing development failures in Africa. But it should be said right at the outset that aid may, in fact, be quite a small part of the whole explanation of the development path of Africa. Sachs and Warner (1997) emphasise the burden of geography and poor policies. Basil Davidson (1992) points to the central role played by the Congress of Berlin and various post-WWI adjustments, which drew and redrew the colonial map, and hence the post-independence map, in a way that made no historic, geographic or ethnic sense. This, according to the title of Davidson's book, is *The Black Man's Burden*, and the instability which it has bred has been a root cause of the failure of African development (the subtitle of Davidson's book is 'Africa and the Curse of the Nation State'). In a more standard econometric work, Easterly and Levine (1997) confirm the importance of ethnic fragmentation in explaining Africa's poor performance. Others, less convincingly (think again about the Ghana–Malaysia comparison), have blamed world markets and Africa's specialisation in primary commodities at independence as structural features which have inhibited African development. And so on. Despite the natural tendency among those discussing aid – supporters and critics alike – to talk up aid as a key determinant of development, it is only a part, and perhaps a small part, of the overall picture of why development has failed in Africa so far.

This being said, the accounts of aid failure in Africa are legion. They range from journalistic reports to detailed academic studies. From Mobutu's money flowing to Swiss bank accounts to the rusting blue East German tractors in villages in Ghana, anecdotal accounts abound of the ineffectiveness of aid flows in achieving their objectives of helping development and growth. To be fair, these have to be set against many individual successes that all of us also know about. And this is why a higher level of aggregation and a broader perspective is needed in such analysis. This is provided by a whole slew of sector studies which evaluate past interventions in specific areas in the past. Rural credit is back in vogue today as an intervention sector. But it is forgotten that there were major interventions in this area in the 1960s and 1970s, when agencies attempted to channel credit to rural small holders through apex agencies which on-lent to rural banks and then on to co-operatives and the like. There were individual successes, of course, but by and large these efforts have been judged to be failures. Take another example, infrastructure. Roads are back in fashion, but it should not be forgotten that billions of dollars in aid, and in local resources, have been poured into African infrastructure – but it has all been washed away.

These sectoral experiences are confirmed by analysis at country level. It has been estimated that if all of the aid that flowed into Zambia between 1961 and 1993 had been invested at a normal rate of return, Zambia's per capita GDP would have been at least 30 times what it is today (Easterly 1997). The failure of very high levels of aid in Mozambique is discussed quite openly now (Wuyts 1996). More recently, there have been exercises that have taken a cross-country perspective, and shown, essentially, that there is no association between aid flows and improvements in development indicators. These studies are typical for all countries in the world, and it may of course be that the results do not apply to Africa but, given the results and given ground level experience, this seems unlikely.

The most cited recent work in this cross-country tradition is that of Burnside and Dollar (1997), which addresses some of the econometric problems with the earlier work, and produces more nuanced results (another often cited author is Boone 1994, 1996, see also Easterly 1997). This work finds, like most of the earlier literature, no relationship between aid flows and growth in per capita GDP (or other indicators of development). But it goes on to look deeper into the issue by estimating three relationships: (i) the relationship between growth, aid, 'a good macroeconomic policy environment', and a number of other standard variables, (ii) an aid allocation equation giving the relationship between aid flows to a country and a number of country-specific variables, especially the macroeconomic policy environment variable and (iii) a relationship between the macroeconomic policy environment and aid flows. While much can be said about the details of the data and estimation techniques, the results are illuminating, and sobering. Burnside and Dollar (1997) find, from the first estimated relationship, that when aid flows into good policy environments it helps growth. However, the second relationship reveals why there is no simple correlation between aid and growth; aid does not flow to countries with good policy environments. But, it might be argued, there need be no relationship between aid flow and policy environment if aid flows initially to bad policy environments as an inducement or support for them to improve. This is where the third relationship comes in; it is found that aid does not induce good policy environments to emerge at all!

Aid conditionality

The last two findings – that aid does not flow into good policy environments, and that when it flows into poor policy environments it does not induce them to change – are devastating, in view of the fact that the international community, led by the Bretton Woods Institutions, is meant to have been applying conditionality to its aid flows, specifically to direct aid towards good policy environments and to encourage (through the carrot of more aid, and the stick of reduced aid) these policy environments to emerge. And the debates since the mid-1980s have been about nothing if not conditionality! The discussion has been confusing, perhaps confused. There are those, like Burnside and Dollar (1997), who draw the inference from their work that if only aid were channelled to environments with sound macroeconomic policy, it would spur growth and development. But then there are those who reject at least some of the detail of 'a good macroeoconomic policy environment' but nevertheless believe that conditionality with a different set of conditions is what is needed. To quote one of the best known proponents of this view:

> Can and should aid be used to put pressure on governments to reform their spending policies in favor of the poor? Oxfam believes that new forms of conditionality could help to bring about positive policy reforms. . . . Governments and donors could, in principle, agree on incremental steps for raising investment in primary health care, basic education, and the provision of water and sanitation. . . . Most donors reject such an approach on the grounds that it would undermine the national sovereignty of developing country governments. They have been considerably less reluctant about eroding sovereignty in other areas; through their structural adjustment programs, donors have obliged governments to impose fees for primary education and basic health facilities, to devalue their currencies, set interest rates at levels dictated by the IMF, privatise whole industries, and liberalise markets.
>
> (Oxfam 1995)

Thus the Oxfam view is that conditionality could work – but it should be based on the right sort of conditions. Of course, which conditions are right depends on one's view of alternative development paradigms (see Gwin and Nelson 1997, for a discussion of emerging consensus on at least some aspects of the development paradigm). The Oxfam critique is that the wrong sorts of conditions have been 'imposed'. But, in fact, the Burnside–Dollar study shows that, whatever the terms of the formal aid agreements, even these conditions have simply not been implemented – and yet the aid has flowed. Oxfam itself gives an example of the failure of conditionality, this time on public expenditure, of the sort they support:

> Another problem is that the evaluation procedures [of the World Bank] confuse the terms of the adjustment agreements with their implementation. For example, the structural adjustment program in Zimbabwe is counted as poverty-focused, partly on the grounds that it provided for the restoration of current expenditures on health and education as a condition for releasing funds. In the event, even though expenditure under both budget heads fell sharply under the adjustment program, funds were released.
>
> (Oxfam 1995)

In fact, the Operations Evaluation Department of the World Bank pointed to precisely this problem, only more generalised (World Bank 1992c). They concluded that although compliance rates on conditions were below 50 per cent, tranche release rates were close to 100 per cent. Mosley *et al.* (1995a) make precisely the same point in a more academic analysis. These studies, and Oxfam's own cautions above, suggest that the problem is not simply what the conditions are (although there is debate enough to be had on that score!); it is that conditionality of whatever type has failed in Africa (for an overview of this failure, see Collier 1997)

The weakness of strength

On the face of it, the suggestion that conditionality has failed in Africa is strange indeed. Is not the situation one of enormously unequal power between donors and recipients? Surely, Africa's aid dependence makes it a mere pawn in an international great game where every whim of donor agencies, especially those of the Bretton Woods institutions, is immediately complied with? Certainly, the writings of some commentators suggest this:

> Virtually every external support to any African country, including debt rescheduling and relief, became dependent on the award of a certificate of good behavior by these institutions. Such an award was and is dependent upon adherence to SAP and their conditionalities. Consequently, independent policy making and national economic management were considerably diminished and narrowed in Africa.
>
> (Adedeji 1995)

The above is representative of a major strand of thinking and writing on aid in Africa. I will presently argue that independence of policymaking has indeed been undermined in Africa as the result of the aid nexus, but it should be clear from the empirical results of Burnside and Dollar (1997), the work of Mosley *et al.* (1995a) and Oxfam (1995) and other people's ground-level experiences, that the issue is considerably more subtle than imposition of conditionality – in fact, the evidence is that aid flows continue even when conditionality is violated, which happens frequently. Rather, I will argue that the real issue is one of an unhealthy interaction between donor and recipient processes which propagate aid dependence but are not so simple as to be characterised as the strength of the donors and the weakness of the recipients. In fact, there is strength in the weakness of the recipients and, above all, weakness in the strength of the donors.

How can the strong be weak? It is of course true that representatives of the aid agencies in Africa, those who 'parachute in' for missions of a few days and those who are resident locally, are the symbols of the power of the donor agencies. They stay in the big hotels (or big houses), are driven around, and demand to see policymakers at the drop of a hat. As they travel in convoys of four wheel drives to inspect projects funded by their agencies, and as they mingle on the diplomatic cocktail circuit, the resentment they evoke in the local population should not be underestimated. But, when it comes to it, these symbols of strength hide fundamental weaknesses that arise from the inner logic and dynamic of the aid process and donor agency imperatives.

I want to illustrate this weakness of strength with events that unfolded in 1992–3 in Ghana. Up to 1992, Ghana had been called the 'star pupil' of the Bretton Woods institutions, with an adjustment programme proclaimed by the IMF and the World Bank as perhaps the most successful in Africa (for a perspective on the programme at this time, see Kanbur 1995). But in 1992 Ghana consummated its transition to democracy and, in the process, the government gave in to pressures to grant enormous pay increases to civil servants and the military. In late 1992, in advance of the elections, an 80 per cent across-the-board pay increase, backdated, was announced. As a result, the budgetary conditionality in the World Bank's then current structural adjustment credit was violated, and the impending tranche release was suspended. Through its own tranche, and through co-financing tied to it, the World Bank found itself holding up as much as one eighth of the annual import bill of the country.

One would think that holding one eighth of the annual import bill of a poor cash-strapped economy would give enormous leverage to the World Bank and the donors to dictate terms to the Ghanaians. In fact, as the representative of the World Bank on the ground, I came under pressure from several sources, some of them quite surprising, to release the tranche with minimal attention to conditionality. There was a steady stream of private sector representatives, domestic and foreign, arguing for release of the tranche both because of fears of what macroeconomic disruption would do to the business climate in general, and also because some of them had specific contracts with the government which were unlikely to be paid on time if the government did not in turn get the money from the World

Bank and other donors. Next in line, were the bilateral donors – even those who had tied themselves to the presumably greater discipline of the World Bank by co-financing. Some of these had 'fiscal year' concerns – they feared the consequences within their agencies of not releasing the funds in the fiscal year for which they were slated. Others worried about a melt down of the economy if the tranche was not released. Yet others found their projects slowing up because government counterpart funds were not available, and many project agreements stipulate that donor money flows in a fixed relationship to government contributions. Rather like private sector con- tractors, these aid agency personnel were dependent upon the government releasing enough resources for the success of their specific projects, and this money would not come, or not come soon enough, if the tranche release was delayed. I include in this list of donors the World Bank itself – implementation of old projects, and development of new ones, would be severely affected so long as the impasse lasted.

In the end, the impasse lasted till early 1993, when a new budget was announced with at least some measures to counter the ballooning budget deficit, and the tranche was released. What is important about this episode are not the specifics but the generics – in the specific case the government argued, with good reason I believe, that the budget busting pay rise was essential to ensure a peaceful transition to democracy, and once the deficit was there it made sense not to compound the problem by too rapid a fiscal adjustment in the other direction. And what is important for this chapter are the generics on conditionality and the pressures surrounding it; there are many other issues, to do with the design of adjustment programmes, which are also important but are not discussed here (on these, see Kanbur 1999).

The key point I want to illustrate is that of a fundamental time incon- sistency. Conditionality can be introduced on paper with much pomp and circumstance, but when push comes to shove, all of the pressures, mostly from the donor side, are to look the other way when conditionality is viol- ated. Some of these pressures are in the nature of the problem. They come, paradoxically, precisely from the fact that donors control so much in the way of funds that to stop these, at any rate to stop them sharply, would cause major chaos in the economy. In some instances, like the social sector expen- ditures case mentioned by Oxfam above, there is what has been called the 'samaritan's dilemma' (see Coate 1995 and Svensson 1997); the government didn't spend enough on the poor and thus violated conditionality, but imposing sanctions might well mean a 'double whammy' for the poor.

But in other instances it is, again only apparently paradoxically, in the donor's direct self-interest not to impose the sanction of aid withdrawal when conditionality is violated. The most obvious case of this is political clientelism. How else can one explain the repeated tranche releases to Zaire and Senegal in the 1980s and early 1990s, for example, despite continued failure to comply with adjustment conditionality, except in terms of pressure from the United States and France? Other cases arise when heavy debt servicing (to the World Bank, the IMF, donor governments and private creditors) is involved; without the inflow, the outflow of debt servicing might be interrupted. Côte d'Ivoire is an example of a country where these forces have been at play.

Finally, there is the imperative of aid agencies to keep relations with recipients on a 'normal' footing, since it is only in such circumstances that aid flows can continue. The incentives in aid agencies are ultimately driven by keeping aid flows going, and implementing sanctions when conditionality is violated not only stops the specific aid flows in question, but also puts in jeopardy the preparation of future aid projects and programmes, on which depend the livelihoods and careers of agency staff as well as the image of the agency in the eyes of its political masters. Thus those who appear powerful as they are driven around African capitals, no matter what petty power they may exercise in their interaction with local functionaries, are in fact quite weak because of the systemic imperative to keep aid flowing; the best of the functionaries on the other side know this, and use the strength of their weakness. Of course, none of this is to deny that many individuals have noble motives and achieve impossible things in their interaction across the donor–recipient table, but it is the systemic forces which are the key. And, of course, sometimes donors do say enough is enough; they did stop giving aid to Mobutu, once the cold war was over. But more often than not there is an elaborate minuet that is danced over and over again:

> Over the past few years Kenya has performed a curious mating ritual with its aid donors. The steps are: one, Kenya wins its yearly pledges of foreign aid. Two, the government begins to misbehave, back-tracking on reform and behaving in an authoritarian manner. Three, a new meeting of donor countries looms with exasperated foreign governments preparing their sharp rebukes. Four, Kenya pulls a placatory rabbit out of the hat. Five, the donors are mollified and the aid is pledged. The whole dance starts again.
>
> (*The Economist* 1995)

The basic point is that donors and recipients are so enmeshed, at the level of governments, agencies and individuals, that it is actually not clear where the strengths and weaknesses lie. It is the system as a whole which is dysfunctional. Conditionality is no doubt 'imposed' on unwilling recipients at the time of signing a document, but the recipients know, the donors know, and in fact everybody knows, that these are paper conditions; the outcome will be driven by the need of both sides to maintain normal relations and the flow of aid. It is not clear how else one can explain the results of Burnside and Dollar (1997), Mosley *et al.* (1995a) and Killick (1995), among others, that not only have aid flows not helped in the development of Africa, they have not even helped in the development of policies they were meant to be conditional on.

Principal–agent analysis

Perhaps not surprisingly, the theory of donor–recipient relationships, as developed in the economic literature deriving from principal–agent analysis, reflects the realities described above. The standard way in which the relationship is modelled is in terms of a Stackleberg leader–follower interaction. The donor is the leader, and decides on the level of aid. The recipient is the follower who, taking as given the level of aid, decides on actions (for example, public expenditure patterns, or tariff structures) which affect outcomes for the recipient (access of the poor to education, economic growth). But the donor also values these outcomes and chooses the aid level to influence the choice of actions by the recipient and hence the outcomes for the recipient. The level of aid is thus chosen to maximise the donor's preferences, subject to the reaction function of the recipient, which in turn comes out of the recipient's preferences and shows the actions the latter would choose for each level of aid.

The simplest versions of the theory assume the donor and the recipient to be unitary entities (governments, say), represented only by a set of preferences. In most models it is assumed that the donor is more concerned with the poor than is the recipient. But, in general, all that is needed is that the two sets of preferences are different. The donor can then induce different actions by offering different levels of unconditional aid. However, the donor can clearly do better by offering a schedule of different levels of aid for different actions undertaken by the recipient. In other words, the donor can do better by aid conditionality, by pricing out aid in terms of the actions taken. The recipient may prefer unconditional aid but there is no choice. Conditionality makes the donor better off as measured by the donor's preferences and if, as is assumed, the donor cares more for the poor than the poor's own government, conditionality will improve the lot of the poor. This is the Oxfam (1995) argument for conditionality quoted above.

But can the conditionality be enforced? Suppose, after the aid is released, the recipient goes back to pre-aid actions. What recourse does the donor have? To cut off aid is one option, but to model this we have to introduce a time structure into the simple model. I follow the interesting work of Svensson (1997) in this exposition. Consider the following timing structure. First, the donor calls out the aid-action conditionality schedule. Second, the recipient decides on the action given this schedule. Third, the action leads to an outcome, but with a stochastic component reflecting risks of various types. Fourth, the donor releases the aid. It should be clear that everything hinges on what happens at the fourth stage; whether the donor in fact sticks to the aid conditionality schedule and releases aid according to the actions taken in the second stage, and is not tempted to make *ex post* adjustments either in the face of the stochastic shock or, irrespective of the action taken by the recipient, when the unpalatable outcome emerges.

Because if that were the case, the recipient would know this and adjust action accordingly, so that the outcome for the donor would be worse than if the donor had stuck to the original schedule.

Conditionality is a 'commitment technology' which overcomes the time inconsistency problem inherent in these problems, but only if it is strictly adhered to. The institutional question then is, what are the mechanisms that ensure that conditionality is adhered to? I have argued that, in fact, conditionality is not adhered to in practice, and the institutional dimension of the donor–recipient relationship is the key to this failure. One standard suggestion in the theoretical literature is for the donor to cede respons-ibility to an intermediary who is, and is known to be, 'tougher' in the face of conditionality violations, and will not be prone to the influences of the samaritan's dilemma, or to other distractions. Paradoxically, by being tougher, the intermediary comes closer to achieving the donor's own objectives once all the repercussions of interaction with the recipient are played through. In the aid arena, the Bretton Woods institutions are meant to have been such tough intermediaries, and certainly that is the image that they have probably succeeded in conveying. But, as we have seen, the reality is somewhat different. If anything, these institutions are liable to free riding by the great powers, seeking leniency on behalf of their clients, and thus weaken the resolve on conditionality.

In another part of the theoretical literature, the recipient is modelled not as a unitary government, but as a combination of interest groups interacting amongst themselves. The aid flow then influences this process of domestic political economy, strengthening the hand of one group against another, ensuring that some actions are more likely to be taken, and hence some outcomes are more likely. Adam and O'Connell (1997) and Coate and Morris (1996) are good examples of recent such work. One issue is on the sustainability of policies adopted in this way. If aid is needed to support an interest group which in turn supports a particular policy that the donor likes, then what happens when the aid is withdrawn? Will the policy reverse itself and thus be unsustainable? Coate and Morris (1996) show that to make sense of the political economy arguments ('strengthen-ing the hand of the reformers', for example) we need, *inter alia*, a political economy model that allows for irreversibilities in equilibrium outcomes. While the model can be, and has been, developed theoretically, the issue is the extent to which in reality the aid tail can wag the domestic political economy dog, and do so irreversibly! Certainly the evidence to date in Africa is not encouraging, if the failure of attempted conditionality is anything to go by.

The institution of aid dependence

I have argued that some of the standard critiques of donor–recipient relations in Africa capture only part of the truth. It is true that donors have strength because they bring enormous resources. But I have argued that this is also a source of their weakness, explaining why resource flows continue despite widespread violations of conditionality. The relationship between recipient and donor is more subtle than this, with each needing the other, given the particular institutional structures and imperatives involved (for an argument in similar spirit, see van de Walle 1998).

At the same time, there is no doubt in my mind that Africa suffers from aid dependence, by which I do not mean that Africans have to jump to every whim of the donors. While this is true, and obnoxiously so, in the small, I hope to have shown that in the large and overall, the 'short leash' is one which pulls donors and recipients alike. No, what I mean by saying that Africa suffers from aid dependence is that far too much of the time its policymaking and implementation energies are devoted to interacting with external donor agencies, many times to use the 'weakness of strength' ploy against the donors, more often simply doing routine business of reporting to donors, servicing donor consultants, and keeping things 'normal' (just as on the donor side, where 'normality' of relations is prized). Killick (1995) has documented how much time the leading policymakers spend negotiating with donors, on debt issues but also on the normal business of keeping aid flows going. Wuyts (1996) gives specifics for Mozambique, where there are 405 projects in the Ministry of Health alone and administrative costs run to 30 to 40 per cent of project funds. Separate reporting requirements for each donor, and separate links between parts of different aid agencies and their counterparts in the various ministries, mean that much time, energy and political capital is spent in gaming with external actors.

In my view, the real cost to Africa of the current aid system is thus the fact that it wastes much national energy and political capital in interacting with donor agencies, and diverts attention from domestic debate and consensus building. As I have argued, donor conditionality is not, in the end, fully satisfied. And, in the end, the aid flows anyway. But the process leading up to this outcome is debilitating in the extreme. It is not so much that it undermines, ultimately, the logic of domestic political economy. It just represents a long and tedious distraction, and leaves the impression that the government dances to the tune of the donors, which in turn affects the domestic political economy. Sensible policy measures are often opposed simply on the grounds that they were allegedly recommended by the donors, for example.

Is all of the above independent of the volume of foreign aid? Hardly. The institution of aid dependence is linked very much to the need of donor agencies to disburse large volumes of funds while supposedly keeping accountability for these funds to donor country taxpayers; this is what leads to separate project units of the type seen in Mozambique, where foreign grants amounted to around 35 per cent of GDP in the early 1990s, and it is what leads to pages of conditionality in adjustment programmes, which will not be met anyway. It is a tautology to say that were the current volume of aid delivered more effectively, it would have a better impact on growth and development. But my hypothesis is that the volume of aid, in and of itself, is a key feature of the dysfunctional aid institutions and relationships we currently see in Africa. My arguments are to do with the institution of aid dependence, but there are also more standard arguments on the macro-economic impact of high volumes of aid, as in Elbadawi (1998) or Younger (1992).

The debt question

In Africa, the debt question is intimately tied up with aid and condition-ality. There has been much discussion of this topic lately, in the lead up to the World Bank–IMF debt relief proposal for the Heavily Indebted Poor Countries (HIPCs). The HIPCs are 41 countries, of which 34 are from sub-Saharan Africa. In what follows, figures will be for the HIPCs as a whole (taken from Claessens *et al.* 1997). For these countries, the median debt to exports ratio (after allowing for concessionality of debt) was 340 per cent. Of the total debt, private creditors were owed 17 per cent, official bilateral creditors 64 per cent and multilaterals 19 per cent. This is very different from the Latin American debt crisis of the 1980s, where the bulk of the debt owed was to private creditors. Another big difference is that, unlike their Latin American counterparts in the 1980s, in the 1990s the HIPCs continued to receive large positive net transfers from the international donor/creditor community. The median net transfers to HIPCs were about 11 per cent of GDP on average over the 1990–4 period. Notice that this is *net*, in other words, it is calculated *after* debt service payments. Compare this to the average net transfers *to* creditors by Mexico of 5 per cent of GDP over the 1984–8 period.

What exactly is the debt problem in Africa? Many commentators have highlighted debt service *outflows*:

> Between 1990 and 1993, the region transferred $13.4 bn annually to its external creditors. This is four times as much as governments in the region spent on health services. In fact, it is more than their combined spending on health and education. It is also substantially in excess of the $9 bn a year which Unicef estimates as the total cost of meeting basic human needs for health, nutrition, education, and family planning.
>
> (Oxfam 1995)

Let us start by noting that, in fact, Africa receives large *net* inflows, even after allowing for debt servicing. Of course, if the debt servicing was not there, *and the inflows did not decrease*, then net aid to Africa would increase, quite substantially. This raises several issues. First, the assumption is that an increase in net aid inflows would be good for Africa. This is questionable, given the established difficulties of enforcing conditionality, and the argument in this chapter that the volume of aid is a key determinant of the current dysfunctionality of the aid system. Second, the assumption is that the net inflows will remain unchanged when debt servicing ends. This is highly unlikely, since in fact, as argued above, and in Claessens *et al.* (1997), much of the aid inflows is motivated simply to ensure 'normal relations' with regular debt servicing.

Of course, as has been argued by many analysts, African debt is a charade; it will not be repaid and, as the large net inflows to Africa demonstrate, it is not in fact being repaid. For their own reasons – to do with the institutional importance of avoiding certain types of balance sheet adjustments – the official donors, who are also the main creditors, are putting money in so that the debt can be serviced. It is important, however, to bring the appropriate perspective on the real nature of the debt problem. The debt problem is not, I would argue, a problem of too low a level of aid to Africa; if anything, the levels of aid are too high relative to the current institutional structures for absorbing them. Rather, the debt problem is three-fold. First, the *stock* of debt does indeed act as a drag on private investment and on the political economy of policy reform, since it can be argued that the costs of reform will be borne by the local population but the benefits will accrue to foreign creditors (for a discussion of this and other analytical issues on debt and development, see the papers in Iqbal and Kanbur 1997). Second, the merry-go-round of constant debt rescheduling, and the negotiations to keep gross inflows sufficient to fund debt servicing outflows, takes up the time, energy and political capital of key policymakers and technocrats. Third, and relatedly, large outflows and matching large inflows lead to the institution of aid dependence in the polity, in the sense this was defined in the last section.

For these reasons, I believe that deep debt relief is needed and appropriate for Africa, and I would support this independently of what might happen to net flows after debt relief. In fact, I believe that donor agencies will be better able to stand firm on conditionality (whether of the Burnside–Dollar or Oxfam variety), since worries on debt servicing have been one of the reasons for the failure to enforce conditionality. Thus worries on the 'moral hazard' consequences of debt relief are misplaced; the moral hazard is as much on the donor as on the recipient side. The World Bank–IMF HIPC debt relief inititative (described in Boote *et al.* 1997) was probably the best that could have been achieved politically at the time, given the concerns of major donor countries on moral hazard and on the possibilities of demands for debt relief from countries outside the HIPC net. But it was clearly too timid an attempt at resolving one of the key determinants of African aid dependence, and its current implementation leaves much to be desired. In any event, the problems of conditionality discussed here apply equally well to conditional debt relief.

Conclusion: what to do?

This chapter has presented a somewhat pessimistic diagnosis of the current nexus of aid, conditionality and foreign debt in Africa. It can, however, be argued that this diagnosis reflects a disastrous past rather than emerging realities. With the cold war gone, and the democratic transition beginning in Africa, surely the parameters are now different? While this is true, I believe that purposive reform, undertaken pro-actively, is what is needed to make the most of the favourable trends (I have restricted myself in this chapter to conventional foreign aid, not addressing the issue of growing levels of humanitarian aid).

Based on the diagnosis presented here, I think that four related factors will be central in any reform process. First, it will be important for there to be more of an arm's length relationship between donors and recipients; the current system's dysfunctionality arises in part from the fact that donors are involved too intrusively in a country, in the name of aid effectiveness. Second, and relatedly, donors (and recipients) will have to develop a new toughness in standing firm on conditionalities; the incentive systems in donor agencies and recipient countries will have to be modified. Third, deep debt relief will be an important step on the road to achieving greater toughness and more of an arm's length relationship on aid flows. Fourth and finally, if the above reforms lead to a fall off in the volume of foreign aid, or even require such a fall off, then so be it; donors and recipients should obsess less about the volume of aid and more about the consequences of aid dependence (in the sense characterised in this chapter) for aid effectiveness.

Of course, these basic principles will need to be translated into pragmatic and workable steps. This is not the place to discuss such details. A start is made in this direction in Kanbur (1998), and some concrete steps for a specific agency (which may not necessarily agree in full with the diagnosis presented here) are discussed in World Bank (1998g).

Note

*   The perspectives set out in this chapter arise largely as the result of my experiences as the World Bank's resident representative in Ghana from 1992 to 1994, and then as chief economist of the Africa Region of the World Bank from 1994 to 1996, during which time I also served on the joint World Bank–IMF task force which developed the Heavily Indebted Poor Countries (HIPC) debt relief initiative. I am indebted to Kwesi Botchwey, former Finance Minister of Ghana, for discussion and debate over many years on these topics – I have benefited greatly from our discussions, even when we have disagreed. The ideas in this chapter were presented to seminars at Cornell University, the University of Minnesota, the University of Vermont and Vanderbilt University during academic year 1997–8. The paper is part of a broader project on the future of multilateral development assistance, which is being conducted under the auspices of the Overseas Development Council. I am grateful to Raji Jayaraman and David Pottebaum for research assistance.

19 Political economy of foreign aid

*Raymond F. Hopkins**

Introduction

The future of foreign aid is precarious. With aid in decline, violence in developing countries' on the rise, and Western countries' interests in global outreach increasingly uncertain, a new formula for relations between donors and aid receiving countries is evolving. Countries with the greatest need are also the ones most troubled by weak institutions and political upheavals. Such recipients need more effective governments. This demand is voiced in this volume and elsewhere. It fuels aid in support of state strengthening. The rise of aid for capacity building, governance and democracy, however, poses a major dilemma. On the one hand, institutional weakness is recognised as a major barrier to aid effectiveness. On the other hand, donor efforts to link aid to improved governance compete with recipients' preferences to protect existing privileges. Weak states do not readily use aid to improve their polities or economy. The central task for the changing aid regime is to develop strategies to resolve this dilemma. The post-cold war aid regime requires a formula for aid that goes beyond conventional economic liberalism to support the strengthening of states burdened with failed institutions.

As noted in Chapter 3, the share of GNP that rich countries contribute to official development assistance is in decline, in some states for over 20 years. In spite of the increased generosity of some states, since 1992 net aid disbursements from OECD states dropped, falling from over $62 billion to less than $50 billion in 1997. Not surprisingly, this decline has spawned interest in what caused it and what will happen in the future. This chapter addresses these questions. Drawing on the earlier contributions to the volume, it explores conditions influencing future bilateral and multilateral aid, with principal attention to large donor states, since their outlooks shape their own as well as multilateral flows.

In addressing these questions, this chapter focuses principally on political explanations. Previous chapters mainly addressed the economic dimensions of aid. They asked how its performance as an instrument for development could be improved. Only occasional attention was paid to political economy issues, such as how politics influences the allocations and results of aid. Yet some grasp of why richer countries are willing to transfer resources to poor countries is essential to any credible forecast about future aid flows. Further, since aid supplies are contingent on results, and on the willingness of recipients to accede to aid conditions, the political motivations of those in control of recipient governments, as well as those with power in donor states, must be considered. Together these factors determine the allocation and use of aid.[1] In considering the causes of aid, and reflecting on what causal conditions support foreign aid, political economy perspectives are useful. A political economy perspective treats aid as a policy action of donors, to be explained by political and economic goals. These, in turn, are products of culture, institutions, power distribution and the dynamics of competitive interests (Gilpin 1987, Nelson 1990, Cassen *et al.* 1994 and Schraeder *et al.* 1998).

There are various traditions in political economy, ranging from economic determinism and rational choice modelling to idea-grounded social constructivism (Mueller 1997, Bates 1998 and Staniland 1985). This essay draws on at least three approaches. In one, foreign aid is determined by the economic interests of powerful groups within donor countries. Executive and legislative branches make economic policy with a view to its implications for their power. The second approach explains aid (bilateral and multilateral) as an effort to maximise benefits to donor states, deriving preferences for them from their situation in the international system. In the third, aid is the outcome of bargaining among units, a kind of political market made up of donor aid bureaucracies, multilateral aid agencies and recipient government officials. All three help explain donor motivations. Since preference formation and estimation is controversial, this essay relies little on formal models or deductions from assumed interests. It uses historical language to speak of motivations and goals (not preferences and strategies), particularly for donors. Motivations are discussed as emergent properties from social context.

In the first approach, groups within states – e.g. parties, sectors, firms and NGOs – press for various policies. Empirical evidence about how various unbundled components of a state see their interests affected by aid is the basis for explaining aid outcomes. Political leaders, interacting within executive and legislative branches, set policy on levels and allocations of aid. Bureaucracies and personalities seek to improve their situation by strategic uses of aid; patronage and short-term solutions often dominate choices (Nelson and Eglinton 1993 and van de Walle 1998).

In the second approach, the state is a unified actor with interests. These interests arise from a state's position in world affairs and its cultural values. Aid is used to advance interests, whether diplomatic, commercial or cultural. Because donors pursue multiple goals, and these vary over time and among donors, it is difficult to generalise about the weight these goals play in explaining aid. For example, economic gains seem important in Japanese aid, political goals in French aid and global welfare improvement in Nordic aid (Chapter 3).

In the third approach, producers and consumers of foreign aid set terms (prices) by bargaining. Units remain state or government agencies, but in interaction. Donors want a bundle of outcomes in return for their aid. One outcome is from other donors. In this context they want burden sharing and co-ordination to achieve common goals. Among recipients, donors want compliance with their conditions. Recipients, of course, want aid without conditions. Donor–recipient exchanges can be considered strategic results of co-operative bargaining games. Acceptable outcomes for players are aid arrangements within each player's win set, varying according to which side pulls the other closest to its preferred position (Putnam 1988).

As world political conditions change, foreign aid changes: both its size and purposes. There has never been a pure economic development assistance regime. Rather, foreign policy has created and sustained various aid regimes among donors (Grant and Nijman 1998). Until 1990, cold war concerns provided a core motivation for aid. Recipient states did not fail because it was in the interests of the cold war combatants that they not fail. Development was a secondary concern; rentier elites were not obliged to account to donors for aid effectiveness in terms of economic or political improvements. Now that the cold war is over, foreign policy is more geared towards international public goods, including containing international 'bads'. Ironically, international public 'bads' have multiplied as states once propped-up by strategically motivated aid are now openly failing. This situation provides a new focus for aid efforts. Donors should intervene in crisis situations (see Chapter 17), so as to contain negative externalities and gear their assistance in normal times to institution building. In the short term, the donor objective is not higher economic growth in aid recipients; if it were, aid would go to countries with competent states and good policies, ones already relatively rich and able to attract private investment.[2] The priority for aid in the first decade of the twenty-first century should be for institutionalising political stability, seeking the best package of long-term reduction in political crises and better future economic growth among states too risky for private sector funds. It is not an easy task.

Explaining the decline in aid

Explaining the change in aid volumes, and especially its decline in the 1990s, begins with recalling how the system of foreign aid evolved over its first 50 years, as reviewed in Chapters 1 and 3. The institutionalisation of foreign aid after the Second World War occurred in a context of the cold war. Welfare principles dominated economic policies of donors (Noel and Therien 1995). Strategic political considerations were the major force shaping aid allocations, at least bilateral ones (Wood 1986 and Ruttan 1996). While moral concerns underlay aid, especially emergency relief, this motivation was never paramount, certainly not in a sustainable fashion.[3] These founding principles and regime features changed. The demise of the United States as a hegemonic donor was reflected in the drop of US aid as a percentage of US GNP, from over 2 per cent in 1950 (not shown in the figure), to about 0.6 per cent in 1960–2, and only 0.08 per cent in 1997 (see Figure 19.1).[4]

Multilateral agencies played a growing role in the regime, as the World Bank and the UNDP facilitated co-ordination in aid administration, while the Development Assistance Committee (DAC) of the OECD encouraged more generous giving among its member countries, along with establishing guidelines for what counted as aid. From the 1960s to 1992, the amount of official development assistance rose steadily, even taking inflation into account (see Chapter 3). It centred increasingly on impoverished countries, as successful developing states in Latin America and Asia 'graduated' as recipients. Japanese and European aid especially increased, surpassing US contributions. Equitable development and economic reform became more central principles for justifying aid. Then, following the end of the cold war, with the collapse of the Soviet Union in 1991, funding peaked and declined.

The decline in foreign aid occurred for six reasons. First, the end of the cold war made it less important. Second, globalisation attenuated aid tied to colonial interests. Third, growing budget pressures squeezed donor resources. Fourth, disappointment with the effectiveness of aid weakened popular support. Fifth, donor country special interest coalitions supporting aid unravelled. Finally, neo-liberal philosophies challenged some of the intellectual foundations of aid. A brief elaboration of these reasons follows.

Cold war ending

The end of the cold war reduced both aid and the ability of recipients to manoeuver among donors. In donors most engaged in the cold war struggle, particularly the United States and the Soviet Union, domestic support for aid evaporated with the end of the global ideological clash. Predictably, among OECD members, the largest declines in aid since 1992 are reported for the United States, followed by close military allies Germany, Japan and Australia. The declines in aid from 1992 to 1998 for each of the OECD countries corresponds fairly well to a rank ordering of countries in terms of the intensity of their involvement in cold war activities. The erosion of cold war motivations did not affect all of these donors. In the 1980s, for example, nonaligned states, such as Finland and Switzerland, did not use aid for strategic purposes. They also avoided substantial decline in the 1990s. Nominal cold war alignments, moreover, such as NATO membership, are not a good proxy for strategic motivation of foreign aid. Those states that accepted (and have reached and surpassed) the UN aid volume target (0.7 per cent of donor GNP) in their national policy, had both

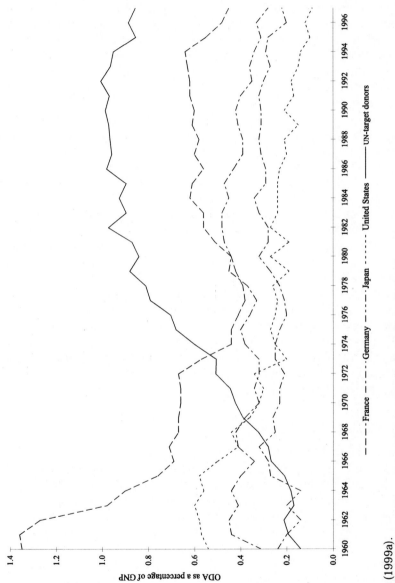

Source: OECD (1999a).

Note: UN-target donors are Denmark, Norway, the Netherlands and Sweden.

Figure 19.1 Net ODA disbursements as a percentage of donor GNP, selected donors, 1960–97.

the least decline in terms of aid volume (Figure 19.2), in terms of their relative aid effort (Figure 19.1) and the least responsibility for the cold war world structure.[5]

Aid from China and Russia, and other former communist states, also declined. These states give little or no aid today. This decline, likewise, is a function, at least partially, of the cold war's demise. Many of these states have become aid recipients. Their role in the aid drama today stands in striking comparison to their role in the 1955–80 era. Once significant contributors to the aid regime (Schraeder *et al.* 1998), these states now absorb billions of aid monies in efforts to transform their economies from command to market based ones and to encourage their peaceful transition into a global liberal economy (Grant and Nijman 1998). The rise in aid to these recipients basically absorbed aid increases after 1989; from the mid-1990s this put pressure on the availability of development aid for traditional poor countries.[6]

The case of aid to the Horn of Africa is instructive. In spite of large needs, foreign aid has declined. From the 1960s to the 1980s, cold war alliances were the major factor shaping aid flows to that area. In the 1980s Somalia and Sudan received large amounts of US aid as a product of alignments. Ethiopia, following the rise to power there of Marxist military leaders, lost foreign aid from the West. Today, global alliances do not mobilise or direct aid.

In sum, the end of the cold war both reduced support for aid and loosened constraints on its use. From 1948 until 1991, the great risk to security from a war between the two large alliances caused each side to mobilise and use aid as a tool to shape relations with other states. Aid continues today for other reasons.[7] As security-based incentives declined, overall aid did not fall immediately; and for certain donors with commercial or global welfare interests aid grew.

Dying patron–client ties

A second reason for declining aid levels is the atrophying of international patron–client relations. Globalisation of economic and cultural production has subordinated links originating in earlier colonial ties and spheres of influence. For great powers, these ties, which pre-date the cold war, were important in justifying and allocating aid in the 1950s and 1960s. The desire of France and Britain to maintain economic and cultural links with former colonies, and similar desires by the United States with respect to areas it formerly governed or strongly controlled, such as the Philippines, Liberia and Panama, encouraged aid that could provide direct budgetary support to friendly governments. The French focus on states in West Africa is particularly revealing. French ties to West Africa were not part of a strategic alliance, but represented the protection of historical investments in overseas peoples and expatriate residents. Aid supported a network of

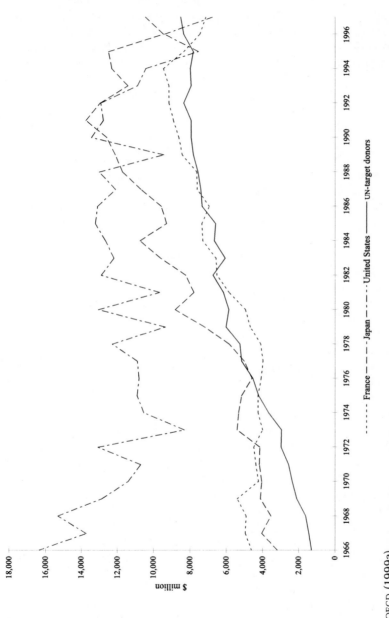

Source: OECD (1999a).

Note: UN-target donors are Denmark, Norway, the Netherlands and Sweden.

Figure 19.2 Net ODA disbursements, selected donors, 1966–97.

commercial and cultural links. The aim was to build political stability in those countries with which France shared historical and linguistic identities (Schraeder *et al.* 1998). A review of aid to six West African states in 1987–91 by the French ministry of co-operation concluded that 'France's development aid contributed to the reproduction of social economic and political systems that are clientist and predatory.' (quoted in Lancaster 1999: 121).

In the 1990s these culturally based political and economic links have weakened as donor country firms responded to global and Europe-wide market imperatives. Popular interest in these overseas locales also waned as global humanitarian opportunities captured the attention of large NGOs. A residue of support for client-maintenance remains; French aid continues to be concentrated, for example. The United States continues to give aid to countries with special ties, but without emphasis on maintaining solidarity of customs. A decline in client-oriented aid is notable in the case of the United Kingdom. It has loosened its targeting of aid to former colonies, reacting to a vocal development lobby and strong support of the Labour party. Portugal and the Netherlands also have historical ties that promote aid. Other donors have developed a target group of countries based on shared political philosophy, as in the case of Nordic states with Tanzania. The special sentiments linking particular donors and recipients, whatever their origin, have withered in recent years, especially as experiences of success dropped.

One result of this withering of sentiments is diminished aid to 'client' governments. This, in turn, has reduced aid's role in stabilising these polities. Of course, this role is controversial. Aid to train police and military, or to bolster a particular set of officials, is of debatable value, witness such aid to Vietnam in the 1960s or Somalia and Zaire in the 1970s. Further, in Africa, where aid rose dramatically in the wake of fiscal crises, famines, and devastating civil wars in Uganda, Chad and Mozambique, more aid actually weakened the polity. The proliferation of donors with individual projects created a complex nightmare of planning, oversight, evaluation and negotiation in weak states. Donor demands overwhelmed government capacity.

Some political uses of aid to promote stability continue. For instance, aid still goes to help stabilise countries or regions, such as the Middle East, Eastern Europe or Southern Africa. Some aid may go as a bulwark against terrorism. Such flows are donor specific. Aid from the United States to Egypt and Israel and European aid to Eastern Europe and Russia stand out as examples. Japan's aid to Asia may also play such a role, though it rests more on commercial and regional stability interests. Bilateral aid to prop up particular client states, however, is over (Ruttan 1996 and Lancaster 1999). Furthermore, multilateral aid is harder to use for state support, even though technical assistance from the World Bank or UNDP is specifically designed for capacity building (see also Chapters 6 and 12). While multilateral agencies are often more trusted by recipients, they are less able to exercise political conditionality, certainly overtly. Multilateral agencies have charters and governing bodies with strong respect for putative sovereignty. This inhibits aid used to prop up governments, or to force political reform. Their failure in this task has been broadly assailed (van de Walle 1998).

Tight budgets

A third reason for the decline of aid is budgetary constraints. Many OECD governments reduced their aid in the 1990s, at least from trend levels, a likely consequence of broader efforts to lower government deficits. Both domestic and foreign expenditures came under pressure. Military spending and foreign aid suffered cuts, many in absolute terms. Entitlement programmes expanded, gaining a larger share of allocations, even as benefit levels for such programmes were tightened. Reasons for this tightening varied. Among European countries, the decision to meet the Maastricht treaty's criteria for entering the Euro-currency arrangement required substantial shrinking in budget deficits in the years leading up to January 1999. Slow economic growth made the fiscal cuts required particularly painful. Some were dramatic. In Italy, for example, after large increases in aid, budget pressures in the 1990s, combined with disappointment about fraud and waste in projects, brought about a fall in Italian aid of over 50 per cent. In the United States, aid declines since the 1980s can be linked to tax cuts and legislatively mandated caps on budget expenditures. Once the Clinton administration promoted a balanced budget goal, austerity across a large realm of discretionary expenditures ensued. In Japan, which became the largest single donor in 1992, aid declined by over 30 per cent from 1995 to 1996. The collapse of the balloon economy and the subsequent long recession explain a large part of Japanese aid downturn. The fiscal reform law of December 1997 schedules aid volumes to fall from 1997 levels by 10 per cent a year from 1998–2000. In the face of this austerity, aid from conservative welfare states declined the most and from socialist welfare states the least (Noel and Therien 1995).

Budget constraints also affected non-OECD donors. Falling government revenues in oil-rich Middle East states explain their budget induced decline. These countries, so heavily dependent on export revenues from oil, encountered budget crises in the 1990s as world prices plummeted. Since the Gulf War, the flow of aid from Saudi Arabia, Kuwait and other smaller neighbours has dwindled. At one time, in the 1970s, these donors funded 5–10 per cent of total aid commitments. Today there are few aid donors outside the OECD. The small amounts of aid provided by countries such as Argentina, Taiwan and Brazil are dwarfed by other aid flows.

Poor performance

The fourth reason for the decline in aid volumes is disappointment with performance. Sometimes labelled 'aid fatigue', this factor is best understood as lack of satisfaction that aid is working. Aid has been seen to fail in many countries, especially in Africa. The failure of economic development in some countries, ones increasingly targeted for aid in the 1980s, was particularly disappointing.[8] Some analysts blamed failure on donor governments, pointing out that they had undercut development results by giving priority to other donor state purposes, particularly political and commercial interests.[9] There have long been critics of aid who doubted its efficacy.[10] More recently, critiques have suggested donors were culpable thanks to their support for bad economic policies in earlier years, e.g. helping parastatal development in the 1960s and 1970s, coupled with insufficient attention to the impact of aid on recipient institutions in subsequent years (van de Walle 1998). Other damning attacks on donors arise from dependency theorists. They claim that aid is really provided in order to exploit recipient countries, with the effect of slowing development (Amin 1973 and Seligson and Passe-Smith 1998). This charge still resonates among some donor NGOs and recipient country officials. Finally, after 50 years of experience, there is a massive accumulation of critical evaluations of aid, especially failed projects in Africa. These critiques informed much of the analytical work reviewed in this volume's earlier chapters, including the influential work of the World Bank by Burnside and Dollar (1997) discussed in Chapter 4. In general, flaws in donor motivation, bureaucratic mismanagement and recipient country socio-political distortion of aid objectives were identified. The reaction to perceived aid failure has been to identify better ways to use aid more effectively. As Eric Thorbecke illustrates in Chapter 1, each successive decade has brought efforts to correct and improve aid.

Domestic publics and elites have absorbed some of the scepticism raised by critics (Noel and Therien 1995: 547–48). In Japan, for example, less than half the population in 1996 thought foreign aid benefited 'developing countries' while 15 per cent held it was of no benefit.[11] Fact finding missions by parliamentary bodies have raised concerns about ineffective results and misused resources. In the United States, after years of public discussion of such results, it is not surprising that in 1998 about half the population favoured giving no aid. While only 10 per cent of those considered 'leaders' held this sceptical view, leaders support for aid levels declined (Reilly 1999: 38). The decline in trust of government in many OECD countries might provide a more general reason for some of these views. In fact, for the US population, aid has never been viewed favourably. The portion of the public supporting it in principle ranged from 52 per cent in 1974 to 46 per cent in 1998 (Reilly 1999: 21). Disappointment with aid probably accounts for the downward shift in support for aid among leaders more so than other factors.

Smaller special interest payoffs

A fifth reason for a decline in aid support is that special economic interests in donors are less powerful. It can be argued, indeed is argued, that aid has the most support from groups inside donor countries that derive selective advantage from it. These include firms with investments in recipient countries, or who provide exports tied to aid, and bureaucracies with employees with career interests in aid – including NGOs. There has been an impressive growth in NGOs in the 1980s and 1990s, and they have developed strong ties to aid programmes that help fund them.[12] Their growing strength creates a powerful lobby for continued government allocations (but, as the sixth reason suggests, their success reinforces a presumption that development can be addressed as a private sector responsibility). Business firms with profits linked to guarantees or direct payment from an aid account also actively support aid levels in their home country. The growth of direct foreign investment, the development of alternatives to aid for increasing export sales and trans-corporate co-operation have reduced the salience of aid for most firms operating overseas or who are heavily export dependent. Moreover, there is a vicious cycle at work. Once the aid pie begins to shrink, the fewer domestic economic interests it will serve. In addition, there can be a decline in the lobbying weight of groups that historically supported aid, as their interest or their ability to shape aid declines.

Another reason why aid has weaker special interest constituencies is because the countries receiving aid have changed. As aid has shifted from Asia to Africa, and from fast- to slow-growing countries, the results sought in these recipients promise fewer political and economic benefits for export or financial interests within donors. Aid has less relevance as a way to open recipients' markets if those markets have very small potential. Exporters look to market benefits in large countries such as China or Nigeria, none of which receives significant per capita aid.[13] The decline of aid compared to direct foreign investment also reduced commercial interests' support. The IMF is more effective than aid institutions in promoting their interests. A kind of downward cycle of support results. All these factors have made aid less relevant to donor country firms and bureaucracies.

Ascendent neo-liberal outlook

A sixth, and final, reason for lower aid volumes is the shift to neo-liberal views. In the global climate of opinion, the size and intervention of government has come to be considered excessive. Such views are dominant in western welfare states as well as socialist ones. The United States and Great Britain championed reduction of entitlement spending. This view, first fashionable in the 1980s, became triumphant by the 1990s, as the Soviet Union and China began to adopt market-oriented economic policies.[14] As governments are less trusted and market solutions are celebrated, the use of governments to transfer resources globally has become decreasingly legitimate. Yet some motor for efficient progress is needed. This is increasingly met by the rise in private capital flows and foreign investment, especially by multinational corporations. Such flows have grown remarkably compared with portfolio investment, short-term loans, or aid flows (see Chapter 3 and Stopford 1998). Most of these funds, however, do not reach very poor countries, such as those in Africa, with the greatest gaps between needed and realised public investment. Yet these private flows do reduce support for the public system of aid that had supported international financial flows, especially World Bank lending. With large capital flows occurring outside the Bretton Woods institutions, and with the concessional lending of the World Bank largely targeted to very poor states, such as those in Africa, aspirations about aid launching rapid growth, as it seemed to do for South Korea, Indonesia and Taiwan, have waned. Confidence in aid as an instrument has eroded. Its past association as a successful boost in the early years of Asian state-led development was undercut by the 1997–8 Asian crisis. The neo-liberal creed in extreme form has no place for foreign aid as a public good; aid as charity should be voluntary, not tax based. The NGOs, successfully mobilising private funds, confirm this ideal.

The effect of this shift in ideas is manifest in the programme of various political movements to cut 'welfare' both domestically and internationally. It can also be seen in concern about the unsustainability of national entitlement policies. Deep scepticism about state solutions pervades analyses by individual states and multilateral agencies, such as the OECD and the World Bank. The solution to past aid failures is more market-oriented solutions. Ironically, privatisation as a solution does not exclude public funds to assist this process, even though logically this requires state management of the process (see Chapter 12 and Kahler 1990). Thus a broad shift in world views about aid emerges from the ascendance of a neo-liberal orientation. In donor countries, a decline in national welfare has been matched by a decline in foreign aid (Noel and Therien 1995). Such judgments have been reinforced by the analysis of aid failures.

Four donor motivations

What support for aid is likely to exist among donors for such future directions? Coalitions of internationally oriented populace, mobilised by political parties and the advocacy of NGOs, will be particularly necessary to sustain aid, especially as development imperatives supplant earlier political ones. However, aid targeted on development goals must also relate to the self-interested motivations of donors. We know that the goals of donors in the contemporary state system have complex economic underpinnings. The political context faced by donors has great uncertainty about security and economic 'interests', as conventionally defined. Foreign policy goals centre on combating immediate disturbances, such as conflicts, emergencies and global environmental threats. The difficulty in pursuing these goals suggests that a collective action problem is the basic barrier to sustainable aid. Benefits of aid are so dispersed that donor political interests are hard to marshal. Costs, such as taxes, are visible and divisible in comparison.

How to overcome the collective action problem is complicated, to say the least; paths to doing so will vary according to the political system of various donors and the assets available to mobilise populations within their existing national creeds.

Donors have four motivations for sustaining aid. These provide opportunities in various donors for mobilising support, domestically and transnationally. They also represent desiderata shaping aid size, packaging and effectiveness. These are: (i) the pursuit of global public goods, (ii) economic development benefits for donors, (iii) domestic special interests and (iv) increased willingness of recipients to accept conditionality. The first will draw on collective benefits from reduced violence, disease and pollution. The second will build on national self-interest in gains from trade and investment thanks to economic development. The third rests on interest group pressures and bureaucracies that organise and serve these. The last rests on what recipient countries are willing to do to get aid; they are likely to pay higher prices in terms of loss of implementing conditionality.

Global public goods

In the 1990s, threats to political and economic values emerged from the rise in wars and conflicts (Chapter 17), the financial instability in global markets seen in the Asian crises (Chapter 14) and the increase in pollutants and diseases which flow across borders (Chapter 11). Donor countries have an interest in reducing these threats. A more benign and secure global environment is a key donor goal to which aid can be attached. This goal is now widely cited by donors, both in general and in announcing specific commitments. The World Bank and many bilateral donors have a growing portfolio of projects to improve the environment, to secure better governance and to support strengthening financial sector regulatory capacity. An intellectual foundation for these initiatives rests on a recognition of the importance of public sector institutions in providing frameworks. The domination of neo-liberal ideas, eschewing public sector intervention, is hence challenged by these global concerns (Gray 1998). The pendulum swinging toward neo-liberal philosophy has probably reached its apogee. Hence, the scepticism about aid it encouraged, seeing aid as an inappropriate welfare transfer, is offset by concern about international market failures, including states in collapse. Global public goods encourage aid as a way to build constraints against market excesses.

A wide variety of practices threaten global welfare. Dumping wastes in the ocean, cutting tropical forests, releasing carbon emissions into the atmosphere are all understood to create shared environmental losses to people around the world. The spread of infectious disease and other public health hazards also are preventable losses. Industrialisation and population pressures exacerbate these global 'bads', while the absence of regulatory mechanisms permits them. Some international paths to collective action have been designed, both through international treaties and via transnational politics, the latter via international NGOs that support environmental lobbying by local affiliates. Donor publics seeking these collective goods recognise aid as a tool. Its role includes reducing transaction costs of negotiations and inducing co-operation instead of free riding by having rich countries bear some of the costs of jointly beneficial actions by developing countries.

Analytically, there is an appealing case for increasing the supply of global public goods, from research to the environmental regulation, from financial arrangements to conflict reduction. A recent World Bank *World Development Report* (World Bank 1997a) stressed the role of the state for welfare improving action. With the rise in refugees and hot money, interest in dampening destabilising flows of people and money is high. Donor government budgets have grown by billions of dollars to control the substantial rise in the last decade of flows of people and illegal substances that have fostered efforts to strengthen border controls, at least in Europe and the United States. Among political elites in donor states enhanced aid may also be attractive as a way to use international agreements to leverage desired national policies, for example, on trade or regulation of illegal economic activity.

With the waning of the cold war, defects in state institutions and their performance on issues of protecting natural resources and the environment have gained general visibility and mass appeal. Calls for intervention to offset bad effects in developing countries are striking. In addition, health threats, gender equity, pollution, hunger and poverty related suffering has built broad coalitions in donor states, spurred on by NGO actions, international conferences and trans-governmental co-operation.[15]

Economic development

A second goal motivating donors is the benefits they derive from economic development in recipient states. The earlier chapters in this volume make a strong case that aid has been, or at least can be, effective in promoting development. For the donor state as a whole, looking at its reasons to commit both bilateral and multilateral funds, there is near universal recognition that development will be linked to trade enhancement and expanded, more secure overseas investment opportunities. To care about such benefits, confidence in the efficacy of aid and development is needed. One explanation for earlier failures in development has been that foreign governments were, at least as perceived by public opinion in donor countries, resisting aid objectives. Tying success to adaptive and monitored project objectives and relating these to the prospect of accelerating development, are measures by which the decline in aid can be limited. Support for aid is also greater if the recipients are viewed as worthy. Success in achieving development in aid concentrated on 'worthy' states can reverse cynicism that has grown around the process (Kapur 1998 and Grant and Nijman 1998). Amending aid practices to realise greater effectiveness involves greater country targeting, capacity building and improvement of bureaucratic management, as was earlier proposed as a supportable target when linked to economic performance (Chapters 1, 5–9 and Lancaster 1999).

The exact importance of economic development, to donors at least, is difficult to measure through gains from trade from poor country recipients.[16] Among OECD states, the share of trade with such aid target states is small and not growing. The financial exposure of debt in these states is likewise small, even though these are countries with the highest debt burden relative to their economies. Economic development goals for aid may be inversely proportional to the size of a recipient. Were per capita aid to become significantly larger in countries with large populations – China or India, for example – the consequences for donor economies from aid accelerated growth would weigh far heavier. Aid could also be linked to smoothing global firm alliances. Political resistance in these countries makes this unlikely; hence the weight of development benefits are likely to come from accelerated growth in smaller countries. Moreover, the participation of these states in global economic affairs has diffuse value. In recent years, donors encouraged adoption of economic rules that are conducive to global capitalist growth and to increased trade, by these states. Membership of WTO virtually doubled (Chapter 16). Countries such as France and the Nordic states abandoned support for state centred development models. This convergence of policy thinking on economic issues lowers global transaction costs. Aid reinforces this great transformation. Economic growth also improves realisation of donor goals for political performance (Przeworski and Limongi 1997).

In sum, the shift of aid toward the most difficult development cases reduces direct benefits to the donor economies, but increases gains from a reduction of global burdens and threats which can be avoided by growth. Narrow donor interests distorting aid flows are sometimes blamed for poor performance. Past failures of aid have been explained by the allocation and absorption of aid according to non-economic factors that undermine its desired effectiveness on development. The appeal of developmentally focused aid in coming years is that it could escape this distortion, accepting that aid to weak states must be multi-dimensional to be effective.

Domestic coalitions

We have noted how unbundling the nation-state as a unit allows us to see how special interests within countries form coalitions to support various aid policies. These interests are substantial; the problem is putting together coalitions supporting diffuse goals. Virtually all donors link aid to domestic exports: either for commodities or services such as technical assistance. Inside donor countries, firms then compete to protect their share of benefits from a dwindling aid appropriation. Firms and sectors that see foreign aid expanding their incomes, lobby for aid appropriations. This varies depending on the influence such groups command and the salience of aid for their profitability. Organised labour, for example, long a supporter of aid in OECD domestic politics, has gradually withdrawn support, especially as trade with developing countries is perceived as bringing pressure to keep wages low. Sectoral influence on aid policy is nicely illustrated by food aid. This aid flow (discussed in Chapter 8) has long enjoyed strong farm sector support, most visibly in the United States. As the power of the farm lobby's voting bloc has declined (as there are fewer farm voters and legislators), and as their interest in subsidising exports moved toward the solution of trade negotiations to gain more market access abroad, farm sector support of aid weakened. In the case of food aid, humanitarian groups have become more important. While farm interests still join forces in support of appropriations for this tied form of aid, their importance has waned. Getting rid of US and EU surpluses unduly drove the size and allocation of food aid and distorted aid effectiveness. This is one reason Colding and Pinstrup-Andersen (Chapter 8) propose giving the World Food Programme (WFP) a larger role in food aid management, because as a UN body it is less subject to disposal pressures. The risk in cutting ties with special interests, however, is that as selective benefits are lost, groups inside donors will lose interest in aid. This has occurred, as we noted, with regard to food aid; it is also the case with respect to financial sector support for aid (Haggard *et al.* 1993).

Domestic coalitions then explain differential support for types of aid; and they partially account for the variety of support aid enjoys among donors. Generally, the larger the aid package, the more benefits can accrue to specific firms or sectors in a donor country, and the more intensely these groups will build winning coalitions in budgetary struggles over scarce resources. Often support coalitions form around particular components of aid that directly affect them. Universities lobby for the research and institutional strengthening lines in aid budgets. Contracting firms bid for airports and phone systems. Once shares of aid budgets are settled, however, these various special interests support the overall appropriation.[17]

Non-governmental organisations, such as church organisations and political parties, are the most frequently used vehicles for articulating equity demands. Such groups have been strong advocates in donor countries for generous foreign aid. Thus, interest group politics is not exclusively grounded in selective economic gains. Every donor's culture is saturated with various demands for justice, duties to others, requirements for national rectitude. Foreign aid from OECD states is justified by various formulas by which national responsibilities are met by providing aid. Among these are concerns for international welfare (or distributive justice) and for burden sharing among donors. In socialist welfare states, aid objectives continue to be especially visible in support of aid for reasons of national philosophy (Noel and Therien 1995).

One player among such coalitions is the aid bureaucracy itself. Bureaucratic interests exist for all established agencies, which quite naturally seek to maintain themselves.[18] Managing aid is a profession, and it attracts people committed to its goals. Not surprisingly they lobby to protect or increase their resources. Like physicians, they have a body of received wisdom about how to achieve the goals of aid, usually development. Multilateral institutions do this quite openly, with national citizens testifying to parliaments on behalf of appropriations. They promote allocations to their work by speeches, reports, and mobilisation of support from allies in other parts of government and the private sector. These bureaucracies have a limited ability to shape appropriations. This is true for both domestic based government bureaus and multilateral agencies. Indeed, many government branches – foreign affairs, trade, commerce and intelligence ministries, for example – weigh in to support aid. For them it is a complementary resource for carrying out their tasks. Multilateral agencies, such as the World Bank and UNDP have officials who pursue aid promotion interests. They have lobbied through legislative testimony and personal networks in their home countries.

Increased concessions from recipients

A final motivation for donors is increased influence for each aid dollar. Historically, some recipient countries have shopped wantonly for aid, while others accepted aid only if it fitted with their own plans and preferences. Over time, however, except for the rapidly growing countries of Asia, recipients have moved toward offering more concessions to donor preferences. Attitudes are far more accommodating compared to 20 years ago. One reason for this is the loss of an option to switch among donors; with the end of aid from the Communist bloc this has largely disappeared.[19] The ease with which Indonesia, Egypt and India resisted aid and policy pressures from the West in the 1960s is over. Especially in Africa, recipient countries have become supplicants, trotting out a range of projects in hope to capture aid (Lancaster 1999).

As a result, donors can now bargain for more. Even elements crucial to power maintenance, such as corruption, may be open to concessions. Gaining support for international positions is less salient to donors compared to aid regimes of earlier years. They can now ask a higher policy and institutional price for their money. What donors can now demand in such circumstances, in return for aid, is for these standard ways of corruption to end. This is no easy request. Corruption, associated with over-billing and capital flight, can become institutionalised in the aid receiving country to the point that it would be hard to avoid a diversion of aid. However, corrupt predatory states now have difficulty raising revenues to pay the costs of government. Hence, government requires financing from foreign aid. In spite of donor policies eschewing the financing of 'recurrent' costs, this avenue opens a powerful path to address the state strengthening target. Given the importance of state institutions for development, as suggested, donor agencies may attempt to ensure future sustainability by demanding political reform of institutions (North 1998).

Of course, changes in recipient attitudes are not simply bought by aid. When first China and, by the 1990s, Russia became recipients, their orientations toward aid and development strategies had first shifted, thanks to internally driven forces. Official policy favoured market-oriented economic policy; aid was to support political liberalisation as defined by the recipient. Another event raising the malleability of recipients has been a rise in natural and man-made emergencies. These created growing demands for emergency aid. A third factor encouraging recipients to accept greater conditions was the end of options in finding alternative sources of aid. When famine came to North Korea in 1995 it led to large flows of aid from Western governments, mostly through the UN. Resistance to external influence abated, at least partially.

In review, the last reason for sustaining or increasing donor motivation for aid is that recipients will concede more in return. Broad concessions are possible, including an assault on society-wide corruption, an end to human and property rights violations, and the use of regulatory capacity to expose illegal public and private actions, such as tax evasion. The failures reported by Elliot Berg in Chapter 12 occurring in the privatisation process illustrate the importance of such changes. Another area in which recipients might offer higher concessions is in the regulation of finance and the environment. Weak state authority has failed to cope with the rapid changes; opportunities for predation in the globalised economy's financial and raw materials markets grow (Ascher and Healy 1990). Indifference by the aid regime to these problems, will leave the lessons of past aid unused. The result will be a further decline in moral anchors and, in the absence of norms for living in a highly monetised society, anomie and a climate for corruption and social conflict will prevail.

Strategies for aid sustainability

The shift in the organising rationale for aid – from cold war rivalry, North–South paternalism and state-led development to globalisation and market-oriented growth – has contributed, along with tumbling aid levels, to a weakening of global authority (Hopkins 1995). This also unleashed new economic interests and cross-national alignments that affected bargaining within the aid regime. The underpinnings of aid, institutionalised in the post-WWII era, will not continue on inertia alone. Future aid will necessarily be linked to these changes. Or it will disappear. In response to this challenge, new and more complex formulas for aid have been put forward (Chapters 1 and 16–18 and World Bank 1997a, 1998b). They stress using aid effectively to build governance while expanding market activity.

What prospects are there for this emerging future aid regime? Three targets for aid have wide appeal among diverse elements in the donor and recipient communities. These are (i) state strengthening, (ii) improved market management and (iii) emergency safety nets. These targets are recommended as problems for promoting future aid. Moreover, motivations of donors are favourably predisposed to these targets, since they appeal to overlapping transnational coalitions and can be linked with benefits, as argued earlier.

Previous chapters provide background for this claim. Several of this volume's authors – e.g. Irma Adelman in Chapter 2 and Tony Addison in Chapter 17 – see the deterioration of states as a major obstacle to development. While aid effectiveness can be undermined by a poor set of policies, the right policy environment is a chimera without a functioning state. After all, a state's key role is to set up conditions for markets to operate. In particular, developing country markets are recognised as imperfect (Chapters 12 and 14). So reforming markets is a second target. Finally, with widespread poverty and growing instability, refugees and internally displaced peoples have grown. Aid linked to emergency needs commands priority. This target represents a politically sustainable path for reinforcing international safety nets. It is an insurance mechanism to protect vital human and physical capital. The increased share of aid going to emergencies is likely to continue, since the conditions creating these emergencies continue with the growth of failed states and the large impact of natural disasters on crowded, ecologically vulnerable populations. Below, these three aid targets are considered in more detail.

Strengthening states

Political goals are important. There has been a continuous growth in the number of wars, especially civil wars, since 1950. The rise of internal wars has spilled across borders, involving neighbouring states and even out-of-region participants. The Balkans and the Great Lakes region of Africa are the most striking instances. The involvement of the UN in Somalia, Cambodia and Southern Africa, and of NATO in the Balkan wars, suggests that containing armed conflict is a rising goal of Western states, especially when refugees threaten to destabilise surrounding states. This goal is only weakly undertaken in Africa, however, as Congo (Kinshasa) has become the locus for nine countries and a dozen transnational insurgent groups to engage in fighting.[20]

From about 10 wars ongoing during 1945–55, there were perhaps 50 wars being waged in the 1990s, most of them internal wars, and with enormous total death rates. This growth, encompassing conflicts from Sri Lanka and Afghanistan to Liberia and Colombia, is due to complex factors, including the prolonged duration of fighting, which became chronic in many areas. The prospect is that peace will be short-lived in areas afflicted with these semi-legitimate, semi-sovereign states. This creates a case for targeting aid to the task of nurturing peaceful conditions in such anarchic conditions, as was made by Tony Addison (Chapter 17). He sees a continuing role in areas where 'incomplete peace' lurks. The first concern is to improve the operation of polities so that ethnic rivalry, or the quick wealth from capturing resource rents, does not spawn conflict. Domestic conflicts endanger food supplies, basic institutions, and are a barrier to any long-term development (de Soysa and Gleditsch 1999). A second goal of targeting state failures is to discourage internal wars from generating refugees, promoting terrorist movements and increasing threats to stability, all of which can spread elsewhere. Exigencies of change, including ethnic conflict, nationalism, and globalisation, have caused the rise in conflict. The Rwanda case highlights failures of past aid to create conditions for peace. Peter Uvin argues that when civil war flared in 1991–2, structural adjustment-based aid utterly failed to address growing political rifts. Projects focused on food production, family planning, education and health, were judged against narrow technical benchmarks. Five billion dollars of foreign aid, delivered over 15 years, condoned official racism, ethnic identity cards, corruption, violence, hatred and human right abuses (Uvin 1998). Responsible government criteria as aid requirements, if credible and even modestly effective, would have averted this calamity.

Strengthening state institutions is also a prerequisite for securing increasingly important global collective goods. Within the current world system, stability, predictability and recognition of rights are necessary properties of a state if environmental damage and international crime is to be confronted (Mittelman and Johnston 1999). The absence of terrorist threats, for example, can be linked to expected state compliance with rules that discourage and penalise terrorism. On the positive side, the aim is to make it possible for developing countries to deliver global goods on environment, human rights, migration control and health. Weak conflict-ridden states are the worst resource exploiters and make the largest mess for others. Efforts to strengthen such countries are supported by neighbouring states, by donor states' foreign affairs ministries, military institutions and attentive publics and by environmental and humanitarian NGOs. State strengthening efforts relate to governance/democracy projects, technical assistance for capacity building and basic budget support.

Managing such aid successfully, however, is difficult (Lancaster 1999). Agreement on broad goals is not easily transferred into effective aid projects in this area of capacity building and state formation. The major question facing such aid use is not 'what' but 'how'. For example, if ensuring rule-of-law rights are core elements in a successful state, then how is this achieved? Will assistance to judiciary organisations or police work? Strengthening government institutions with technical support and by privatisation, for example, are widely endorsed as ways to improve public sector performance. Yet Elliott Berg's review of public enterprise reform (Chapter 12) and Channing Arndt's discussion of technical assistance (Chapter 6) suggest a paucity of success in strengthening efforts. Lessons for effective aid reviewed earlier suggest that direct aid to officials and institutions may not work. If so, indirect aid to incumbent officials which strengthen them politically may be the best strategy (Kapur 1998 and Lancaster 1999). This strategy aims to improve intangible goods, such as legitimacy. Conceivably, infrastructure projects can achieve this, while constraining corrupt officials through using the aid to exact conditions making it harder for them to hide their money. Bank transparency around the world could also work to stop international opportunities for money laundering and tax evasion which plague states with bankrupt treasuries. So external pressures are needed, in order to prevent domestic rent-seeking or other self-serving tendencies by public or private agencies and these can be achieved through tough bureaucratic norms within OECD countries as well as using aid to provide external sanctions.

Similarly, the importance of the rule-of-law within countries is a logical part of this target, but we need research help. The design of contextually sensitive and effective projects, including how they should relate to government, is a challenge. Deepening authoritative expectations is a complex task and may require long-term adaptive aid financing. Too little is said regarding its importance in the international context and in creating conditions for effective state regulation, to achieve, among other goals, the creation of private market guarantees and sensible privatisation of state enterprises (Chapters 12 and 13). Stable expectations, based on a reliable civil service, are as crucial as a country's laws, if the aim of aid is to promote economic stability.

Market management

The second promising direction for future aid is to target market construction and financial management. This is the next stage of structural adjustment. The barriers to privatisation and good policies identified in various earlier chapters need to be tackled. The chapter by Irma Adelman, for example, affirms that the desiderata of efficient markets – information, free participation, multiple actors – do not occur readily. State oversight, regulatory mechanisms and provision of corrective ingredients, such as information, are important elements in constructing markets. Markets are not self-provisioning. They require external resources and constraints. The imperfections in markets, dramatised for Asian countries in financial crises of 1997–9, are striking. Aid can be targeted to address these imperfections, certainly in those countries with multiple banking problems, and with heavy debt. Financial markets are of special concern for securing improved frameworks, both to control panic instability and to resolve excessive indebtedness. The pattern of debt crises and economic downturn in the 1990s moved from Mexico to affect a wide array of countries from Indonesia to Russia. And the deep indebtedness of Africa festers, as the failure of debt forgiveness programmes for the most heavily indebted poor states has failed.[21] The most poignant cases exist in Africa. The World Bank, the IMF and the UN agencies have all stressed the need for national governments to take the lead and initiate economic management that addresses their imbalances of globalisation. The basic taxation capacity of many countries is so crippled that they skew their economies toward taxing too heavily the most productive sectors, such as exports, as they are the easiest to reach. This distorts markets, and is unnecessary. Policies can be adopted that involve little bureaucratic cost and more decentralised arrangements (Chapters 12–15). The revenue base for governments could be improved if national level corruption, both official and private, could be lowered.[22]

Poverty and emergency safety nets

The third target for aid is poverty and emergency safety nets. This theme coincides with commitments to poverty reduction at the OECD and the World Bank. Poverty is connected emotionally to emergency relief. International relief assistance plays the role of a safety net for the poorest countries and peoples. The rise in emergency aid coincides with the return to a poverty focus, which had been the central goal of aid in the 1970s prior to policy reform or the structural adjustment ascendance. The treatment of emergency aid as a special, unfortunate use of funds would be replaced by eliminating the emergency to development continuum in aid design. The targets are those poor vulnerable people whose climb from poverty can be set back decades by emergencies. Rescuing them with international assistance, when recipient countries lack the resources to do this, can be linked to long-term strategies both analytically and institutionally. For example, in Bangladesh in 1998, the worst flood in the twentieth century threatened the well-being of 30 million poor and caused $1.5 billion worth of damage. Aid provided by dozens of international agencies protected these endangered people from ruinous effects. The aid was channelled through (and strengthened poverty-oriented) local institutions, both state agencies and non-governmental ones, such as the Grameen Bank. It supported local safety nets and averted the worst consequences of the flood for Bangladesh's most impoverished populations (Kahn 1999). Early warning systems for emergencies also offer a link between information about the conditions of the poor, their needs, and their abilities to adapt to new opportunities following a shock to their lives, a consideration that may offset the rapid expansion of information that otherwise increases rich and poor divides (World Bank 1998b: ch. 8).

Summing up

The three targets discussed above: (i) state strengthening, (ii) market management and (iii) poverty and emergency safety net guarantees all relate to diffuse goals: global goods and economic justice. There is no simple design for aid-use in pursuing these targets, as earlier chapters made clear. Aid channels and modalities to impact these are necessarily context dependent, including emergency aid to protect human capital. What does appear true is that such aid may be more intrusive of sovereignty than previous aid.

Strengthening states appeals broadly to popular concern about threats from the international sphere. Reilly (1999) found that international terrorism, for example, seen as out of control in weak states, was the most frequently cited threat to the United States according to the American public. Support for using aid to improve markets can be found among the development banks, private international financial and corporate institutions, and their government allies in ministries of finance, trade, commerce and legislative bodies. Support for the twin aid goals – sustainable reduction of poverty and emergency responses – involves helping the most vulnerable and comes from the same coalitions generally. It is the poorest, after all, who are most endangered by disasters (natural or man-made). Support for long-term poverty reduction through institutions such as the Grameen Bank is popular with the same groups: NGOs, political parties and foundations concerned about global inequities. These coalitions support emergency humanitarian relief and are frequently the most effective advocates of poverty-oriented aid. Even though emergency aid is criticised as a 'Band-Aid', unsustainable, and even counter to long-term goals, it is supported by the same humanitarian sentiments that put poverty at the top of the aid policy agenda.

Conclusions: future conditions

> Development – economic, social, and sustainable – without an effective state is impossible.
>
> (World Bank 1997a: 18)

A major condition for sustainability of future aid is a belief in its efficacy. Such a belief rests on seeing improvements linked to aid. And this, in turn, is affected by what donors and recipients want improved. Complex social processes shape aid use, including the administrative management of donors and the policies and state machinery of recipients. As noted throughout this volume, state institutions make a big difference in development. Adelman emphasised that 'a government with substantial autonomy, capacity and credibility is required for successful long-term economic growth.' (Chapter 2). North (1990) shares this view, asserting that institution of formal rules, informal norms and enforcement probabilities determine economic growth. He finds a pressing need to understand how third world and East European polities operate in order to promote development through informal constraints. The focus on institutions in this volume pushes future aid toward attention to informal rules that affect states, markets and vulnerabilities of the poor.

Many aid receiving candidates are anarchical states. In Africa and the post-communist world, terms such as patrimonial, shadow, rent-seeking, semi-sovereign, mafia-like and corrupt have been used to characterise the polity. These two areas have been the major foci for aid in the 1990s. Most of the 50–odd wars of this decade are internal and occur in these two areas. Thus the basic capacity of states to deliver security is problematic. As noted in Chapter 17, aid can play a vital role in rescuing peoples from the damage of conflict. It also can assist state formation, helping build administrative structure and analytical or steering capacity. The vital role these play in development processes has been stressed in earlier chapters (e.g. Chapter 2). Aid to these countries, aimed at state reform, may require unconventional development assistance packages. State strengthening would focus on core functions: legitimate force to uphold order, tax collection to finance public goods, technical assistance to enhance military and tax collection skills and controls to limit corruption, encourage civic norms and expand accountability. These and other governance elements need deepening. Withholding aid has been the major tool for political conditionality. This does not work very well because of pressures to release funds already earmarked. Given this problem, and the desire to aid weak states, one goal of aid must be to acknowledge ends that maximise its relation to political performance and minimise the ability of predatory officials to hijack it for private purposes.

For both rich and poor countries, state failure promises to be the greatest threat in coming decades. Openness and sound economic policies are largely irrelevant in situations where capital flight dominates private market financial calculations. For states to 'own' a set of policies, including use of aid, there must first be a state structure. Aid to provide a transition from anarchy must precede aid for a transition to a stable development path. From the states of the former Soviet Union to the collapsed governments in Africa, there is a growing vacuum of political order – a vacuum that aid undertakings are challenged to fill. Aid for political construction requires delicate balancing in which the trade-off between conditionality and ownership is acknowledged. This dilemma is still to be resolved. Yet it must be, so that countries with the greatest needs, often ones most troubled by political upheavals, will not continue to be the ones least able to absorb aid efficiently. Resolutions of the dilemma relate to the three targets for aid discussed earlier. To the extent these targets grow among donor motivations, they will point directly to behavioural obstacles for aid effectiveness, such as corrupt or merely under-skilled human capital. This theme is easier to observe than address. A major future task for research on aid effectiveness is to explain how recipient governments can realise stronger capacity as well as some authentic 'ownership' of their work as a result of aid. Reducing failures of political institutions in recipients requires prescriptions with greater specificity. We need to know how aid can effect real improvements in politics.

This chapter has looked at changing donor motivations and asked what can and should shape future aid. With decay in recipient country institutions a problem, with a rise in support for global goods, such as environmental protection, and with donors enjoying increased scope to demand concessions from aid recipients, targeting aid to save failing political institutions commands and deserves broad support.

Notes

* The author is most grateful for research assistance and advice by Sandip Sukhtankar of Swarthmore College, and to the wisdom provided by two extremely helpful commentaries, Professors Finn Tarp and Steven O'Connell.

1 Most political economy interest addressed in this book focused on how recipient government behaviour affected aid's impact (see Chapters 2 and 18). The most persistent theme by the World Bank and scholars in the 1990s has been how 'good policies' in recipients were crucial to aid effectiveness. Ravi Kanbur notes that in donor–recipient relationships the 'donor is the leader, and decides on the level of aid. The recipient is the follower who, taking as the given the level of aid, decides on actions. . . . The level of aid is thus chosen to maximise the donor's preferences, subject to the reaction function of the recipient. . . .' (Chapter 18).

2 The major debate addressed in Chapter 4 about aid effectiveness is relevant here. Hansen and Tarp's view that aid works even in an unfavourable policy environment implies that targeting vulnerable peoples even in weak states remains a meaningful donor strategy when poverty alleviation is the overriding goal of aid policy.

3 Lumsdaine (1993) suggests altruism has become ascendant, but various studies suggest this has been, at best, a secondary motive (Chapter 3, Alesina and Dollar 1998, McGillivray and White 1993a, Noel and Therien 1995, White 1974 and Wall 1973).

4 Even excluding Marshall Plan funds, US aid in the 1990s was many times higher.

5 NATO members, such as Norway, Denmark and the Netherlands, along with Sweden maintained high levels of aid relative to their GNP, having adopted the UN target for development in national legislation. These four countries are thus denoted UN-target donors in Figure 19.2.

6 In 1992–6 Russia and China received $9 and $16 billion of aid, respectively, amounting to about 10 per cent of all aid during this period (not even counting the growing aid to East Europe and former states of the Soviet Union).

7 Once aid became institutionalised as a practice in international affairs, the regime developed an inertial force of its own. Multiple purposes sustained it (see Chapters 1–4, Lancaster 1999 and Schraeder *et al.* 1998). In classic fashion, by creating international institutions and organisations for aid, the practice of aid has been continued even as older motives for it have weakened (Keohane 1998). The effort of DAC to develop a new rationale for donors, focusing on poverty reduction and co-operation in aid implementation, is such an institutional

adaptation. The bureaucratic reorganisation of bilateral aid agencies, the World Bank and UN development organisations, including their wide adoption of impact criteria to assess aid, are further evidence of adaptive institutional change (see Chapter 18 for further discussion).

8 The concern with disappointment is widely discussed (e.g. Cassen *et al.* 1994, van de Walle 1998, Lancaster 1999 and Chapters 1–4).

9 Political motivations distorting aid effectiveness is a frequent conclusion in economic analyses of aid donor motivations, as noted in Chapter 4 and by Alesina and Dollar (1998).

10 See Bauer (1973) or Boone (1994, 1996).

11 Information obtained from the Web site of JICA (Japan International Co-operation Agency), retrieved in 1999 from the World Wide Web: http://www. jica.go.jp.

12 From an effectiveness perspective, these organisations offer a myriad of advantages and problems in their role in the aid process (e.g. Weiss and Gordenker 1996 and Hulme and Edwards 1997).

13 Aid is targeted to countries largely outside the group of states with rising salience for international politics (see Stremlau 1994 and Chase *et al.* 1998).

14 Fukayama (1992) notes the triumph of liberalism. The widespread and pervasive influence of anti-state and market promoting ideology is explicated in Gray (1998) and Grant and Nijman (1998).

15 Princen and Finger (1994) detail the efforts of this environmental coalition. The advocacy group Bread for the World cites a network of 41 international NGOs that have become powerful advocates on these issues (BFWI 1999).

16 Economic models can capture some aspects of gain, including links of aid to trade patterns (Schraeder *et al.* 1998), but indirect gains from positive externalities of growth, such as unwanted economic migration or cross-border crime, are elusive to estimation.

17 Aid then can be an important resource for particular donor country actors, both private businesses and non-profit humanitarian organisations. These private sector international actors lobby both home and 'partner' country governments to win contracts for providing 'public' goods, e.g. telecommunications or consulting services. In emergencies, for example, there is a group of firms that specialise in the rapid delivery of supplies such as vehicles and camp provisions. Foreign aid is visible pursuit for agencies with fairly hard target allocations at stake. Ravi Kanbur notes the power of such contractor groups in lobbying the World Bank and bilateral donors for releasing committed funds in spite of Ghana's failure to meet agreed conditions for aid (Chapter 18). Aid has subsidised the contracts of national firms doing business with foreign governments and it has rewarded foreign governments for favourable treatment of national firms. Inside donor countries, similar benefits occur. In Canada, for instance, the CIDA is quite explicit about its aid supporting 36,000 employees and notes that 70 per cent of aid is spent in Canada. Universities and research institutes are another part of the pro-aid coalition in most donor countries. More than half of French aid is tied to domestic enterprises and Japan has used its aid to fund joint ventures and public works requiring employment of Japanese firms.

18 The impetus of bureaucracies to maintain or expand their role is a major theme in political analysis, well explained by Lancaster (1999).

19 As cold war rivalry subsided, it created a permissive environment that increased the bargaining strength of remaining donors. The imposition of structural adjustment conditionality in Africa in the 1980s was facilitated by this weakening of manoeuver room for recipients (van de Walle 1998). With no pressures from competing rivals, aid has been delinked from prestige or alliance

considerations. Economic need and prospective performance rise in comparative salience.

20 In 1998-9 the Congo experienced an internal armed conflict with the added fighting among nine armies, eight from neighbouring states: Rwanda, Uganda, Burundi, Angola, Namibia, Sudan, Chad and Zimbabwe.

21 The *New York Times* (1999) reported that only two of 29 eligible countries under the World Bank–IMF Heavily Indebted Poor Countries (HIPC) debt relief initiative had received debt relief after the plan had been announced two and a half years earlier. The World Bank promoted debt relief as a way to fight poverty, and estimated that the cost to donors of waiting one year grew by 30 per cent.

22 African Finance Ministers recognised the dramatic negative impact of capital flight on development, and resolved to 'take the necessary steps to stem and reverse capital flight, including preventing macroeconomic policy lapses or policy inconsistencies, which are likely to trigger, or contribute to capital flight' (ECA 1999).

References

The term 'processed' refers to informally reproduced works that may not be commonly available through library systems.

AAWORD (Association of African Women for Research and Development) (1982) 'The Experience of the Association of African Women for Research and Development (AAWORD)', *Development Dialogue* (1–2): 101–13.

ABD (Aid Book Database) (1999), Statistical annexes on trends in aid flows, prepared by Peter Hjertholm, Development Economics Research Group (DERG), Institute of Economics, University of Copenhagen (available at www.econ.ku.dk/derg/pub.htm).

Ablo, E. and Reinikka, R. (1998) *Do Budgets Really Matter? Evidence from Public Spending on Education and Health in Uganda*, Policy Research Working Paper 1926, Washington, D.C.: World Bank.

Adam, C. and O'Connell, S. (1997) *Aid, Taxation and Development: Analytical Perspectives on Aid Effectiveness in Sub-Saharan Africa*, Working Paper WPS/95-5, Centre for the Study of African Economies, University of Oxford.

Adams, W.M. (1990) *Green Development: Environment and Sustainability in the Third World*, London and New York: Routledge.

Addison, T. and de Sousa, C. (1999) 'Economic Reform and Economic Reconstruction in Mozambique', in O. Morrissey and M. McGillivray (eds) *Structural Adjustment in Developing Countries*, Basingstoke: Macmillan.

Adedeji, A. (1995) 'An African Perspective on Bretton Woods', in M. ul Haq, R. Jolly, P. Streeten and K. Haq (eds) *The UN and Bretton Woods Institutions: New Challenges for the Twenty First Century*, New York: St. Martin's Press.

Adelman, I. (1999) 'State and Market in the Economic Development of Korea and Taiwan', in E. Thorbecke and H. Wan (eds) *Taiwan's Development Experience: Lessons on Roles of State and Market*, Norwell: Kluwer Academic.

Adelman, I. and Morris, C.T. (1967) *Society, Politics and Economic Development: A Quantitative Approach*, Baltimore: Johns Hopkins University Press.

AFDB (1998) *Annual Report*, Abidjan: African Development Bank.

Afshar, H. (ed.) (1991) *Women, Development and Survival in the Third World*, London: Longman.

—— (ed.) (1998) *Women and Empowerment: Illustrations from the Third World*, New York: St. Martin's Press.

Agarwal, S., Lee, K. and Tian, N. (1999) *Trends in International Development Funding*, report prepared for the Center for International Development at the Research Triangle Institute, Terry Sanford Institute of Public Policy, Duke University, Durham.

Aghion, P. and Howitt, P. (1998) *Endogenous Growth Theory*, Cambridge: MIT Press.

Ahmed, N. (1971) 'A Note on the Haavelmo Hypothesis', *Review of Economics and Statistics* 53(4): 413–4.

Alesina, A. and Weder, B. (1999) *Do Corrupt Governments Receive Less Foreign Aid?*, NBER Working Papers 7108, Cambridge: National Bureau of Economic Research.

Alderman, H. and Garcia, M. (1993) *Poverty, Household Food Security and Nutrition in Rural Pakistan*, IFPRI Research Report 96, Washington, D.C.: International Food Policy Research Institute.

Alesina, A. and Dollar, D. (1998) *Who Gives Foreign Aid to Whom and Why?*, NBER Working Papers 6612, Cambridge: National Bureau of Economic Research.

Amin, S. (1973) *Neo-Colonialism in West Africa*, New York: Monthly Review Press.

Anderson, K. and Tyers, R. (1990) 'How Developing Countries Could Gain from Agricultural Trade Liberalization in the Uruguay Round', in I. Goldin and O. Knudsen (eds) *Agricultural Trade Liberalization: Implications for Developing Countries*, Paris: Organisation for Economic Co-operation and Development.

Annan, K. (1998) 'The Causes of Conflict and the Promotion of Durable Peace and Sustainable Development in Africa: Report of the United Nations Secretary-General to the Security Council', in NGLS (ed.) *Conflict, Peace and Reconstruction*, Geneva: United Nations Non-Governmental Liaison Service.

Areskoug, K. (1969) *External Public Borrowing: Its Role in Economic Development*, New York: Praeger.

—— (1973) 'Foreign-Capital Utilization and Economic Policies in Developing Countries', *Review of Economics and Statistics* 55(2): 182–9.

Argyle, B. D. (1983) 'Development Assistance, National Policies, and Lender Type and Performance', in J.D. von Pischke, D.W. Adams and G. Donald (eds) *Rural Financial Markets in Developing Countries: Their Use and Abuse*, Baltimore: Johns Hopkins University Press.

Arndt, T.C. (1996) *Three Essays in the Efficient Treatment of Randomness*, PhD Dissertation, Department of Agricultural Economics, Purdue University.

Aryeetey, E. (1996) 'Rural Finance in Africa: Institutional Developments and Access for the Poor', in M. Bruno and B. Pleskovic (eds) *Annual World Bank Conference on Development Economics, 1996*, Washington, D.C.: World Bank.

Ascher, W. and Healy, R. (1990) *Resource Policymaking in Developing Countries*, Durham: Duke University Press.

ASDB (1998) *Annual Report*, Manila: Asian Development Bank.

Avramovic, D. *et al.* (1964) *Economic Growth and External Debt*, Baltimore: Johns Hopkins University Press (for the World Bank).

Aziz, J. and Wescott, R. (1997) *Policy Complementarities and the Washington Consensus*, IMF Working Paper 97/118, Washington, D.C.: International Monetary Fund.

Babbitt, E. (1999) 'Ethnic Conflict and the Pivotal States', in R. Chase, E. Hill, and P. Kennedy (eds) *The Pivotal States: A New Framework for US Policy in the Developing World*, New York: W.W. Norton & Company.

Bacha, E.L. (1990) 'A Three-Gap Model of Foreign Transfer and the GDP Growth in Developing Countries', *Journal of Development Economics* 32(2): 279–96.

Baden, S. and Goetz, A.M. (1997) 'Who Needs [Sex] When You Can Have [Gender]? Conflicting Discourses on Gender at Beijing', in K.A. Staudt (ed.) *Women, International Development and Politics: The Bureaucratic Mire*, Philadelphia: Temple University Press.

Balasubramanyam, V.N. (1993) 'Economics of the Brain Drain: The Case for a Tax on Brains', in V.N. Balasubramanyam and J.M. Bates (eds) *Topics in Policy Appraisal: Case-Studies in Economic Development*, vol. 2, New York: St. Martin's Press.

Baldwin, R. (1997a) 'The Causes of Regionalism', *The World Economy* 20(5): 865–88.

—— (1997b) 'Review of Theoretical Developments of Regional Integration', in A. Oyejide, I. Elbadawi and P. Collier (eds) *Regional Integration and Trade Liberalization in Sub-Saharan Africa, vol. 1: Framework, Issues and Methodological Perspectives*, Basingstoke: Macmillan.

Barber, B. (1997) 'Feeding Refugees, or War?', *Foreign Affairs* 76(4): 8–14.

Bardhan, P. (1989) *The Economic Theory of Agrarian Institutions*, Oxford: Clarendon Press.

Barnes, S. (1998) 'NGOs in Peace-Keeping Operations: Their Role in Mozambique', *Development in Practice* 8(3): 309–22.

Barrett, C.B. (1998) 'Food Aid: Is It Development Assistance, Trade Promotion, Both or Neither?', *American Journal of Agricultural Economics* 80(3): 566–71.

Barro, R.J. and Sala-i-Martin, X. (1995) *Economic Growth*, New York: McGraw-Hill.

Barro, R.J., Mankiw, N.G. and Sala-i-Martin, X. (1995) 'Capital Mobility in Neoclassical Models of Growth', *American Economic Review* 85(1): 103–15.

Bates, R.H. (1998) 'The Political Framework for Agricultural Policy Decisions', in C.K. Eicher and J.M. Staatz (eds) *International Agricultural Development*, Baltimore: Johns Hopkins University Press.

Bauer, P. (1973) *Dissent on Development*, Cambridge: Harvard University Press.

Bautista, R. and Valdes, A. (eds) (1993) *The Bias Against Agriculture: Trade and Macroeconomic Policies in Developing Countries*, San Francisco: Institute for Contemporary Studies Press (for the International Center for Economic Growth and the International Food Policy Research Institute).

Bennett, A. (1994) *Performance Contracting for Public Enterprises*, papers presented at an expert group meeting, New York, 26–7 April 1994, New York: United Nations Department for Development Support and Management Services.

Berg, E.J., (1993) *Rethinking Technical Co-operation: Reforms for Capacity Building in Africa*, New York: United Nations Development Programme.

—— (1997) 'Dilemmas in Donor Aid Strategies', in C. Gwin and J.M. Nelson (eds) *Perspectives on Aid and Development*, ODC Policy Essay 22, Washington, D.C.: Overseas Development Council.

Bevan, D., Collier, P. and Gunning, J.W. (1992) 'Anatomy of a Temporary Trade Shock: The Kenyan Coffee Boom of 1976–9', *Journal of African Economies* 1(2): 271–305.

BFWI (1999) *The Changing Politics of Hunger: Hunger 1999*, Silver Spring: Bread for the World Institute.

Bhagwati, J.N. (1967) *The Tying of Aid*, UNCTAD Secretariat TD-7/Supplement 4, Geneva: United Nations Conference on Trade and Development.

—— (1993) 'Multilateralism and Regionalism', in J. de Melo and A. Panagariya (eds) *New Dimensions in Regional Integration*, Cambridge: Cambridge University Press (for the Centre for Economic Policy Research).

Bienen, H. (1988) 'Nigeria: From Windfall Gains to Welfare Losses?', in A. Gelb *et al. Oil Windfalls: Blessing or Curse?*, New York: Oxford University Press (for the World Bank).

Binh, T.N. and McGillivray, M. (1993) 'Foreign Aid, Taxes and Public Investment: A Comment', *Journal of Development Economics* 41(1): 173–6.

BIS (1998) *International Banking and Financial Market Developments*, Basle: Bank for International Settlements.

Blake, A., Rayner, A.J. and Reed, G. (1998) Decomposition of the Effects of the Uruguay Round, CREDIT Research Paper 96/16, Centre for Research in Economic Development and International Trade, University of Nottingham.

BMZ (1994) *Financial System Development: Promotion of Savings and Credit*, policy paper, Berlin: Bundesministerium für Wirtschaftliche Zusammenarbeit und Entwicklung (Federal Ministry for Economic Co-operation and Development).

Boone, P. (1994) *The Impact of Foreign Aid on Savings and Growth*, processed, London School of Economics.

—— (1996) 'Politics and the Effectiveness of Foreign Aid', *European Economic Review* 40(2): 289–329.

Boote, A., Kilby, F., Thugge, K. and von Trotsenburg, A. (1997) 'Debt Relief for Low-Income Countries and the HIPC Debt Initiative', in Z. Iqbal and R. Kanbur (eds) *External Finance for Low-Income Countries*, Washington, D.C.: International Monetary Fund.

Booth, K.M. (1998) 'National Mother, Global Whore, and Transnational Femocrats: The Politics of AIDS and the Construction of Women at the World Health Organization', *Feminist Studies* 24(1): 115–39.

Borensztein, E. (1990) 'Debt Overhang, Credit Rationing and Investment', *Journal of Development Economics* 32(2): 315–35.

Bornschier, V., Chase-Dunn, C. and Rubinson, V. (1978) 'Cross-National Evidence of the Effects of Foreign Investment and Aid on Economic Growth and Inequality: A Survey of Findings and a Re-analysis', *American Journal of Sociology* 84(3): 651–83.

Boserup, E. (1970) *Women's Role in Economic Development*, New York: St. Martin's Press.

Bourginon, F., de Melo, J. and Morrison, C. (eds) (1991) 'Special Issue: Adjustment with Growth and Equity', *World Development* 19(11).

Boyce, J.K. (1996) 'El Salvador's Adjustment Toward Peace: An Introduction', in J.K. Boyce (ed.) *Economic Policy for Building Peace: The Lessons of El Salvador*, Boulder: Lynne Rienner.

Boyd, C.G. (1998) 'Making Bosnia Work', *Foreign Affairs* 77(1): 42–55.

Bremer, J., Bell, C. and McKean, C. (1994) *Export and Investment Promotion Services: Service Use and its Impact on Export Performance*, Report no. PN-AAX-278, Washington, D.C.: US Agency for International Development.

Brogan, P. (1998) *World Conflicts*, London: Bloomsbury.

Brown, S. (1990) *Foreign Aid and Tractors*, New York: New York University Press.

Browning, M. and Lusardi, A. (1996) 'Household Saving: Micro Theories and Micro Facts', *Journal of Economic Literature* 34(4): 1797–1855.

Brunetti, A., Kisunko, G. and Weder, B. (1997) *Economic Growth with 'Incredible' Rules: Evidence from a Worldwide Private Sector Survey*, background paper for World Development Report 1997, Washington, D.C.: World Bank.

Bulmer-Thomas, V. (ed.) (1998) 'Special Section: Regional Integration in Central America', *World Development* 26(2): 311–62.

Bulvinic, M. (1983) 'Women's Issues in Third World Poverty: A Policy Analysis', in M. Bulvinic, M. Lycette and W. McGreevey (eds) *Women and Poverty in the Third World*, Baltimore: Johns Hopkins University Press.

Burnside, C. and Dollar, D. (1997) *Aid, Policies and Growth*, Policy Research Working Papers 1777, Washington, D.C.: World Bank.

Buyck, B. (1991) *The Bank's Use of Technical Assistance for Institutional Development*, Policy, Research, and External Affairs Working Papers 578, Washington, D.C.: World Bank.

Cagatay, N., Elson, D. and Grown, C. (1995) 'Gender, Adjustment and Macro-economics: Introduction', *World Development* 23(11): 1827–36.

Cairns, E. (1997) *A Safer Future: Reducing the Human Cost of War*, Oxford: Oxfam.

Camdessus, M. (1997) *Old Battles and New Challenges: A Perspective on Latin America*, Washington, D.C.: International Monetary Fund.

Carvalho, S. and White H. (1996) *Implementing Projects for the Poor: What Has Been Learned?*, processed, Washington, D.C.: World Bank.

Cassels, A. (1997) *A Guide to Sector-Wide Approaches for Health Development: Concepts, Issues and Working Arrangements*, Geneva: World Health Organisation.

Cassen, R. *et al.* (1994) *Does Aid Work?*, Oxford: Clarendon Press.

CCPDC (1997) *Preventing Deadly Conflict*, final report of the Carnegie Commission on Preventing Deadly Conflict, New York: Carnegie Corporation.

CDC (1998) *Annual Report*, London: Commonwealth Development Corporation.

CEC (1996) *Green Paper on Relations Between EU and the ACP Countries on the Eve of the 21st Century*, Brussels: Commission of the European Communities.

Chandler, D. (1998) 'Democratization in Bosnia: The Limits of Civil Society Building Strategies', *Democratization* 5(4): 78–102.

Chang, C.C., Fernandez-Arias, E. and Serven, L. (1998) *Measuring Aid Flows: A New Approach*, processed, Washington, D.C.: World Bank.

Chase, R., Hill, E. and Kennedy, P. (eds) (1998). *The Pivotal States: A New Framework for US Policy in the Developing World*, New York: W.W. Norton & Company.

Chaves, R. A. and Gonzalez-Vega, C. (1996) 'The Design of Successful Rural Financial Intermediaries: Evidence from Indonesia', *World Development* 24(1): 65–78.

Chenery, H.B. (1953) 'Application of Investment Criteria', *Quarterly Journal of Economics* 67(February): 76–96.

—— (1960) 'Patterns of Industrial Growth', *American Economic Review* 50(4): 624–54

Chenery, H.B. and Eckstein, P. (1970) 'Development Alternatives for Latin America', *Journal of Political Economy* 78(4): 966–1006.

Chenery, H.B. and Strout, A.M. (1966) 'Foreign Assistance and Economic Development', *American Economic Review* 56(4): 679–733.

Chenery, H.B. and Taylor, L. (1968) 'Development Patterns: Among Countries and Over Time', *Review of Economics and Statistics* 50(4): 391–416.

Chenery, H.B. Ahluwalia M.S., Bell, C.L.G., Duloy, J.H. and Jolly, R. (eds) (1974) *Redistribution with Growth*, New York: Oxford University Press.

Chibber, A. (1998) 'Institutions, Policies and Development Outcomes', in R. Picciotto and E. Wiesner (eds) *Evaluation and Development: The Institutional Dimension*, New Brunswick and London: Transaction Publishers (for the World Bank).

Chowdhry, G. (1995) 'Engendering Development? Women in Development (WID) in International Development Regimes', in M.H. Marchand and J.L. Parpart (eds) *Feminism/Postmodernism/Development*, London and New York: Routledge.

Christen, R.P., Rhyne, E. and Vogel, R. (1994) *Maximising the Outreach of Microfinance: An Analysis of Successful Microfinance Programs*, Programs and Operations Assessment Report 10, Washington, D.C.: US Agency for International Development.

CIDA (1993) *Jamaica Export Promotion (CANEXPORT) Project*, Toronto: Canadian International Development Agency.

Cissé, N.D. (1994) *The Impact of Performance Contracts on Public Enterprise Performance*, paper presented at a World Bank conference on 'Changing Role of the State: Strategies for Reforming Public Enterprises', Washington, D.C.: World Bank.

Claessens, S., Detragiache, E., Kanbur, R. and Wickham, P. (1997) 'HIPCs' Debt: Review of the Issues', *Journal of African Economies* 6(2): 231–54.

Clarke, W. and Herbst, J. (1997) *Learning from Somalia: The Lessons of Armed Humanitarian Intervention*, Boulder: Westview Press.

Clay, E. and Benson, C. (1990) 'Aid for Food: Acquisition of Commodities in Developing Countries for Food Aid in the 1980s', *Food Policy* 15(1): 27–43.

Clay, E., Dhiri, S. and Benson, C. (1996) *Joint Evaluation of European Union Programme Food Aid: Synthesis Report and Summary of Synthesis Report*, study commissioned by the Working Group of Heads of Evaluation Service (Development) of the European Union, London: Overseas Development Institute.

Coate, S. (1995) 'Altruism, the Samaritan's Dilemma, and Government Transfer Policy', *American Economic Review* 85(1): 46–57.

Coate, S. and Morris, S. (1996) *Policy Conditionality*, processed, Department of Economics, University of Pennsylvania.

Cohen, D. (1996) *The Sustainability of African Debt*, World Bank Policy Research Paper 1621, Washington, D.C.: World Bank.

Cohen, M.J. and Pinstrup-Andersen, P. (1998) *Food Security and Conflict*, Washington, D.C.: International Food Policy Research Institute.

Collier, P. (1997) 'The Failure of Conditionality', in C. Gwin and J.M. Nelson (eds) *Perspectives on Aid and Development*, ODC Policy Essay 22, Washington, D.C.: Overseas Development Council.

Collier, P. and Dollar, D. (1999) *Aid Allocation and Poverty Reduction*, Policy Research Working Papers 2041, Washington, D.C.: World Bank.

Collier, P. and Gunning, J.W. (1997) *Explaining African Economic Performance*, Working Paper WPS/97-2.2, Centre for the Study of African Economies, University of Oxford.

Collier, P., Guillaumont, P. Guillaumont, S. and Gunning, J.W. (1997) 'The Future of Lomé: Europe's Role in African Growth', *The World Economy* 20(3): 285–305.

Commander, S., Davoodi, H. and Lee, U.J. (1996) *The Causes and Consequences of Government for Growth and Well-being*, background paper for World Development Report 1997, Washington, D.C.: World Bank.

Commonwealth Secretariat (1989) *Engendering Adjustment for the 1990s*, London: Commonwealth Secretariat.

Cooper, R.N. and Sachs, J.D. (1985) 'Borrowing Abroad: The Debtor's Perspective', in G.W. Smith and J.T. Cuddington (eds) *International Debt and the Developing Countries*, Washington, D.C.: World Bank.

Corbo, V. and Fischer, S. (1995) 'Structural Adjustment, Stabilisation and Policy Reform: Domestic and International Finance', in J. Behrman and T.N. Srinivasan (eds) *Handbook of Development Economics*, vol. 3b, Amsterdam: Elsevier.

Corbo, V., Fischer, S. and Webb, S.B. (eds) (1992) *Adjustment Lending Revisited: Policies to Restore Growth*, Washington, D.C.: World Bank.

Corden, W.M. and Neary, P.J. (1982) 'Booming Sector and De-Industrialisation in a Small Open Economy', *Economic Journal* 92(368): 825–48.

Cornia, G., Jolly, R. and Stewart, F. (1987) *Adjustment with a Human Face: Protecting the Vulnerable and Promoting Growth*, Oxford: Clarendon Press.

Cox, A., Healey J., Hoebink, P. and Voipio, T. (2000) *European Development Co-operation and the Poor*, Basingstoke: Macmillan.

Cramer, C. and Weeks, J. (1998), 'Conditionality and Conflict Reduction', in F. Stewart, W. Nafziger and R. Vayrynen (eds) *Economic Causes of Conflict*, Oxford: Oxford University Press.

Crisp, J. (1998) *The 'Post-Conflict' Concept: Some Critical Observations*, Geneva: United Nations High Commissioner for Refugees.

Cropper, M. and Griffiths, C. (1994) 'The Interaction of Population Growth and Environmental Quality', *American Economic Review* 84(2): 250–4.

Curto, S. (1998) Review of Social Policy in Selected Fund Programs, processed, Kiel: Institut für Weltwirtschaft.

Danida (1995) *Review of the Danish PSD Programme*, Copenhagen: Ministry of Foreign Affairs.

—— (1998a) *Guidelines for Sector Programme Support*, Copenhagen: Ministry of Foreign Affairs.

—— (1998b) *Support for Rural Financial Services*, Technical Working Paper, Copenhagen: Ministry of Foreign Affairs.

Dasgupta, P. and Mäler, K.G. (1995) 'Poverty, Institutions and the Environmental Resource Base', in J. Behrman and T.N. Srinivasan (eds) *Handbook of Development Economics*, vol. 3, Amsterdam: Elsevier.

Datta-Mitra, J. (1997) *Fiscal Management in Adjustment Lending*, Operations Evaluation Study, Washington, D.C.: World Bank.

Davidson, B. (1992) *The Black Man's Burden: Africa and the Curse of the Nation State*, New York: Times Books.

Dean, J., Desai, S. and Riedel, J. (1994) *Trade Policy Reform in Developing Countries Since 1985: A Review of the Evidence*, World Bank Discussion Papers 267, Washington, D.C.: World Bank.

de Groot, J. (1991) 'Conceptions and Misconceptions: The Historical and Cultural Context of Discussion on Women and Development', in H. Afshar (ed.) *Women, Development and Survival in the Third World*, London: Longman.

de Janvry, A., Sadoulet, E. and Thorbecke, E. (1993) 'Introduction to State, Market, and Civil Organizations: New Theories, New Practices, and Their Implications for Rural Development', *World Development* 21(4): 565–75.

Demery, L. and Squire, L. (1996) 'Macroeconomic Adjustment and Poverty in Africa: An Emerging Picture', *World Bank Research Observer* 11(1): 39–59.

Demery, L. and Walton, M. (1998) *Are Poverty Reduction and Other 21st Century Social Goals Attainable?*, Washington, D.C.: World Bank.

Dervis, K., de Melo, J. and Robinson, S. (1982) *General Equilibrium Models for Developing Countries*, London: Cambridge University Press.

DeSombre, E.R. and Kauffman, J. (1996) 'The Montreal Protocol Multilateral Fund: Partial Success Story', in R.O. Keohane and M.A. Levy (eds) *Institutions for Environmental Aid: Pitfalls and Promise*, Cambridge: MIT Press.

de Soysa, I. and Gleditsch, N.P. (1999) *To Cultivate Peace – Agriculture in a World of Conflict*, PRIO Report 1/99, Oslo: International Peace Research Institute.

de Waal, A. (1997) *Famine Crimes: Politics and the Disaster Relief Industry in Africa*, Oxford: James Curry and Bloomington: Indiana University Press (for Africa Rights and the International Africa Institute).

DFID (1997) *Eliminating World Poverty: A Challenge for the 21st Century*, White Paper, London: Department For International Development.

—— (1999) *Statistics on International Development 1993/94–1997/98*, London: Department For International Development.

Dia, M. (1993) *A Governance Approach to Civil Service Reform in Sub-Saharan Africa*, World Bank Technical Paper 225, Washington, D.C.: World Bank.

Diamond, P.A. and Hausman, J.A. (1994) 'Contingent Valuation: Is Some Number Better than No Number?', *Journal of Economic Perspectives* 8(4), 45–64.

Díaz-Alejandro, C.F. (1981) 'Southern Core Stabilization Plans', in W.R. Cline and S. Weintraub (eds) *Economic Stabilization in Developing Countries*, Washington, D.C.: Brookings Institution.

Dichter, T. W. (1996) 'Questioning the Future of NGOs in Microfinance', *Journal of International Development* 8(2): 259–69.

Dixon, J.A., Scura, L.F., Carpenter, R.A. and Shernan, P.B. (1994) *Economic Analysis of Environmental Impacts*, London: Earthscan.

Dowling, M. and Hiemenz, U. (1982) *Aid, Savings and Growth in the Asian Region*, Economic Office Report Series 3, Manila: Asian Development Bank.

Duffield, M. (1998) *Aid Policy and Post-Modern Conflict: A Critical Review*, Relief and Rehabilitation Network Newsletter 11, London: Overseas Development Institute.

—— (1999) *Internal Conflict: Adaptation and Reaction to Globalisation*, Corner House Briefing 12, Sturminster Newton: The Corner House.

Durbarry, R., Gemmell, N. and Greenaway, D. (1998) *New Evidence on the Impact of Foreign Aid on Economic Growth*, CREDIT Research Paper 98/8, Centre for Research in Economic Development and International Trade, University of Nottingham.

Dziobek, C. and Pazarbasioglu, C. (1997) *Lessons from Systemic Bank Restructuring: A Survey of 24 Countries*, IMF Working Paper WP/97/161, Washington, D.C.: International Monetary Fund.

Easterly, W. (1997) *The Ghost of Financing Gap: How the Harrod–Domar Growth Model Still Haunts Development Economics*, processed, Washington, D.C.: World Bank.

Easterly, W. and Levine, R. (1997) 'Africa's Growth Tragedy: Policies and Ethnic Divisions', *Quarterly Journal of Economics* 112(4): 1203–50.

EBRD (1997) *Transition Report 1997: Enterprise Performance and Growth*, London: European Bank for Reconstruction and Development.

EC (1997) *Long-Term Prospects: Grains, Milk, and Meat Markets*, CAP 2000 Working Document, Brussels: European Commission.

ECA (1999) *Economic Report on Africa 1999: The Challenges of Poverty Reduction and Sustainablity*, Addis Ababa: Economic Commission for Africa (United Nations).

Eckstein, A. (1957) 'Investment Criteria for Economic Development and the Theory of Intertemporal Welfare Economics', *Quarterly Journal of Economics* 71(1): 56–85.

EDFI (1998) *Annual Report*, Brussels: European Development Finance Institutions.

Edwards, S. (1998) 'Openness, Productivity and Growth: What Do We Really Know?', *Economic Journal* 108(447): 383–98.

Elbadawi, I. (1998) *External Aid: Help or Hindrance to Export Orientation in Africa*, processed, Nairobi: African Economic Research Consortium.

Elson, D. (1995) 'Gender Awareness in Modelling Structural Adjustment', *World Development* 23(11): 1851–68.

—— (1998) 'Talking to the Boys: Gender and Economic Growth Models', in C. Jackson and R. Pearson (eds) *Feminist Visions of Development: Gender Analysis and Policy*, London and New York: Routledge.

Elson, D. and Evers, B. (1996) *Gender Aware Country Economic Reports: Uganda*, Working Paper 2, Gender and Development Economics Unit (GENECON), Graduate School of Social Sciences, University of Manchester.

Engberg, U. and Stubbs, P. (1999) *Social Capital and Integrated Development: A Civil Society Grants Programme in Travnik, Bosnia-Herzegovina*, Developments in Global Social Policy Occasional Paper 2, Globalism and Social Policy (GASPP), National Research and Development Centre for Welfare and Health (STAKES), Helsinki and Centre for Research on Globalisation and Social Policy, Department of Sociological Studies, University of Sheffield.

Evenson, R.E. and Westphal, L.E. (1995) 'Technological Change and Technology Strategy', in J. Behrman and T.N. Srinivasan (eds) *Handbook of Development Economics*, vol. 3a, Amsterdam: Elsevier.

Fairman, D. (1996) 'The Global Environment Facility: Haunted by the Shadow of the Future', in R.O. Keohane and M.A. Levy (eds) *Institutions for Environmental Aid: Pitfalls and Promise*, Cambridge: MIT Press.

FAO (various issues) *Food Outlook*, Rome: Food and Agriculture Organization.

FDI (1992) *Private Sector Development: Lessons of Experience and Prospects for the Future: A Survey of Multi and Bilateral Aid Agencies Prepared for Danida*, Copenhagen: Federation of Danish Industries.

Fei, J.C.H. and Paauw, D.S. (1965) 'Foreign Assistance and Self-Help: A Reappraisal of Development Finance', *Review of Economics and Statistics* 47(3): 251–67.

Fei, J.C.H. and Ranis, G. (1964) *Development of the Labor Surplus Economy*, Homewood: Irwin.

Ferguson, P.R. and Ferguson, G.J (1988) *Industrial Economics: Issues and Perspectives*, Basingstoke: Macmillan.

Feyzioglu, T., Swaroop, V. and Zhu, M. (1998) 'A Panel Data Analysis of the Fungibility of Foreign Aid', *World Bank Economic Review* 12(1): 29–58.

Fieldhouse, D.K. (1983) *Black Africa 1945–1980: Economic Decolonization and Arrested Development*, London: Allen and Unwin.

Fielding, D. (1997) 'Modelling the Determinants of Government Spending in Sub-Saharan Africa', *Journal of African Economies* 6(3): 377–90.

Fine, J. and Yeo, S. (1997) 'Regional Integration in Sub-Saharan Africa: Dead End or a Fresh Start?', in A. Oyejide, I. Elbadawi and P. Collier (eds) *Regional Integration and Trade Liberalization in Sub-Saharan Africa, vol. 1: Framework, Issues and Methodological Perspectives*, Basingstoke: Macmillan.

Fitzpatrick, J. and Hansch, S. (1990) *Food Aid Cost Effectiveness*, Rome: Food and Agriculture Organization of the United Nations.

Forss, K., Carlsen, J., Froyland, E., Sitari, T. and Vilby, K (1990) *Evaluation of the Effectiveness of Technical Assistance Personnel Financed by Nordic Countries*, Copenhagen: Ministry of Foreign Affairs.

Fox, K., Sengupta, J.K. and Thorbecke, E. (1972) *The Theory of Quantitative Economic Policies*, Amsterdam: North-Holland.

Franco-Rodriguez, S., Morrissey, O. and McGillivray, M. (1998) 'Aid and the Public

Sector in Pakistan: Evidence with Endogenous Aid', *World Development* 26(7): 1241–50.

Franz, W.E. (1996) 'The Scope of Global Environmental Financing: Cases in Context, in R.O. Keohane and M.A. Levy (eds) *Institutions for Environmental Aid: Pitfalls and Promise*, Cambridge: MIT Press.

Fraser, N. (1997) *Justice Interruptus: Critical Reflections on the 'Post Socialist' Condition*, London and New York: Routledge.

Frischmuth, C. (1997) *Gender is Not a Sensitive Issue: Institutionalising a Gender-Oriented Participatory Approach in Siavonga, Zambia*, SARL Gatekeeper Series 72, Sustainable Agriculture and Rural Livelihoods Programme, London: International Institute for Environment and Development.

Fry, M. J. (1995) *Money, Interest, and Banking in Economic Development*, Baltimore: Johns Hopkins University Press.

Fukayama, F. (1992) *The End of History and the Last Man*, New York: The Free Press.

Fukuda-Parr, S. (1996) 'Beyond Rethinking Technical Co-operation: Priorities for Capacity Building and Capacity Utilisation in Africa', *International Journal of Technical Co-operation* 2(2): 145–7.

Galenson, W. and Leibenstein, H. (1955) 'Investment Criteria, Productivity and Economic Development', *Quarterly Journal of Economics* 69(3): 343–70.

Gallagher, M. (1994) 'Government Spending in Africa: A Retrospective of the 1980s', *Journal of African Economies* 3(1): 62–92.

Gang, I.N. and Khan, H.A. (1991) 'Foreign Aid, Taxes, and Public Investment', *Journal of Development Economics* 34(1–2): 355–69.

Garson, J. (1996) *Microfinance: A Donor Perspective*, United Nations Capital Development Fund, New York: United Nations Development Programme.

GATT (1993) *An Analysis of the Proposed Uruguay Round Agreement with Particular Emphasis on Aspects of Interest to Developing Countries*, Geneva: General Agreement on Tariffs and Trade Secretariat.

Gelb, A. and P. Honohan (1991) 'Financial Sector Reform', in V. Thomas, A. Chhibber, M. Dailami and J. de Melo (eds) *Restructuring Economies in Distress: Policy Reform and the World Bank*, New York: Oxford University Press (for the World Bank).

German, T. and Randel, J. (1998) 'Targeting the End of Absolute Poverty; Trends in Development Co-operation', in J. Randel and T. German (eds) *The Reality of Aid 1998/1999: An Independent Review of Poverty Reduction and Development Assistance*, London: Earthscan Publications for Eurostep (European Solidarity Towards Equal Participation of People) and ICVA (International Council of Voluntary Agencies).

Ghate, P. B. (1992) 'Interaction Between the Formal and Informal Financial Sectors: The Asian Experience', *World Development* 20(6): 859–72.

Gibbon, P., Havnevik, K. and Hermele, K. (1993) *A Blighted Harvest: The World Bank and African Agriculture in the 1980s*, London: James Currey and Trenton: Africa World Press.

Gillis, M., Perkins, D.H., Roemer, M. and Snodgrass, D.R. (1996) *Economics of Development*, New York: W.W. Norton & Company.

Gilpin, R. (1987) *The Political Economy of International Relations*, Princeton: Princeton University Press.

Glewwe, P. and van der Gaag, J. (1990) 'Identifying the Poor in Developing Countries: Do Different Definitions Matter?', *World Development* 18(6): 803–14.

Goetz, A.M. (1996) *Local Heroes: Patterns of Field Worker Discretion in Implementing GAD Policy in Bangladesh*, IDS Discussion Paper 358, Institute of Development Studies, University of Sussex.

—— (ed.) (1997) *Getting Institutions Right for Women in Development*, London and New York: Zed Books.

Goldstein, M. and Turner, P. (1996) *Banking Crises in Emerging Economies: Origins and Policy Options*, Economic Papers 46, Basle: Bank for International Settlements.

Goodhand, J. and Hulme, D. (1997) *NGOs and Peace Building in Complex Political Emergencies: An Introduction*, NGOs and Complex Political Emergencies Working Paper 1, Oxford: International NGO Training and Research Centre.

Goodland, R. (1996) *What is Environmental Sustainability in the Energy Sector? The 'Big Dams' Debate*, paper presented at a conference at the Agricultural University of Sweden, Uppsala, June 1996.

Gordon, A.A. (1996) *Transforming Capitalism and Patriarchy*, Boulder and London: Lynne Rienner.

Gould, J., Takala, T. and Nokkala, M. (1998) *How Sectoral Programs Work: An Analysis of Education and Agriculture Sector Programs in Zambia, Ethiopia, Mozambique and Nepal*, Policy Papers 1/1998, Institute of Development Studies, University of Helsinki.

Gourevitch, P. (1998a) *We Wish to Inform You That Tomorrow We Will be Killed with Our Families: Stories from Rwanda*, New York: Farrar, Straus and Giroux.

—— (1998b) 'The Genocide Fax', *The New Yorker* (May 11): 42–6.

Grabher, G. (ed.) (1993) *The Embedded Firm: On the Socioeconomics of Industrial Networks*, London and New York: Routledge.

Graham, C. and O'Hanlon, M. (1997) 'Making Foreign Aid Work', *Foreign Affairs* 76(4): 8–14.

Grant, J. P. (1990) *The State of the World's Children 1990*, Oxford: Oxford University Press (for Unicef).

Grant, R. and Nijman, J. (eds) (1998) *The Global Crisis In Foreign Aid*, Syracuse: Syracuse University Press.

Gray, J. (1998) *False Dawn: The Delusions of Global Capitalism*, London: Granta Books.

Greenaway, D. (1993) 'Liberalizing Foreign Trade Through Rose-Tinted Glasses', *Economic Journal* 103(416): 208–22.

—— (1999) Multilateralism, Minilateralism and Trade Expansion, processed, background paper for Asian Development Bank Study of Asia's Exports.

Greenaway, D. and Morrissey, O. (1993) 'Structural Adjustment and Liberalisation in Developing Countries: What Lessons Have We Learned?', *Kyklos* 46(2): 241–61.

—— (1994) 'Trade Liberalisation and Economic Growth in Developing Countries', in S.M. Murshed and K. Raffer (eds) *Trade Transfers and Development*, London: Edward Elgar.

Greenaway, D., Morgan, C.W. and Wright, P. (1998) 'Trade Reform, Adjustment and Growth: What Does the Evidence Tell Us?', *Economic Journal* 108(450): 1547–61.

Greene, J.E. and Khan, M.S. (1990) *The African Debt Crisis*, AERC Special Paper 3, Nairobi: African Economic Research Consortium.

Greene, J.E. and Villanueva, D. (1990) *Private Investment in Developing Countries: An Empirical Analysis*, IMF Working Paper WP/90/40, Washington, D.C.: International Monetary Fund.

Griffin, K.B (1970) 'Foreign Capital, Domestic Savings and Economic Development', *Bulletin of the Oxford University Institute of Economics and Statistics* 32(2): 99–112.

Griffin, K.B. and Enos, J.L. (1970) 'Foreign Assistance: Objectives and Consequences', *Economic Development and Cultural Change* 18(3): 313–27.

Grindle, M.S. and Hilderbrand, M.E. (1995) 'Building Sustainable Capacity in the Public Sector: What Can Be Done?', *Public Administration and Development* 15(5): 441–63.

Grootaert, C. and Kanbur, R. (1995) 'The Lucky Few amidst Economic Decline: Distributional Change in Côte d'Ivoire as Seen Through Panel Data Sets, 1985–88', *Journal of Development Studies* 31(4): 603–19.

Grossman, G.M. and Krueger, A.B. (1995) 'Economic Growth and the Environment', *Quarterly Journal of Economics* 110(2): 353–77.

Groth, C. (1990) *Noter til økonomisk vækst* (Notes on Economic Growth), vol. 1–2, Memo 14 and 27, Institute of Economics, University of Copenhagen (in Danish).

Guillamont, P. and Chauvet, L. (1999) *Aid and Performance: A Reassessment*, Working Paper 9910, Clermont-Ferrand: Centre d'Etudes et de Recherches sur le Développement International (CERDI), Université d'Auvergne.

Gupta, K.L. (1970) 'Foreign Capital and Domestic Savings: A Test of Haavelmo's Hypothesis with Cross-Country Data: A Comment', *Review of Economics and Statistics* 52(2): 214–6.

—— (1975) 'Foreign Capital Inflows, Dependency Burden, and Saving Rates in Developing Countries: A Simultaneous Equation Model', *Kyklos* 28(2): 358–74.

Gupta, K.L. and Islam, M.A. (1983) *Foreign Capital, Savings and Growth – An International Cross-Section Study*, Dordrecht: Reidel Publishing Company.

Gupta, P.S. (1975) *Imperialism and the British Labour Movement 1914–64*, Basingstoke: Macmillan.

Gwin, C. and Nelson, J.M. (eds) (1997) *Perspectives on Aid and Development*, ODC Policy Essay 22, Washington, D.C.: Overseas Development Council.

Hadjimichael, M.T. and Ghura, D. (1995) *Public Policies and Private Investment in Sub-Saharan Africa: An Empirical Investigation*, IMF Working Paper WP/95/19, Washington, D.C.: International Monetary Fund.

Hadjimichael, M.T., Ghura, D., Mühleisen, M., Nord, R. and Uçer, E.M. (1995) *Sub-Saharan Africa: Growth, Savings, and Investment, 1986–93*, Occasional Papers 118, Washington, D.C.: International Monetary Fund.

Haggard, S., Lee, C.H. and Maxfield, S. (eds) (1993) *The Politics of Finance in Developing Countries*, Ithaca: Cornell University Press.

Halevi, N. (1976) 'The Effects on Investment and Consumption of Import Surpluses of Developing Countries', *Economic Journal* 86(344): 853–8.

Hanmer, L., Pyatt, G. and White, H. (1996) *Poverty in Sub-Saharan Africa: What can we Learn from the World Bank's Poverty Assessments?*, The Hague: Institute of Social Studies.

Hansen, H. and Tarp, F. (1999) *The Effectiveness of Foreign Aid*, processed, Development Economics Research Group, Institute of Economics, University of Copenhagen.

Hansen, S. (1989) 'Debt for Nature Swaps: Overview and Discussion of Key Issues', *Ecological Economics* 1(1): 77–93.

Hardiman, M. and Midgley, J. (1982) *The Social Dimensions of Development*, London: Wiley.

Harris, J.R. and Todaro, M.P. (1970) 'Migration, Unemployment and Development: A Two-Sector Analysis', *American Economic Review* 60(1): 126–42.

Harrold, P. (1995) *The Broad Sector Approach to Investment Lending: Sector Investment Programs*, World Bank Discussion Papers 302, Washington, D.C.: World Bank.

Hayter, T. and Watson, C. (1985) *Aid: Rhetoric and Reality*, London: Pluto Press.

Heiberg, A.N. (1998) *The Humanitarian Challenge in a World of Conflict: The Plight of Land-mine Victims*, Fridtjof Nansen Memorial Lecture 1998, Tokyo: United Nations University.

Heller, P.S. (1975) 'A Model of Public Fiscal Behavior in Developing Countries: Aid, Investment, and Taxation', *American Economic Review* 65(3): 429–45.

Heltberg, R. (1995) 'Biologisk mangfoldighed og udvikling' (Development and Biological Diversity), *Nationaløkonomisk Tidsskrift* 133(3): 236–51 (in Danish).

Hemphill, W. (1974) 'The Effects of Foreign Exchange Receipts on Imports of Less Developed Countries', *International Monetary Fund Staff Papers* 21(3): 637–77.

Henderson, D. and Loxley, J. (1997) *The African Economic Research Consortium: An Evaluation and Review*, AERC Special Paper 25, Nairobi: African Economic Research Consortium.

Herbst, J. (1998) 'African Armies and Regional Peacekeeping: Are There African Solutions to African Problems?', in R. Rotberg and G. Mills (eds) *War and Peace in Southern Africa*, Washington, D.C.: Brookings Institution Press and the World Peace Foundation.

Hernandez-Cata, E. (1988) *Issues in the Design of Growth Exercises*, IMF Working Paper WP/88/65, Washington, D.C.: International Monetary Fund.

Hill, C.B. (1991) 'Managing Commodity Booms in Botswana', *World Development* 19(9): 1185–96.

Hirshman, A.O. (1958) *The Strategy of Economic Development*, New Haven: Yale University Press.

Hirshman, M. (1995) 'Women and Development: A Critique', in M.H. Marchand and J.L. Parpart (eds) *Feminism/Postmodernism/Development*, London and New York: Routledge.

Hjertholm, P. (1997a) *An Inquiry Into the Fiscal Dimension of External Debt: The Case of Sub-Saharan Africa*, Ph.D. Thesis, Red Series 43, Institute of Economics, University of Copenhagen.

—— (1997b) *Den private og offentlige sektor i u-landenes økonomiske udvikling* (The Private and Public Sector in the Economic Development of Developing Countries), background paper prepared for the Danish Ministry of Foreign Affairs (Danida), Institute of Economics, University of Copenhagen (in Danish).

Hjertholm, P. and White, H. (2000) *Survey of Foreign Aid: History, Trends and Allocation*, Discussion Papers 00–04, Institute of Economics, University of Copenhagen.

Hjertholm, P., Laursen, J. and White, H. (2000) *Macroeconomic Issues in Foreign Aid*, Discussion Papers 00–05, Institute of Economics, University of Copenhagen.

Hodgson, D. and Watkins, S.C. (1997) 'Feminists and Neo-Malthusians: Past and Present Alliances', *Population and Development* Review 23(3): 469–523.

Hoffman, S. (1999) *World Disorders: Troubled Peace in the Post-Cold War Era*, Lanham: Rowman and Littlefield.

Holden, S.T., Shiferaw, B. and Wik, M. (1998) 'Poverty, Market Imperfections and Time Preferences: Of Relevance for Environmental Policy?', *Environment and Development Economics* 3(1): 105–30.

Hopkins, R.F. (1995) 'Anomie, System Reform, and Challenges to the UN System', in M.J. Esman and S. Telhami (eds) *International Organizations and Ethnic Conflict*, Ithaca: Cornell University Press.

Hulme, D. and Edwards M. (1997) *NGOs, States and Donors: Too Close for Comfort?*, New York: St. Martin's Press.

Humphrey, J. and Schmitz, H (1995) *Principles for Promoting Clusters and Networks of SMEs*, Vienna: United Nations Industrial Development Organization.

Hunt, K. (1999) 'Bosnian Women's Initiative: Making a Difference', *The Forced Migration Monitor* 27(January): 1–6.

Huther, J., Roberts, S. and Shah, A. (1998) *Public Expenditure Reform under Adjustment Lending: Lessons from World Bank Experience*, World Bank Discussion Papers 382, Washington, D.C.: World Bank.

IFC (1998) *Annual Report*, Washington, D.C.: International Finance Corporation.

IFPRI (1998) 'The Changing Outlook for Food Aid', *News and Views* (November: 1–6), 2020 Vision Initiative, Washington, D.C.: International Food Policy Research Institute.

IFU (1998) *Annual Report*, Copenhagen: Industrialization Fund for Developing Countries.

—— (1999) *30 Years Report*, Copenhagen: Industrialization Fund for Developing Countries.

Ignatieff, M. (1998) *The Warrior's Honor: Ethnic War and the Modern Conscience*, London: Chatto and Windus.

IIC (1998) *Annual Report*, Washington, D.C.: Inter-American Investment Corporation.

ILO (1973) *Employment, Income and Equality: A Strategy for Increasing Productive Employment in Kenya*, Geneva: International Labour Organization.

IMAC (1996), *Accountability and Financial Management Issues in Sectoral Assistance Programmes*, presentation notes, Washington, D.C.: Institute for Management and Accounting.

IMF (1998) *The IMF's Response to the Asian Crisis*, Factsheet, April 1998, External Relations Department, Washington, D.C.: International Monetary Fund.

Iqbal, Z. and Kanbur, R. (eds) (1997) *External Finance in Low-Income Countries*, Washington, D.C.: International Monetary Fund.

Jackson, C. (1998) 'Rescuing Gender from the Poverty Trap', in C. Jackson and R. Pearson (eds) *Feminist Visions of Development: Gender, Analysis and Policy*, London and New York: Routledge.

Jahan, R. (1995) *The Elusive Agenda: Mainstreaming Women in Development*, London and New York: Zed Books.

—— (1997) 'Mainstreaming Women in Development: Four Agency Approaches', in K.A. Staudt (ed.) *Women, International Development, and Politics: The Bureaucratic Mire*, Philadelphia: Temple University Press.

Jakobeit, C. (1996) 'Nonstate Actors Leading the Way: Debt-for-Nature Swaps', in R.O. Keohane and M.A. Levy (eds) *Institutions for Environmental Aid: Pitfalls and Promise*, Cambridge: MIT Press.

Jansson, T. and Wenner, M.D. (1997) *Financial Regulation and its Significance for Microfinance in Latin America and the Caribbean*, Washington, D.C.: Inter-American Development Bank.

Jaquette, J. S. and Staudt, K.A. (1985) 'Women as "At Risk" Reproducers: Biology, Science, and Population In us Foreign Policy', in V. Sapiro (ed.) *Women, Biology, and Public Policy*, Beverly Hills: Sage Publications.

Jayarajah, C.A.B. and Branson, W.H. (1995) *Structural and Sectoral Adjustment: World Bank Experience, 1980–92*, Operations Evaluation Study, Washington, D.C.: World Bank.

Jaycox, E.V.K., (1993) *Capacity Building: The Missing Link in African Development*, address to the African–American Institute Conference, May 20 1993.

Jodha, N.S. (1989) 'Social Science Research on Rural Change: Some Gaps', in P. Bardhan (ed.) *Conversations Between Economists and Anthropologists: Methodological Issues in Measuring Economic Change in Rural India*, New Delhi: Oxford University Press.

Johnston, B.F. and Kilby, P. (1975) *Agriculture and Structural Transformation*, London: Oxford University Press.

Jones, S. (1997) *Sector Investment Programmes in Sub-Saharan Africa: Review of Issues and Experience*, Oxford: Oxford Policy Management.

Kabeer, N. (1997) *Reversed Realities: Gender Hierarchies in Development Thought*, London and New York: Verso.

Kahler, M. (1990) 'Orthodoxy and its Alternatives: Explaining Approaches to Stabilization and Adjustment', in J. Nelson (ed.) *Economic Crisis and Policy Choice: The Politics of Economic Adjustment in the Third World*, Princeton: Princeton University Press.

Kahn, O. (1999) *Bangladesh Floods 1998 and Food Security*, paper prepared for Harvard University Conference on Natural Disasters in Asia, May 1999, Cambridge.

Kanbur, R. (1995) 'Welfare Economics, Political Economy, and Policy Reform in Ghana', *African Development Review* 7(1): 35–49.

—— (1998) *A Framework for Thinking Through Reduced Aid Dependence*, paper presented to the Overseas Development Council/AERC Collaborative Research Workshop on Transition to Less Aid Dependence in Africa, Nairobi: African Economic Research Consortium.

—— (1999) 'Prospective and Retrospective Conditionality: Practicalities and Fundamentals', in P. Collier and C. Pattillo (eds) *Investment and Risk in Africa*, forthcoming, Basingstoke: Macmillan.

Kapur, D. (1998) *A Critique of the 1997 World Development Report*, processed, Harvard University.

Kardam, N. (1997) 'The Adaptability of International Development Agencies: The Response of the World Bank to Women in Development', in K.A. Staudt (ed.) *Women, International Development, and Politics: The Bureaucratic Mire*, Philadelphia: Temple University Press.

Karl, M. (1995) *Women and Empowerment: Participation and Decision Making*, London and New York: Zed Books.

Katona-Apte, J. (1986) A Commodity-Appropriateness Evaluation of Four WFP Projects: A Brief Exposition', in M.J. Forman (ed.) *Nutritional Aspects of Project Food Aid*, Geneva: United Nations Administrative Committee on Co-ordination, Sub-Committee on Nutrition.

—— (1993) 'Issues in Food Aid and Nutrition', in *Nutritional Issues in Food Aid*, ACC/SCN Nutrition Policy Papers 12, Geneva: United Nations Administrative Committee on Co-ordination, Sub-Committee on Nutrition.

Kayizzi-Mugerwa, S. (1990) 'Zambia: A Note on the Macroeconomic Impacts of Copper Prices', *Eastern Africa Economic Review* 6(2): 143–7.

Keohane, R. (1998) 'International Institutions: Can Interdependence Work', *Foreign Policy* 110(Spring): 82–96.

Khan, A.E. (1951) 'Investment Criteria in Development Programs', *Quarterly Journal of Economics* 65(February): 38–61.

Khan, H.A. and Hoshino, E. (1992) 'Impact of Foreign Aid on the Fiscal Behaviour of LDC Governments', *World Development* 20(10): 1481–8.

Kharas, H. (1981) *The Analysis of Long-Run Creditworthiness: Theory and Practice*, World Bank Domestic Finance Study 73, Washington, D.C.: World Bank.

Killick, T. (1995) 'Conditionality and the Adjustment–Development Connection', *Pakistan Journal of Applied Economics* 11(1–2): 17–36.

—— (1998a) *Aid and the Political Economy of Policy Reform*, London and New York: Routledge.

—— (1998b) *Adjustment, Income Distribution and Poverty in Africa: A Research Guide*, processed, Nairobi: African Economic Research Consortium.

Kim, J.I. and Lau, L.J. (1994) 'The Sources of Economic Growth of East-Asian Newly Industrialized Countries', *Journal of the Japanese and International Economies* 8(3): 235–71.

Klitgaard, R. (1997) 'Cleaning Up and Invigorating the Civil Service', *Public Administration and Development* 17(5): 487–509.

Knudsen, C. (1991) *Økonomisk metodologi, vol. 1: Videnskabsidealer & forklaringstyper*, Copenhagen: DJØF Publishing (in Danish).

Korten, F.F. (1994) 'Questioning the Call for Environmental Loans: A Critical Examination of Forestry Lending in the Philippines', *World Development* 22(7): 971–81.

Krugman, P.R. (1993) 'Regionalism versus Multilateralism: Analytical Notes', in J. de Melo and A. Panagariya (eds) *New Dimensions in Regional Integration*, Cambridge: Cambridge University Press (for the Centre for Economic Policy Research).

—— (1994) 'The Myth of Asia's Miracle', *Foreign Affairs* 73(6): 62–78.

Kumar, K. (1998) 'Postconflict Elections and International Assistance', in K. Kumar (ed.) *Postconflict Elections, Democratization and International Assistance*, Boulder and London: Lynne Rienner.

Kuyvenhoven, A. (1978) *Planning with a Semi-input–output Method*, processed, Liden.

Kuznets, S. (1958) 'Underdeveloped Countries and the Pre-Industrial Phase in the Advanced Economies', in A.N. Agarwala, and S.P. Singh (eds) *The Economics of Underdevelopment*, Bombay: Oxford University Press.

—— (1966) *Modern Economic Growth*, New Haven: Yale University Press.

Lafay, J-D. and Lecaillon, J. (1993) *The Political Dimension of Economic Adjustment*, OECD Development Centre Studies, Paris: Organisation for Economic Co-operation and Development.

Lall, S. (1993) 'Technological Development, Technology Impacts and Industrial Strategy: A Review of the Issues', *Industry and Development* 34: 1–36.

Lancaster, C. (1999) *Foreign Aid and Development in Africa*, Chicago: University of Chicago Press.

Landell-Mills, P. (1981) 'Structural Adjustment Lending: An Overview', *Finance and Development* 18(1): 17–21.

Landes, D.S. (1998) *The Wealth and Poverty of Nations: Why Some Are So Rich and Some So Poor*, New York and London: W.W. Norton & Company.

Larsen, A.F. (1989) *Usambara: Afrika's Grönne Magnet*, Copenhagen: MS Press (in Swedish).

Larsson, K.A. (1994) *Structural Adjustment, Aid and Development*, Stockholm: SIDA.

Leamer, E.E. (1985) 'Sensitivity Analysis Would Help', *American Economic Review* 75(3): 308–13.

Lee, H. and Roland-Holst, D. (1997) 'The Environment and Welfare Implications of Trade and Tax Policy', *Journal of Development Economics* 52(1): 65–82.

Lefebvre, J.A. (1991) *Arms for the Horn: US Security Policy in Ethiopia and Somalia, 1953–1991*, Pittsburgh: University of Pittsburgh Press.

Leibenstein, H. (1957) *Economic Backwardness and Economic Growth*, New York: Wiley.

Lele, U. (ed.) (1991) *Aid to African Agriculture: Lessons From Two Decades of Donors' Experience*, Baltimore: Johns Hopkins University Press (for the World Bank).

Lensink, R. (1996) *Structural Adjustment in Sub-Saharan Africa*, London: Longman.

Levy, V. (1987) 'Does Concessionary Aid Lead to Higher Investment Rates in Low-Income Countries?', *Review of Economics and Statistics* 69(1): 152–6.

—— (1988) 'Aid and Growth in Sub-Saharan Africa: The Recent Experience', *European Economic Review* 32(9): 1777–95.

Lewis, W.A. (1954) 'Economic Development with Unlimited Supplies of Labour', *The Manchester School* 22(2): 139–91.

Lienert, I. and Modi, J.R. (1997) *A Decade of Civil Service Reform in Sub-Saharan Africa*, IMF Working Paper WP/97/179, Washington, D.C.: International Monetary Fund.

Lindauer, D.L. and Nunberg, B. (eds) (1994) *Rehabilitating Government: Pay and Employment Reform in Africa*, Washington, D.C.: World Bank.

Little, I.M.D. and Mirrlees, J. (1974) *Project Appraisal and Planning for Developing Countries*, New York: Basic Books.

Longwe, S.H. (1991) 'Gender Awareness: The Missing Element in the Third World Development Project', in T. Wallace and C. March (eds) *Changing Perceptions: Writings on Gender and Development*, Oxford: Oxfam.

Lucas, R.E. (1988) 'On the Mechanics of Economic Development', *Journal of Monetary Economics* 22(1): 3–42.

Lummis, C.D. (1993) 'Equality', in W. Sachs (ed.) *The Development Dictionary: A Guide to Knowledge as Power*, Johannesburg: Witwatersrand University Press.

Lumsdaine, D. (1993) *Moral Vision in International Politics: The Foreign Aid Regime, 1949–1989*, Princeton: Princeton University Press.

Luttwak, E. (1999) 'Give War a Chance', *Foreign Affairs* 78(4): 36–44.

Lyakurwa, W., McKay, A. Ng'eno, N. and Kennes, W. (1997) 'Regional Integration in Sub-Saharan Africa: A Review of Experiences and Issues', in A. Oyejide, I. Elbadawi and P. Collier (eds) *Regional Integration and Trade Liberalization in Sub-Saharan Africa, vol. 1: Framework, Issues and Methodological Perspectives*, London: Macmillan.

McDonald, D.C. (1982) 'Debt Capacity and Developing Country Borrowing: A Survey of the Literature', *International Monetary Fund Staff Papers* 29(4): 603–46.

McGillivray, M. (1999) 'Aid and Public Sector Fiscal Behaviour in Developing Countries', *Review of Development Economics* 4(2).

McGillivray, M. and Morrissey, O. (1998) *What Do We Know About the Impact of Aid on Economic Growth*, paper prepared for the CREDIT 10th Anniversary Conference, 17 September 1998, Centre for Research in Economic Development and International Trade, University of Nottingham.

—— (1999a) *The New Macroeconomics of Aid: A Review of Recent Theories and Empirical Evidence*, provisional draft paper prepared for session of the Aid Policy and

Performance Working Group at the 9th General Conference of the European Association of Development Research and Training Institutes (EADI) entitled 'Europe and the South in the 21st Century: Challenges for Renewed Co-operation', 22–25 September 1999, Paris.

—— (eds) (1999b) *Evaluating Economic Liberalization*, Basingstoke: Macmillan.

—— (2000) 'Aid Fungibility', in *Assessing Aid:* Red Herring or True Concern?, *Journal of International Development* 12(3): 413–28.

McGillivray, M. and White, H. (1993a) *Explanatory Studies of Aid Allocation Among Developing Countries: A Critical Survey*, ISS Working Paper 148, The Hague: Institute of Social Studies.

—— (1993b) *Developmental Criteria for the Allocation of Aid and Assessment of Donor Performance*, processed, Deakin University, Geelong and Institute of Social Studies, the Hague.

—— (1993c) *Aid Principles and Policy: An Operational Basis for the Assessment of Donor Performance*, processed, Deakin University, Geelong and Institute of Social Studies, the Hague.

McKay, A. (1997) 'Poverty Reduction Through Economic Growth: Some Issues' *Journal of International Development* 9(4): 665–73.

McKay, A., Morrissey, O. and Vaillant, C. (1997) 'Trade Liberalisation and Agricultural Supply Response: Issues and Some Lessons', *European Journal of Development Research* 9(2): 129–47.

McKean, C. and Fox, J. (1994) *Export and Investment Promotion Services: Do They Work?*, Report no. PN-AAX-279, Washington, D.C.: US Agency for International Development.

Madsen, B. (1998) *Rural Water Supply Rehabilitation, Sustainable Maintenance and Sanitation in Cuddalore and Villupuram Districts of the State of Tamil Nadu, India: Measurement, Assessment and Reporting of Qualitative Aspects of Participation and Empowerment in Project Activities*, Copenhagen: Ministry of Foreign Affairs.

Majd, M.G. (1989) 'The Oil Boom and Agricultural Development: A Reconsideration of Agricultural Policy in Iran', *Journal of Energy and Development* 15(1): 125–40.

Mäler, K.G. (1990) 'International Environmental Problems', *Oxford Review of Economic Policy* 6(1): 80–108.

Mankiw, N.G., Romer, D. and Weil, D.N. (1992) 'A Contribution to the Empirics of Economic Growth', *Quarterly Journal of Economics* 107(2): 407–37.

Manne, A.S. (1974) 'Multi-Sector Models for Development Planning, A Survey', *Journal of Development Economics* 1(1): 43–69.

Marchand, M.H. (1995) 'Latin American Women Speak on Development: Are We Listening Yet?', in M.H. Marchand and J.L. Parpart (eds) *Feminism/Postmodernism/Development*, London and New York: Routledge.

Maren, M. (1997) *The Road to Hell: The Ravaging Effects of Foreign Aid and International Charity*, New York: The Free Press.

Marshall, K. (1998) *From War and Resettlement to Peace Development: Some Lessons from Mozambique and UNHCR and World Bank Collaboration*, HIID Development Discussion Paper 633, Harvard Institute for International Development, Harvard University.

Martin, W. and Winters, A. (1996) *The Uruguay Round and the Developing Countries*, Cambridge: Cambridge University Press.

Massell, B.F., Pearson, S.R. and Fitch, J.B. (1972) 'Foreign Exchange and Economic

Development: An Empirical Study of Selected Latin American Countries', *Review of Economics and Statistics* 54(2): 208–12.

Masson, P.R., Bayoumi, T. and Samiei, H. (1998) 'International Evidence on the Determinants of Private Saving', *World Bank Economic Review* 12(3): 483–501.

Masters, W.A., Bedingar, T. and Oehmke, J.F (1998) 'The Impact of Agricultural Research in Africa: Aggregate and Case Study Evidence', *Agricultural Economics* 19(1–2): 81–6.

Matthews, A. (1998) *International Development Assistance and Food Security*, Trinity Economic Papers, Policy Papers 98–2, Dublin: Trinity College.

Maxwell, S.J. (1996) 'Apples, Pears and Poverty Reduction: An Assessment of British Bilateral Aid', *IDS Bulletin* 27(1): 109–21.

Maxwell, S.J. and Singer, H.W. (1979) 'Food Aid to Developing Countries: A Survey', *World Development* 7(3): 225–47.

Mehta, M. (1991) 'Gender, Development and Culture', in T. Wallace and M. Candida (eds) *Changing Perceptions: Writings on Gender and Development*, Oxford: Oxfam.

Meier, P., Munasinghe, M. and Siyambalapitiya, T. (1996) 'Energy Sector Policy and the Environment: A Case Study of Sri Lanka', in M. Munasinghe (ed.) *Environmental Impacts of Macroeconomic and Sectoral Policies*, Washington, D.C.: World Bank.

Michaely, M. (1981) 'Foreign Aid, Economic Structure, and Dependence', *Journal of Development Economics* 9(3): 313–30.

Michalopoulos, C. and Sukhatme, V. (1989) 'The Impact of Development Assistance: A Review of the Quantitative Evidence', in A.O. Krueger (ed.) *Aid and Development*, Baltimore: Johns Hopkins University Press.

Mikesell, R.F. and Williams, L. (1992) *International Banks and the Environment: From Growth to Sustainability – An Unfinished Agenda*, San Francisco: Sierra Club Books.

Milner, C. and Morrissey, O. (1999) 'Measuring Trade Liberalisation', in M. McGillivray and O. Morrissey (eds) *Evaluating Economic Liberalization*, Basingstoke: Macmillan.

Mittelman, J.H. and Johnston, R. (1999) 'The Globalization of Organized Crime, the Courtesan State, and the Corruption of Civil Society', *Global Governance* 5(1): 103–26.

Mkandawire, T. (1998) *Notes on Consultancy and Research in Africa*, CDR Working Papers 98.13, Copenhagen: Centre for Development Research.

Mohamad, M.B. (1995) Statement at the United Nations Summit for Social Development, Copenhagen, March.

Mohanty, C.T. (1991) 'Introduction: Cartographies of Struggle: Third World Women and the Politics of Feminism', in C.T. Mohanty, A. Russo and L. Torres (eds) *Third World Women and The Politics of Feminism*, Bloomington: Indiana University Press.

Moïsi, D. (1999) 'Dreaming of Europe, *Foreign Policy* 115(Summer): 44–59.

Molyneux, M. (1985) 'Mobilization Without Emancipation? Women's Interests, the State, and Revolution in Nicaragua', *Feminist Studies* 11(2): 227–54.

Montagnon, P. (1998) *Credit where Credit is due: Bringing Microfinance into the Mainstream*, Series Monograph 30, London: Centre for the Study of Financial Innovation.

Moore, M. (1997) *Aid and Tax Effort in Developing Countries*, processed, Institute of Development Studies, University of Sussex.

Moran, C. (1989) 'Imports under a Foreign Exchange Constraint', *World Bank Economic Review* 3(1): 279–95.

Morra, L. and Thumm, U. (1997) *1995 Evaluation Results*, vol. 1–2, Washington, D.C.: World Bank.

Morris, C.T. and Adelman, I. (1988) *Comparative Patterns of Economic Development, 1850–1914*, Johns Hopkins Studies in Development Series, Baltimore and London: Johns Hopkins University Press.

—— (1989) 'Nineteenth-Century Development Experience and Lessons for Today', *World Development* 17(9): 1417–32.

Morrissey, O. (1996) 'Politics and Economic Policy Reform: Trade Liberalisation in Sub-Saharan Africa', *Journal of International Development* 7(4): 599–618.

Morrissey, O. and White, H. (1996) 'Evaluating the Concessionality of Tied Aid', *Manchester School of Economic and Social Studies* 64(2): 208–26.

Moser, C.O.N. (1989) 'Gender Planning in the Third World: Meeting Practical and Strategic Gender Needs', *World Development* 17(11): 1799–1825.

—— (1993) Gender Planning and Development: Theory, Practice and Training, London and New York: Routledge.

Mosley, P. (1980) 'Aid, Savings and Growth Revisited', *Oxford Bulletin of Economics and Statistics* 42(2): 79–95.

—— (1987) *Overseas Aid: Its Defence and Reform*, Brighton: Wheatsheaf Books.

—— (1996) 'The Failure of Aid and Adjustment Policies in Sub-Saharan Africa: Counter-Examples and Policy Proposals', *Journal of African Economies* 5(3): 406–43.

—— (1998) *Globalization, Economic Policy and Convergence*, paper prepared for Group of 24, to be published by UNCTAD.

Mosley, P. and Hudson, J. (1998) *Has Aid Effectiveness Increased?*, processed, International Development Centre, University of Reading and University of Bath.

Mosley, P., Hudson, J. and Horrell, S. (1987) 'Aid, the Public Sector and the Market in Less Developed Countries', *Economic Journal* 97(387): 616–41.

—— (1992) 'Aid, the Public Sector and the Market in Less Developed Countries: A Return to the Scene of the Crime', *Journal of International Development* 4(2): 139–50.

Mosley, P., Harrigan, J. and Toye, J. (1995a) *Aid and Power: The World Bank and Policy-Based Lending*, vol. 1–2, London and New York: Routledge.

Mosley, P., Subasat, T. and Weeks, J. (1995b) 'Assessing Adjustment in Africa', *World Development* 23(9): 1459–73.

Mueller, D.C. (1997) *Perspectives on Public Choice: A Handbook*, New York: Cambridge University Press.

Munasinghe, M., Cruz, W. and Warford, J.J. (1996) 'The Environmental Impact of Economywide Policies: Some Recent Evidence', in M. Munasinghe (ed.) *Environmental Impacts of Macroeconomic and Sectoral Policies*, Washington, D.C.: World Bank.

Musonda, F.M. and Luvanda, E. (1991) 'The Consequences of the 1976–77 Coffee Boom on the Tanzanian Economy: A Test of the Dutch Disease Model', *Eastern Africa Economic Review* 7(2): 1–16.

Nabli, M.K. and Nugent, J.B. (1989) 'The New Institutional Economics and Its Applicability to Development', *World Development* 17(9): 1333–47.

Nalo, D.S.O. (1993) 'Constraints to Growth in Developing Countries and the Three-Gap Model', *Eastern Africa Economic Review* 9(2): 247–64.

Naudet, J.D. (forthcoming) *Trouver des Problèmes aux Solutions: Vingt Ans d'Aide au Sahel*, processed.

Ndulu, B.J. (1991) 'Growth and Adjustment in Sub-Saharan Africa', in A. Chhibber and S. Fischer (eds) *Economic Reform in Sub-Saharan Africa*, Washington, D.C.: World Bank.

Nellis, J.R. (1988) *Contract-Plans and Public Enterprise Performance*, Policy, Planning, and Research Working Papers 118, Washington D.C: World Bank.

Nellis, J.R. and Kikeri, S. (1989) 'Public Enterprise Reform: Privatisation and the World Bank', *World Development* 17(5): 659–72.

Nelson, J.M. (ed.) (1990) *Economic Crisis and Policy Choices: The Politics of Economic Adjustment in the Third World*, Princeton: Princeton University Press.

Nelson, J.M. and Eglinton, S.J. (1993) *Global Goals, Contentious Means: Issues of Multiple Aid Conditionality*, Washington, D.C.: Overseas Development Council.

Nelson, R. and Winter, S. (1982) *An Evolutionary Theory of Economic Change*, Cambridge: Harvard University Press (Belknap).

Newlyn, W.T. (1973) 'The Effect of Aid and Other Resource Transfers on Savings and Growth in Less Developed Countries: A Comment', *Economic Journal* 83(331): 867–69.

New York Times (1999) 'Debt-Relief Plan Is Flawed, 5 Nations Say', April 24th.

Noel, A. and Therien, J-P. (1995) 'From Domestic to International Justice: The Welfare State and Foreign Aid', *International Organization* 49(3): 523–53.

North, D.C (1990) *Institutions, Institutional Change and Economic Performance*, The Political Economy of Institutions and Decisions Series, New York: Cambridge University Press.

—— (1998) 'Economic Performance Through Time', in C.K. Eicher and J.M. Staatz (eds) *International Agricultural Development*, Baltimore: Johns Hopkins University Press.

Nunberg, B. (1994) 'Experience with Civil Service Pay and Employment Reform: An Overview', in D.L. Lindauer and B. Nunberg (eds) *Rehabilitating Government: Pay and Employment Reform in Africa*, Washington, D.C.: World Bank.

—— (1997) *Re-Thinking Civil Service Reform: An Agenda for Smart Government*, processed, Poverty and Social Policy Department, Washington, D.C.: World Bank.

Nurkse, R. (1953) *Problems of Capital Formation in Underdeveloped Countries*, New York: Oxford University Press.

Nyatepe-Coo, A.A. (1994) 'Dutch Disease, Government Policy and Import Demand in Nigeria', *Applied Economics* 26(4): 327–36.

Nye, J.S. (1999) 'Redefining the National Interest', *Foreign Affairs* 78(4): 22–35.

Nyoni, T.S. (1998) 'Foreign Aid and Economic Performance in Tanzania', *World Development* 26(7): 1235–40.

ODI (1998) *The State of the International Humanitarian System*, ODI Briefing Paper 1998 (1), London: Overseas Development Institute.

ODM (1975) *More Aid for the Poorest*, White Paper, London: Overseas Development Ministry.

OECD (1985) *Twenty-five Years of Development Co-operation: A Review–Development Assistance Committee 1985 Report*, Paris: Organisation for Economic Co-operation and Development.

—— (1991) *Principles for New Orientations in Technical Co-operation*, Paris: Organisation for Economic Co-operation and Development.

—— (1992a) *Development Assistance Manual: DAC Principles for Effective Aid*, Paris: Organisation for Economic Co-operation and Development.

—— (1992b) *Guidelines for Aid Agencies on Global Environmental Problems*, DAC Guidelines on Aid and Environment 4, Paris: Organisation for Economic Co-operation and Development.

—— (1994) *Development Co-operation – Development Assistance Committee 1993 Report*, Paris: Organisation for Economic Co-operation and Development.

—— (1995) *Private Sector Development: A Guide to Donor Support*, Paris: Organisation for Economic Co-operation and Development.

—— (1996a) *Shaping the 21st Century: The Contribution of Development Co-operation*, Paris: Organisation for Economic Co-operation and Development.

—— (1996b) *Development Co-operation – Development Assistance Committee 1995 Report*, Paris: Organisation for Economic Co-operation and Development.

—— (1997) *Development Co-operation – Development Assistance Committee 1996 Report*, Paris: Organisation for Economic Co-operation and Development.

—— (1998a) *Geographical Distribution of Financial Flows to Aid Recipients*, CD-ROM, Paris: Organisation for Economic Co-operation and Development.

—— (1998b) *Review of the International Aid System in Mali*, Special Meeting on the Mali Aid Review, 2–3 March 1998, Paris: Organisation for Economic Co-operation and Development.

—— (1998c) *DAC Source Book on Concepts and Approaches Linked to Gender Equality*, Paris: Organisation for Economic Co-operation and Development.

—— (1998d) *DAC Guidelines for Gender Equality and Women's Empowerment in Development Co-operation*, Paris: Organisation for Economic Co-operation and Development.

—— (1999a) *DAC On-line Database* (at www.oecd.org/dac), Paris: Organisation for Economic Co-operation and Development.

—— (1999b) *DAC Scoping Study of Donor Poverty Reduction Policies and Practice: Synthesis Report*, Paris: Organisation for Economic Co-operation and Development.

Ojo, K.O. and Oshikoya, T.W. (1995) 'Determinants of Long-Term Growth: Some African Results', *Journal of African Economies* 4(2): 163–91.

Olsen, O.E. (1995) *Small Steps Towards Great Changes? Enterprise Development in Aid Supported Technology Transfer Projects*, Norwegian University of Science and Technology, Trondheim.

Onafowora, O. and Owoye, O. (1998) 'Can Trade Liberalization Stimulate Economic Growth in Africa', *World Development* 26(3): 497–506.

Osakwe, P.N. (1998) *Food Aid Delivery, Food Security, and Aggregate Welfare in a Small Open Economy: Theory and Evidence*, Working Paper 98–1, Ottawa: Bank of Canada.

Oshikoya, T.W. (1994) 'Macroeconomic Determinants of Domestic Private Investment in Africa: An Empirical Analysis', *Economic Development and Cultural Change* 42(3): 573–96.

Over, A.M. (1975) 'An Example of the Simultaneous-Equation Problem: A Note on Foreign Assistance: Objectives and Consequences', *Economic Development and Cultural Change* 23(4): 751–6.

Overholt, C., K. Cloud, Anderson, M.B. and Austin, J. (1985) 'Women in Development: A Framework for Project Analysis', in C. Overholt, K. Cloud, M.B. Anderson and J. Austin (eds) *Gender Roles in Development Projects*, West Hartford: Kumarian Press.

Oxfam (1995) *The Oxfam Poverty Report*, Oxford: Oxfam.

—— (1997) *The Importance of Engagement: A Strategy for Reconstruction in the Great Lakes Region*, Oxford: Oxfam.

Oyejide, A., Elbadawi, I. and Collier, P. (eds) (1997) *Regional Integration and Trade Liberalization in Sub-Saharan Africa, vol. 1: Framework, Issues and Methodological Perspectives*, Basingstoke: Macmillan.

Pack, H. and Pack, J.R. (1993) 'Foreign Aid and the Question of Fungibility', *Review of Economics and Statistics* 75(2): 258–65.

Panayotou, T. (1994) 'Conservation of Biodiversity and Economic Development: The Concept of Transferable Development Rights', *Environmental and Resource Economics* 4(1): 91–110.

Panayotou, T. and Hupé, K. (1996) 'Environmental Impacts of Structural Adjustment Programs: Synthesis and Recommendations', in M. Munasinghe (ed.) *Environmental Impacts of Macroeconomic and Sectoral Policies*, Washington, D.C.: World Bank.

Pant, P. (1974) 'Perspective of Development: 1961–1976: Implications of Planning for a Minimum Level of Living: A Decade of Development', in T.N. Srinivasan and P.K. Bardhan (eds) *Poverty and Income Distribution in India*, Calcutta.

Papageorgiou, D., Michaely, M. and Choksi, A. (1991) *Liberalizing Foreign Trade*, vol. 1–7, Oxford: Basil Blackwell.

Papanek, G.F. (1972) 'The Effect of Aid and Other Resource Transfers on Savings and Growth in Less Developed Countries, *Economic Journal* 82(327): 934–50.

—— (1973) 'Aid, Foreign Private Investment, Savings, and Growth In Less Developed Countries', *Journal of Political Economy* 81(1): 120–30.

Parpart, J.L. (1995a) 'Deconstructing the Development "Expert:" Gender, Development and the "Vulnerable Groups"', in M.H. Marchand and J.L. Parpart (eds) *Feminism/Postmodernism/Development*, London and New York: Routledge.

—— (1995b) 'Post-Modernism, Gender and Development', in J. Crush (ed.) *Power of Development*, London and New York: Routledge.

Parpart, J.L. and Marchand, M.H. (1995) 'Exploding the Canon: An Introduction/ Conclusion', in M.H. Marchand and J.L. Parpart (eds) *Feminism/Postmodernism/Development*, London and New York: Routledge.

Parpart, J.L., Rai, S.M. and Staudt, K.A. (eds) (2000) *Rethinking Empowerment and Development in a Global/Local World: Gendered Perspectives*, forthcoming, London and New York: Routledge.

Parsons, A. (1995) *From Cold War to Hot Peace: UN Interventions 1947–1995*, London: Penguin.

Paul, D. (1997) *Aiding and Abetting*, War Report 51, London: Institute for War and Peace Reporting.

Pearce, D.W. and Warford, J.J. (1993) *World Without End: Economics, Environment and Sustainable Development*, New York: Oxford University Press (for the World Bank).

Pedersen, K.R. (1996) 'Aid, Investment and Incentives', *Scandinavian Journal of Economics* 98(3): 423–38.

Pedersen, R.J. (1994) *Survey af virksomhed-til-virksomhed teknologisamarbejdsprogrammer mellem små og mellemstore virksomheder i i- og u-lande* (Survey of Business-to-Business Technological Co-operation Programmes Between Small and Medium-Sized Companies in Industrial and Developing Countries), Copenhagen: Danish Federation of Small and Medium-Sized Enterprises (in Danish).

Persson, T. and Tabellini, G. (1990) *Macroeconomic Policy, Credibility, and Politics*, New York and Melbourne: Harwood.

Pfannenschmidt, S., McKay, A. and McNeill, E. (1997) *Through a Gender Lens: Resources for Population, Health and Nutrition Projects*, Washington, D.C.: Family Health International (for US Agency for International Development).

Pinstrup-Andersen, P. (1988) *Food Subsidies in Developing Countries: Costs, Benefits, and Policy Options*, Baltimore: Johns Hopkins University Press (for the International Food Policy Research Institute).

Pinstrup-Andersen, P., Lundberg, M. and Garrett, J.L. (1995a) *Foreign Assistance to Agriculture: A Win-Win Proposition*, IFPRI Food Policy Report, Washington, D.C.: International Food Policy Research Institute.

Pinstrup-Andersen, P. Pelletier, D. and Alderman, H. (1995b) 'Enhancing Child Growth and Nutrition: Lessons for Action', in P. Pinstrup-Andersen, D. Pelletier, and H. Alderman (eds) *Child Growth and Nutrition in Developing Countries: Priorities for Action*, Ithaca: Cornell University Press.

Pinstrup-Andersen, P. and Garrett, J.L. (1996) *Rising Food Prices and Falling Grain Stocks: Short-Run Blips or New Trends?*, 2020 Brief 30, 2020 Vision Initiative, Washington, D.C.: International Food Policy Research Institute.

Pinstrup-Andersen, P., Pandya-Lorch, R. and Rosegrant, M.W. (1997) *The World Food Situation: Recent Developments, Emerging Issues, and Long-Term Prospects*, IFPRI Food Policy Report, Washington, D.C.: International Food Policy Research Institute.

Porter, M.E. (1990) *The Competitive Advantages of Nations*, Basingstoke and New York: Macmillan.

Pradhan, S. (1996) *Evaluating Public Spending: A Framework for Public Expenditure Reviews*, World Bank Discussion Paper 323, Washington, D.C.: World Bank.

Princen, T. and Finger, M. (1994) *Environmental NGOs in World Politics: Linking the Local and the Global*, London and New York: Routledge.

Przeworski, A. and Limongi, F. (1997) 'Modernization: Theories and Facts', *World Politics* 49(2): 155–83.

Putnam, R. (1988) 'Diplomacy and Domestic Politics: The Logic of Two-Level Games', *International Organization* 42(3): 427–60.

Quisumbing, A.R., Brown, L.R., Feldstein, H.S., Haddad, L. and Peña, C. (1995) *Women: The Key to Food Security*, IFPRI Food Policy Report, Washington, D.C.: International Food Policy Research Institute.

Radcliffe, S.A. and Westwood, S. (1993) *Viva: Women and Popular Protest in Latin America*, London and New York: Routledge.

Rahman, A. (1968) 'Foreign Capital and Domestic Savings: A Test of Haavelmo's Hypothesis with Cross-Country Data', *Review of Economics and Statistics* 50(1): 137–8.

Ramsbotham, O. and Woodhouse, T. (1996) *Humanitarian Intervention in Contemporary Conflict*, Cambridge: Polity Press.

Rathgeber, E.M. (1995) 'Gender and Development in Action', in M.H. Marchand and J.L. Parpart (eds) *Feminism/Postmodernism/Development*, London and New York: Routledge.

Rattsø, J. and Torvik, R. (1999) 'The Macroeconomics of Foreign Aid in Sub-Saharan Africa: Dutch Disease Effects Reconsidered', in K.L. Gupta (ed.) *Foreign Aid: New Perspectives*, Boston: Kluwer.

Ray, D. (1998) *Development Economics*, Princeton: Princeton University Press.

RDI (Relief and Development Institute) (1987) *A Study of Triangular Transactions and Local Purchases in Food Aid*, Occasional Paper 11, Rome: World Food Programme.

Reed, D. (1992) *Structural Adjustment and the Environment*, London: Earthscan.

—— (1996) 'Environmental Impacts of Structural Adjustment: The Social Dimension', in M. Munasinghe (ed.) *Environmental Impacts of Macroeconomic and Sectoral Policies*, Washington, D.C.: World Bank.

Reed, D. and Sheng, F. (1998) *Macroeconomic Policies, Poverty and The Environment*, Discussion Paper, Macroeconomics for Sustainable Development Program Office (MPO), Washington, D.C.: World Wildlife Fund.

Reilly, B. and Reynolds, A. (1999) *Electoral Systems and Conflict in Divided Societies*, Washington, D.C.: National Academy Press.

Reilly, J.E. (ed.) (1999) *American Public Opinion and US Foreign Policy 1999*, Chicago: Chicago Council on Foreign Relations.

Reisen, H. and van Trotsenburg, A. (1988) *Developing Country Debt: The Budgetary and Transfer Problem*, OECD Development Centre Studies, Paris: Organisation for Economic Co-operation and Development.

Reutlinger, S. (1984) 'Project Food Aid and Equitable Growth: Income-Transfer Efficiency First!', *World Development* 12(9): 901–11.

Reutlinger, S. and Katona-Apte, J. (1987) 'The Nutritional Impact of Food Aid: Criteria for the Selection of Cost-Effective Foods', in J.P. Gittinger, J. Leslie and C. Hoisington (eds) *Food Policy: Integrating Supply, Distribution, and Consumption*, Baltimore: The Johns Hopkins University Press (for the World Bank).

Richey, L. (2000) 'Demographic "Development" and Feminist Agenda: Depoliticizing Gender in a Tanzanian Family Planning Project', in J.L. Parpart, S.M. Rai and K.A. Staudt (eds) *Rethinking Empowerment and Development in a Global/Local World: Gendered Perspectives*, forthcoming, London and New York: Routledge.

Riddell, R. (1987) *Foreign Aid Reconsidered*, London: James Curry.

Robinson, M.S. (1997) *Introducing Savings in Microcredit Institutions: When and How?*, Focus Note 8, Consultative Group to Assist the Poorest – A Micro-Finance Program (CGAP), Washington, D.C.: World Bank.

Robinson, S. (1971) 'Sources of Growth in Less Developed Countries: A Cross-Section Study', *Quarterly Journal of Economics* 85(3): 391–408.

Rock, M. (1993) *Can Export Services Assistance Make a Difference? The Korean Experience*, Report PN-AAX-264, Washington, D.C.: US Agency for International Development.

Rock, R. and Otero, M. (1997) *From Margin to Mainstream: The Regulation and Supervision of Microfinance*, Monograph Series 11, Somerville: Accion International.

Rodrik, D. (1990) 'How Should Structural Adjustment Programs Be Designed?', *World Development* 18(7): 933–47.

—— (1999) *The New Global Economy and Developing Countries: Making Openness Work*, ODC Policy Essay 24, Washington, D.C.: Overseas Development Council.

Romer, P. (1990) 'Endogenous Technological Change', *Journal of Political Economy* 98(5, part 2): S71–102.

Rosegrant, M.W., Agcaoili-Sombilla, M. and Perez, N.D. (1995) *Global Food Projections to 2020: Implications for Investment*, Food, Agriculture, and the Environment Discussion Paper 5, Washington, D.C.: International Food Policy Research Institute.

Rosenstein-Rodan, P.N. (1943) 'Problems of Industrialisation of Eastern and South-Eastern Europe', *Economic Journal* 53(210): 202–11.

—— (1961) 'International Aid for Underdeveloped Countries', *Review of Economics and Statistics* 43(2): 107–38.

Rostow, W.W. (1956) 'The Take-Off into Self-Sustained Growth', *Economic Journal* 66(March): 25–48.

Rowlands, J. (1997) *Questioning Empowerment: Working with Women in Honduras*, Oxford: Oxfam.

Ruttan, V.W. (1996) *United States Development Assistance Policy*, Baltimore: Johns Hopkins University Press.

—— (1998) 'Does Food Aid Have a Future?', *American Journal of Agricultural Economics* 80(3): 566–71.

Sachs, J.D. and Warner, A.M. (1995) 'Economic Reform and the Process of Global Integration', *Brookings Papers on Economic Activity* 1: 1–95.

—— (1997) 'Sources of Slow Growth in African Economies', *Journal of African Economies* 6(3): 335–76.

Sahn, D.E. (1992) 'Public Expenditures in Sub-Saharan Africa During a Period of Economic Reforms', *World Development* 20(5): 673–93.

—— (1994) 'The Impact of Macroeconomic Adjustment on Incomes, Health and Nutrition: Sub-Saharan Africa in the 1980s', in G.A. Cornia and G.K. Helleiner (eds) *From Adjustment to Development in Africa: Conflict, Controversy, Convergence, Consensus?*, New York: St. Martin's Press and Basingstoke: Macmillan.

Sahn, D.E., Dorosh, P. and Younger, S. (1996) 'Exchange Rate, Fiscal and Agricultural Policies in Africa: Does Adjustment Hurt the Poor?', *World Development* 24(4): 719–47.

Sala-i-Martin, X. (1997) 'I Just Ran Two Million Regressions', *American Economic Review* 87(2): 178–83.

Saran, R. and Konandreas, P. (1991) 'An Additional Resource? A Global Perspective on Food Aid Flows in Relation to Development Assistance', in E. Clay and O. Stokke (eds) *Food Aid Reconsidered*, London: Frank Cass.

Sarel, M. (1996) 'Nonlinear Effects of Inflation on Economic Growth', *International Monetary Fund Staff Papers* 43(1): 199–215.

Schadler, S., Rozwadowski, F., Tiwari, S. and Robinson, D.O. (1993) *Economic Adjustment in Low-Income Countries: Experience Under the Enhanced Structural Adjustment Facility*, Occasional Papers 106, Washington, D.C.: International Monetary Fund.

Schalkwyk, J., Thomas, H. and Beth, W. (1996) *Mainstreaming: A Strategy for Achieving Equality Between Women and Men – A Think Piece*, Stockholm: Swedish International Development Co-operation Agency.

Schraeder, P.J., Hook, S.W. and Taylor, B. (1998) 'Clarifying the Foreign Aid Puzzle: A Comparison of American, Japanese, French and Swedish Flows', *World Politics* 50(2): 294–323.

Scott, C.V. (1995) *Gender and Development: Rethinking Modernization and Dependency Theory*, Boulder and London: Lynne Rienner.

Seligson, M.A. and Passe-Smith, J.T. (eds) (1998) *Development and Underdevelopment: The Political Economy of Global Inequality*, Boulder: Lynne Rienner.

Sen, G. and Grown, C. (1987) *Development Crises and Alternative Visions: Third World Women's Perspectives*, New York: Monthly Review Press.

Shaaeldin, E. (1988) 'Sources of Industrial Growth in Kenya, Tanzania, Zambia and Zimbabwe', *Eastern Africa Economic Review* 4(2): 21–31.

Shafik, N. and Bandyopadhyay, S. (1992) *Economic Growth and Environmental Quality:*

Time Series and Cross-Country Evidence, processed, background paper for World Development Report 1992, Washington, D.C.: World Bank.

Sharpless, J. (1997) 'Population Science, Private Foundations, and Development Aid: The Transformation of Demographic Knowledge in the United States, 1945–1965', in F. Cooper and R. Packard (eds) *International Development and the Social Sciences*, Berkeley and London: University of California Press.

Shaw, D.J. and Singer, H.W. (1996) 'A Future Food Aid Regime: Implications of the Final Act of the Uruguay Round', *Food Policy* 21(4–5): 447–60.

Shirley, M.M. and Nellis, J.R. (1991) *Public Enterprise Reform: The Lessons of Experience*, Economic Development Institute (EDI) Development Study, Washington, D.C.: World Bank.

Shirley, M.M and Xu, L.C. (1997) *Information, Incentives and Commitment. An Empirical Analysis of Contracts Between Government and State Enterprises*, Policy Research Working Paper 1769, Washington D.C.: World Bank.

Sida (1995) *Sector Programme Support: Background Document to Sida Strategy*, Stockholm: Swedish International Development Co-operation Agency.

—— (1996) *Aid Dependency: Causes, Symptoms and Remedies*, Stockholm: Swedish International Development Co-operation Agency.

—— (1997) *Financial Sector Development*, Sida Task Force report, Stockholm: Swedish International Development Co-operation Agency.

Simmons, P. (1997) '"Women in Development:" A Threat to Liberation', in M. Rahnema and V. Bawtree (eds) *The Post-Development Reader*, London and New York: Zed Books.

Simonsen, M.H. (1985) 'The Developing-Country Debt Problem', in G.W. Smith and J.T. Cuddington (eds) *International Debt and the Developing Countries*, Washington, D.C.: World Bank.

Singer, H.W. (1965) 'External Aid: For Plans or Projects?', *Economic Journal* 75(September): 539–45.

Singer, H.W. and Ansari, J. (1988) *Rich and Poor Countries: Consequences of International Disorder*, London: Uwin Hyman.

Singh, R.D. (1985) 'State Intervention, Foreign Economic Aid, Savings and Growth in LDCs: Some Recent Evidence', *Kyklos* 38(2): 216–32.

Snyder, D.W. (1990) 'Foreign Aid and Domestic Savings: A Spurious Correlation?', *Economic Development and Cultural Change* 39(1): 175–81.

—— (1993) 'Donor Bias Towards Small Countries: An Overlooked Factor in the Analysis of Foreign Aid and Economic Growth', *Applied Economics* 25(4): 481–8.

Srinivasan, T.N. (1989) 'Food Aid: A Cause of Development Failure or an Instrument for Success?', *World Bank Economic Review* 3(1): 39–65.

Stamp, P. (1990) *Technology, Gender and Power in Africa*, Ottawa: International Development Research Centre.

Standing, H. (1997) 'Gender and Equity in Health Sector Reform Programmes: A Review', *Health Policy and Planning* 12(1): 1–18.

Staniland, M. (1985) *What is Political Economy? A Study of Social Theory and Underdevelopment*, New Haven: Yale University Press.

Staudt, K.A. (ed.) (1997) *Women, International Development, and Politics: The Bureaucratic Mire*, Philadelphia: Temple University Press.

—— (1998) *Policy, Politics and Gender: Women Gaining Ground*, West Hartford: Kumarian Press.

Stein, J. (1997) *Empowerment and Women's Health: Theory, Method and Practice*, London and New York: Zed Books.

Stewart, F. (1998) 'Food Aid During Conflict: Can One Reconcile Its Humanitarian, Economic, and Political Economy Effects?', *American Journal of Agricultural Economics* 80(3): 560–5.

Stiglitz, J.E. (1998) *More Instruments and Broader Goals: Moving Toward the Post-Washington Consensus*, WIDER Annual Lectures 2, Helsinki: World Institute for Development Economics Research.

Stoneman, C. (1975) 'Foreign Capital and Economic Growth', *World Development* 3(1): 11–26.

Stopford, J. (1998) 'Multinational Corporations', *Foreign Policy* 113(Winter): 12–24.

Stremlau, J. (1994) 'Clinton's Dollar Diplomacy', *Foreign Policy* 97(Winter): 18–35.

Svensson, J. (1997) *When is Foreign Aid Policy Credible? Aid Dependence and Conditionality*, processed, Washington, D.C.: World Bank.

Swamy, A., Knack, S., Young, L. and Azfar, O. (1999) *Gender and Corruption*, Draft IRIS Working Paper, Center for Institutional Reform and the Informal Sector, University of Maryland.

Swedberg, R. (ed.) (1993) *Explanations in Economic Sociology*, New York: Russell Sage Foundation.

Taylor, L. (1983) *Structuralist Macroeconomics*, New York: Basic Books.

—— (1991) *Foreign Resource Flows and Developing Country Growth*, Research for Action Study 8, Helsinki: World Institute for Development Economics Research.

—— (ed.) (1993) *The Rocky Road to Reform: Adjustment, Income Distribution, and Growth in the Developing World*, Cambridge: MIT Press.

Tendler, J. (1975) *Inside Foreign Aid*, Baltimore: Johns Hopkins University Press.

The Economist (1994) 'Down the Rathole', December 10th.

—— (1995) 'Aid for Kenya. Stop, Go', August 19th.

—— (1998) 'Making Aid Work', November 14th.

—— (1999) 'How to Make Aid Work', June 14th.

Thorbecke, E. (ed.) (1969) *The Role of Agriculture in Economic Development*, New York: Columbia University Press.

—— (1991) 'Adjustment, Growth and Income Distribution in Indonesia', *World Development* 19(11): 1595–614.

—— (1993) 'Impact of State and Civil Institutions on the Operation of Rural Market and Non-Market Configurations', *World Development* 21(4): 591–605.

—— (1996) *The AERC Research Programme: An Evaluation*, AERC Special Paper 21, Nairobi: African Economic Research Consortium.

Tisdell, C.A. (1991) *Economics of Environmental Conservation: Economics for Environmental and Ecological Management*, Amsterdam: Elsevier.

Tobin, J. (1974) *The New Economics One Decade Older*, The Janeway Lectures on Historical Economics, Princeton: Princeton University Press.

Tong, R. (1989) *Feminist Thought: A Comprehensive Introduction*, Boulder: Westview Press.

Toye, J. and Jackson, C. (1996) 'Public Expenditure and Poverty Reduction: Has the World Bank Got It Right?', *IDS Bulletin* 27(1).

Tsikata, T.M. (1998) *Aid Effectiveness: A Survey of the Recent Empirical Literature*, IMF Papers on Policy Analysis and Assessments PPAA/98/1, Washington, D.C.: International Monetary Fund.

UN (1995a) *The Copenhagen Declaration and Programme of Action*, New York: United Nations.

——— (1995b) *Report of United Nations Fourth World Conference on Women*, New York: United Nations.

UNCTAD (1990) *Agricultural Trade Liberalization in the Uruguay Round: Implications for Developing Countries*, Geneva: United Nations Conference on Trade and Development.

——— (1995) *Commodity Yearbook 1995*, Geneva: United Nations Conference on Trade and Development.

——— (1996) *Handbook of International Trade and Development Statistics*, Geneva: United Nations Conference on Trade and Development.

UNDP (1997a) *Capacity Development*, Technical Advisory Paper 2, New York: United Nations Development Programme.

——— (1997b) *Human Development Report 1997*, New York: United Nations Development Programme.

UNEP (1997) *Global Environment Outlook-1: Global State of the Environment Report 1997*, Nairobi: United Nations Environment Programme.

UNFPA (1998) *Gender, Population and Development Themes in United Nations Conferences 1985–1995*, New York: United Nations Population Fund.

Unicef (1998) *News in Brief* (December), London: United Kingdom Committee for United Nations Childrens Fund.

——— (1999) *News in Brief* (January), London: United Kingdom Committee for United Nations Childrens Fund.

USDA (1995) *Food Aid Needs and Availabilities: Projections for 2005*, Washington, D.C.: United States Department of Agriculture.

Uvin, P. (1998) *Aiding Violence: The Development Enterprise in Rwanda*, West Hartford: Kumarian Press.

van de Walle, N. (1989) 'Privatization in Developing Countries: A Review of the Issues', *World Development* 17(5): 601–15.

——— (1998) *Managing Aid to Africa: The Rise and Decline of the Structural Adjustment Regime*, paper prepared for AERC Workshop, May 1998, Nairobi: African Economic Research Consortium.

van de Walle, N. and Johnston, T.A. (1996) *Improving Aid to Africa*, Policy Essay 21, Washington, D.C.: Overseas Development Council.

van der Windt, N. (1995) *Strengthening Budget Management in SPA Countries*, Rotterdam: Netherlands Economic Institute.

van Wijnbergen, S. (1985) *Aid, Export Promotion and the Real Exchange Rate: An African Dilemma*, CEPR Discussion Paper 88, London: Centre for Economic Policy Research.

——— (1986) 'Macroeconomic Aspects of the Effectiveness of Foreign Aid: On the Two-Gap Model, Home Goods Disequilibrium and Real Exchange Rate Misalignment', *Journal of International Economics* 21(1–2): 123–36.

Viner, J.N. (1950) *The Customs Union Issue*, New York: Carnegie Endowment for International Peace.

Visvanathan, N. (1997) 'Introduction to Part 1', in N. Visvanathan, L. Duggan, L. Nisonoff and N. Wiegersma (eds) *The Women, Gender and Development Reader*, London and New York: Zed Books.

Vogel, R.C. (1994) *Other People's Money: Regulatory Issues Facing Microenterprise Finance Programs*, processed, Arlington: International Management and Communications Corporation.

Voivodas, C.S. (1973) 'Exports, Foreign Capital Inflow and Economic Growth', *Journal of International Economics* 3(4): 337–49.

von Braun, J. and Huddleston, B. (1988) 'Implications of Food Aid for Price Policy in Recipient Countries', in J.W. Mellor and R. Ahmed (eds) *Agricultural Price Policy for Developing Countries*, Baltimore: Johns Hopkins University Press (for the International Food Policy Research Institute).

von Braun, J., Teklu, T. and Webb, P. (1991) *Labor-Intensive Public Works for Food Security: Experience in Africa*, Working Papers on Food Subsidies 6, Washington, D.C.: International Food Policy Research Institute.

von Stauffenberg, D. (1996) *A Rating Agency for the Microfinance Industry*, paper presented at Establishing a MicroFinance Industry: Proceedings of the 4th MicroFinance Network Annual Conference, 1996, Toronto.

Wall, D. (1973) *The Charity of Nations: The Political Economy of Foreign Aid*, New York: Basic Books.

Wallace, T. (1998) 'Institutionalising Gender in UK NGOs', *Development in Practice* 8(2): 159–71.

Wallensteen, P. and Sollenberg, M. (1997) 'The End of International War? Armed Conflict 1989–1996', *Journal of Peace Research* 34(3): 339–58.

WCED (1987) *Our Common Future*, Oxford: Oxford University Press (for the World Commission on Energy and Development).

Weeks, J. (1997) 'Analysis of the Demery and Squire "Adjustment and Poverty" Evidence', *Journal of International Development* 9(6): 827–36.

Weiss, T.G. (1999) *Military–Civilian Interactions: Intervening in Humanitarian Crises*, Lanham: Rowman and Littlefield.

Weiss, T.G. and Gordenker, L. (eds) (1996) *NGOs, the UN, and Global Governance*, Boulder: Lynne Reinner.

Weisskopf, T.E. (1972) 'The Impact of Foreign Capital Inflow on Domestic Savings in Underdeveloped Countries', *Journal of International Economics* 2(1): 25–38.

WFP (1998) *1997 Food Aid Flows*, Food Aid Monitor, special issue, Rome: World Food Programme.

White, H. (1992a) 'The Macroeconomic Impact of Development Aid: A Critical Survey', *Journal of Development Studies* 28(2): 163–240.

—— (1992b) 'What Do We Know About Aid's Macroeconomic Impact? An Overview of the Aid Effectiveness Debate', *Journal of International Development* 4(2): 121–37.

—— (1993) 'Aid and Government: A Dynamic Model of Aid, Income and Fiscal Behaviour', *Journal of International Development* 5(3): 305–12.

—— (1994) 'Foreign Aid, Taxes and Public Investment: A Further Comment', *Journal of Development Economics* 45(1): 155–63.

—— (1998) *Aid and Macroeconomic Performance*, Basingstoke: Macmillan.

—— (1999a) *Swedish Programme Aid: An Evaluation*, Stockholm: Swedish International Development Co-operation Agency.

—— (1999b) 'Aid and Economic Reform', in S. Kayizzi-Mugerwa (ed.) *The African Economy*, London and New York: Routledge.

White H. and McGillivray, M. (1995) 'How Well is Aid Allocated? Descriptive Measures of Aid Allocation: A Survey of Methodology and Results', *Development and Change* 26(1): 163–83.

White, H. and Wignaraja, G. (1992) 'Exchange Rates, Trade Liberalization and Aid: The Sri Lankan Experience', *World Development* 20(10): 1471–80.

White, H. and Woestman, L. (1994) 'The Quality of Aid: Measuring Trends in Donor Performance', *Development and Change* 25(3): 527–54.

White, J.A. (1974) *The Politics of Foreign Aid*, New York: St. Martin's Press.

White, O.C. and Bhatia, A. (1998) *Privatization in Africa*, Washington, D.C.: World Bank.

Wiggins, S. (1985) 'Planning and Management of Integrated Rural Development in Drylands: Lessons from Kenya's Arid and Semi-Arid Lands Programmes', *Public Administration and Development* 5(2): 91–108.

Wilensky, H. and Lebaux, C. (1965) *Industrial Society and Social Welfare*, New York: Free Press.

Williams, M. (1991) *Evaluation of National Technical Co-operation Assessment and Programmes (NatCAP)*, volume 1, New York: United Nations Development Programme.

Williamson, J. (1993) 'Democracy and the "Washington Consensus"', *World Development* 21(8): 1329–36.

Williamson, O. (1991) *Comparative Economic Organization: The Analysis of Discrete Structural Alternatives*, working paper, Washington, D.C.: Institute for Policy Reform.

Williamson, O. (1994) 'The Institutions of Governance of Economic Development and Reform', in M. Bruno and B. Pleskovic (eds) *Proceedings of the World Bank Annual Conference on Development Economics, 1994*, Supplement to The World Bank Economic Review and The World Bank Research Observer (1995): 171–97.

Wintrobe, R. (1998) *The Political Economy of Dictatorship*, Cambridge: Cambridge University Press.

Wood, A. (1997) 'Openness and Wage Inequality in Developing Countries: The Latin American Challenge to East Asian Conventional Wisdom', *World Bank Economic Review*, 11(1): 33–57.

Wood, R.E. (1986) *From Marshall Plan to Debt Crisis: Foreign Aid and Development Choices in the World Economy*, Berkeley: University of California Press.

World Bank (1981) *Accelerated Development in Sub-Saharan Africa: An Agenda for Action*, Washington, D.C: World Bank.

—— (1988) *Adjustment Lending: An Evaluation of Ten Years of Experience*, Washington, D.C: World Bank.

—— (1989) *World Development Report 1989*, New York: Oxford University Press (for the World Bank).

—— (1990a), *World Development Report 1990*, New York: Oxford University Press (for the World Bank).

—— (1990b) *Adjustment Lending: Policies for Sustainable Growth*, Washington, D.C: World Bank.

—— (1991a), *World Development Report 1991*, New York: Oxford University Press (for the World Bank).

—— (1991b) *Report of the Technical Assistance Review Task Force*, Washington, D.C: World Bank.

—— (1992a) *Adjustment Lending and Mobilization of Public and Private Resources for Growth*, Washington, D.C: World Bank.

—— (1992b) *World Development Report 1992*, New York: Oxford University Press (for the World Bank).

—— (1992c) *World Bank Structural and Sectoral Adjustment Operations: The Second OED Review*, Operations Evaluation Department Report 10870, Washington, D.C: World Bank.

—— (1993a) *The East Asian Miracle*, Washington, D.C: World Bank.

—— (1993b) *Putting the Private Sector on Track*, Findings 9, Africa Region, Washington, D.C: World Bank.

—— (1994a) *Adjustment in Africa: Reforms, Results, and the Road Ahead*, Oxford: Oxford University Press (for the World Bank).

—— (1994b) *World Bank Assistance to Privatization in Developing Countries*, Operations Evaluation Study, Washington, D.C: World Bank.

—— (1995) *Bureaucrats in Business: The Economics and Politics of Government Ownership*, New York: Oxford University Press (for the World Bank).

—— (1996a) *Taking Action for Poverty Reduction in Sub-Saharan Africa*, Africa Region Task Force report, Washington, D.C.: World Bank.

—— (1996b) *World Bank Lending for Large Dams: A Preliminary Review of Impacts*, Operations Evaluation Study, Washington, D.C: World Bank.

—— (1996c) *Sustainable Banking with the Poor. A Worldwide Inventory of Microfinance Institutions*, Washington, D.C: World Bank.

—— (1996d) *Sri Lanka: Economic Restructuring Credit and Public Manufacturing Enterprises Adjustment Credit*, Report No. 15820, Washington, D.C.: World Bank.

—— (1997a) *World Development Report 1997*, New York: Oxford University Press (for the World Bank).

—— (1997b) *Special Programme of Assistance for Africa (Phase Four): Building for the 21st Century*, Washington, D.C: World Bank.

—— (1997c) *Annual Report 1997*, Washington, D.C: World Bank.

—— (1997d) *Global Development Finance 1997*, Washington, D.C: World Bank.

—— (1997e) *A Framework for World Bank Involvement in Post-Conflict Reconstruction*, Oxford: Oxford University Press (for the World Bank).

—— (1998a) *Assessing Aid: What Works, What Doesn't, and Why*, Oxford: Oxford University Press (for the World Bank).

—— (1998b), *World Development Report 1998*, New York: Oxford University Press (for the World Bank).

—— (1998c) *Independent Evaluation of the SPA as a Mechanism to Promote Adjustment and Development in Sub-Saharan Africa*, Washington, D.C: World Bank.

—— (1998d) *The Impact of Public Expenditure Reviews: An Evaluation*, Operations Evaluation Study, Washington, D.C: World Bank.

—— (1998e), *Public Expenditure Management Handbook*, Washington, D.C: World Bank.

—— (1998f) *Mainstreaming Gender and Development in the World Bank: Progress and Recommendations*, Washington, D.C: World Bank.

—— (1998g) *Partnerships for Development: Proposed Actions for the World Bank*, Washington, D.C: World Bank.

—— (1998h) *Macedonia – Joint Country Assistance Strategy*, Report No. 18162, Washington, D.C: World Bank.

—— (various issues) *Annual Report*, Washington, D.C: World Bank.

Wuyts, M. (1996) 'Foreign Aid, Structural Adjustment and Public Management: The Mozambican Experience', *Development and Change* 27(4): 717–49.

Yaron, J. (1992) *Successful Rural Finance Institutions*, World Bank Discussion Paper 150, Washington, D.C.: World Bank.

Young, A. (1995) 'The Tyranny of Numbers: Confronting the Statistical Realities of the East-Asian Growth Experience', *Quarterly Journal of Economics* 110(3): 641–80.

Young, K. (1997) 'Gender and Development', in N. Visvanathan, L. Duggan, L. Nisonoff and N. Wiegersma (eds) *The Women, Gender and Development Reader*, London and New York: Zed Books.

Younger, S.D. (1992) 'Aid and the Dutch Disease: Macroeconomic Management When Everybody Loves You', *World Development* 20(11): 1587–97.

Zank, N. (1990) 'Privatization and Deregulation in the LDC Financial Sector: An AID Perspective', in D.J. Gayle and J. N. Goodrich (eds) *Privatization and Deregulation in Global Perspective*, London: Pinter.

Zietz, J. and Valdes, A. (1990) 'International Interactions in Food and Agricultural Policies: Effects of Alternative Policies', in I. Goldin and O. Knudsen (eds) *Agricultural Trade Liberalization: Implications for Developing Countries*, Paris: Organisation for Economic Co-operation and Development.

Index